3 vol

A CATALOGUE OF
HORACE WALPOLE'S LIBRARY

A CATALOGUE OF

HORACE WALPOLE'S LIBRARY

By ALLEN T. HAZEN

With

HORACE WALPOLE'S LIBRARY

By WILMARTH SHELDON LEWIS

VOLUME III

Numbers 3178–4019 and Indexes

LONDON

OXFORD UNIVERSITY PRESS

NEW HAVEN · YALE UNIVERSITY PRESS

1969

Library of Congress catalog card number: 65–11182
Standard book number: 19 625721 2

Set in Baskerville type,
and printed in the United States of America by
Connecticut Printers, Inc., Hartford, Conn.

Distributed in the United Kingdom and British Commonwealth,
excluding Canada, by Oxford University Press, London; in
Canada by McGill-Queen's University Press, Montreal; and
in Mexico by Centro Interamericano de Libros
Académicos, Mexico City.

THE CURTIS SEAMAN READ
MEMORIAL PUBLICATION FUND

This is the final work published by the Yale University Press on the Fund established in memory of Curtis Seaman Read in 1920. Born on August 21, 1893, the son of William A. and Caroline (Seaman) Read, he was a member of the Class of 1918, Yale College, leaving in his junior year to enter the United States Naval Reserve Flying Corps, in which he qualified as a Naval Aviator with an Ensign's commission. He was killed on active service near Dunkirk, France, in February, 1918.

This memorial was established by his fourteen classmates in the Scroll and Key Society of Yale College to express the love and honor in which they held him.

The seven surviving members now devote the principal of the Fund to help defray the publication costs of this work, which has been of special interest to one of them for more than forty years.

CONTENTS OF THE THIRD VOLUME

The Library in the Offices (*cont.*)   1

The Round Tower   111

Appendix 1.   False Attributions   267

Appendix 2.   Books given away by Walpole   283

Appendix 3.   Books owned by Walpole when at
     Eton and Cambridge   289

Index of Binders   293

Index of Owners   295

General Index   329

Noteworthy in Press S were the 22 volumes of 'Poems of the Reign of George the 3d,' presumably moved to the Offices in 1792. Previously they may have been in the Cottage.

Other books in Press S were all in quarto, rather miscellaneous in nature. But HW's continuing interest in local history and topography is clearly reflected by the books shelved here. The 'Poems' are here recorded at the end of Press S for convenience.

BAKER, JAMES   3178
A picturesque guide through Wales and the Marches. [London?] 1794.
  Two volumes, 4to.
  Not in MC.
  SH SALE, v.58 (with Tindal), to Strong, £1.1.0.

BUTLER, SAMUEL   3179
Hudibras. Edited by Treadway Russell Nash. London, 1793. Three
  volumes, 4to.
  Not in MC.
  SH SALE, v.59, to Pickering, £3.
  ☞ The sale catalogue says 'very fine impressions of the plates, after
Hogarth.' Two hundred copies were printed.

[CAVAN, RICHARD LAMBART, Earl of]   3180
*A new system of military discipline, founded upon principle. By a
  General Officer.* London, 1773. 4to.
  Not in MC.
  SH SALE, v.67 (with Cozens, Lucas, Napier, Tresham, and Wood), to
Thorpe, £1.19.0. When sold at Sotheby's, 30 June 1858 (Bliss Sale, Part
1), lot 831, it was described as having HW's BP and his identification of the
author as Lord Cavan; sold to Arthur, 6d.

CELLINI, BENVENUTO   3181
Life. Written by himself and translated by Thomas Nugent. London,
  1771. Two volumes, 8vo.
  Not in MC.
  SH SALE, v.47 (with 8 *non*-Walpolian volumes), to Pickering, 15/–.

[1]

☞ The sale catalogue reads 'The Life of Benvenuto Cellini, 2 vols. 8vo.' Since all eight volumes sold with this were almost certainly *post*-1797, the Cellini may have been also; but one would expect that HW might have wanted this translation by Nugent. That he read it is clear from his question to the Earl of Strafford, 20 June 1771: 'Have you read the Life of Benvenuto Cellini, my Lord? I am angry with him for being more distracted and wrong-headed than my Lord Herbert.'

3182 CHARLTON, LIONEL

The history of Whitby, and of Whitby Abbey. York, 1779. 4to.

Not in MC.

SH SALE, v.52 (with Ledwich, Pole, and Watson), to Newman, Holborn, £2.12.6.

☞ Entered in the sale catalogue as 'Carleton.'

3183 COOK, JAMES

A voyage towards the South Pole and round the world [Second Voyage]. London, 1777. Two volumes, 4to.

Not in MC.

SH SALE, v.56, to — Jackson, Esq., £1.1.0.

☞ The sale catalogue reads only 'Cook's Voyages, 4to, fine impressions of the plates, 2.' This first edition of the Second Voyage seems the likeliest; HW wrote to Lady Ossory about the Third Voyage, 19 June 1784: 'Captain Cook's *Voyage* I have neither read nor intend to read. . . . My brother's death has made me poor, and I cannot now afford to buy everything I see.' Furthermore, the First Voyage was published in one volume, 1771, or in three volumes, by Hawkesworth in 1773 (in Press O, No. 2869 *above*); and the Third Voyage was also in three volumes, 1784.

3184 [COZENS, ZECHARIAH]

A tour through the Isle of Thanet. London, 1793. 4to.

Not in MC.

SH SALE, v.67 (with Cavan, Lucas, Napier, Tresham, and Wood), to Thorpe, £1.19.0.

☞ Not found in the SH SALE records is another book of local topography, George Hadley's *New and complete history of Kingston on Hull*, published in parts 1788–91, 4to. In his letter to Lady Ossory, 20 November 1796, HW wrote: 'Three days ago I received a portly quarto inscribed *History of Kingston on Hull*.' Since the work was only a bookseller's compilation, HW perhaps chose not to preserve it.

DALRYMPLE, Sir DAVID, Lord Hailes   3185

Annals of Scotland. Edinburgh, 1776–9. Two volumes, 4to.

Not in MC.

SH SALE, v.62 (with Sir John Dalrymple's *Memoirs of Great Britain*), to Strong, £2.

☞ *See* HW to Dalrymple, 12 March 1779: 'I have received this moment from your bookseller, Sir, the valuable present of the second volume of your *Annals*.'

DALRYMPLE, Sir JOHN   3186

Memoirs of Great Britain and Ireland. Edinburgh and London, 1771–88. Three volumes, 4to.

'Calf, gilt, with notes by HW.' Not in MC.

SH SALE, v.62 (with Sir David Dalrymple's *Annals*), to Strong, £2; Sotheby's, 20 February 1854 (a Collector, i.e., Rev. Charles Henry Crawford), lot 157, to Upham, £2.5.0; offered by Willis & Sotheran, 1866, lot 2906, for £1.1.0. (The third volume was apparently missing in 1866.)

☞ In a letter to Mason, 21 July 1772, HW classed this with a variety of dull antiquarian or occasional pieces, and reflected: 'What a figure will this our Augustan age make.' On the publication of the 2d volume, he wrote an angry letter to Mason, 2 March 1773, because of the charges against Algernon Sidney.

DUNSFORD, MARTIN   3187

Historical memoirs of the town and parish of Tiverton. Exeter, 1790. 4to.

Not in MC.

SH SALE, v.53 (with Hutchinson, Wallis, and Whitaker), to Longman, £2.15.0.

GIBBON, EDWARD   3188

The history of the decline and fall of the Roman Empire. London, 1776–88. Six volumes, 4to.

Rebound in half calf. The first volume is inscribed 'From the author,' not in Gibbon's hand. BP² in Volumes 1–5. Numerous notes by HW in the first volume and one note in the last volume. Not in MC.

SH SALE, v.64 (with the *Miscellaneous Works*), to Dr. Gray, Dean's-yard, £3.5.0; Sotheby's, 14 November 1930 (Findlay Sale), lot 950, to Quaritch, £104; Sotheby's, 29 March 1939 (Harmsworth Sale), lot 449, to Robinson for Lord Rothschild, £135. In Lord Rothschild's Catalogue, No. 942.

☞ Gibbon presented the first volume to HW in February 1776, and received two letters of thanks and praise in return; HW also praised Gibbon highly in a letter to Mason, 18 February 1776. In 1778, when Gibbon was planning his *Vindication* in reply to H. E. Davis's *Examination*, HW sent his copy of Davis to Gibbon, 'because I scribbled my remarks. I do not send them with the impertinent presumption of suggesting a hint to you, but to prove I did not grudge the trouble of going through such a book when you desired it, and to show how little struck me as of any weight. . . .'

The subject matter of Volumes 2 and 3 interested HW less: *see* his letters to Mason, 27 January 1781, concerning his interview with Gibbon; and 3 March 1781: 'Mr. Gibbon has treated [people] with his vast two volumes. I have almost finished the last, and some parts are more entertaining than the other, and yet it has tired me, and so I think it did himself. . . . He has made me a present of these volumes, and I am sure I shall have fully paid for them when I have finished them. . . . I was charmed, as I owned, with the enamel of the first volume, but I am tired by this rhetoric diction, and wish again for Bishop Burnet's *And so.*'

He enjoyed the last three volumes, however, especially the sixth volume. He wrote to Thomas Barrett, 5 June 1788: 'I finished Mr. Gibbon a full fortnight ago, and was extremely pleased. It is a most wonderful mass of information. . . . Mahomet and the Popes were gentlemen and good company.' And in rebuttal of Lady Ossory, he wrote to her, 8 November 1789: 'Mr. Gibbon never tires me,' when he was thinking of the sixth volume.

3189 GIBBON, EDWARD

Miscellaneous works. Edited by John Baker Holroyd, Earl of Sheffield. London, 1796. Two volumes, 4to.

Not in MC.

SH SALE, v.64 (with *Decline and Fall*), to Dr. Gray, Dean's-yard, £3.5.0.

3190 GILLIES, JOHN, Translator

The orations of Lysias and Isocrates. London, 1778. 4to.

Not in MC.

SH SALE, v.66 (with his *History*), to Pickering, 10/–.

3191 GILLIES, JOHN

The history of ancient Greece. London, 1786. Two volumes, 4to.

Not in MC.

SH SALE, v.66 (with his *Orations of Lysias*), to Pickering, 10/–.

☞ Gillies is mentioned by HW in his letters to Lady Ossory, 10 and 24 February 1789.

GILLINGWATER, EDMUND   3192

An historical account of the town of Lowestoft. London [1790]. 4to.

'Boards, uncut, with Orford BP.' Not in MC.

SH SALE, v.60 (with Jones, Parsons, Seward, and Walker), to Thorpe, £3.5.0; offered in Thorpe's Supplement for 1842, lot 12449, for 15/–.

HUTCHINSON, WILLIAM   3193

The history of the County of Cumberland, and some places adjacent. Carlisle, 1794. Three volumes, 4to.

Not in MC.

SH SALE, v.53 (with Dunsford, Wallis, and Whitaker), to Longman, £2.15.0.

☞ The sale catalogue lists three volumes, although the work was published in two. It seems likely that the extra volume here was actually the lost third volume (1794) of Hutchinson's Durham, in Press X, No. 3329 *below.*

JONES, Sir WILLIAM   3194

Sacontalá; or the fatal ring, an Indian drama. Translated from Kālidāsa. London, 1790. 4to.

'Boards, uncut.' Not in MC.

SH SALE, v.60 (with Gillingwater, Parsons, Seward, and Walker), to Thorpe, £3.5.0; offered in Thorpe's Supplement for 1842, lot 12645, for 12/–.

LEDWICH, EDWARD   3195

The antiquities of Ireland. Dublin, 1790. 4to.

Not in MC.

SH SALE, v.52 (with Charlton, Pole, and Watson), to Newman, Holborn, £2.12.6.

☞ Since the sale catalogue says only 'Antiquities of Ireland,' this may possibly have been one volume of Francis Grose's *Antiquities,* edited in 1791 by Ledwich; but Grose's work is probably what was in vii.1, in the Closet in the Round Tower.

3196 LUCAS, HENRY

Poems to Her Majesty. London, 1779. 4to.

Not in MC.

SH SALE, v.67 (with Cavan, Cozens, Napier, Tresham and Wood), to Thorpe, £1.19.0.

☞ Included in the volume was his tragedy, the *Earl of Somerset.* This volume of poems looks odd in Press S, but perhaps it was attracted by the 'Poems of George 3d' or perhaps its size alone determined its position among other works in quarto. Tresham, No. 3211 *below,* was similarly either misplaced or unexpectedly placed.

Although the book does not appear in any records of the sale, Dr. Lort sent to HW the proposals for Anne Penny's *Poems,* published by subscription in 1780, in 4to (Lort's letter, 18 May 1779). The printed list of subscribers includes 'The Honourable Horace Walpole,' who may have been not HW but his young cousin Horatio (1752–1822). But the book included lines 'Written upon viewing the seat of the Honourable Horace Walpole,' and a subscription would have been appropriate.

3197 MACAULAY, Mrs. CATHARINE, later Mrs. Graham

The history of England from the accession of James I. London, 1763–83. Nine volumes, 4to.

Press-mark C.5.33 in MC, entered by HW. The number of volumes was corrected up to five, in 1771; Kirgate later added in the margin: 'Library in the Offices.'

SH SALE, v.51, to Newman, Holborn, £2.2.0.

☞ Published in eight volumes, but the sale catalogue lists nine. The extra volume was no doubt her *History of England from the Revolution . . . in a series of letters to Dr. Wilson,* Bath, 1778, of which HW wrote to Mason, 16 March 1778: 'I ran through the book, had forgotten it, and only recollect it now to answer your question.'

At first HW spoke of the author with general approval; he wrote to Mason, 29 December 1763: 'Have you read Mrs. Macaulay? . . . It is the most sensible, unaffected, and best history of England that we have had yet.' But later he was more disturbed by her prejudice and her carelessness. He made a few notes from the fourth volume in his 'Book of Materials,' *ca.* 1768, and in 1783 he included her in a short list of 'Ladies and Gentlewomen distinguished by their writings, learning, or talents.' To Mason, 16 March 1778, he apologized for having given her a letter of introduction, apparently to Mme. du Deffand; to Mason, 3 February 1781, he merely mentioned the fact that Volumes 6 and 7 had appeared.

[6]

Possibly Mrs. Macaulay gave the books to HW, since a Kirgate letter of 16
July 1783 (just after the last volume appeared) inquired after Mrs.
Macaulay's address (HW to Mason, 3 Feb. 1781, n. 15).

MACPHERSON, JAMES 3198

*The history of Great Britain from the Restoration to the accession of
the House of Hanover.* London, 1775. Two volumes, 4to.

'Boards.' Not in MC.
SH SALE, v.65 (with his *Original Papers*), to Pickering, 10/–.

MACPHERSON, JAMES 3199

*Original papers; containing the secret history of Great Britain, from
the Restoration to the accession of the House of Hanover.* London, 1775. Two volumes, 4to.

'Boards.' Not in MC.
SH SALE, v.65 (with his *History*), to Pickering, 10/–. The four volumes
were offered in Payne & Foss's Catalogue for 1845, lot 607, for £3.3.0.

☞ *See* HW to Mason, 3 April 1775: 'For Macpherson, I stopped dead
short in the first volume; never was such a heap of insignificant trash and
lies. . . .' *See also* his exclamation to Mason, [November 1776]: 'When
one's pen can sink to him, it is time to seal one's letter.'

MARTIN, THOMAS 3200

The history of the town of Thetford. Edited by Richard Gough. London, 1779. 4to.

'Boards, uncut, with HW's BP and a few notes.' Not in MC.
SH SALE, v.54 (with Newcome, Williams, Worsley, and Wyndham), to
Strong, £2; offered in Thorpe's Supplement for 1842, lot 12763, for £1.1.0.

☞ Another copy was in Press O, No. 2902 *above*.

NAPIER, ARCHIBALD, 1st Baron Napier 3201

Memoirs of Archibald first Lord Napier: written by himself. Edinburgh, 1793. 4to.

Not in MC.
SH SALE, v.67 (with Cavan, Cozens, Lucas, Tresham, and Wood), to
Thorpe, £1.19.0.

3202 NEWCOME, PETER

The history of the . . . Abbey of St. Alban. London, 1793. 4to.

Not in MC.
SH SALE, v.54 (with Martin, Williams, Worsley, and Wyndham), to Strong, £2.

☞ *Apparently HW had two copies, the second in Press T, No. 3248 below.*

3203 PARSONS, PHILIP

The monuments and painted glass of . . . Kent. Canterbury, 1794. 4to.

'Boards, uncut, with Orford BP.' Not in MC.
SH SALE, v.60 (with Gillingwater, Jones, Seward, and Walker), to Thorpe, £3.5.0; offered in Thorpe's Supplement for 1842, lot 12924, for £2.12.6.

3204 PHILLIPS, THOMAS

The history and antiquities of Shrewsbury. Shrewsbury, 1779. 4to.

Not in MC.
SH SALE, v.61 (with Rowlands, Swinden, and Throsby), to Thorpe, £2.5.0.

3205 POLE, Sir WILLIAM

Collections towards a description of the County of Devon. London, 1791. 4to.

Not in MC.
SH SALE, v.52 (with Charlton, Ledwich, and Watson), to Newman, Holborn, £2.12.6.

☞ *The first edition of the sale catalogue reads: 'Poole's Collections towards the history of Devonshire,' and the later editions correct 'Poole' to 'Polwhele.' The corrector therefore thought of Richard Polwhele's History of Devonshire, 3 volumes, 1793–97; but the title is so much closer to Pole's work that I think Polwhele was a hurried bookseller's attempt to correct 'Poole.' Polwhele was in Press O, No. 2929 above.*

ROWLANDS, HENRY   3206

Mona antiqua restaurata, an archaeological discourse on the anti-quities, natural and historical, of the Isle of Anglesey. The 2d edition. London, 1766. 4to.

'Calf, with HW's BP.' Not in MC.

SH SALE, v.61 (with Phillips, Swinden, and Throsby), to Thorpe, £2.5.0; offered by Lasbury (assistant to the late William Strong) in 1848 for £1.1.0, and in 1849 for 18/–.

☞ The sale catalogue reads 'Rowland's History and Antiquities of Anglesea.' The supplement by Nicholas Owen, 1775, was in C.6 in the Main Library, No. 513 *above.*

SEWARD, ANNA   3207

Elegy on Captain Cook. London, 1780. 4to.

Not in MC.

SH SALE, v.60 (with Gillingwater, Jones, Parsons, and Walker), to Thorpe, £3.5.0.

☞ Mann sent four copies of Michel Angelo Gianetti's *Elogio del Capi-tano Cook* (with English translation by Robert Merry), Florence 1785, for which HW thanked Mann, 28 March 1786. On 21 June 1786, HW sent one copy of Gianetti to Richard Gough; but no doubt at least one of the other three copies was in some miscellaneous lot in 1842.

SWINDEN, HENRY   3208

The history and antiquities of Great Yarmouth in the County of Norfolk. Norwich, 1772. 4to.

Not in MC.

SH SALE, v.61 (with Phillips, Rowlands, and Throsby), to Thorpe, £2.5.0.

☞ Another copy was in Press O, No, 2962 *above.*

THROSBY, JOHN   3209

Select views in Leicestershire. Leicester, 1790–2. Two volumes, 4to.

Not in MC.

SH SALE, v.61 (with Phillips, Rowlands, and Swinden), to Thorpe, £2.5.0.

☞ Entered in the sale catalogue, by an easy confusion, as Thoresby.

3210 TINDAL, WILLIAM

The history and antiquities of the Abbey and Borough of Evesham.
Evesham, 1794. 4to.

'Boards, uncut.' Not in MC.

SH SALE, v.58 (with Baker), to Strong, £1.1.0; offered in Strong's Catalogue for 1843, lot 1502, for 10/6.

☞ *See* HW's comment about Tindal's book to Robert Nares, 12 October 1794: 'I can confidently say it deserves to be highly commended. . . . I am fond of English local history, a study, if it may be called so, that requires little but patience and a memory for trifles. . . .'

3211 [TRESHAM, HENRY]

The sea-sick minstrel; or maritime sorrows. A poem. London, 1796.
4to.

Not in MC.

SH SALE, v.67 (with Cavan, Cozens, Lucas, Napier, and Wood), to Thorpe, £1.19.0.

3212 WALKER, JOSEPH COOPER

Historical memoirs of the Irish bards. London, 1786. 4to.

'Boards, uncut.' Not in MC.

SH SALE, v.60 (with Gillingwater, Jones, Parsons, and Seward), to Thorpe, £3.5.0; offered in Strong's Catalogue for 1843, lot 1565, for 18/–.

☞ Three books from this lot were offered by Thorpe, but Strong describes Walker's *Irish Bards* as 'from the SH collection.'

3213 WALLIS, JOHN, A.M.

The natural history and antiquities of Northumberland. London, 1769. Two volumes, 4to.

Not in MC.

SH SALE, v.53 (with Dunsford, Hutchinson, and Whitaker), to Longman, £2.15.0.

3214 WARTON, THOMAS

History of English poetry. London, 1774–81. Three volumes, 4to.

'Boards, uncut, with interesting notes by HW.' Not in MC.

SH SALE, v.63 (with Watson), to Thorpe, £2.12.6; offered in Thorpe's Supplement for 1842, lot 13391, for £4.4.0.

☞ *See* HW's letters to Mason, 23 March 1774: 'I have just got Mr. Warton's *Life* of poetry, and it seems delightfully full of things I love'; 6 April 1774: 'At present I am immersed in Warton's *History of Poetry* . . .'; and 7 April 1774: 'Well, I have read Mr. Warton's book. . . . I never saw so many entertaining particulars crowded together with so little entertainment and vivacity. The facts are overwhelmed by one another, as Johnson's sense is by words: they are all equally strong. . . .' Of the second volume, HW wrote to Mason, 8 April 1778: 'I have dipped into Mr. Warton's second volume, which seems more unentertaining than the former. I perceive he excommunicates Rowley totally'; 18 April 1778: 'I have very near finished Warton, but, antiquary as I am, it was a tough achievement. . . . The latter chapters, especially on the progress and revival of the theatre, are more entertaining; however, it is very fatiguing to wade through the muddy poetry of three or four centuries that had never a poet.' Of the third volume, he wrote to Mason, 9 March 1781: 'I am now embarked in . . . Mr. Warton's third volume. This is the third immense history of the life of poetry, and still poetry is not yet born, for Spenser will not appear till the fourth tome. I perceive it is the certain fate of an antiquary to become an old fool. . . .'

WATSON, JOHN   3215

The history and antiquities of the parish of Halifax, in Yorkshire.
London, 1775. 4to.

Not in MC.

SH SALE, v.52 (with Charlton, Ledwich, and Pole), to Newman, Holborn, £2.2.0.

WATSON, ROBERT   3216

History of the reign of Philip the Second, King of Spain. London, 1777. Two volumes, 4to.

Not in MC.

SH SALE, v.63 (with Warton), to Thorpe, £2.12.6; probably the copy offered, but not identified as HW's, in Thorpe's Supplement for 1842, lot 13396, for £1.1.0.

☞ *See* HW to Lady Ossory, 23 December 1776: 'I am reading the *Life of Philip II*, by a professor of St. Andrews. I sent for it to see how a Scotchman would celebrate the barbarities of Philip, Cardinal Granville, and the Duke of Alva, in the United Provinces; but to my utter astonishment the man does not . . . fall in love with his hero. On the contrary, he is so just and explicit, that I believe even Dr. Franklin would admit him to kiss his hand. But I have read only the first volume.'

3217 WHITAKER, JOHN

The history of Manchester. London, 1771. 4to.

Not in MC.

SH SALE, v.53 (with Dunsford, Hutchinson, and Wallis), to Longman, £2.15.0.

3218 WILLIAMS, DAVID

The history of Monmouthshire. With plates by John Gardnor. London, 1796. 4to.

'Boards, uncut, with Orford BP.' Not in MC.

SH SALE, v.54 (with Martin, Newcome, Worsley, and Wyndham), to Strong, £2; offered in Thorpe's Supplement for 1842, lot 13411, for £2.2.0.

3219 WOOD, ANTHONY À

The history and antiquities of the Colleges and Halls in the University of Oxford. Edited by John Gutch. Oxford, 1786. 4to.

Not in MC.

SH SALE, v.67 (with Cavan, Cozens, Lucas, Napier, and Tresham), to Thorpe, £1.19.0.

☞ *See* HW to Lord Strafford, 29 August 1786: 'I have just been reading a new published History of the Colleges in Oxford, by Anthony Wood. . . .' And he made a number of extracts in his 'Book of Materials,' particularly about the works of art in the colleges.

3220 WORSLEY, Sir RICHARD

The history of the Isle of Wight. London, 1781. 4to.

'Blue morocco by Hayday; a few notes by HW.' Not in MC.

SH SALE, v.54 (with Martin, Newcome, Williams, and Wyndham), to Strong, £2; Sotheby's, 14 May 1847 (Eyton Sale), lot 207, to Newman, £1.11.6.

☞ *See* HW to Mason, 14 June 1781: 'I have been reading another courtier's book, Sir Richard Worsley's *History of the Isle of Wight.* It is dedicated to the King, and to himself too, for I see no reason for his writing it, but to call himself *Right Honourable.* . . .' Two days later he described the book to Cole: 'with many views poorly done enough.'

WYNDHAM, HENRY PENRUDDOCKE   3221

A tour through Monmouthshire and Wales. The 2d edition. Salisbury, 1781. 4to.

'Boards, uncut.' Not in MC.

SH SALE, v.54 (with Martin, Newcome, Williams, and Worsley), to Strong, £2; offered in Thorpe's Supplement for 1842, lot 13438, for £1.1.0.

☞ Thorpe quotes a note by HW: 'This is a sensible, impartial, and unaffected account.' A copy of the first edition was sold in Press Y, No. 3481 *below*.

POEMS   3222

Poems published in the Reign of King George the Third. Twenty-two volumes, containing 344 pieces, in 4to.

Calf, gilt, with HW's arms on sides of all volumes. Press-mark S.3 in each volume; in or about 1792, this set and the *London Chronicle* would therefore seem to have been installed in adjacent presses in the new Library in the Offices, and press-marks were then entered in the volumes: R.3 for the *London Chronicle* (No. 538 *above*) and S.3 for the Poems. Special title-pages (printed at the SH Press) in Volumes 1–8. Bookplate of Henry Labouchere, later Lord Taunton, in each volume.

SH SALE, v.57, to Thorpe, £8.18.6; offered in Thorpe's Supplement for 1842; Sotheby's, 2 December 1920 (Stanley Sale, i.e. books sold by Lord Taunton's grandson), lot 453, to Pickering, £230; offered in Pickering's Catalogue 194, for £375; given by Augustin H. Parker, 1924, to Harvard.

☞ Since HW did not keep strict chronological order in binding these volumes, it has seemed convenient to alphabetize each volume at the cost of separating a few related pieces. The contents follow:

Volume 1.   (1) *The Anti-Rosciad. By the Author.* 1761. An attempt to defend the actors against Churchill's *Rosciad*; published by Kearsley.

(2) CHURCHILL, CHARLES. *The apology. Addressed to the Critical Reviewers.* 1761. A few identifications by HW.

(3) [CHURCHILL, CHARLES] *Night. An epistle to Robert Lloyd.* 1761 [i.e. 1762]. The author is identified by HW on the title-page.

(4) CHURCHILL, CHARLES. *The Rosciad.* The 6th edition. 1762. Names filled in and many identifications by HW.

(5) *The Churchilliad: or, a few modest questions proposed to the Reverend Author of the Rosciad.* 1761.

(6) CUMBERLAND, RICHARD. *The banishment of Cicero. A tragedy.* 1761. Author's signature on the half-title.

3222   (7) [Garrick, David] *The Fribbleriad.* 1761. Note by hw on the title: 'said to be written by Mr. Garrick.' One identification by hw.

(8) Glover, Richard. *Medea. A tragedy.* 1761.

(9) Keate, George. *An epistle from Lady Jane Grey.* 1762. Date of publication marked by hw on the title-page: 'February 23d.' Ten years later, when hw was compiling some notes on Mary Lepel, Lady Hervey, he recorded that both his own *Anecdotes* and Keate's *Epistle* had been dedicated to her.

(10) Lloyd, Robert. *An epistle to C. Churchill.* 1761. One identification by hw.

(11) Murphy, Arthur. *The examiner, a satire.* 1761. Dated 'November' by hw on the title-page, and a number of identifications by him.

(12) Murphy, Arthur. *An ode to the Naiads of Fleet-Ditch.* 1761. One identification by hw.

(13) *The Rosciad of C–v–nt-g–rd–n.* 1762. Doubtfully attributed to Henry James Pye. Blanks in the text filled in by hw.

(14) [Thompson, Edward] *The Meretriciad.* 1761. A few identifications by hw.

(15) *Truth, in rhyme: addressed to a certain Noble Lord.* 1761. Marked by hw on the title-page: 'By David Mallet, Esq.,' and dated 'April.'

(16) Whitehead, William. *A charge to the poets.* 1762. Date of publication 'March 15' by hw; also one identification.

Volume 2.   (1) [Garrick, David] *The farmer's return from London. An interlude.* 1762. One allusion identified by hw, who also identified Garrick as author.

(2) Gray, Thomas. *Elegia scripta in coemeterio rustico Latinè reddita.* Translated by Christopher Anstey. Cambridge, 1762. With identification by hw of the translator on the title-page.

(3) [Jerningham, Edward] *The nunnery. An elegy in imitation of the Elegy in a Church-Yard.* The 2d edition. [1763?] The title-page marked by hw: 'By Mr. Jernegan.'

(4) Macdonald, Donald, *pseud. Three beautiful and important passages omitted by the translator of Fingal. Translated and restored by Donald Macdonald.* 1762. The identification by hw, 'By Mr. Hall,' i.e. Hall Stevenson, is very probably correct.

(5) Macpherson, James. *Fingal, an ancient epic poem.* 1762. Although hw thanked Dalrymple, 28 June 1760, for sending him Macpherson's *Fragments of ancient poetry*, 1760, in 8vo, the volume does not appear in the sh records.

(6) [STEVENSON, JOHN HALL] *Crazy tales.* 1762. The title-page marked by 3222 HW: 'By Anthony Hall, Esq.' i.e., John Hall Stevenson; also a few identifications.

Volume 3.   (1) CHURCHILL, CHARLES. *The ghost.* The 2d edition. 1762. The third book has separate title-page but continuous pagination. Identifications throughout by HW.

(2) MASON, WILLIAM. *Elegies.* 1763. Identifications by HW.

(3) *The Minister of state; a satire.* 1762. A few identifications by HW.

(4) OGILVIE, JOHN. *Poems on several subjects.* 1762.

Volume 4.   (1) BROWN, JOHN. *The cure of Saul. A sacred ode.* 1763. With HW's note: 'Set to music and performed twice.' He also noted the date of publication, 'Feb. 26.'

(2) BROWNE, Sir WILLIAM. *Ode, in imitation of Horace.* 1763. With HW's identification of John, Lord Montagu, to whom the poem was dedicated.

(3) CHURCHILL, CHARLES. *The prophecy of famine.* 1763. Dated by HW 'January 20th'; some identifications. Inserted in it is a folded broadside, *The staff of Gisbal*, a satire on John Stuart, 3d Earl of Bute.

(4) GRAHAM, GEORGE. *Telemachus, a mask.* 1763. With HW's note on the title: 'Never acted.'

(5) [JERNINGHAM, EDWARD] *The Magdalens: an elegy. By the author of the Nunnery.* 1763. With HW's identification of the author, 'Mr. Jernegan,' and he noted the date of publication, 'January 22d.' In his 'Book of Materials,' *ca.* 1772, when he was compiling notes about Mary Lepel, Lady Hervey, HW recorded that this poem was dedicated to her.

(6) KEATE, GEORGE. *The Alps, a poem.* 1763. Dated 'April' by HW.

(7) MACPHERSON, JAMES. *Temora, an ancient epic poem.* 1763.

(8) SCOTT, JAMES. *Every man the architect of his own fortune: or the art of rising in the Church.* 1763. A few identifications by HW.

(9) [STEVENSON, JOHN HALL] *A pastoral cordial, or, an anodyne sermon.* 1763. Marked by HW on the title-page, 'By Mr. Hall,' i.e. Hall Stevenson, and dated 'January'; he also identified several allusions.

(10) THORNTON, BONNELL. *An ode on Saint Caecilia's Day, adapted to the ancient British musick.* 1763. The date of publication, 'June,' marked by HW.

Volume 5.   (1) [BENTLEY, RICHARD] *Patriotism, a mock heroic.* 1763. With HW's note 'By Mr. Bentley' on the title, date of publication, 'November,' and some marginal notes. His copy of the 2d edition, in 8vo, is now at Farmington in the octavo 'Poems of George the 3d.'

3222 (2) CHURCHILL, CHARLES. *The author.* 1763. Dated 'December' by HW, and a few identifications by him.

(3) CHURCHILL, CHARLES. *The conference.* 1763. Dated 'November 25th' by HW, and a few identifications by him.

(4) CHURCHILL, CHARLES. *The duellist.* 1764. Dated 'Jan. 20th' by HW, and many identifications by him. To Lord Hertford, 22 January 1764, HW described this poem as the finest and bitterest of Churchill's works.

(5) CHURCHILL, CHARLES. *An epistle to William Hogarth.* 1763. Three engravings by Hogarth inserted, and numerous notes by HW.

(6) CHURCHILL, CHARLES. *The ghost. Book IV.* (Paged and signed to follow Book III.) 1763. Numerous identifications by HW.

(7) [CORYATE, GEORGE] *Descriptio Angliae, et descriptio Londini.* 1763. Note on the title, apparently by Dr. Ducarel: 'The original MS is in the library of Rob. Lumley Kingston, Esq., F.S.A., of Dorchester.' With HW's identification of the publisher, i.e. editor, as Dr. Ducarel.

(8) *The Crisis. An ode, to John Wilkes, Esq.* 1763. With HW's date of publication, 'November,' and a few identifications by him.

(9) *Ingratitude. A poem. Inscribed to the most grateful of mankind.* 1764. With HW's date on the title, 'February,' and extensive notes by him.

(10) [JERNINGHAM, EDWARD] *The nun, an elegy. By the author of the Magdalens.* 1764. Identification by HW on the title: 'Edward Jernegan, Esq., 2d son of Sr. George Jernegan'; and date of publication, 'January 28th.'

(11) *The Three conjurors, a political interlude. Stolen from Shakespeare.* Dedicated to Wilkes. [1763?] Identifications by HW.

(12) *Verses addressed to no Minister* [i.e. William Pitt]. 1763. Date of publication on the title-page, 'September,' and a few identifications by HW.

Volume 6.   (1) CHURCHILL, CHARLES. *The candidate.* 1764. Dated 'May 11th' by HW, and his identifications and notes throughout.

(2) CHURCHILL, CHARLES. *The farewell.* 1764. Dated 'June 18th' by HW, and a few identifications by him.

(3) CHURCHILL, CHARLES. *Gotham.* Books I–III (with separate title-pages). 1764. Dated February 21st, March 26th, and August 10th, respectively, by HW, and some notes by him in Book I.

(4) CHURCHILL, CHARLES. *Independence.* 1764. Dated 'September 29th' by HW, and numerous identifications by him.

(5) CHURCHILL, CHARLES. *The times.* 1764. Dated 'Sept. 4' by HW, and a 3222
few identifications. When Churchill died, HW sent to Mann a careful
critique of his poetry, 15 November 1764.

(6) [GENTLEMAN, FRANCIS] *The general. A poem. . . . By the author of
A trip to the moon.* 1764. With HW's date of publication, 'August,' and a
few identifications by him.

(7) GOLDSMITH, OLIVER. *The traveller, or a prospect of society.* 1765.
Dated 'December' by HW, who changed the imprint to 1764.

(8) [JERNINGHAM, EDWARD] *An elegy written among the ruins of an abbey.
By the author of the Nun.* 1765. Dated 'March 23d' by HW.

(9) KEATE, GEORGE. *The ruins of Netley Abbey.* 1764. Dated 'March 30th'
by HW.

(10) [KEATE, GEORGE] *The Temple-student: an epistle to a friend.* 1765.
On the title-page HW identified the author and dated it, but the binder
cropped the date.

(11) [KELLY, HUGH] *An elegy to the memory of the Right Honourable
William* [Pulteney], *late Earl of Bath.* 1765. Date of publication, 'January 11th,' by HW.

(12) POTTER, JOHN. *The choice of Apollo: a serenata. . . . The music composed by Mr. William Yates.* 1765. With HW's note on the title: 'Acted
Mar. 11th.'

(13) SHIRLEY, WILLIAM. *Electra, a tragedy.* 1765. Dated 'May' by HW.

(14) [STEVENSON, JOHN HALL] *A pastoral puke. A second sermon preached
before the people called Whigs. By an Independent.* 1764. A few identifications by HW, and his identification of the author: 'By Anthony
Hall, Esq.' i.e., Hall Stevenson. Date of publication, 'April 12th,' by
HW.

(15) [STEVENSON, JOHN HALL, *supposed author*] *The sick monkey, a
fable.* [Addressed to Garrick.] 1765. Dated 'May' by HW, and identified
as 'By Antony Hall, Esq.' It is perhaps as likely that Garrick wrote the
satire himself, as a device to disarm criticism, but HW may have had some
knowledge of Hall Stevenson's authorship.

(16) [THOMPSON, Captain EDWARD] *The soldier. A poem. Inscribed to the
Honourable General Conway.* 1764. Identified by HW as 'By an Officer,'
and dated 'August'; a few identifications in text.

(17) *The Trial for murder, or, the siege of Calais besieg'd.* 1765.

(18) [WALPOLE, Sir EDWARD] *A poem on satire.* 1764. Marked by HW:
'Published January 31st 1765'; and in his 'Book of Materials,' January
1765, he carefully identified this as written by his brother.

3222 Volume 7.   (1) [ADAIR, JAMES MAKITTRICK] *The Methodist and mimick. A tale, in Hudibrastick verse. By Peter Paragraph.* 1766.

(2) AKENSIDE, MARK. *An ode to the late Thomas Edwards, Esq. Written in the year M.DCC.LI.* 1766. Pot folio, but leaves folded by the binder. Dated 'May 2d' by HW.

(3) ANSTEY, CHRISTOPHER. *The new Bath guide: or, memoirs of the B—R—D* [Blunderhead] *family.* 1766. Dated 'May' by HW, and he identified the author. His copy of the 2d edition is in his octavo volume of 'Poems of George 3d,' now WSL.

(4) *Anti-Thespis: or, a vindication of the principal performers at Drury-Lane Theatre.* 1767. With HW's date of publication, 'January 16th.'

(5) [BROWN, JOHN] *Ode to the Legislator Elect of Russia, on his being prevented from entering on his high office of civilization, by a fit of the gout.* 1766. A satire on 'Estimate' Brown, just before his sudden death. Dated 'August' by HW, and he identified the subject as 'Dr. Brown.'

(6) CASWALL, GEORGE. *The trifler. A satire.* 1767. Dated 'December' and imprint changed to 1766 by HW. Two identifications by him.

(7) [JERNINGHAM, EDWARD] *Yarico to Inkle, an epistle. By the author of the Elegy written among the ruins of an Abbey.* 1766.

(8) [KELLY, HUGH] *Thespis: or, a critical examination into the merits of all the principal performers belonging to Drury-Lane Theatre.* 1766. With HW's identification on the title: 'By Mr. Kelly,' and his date, 'November.'

(9) [MICKLE, WILLIAM JULIUS] *Pollio: an elegiac ode. Written in the wood near R— Castle, 1762.* Oxford, 1766.

(10) [PITT, WILLIAM, Earl of Chatham] *E--L of CH----M's apology.* 1766. A satire on Pitt's peerage. Dated 'November' by HW, and some identifications by him.

(11) [PITT, WILLIAM, Earl of Chatham] *An elegy on the late Rt. Hon. W......P..., Esq.* 1766. A satire on Pitt's peerage. With HW's publication date, 'August.'

(12) *The Rational Rosciad. . . . I. On the stage in general and particular. . . . II. On the merits of the principal performers. . . . By F— B— L—.* 1767. Dated 'February' by HW.

(13) *The Scourge, a satire. Part I.* 1765. A few identifications by HW.

(14) STAMMA, LOUIS. *The Kellyad: or a critical examination into the merits of Thespis.* 1767. With HW's date of publication, 'January 16th.' The *Monthly Review* suggested that the name is a pseudonym.

(15) *The Tears of Twickenham*. 1766. A satire on George Grenville. Dated   3222
'April 29' by HW, and a few identifications. Lysons, in his *Environs of London*, iii.511, attributed the authorship to John Cosens.

(16) WODHULL, MICHAEL. *The equality of mankind*. Oxford, 1765. A few identifications by HW.

Volume 8.   (1) [ANSTEY, CHRISTOPHER] *On the much lamented death of the Marquis of Tavistock* [Francis Russell]. 1767. Dated 'April the 1st' and the author identified by HW; also two notes.

(2) [ANSTEY, CHRISTOPHER] *The patriot*. 1767. Dated 'Dec. 5th' and the author identified by HW, with a few other identifications.

(3) [BENTLEY, RICHARD] *Philodamus. A tragedy*. 1767. Dated 'April the 21st' and the author identified by HW.

(4) BROWNSMITH, JOHN. *The rescue: or, Thespian scourge. Being a critical enquiry into the merit of a poem, intituled Thespis. . . . Written in Hudibrastic verse*. 1767. Dated 'February 20th' by HW.

(5) [COWPER, Dr. WILLIAM, of Chester] *Il Penseroso. An evening's contemplation in St. John's Church-yard, Chester*. 1767. Dated 'April 16th' by HW.

(6) JAGO, RICHARD. *Edge-Hill, or, the rural prospect delineated and moralized*. 1767. Dated 'May 2d' by HW. His name is not in the list of subscribers.

(7) [JERNINGHAM, EDWARD] *Il Latte. An elegy*. 1767. Dated 'February 23d' and author identified, 'By Mr. Jernegan,' by HW.

(8) KELLY, D. *Molly White: or the bride bewitched*. 1767.

(9) KELLY, HUGH. *Thespis: or, a critical examination into the merits of all the principal performers belonging to Covent-Garden Theatre. Book the Second*. 1767. Dated 'February 12th' by HW, and one identification.

(10) *Momus, a poem; or a critical examination into the merits of the performers . . . at the Theatre Royal in the Hay-market*. [1767?] Attributed doubtfully to George Saville Carey. Dated 'July' by HW, and he made three identifications.

(11) *The Rise and progress of the present taste in planting parks, pleasure grounds, gardens, &c*. Addressed to Charles Ingram, Viscount Irwin. 1767. A few identifications by HW, who dated it 'June 3d.' He alluded to this poem in his *Essay on Modern Gardening*.

(12) *The Vanity of human life, a monody. Sacred to the memory of . . . Francis Russel, Marquis of Tavistock*. 1767. Dated 'April 16th' by HW.

Volume 9.   (1) [ANSTEY, CHRISTOPHER] *Appendix to the Patriot*. Cambridge, 1768. Paged to follow the *Patriot*. Author identified by HW.

3222   (2) [CARTWRIGHT, EDMUND] *Constantia, an elegy.* 1768. Dated 'September' by HW.

(3) *An Epistle from N———y P—————s to his Grace the Duke of G—————n* [Nancy Parsons, later Viscountess Maynard, to the Duke of Grafton]. 1769.

(4) *Friendship: a poem.* 1769. Included is a letter presenting the poem to HW, and asking that his reply be addressed to F. W.

(5) [GRAY, THOMAS] *Ode performed in the Senate-house at Cambridge, ... at the installation of His Grace Augustus-Henry Fitzroy, Duke of Grafton. ... Set to music by Dr. Randal.* The 2d edition. Cambridge, 1769. William Cole sent this 2d edition (the first edition being exhausted) on 3 August 1769.

(6) JAGO, RICHARD. *Labour, and genius.* 1768. Dated 'March 28th' by HW.

(7) JERNINGHAM, EDWARD. *Amabella, a poem.* 1768. Dated 'February 15th' by HW.

(8) KEATE, GEORGE. *Ferney: an epistle to Monsr. de Voltaire.* 1768. Dated 'January 29th' by HW.

(9) KEATE, GEORGE. *Netley Abbey.* The 2d edition. 1769.

(10) KENRICK, WILLIAM. *An epistle to G. Colman.* 1768. Dated 'February 22d' by HW, and one identification by him.

(11) *The Masquerade; a poem.* To Christian VII, King of Denmark. 1768. Dated 'November' by HW, who identified the author as 'Mr. Griffith' and added several notes.

(12) *An Ode upon the present period of time.* To George Grenville. 1769. Attributed by HW to Henry Seymour (*d.* 1805).

(13) *A Pindarick ode on painting. Addressed to Joshua Reynolds, Esq.* 1767. Dated 'May 16th' by HW, and one note by him. The author was Thomas Morrison: *see* Augustan Reprint, ed. F. W. Hilles, 1952.

(14) [STEVENSON, JOHN HALL] *Makarony fables.* 1768. Dated 'January 19th' by HW, and identified as 'By Mr. Ant. Hall,' i.e. Hall Stevenson; a few identifications by HW.

(15) THORNTON, BONNELL. *The battle of the wigs.* 1768. With HW's date of publication, 'February 13th 1768'; since the title-page and 'Advertisement' are wanting, he also added Thornton's name on the half-title.

Volume 10.   (1) *Anti-Midas: A Jubilee preservative.* 1769. A defence of Garrick's *Ode.* Dated 'December 16th' by HW.

(2) *The Auction a poem.* 1770. Dated 'February' by HW.

(3) [CAREY, GEORGE SAVILLE] *The magic girdle: a burletta.* 1770. Dated 'July' by HW.

(4) [CHURCHILL, W.] *The temple of corruption, a poem.* 1770. (The 3222
name 'W Churchill' is in MS on title.) Dated 'Feb. 8th' by HW.

(5) *An epistle to Lord Holland.* 1769. Dated 'Feb. 8th' by HW; and a few
identifications.

(6) [GARRICK, DAVID] *An ode upon dedicating a building and erecting a
statue, to Shakespeare, at Stratford.* 1769. The author is identified by
HW, and the poem dated 'September.'

(7) GOLDSMITH, OLIVER. *The deserted village.* 1770. Dated 'May 28' by
HW.

(8) [JERNINGHAM, EDWARD] *The deserter: a poem.* 1770. Dated 'January
29th' by HW.

(9) *The Ode on dedicating a building, and erecting a statue, to Le Stue,
cook to the Duke of Newcastle.* Oxford, 1769. A parody of Garrick's
Ode.

(10) *Ode to Palinurus.* 1770. A political satire. Dated 'March 15th' by HW,
and some identifications.

(11) [SHEPHERD, RICHARD] *Hector, a dramatic poem.* 1770. Dated 'March
16th' by HW.

(12) [STEVENSON, JOHN HALL] *Fables for grown gentlemen, for the year
1770.* 1770. Dated 'January' by HW, and some notes by him; he identified the author as 'Antony Hall, Esq.'

(13) [THOMPSON, EDWARD] *Trinculo's trip to the Jubilee.* 1769. Dated
'November' by HW.

Volume 11.   (1) [BEATTIE, JAMES] *The minstrel: or, the progress of
genius. A poem. Book the First.* 1771. With HW's note on the title: 'By
Mr. Beattie.'

(2) [CAREY, GEORGE SAVILLE] *The noble pedlar: a burletta.* 1770.

(3) [CARTWRIGHT, EDMUND] *Armine and Elvira, a legendary tale.* 1771.
With HW's notes on the title: 'By Mr. Jerningham, May'; but Cartwright
is almost certainly the author.

(4) *An Elegy written in Covent-Garden.* [1771?] Dated 'March 1771' by
HW. A parody of Gray.

(5) *The Exhibition in Hell; or, Moloch turn'd painter.* [1771?] Dated
'Feb. 15, 1771' by HW.

(6) JERNINGHAM, EDWARD. *The funeral of Arabert, Monk of La Trappe.*
1771. Dated 'March' by HW.

(7) LANGHORNE, JOHN. *The fables of Flora.* The 3d edition. 1771.

(8) LOVE, JAMES. *Cricket. An heroic poem.* 1771. Dated 'March' by HW.

(9) *The Magnet. A musical entertainment.* 1771. Dated 'June' by HW.

3222   (10) [Percy, Thomas, Bishop] *The hermit of Warkworth*. 1771. With HW's note 'Dr. Percy' at the end of the dedicatory poem.

(11) Smith, George. *Six pastorals*. 1770.

(12) *The Triumphs of Bute. A poem*. 1770. A satire on the Earl of Bute.

Volume 12.   (1) Carlisle, Frederick Howard, 5th Earl of. *Poems*. The 3d edition. 1773.

(2) [Chatterton, Thomas] *The execution of Sir Charles Bawdin*. 1772. Dated 'May 15th' by HW. He wrote to Mason, 25 May 1772: 'Somebody, I fancy Dr. Percy, has produced a dismal dull ballad, called *The Execution of Sir Charles Bawdin*, and given it for one of the Bristol poems, called Rowley's—but it is a still worse counterfeit than those that were first sent to me.'

(3) [Delamayne, Thomas Hallie] *The patricians. . . . By the author of the Senators*. 1773. Dated 'February' by HW, and numerous identifications by him.

(4) [Delamayne, Thomas Hallie] *The senators*. 1772. Dated 'May 2d' by HW, and numerous identifications by him.

(5) [Delamayne, Thomas Hallie] *The senators*. The 2d edition. 1772. Numerous identifications by HW.

(6) *An Epistle from Mrs. B[ail]y to His R[oya]l H[ighne]ss the D[uke] of C[umberlan]d: or, Beauty scourging rank*. 1772. Dated 'January' by HW; some identifications by him.

(7) *An Irregular ode, occasioned by the death of Mr. Gray*. 1772. Dated 'January 8th' by HW.

(8) Jerningham, Edward. *Faldoni and Teresa*. 1773. Dated 'February' by HW.

(9) Mason, William. *The English garden: a poem. Book the First*. 1772. Dated 'February 10th' by HW, and numerous marginal markings by him. Mason told Alderson that a thousand copies of this first edition 'went off' in a week.

(10) [Mason, William] *An heroic epistle to Sir William Chambers*. 1773. Dated 'February' by HW, and numerous identifications by him.

(11) [Maude, Thomas] *Wensley-Dale; or rural contemplations*. The 2d edition. Published for the benefit of the General Infirmary at Leeds. 1772.

(12) *The Theatres. A poetical dissection. By Sir Nicholas Nipclose, Baronet*. 1772. Dated 'December 1771' by HW.

(13) [Walpole, Sir Edward] *A sketch of the times, for A. D. 1769, corrected and enlarged: and now reprinted for A. D. 1771*. 1771. Laid in

HW's MS *Journal of . . . George the 3d* is a copy of the original edition of 3222
1769, with a few notes by HW.

Volume 13.   (1) [ANSTEY, CHRISTOPHER] *The priest dissected.* Bath
[1774]. Dated 'June 1774' by HW.

(2) BEATTIE, JAMES. *The minstrel. . . . The Second Book.* 1774.

(3) *Charity: a poetical essay.* 1774. Note by HW 'Supposed to be written by
[Charles Manners] the Marquis of Granby.'

(4) CLARE, JOHN FITZGIBBON, Earl of. *Verses addressed to the Queen, with a
New Year's gift of Irish manufacture.* 1775. Dated 'January 7th' by HW.

(5) [COURTENEY, JOHN] *The rape of Pomona.* The 2d edition. 1773. Some
identifications by HW.

(6) *Female artifice; or, Charles F-x outwitted.* 1774. A satire on Charles
James Fox, who had hoped to marry an heiress. Dated 'February' by HW,
who also identified the go-between as Mrs. Grieve.

(7) *La Fête champêtre.* The 2d edition. 1774. A satire on the party given
at the Oaks by Edward Smith-Stanley, later Earl of Derby, in honor of
his approaching marriage: HW wrote Mann, 8 June 1774, that it would
cost £5000; on 19 June he wrote Sir William Hamilton, apparently in
deliberate exaggeration, that it had cost half a million. Some identifications by HW.

(8) [FIELDING, —] *The asylum. A poem. By a gentleman.* 1773. Identified
by HW as by a 'son of Henry Fielding, author of *Tom Jones*, &c.' The
poem is dedicated to Sir John Fielding.

(9) *The Genius of Britain. An ode. In allusion to the present times.* 1775.
Dated 'February 14th' by HW.

(10) GOLDSMITH, OLIVER. *Retaliation: a poem.* 1774. Dated 'April 19th' by
HW, and some identifications by him.

(11) [GOLDSMITH, OLIVER] *An impartial character of the late Doctor Goldsmith, with a word to his encomiasts.* 1774. A few blanks filled in by
HW.

(12) *The Graces: a poetical epistle from a gentleman to his son.* 1774. By
William Woty. Identified by HW: 'A satire on Lord Chesterfield's
Letters.' Some identifications by HW.

(13) HULL, THOMAS. *Richard Plantagenet; a legendary tale.* 1774.

(14) [JERNINGHAM, EDWARD] *The Swedish curate.* 1773. Dated 'May' by
HW. Dedicated to HW.

(15) KEATE, GEORGE. *The monument in Arcadia: a dramatic poem.* 1773.
Dated 'May' by HW, and one identification by him.

3222   (16) *Kien Long. A Chinese imperial eclogue. Translated . . . and inscribed by the translator to the author of an Heroic Epistle to Sir William Chambers.* 1775. A satire. Dated 'February 14th' by HW.

(17) MARRIOTT, GEORGE. *The Jesuit. An allegorical poem.* 1773. Dated 'May' by HW.

(18) [MASON, WILLIAM] *An heroic postscript to the public, occasioned by their favourable reception of a late Heroic Epistle.* 1774. Dated 'February 10th' by HW, and a few identifications by him.

(19) *A Mob in the pit: or, lines addressed to the D—ch—ss of A— — — — —ll.* 1773. On Elizabeth Gunning, Duchess of Argyle. Dated 'May' by HW, and numerous identifications by him.

(20) *The Muses and graces on a visit to Grosvenor Square. Being a collection of original songs sung by the maskers, at Mrs. Crewe's elegant ball, Tuesday, March 21, 1775.* 1775. Ballads by Lady Craven, Mrs. Crewe, and others. Notes by HW, who identified the authors as 'Dr. Thomas Frankland,' i.e., Thomas Francklin, Sir Charles Bingham, Lady Craven, &c.

(21) [NUGENT, ROBERT, Viscount Clare and later Earl Nugent] *Faith: a poem.* 1774. Identified by HW: 'By Robert Nugent, Viscount Clare' and dated 'March' by him.

(22) OBEREA, *pseud. An epistle from Oberea, Queen of Otaheite, to Joseph Banks.* 1774. Possibly by John Scott, of Amwell.

(23) *An Ode, sacred to the memory of the late Right Honourable George Lord Lyttelton.* 1773. Dated 'September' by HW.

(24) *The Pantheon, a poem.* 1773. A satire. Dated 'August' by HW, and numerous identifications by him.

(25) [PILON, FREDERICK] *The drama, a poem.* 1775. Also attributed, less probably, to Hugh Downman. Dated 'March' by HW.

(26) *The Silver tail, a tale. In two heroic epistles, from Mr. S—z, of the Exchequer, to Signora A**j**e; with Signora A***j**'s answer to Mr. S***z.* 1775. On the tax controversy between Charles Schutz and Lucrezia Agujari. Several notes by HW.

(27) *Verses addressed to the —. With a New Year's gift of Irish potatoes. By Lord knows who.* 1775. A parody of Lord Clare's poem *above*. Dated 'February 14th' by HW.

Volume 14.   (1) CUMBERLAND, RICHARD. *Odes.* 1776. Dated 'March' by HW. In his 'Book of Materials,' 1776, HW recorded that the book was dedicated to George Romney, and then later he forgetfully made a second, similar note. A few marginal markings by HW.

(2) [DAY, THOMAS] *The devoted legions.* 1776. On the American War.   3222
Dated 'February' by HW.

(3) [DUNCOMBE, JOHN] *A parody on Gray's Elegy. By an Oxonian.* 1776.
Dated 'March' by HW.

(4) GOLDSMITH, OLIVER. *The haunch of venison.* 1776. Two notes by HW.

(5) GRAY, THOMAS. *The bard.* Translated into Latin [by Rev. R. Williams]. Chester, 1775.

(6) GRAY, THOMAS. [*The bard*] *Ode Pindarica, pro Cambriae vatibus
Latino carmine reddita.* Cambridge, 1775. With HW's identification of
the translator, Edward Burnaby Greene, 'now a rich brewer in Westminster.' Cole sent these two translations of the *Bard* to HW, 24 December 1775, and told him that Greene was a rich brewer.

(7) GRAY, THOMAS. *The Latin odes of Mr. Gray, in English verse, with an
Ode on the death of a favourite spaniel.* 1775. With HW's identification
of the author, Edward Burnaby Greene, and date of publication,
'December.'

(8) JERNINGHAM, EDWARD. *The fall of Mexico.* 1775.

(9) [MAN, HENRY] *Cloacina; a comi-tragedy.* 1775. Dated 'May 1st' by
HW, with numerous identifications by him.

(10) MASON, WILLIAM. *The English garden. Book the Second.* [York,
1776] This was a privately printed edition, with no title-page. In his
letter of 20 May 1776 HW thanked Mason for it; the published edition
appeared in April 1777.

(11) [MASON, WILLIAM] *Ode to Mr. Pinchbeck, upon his newly invented
patent candle-snuffers. By Malcolm M'Greggor, [pseud.]* 1776. Dated
'May' by HW, and identifications by him.

(12) [MASON, WILLIAM] *Pro-Pinchbeck's answer to the Ode.* 1776.

(13) [MAURICE, THOMAS] *Hagley. A descriptive poem.* Oxford, 1776.
Dated 'December' by HW.

(14) MAURICE, THOMAS. *Netherby: a poem.* Oxford, 1776.

(15) MORE, HANNAH. *Sir Eldred of the Bower, and the Bleeding Rock.*
1776. Dated 'December 22d 1775' by HW.

(16) [PENTYCROSS, THOMAS] *Wittenham-Hill, a poem.* 1776. Title-page
marked by HW: 'By Mr. Pentycross.'

(17) POPE, ALEXANDER. *Poema Alexandri Pope De Homine, Jacobi Thomson, & Thomae Gray selecta carmina.* Translated by Giovanni Costa.
Padua, 1775.

(18) [PRATT, SAMUEL JACKSON] *The Tears of genius: an elegy. By Courtney Melmoth, [pseud.].* The 2d edition. 1775.

3222 (19) REEVE, JOSEPH. *Ugbrooke Park: a poem.* 1776.

(20) SCOTT, JOHN, of Amwell. *Amwell: a descriptive poem.* 1776. Dated 'April 5th' by HW; he wrote Mason, 8 April 1776: 'I bought yesterday a poem in blank verse called *Amwell. . . .*'

(21) SHERIDAN, RICHARD BRINSLEY. *Songs, duets, trios, &c. in the Duenna.* The 15th edition. 1776.

(22) *Sonnets, printed for the author.* [1776?]

(23) [WHITEHEAD, WILLIAM] *Variety. A tale, for married people.* 1776. Marked on the title-page 'By William Whitehead,' and dated 'February' by HW. In his 'Book of Materials,' *ca.* 1776, HW noted that the poem contains a 'just compliment to Mr. Wyat [James Wyatt] on the Pantheon.'

Volume 15.   (1) [ANSTEY, CHRISTOPHER] *Ad C. W. Bampfylde, Arm: epistola poetica familiaris.* Bath, 1776.

(2) ANSTEY, CHRISTOPHER. *An election ball in poetical letters from Mr. Inkle.* The 2d edition. Bath, 1776.

(3) BEAVAN, EDWARD. *Box-Hill: a descriptive poem.* 1777.

(4) [BURGESS, THOMAS, Bishop] *Bagley; a descriptive poem.* Oxford, 1777.

(5) [BURNET, Sir THOMAS] *Verses written on several occasions between the years 1712 and 1721.* 1777. With HW's identification on the title: 'By Judge Burnet'; and a few identifications by him. In his 'Book of Materials,' *ca.* 1780, HW commented that Burnet was a poet but not a great one.

(6) [COMBE, WILLIAM] *The diaboliad.* 1777. Dated 'January,' with HW's identification of the author, and other identifications. In his 'Book of Materials' HW described Combe's career briefly and recorded some anecdotes.

(7) [COMBE, WILLIAM] *Additions to the diaboliad.* 1777. Some identifications by HW.

(8) [COMBE, WILLIAM] *The diaboliad. Part the Second.* 1778. Identifications by HW.

(9) [COMBE, WILLIAM] *The diabo-lady: or, a match in Hell.* 1777. Identifications by HW. In his 'Book of Materials' HW inserted with approval a satirical attack on Combe printed in the *General Advertiser* by Richard Griffith.

(10) [COMBE, WILLIAM] *The Duchess of Devonshire's cow; a poem.* 1777.

(11) [COMBE, WILLIAM] *The first of April: or, the triumphs of folly.* A new edition. 1777. One identification by HW.

[26]

(12) [COMBE, WILLIAM] *An heroic epistle to the noble author of the* 3222
Duchess of Devonshire's cow. 1777.

(13) [COMBE, WILLIAM] *A poetical epistle to Sir Joshua Reynolds.* 1777.

(14) [COMBE, WILLIAM] *The justification: a poem.* 1777.

(15) CRAWFORD, CHARLES. *Richmond Hill. A poem.* 1777.

(16) DODINGTON, GEORGE BUBB. *A poetical epistle from the late Lord Mel-*
combe to the Earl of Bute: with corrections by the author of the Night
Thoughts. 1776. Dated 'April 8th' by HW, but his letter to Mason, 18 February 1776, shows that he had read the poem, and it was in fact published 13 February. The title-page is dirty, so that HW may have left the
poem unprotected for some time, and then added the wrong date somewhat later.

(17) [ELLIS, GEORGE] *Bath: its beauties, and amusements.* [Bath?] 1776.
With HW's identification of the author, and two notes by him.

(18) [GRAHAM, JAMES, Editor] *Six odes, presented to . . . Mrs. Catharine*
Macaulay, on her birthday. Bath [1777]. One note by HW.

(19) [MORE, HANNAH] *Ode to Dragon, Mr. Garrick's house-dog.* 1777.

(20) *Poetical excursions in the Isle of Wight.* 1777.

(21) [PRESTON, WILLIAM] *An heroic epistle from Donna Teresa Pinna y*
Ruiz, of Murcia, to Richard Twiss. Printed from the Dublin 3d edition,
1777. (With his *Heroic answer from Richard Twiss at Rotterdam.*)
Satires on Twiss's *Travels.*

(22) *The Prospect from Malvern Hill: or, liberty bewailing her injuries in*
America. A poem. By a Gentleman of the Inner Temple. 1777. The
dedication is signed: M. D—.

(23) SINGLETON, JOHN. *A description of the West-Indies.* 1776.

(24) STRONG, ADAM, *pseud. The electrical eel; or, Gymnotus electricus.*
The 3d edition. 1777. Perhaps by the journalist James Perry.

(25) *Venus attiring the Graces. Address to —.* 1777. Marked by HW: 'To
the Duchess of Queensberry,' and dated 'May.'

(26) [WHITEHEAD, WILLIAM] *The goat's beard. A fable.* 1777. Author
identified by HW, and dated 'February 13th' by him. Two identifications.

Volume 16.   (1) [CARTWRIGHT, EDMUND] *The Prince of Peace; and other*
poems. 1779.

(2) [COMBE, WILLIAM] *The auction: a town eclogue.* The 2d edition. 1778.

(3) [COMBE, WILLIAM] *The world as it goes, a poem.* The 2d edition. 1779.
Numerous identifications by HW.

(4) *The Court of adultery: a vision.* A new edition, 1778.

3222 (5) [FOOTE, SAMUEL] *An elegy on the death of Samuel Foote, Esq. By Boschereccio.* 1778.

(6) [GERMAIN, Lord GEORGE] *An epistle to the Right Honourable Lord G————G——————.* 1778.

(7) [HAYLEY, WILLIAM] *A poetical epistle to an eminent painter.* 1778. Author identified by HW; in his 'Book of Materials,' HW noted that the painter was George Romney.

(8) HEARD, WILLIAM. *A sentimental journey to Bath, Bristol, and their environs; a descriptive poem.* 1778. Dedicated to Hannah More. The name of HW is not listed as a subscriber.

(9) *The Injured islanders: or, the influence of art upon the happiness of nature.* 1779. Because of its subject, the poem has been attributed to Captain Samuel Wallis. The preface is written from Trinity College, Dublin.

(10) JERNINGHAM, EDWARD. *The ancient English wake.* 1779. Dated 'November' by HW.

(11) *An Heroic epistle to an unfortunate monarch, by Peregrine the Elder.* 1778. Dated 'March' by HW. A satire on George III.

(12) [LUCAN, MARGARET BINGHAM, Countess of] *Verses on the present state of Ireland. By a Lady.* 1778. With HW's note: 'By Lady Lucan.'

(13) MASON, WILLIAM. *The English garden. Book the Third.* 1779. One identification, and a few marginal markings by HW.

(14) [MASON, WILLIAM] *An epistle to Dr. Shebbeare. . . . By Malcolm MacGreggor.* The 4th edition. 1777.

(15) MASON, WILLIAM. *Ode to the naval officers of Great Britain.* 1779.

(16) *Matrimonial overtures, from an enamour'd lady, to Lord G————G–rm——ne.* 1778. A satire.

(17) *A Ride and walk through Stourhead.* 1780. The imprint in error is MDCCLXIXX.

(18) ROUSSEAU, JEAN JACQUES. *Pygmalion, a poem.* Translated from the French. 1779.

(19) *Royal perseverance. A poem. Humbly dedicated to that Prince, whose piety, clemency . . . are the admiration of all mankind.* 1778. A satire on George III.

(20) *Ruin seize thee, ruthless King! A Pindaric ode, not written by Mr. Gray.* 1779. Dated 'December' by HW, and a few identifications.

(21) *The Scotch hut, a poem, addressed to Euphorbus; or, the Earl of the Grove.* 1779. A satire on Thomas Villiers, Earl of Clarendon. Some identifications by HW.

(22) [SHERIDAN, RICHARD BRINSLEY] *Verses to the memory of Garrick,* 3222
spoken as a monody at the Theatre Royal in Drury-Lane. 1779. Identified by HW as spoken 'By Mrs. Yates,' and dated 'March.'

(23) [TICKELL, RICHARD] *Epistle from the Honourable Charles Fox,*
partridge-shooting, to the Honourable John Townshend, cruising. 1779.
Identifications by HW, and dated 'November.'

(24) [TICKELL, RICHARD] *The project. A poem.* 1778. Dated 'February' by HW, with his notes and identifications.

(25) TICKELL, RICHARD *The wreath of fashion.* 1778. Dated 'April' by HW, with his notes and identifications. He wrote to Mason, 18 April 1778: 'There is a pretty poem just published called *The Wreath of Fashion*: it is written by one Tickell. . . . He wrote this winter another poem at least as good, called *The Project. . . .*'

(26) *Windsor: an ode; sacred to the birth-day of her Royal Highness,*
Charlotte Augusta Matilda. [Brentford] 1778. Author identified by HW as 'Dr. Cosins, Minister of Teddington.'

Volume 17.   (1) [ANSTEY, CHRISTOPHER] *Speculation; or, a defence of*
mankind. 1780. Dated 'February' by HW.

(2) *Catiline's conspiracy: a mirror of the times.* 1780. A few identifications by HW.

(3) [CRABBE, GEORGE] *The library. A poem.* 1781. Some notes by HW, and his identification: 'By Mr. Crab, bred an apothecary.'

(4) FEILDING, CHARLES JOHN. *The brothers, an eclogue.* 1781.

(5) HAYLEY, WILLIAM. *An essay on history.* 1780. A few comments by HW.

(6) HAYLEY, WILLIAM. *Ode, inscribed to John Howard.* 1780.

(7) HAYLEY, WILLIAM. *The triumphs of temper.* 1781. Marginal markings by HW. He had no great opinion of Hayley; *see, inter alia,* his letter to Mason, 25 June 1782: 'For Mr. Hayley himself, though he chants in good tune, . . . he has, I think, no genius, no fire, and not a grain of originality, the first of merits (in my eyes) in these latter ages. . . .' In an earlier letter, 3 March 1781, he complained that Hayley had no more ear or imagination than the Monthly Reviewers who called him a great poet.

(8) *Hobby-horses. Read at Bath-Easton.* 1780. Attributed to a Miss Winford. Dated 'March' by HW.

(9) [JENYNS, SOAME] *An ode.* 1780. With HW's note: 'Said to be written by Soame Jenyns,' and dated 'May.' He described it, in his letter to Mason, May 1780, as a 'paltry performance.'

3222 (10) KEATE, GEORGE. *An epistle to Angelica Kauffman.* 1781. Dated 'Febr. 27th' by HW, who also entered it in his 'Book of Materials.'

(11) [LYTTELTON, THOMAS, 2d Baron Lyttelton] *Poems by a young nobleman, of distinguished abilities, lately deceased.* 1780. A few identifications by HW. He wrote Mason, 4 January 1780: 'Some foolish friend . . . has published some paltry poems of the last Lord Lyttelton, that appear genuine, and discover no parts, which I have long believed he had not. There is a prefatory defence of his character, the badness of which the officious editor comprises in the love of women and gaming, and which were virtues compared with his other faults.'

(12) [MADAN, MARTIN] *An heroic epistle to the Rev. Martin M—d—n, author of a late treatise on polygamy.* 1780. A satire.

(13) *Poems fit for a bishop; which two bishops will read.* 1780. Attributed doubtfully to — Ellison. Dated 'February' by HW, who identified the two bishops as John Hinchliffe, Bishop of Peterborough, and Jonathan Shipley, Bishop of St. Asaph; both were friends of America.

(14) *Poetical epistle from Florizel* [George, *later* George IV] *to Perdita* [Mrs. Mary Robinson]: *with Perdita's answer.* 1781. Some identifications by HW.

(15) RYVES, ELIZABETH. *Ode to the Rev. Mr. Mason.* 1780.

Volume 18.   (1) [BAYNES, JOHN] *An archaeological epistle to the Reverend . . . Jeremiah Milles.* 1782. Dated 'March' by HW.

(2) [BULL, RICHARD] *Lines sent to Lady Miller's vase.* 1781. Identifications by HW; and notes apparently by Bull.

(3) DANTE ALIGHIERI. *The Inferno of Dante.* Translated by Charles Rogers. 1782. Dedicated to Sir Edward Walpole. When he castigated epic poetry in his letter to Mann, 25 June 1782, HW perhaps included Dante because he had just seen Rogers's *Inferno:* he asserted that Dante was 'extravagant, absurd, disgusting, in short a Methodist parson in Bedlam.'

(4) HAYLEY, WILLIAM. *An essay on epic poetry.* 1782. Scattered notes and markings by HW.

(5) [JERNINGHAM, EDWARD] *Honoria: or the Day of All Souls.* 1782. Identification of author by HW, 'by Mr. Jerningham.'

(6) JONES, Sir WILLIAM. *The muse recalled, an ode.* Strawberry Hill, 1781.

(7) [MASON, WILLIAM] *The dean and the 'squire.* 1782. Dated 'May' by HW, and some identifications by him.

(8) [MASON, WILLIAM] *The English garden: a poem, in four books.* York, 1781. General title, and the fourth book.

(9) MASON, WILLIAM. *Ode to the Honourable William Pitt.* 1782. Dated   3222
'May 28th' by HW.

(10) MICKLE, WILLIAM JULIUS. *Almada Hill: an epistle from Lisbon.* Oxford, 1781.

(11) *Orpheus, priest of nature, and prophet of infidelity.* The 2d edition. 1782. A satire on the Reverend David Williams.

(12) ROBINSON, POLLINGROVE. *The beauties of painting.* 1782. Dated 'May' by HW, who added an exclamatory marginal tick on p. 3 and a few other markings on the early pages.

(13) SEWARD, ANNA. *Poem to the memory of Lady Miller.* 1782.

(14) [STRATFORD, THOMAS] *The first book of Fontenoy, a poem.* 1782. On the title-page HW identified the author as 'an Irish clergyman' and dated it 'November.' He subscribed to ten copies in order to help the author; *see* his letter to Mason, 14 April 1782, for amusing comments on Stratford. He also sent a copy to Mrs. Garrick, who had subscribed; his letter to Mrs. Garrick speaks of 'Mrs. Stratford's poem,' because Agnes Stratford had seen her brother's poem through the press.

(15) [WARTON, THOMAS] *Verses on Sir Joshua Reynolds's painted window at New-College, Oxford.* 1782. Dated 'May 8th' by HW, and recorded in his 'Book of Materials.'

Volume 19.   (1) [BENTLEY, RICHARD] *Philodamus. A tragedy.* [1782]. With HW's note: 'By Richard Bentley, Esq. When performed it was reduced to four acts.' Originally produced and printed in 1767; *see* Volume 8 *above.*

(2) *The Christmas tale, a poetical address and remonstrance to the young Ministry.* 1784. Dated 'January' by HW, and identifications by him.

(3) COLLS, JOHN HENRY. *The poet, a poem; addressed to Mr. Jerningham.* 1785.

(4) CRABBE, GEORGE. *The news-paper: a poem.* 1785.

(5) CRABBE, GEORGE. *The village: a poem.* 1783.

(6) [HOBHOUSE, THOMAS] *Kingsweston Hill. A poem.* 1785.

(7) HORATIUS FLACCUS, QUINTUS. *The art of poetry.* Translated by George Colman, the Elder. 1783. Colman presented his work to HW, who thanked him on 10 May with extremely favorable comments. Some notes by HW. The draft of HW's letter has been inserted in the first volume of this set.

(8) IRWIN, EYLES. *Occasional epistles. Written during a journey from London to Busrah, in the Gulf of Persia.* 1783. Dated 'June' by HW. Addressed to William Hayley.

3222   (9) JERNINGHAM, EDWARD. *The rise and progress of the Scandinavian poetry*. 1784.

(10) JODRELL, RICHARD PAUL. *The knight and friars; an historick tale*. 1785. Dated 'February' by HW.

(11) *Ode to Lansdown-Hill, with notes, mostly relative to the Granville family; to which are added, two letters of advice from George* [Granville] *Lord Lansdown, Anno MDCCXI, to William Henry* [Grenville] *Earl of Bath*. 1785.

(12) SARGENT, JOHN. *The mine: a dramatic poem*. 1785. Another edition is listed *above*, No. 2951.

(13) TASKER, WILLIAM. *Annus mirabilis; or, the eventful year eighty-two*. Exeter [1783].

(14) *The Voluntary exile, a political essay*. 1784. Some identifications by HW.

(15) WARTON, THOMAS. *Verses on Sir Joshua Reynolds's painted window at New-College Oxford*. The 2d edition. 1783. A copy of the 1st edition is in Volume 18.

(16) [WHARTON, CHARLES HENRY] *A poetical epistle to His Excellency George Washington . . . from an inhabitant of the State of Maryland*. Annapolis printed 1779; London reprinted, 1780.

Volume 20.   (1) BOYCE, THOMAS. *Harold; a tragedy*. 1786.

(2) CARLISLE, FREDERICK HOWARD, 5th Earl of. *The father's revenge, a tragedy*. 1783. On 10 April 1790, HW wrote to thank Lord Carlisle for sending him a copy of his verses, *To Sir Joshua Reynolds on his late resignation*, 1790; but this pamphlet has not been traced in the SH records.

(3) HOYLAND, FRANCIS. *Odes*. Edinburgh, 1783.

(4) [JERNINGHAM, EDWARD] *Lines written in the album, at Cossey-Hall, Norfolk, the seat of Sir William Jerningham*. 1786. Author identified by HW, and one identification.

(5) JODRELL, RICHARD PAUL. *The Persian heroine, a tragedy*. The 2d edition. 1786.

(6) [KNIGHT, SAMUEL] *Elegies and sonnets*. 1785. Presentation copy to HW, who wrote on title: 'by Mr. Knight of Milton in Cambridgeshire.' *See* his letter to Pinkerton, 26 June 1785.

(7) MORE, HANNAH. *Florio . . . and, the Bas Bleu*. 1786. *Florio* is dedicated to HW. Identifications in the *Bas Bleu* by HW.

(8) [WARWICK, THOMAS] *Abelard to Eloisa: a poetic epistle*. 1782. Emendations in MS, apparently by the author.

(9) [WILLIAMS, JOHN] *The children of Thespis. Part First.* 1786. A few   3222
identifications by HW.

(10) [WOLCOT, JOHN] *The Lousiad: an heroi-comic poem.* Canto I. By
Peter Pindar, *pseud.* 1785. Author identified by HW as 'Dr. Woolcot.'

(11) [WOLCOT, JOHN] *A poetical and congratulatory epistle to James Boswell.* By Peter Pindar, *pseud.* 1786.

(12) YEARSLEY, ANN. *Poems, on several occasions.* 1785. Dated 'June' by
HW; he identified two references to Hannah More, but made no comment on the poem (dated December 1784) addressed to him in honor
of his *Castle of Otranto.* The name of HW is included in the long list of
subscribers. He wrote to Hannah More, 14 October 1787: 'With fifty
times the genius of a Yearsley, you are void of vanity.' He also commented on Ann Yearsley in an earlier letter to Hannah More, 13
November 1784.

Volume 21.   (1) ARISTOPHANES. *The frogs, a comedy.* Translated by
Charles Dunster. Oxford [1785].

(2) *Chatsworth: a poem; dedicated by permission to Her Grace the Duchess
of Devonshire.* [1788].

(3) FITZGERALD, GEORGE ROBERT. *The riddle.* With notes by William Bingley. [1787]. A satire.

(4) KEATE, GEORGE. *The distressed poet.* 1787.

(5) [KEATE, GEORGE] *A probationary ode for the laureatship. With notes
... by the editor.* 1787. A satire on Keate. One note by HW.

(6) MAVOR, WILLIAM FORDYCE. *Blenheim, a poem.* 1787.

(7) [WILLIAMS, JOHN] *The children of Thespis. A poem. By Anthony
Pasquin, [pseud.] Part the Second.* 1787. Some identifications by HW.

(8) [WOLCOT, JOHN] *An apologetic postscript to Ode upon Ode.* By Peter
Pindar, *pseud.* 1787.

(9) [WOLCOT, JOHN] *Bozzy and Piozzi, or the British biographers.* 1786.

(10) [WOLCOT, JOHN] *Instructions to a celebrated laureat.* 1787. Dated
'July' by HW.

(11) [WOLCOT, JOHN] *The Lousiad. An heroi-comic poem.* Canto II. 1787.
A few identifications by HW.

(12) [WOLCOT, JOHN] *Ode upon ode; or a peep at St. James's.* 1787. Dated
'February' by HW, and identifications and markings by him.

(13) WRIGHT, J. *Elegia scripta in sepulchreto rustico, Latine reddita, a J.
Wright, cui subjiciuntur alia poemata.* 1786. 'J. Wright' is perhaps a
pseudonym for William Gifford.

3222 Volume 22.   (1) *Begum B—rke to Begum Bow, a poetical rhapsody.* 1789. A satire on Edmund Burke.

(2) [CONWAY, HENRY SEYMOUR, General] *Elegy on the death of Miss Caroline Campbell.* [1789]. Marked by HW: 'By General Conway, 1789.'

(3) [CROWE, WILLIAM] *Lewesden Hill a poem.* Oxford, 1788. Dated 'February' by HW; and one identification by him.

(4) [JERNINGHAM, EDWARD] *Enthusiasm: a poem.* 1789.

(5) [JERNINGHAM, EDWARD] *Lines on a late resignation at the Royal Academy.* 1790. On Sir Joshua Reynolds.

(6) [JERNINGHAM, EDWARD] *Lines written in the album, at Cossey-Hall, Norfolk, the seat of Sir William Jerningham.* 1786. Author and his mother identified by HW; another copy is in Volume 20 *above*.

(7) [MERRY, ROBERT] *Diversity. A poem. By Della Crusca.* 1788.

(8) [MORE, HANNAH] *Slavery, a poem.* 1788. One identification by HW.

(9) [MUNDY, FRANCIS NOEL CLARKE] *Needwood forest.* Lichfield, [1776?] Identification of author and one identification by HW; a few corrections in MS, apparently by the author.

(10) [O'BRYEN, DENIS] *Lines written at Twickenham.* 1788.

(11) *The Sick Laureat, or Parnassus in confusion.* 1789. Some identifications by HW.

(12) [TOWNSHEND, Lord JOHN] *Jekyll: a political eclogue.* 1788. Two identifications by HW; also marked by HW on the title: 'By Lord John Townshend,' and dated 'February.' The poem was included in the *Rolliad;* it has also been attributed to Joseph Richardson.

(13) WHITE, JAMES. *Conway Castle; a poem.* 1789.

(14) [WILLIAMS, JOHN] *The children of Thespis: a poem. Part the Third.* By Anthony Pasquin, *pseud.* 1788. Dated 'March' by HW.

(15) [WOLCOT, JOHN] *A benevolent epistle to Sylvanus Urban, alias Master John Nichols.* By Peter Pindar, *pseud.* 1790. Dated 'April' by HW.

(16) [WOLCOT, JOHN] *Expostulatory odes to a great duke, and a little lord.* 1789.

(17) [WOLCOT, JOHN] *Brother Peter to Brother Tom* [Thomas Warton]. 1788.

(18) [WOLCOT, JOHN] *Peter's pension.* 1788.

(19) [WOLCOT, JOHN] *Peter's prophecy.* 1788.

(20) [WOLCOT, JOHN] *A poetical epistle to a falling minister* [William Pitt, the Younger]. 1789. Dated 'February' by HW, and a few identifications by him.

(21) [WOLCOT, JOHN] *Sir Joseph Banks and the Emperor of Morocco.* 1788.

(22) [WOLCOT, JOHN] *Subjects for painters.* 1789.

PRESS T

The books shelved in Press T, as they were sold in 1842, were a somewhat miscellaneous group: included were antiquities, bibliography, history, topography, and travels, all of continuing interest to Walpole. Also sold in this group were such unrelated works as Butler's *Analogy,* Johnson's *Letters,* a translation of Lucian, Alexander Monro's medical writings, Smith's *Wealth of Nations,* and Whitehead's *Poems.* Press T must therefore have been planned only as miscellaneous current publications.

Archaeologia; or miscellaneous tracts relating to antiquity. Published   3223
    by the Society of Antiquaries. London, 1770–96. Twelve volumes, 4to.

Rebound in half calf. BP² early state, in Volumes 1–3, 5; later state in Volumes 6–10; Orford seal, type 2, in Volume 11. Not in MC.

SH SALE, v.78, to — Barnard, Esq., £17.17.0; purchased as part of a complete set in 1925 by the University of Chicago Library (for the Oriental Institute's library at Luxor, Egypt); University of Chicago Library, 1947, to WSL, in exchange for another set.

☞ Notes and markings by HW throughout, in the articles of special interest to him. In Volume 2, the notes to Masters's 'Remarks on Mr. Walpole's *Historic Doubts,*' which served as the basis of HW's reply, have been so much erased as to be unrecoverable. The article by Dean Milles, at the end of Volume 1, has no annotation.

ASTLE, THOMAS   3224

The origin and progress of writing. London, 1784. Royal 4to.

Original boards, uncut, now rebacked. BP² later state. Press-mark T.2. Not in MC. Bookplate of Henry A. Bulwer.

SH SALE, v.75 (with King, Wallace, and Whitehead), to Pickering, 18/–; offered in Thorpe's Supplement for 1842, lot 11945, for £2.2.0; Vancouver Public Library, June 1954, to WSL, by exchange.

☞ Scattered markings by HW, and two notes. The more interesting note (p. 174) is appended to Astle's application of the word 'elegant' to Dr. Middleton's translation of one of Cicero's letters; HW says 'I think this is a most inelegant translation,' and he then itemizes his objections to numerous expressions.

3225 AYSCOUGH, SAMUEL

A catalogue of the manuscripts preserved in the British Museum. London, 1782. Two volumes, 4to.

Not in MC.
SH SALE, v.76 (with Hardwicke and Monro), to Pickering, £1.2.0; offered in Thorpe's Supplement for 1842, lot 11955, for £1.11.6.

☞ Thorpe describes it as a 'fine clean copy, with a few MS notes by HW.'

3226 BLOMEFIELD, FRANCIS

Collectanea Cantabrigiensia. Norwich, 1751. 4to.

Not in MC.
SH SALE, v.72 (with Denne, Herbert, Marshall, Pegge, Pool, Southgate, Weston, and one *non*-Walpolian book), to Pickering, 16/–; probably the copy offered, but not identified as HW's, in Thorpe's Supplement for 1842, lot 12016, for £1.11.6.

☞ Another copy was in E.4, No. 649 *above*.

3227 BROMLEY, Sir GEORGE

A collection of original royal letters written by King Charles the First and Second, King James the Second. . . . London, 1787. 8vo.

'Boards, uncut' in 1842; now rebound in mottled calf. BP² later state. Not in MC. Bookplate of J. W. Lloyd, of Kington, Herefordshire.
SH SALE, v.71 (with Butler, Franklin, Johnson, Pinkerton, Saint-Simon, Thunberg, and Warton), to Strong, 18/–; offered in Strong's Catalogue for 1843, lot 143, for 7/6; Blackwell, June 1932, to WSL, 15/–.

☞ Three engravings added, but probably not by HW. One characteristic marginal cross on p. 80; and the correct BP seems to authenticate this copy.

BUTLER, JOSEPH, Bishop   3228

The analogy of religion, natural and revealed. London, 1785. 8vo.

'Boards, uncut.' Not in MC.

SH SALE, v.71 (with Bromley, Franklin, Johnson, Pinkerton, Saint-Simon, Thunberg, and Warton), to Strong, 18/–; offered in Strong's Catalogue for 1843, lot 186, for 9/–.

☞ First published in 1736.

CLARENDON, EDWARD HYDE, 1st Earl of   3229

State papers. Edited by Richard Scrope. Oxford, 1767. Three volumes, 8vo.

Not in MC.

SH SALE, v.69 (with Jortin and Madan), to Pickering, £1.2.0.

☞ Although HW owned the continuation of 1786 in folio (sold in C.1 in the Main Library, No. 426 *above*) and mentioned the folios of 1767–73 in his 'Book of Materials,' the description here of three volumes sold with other octavos seems sufficient to identify this as the octavo edition of 1767.

CLAVIÈRE, ETIENNE DE, and BRISSOT DE WARVILLE, JEAN   3230
PIERRE

Considerations on the relative situation of France and the United States of America. London, 1788. 8vo.

'Boards.' Not in MC.

SH SALE, v.70 (with Dagge, Harris, Macaulay, *Observer*, Owen, Piozzi, Rivers, Wallis, and Warburton), to Pickering, 18/–; offered in Strong's Catalogue for 1843, lot 287, for 6/–; Fletcher, 7 April 1846 (Britton Sale, Part 4), lot 255, to Wilks, 1/6.

COOKSEY, RICHARD   3231

Essay on the life and character of John Lord Somers. Worcester, 1791. 4to.

Not in MC.

SH SALE, v.74 (with Dalrymple, Ridley, and Russell), to Strong, £1.2.0; probably the copy offered, but not identified as HW's, in Thorpe's Supplement for 1842, lot 13169, for 6/–.

3232 [DAGGE, HENRY]

Considerations on criminal law. London, 1772. 8vo.

'Boards, with HW's BP and MS notes.' Not in MC.

SH SALE, v.70 (with Clavière, Harris, Macaulay, *Observer*, Owen, Piozzi, Rivers, Wallis, and Warburton), to Pickering, 18/–; offered in Strong's Catalogue for 1843, lot 479, for 6/–; Fletcher, 7 April 1846 (Britton Sale, Part 4), lot 319, to R. Smith, 1/6.

☞ The sale catalogue has only 'Criminal Law'; both Strong and Fletcher, by a not astonishing confusion with the *Principles of Penal Law* of 1771, attribute the book to William Eden, Lord Auckland; possibly a MS attribution was at fault. The new edition of 1774 was in Press O, No. 2831 *above.* Dagge was HW's lawyer.

3233 DALRYMPLE, WILLIAM

Travels through Spain and Portugal. London, 1777. 4to.

Not in MC.

SH SALE, v.74 (with Cooksey, Ridley, and Russell), to Strong, £1.2.0; probably the copy offered, but not identified as HW's, in Thorpe's Supplement for 1842, lot 12259, for 10/6.

3234 DENNE, SAMUEL

Historical particulars of Lambeth Parish and Lambeth Palace. London, 1795. 4to.

Not in MC.

SH SALE, v.72 (with Blomefield, Herbert, Marshall, Pegge, Pool, Southgate, Weston, and one *non*-Walpolian book), to Pickering, 16/–; probably the copy offered, but not identified as HW's, in Thorpe's Supplement for 1842, lot 12281, for £1.11.6.

☞ Issued as No. 5 or part of Volume 10 of the continuation of Nichols's 'Bibliotheca topographica Britannica.'

3235 FRANKLIN, BENJAMIN

Works. Volume 2. London, 1793. 8vo.

Not in MC.

SH SALE, v.71 (with Bromley, Butler, Johnson, Pinkerton, Saint-Simon, Thunberg, and Warton), to Strong, 18/–.

☞ This seems the most probable explanation of the entry: 'Franklin, vol. 2.'

HARDWICKE, PHILIP YORKE, 2d Earl of, Editor   3236

Miscellaneous state papers, from 1501 to 1726. London, 1778. Two
  volumes, 4to.

Rebound in half calf, *ca.* 1860. BP² early state, in first volume. Not
in MC. Bookplate of Lord Rosebery, and an unidentified plate.

SH SALE, v.76 (with Ayscough and Monro), to Pickering, £1.2.0; offered
in Thorpe's Supplement for 1842, lot 12505, for £6.6.0; and in his Catalogue for 1844, lot 68, for £5.5.0; priced at £4.4.0 in 1845 and 1846 by
Thorpe; Puttick, 29 April 1852 (Miscellaneous Sale), lot 144, to Lilly,
13/–; Sotheby's, 26 June 1933 (Rosebery Sale), lot 1309, to Walter Hill,
£31; Hill, September 1934, to WSL, $150.

☞ Numerous notes and corrections by HW in both volumes; he recorded one Shirley reference in his 'Book of Materials.' He wrote to Cole, 5
March 1781: 'Nothing upon earth ever was duller than the three heavy
tomes his Lordship [Hardwicke] printed of Sir Dudley Carleton's Negotiations, and of what he called state-papers.' *See also* his earlier letter to
Cole, 23 April 1778.

HARRIS, JAMES   3237

Philological inquiries. London, 1781. Three parts in two volumes,
  8vo.

Not in MC.

SH SALE, v.70 (with Clavière, Dagge, Macaulay, *Observer*, Owen, Piozzi,
Rivers, Wallis, and Warburton), to Pickering, 18/–.

☞ *See* HW to Mason, 6 May 1781: 'There are published two more volumes of Harris of Salisbury—paltry things indeed! He dwells on Aristotle's
old hackneyed rules for the drama, and the pedantry of a beginning,
middle, and end. Harris was one of those wiseacres whom such wiseacres
as himself cried up for profound; but he was more like the scum at the
top of a well.'

HERBERT, EDWARD, Baron Herbert of Cherbury   3238

A dialogue between a tutor and his pupil. London, 1768. 4to.

Not in MC.

SH SALE, v.72 (with Blomefield, Denne, Marshall, Pegge, Pool, Southgate, Weston, and one *non*-Walpolian book), to Pickering, 16/–.

JOHNSON, SAMUEL   3239

Letters. Edited by Mrs. Piozzi. London, 1788. Two volumes, 8vo.

'Boards, uncut, with one note by HW.' Not in MC.

SH SALE, v.71 (with Bromley, Butler, Franklin, Pinkerton, Saint-Simon, Thunberg, and Warton), to Strong, 18/–; offered in Strong's Catalogue for 1843, lot 842, for 12/–; Fletcher, 8 April 1846 (Britton Sale, Part 4), lot 555, to Vale, 4/–.

3240 JORTIN, JOHN

Remarks on ecclesiastical history. London, 1767–73. Four volumes, 8vo.

Not in MC.

SH SALE, v.69 (with Clarendon and Madan), to Pickering, £1.2.0.

☞ The first volumes were originally published in 1751-2-4, but these three were reprinted in two volumes in 1767. The sale catalogue reads: 'Jortan's Remarks on Ecclesiastical Mystery.'

3241 KING, EDWARD

Morsels of criticism, tending to illustrate some few passages in the Holy Scriptures upon philosophical principles. London, 1788. 4to.

Not in MC.

SH SALE, v.75 (with Astle, Wallace, and Whitehead), to Pickering, 18/–; probably the copy offered, but not identified as HW's, in Thorpe's Supplement for 1842, lot 12663, for 18/–.

☞ On 26 January 1788, HW wrote to King to thank him 'for the honour he has done him by his valuable present, which Mr. Walpole is sure he shall read with great pleasure and instruction.' Despite the book's absurdities, King published a second part in 1800.

3242 LUCIAN, of Samosata

Works. Translated by Thomas Francklin. London, 1780. Two volumes, 4to.

Not in MC.

SH SALE, v.77 (with Smith), to Pickering, 10/6.

3243 MACAULAY, Mrs. CATHARINE, later Mrs. Graham

A treatise on the immutability of moral truth. London, 1783. 8vo.

'Boards.' Not in MC.

SH SALE, v.70 (with Clavière, Dagge, Harris, *Observer*, Owen, Piozzi, Rivers, Wallis, and Warburton), to Pickering, 18/–; offered in Strong's Catalogue for 1843, lot 627, for 4/6.

[MADAN, MARTIN]   3244

Thelyphthora; or, a treatise on female ruin. London, 1780. Two
   volumes, 8vo.

Rebound in calf with crest of Hudson Gurney (1775–1864) stamped on
sides and spine; Volume I now rebacked. BP¹ inserted on verso of the title-
page in Volume I. Not in MC.

SH SALE, v.69 (with Clarendon and Jortin), to Pickering, £1.2.0;
Maggs, July 1949, to WSL, £11.11.0.

☞ The sale catalogue reads 'Maden on Polygamy,' the way the work
is commonly known. The BP has of course been removed from some other
position, and it is the wrong plate for 1780; yet one MS note on p. 113 is
certainly by HW. Possibly Gurney or his binder in dealing with several
books reapplied the wrong plate. Or perhaps a bookplate was merely inserted in the book in 1842 or later because it came from SH.

[MARSHALL, WILLIAM]   3245

A review of the Landscape, a didactic poem [by Richard Payne
   Knight]. London, 1795. 8vo.

Not in MC.

SH SALE, v.72 (with Blomefield, Denne, Herbert, Pegge, Pool, Southgate, Weston, and one *non*-Walpolian book), to Pickering, 16/–; probably
the copy offered, but not identified as HW's, in Thorpe's Supplement for
1842, lot 12668, for 7/6.

MONRO, ALEXANDER   3246

Works. Edinburgh, 1781. 4to.

Not in MC.

SH SALE, v.76 (with Ayscough and Hardwicke), to Pickering, £1.2.0;
probably the copy offered, but not identified as HW's, in Thorpe's Supplement for 1842, lot 12812, for 18/–.

MURPHY, JAMES CAVANAH   3247

Travels in Portugal . . . in the years 1789 and 1790. London, 1795.
   4to.

Not in MC.

SH SALE, v.73 (with Newcome and Toulmin), to Pickering, 10/–.

☞ In his 'Book of Materials,' HW commented on one passage in Murphy, on English architects in Spain, and he quoted a passage in a letter to Mary Berry, 22 November 1795. A second copy was in Press O, No. 2910 *above*.

3248 NEWCOME, PETER
The history of the . . . Abbey of St. Alban. London, 1793. 4to.
    Not in MC.
    SH SALE, v.73 (with Murphy and Toulmin), to Pickering, 10/–.
    ☞ Probably a second copy; the first was in Press S, No. 3202 *above*.

3249 *The Observer.* By Richard Cumberland. Volume I. London, 1785. 8vo.
    Rebound in sprinkled calf. BP² later state (at end of the Table of Contents). Not in MC.
    SH SALE, v.70 (with Clavière, Dagge, Harris, Macaulay, Owen, Piozzi, Rivers, Wallis, and Warburton), to Pickering, 18/–; probably this volume sold by English, 17 October 1849 (Pigott Sale), lot 478; Birrell & Garnett, May 1926, to WSL, 30/–.
    ☞ Several identifications and notes by HW, and numerous marginal markings. Another volume of the *Observer* was in X, No. 3357 *below*.

3250 OWEN, HENRY
Sixteen sermons on various subjects. London, 1797. 8vo.
    'Boards.' Not in MC.
    SH SALE, v.70 (with Clavière, Dagge, Harris, Macaulay, *Observer*, Piozzi, Rivers, Wallis, and Warburton), to Pickering, 18/–; offered in Strong's Catalogue for 1843, lot 1128, for 5/–.

3251 PASTON LETTERS
Original letters . . . of the Paston family. Edited by Sir John Fenn. London, 1787–9. Four volumes, 4to.
    'Boards, uncut.' Not in MC.
    SH SALE, v.79, to Thorpe, £5.15.6; offered, with the fifth volume not HW's, in Thorpe's Supplement for 1842, lot 12379, for £9.9.0.
    ☞ A volume with letters of thanks from friends to whom Fenn had presented copies of the first two volumes, sold in 1896, included a letter and a card from HW. Much earlier, 15 May 1782, HW expressed his pleasure in a

letter by William of Worcester, and urged Fenn to prepare the Paston letters for publication; and Fenn in his Introduction acknowledges HW's help. Thorpe describes the four volumes as presentation copies to HW.

PEGGE, SAMUEL   3252
Life of Robert Grosseteste, Bishop of Lincoln. London, 1793. 4to.

'Boards, uncut.' Not in MC.

SH SALE, v.72 (with Blomefield, Denne, Herbert, Marshall, Pool, Southgate, Weston, and one *non*-Walpolian book), to Pickering, 16/–; offered in Thorpe's Supplement for 1842, lot 12936, for £2.12.6.

PINKERTON, JOHN   3253
An enquiry into the history of Scotland. London, 1789. Two volumes, 8vo.

Boards, uncut, presentation copy from the author. BP² later state. Press-mark T.3. Not in MC.

SH SALE, v.71 (with Bromley, Butler, Franklin, Johnson, Saint-Simon, Thunberg, and Warton), to Strong, 18/–; English, 17 October 1849 (Pigott Sale), lot 494; Sotheby's, 24 April 1903 (Brown Sale), lot 1717, to Dobell, 14/–; Goodspeed, December 1956, to WSL, $65.

☞ Walpole seems to have examined much of the first volume, but he found it difficult reading. He thanked Pinkerton in a carefully phrased letter, 31 July 1789, and then had to defend himself in a second letter, 14 August, because Pinkerton was offended by the first. There are marginal markings in both volumes.

PIOZZI, HESTER LYNCH (THRALE)   3254
British synonymy. London, 1794. Two volumes, 8vo.

'Boards, with notes by HW.' Not in MC.

SH SALE, v.70 (with Clavière, Dagge, Harris, Macaulay, *Observer*, Owen, Rivers, Wallis, and Warburton), to Pickering, 18/–; offered in Strong's Catalogue for 1843, lot 1195, for 7/6; Fletcher, 9 April 1846 (Britton Sale, Part 4), lot 748, to Bentley, 1/–.

POOL, ROBERT, and CASH, JOHN   3255
Views of the most remarkable public buildings . . . in the City of Dublin. Dublin, 1780. Post 4to.

Original boards, uncut. Large SH fleuron on Errata leaf. Press-mark largely obliterated but seems to be T.3. Not in MC.

SH SALE, V.72 (with Blomefield, Denne, Herbert, Marshall, Pegge, South-gate, Weston, and one *non*-Walpolian book), to Pickering, 16/–; offered in Thorpe's Supplement for 1842, lot 13003, for £1.8.0; priced at 18/– by Thorpe in 1846; I. Kyrle Fletcher, October 1946, to WSL, £10.10.0.

☞ One identification and three corrections by HW.

3256 RIDLEY, GLOCESTER

The life of Dr. Nicholas Ridley, sometime Bishop of London. London, 1763. 4to.

Not in MC.

SH SALE, V.74 (with Cooksey, Dalrymple, and Russell), to Strong, £1.2.0; probably the copy offered, but not identified as HW's, in Thorpe's Supplement for 1842, lot 13061, for 15/–.

3257 [RIVERS, GEORGE PITT, Baron]

Letters to a young nobleman upon various subjects, particularly on government and civil liberty. London, 1784. 8vo.

'Boards, uncut, with HW's note identifying the author.' Not in MC.

SH SALE, V.70 (with Clavière, Dagge, Harris, Macaulay, *Observer*, Owen, Piozzi, Wallis, and Warburton), to Pickering, 18/–; offered in Strong's Catalogue for 1843, lot 1197, for 7/6; Fletcher, 8 April 1846 (Britton Sale, Part 4), lot 574, to Bright, 1/–.

3258 RUSSELL, RACHEL, Baroness Russell

Letters. Edited by Thomas Sellwood. London, 1773. 4to.

Not in MC.

SH SALE, V.74 (with Cooksey, Dalrymple, and Ridley), to Strong, £1.2.0; probably the copy in original boards offered, but not identified as HW's, in Thorpe's Supplement for 1842, lot 13102, for 10/6.

☞ *See* HW to Mason, 15 May 1773: 'Lady Russell's *Letters*, too, I have seen formerly. . . . I am much surprised in this our day that the Duchess gives leave for the publication.' He had seen them in MS in 1751: *see* his letter to Mann, 14 October 1751, when he praised them and expressed the hope that they might be printed.

A copy in 'original calf,' with the name 'Walpole' on the title, was offered as the SH copy by Rosenthal in December 1945. But HW's copy was presumably in boards, and in 1773 the signature 'Walpole' could only be that of HW's cousin, Horatio, Lord Walpole (1723–1809).

In 1936, Mr. A. N. L. Munby saw in a private library a copy of the fifth edition, 1793, 8vo, with HW's BP. But it is unlikely that HW bought a later edition, and this bookplate was presumably an insertion.

SAINT-SIMON, LOUIS DE ROUVROY, Duc de   3259
Mémoires. Edited by J. L. G. Soulavie. Londres [i.e. Paris?], 1788.
   Two volumes, 8vo.
   Not in MC. Perhaps misplaced with the books in English.
   SH SALE, v.71 (with Bromley, Butler, Franklin, Johnson, Pinkerton, Thunberg, and Warton), to Strong, 18/–.
   ☞ Published in three volumes: the third volume was misplaced in X, No. 3371 *below*. In his letter to Lady Ossory, 19 October 1788, HW summarizes the history of this MS, and says he has so far had a glimpse of one volume only: possibly the volumes were never reunited on his shelves.

SMITH, ADAM   3260
An inquiry into the nature and causes of the wealth of nations. London, 1776. Two volumes, 4to.
   Not in MC.
   SH SALE, v.77 (with Lucian), to Pickering, 10/6.
   ☞ In his 'Book of Materials,' 1787, HW classes this with Harte's *Gustavus Adolphus* and Hancarville's *Progress of the Arts* as 'the three worst books, considering the quantity of valuable matter that they contain, that ever were written for bad style, bad method, bad arrangement, anticipation, and repetition.'

SOUTHGATE, RICHARD   3261
Museum Southgatianum: being a catalogue of the collection of books, coins, medals, and natural history. London, 1795. 8vo.
   'Large paper, uncut.' Not in MC.
   SH SALE, v.72 (with Blomefield, Denne, Herbert, Marshall, Pegge, Pool, Weston, and one *non*-Walpolian book), to Pickering, 16/–; Sotheby's, 19 April 1844 (Eyton Sale), lot 435, to Merridan, 2/6.

THUNBERG, CARL PETER   3262
Travels in Europe, Africa, and Asia. Volume 4. London, 1795. 8vo.
   Not in MC.
   SH SALE, v.71 (with Bromley, Butler, Franklin, Johnson, Pinkerton, Saint-Simon, and Warton), to Strong, 18/–.
   ☞ The sale catalogue records it as 'Thunberg's Travels, vol. 4.'

3263 Toulmin, Joshua

The history of the town of Taunton. London, 1791. 4to.

Not in MC.

SH SALE, v.73 (with Murphy and Newcome), to Pickering, 10/–.

3264 Wallace, George

Thoughts on the origin of feudal tenures, and the descent of ancient peerages, in Scotland. Edinburgh, 1783. 4to.

'Boards, uncut; presentation copy to HW.' Not in MC.

SH SALE, v.75 (with Astle, King, and Whitehead), to Pickering, 18/–; offered in Thorpe's Supplement for 1842, lot 13340, for 18/–.

☞ The sale catalogue calls him Wallis. For the 2d edition, 1785, *see* No. 3154, in Press Q *above*.

3265 Wallis, John, D.D.

Sermons.... To which are prefixed memoirs of the author. Edited by Charles Edward de Coetlogon. London, 1791. 8vo.

'Boards, uncut.' Not in MC.

SH SALE, v.70 (with Clavière, Dagge, Harris, Macaulay, *Observer*, Owen, Piozzi, Rivers, and Warburton), to Pickering, 18/–; offered in Strong's Catalogue for 1843, lot 1572, for 6/6.

3266 Warburton, William, Bishop

Supplemental volume of Bishop Warburton's Works. Edited by Richard Hurd. London, 1788. 8vo.

Not in MC.

SH SALE, v.70 (with Clavière, Dagge, Harris, Macaulay, *Observer*, Owen, Piozzi, Rivers, and Wallis), to Pickering, 18/–.

☞ A second copy was sold in Press Y, No. 3477 *below*.

3267 Warton, Joseph

An essay on the writings and genius of Pope. Volume 2. London, 1782. 8vo.

Rebound in calf before 1860, now rebacked. BP² early state. No pressmark preserved. Not in MC.

SH SALE, v.71 (with Bromley, Butler, Franklin, Johnson, Pinkerton, Saint-Simon, and Thunberg), to Strong, 18/–; offered in Strong's Catalogue for 1843, lot 1210, for 12/–; Sotheby's, 24 April 1860 (Mitford Sale), lot 2814, to Pickering, 16/–; now in the British Museum.

☞ Some notes by HW. The first volume, 1756, was in K.9, No. 2033 *above*. In his letter to Mason, 7 February 1782, HW alluded to the new volume.

WESTON, STEPHEN   3268

Letters from Paris. London, 1792–3. Two volumes, 8vo.

'Boards, uncut, with Orford BP.' Not in MC.

SH SALE, v.72 (with Blomefield, Denne, Herbert, Marshall, Pegge, Pool, Southgate, and one *non*-Walpolian book), to Pickering, 16/–; offered in Thorpe's Supplement for 1842, lot 13399, for 7/6.

WHITEHEAD, PAUL   3269

Poems and miscellaneous compositions. Edited by Edward Thompson. London, 1777. 4to.

Not in MC.

SH SALE, v.75 (with Astle, King, and Wallace), to Pickering, 18/–; probably the copy offered, but not identified as HW's, in Thorpe's Supplement for 1842, lot 13408, for 7/6.

PRESS V

Only one book with this press-mark has been recovered, but the grouping seems to suggest that Press V held folios only, some forty volumes in all. Many of these were books of prints such as might have been shelved in the Round Tower, but the rest can best be described as miscellaneous volumes in folio.

AQUINO, CARLO D'   3270

Sacra exequialia, in funere Jacobi II. Rome, 1702. Folio.

'Calf.' Not in MC.

SH SALE, v.84 (with Sainte-Marthe and Sandford), to H. G. Bohn, £3.10.0; offered in Bohn's Catalogue for 1847 (Prints), p. 159, for £1.1.0.

☞ Another copy was in C.6, No. 494 *above*.

BLOME, RICHARD   3271

Britannia; or a geographical description of the kingdoms of England, Scotland, and Ireland. London, 1673. Folio.

Not in MC.

SH SALE, v.81 (with Collier), to Thorpe, £1; probably the copy offered,

but not identified as hw's, in Thorpe's Supplement for 1842, lot 12015, for £1.11.6.

☞ The sale catalogue reads 'Bloom's Geographical History of Great Britain, with the plates coloured.'

3272 COLLIER, JEREMY

The great historical, geographical, genealogical, and poetical diction-ary. The 2d edition. London, 1701–16. Four volumes, folio.

Not in MC.

SH SALE, v.81 (with Blome), to Thorpe, £1; probably the copy offered, but not identified as hw's, in Thorpe's Supplement for 1842, lot 12216, for £1.1.0.

☞ Based on the dictionary of Louis Moréri. The first edition in English was published in 1694. To the second edition of 1701, in two volumes, Collier added a *Supplement* in 1705 and an *Appendix* in 1716; these seem to have been included in hw's set.

3273 DAVENANT, Sir WILLIAM

Works. London, 1673. Folio.

Not in MC.

SH SALE, v.85 (with Fougasses and Ogilby), to Newman, Holborn, £1.5.0.

☞ Another copy was in G.2, No. 1108 *above*.

3274 DUCAREL, ANDREW COLTEE

Anglo-Norman antiquities considered. London, 1767. Folio.

'Boards.' Not in MC.

SH SALE, v.83 (with Fryer, Kingston, and Speer), to Thorpe, 10/6; offered in Payne & Foss Catalogue for 1845, lot 308, for £1.1.0.

☞ On 25 April 1767, hw wrote Ducarel to thank him for 'the obliging favour of his most curious and valuable work, which Mr. Walpole has read with the greatest pleasure and satisfaction.' In his 'Book of Materials,' *ca.* 1767, hw made several notes from Ducarel's book.

3275 ENGLAND. PARLIAMENT

Journals of the House of Commons, 1558–1729. London. Twenty-four volumes, folio.

Entered in MC, but press-mark and number of volumes obliterated. Marked in margin by Kirgate: 'In the Library in the Offices.'

SH SALE, v.80, to Thorpe, £2.

☞ In his 'Book of Materials,' *ca.* 1763, HW made one note from the eleventh volume, and he used this in the 2d edition of his *Anecdotes.* He also cited the Commons *Journals* elsewhere in his *Anecdotes* and once in *R&NA.* The printing was done by Richardson, over a ten-year period beginning in 1742; the series covered the years from 1547–1741, and was then continued. The dates listed above are from the sale catalogue. The set, which apparently began with Elizabeth's reign, must have had two or three volumes of indexes to make up the 24.

FOUGASSES, THOMAS DE   3276
The general historie of Venice. Translated by W. Shute. London, 1612. Two volumes, folio.

Not in MC.

SH SALE, v.85 (with Davenant and Ogilby), to Newman, Holborn, £1.5.0.

FRYER, JOHN   3277
A new account of East India and Persia. London, 1698. Folio.

Not in MC.

SH SALE, v.83 (with Ducarel, Kingston, and Speer), to Thorpe, 10/6; offered in the Payne & Foss Catalogue for 1845, lot 378, for 18/–.

KINGSTON, EVELYN PIERREPONT, 1st Duke of   3278
Catalogus bibliothecae Kingstonianae. [London, 1726?] Folio.

Not in MC.

SH SALE, v.83 (with Ducarel, Fryer, and Speer), to Thorpe, 10/6.

LE MOYNE, PIERRE   3279
The gallery of heroick women. Translated by John Paulet, 5th Marquess of Winchester. London, 1652. Folio.

Not in MC.

SH SALE, v.82 (with Solis), to Jones, 10/–.

OGILBY, JOHN   3280
The entertainment of . . . Charles II in his passage through the City of London. London, 1662. Folio.

Not in MC.

SH SALE, v.85 (with Davenant and Fougasses), to Newman, Holborn, £1.5.0.

☞ This may have been the edition of 1661 or of 1685, the titles of which are slightly different; the sale catalogue reads: 'Ogleby's Account of King Charles the Second's Entertainment in London.' An earlier copy was in E.1, No. 575 *above*.

3281 SAINTE-MARTHE, SCÉVOLE DE and LOUIS DE

A genealogical history of the kings of Portugal. Translated by Francis Sandford. London, 1662. Folio.

Not in MC.

SH SALE, v.84 (with Aquino and Sandford), to H. G. Bohn, £3.10.0.

☞ The copy offered in Bohn's Catalogue for 1847 (Heraldry), p. 298, for £1.10.0, is described as a fine copy in old calf, with autograph of Narcissus Luttrell, with no mention of HW. Another copy was in Press B.2, No. 250 *above*.

3282 SANDFORD, FRANCIS

The order and ceremonies used for and at the solemn interment of . . . George, Duke of Albemarle. [London, 1670] Folio.

Old mottled calf, rebacked; the new end-papers were removed and HW's press-marks found underneath. BP² early state. Press-mark C.3.29, altered to V.1 in book, but not altered in MC. Armorial bookplate of John Holland, and his name on end-paper: Hogarth made this plate, *ca.* 1720, for John Holland, the heraldic painter.

SH SALE, v.84 (with Aquino and Sainte-Marthe), to H. G. Bohn, £3.10.0; perhaps the copy offered in Bohn's Catalogue for 1847 (Prints), p. 159, for £3.3.0; H. A. Feisenberger of London, 'from Sir Oliver Welby of Denton Manor in Lincolnshire,' October 1952, to WSL, £27.

☞ Added to the volume, probably by Holland or HW, are a broadside on the funeral of the Duke of Marlborough in 1722; the *London Gazette*, 11 August 1722, containing an account of the funeral; an account of the funeral of Queen Caroline in 1737; and several prints. Two identifications by HW in the account of the funeral of Queen Caroline.

3283 SOLIS Y RIBADENEYRA, ANTONIO DE

The history of the conquest of Mexico. Translated by Thomas Townsend. London, 1724. Folio.

Not in MC.

SH SALE, v.82 (with Le Moyne), to Jones, 10/–.

SPEER, JOSEPH SMITH   3284

The West-India pilot. London, 1766. Folio.

Not in MC.

SH SALE, v.83 (with Ducarel, Fryer, and Kingston), to Thorpe, 10/6.

PRESS X

The rather miscellaneous lots sold in the Fifth Day at the beginning
(lots 1–31) and end (lots 196–249) have been arbitrarily assigned to
Presses X and Y respectively, in continuation of the alphabetized
sequence of Presses in the Library in the Offices. Those at the end,
now grouped under Press Y, were remainders from the SH Press, books
of prints, and other oddments; they were not included in the first
edition of the sale catalogue. Those at the beginning, now grouped
under Press X, seem to be chiefly periodical sets, and the large group
of books brought to the Library in the Offices after 1797 from Press
D of the Main Library. In addition, about a dozen books were brought
here, also after 1797, from Press A.2. (One other book from A.2 was in
Press N and one in Press R, perhaps misplaced there.) Proof that the
moves from Press D and from Press A.2 were made after 1797 is
not absolute but nevertheless convincing: Mrs. Damer marked opposite Hume's *History* (No. 3328) in MC '4 vols. only in D.4,' so that
the Hume must have been in the Main Library when she and Kirgate
read the shelves in 1797; and Kirgate presumably entered Sir Dudley
Carleton's *Letters* (No. 3310) as A.2.25 in 1797.

Five books sold in Press X that have been recovered have the
press-mark T.4, perhaps moved after 1797 or even in 1842.

In the first edition of the sale catalogue, lot 8 contained 40 volumes; when this was recatalogued in April, 21 unnamed volumes
were removed (perhaps to Press Y), so that only 19 volumes were
actually sold in lot 8.

[ALLETZ, PONS AUGUSTIN]   3285

*Histoire des singes et autres animaux curieux, dont l'instinct et l'in-
    dustrie excitent l'admiration des hommes.* Paris, 1752. 12mo.

Not in MC. Purchased in Dr. Lort's Sale, in April 1791, lot 4334 (with
Molé *below*), for 7/6.

SH SALE, v.6 (with Devienne, *Esprit*, Gherardo, Lavallée, Louis XIV,
Molé, Villars, and Walpole), to Pickering, 7/–.

3286 *Annalium.* One volume, 8vo.

> Not certainly identified.
>
> SH SALE, v.8 (with 18 other volumes), to Boone, £2.6.0.
>
> ☞ An edition of Tacitus is a tempting guess, but this lot contained no other classics. Possibly it was William Fleetwood's *Annalium tam Regum Edwardi quinti . . . quam Henrici octavo . . . elenchus.* London, 1579. A copy of this book, in 19th-century morocco by Mackenzie, was sold at Sotheby's, 2 December 1920 (E. A. V. Stanley Sale), lot 189, to Quaritch for Sir Leicester Harmsworth; sold in a collection to the Folger Library, 1938. There is no visible sign of a Walpolian connection in the volume now; but Messrs. Quaritch identified it in a letter to WSL, 21 May 1938, as from HW's library, without citing proof. A bookplate has been removed from Mackenzie's marbled end-paper.

3287 BARRINGTON, DAINES

Miscellanies. London, 1781. 4to.

> 'Boards, uncut.' Not in MC.
>
> SH SALE, v.13 (with Beattie, Hanway, and Martialis), to Thorpe, 5/–; offered in Strong's Catalogue for 1843, lot 69, for 12/–.
>
> ☞ Other items in this lot were offered by Thorpe, but Strong's Catalogue describes this as from HW's collection.

3288 BAUDEAU, NICOLAS

Les idées d'un citoyen. 8vo.

> Not in MC.
>
> SH SALE, v.7 (with Bernard, Boutet, Charlotte Elizabeth, Choiseul, Descamps, Dutens, La Live, Molière, *Observer*, Richelieu, Rousseau, Saint-Simon, Senebier, Suetonius, and Voltaire), to Pickering, 12/–.
>
> ☞ The sale catalogue has only 'Idées d'un Citoyen.' Numerous titles begin in this way, but it is likely that HW owned one of four pamphlets with this title by Baudeau, perhaps 'Les idées . . . sur l'état actuel du royaume de France,' Paris, 1787.

3289 BEATTIE, JAMES

Dissertations moral and critical. London, 1783. 4to.

> 'Boards, uncut, a few notes by HW, and his BP.' Not in MC.
>
> SH SALE, v.13 (with Barrington, Hanway, and Martialis), to Thorpe, 5/–; offered in Thorpe's Supplement for 1842, lot 11978, for 7/6.

☞ *See* HW to Mason, 9 June 1783: 'I have been reading some more of those pinchbeck encomiums in Beattie's new volume. . . . I have waded through many a silly book in my day, as my eyes know to their sorrow, but, poor souls, they never had a more cruel penance imposed on them than this quarto of Beattie, though they did read the whole reign of Henry II [Lyttelton], all Cumberland's works in metre and out of metre, all the *Archaeologias*, and many other reverend bodies of antiquity and heraldry. . . . I have got through one hundred and nine pages, but, dearly as I love quartos, I doubt I shall never compass the other five hundred and fifty pages. . . .'

BENTIVOGLIO, GUIDO, Cardinale   3290

Historicall relations of the United Provinces and Flanders. Translated by Henry Carey, Earl of Monmouth. London, 1652. Folio.

Not in MC.

SH SALE, V.28 (with Capriata and Paruta), to Clarke, Wickham, 10/–.

☞ An extra-illustrated set of *Walpoliana* prepared by James Gibbs in 1875, now in the New York Public Library, has BP[1] inserted in the fifth volume with a note by Gibbs dated 1876 saying it came from the Bentivoglio of 1652 bought at the SH SALE. But *see* Paruta *below*: it is clear that Gibbs reversed the two bookplates.

BERKENHOUT, JOHN   3291

Biographia literaria; or a biographical history of literature. Volume I (no more published). London, 1777. 4to.

Press-mark D.4 in MC; moved with a large group from D to the Library in the Offices.

SH SALE, V.31 (with Boswell, Drinkwater, and Nalson), to Pickering, £1.8.0.

☞ In a letter to Mason, 29 July 1773 HW wrote: 'Has not a Dr. Berkenhout sent to you for lists of your works and anecdotes of your life?' In his 'Book of Materials,' *ca*. 1786, HW recorded one note from Berkenhout.

BERNARD, PIERRE JOSEPH   3292

L'art d'aimer et poésies diverses. [Paris? *ca*. 1795?] 8vo.

'Boards, uncut, with MS note by HW.' Not in MC.

SH SALE, V.7 (with Baudeau, Boutet, Charlotte Elizabeth, Choiseul, Descamps, Dutens, La Live, Molière, *Observer*, Richelieu, Rousseau, Saint-Simon, Senebier, Suetonius, and Voltaire), to Pickering, 12/–; offered in Thorpe's Supplement for 1842, lot 11992, for 3/6.

3293 BOCCALINI, TRAJANO

I ragguagli di Parnasso: or advertisements from Parnassus. Translated by Henry Carey, Earl of Monmouth. London, 1656. Folio.

Press-mark D.3, entered by Kirgate, in MC; moved with a large group from D to the Library in the Offices.

SH SALE, v.20 (with Stirling), to Thorpe, £1.1.0.

☞ The SH copy of the original, reprinted at Amsterdam in 1669, was in L.6, No. 2098 *above.*

3294 BOSWELL, JAMES

The life of Samuel Johnson. London, 1791. Two volumes, 4to.

Bound in calf, rebacked. BP². Press-mark D.4 in MC; moved with a large group from D to the Library in the Offices.

SH SALE, v.31 (with Berkenhout, Drinkwater, and Nalson), to Pickering, £1.8.0; now in the Dyce Collection at the Victoria and Albert Museum.

☞ More than fifty identifications and notes by HW. He sent two paragraphs of interesting commentary on the *Life* and on his opinion of Johnson and Boswell to Mary Berry, 26 May 1791: 'Boswell has done shamefully, particularly against Mrs. Piozzi and Mrs. Montagu and Bishop Percy....'

3295 BOUTET DE MONVEL, JACQUES MARIE

Frédégonde et Brunéhaut, roman historique. London and Paris, 1775. 8vo.

Not in MC.

SH SALE, v.7 (with Baudeau, Bernard, Charlotte Elizabeth, Choiseul, Descamps, Dutens, La Live, Molière, *Observer*, Richelieu, Rousseau, Saint-Simon, Senebier, Suetonius, and Voltaire), to Pickering, 12/-; probably the copy offered, but not identified as HW's, in Thorpe's Supplement for 1842, lot 12817, for 3/-.

☞ For allusions to the old story, both before and after this novel was published, *see* HW's letters to Anne Pitt, 25 December 1765; to Mann, 2 September 1774; and to Lady Ossory, 9 October 1789.

3296 CAPACCIO, GIULIO CESARE

Gli apologi. Venice, 1619. 4to.

Not in MC.

SH SALE, v.8 (with 18 other volumes), to Boone, £2.2.0.

☞ This may have been an earlier edition.

CAPRIATA, PIETRO GIOVANNI   3297

The history of the wars in Italy, 1613 to 1644. Translated by Henry
  Carey, Earl of Monmouth. London, 1663. Folio.

Press-mark A.2.18 in MC; moved with other books to the Library in the
Offices.
SH SALE, v.28 (with Bentivoglio and Paruta), to Clarke, Wickham, 10/-.

[CHARLOTTE ELIZABETH, of Bavaria, Duchesse d'Orléans]   3298

Fragmens de lettres originales. Hamburg and Paris, 1788. Two volumes, 12mo.

Not in MC.
SH SALE, v.7 (with Baudeau, Bernard, Boutet, Choiseul, Descamps,
Dutens, La Live, Molière, *Observer*, Richelieu, Rousseau, Saint-Simon,
Senebier, Suetonius, and Voltaire), to Pickering, 12/-.

☞ *See* HW to the Earl of Strafford, 2 August 1788: 'I have lately been
reading some fragments of letters of the Duchess of Orléans, which are
certainly genuine. . . .'

CHOISEUL-STAINVILLE, ETIENNE FRANÇOIS, Duc de   3299

Mémoires. Paris, 1790. Two volumes, 8vo.

Not in MC.
SH SALE, v.7 (with Baudeau, Bernard, Boutet, Charlotte Elizabeth,
Descamps, Dutens, La Live, Molière, *Observer*, Richelieu, Rousseau,
Saint-Simon, Senebier, Suetonius, and Voltaire), to Pickering, 12/-; prob-
ably the copy offered, but not identified as HW's, in Thorpe's Supplement
for 1842, lot 12781, for 4/6.

☞ In his 'Book of Materials,' *ca.* 1790, HW preserved an account of
the publication of these *Mémoires,* as told to him by M. Barthélemy.

CICERO, MARCUS TULLIUS   3300

Orations against Caius Cornelius Verres. Translated by James White.
  London, 1787. 4to.

Not in MC.
SH SALE, v.12 (with Hayley, Jemmat, Nasmith, Polwhele, and Wild-
man), to Thorpe, £1.1.0; probably the copy offered, but not identified as
HW's, in Thorpe's Supplement for 1842, lot 12196, for 10/6.

3301 Clarke, Edward

Letters concerning the Spanish nation. London, 1763. 4to.

'Neat, with HW's BP.' Press-mark I.3.31, altered to D.2, in MC. (The entry was made by HW, after MC was compiled; D.2 is in Kirgate's hand.) Moved with a large group from D to the Library in the Offices.

SH SALE, v.19 (with Deering, and two works by North), to Thorpe, £2.10.0; offered in Thorpe's Supplement for 1842, lot 12199, for 10/6.

3302 Clarke, Samuel

The lives of sundry eminent persons in this later age. London, 1683. Folio.

Press-mark A.2.10 in MC; moved with other books to the Library in the Offices.

SH SALE, v.30 (with England, Guilford, and Helmont), to Slatter, 14/–.

3303 Consett, Matthew

A tour through Sweden. London, 1789. 4to.

Not in MC.

SH SALE, v.18 (with Huddesford, Owen, and Walker), to Pickering, 5/–.

3304 Coxe, William

Memoirs of . . . Sir Robert Walpole. London, 1798. Three volumes, 4to.

Not in MC, and because of its date of publication not strictly from HW's library. But HW had assisted Coxe in various ways, and this set was perhaps sent to SH by author or publisher.

SH SALE, v.24, to Pickering, £1.10.0.

3305 Deering, Charles

Nottinghamia vetus et nova. Nottingham, 1751. 4to.

'Calf, with HW's BP.' Press-mark E.3.44, entered by HW; altered to D.2 in MC. Moved with a large group from D to the Library in the Offices.

SH SALE, v.19 (with Clarke and two works by North), to Thorpe, £2.10.0; Sotheby's, 29 November 1927 (Sneyd Sale), lot 258.

☞ Another copy was in Press O, No. 2834 *above.*

DEFOE, DANIEL   3306

The history of the Union between England and Scotland. London,
1786. 4to.

Not in MC.

SH SALE, v.16 (with Gough, and two works by Nichols), to Webb &
Co., Leeds, £1.14.0.

DESCAMPS, JEAN BAPTISTE   3307

Voyage pittoresque de la Flandre et du Brabant. Paris, 1769. 8vo.

Purchased by HW at Dr. Lort's sale in April 1791. Not in MC.

SH SALE, v.7 (with Baudeau, Bernard, Boutet, Charlotte Elizabeth,
Choiseul, Dutens, La Live, Molière, *Observer*, Richelieu, Rousseau,
Saint-Simon, Senebier, Suetonius, and Voltaire), to Pickering, 12/–;
probably the copy offered, but not identified as HW's, in Thorpe's Supplement for 1842, lot 12282, for 7/6.

DEVIENNE, CHARLES JEAN BAPTISTE D'AGNEAUX, called Dom 3308

Histoire d'Artois. Paris, 1784–7. Five parts in one volume, 8vo.

Not in MC.

SH SALE, v.6 (with Alletz, *Esprit*, Gherardo, Lavallée, Louis XIV, Molé,
Villars, and Walpole), to Pickering, 7/–.

DOMENICHI, LODOVICO   3309

Facecies et motz subtilz. In French and Italian. Lyons, Granjon, 1559.
8vo.

Old vellum; recased in 1842, with new end-papers. HW's BP not preserved. Press-mark T.4 in Kirgate's hand preserved. Not in MC.

SH SALE, v.8 (with 18 other volumes), to Boone, £2.2.0. This copy is a
duplicate sold by the British Museum in 1769, when it was presumably
acquired by HW. Although the lot is recorded as purchased in 1842 by
Boone, a note on the fly-leaf indicates that Edward Cheney bought the volume soon afterwards. With the plate of Edward Cheney, and his arms
stamped in gold on the sides. Lucien Goldschmidt (from the collection of
Mrs. Benjamin Rogers), April 1962, to WSL, $65.

☞ One leaf, g1, is missing. A few pencilled markings are probably
not by HW.

3310 DORCHESTER, DUDLEY CARLETON, Viscount

Letters from and to Sir Dudley Carleton, Knt. during his embassy in Holland. Edited by Philip Yorke, Viscount Royston and later 2d Earl of Hardwicke. London, 1757. 4to.

Marbled boards, uncut. BP¹. Press-mark A.2.25. (Entered a second time in MC as a folio by Kirgate in error.) Moved with other books to the Library in the Offices.

SH SALE, V.25 (with Pilkington), to Thorpe, £2.5.0; in the Phillipps Collection; Robinson, January 1952, to WSL, $100.

☞ Corrections in MS on two pages by Sir Thomas Phillipps, and a few pencilled notes at the end. The backstrip lettered by HW, and he wrote on the title: 'published by the Lord Viscount Royston.' Opposite the entry in MC he wrote: 'A few only of these were printed for presents.' Lowndes records the number as 20. The work was reprinted in 1775 (50 copies according to Nichols) and 1780. Concerning the 2d edition HW wrote to Cole, 10 December 1775: 'Lord Hardwicke has indeed reprinted his heavy volume of Sir Dudley Carleton's *Dispatches*, and says I was in the wrong to despise it.' He told both Cole and Mason that Lord Hardwicke wanted him to reprint the book at SH.

3311 DRINKWATER, JOHN

A history of the late siege of Gibraltar. London, 1785. 4to.

Not in MC.

SH SALE, V.31 (with Berkenhout, Boswell, and Nalson), to Pickering, £1.8.0.

3312 DUTENS, LOUIS

Des pierres precieuses et des pierres fines. London, 1777. 8vo.

'Sewed, uncut, with note by Lort.' Not in MC. Purchased in Dr. Lort's Sale, April 1791, lot 4229, for 2/6.

SH SALE, V.7 (with Baudeau, Bernard, Boutet, Charlotte Elizabeth, Choiseul, Descamps, La Live, Molière, *Observer*, Richelieu, Rousseau, Saint-Simon, Senebier, Suetonius, and Voltaire), to Pickering, 12/–; offered in Thorpe's Supplement for 1842, lot 12325, for 5/–.

3313 ENGLAND. COURT OF CHANCERY

Select cases in the High Court of Chancery, solemnly argued and decreed by the late Lord Chancellor [Heneage Finch, Earl of Nottingham]. London, 1702. Folio.

Press-mark A.2.11 in MC; moved with other books to the Library in the Offices.

SH SALE, V.30 (with Clarke, Guilford, and Helmont), to Slatter, 14/–.

Esprit des journaux françois et étrangers. Paris, Liège, Brussels,   3314
    1772–. Three volumes, 12mo.
    Not in MC.
    SH SALE, V.6 (with Alletz, Devienne, Gherardo, Lavallée, Louis XIV,
Molé, Villars, and Walpole), to Pickering, 7/–.
    ☞ This review was published for many years; the sale catalogue
defines HW's set only as '3 odd vols.' They seem to have been strays from
the set in Press P, No. 3011 *above.*

FLOREZ, HENRIQUE   3315
Memorias de las Reynas Catholicas. Madrid, 1761. Two volumes, 4to.
    Not in MC.
    SH SALE, V.11 (with Hardinge, Hoblyn, Maittaire, Mirabeau, Waldron,
and Whiston), to Pickering, 10/–.

GHERARDO, PIETRO, *pseud.*   3316
*Histoire de la vie et faits d'Ezzelin III, surnommé da Romano, tyran
    de Padoue.* Translated from Italian. Paris, 1644. 8vo.
    Not in MC.
    SH SALE, V.6 (with Alletz, Devienne, *Esprit*, Lavallée, Louis XIV, Molé,
Villars, and Walpole), to Pickering, 7/–.

GIRALDI CINTIO, GIOVANNI BATTISTA   3317
Hecatommithi, overo cento novelle. Venice, 1593. 4to.
    Not in MC.
    SH SALE, V.8 (with 18 other volumes), to Boone, £2.2.0.

GONZAGA, FRANCESCO, Archbishop   3318
Lettere a prencipi. Edited by Guglielmo Pagnino. Rome, 1658. 8vo.
    Not in MC.
    SH SALE, V.8 (with 18 other volumes), to Boone, £2.2.0.
    ☞ Entered in the sale catalogue as 'Lettere delle Sig. Goazaga.'

3319 [GOUGH, RICHARD]

Anecdotes of British topography. London, 1768. 4to.

Not in MC.

SH SALE, v.16 (with Defoe and two works by Nichols), to Webb & Co., Leeds, £1.14.0.

☞ In a letter to Cole, 27 May 1769, HW wrote that this was 'a delight-ful book in our way.' Cole copied HW's notes and in 1772 sent them to Gough: *see* Cole to HW, 22 June 1772. Cole's own copy of Gough was among his books sold by White in 1784; in the Bliss sale in 1858, lot 1975, Cole's copy, described as having HW's notes copied into it, was purchased by Stewart, £2.11.0. But when the second edition was published in 1780, HW wrote to Cole, 19 May 1780: 'I do not think there was a guinea's worth of entertainment in the first [edition].'

The SH copy of the new edition of 1780 was in A.3 in the Main Library, No. 33 *above*.

3320 [GRAZZINI, ANTONIO FRANCESCO]

Tutti i trionfi, carri, mascherate, o canti carnascialeschi . . . dal tempo del magnifico Lorenzo de' Medici. Cosmopoli [Lucca], 1750. Two volumes, 8vo.

'Calf, with HW's BP.' Not in MC.

SH SALE, v.8 (with 17 other volumes), to Boone, £2.2.0; offered in Nattali's Catalogues for 1848 and 1849, 12/–.

3321 GUILFORD, FRANCIS NORTH, 1st Baron

The late Lord Chief Justice North's argument in the case between Sir William Soames and Sir Samuel Barnardiston. London, 1689. Folio.

Press-mark A.2.9 in MC; moved with other books to the Library in the Offices.

SH SALE, v.30 (with Clarke, England, and Helmont), to Slatter, 14/–.

3322 HANWAY, JONAS

The defects of police the cause of immorality. London, 1775. 4to.

'Boards, uncut, with HW's BP.' Not in MC.

SH SALE, v.13 (with Barrington, Beattie, and Martialis), to Thorpe, 5/–; offered in Thorpe's Supplement for 1842, lot 12503, for 7/6.

HARDINGE, NICHOLAS   3323

Latin verses. London, 1780. 8vo.

'Uncut, with MS notes by author and by HW.' Not in MC.

SH SALE, V.11 (with Florez, Hoblyn, Maittaire, Mirabeau, Waldron, and Whiston), to Pickering, 10/–; offered in Thorpe's Supplement for 1842, lot 12506, for 18/–; Sotheby's, 18 May 1848 (Eyton Sale), lot 719, to Nattali, 1/–. The Eyton Catalogue says 'a few MS notes in the autograph of HW, but without the cancelled leaves, uncut.'

HAYLEY, WILLIAM   3324

Plays in three acts written for a private theatre. London, 1784. 4to.

Not in MC.

SH SALE, V.12 (with Cicero, Jemmat, Nasmith, Polwhele, and Wildman), to Thorpe, £1.1.0; probably the copy offered, but not identified as HW's, in Thorpe's Supplement for 1842, lot 12530, for 15/–.

HELMONT, JAN BAPTISTA VAN   3325

Oriatrike, or physick refined. London, 1662. Folio.

Press-mark A.2.16 in MC; moved with other books to the Library in the Offices.

SH SALE, V.30 (with Clarke, England, and Guilford), to Slatter, 14/–.

HOBLYN, ROBERT   3326

Bibliotheca Hoblyniana. London, 1768. Two volumes, royal 8vo.

Not in MC.

SH SALE, V.11 (with Florez, Hardinge, Maittaire, Mirabeau, Waldron, and Whiston), to Pickering, 10/–.

[HUDDESFORD, GEORGE]   3327

Salmagundi: a miscellaneous combination of original poetry. London, 1791. 4to.

Press-mark D.3 in MC; moved with a large group from Press D to the Library in the Offices.

SH SALE, V.18 (with Consett, Owen, and Walker), to Pickering, 5/–.

3328 HUME, DAVID

The history of England. London, 1754–62. Four volumes, 4to.

Press-mark I.3.18, erased and D.4 superimposed, in MC. The entry says '6 vol. 1762' but Mrs. Damer has marked it '4 vols. only in D.4.' Four volumes are counted in the sale catalogue. The full set of six volumes was first published at intervals from 1754. This set was moved to the Library in the Offices with the other books from D.

SH SALE, v.27 (with Orléans and White), to Pickering, £1.5.0.

☞ There are several references to Hume in HW's 'Book of Materials,' *ca.* 1759 and 1775.

3329 HUTCHINSON, WILLIAM

The history and antiquities of the County Palatine of Durham. Newcastle, 1785–7. Two volumes, 4to.

Press-mark D.4 in MC; moved with a large group to the Library in the Offices.

SH SALE, v.26, to Dr. Gray, Dean's Yard, £1.

☞ The 3d volume, published in 1794, seems perhaps to have been shelved and sold with Hutchinson's *Cumberland*, v.53. *See* Press S, No. 3193 *above.*

3330 JEMMAT, CATHERINE

Miscellanies in prose and verse. London, 1766. 4to.

Not in MC.

SH SALE, v.12 (with Cicero, Hayley, Nasmith, Polwhele, and Wildman), to Thorpe, £1.1.0; probably the copy offered, but not identified as HW's, in Thorpe's Supplement for 1842, lot 12625, for 7/6.

☞ The long list of subscribers includes HW's name.

3331 KNIGHT, ELLIS CORNELIA

Lettere di Marco Flaminio. Translated from English by Baldassar Odescalchi. Rome, 1794. Two volumes, 12mo.

Not in MC.

SH SALE, v.8 (with 17 other volumes), to Boone, £2.2.0.

☞ The English original, in 1792, was dedicated to HW.

LA LIVE DE JULLY, ANGE LAURENT DE   3332
Catalogue historique du cabinet de peinture et sculpture françoise de
  Monsieur de La Live. Paris, 1764. 8vo.

  Not in MC.
  SH SALE, v.7 (with Baudeau, Bernard, Boutet, Charlotte Elizabeth,
  Choiseul, Descamps, Dutens, Molière, *Observer,* Richelieu, Rousseau,
  Saint-Simon, Senebier, Suetonius, and Voltaire), to Pickering, 12/–; prob-
  ably the copy offered, but not specified as HW's, in Thorpe's Supplement
  for 1842, lot 12902, 'boards,' for 5/6.
  ☞ The sale catalogue has only 'Catalogue Historique.'

LANGUET, HUBERT   3333
Epistolae ad Philippum Sydneium. Edited by Sir David Dalrymple.
  Edinburgh, 1776. 8vo.

  Bound in nineteenth-century calf. The label by HW on the paper cover
  is preserved: 'Langueti Epistolae 1776.' Inscribed on fly-leaf: 'From the
  Editor.' BP² early state. Not in MC, and press-mark not preserved by the
  binder.
  SH SALE, v.8 (with 18 other volumes), to Boone, £2.2.0; given by Mr.
  A. N. L. Munby, September 1947, to WSL.

[LAVALLÉE, JOSEPH, Editor]   3334
Voyage dans les départemens de la France, par une Société des artistes
  et de gens de lettres. Paris, 1792. Three volumes, 8vo.

  Not in MC.
  SH SALE, v.6 (with Alletz, Devienne, *Esprit,* Gherardo, Louis XIV, Molé,
  Villars, and Walpole), to Pickering, 7/–.
  ☞ Completed in 1802 in 13 volumes.

LA VALLIÈRE, LOUIS CÉSAR, Duc de   3335
Catalogue des livres de la bibliothèque de feu M. le duc de la Vallière.
  Compiled by Guillaume de Bure. Paris, 1783. Three volumes, 8vo.
  Not in MC.
  SH SALE, v.5 (with Magazines), to Jones, Blackman-Street, 5/–.

  ☞ When Joseph White of London went to Paris to attend the
  sale of the La Vallière MSS, HW gave him some commissions; but he cancelled them later (HW to Thomas Walpole at Paris, 6 January 1784). Perhaps the MSS he had planned to bid on included those that White reported
  to him, in a note from Paris, 11 March 1784: 'The Bedford Missal, King

René's Prayer Book and the greatest part of the MSS were bought by His Majesty. . . . The Guirlande of Julia No. 3247 sold for 14,510 Livres.' On this HW commented: 'The Guirlande de Julie was, I suppose, the dearest book ever sold.'

3336 Le Vassor, Michel, Translator

Lettres et mémoires de François de Vargas [and others] *touchant le Concile de Trent.* Amsterdam, 1699. 8vo.

Not in MC.

SH SALE, v.8 (with 18 other volumes), to Boone, £2.2.0.

3337 Louis XIV, King of France

Galerie de l'ancienne cour, ou mémoires anecdotes pour servir à l'histoire des regnes de Louis XIV et de Louis XV. N.p., 1786. Three volumes, 12mo.

Not in MC.

SH SALE, v.6 (with Alletz, Devienne, *Esprit*, Gherardo, Lavallée, Molé, Villars, and Walpole), to Pickering, 7/–.

☞ This work included extracts from Saint-Simon's *Mémoires*; HW explained the duplication of these extracts, which were printed more completely in 1788 (No. 3259 *above*), in his letter to Lady Ossory, 22 July 1789.

3338 Magazines

It seems convenient to bring the following seven entries together, especially since they were all sold at the beginning of the Fifth Day.

(1) *Annual Register*. Edited at first by Edmund Burke and published by Dodsley. 33 volumes, 8vo. Entered in MC in 1763 as H.4.19, 4 volumes. The total of 33 volumes suggests that HW kept the file only from 1759 to 1790. SH SALE, v.2, to Kimpton, £1.11.6.

(2) *British Critic*, 1793–95. Six volumes, 8vo. SH SALE, v.3 (with *London Magazine*), to Jones, Blackman-Street, 12/–. Edited by HW's correspondents, William Beloe and Robert Nares; HW showed SH to the two men, 30 August 1792.

(3) *European Magazine*, 1782–95. 28 volumes, 8vo. SH SALE, v.4, to Jones, Blackman-Street, 12/–.

(4) *Gentleman's Magazine*, 1731–95. 80 volumes, 8vo. (Published in single volumes annually through 1783, and then two volumes or 'parts' in each year; included were the two volumes of Index of 1789.) Thorpe's description says Volumes 10–51 were half-bound; the rest uncut. SH

SALE, v.1, to Pickering, £7.7.0; offered in Thorpe's Supplement for 1842, lot 12435, for £12.12.0.

(5) *Journal étranger de littérature*. Edited by Le Texier. London, 1777–8. Issued twice a month, 23 numbers in all. According to the SH catalogue, HW's set comprised 33 volumes, perhaps a misprint for 23. The list of subscribers includes HW's name.

(6) *London Magazine*, 1732–47. Sixteen volumes, 8vo. Entered in MC, B.5.1, as 'London Magazines from 1732 to 1747, 16 vol.' Apparently HW never added to this file. Kirgate marked in the margin of MC: 'Library in the Offices.' SH SALE, v.3 (with *British Critic*), to Jones, Blackman-Street, 12/–.

(7) MAGAZINES. Entered in sale catalogue as 'about 100 nos. of magazines.' SH SALE, v.5 (with La Vallière), to Jones, Blackman-Street, 5/–.

MAITTAIRE, MICHAEL   3339
Historia typographorum aliquot Parisiensium. London, 1717. Two volumes bound in one, 8vo.

This copy not in MC.

SH SALE, v.11 (with Florez, Hardinge, Hoblyn, Mirabeau, Waldron, and Whiston), to Pickering, 10/–.

☞ Another copy was in B.3, No. 275 *above*.

MALESPINI, RICORDANO   3340
Historia antica dall' edificazione de Fiorenza. Florence, 1718. 4to.

Not in MC.

SH SALE, v.8 (with 18 other volumes), to Boone, £2.2.0; Sotheby's, 26 July 1884 (Crossley Sale), lot 2329, to Osborne.

☞ First published in 1568. The edition is identified from the Crossley Sale, although that copy may have been HW's other copy in L.3, No. 2081 *above*.

Another book in lot 8 has resisted identification: it is entered in the sale catalogue only as 'La Maria.'

MARTIALIS, MARCUS VALERIUS   3341
Epigrams. Translated by James Elphinston. London, 1782. 4to.

'Boards, uncut, with notes by HW.' Not in MC.

SH SALE, v.13 (with Barrington, Beattie, and Hanway), to Thorpe, 5/–; offered in Thorpe's Supplement for 1842, lot 12762, for 15/–.

3342 METASTASIO, PIETRO ANTONIO DOMENICO BONAVENTURA
[Opere] Six volumes.

>   Not in MC. Possibly a set printed at Paris in 1773.
>   SH SALE, V.10, to Slatter, 12/–.
>
>   ☞ A set of Metastasio in twelve volumes, 1775–83, bound in calf with the French royal arms, was offered by Mr. William P. Wreden in Catalogue 41 (1961); it contained the leather book label of Horace Earl of Orford, i.e., Horatio William (1813–94), 4th Earl of the new creation (lot 198 in the sale of Lord Orford's books at Sotheby's in 1895).

3343 [MIRABEAU, HONORÉ GABRIEL RIQUETTI, Comte de]
Histoire secrète de la cour de Berlin. [Alençon], 1789. Two volumes, 8vo.

>   Not in MC.
>   SH SALE, V.11 (with Florez, Hardinge, Hoblyn, Maittaire, Waldron, and Whiston), to Pickering, 10/–.

3344 [MOLÉ, GUILLAUME FRANÇOIS ROGER]
Histoire des modes françaises. Paris and Amsterdam, 1773. 12mo.

>   Not in MC. Purchased at Dr. Lort's Sale, in April 1791, lot 4333 (with Alletz *above*), for 7/6.
>   SH SALE, V.6 (with Alletz, Devienne, *Esprit*, Gherardo, Lavallée, Louis XIV, Villars, and Walpole), to Pickering, 7/–.

3345 MOLIÈRE, JEAN BAPTISTE POQUELIN DE
One volume, not further identified.

>   SH SALE, V.7 (with 15 other items), to Pickering, 12/–.
>
>   ☞ Any single volume of Molière may be here described, perhaps something like the selections, *Dialogues French and English*, published in London in 1767. The sale catalogue lists only 'Molière.'

3346 NALSON, JOHN
An impartial collection of the great affairs of state. London, 1683. Folio.

>   Not in MC.
>   SH SALE, V.31 (with Berkenhout, Boswell, and Drinkwater), to Pickering, £1.8.0.
>
>   ☞ Published in two volumes, 1682 and 1683. But the sale catalogue lists only one volume and dates it 1683; HW therefore seems to have had only the 2d volume.

NASMITH, JAMES   3347
*Catalogus librorum manuscriptorum quas Collegio Corporis Christi
    legavit Mathaeus Parker.* Cambridge, 1777. 4to.
'Beautiful copy, uncut.' Not in MC.
SH SALE, V.12 (with Cicero, Hayley, Jemmat, Polwhele, and Wildman),
to Thorpe, £1.1.0; Sotheby's, 19 April 1844 (Eyton Sale), lot 559, to Willis,
2/–.

NICHOLS, JOHN, Editor   3348
Bibliotheca topographica Britannica. London, 1780–90. Eight vol-
    umes, 4to.
Not in MC.
SH SALE, V.17, to Slatter, £14.14.0.
☞ Published in parts, with contributions by numerous antiquarians.
From these volumes HW copied a few notes into his 'Book of Materials,' *ca.*
1784 and 1787. According to a contemporary newspaper account of the
sale, the set was uncut.

NICHOLS, JOHN   3349
Biographical and literary anecdotes of William Bowyer. London, 1782.
    4to.
Bound in half calf in the mid-nineteenth century, and now rebacked.
BP² later state. Extra-illustrated by G. Wright, 1844. Bookplate of W. J.
Freer (Major William Jesse Freer, F.S.A.). Sale label, 'No. 5, lot 16,'
preserved on the title-page. Press-mark not preserved, and not in MC.
SH SALE, V.16 (with Defoe, Gough, and Nichols's *Tracts of Bowyer*), to
Webb & Co., Leeds, £1.14.0; B. Halliday, October 1949, to Mr. A. N. L.
Munby for WSL, £12.10.0.
☞ About 40 MS notes by HW. When he reached p. 641, he paused to
refute Bishop Newton's assertion that Bolingbroke had advised Middleton
to publish his treatise on the inutility and inefficacy of prayer; he wrote
a marginal note: 'The contrary was fact, as Mrs. Middleton herself told me.
Lord Bolingbroke advised the Doctor to burn it, but his Lordship kept a
copy of it. HW.' He had noted the same fact thirty years earlier in his anecdotes of Middleton (printed in the Yale Walpole, Vol. 15).

NICHOLS, JOHN   3350
A collection of all the wills . . . of the kings and queens of England.
    London, 1780. 4to.
'Boards, uncut.' Not in MC.

SH SALE, v.15 (with Nichols's *Regulations* and Topham), to Strong, £3.13.6; offered in Strong's Catalogue for 1843, lot 1083, for £1.5.0.

☞ 'With MS notes by HW,' according to Strong's Catalogue.

3351 NICHOLS, JOHN

Collection of ordinances and regulations for the government of the royal household. London, 1790. 4to.

'Boards, uncut.' Not in MC.

SH SALE, v.15 (with Nichols's *Royal Wills* and Topham), to Strong, £3.13.6; offered in Strong's Catalogue for 1843, lot 1085, for £1.18.0; Fletcher, 7 April 1846 (Britton Sale, Part 4), lot 377, to Street, 9/–.

3352 NICHOLS, JOHN, Editor

Miscellaneous tracts by William Bowyer and several of his learned friends. London, 1785. 4to.

Rebound in half calf, probably at the same time as the *Anecdotes of Bowyer.* No BP. Press-mark not preserved. Not in MC. Spine labelled 'SH 1842.'

SH SALE, v.16 (with Defoe, Gough, and Nichols's *Anecdotes of Bowyer*), to Webb & Co., Leeds, £1.14.0; David Low, July 1943, to St. John's College, Cambridge, 21/–; now in the library of St. John's College.

☞ Two notes by HW.

3353 NICHOLS, JOHN

The progresses and processions of Queen Elizabeth. London, 1788. Two volumes, 4to.

Not in MC.

SH SALE, v.14, to Pickering, £2.2.0.

☞ A third volume was published in 1805.

3354 NORTH, ROGER

Examen, or an enquiry into the credit and veracity of a pretended complete history [White Kennet's *History*, 1706]. London, 1740. 4to.

Press-mark I.3.27, altered to D.2, in MC; moved with a large group from D to the Library in the Offices.

SH SALE, v.19 (with Clarke, Deering, and North's *Life*), to Thorpe, £2.10.0; offered with the *Life*, by Strong and in the Britton Sale, 1846.

NORTH, ROGER   3355

The life of the Right Honourable Francis North, Baron of Guilford.
London, 1742. 4to.

Old calf, now repaired. BP[1]. Press-mark I.3.26, altered to D.3 and then
to D.2; moved with a large group from D to the Library in the Offices.

SH SALE, v.19 (with Clarke, Deering, and North's *Examen*), to Thorpe,
£2.10.0; offered in Strong's Catalogue for 1843, lot 1101 (with North's
Examen), for £2.5.0; Fletcher, 9 April 1846 (Britton Sale, Part 4), lot
932 (with North's *Examen*), to Pickering, 16/–; Pratley of Tunbridge
Wells, April 1952, to WSL, £5.5.0.

☞ Bound in is North's *Life of Sir Dudley North and Dr. John North*,
1744.

Numerous pencil markings by HW. In his 'Book of Materials,' *ca.* 1759,
he noted that North's *Life* contained some details of the career of Anne
Clifford, Countess of Dorset. He also referred to this work several times
in his *Anecdotes* and *R&NA*.

NORTHAMPTON, HENRY HOWARD, Earl of   3356

A defensative against the poyson of supposed prophecies. London,
1620. Folio.

'With HW's BP.' Press-mark A.2.20 in MC; moved with other books to
the Library in the Offices.

SH SALE, v.23 (with Paruta and Stair), to Thorpe, 18/–; offered in
Thorpe's Supplement for 1842, lot 12594, for 18/–.

☞ A copy of the edition of 1583 was in A.6, No. 93 *above.*

The Observer. [Essays by Richard Cumberland]. London, 1785–90. 3357
One volume, 8vo.

Not in MC.

SH SALE, v.7 (with 15 other items), to Pickering, 12/–.

☞ The sale catalogue lists 'an odd vol. of the Observer.' A complete set
is usually bound in five volumes.

ORLÉANS, PIERRE JOSEPH D'   3358

Histoire des révolutions d'Espagne. Paris, 1734. Three volumes, 4to.

Press-mark D.4 in MC: entered by HW, but the press-mark is superimposed by Kirgate on an earlier number. Moved with other books to
the Library in the Offices.

SH SALE, v.27 (with Hume and White), to Pickering, £1.5.0.

☞ The entry in the sale catalogue is 'History of the Revolutions in Spain and Portugal, 3.' There are other instances in the sale catalogue of translated titles.

3359 OWEN, THOMAS

The reports of Judge Thomas Owen, wherein are many choice cases. London, 1656. Folio.

Not in MC.

SH SALE, v.18 (with Consett, Huddesford, and Walker), to Pickering, 5/–.

☞ Entered in the sale catalogue as 'Owen's Report.' Since the other books in this group are mostly imprints later than 1763, some other volume may be meant, such as the *Reports of Cases* [in the Court of King's Bench] compiled by Timothy Cunningham and published in 1766 by William Owen, or a *post*-Walpolian *Report* by Robert Owen the Socialist.

3360 PARUTA, PAOLO

The history of Venice. Translated by Henry Carey, Earl of Monmouth. London, 1658. Folio.

Press-mark A.2.26 in MC; moved with other books to the Library in the Offices.

SH SALE, v.28 (with Bentivoglio and Capriata), to Clarke, Wickham, 10/–.

☞ An extra-illustrated set of *Walpoliana* in five volumes prepared by James Gibbs in 1875, now in the New York Public Library, has BP[2] early state inserted in the first volume with a note by Gibbs dated 1876 saying it came from the *History of Venice* of 1658, bought at the SH SALE. But *see* Bentivoglio *above*: Gibbs reversed the two bookplates; the Paruta ought to have had BP[1] and the Bentivoglio BP[2]. It seems unlikely that either volume will now be traced.

3361 PARUTA, PAOLO

Politick discourses. Translated by Henry Carey, Earl of Monmouth. London, 1657. Folio.

Press-mark A.2.27 in MC, added by HW; moved with other books to the Library in the Offices.

SH SALE, v.23 (with Northampton and Stair), to Thorpe, 18/–.

Pilkington, Matthew   3362

The gentleman's and connoisseur's dictionary of painters. London, 1770. 4to.

Not in MC.

SH SALE, V.25 (with Dorchester), to Thorpe, £2.5.0.

Poems   3363

Poems, Odes, and Tracts. Five volumes, 4to.

Press-mark K.1.23, altered to I.3 (to make room for the 'Theatre of George the 3d') in MC; marked in margin: 'some in D.3.' Moved after 1797 with a large group from D to the Library in the Offices.

SH SALE, V.21, to Thorpe, £1.1.0.

☞ Only parts of this collection can be identified. It is entered in MC as 'Poems, Miscellaneous, 7 Vol.' and right under it '1 Vol.' has been added, so that eight volumes in all seem to be recorded in quarto. Perhaps one was left in I.3, sold iii.102, and two were perhaps sold in v.92; if so, five would be left in v.21. (Both iii.102 and v.21 were recorded as purchased by Thorpe.)

Six volumes of Poems were offered by Thomas Rodd in his Catalogue for 1845, lot 7562, and these perhaps included the five volumes of v.21. Rodd describes them as bound in six volumes, calf, with the contents written by HW in each volume. Authors named by Rodd are: Dryden, D'Urfey, Gray, Dodsley, Francklin, Cambridge, Shenstone, Mrs. Killigrew, Lady Mary Wortley Montagu, Akenside, Thomson, Dr. Johnson, West, Mason, Whitehead, Dyer, Churchill, Armstrong, &c.

Presumably these six volumes were broken up. Three pieces now at Farmington may be from them:

(1) [Goldwin, William] *Scotch adventure,* 1746. Pickering & Chatto, January 1940, to WSL, £2.10.0. Note by HW identifying the author on the title.

(2) Montagu, Lady Mary Wortley. *Six town eclogues,* 1747. From the Harmsworth collection; Pickering & Chatto, June 1950, to WSL, £20. It shows traces of having been removed from a calf-bound volume; identifications throughout by HW. He supplied Dodsley with some of the MSS and arranged for the publication of these Eclogues: *see* his letter to Mann, 24 November 1747, and his note in his copy of Dodsley's *Collection* quoted in the Yale Walpole, note 40 to Gray's letter of January 1748.

(3) Waller, Edmund. *Of love.* A half-sheet broadside in two columns, with HW's note indicating that the second column is the poem as 'alter'd by

3363   Coll. Cibber 1755.' It was never bound, but folded and laid loosely in some volume. From the Harmsworth Collection; Pickering & Chatto, June 1950, to WSL, £15.

One of the volumes, now at Harvard, can be identified by the press-marks as having been in this collection at SH: K.1.27, altered to D.3 and then to D.2. BP[1]. Bound in old mottled calf. The binder's title is 'Things about Pope collected by H. Walpole.' With HW's list of contents inside the front cover, and each piece numbered by him. George Daniel bought the volume in 1842, and added notes about the plates; Sotheby's, 25 July 1864 (Daniel Sale), lot 1277, to Lilly, £2; offered in Lilly's Catalogue for 1864, for £3.13.6; bequeathed by Charles Sumner in April 1874 to Harvard.

In addition to various rare plates, this volume includes:

(1) BLAKISTON, Mr. *The Pantheon: a vision.* London, 1747. With HW's note on the half-title: 'By Mr. Blakiston.'

(2) [BROWN, JOHN] *An essay on satire: occasioned by the death of Mr. Pope.* London, 1745. With HW's note on the title: 'By Dr. Browne.'

(3) [MASON, WILLIAM] *Musaeus: a monody to the memory of Mr. Pope, in imitation of Milton's Lycidas.* London, 1747. With HW's note on the half-title: 'By Mr. Mason.'

(4) POPE, ALEXANDER. *Verses on the grotto at Twickenham. Attempted in Latin and Greek.* (With Dodsley's *Cave of Pope.*) London, 1743.

(5) SERLE, JOHN. *A plan of Mr. Pope's garden . . . to which is added, a character of all his writings.* London, 1745. The 'character' is by William Thompson. Some MS notes not by HW.

(6) FÉNELON, FRANÇOIS DE SALIGNAC DE LA MOTHE. *Adventures of Telemachus. The first book.* Translated into English. London, 1738.

(7) *The Jubilade. An ode.* In imitation of Horace, Book IV, Ode 5. London, 1743.

(8) *Honour. A poem.* London, 1743. With HW's note on title, 'By Mr. Nugent'; but usually ascribed to John Brown, on the evidence of the reprint in Dodsley's Collection, 'By the Rev. Mr. Brown.'

(9) *The Crooked six-pence.* London, 1743. A satire on John Philips by James Bramston, who pretended that the poem had been found among Mrs. Katharine Philips's papers.

(10) *The deviliad. An heroic poem.* London, 1744. A satire on Sir Thomas Deveil by a Mr. Taswell.

(11) [AKENSIDE, MARK] *An epistle to Curio.* London, 1744. With HW's note identifying Curio as Lord Bath.

(12) *An Ode, to Mr. Handel.* London, 1745.

(13) *Wit, a poem most humbly inscribed to the . . . Earl of Orford.* London, 1745.

(14) *Jovi Eleutherio: or, an offering to liberty.* London, 1745. By Glocester Ridley.

(15) *Modern virtue. A satire.* London, 1746.

(16) *Plain truth: a satire. Humbly inscribed to the Right Honourable J— — E— — — of G.* London, 1747. Addressed to Lord Granville.

Possibly in this or a similar lot was a volume in 4to now in Lord Walde-grave's collection, bound in calf and labelled 'Poems, &c.' It is a scrapbook containing several hundred prologues and epilogues, and political and theatrical prints. Inside the cover is HW's BP² but the notes in the volume are not by HW, and the plate may be an insertion.

POLWHELE, RICHARD   3364

Historical views of Devonshire. Volume I (no more published). Exeter, 1793. 4to.

Not in MC.

SH SALE, v.12 (with Cicero, Hayley, Jemmat, Nasmith, and Wildman), to Thorpe, £1.1.0; probably the copy offered, but not identified as HW's, in Thorpe's Supplement for 1842, lot 12999, for 10/6.

POPHAM, EDWARD   3365

Illustrium virorum elogia sepulchralia. London, 1778. 8vo.

Not in MC.

SH SALE, v.8 (with 18 other volumes), to Boone, £2.2.0.

☞ Entered only by title in the SH SALE catalogue.

RAGIONAMENTI   3366

One volume, apparently in 4to.

Not in MC.

SH SALE, v.8 (with 18 other volumes), to Boone, £2.2.0.

☞ Entered in sale catalogue as 'Duc [error for Due?] Ragionamenti.' Two possibilities may be suggested:

(1) VASARI, GIORGIO. *Ragionamenti sopra le inventioni da lui dipinte in Firenze . . . insieme con la inventione della pittura.* Florence, 1588. 4to.

(2) BENEDICT XIV, Pope (PROSPERO LAMBERTINI). *Ragionamento* and *Secondo Ragionamento.* Rome, 1715. 4to. Since HW called Pope Benedict 'my friend,' he might have been interested in these early pamphlets, concerning landscaping in Rome.

3367 RANZOVIUS, HENRICUS

Catalogus imperatorum, regum, ac principum qui astrologicam artem amarunt. Antwerp, 1580. 8vo.

Not in MC.

SH SALE, v.8 (with 18 other volumes), to Boone, £2.2.0.

☞ Entered in the sale catalogue only as 'Catalogus Imperatorum,' but presumably a second copy of Ranzovius; the first copy was in H.8, No. 1584 *above.*

3368 RICHELIEU, LOUIS FRANÇOIS ARMAND DU PLESSIS, DUC DE

Mémoires. Edited by Jean Louis Giraud Soulavie. Londres [i.e. Paris?], 1789. 8vo.

Not in MC.

SH SALE, v.7 (with Baudeau, Bernard, Boutet, Charlotte Elizabeth, Choiseul, Descamps, Dutens, La Live, Molière, *Observer*, Rousseau, Saint-Simon, Senebier, Suetonius, and Voltaire), to Pickering, 12/–.

☞ Completed in nine volumes in 1793; HW seems to have had only the single volume.

3369 ROUSSEAU, JEAN JACQUES

Rousseau juge de Jean Jacques. Edited by Sir Brooke Boothby. Lichfield, 1780. 8vo.

Not in MC.

SH SALE, v.7 (with Baudeau, Bernard, Boutet, Charlotte Elizabeth, Choiseul, Descamps, Dutens, La Live, Molière, *Observer*, Richelieu, Saint-Simon, Senebier, Suetonius, and Voltaire), to Pickering, 12/–.

☞ The sale catalogue has only 'Rousseau,' but in a letter to Mason, 31 May 1780, HW wrote: 'There is just published a dialogue of Rousseau, the title of which is *Rousseau juge Jean Jacques*. There are fine strokes of eloquence. . . . Lord Harcourt himself allows it is a very odd book and certainly Rousseau's, and yet I think is sorry it is.'

3370 [RUGGLE, GEORGE]

Ignoramus, Comoedia.

Not in MC.

SH SALE, v.8 (with 18 other volumes), to Boone, £2.2.0.

☞ Entered only as 'Ignoramus' in the sale catalogue. Very probably a different edition from that sold in M.7, No. 2256 *above.* But one may guess that this copy, if it was Ruggle's play, may have been of the edition published in 1789.

SAINT-SIMON, LOUIS DE ROUVROY, DUC de   3371
Mémoires and *Supplément*. Londres [i.e. Paris?], 1788–9. Five volumes, 8vo.

Not in MC.
SH SALE, v.7 (with Baudeau, Bernard, Boutet, Charlotte Elizabeth,
Choiseul, Descamps, Dutens, La Live, Molière, *Observer*, Richelieu,
Rousseau, Senebier, Suetonius, and Voltaire), to Pickering, 12/–.

☞ One volume of the *Mémoires* and four of the *Supplément* were
sold here. The other two volumes of the *Mémoires* were sold in Press
T, No. 3259 *above*, where they had apparently been misplaced.

SENEBIER, JEAN   3372
Catalogue raisonné des manuscrits conservés dans la Bibliothèque
    ... *de Genève*. Geneva, 1779. 8vo.

Rebound. BP and press-mark not preserved. Not in MC. Bookplate of
Cardiff Castle (3d Marquess of Bute).
SH SALE, v.7 (with Baudeau, Bernard, Boutet, Charlotte Elizabeth, Choi-
seul, Descamps, Dutens, La Live, Molière, *Observer*, Richelieu, Rousseau,
Saint-Simon, Suetonius, and Voltaire), to Pickering, 12/–; offered in
Thorpe's Supplement for 1842, lot 12126, for 10/6; given by Mr. A. N. L.
Munby, July 1953, to WSL.

☞ In his 'Book of Materials,' *ca.* 1780, HW commented on a letter of
Calvin mentioned in the *Catalogue*. A few markings and notes by HW,
and his signature, 'Hor. Walpole 1779; this book is curious & well executed.'

SHERLOCK, MARTIN   3373
Consiglio ad un giovane poeta. [Rome, 1779?] 8vo.

Not in MC.
SH SALE, v.8 (with 18 other volumes), to Boone, £2.2.0.

☞ *See* HW to Lady Ossory, 16 November 1780: 'Mr. Sherlock's Italian
is ten times worse than his French, and more bald. He by no means wants
parts, but a good deal more judgment.'

SOPRANI, RAFFAELLO   3374
Vite de pittori, scultori ed architetti Genovesi. Genoa, 1768–9. Two
volumes, 4to.

Original marbled wrappers. BP² early state. Press-mark T.4. (Five
books—Domenichi, Soprani, Tapestries, Ubaldini, and Vasconcellos—

with press-mark T.4 have been recovered; perhaps these were moved at one time, in 1797 or 1842.) Not in MC.

SH SALE, v.9 (with Tapestries, Tractatus, Ubaldini, and Vasconcellos), to Pickering, 10/–; Sotheby's, 23 June 1958 (Lord Vernon Sale), lot 41, to Maggs for WSL, £22.

☞ In his 'Book of Materials,' ca. 1771, HW noted three references to Genoese painters who had lived in England. A few marginal markings by HW, mostly in the first volume.

3375 STAFFORD, THOMAS
Pacata Hibernia. Ireland appeased and reduced, or an historie of the late warres . . . under the government of Sir George Carew. London, 1633. Folio.
Press-mark A.2.5 in MC; moved with other books to the Library in the Offices.
SH SALE, v.29, to Thorpe, £3.5.0; probably the copy offered, but not identified as HW's, in Thorpe's Supplement for 1842, lot 13197, for £5.5.0.

3376 STAIR, JAMES DALRYMPLE, later Viscount
The institutions of the law of Scotland. Edinburgh, 1681. Folio.
Press-mark A.2.21 in MC; moved with other books to the Library in the Offices.
SH SALE, v.23 (with Northampton and Paruta), to Thorpe, 18/–.

3377 STIRLING, WILLIAM ALEXANDER, Earl of
Recreations with the muses. London, 1637. Pot folio.
Old calf, rebacked, with new end-papers. BP[1] now on verso of the title-page. Press-mark A.2.22 in MC; moved with other books to the Library in the Offices. Name on title: 'John Fairfax, November the 26th, 1653.' Bookplate of Beverly Chew.
SH SALE, v.20 (with Boccalini), to Thorpe, £1.1.0; Anderson, 6 November 1918 (Duplicates from Huntington Library), lot 6, $16; gift of Mr. Roland Redmond, March 1942, to the Morgan Library.
☞ A few markings; one pencilled note may be HW's.

3378 SUETONIUS TRANQUILLUS, CAIUS
Les douze Césars. Translated by Jean François de la Harpe. Paris, 1770. Two volumes, 8vo.
Not in MC.

SH SALE, v.7 (with Baudeau, Bernard, Boutet, Charlotte Elizabeth, Choiseul, Descamps, Dutens, La Live, Molière, *Observer*, Richelieu, Rousseau, Saint-Simon, Senebier, and Voltaire), to Pickering, 12/–; probably the copy offered, but not identified as HW's, in Thorpe's Supplement for 1842, lot 13227, for 4/–.

SWIFT, JONATHAN   3379
Works. Edited by John Hawkesworth and (Volume 8) Deane Swift.
   London, 1755–65. Eight volumes, royal 4to.
   Original calf. BP¹. Press-marks K.1.9–16, altered to D.3 and then to
D.2; moved with a large group from D to the Library in the Offices.
   SH SALE, v.22 (with Swift's *Letters*), to Dr. Gray, Dean's Yard, £4.8.0;
Dobell, April 1934, to WSL (with Swift's *Letters*), £25.
   ☞ Scattered markings and identifications by HW, about 30 in all,
throughout. The last two volumes, published 1764–5, have BP² early state;
and the entry in MC is corrected from '6 Vols.' to '8.'

SWIFT, JONATHAN   3380
Letters. Edited by John Hawkesworth and Deane Swift. London,
   1766–68. Four volumes, royal 4to.
   Original calf. No BP. Press-marks D.3, altered to D.2; moved with a
large group from D to the Library in the Offices.
   SH SALE, v.22 (with Swift's *Works*).
   ☞ Many markings and notes by HW, but fewer in the fourth volume.
In his 'Book of Materials,' 15 May 1766, HW wrote: 'I carried to Lady
Suffolk the two new volumes of Swift's correspondence. . . .' And he talked
of them again to Lady Suffolk on July 1st.

TAPESTRIES   3381
Succinte description des tapisseries appartenantes à la . . . Maison
   Delfino à Venise. (In French and Italian) Verona, 1776. 4to.
   Original boards. BP² later state. Press-mark T.4. Not in MC.
   SH SALE, v.9 (with Soprani, Tractatus, Ubaldini, and Vasconcellos), to
Pickering, 10/–; purchased from Pickering, with other SH books, 7 June
1842, by the British Museum.

TOPHAM, JOHN   3382
Liber quotidianus Contrarotulatoris Garderobae, anno regni Regis
   Edwardi primi vicesimo octavo. London, 1787. 4to.
   'Boards, uncut.' Not in MC.

sh sale, v.15 (with two works by Nichols), to Strong, £3.13.6; offered in Strong's Catalogue for 1843, lot 1084, for £1.18.0; Fletcher, 8 April 1846 (Britton Sale, Part 4), lot 684, 7/–.

☞ The volume was published separately by the Society of Antiquaries. Strong catalogued it as a work edited by Nichols.

3383 Tractatus

Tractatus de metro. Cambridge, 1778. 8vo.

Not in mc.
sh sale, v.9 (with Soprani, Tapestries, Ubaldini, and Vasconcellos), to Pickering, 10/–.

☞ This volume, edited by James Nasmith from mss preserved at Corpus Christi College, Cambridge, included *Itineraria* of Simon Simeon and of William of Worcester.

3384 Ubaldini, Petruccio

Descrittione del regno di Scotia. Antwerp [i.e. London, Wolfe], 1588. Folio.

Not in mc.
sh sale, v.9 (with Soprani, Tapestries, Tractatus, and Vasconcellos), to Pickering, 10/–.

☞ Another copy, now wsl, was in C.6, No. 523 *above.*

3385 Ubaldini, Petruccio

Le vite delle donne illustri del regno d'Inghilterra. London, 1591. 4to.

Mottled calf of about 1700, with Seaforth arms on sides, damaged by fire and now rebacked. Signature on title: 'H. Bayntun' and 'Ex libris Kenneth Comitis de Seafort 1686.' (Kenneth Mackenzie, Earl of Seaforth, 1661–1701.) bp² later state. Press-mark T.4; *see* note on Soprani, No. 3374 *above.* Not in mc. Bookplate of Holland House.

sh sale, v.8 (with 18 other volumes), to Boone, £2.2.0; Hodgson's, 13 May 1948 (Holland House Sale), lot 309, to Maggs for wsl, £3.10.0.

☞ A few underlinings by an early owner. Another copy was in M.9, No. 2322 *above.*

VASCONCELLOS, ANTONIO DE   3386

Anacephalaeoses, id est, summa capita actorum regum Lusitaniae . . .
et illorum effigies. Antwerp, 1621. 4to.

Old panelled calf, rebacked. BP[2] later state. Press-mark T.4; *see* note on
Soprani, No. 3374 *above.* Not in MC.

SH SALE, v.9 (with Soprani, Tapestries, Tractatus, and Ubaldini), to
Pickering, 10/–; Sotheby's, 25 March 1854 (Pickering stock, Part 1), lot
1439, to Boone, 9/6; in the Phillipps Collection; Robinson, November
1949, to WSL, $65.

VILLARS, CLAUDE LOUIS HECTOR, Duc de   3387
Vie du maréchal duc de Villars. Edited by Louis Pierre Anquetil.
Paris, 1784. Four volumes, 12mo.

Not in MC.

SH SALE, v.6 (with Alletz, Devienne, *Esprit*, Gherardo, Lavallée, Louis
XIV, Molé, and Walpole), to Pickering, 7/–.

☞ In his 'Book of Materials,' *ca.* 1784, HW noted two passages in which
Villars commented on the Pretender's intrigues and another passage in
which he analyzed Sir Robert Walpole's policy. To Lady Ossory, 19 August
1784, he wrote: 'Have you seen the Memoirs of Marshal Villars, Madam?
The two first volumes have many entertaining passages. The two latter
are a little tedious, but to *me* very interesting, for they abuse my
father.' (This is the same passage he noted in his 'Book of Materials.')

VOLTAIRE, FRANÇOIS MARIE AROUET DE   3388
Fragments sur l'Inde. [Paris?] 1773. 8vo.

'Sewed, uncut, with a few MS corrections by HW.' Not in MC.

SH SALE, v.7 (with Baudeau, Bernard, Boutet, Charlotte Elizabeth,
Choiseul, Descamps, Dutens, La Live, Molière, *Observer*, Richelieu, Rousseau, Saint-Simon, Senebier, and Suetonius), to Pickering, 12/–; offered
in Thorpe's Supplement for 1842, lot 12603, for 5/–.

☞ This defense of General Lally was one of the many French works
sent to HW by Mme. du Deffand; in her letter of 7 November 1773 she
promised to send him the second part.

WALDRON, FRANCIS GODOLPHIN, Editor   3389
The literary museum . . . comprising scarce and curious tracts, poetry,
biography, and criticism. London, 1792. 8vo.

'Boards, uncut, with Orford BP.' Not in MC.

SH SALE, V.11 (with Florez, Hardinge, Hoblyn, Maittaire, Mirabeau, and Whiston), to Pickering, 10/–; offered in Thorpe's Supplement for 1842, lot 13334, for 7/–.

3390 WALKER, JOSEPH COOPER

Historical essay on the dress of the ancient and modern Irish. Dublin, 1788. 4to.

Not in MC.

SH SALE, V.18 (with Consett, Huddesford, and Owen), to Pickering, 5/–.

3391 WALPOLE, HORACE

The Castle of Otranto. 8vo.

Not in MC.

SH SALE, V.6 (with Alletz, Devienne, *Esprit*, Gherardo, Lavallée, Louis XIV, Molé, and Villars), to Pickering, 7/–.

☞ The sale catalogue reads 'Castle of Otranto, in German.' The sale catalogue does sometimes print a translated title, but the use of the English title is a little odd; and since no edition in German is known, I suspect this to have been a copy of the edition printed in English in Berlin in 1794. One of HW's copies of this Berlin edition was offered in Thorpe's Supplement for 1842, lot 12119, 'Castle of Otranto in German, with bookplate as Earl of Orford,' for 7/6; a copy, perhaps from the Round Tower, Press O, 'green morocco, with engraving of his seal [Orford bookplate],' was sold at Sotheby's, 28 November 1883 (Beckford Sale, Part 4), lot 351, to Quaritch, £3.10.0.

3392 WHISTON, WILLIAM

Memoirs. The 3d part. London, 1750. 8vo.

Not in MC.

SH SALE, V.11 (with Florez, Hardinge, Hoblyn, Maittaire, Mirabeau, and Waldron), to Pickering, 10/–.

☞ The first volume, containing parts 1 and 2, was sold in the Glass Closet, No. 2498 *above*.

3393 WHITE, GILBERT

The natural history and antiquities of Selborne. London, 1789. 4to.

Bound in nineteenth-century tree calf by Hayday, now rebacked. BP[2] later state. Press-mark D.4 in MC; moved with a large group from D to the Library in the Offices. Bookplates of Nell Rose and Charles Van Cise Wheeler, of Harold Murdock, and of A. Edward Newton.

sh sale, v.27 (with Hume and Orléans), to Pickering, £1.5.0; Parke-Bernet, 30 October 1941 (Newton Sale), lot 524, to Brick Row for wsl, $55.

☞ One note and a dozen pencilled markings by hw.

WILDMAN, THOMAS   3394

A treatise on the management of bees. London, 1768. 4to.

Not in mc.

sh sale, v.12 (with Cicero, Hayley, Jemmat, Nasmith, and Polwhele), to Thorpe, £1.1.0; probably the copy offered, but not identified as hw's, in Thorpe's Supplement for 1842, lot 13406, for 10/6.

Press Y

These books, not listed at all in the first edition of the sale catalogue, seem to have been catalogued as an afterthought. William Forster, Robins's assistant and cataloguer, in a letter now wsl, speaks of the remainders from the sh Press and other papers as having been 'found after the catalogue was made' in a cupboard in hw's bedroom. But at least four books (Dudin, Rubens, Vries, and hw's *Miscellaneous Antiquities*) included here were originally listed in the first edition of the sale catalogue among the books in the Round Tower.

Certain volumes included here were listed in the Main Library in Press C in 1763, and may have been moved to the Round Tower about 1790; they were perhaps overlooked when the first edition of the sale catalogue was prepared. Other similar volumes were still in the Main Library in 1797, but they also were unlisted in the first edition of the sale catalogue in 1842.

Finally, although the evidence on this point is not conclusive, I suspect that many of the volumes here listed in Press Y were brought by Mrs. Damer from the little library in the Cottage; hw records that there were volumes of prints in the little library. Two books sold in Press Y that have been recovered in original bindings (Marlow, Rigacci) have no press-marks, as if they had been kept by hw in a part of his library not organized with lettered shelves; since these two books are not likely to have been moved out of the Glass Closet (where press-marks were not used) after 1797, they seem likely to have been in the Cottage until 1797.

3395 AMSTERDAM

Le guide ou nouvelle description d'Amsterdam. Amsterdam, 1753. 8vo.

'Uncut, with autograph of Dr. Lort.' Purchased by HW at Dr. Lort's sale in April 1791, lot 4080, for 1/6. Press-mark B.9, entered by Kirgate, in MC; apparently moved with other volumes to the Library in the Offices.

SH SALE, v.244 (with Bray, Catalogues, Cumberland, Dyde, Mensaert, Strange, and Wyndham), to Rodd, £1.4.0; offered in Thorpe's Supplement for 1842, lot 12484, for 3/6.

3396 ASTLE, THOMAS

An account of the seals of the kings, royal boroughs, and magnates of Scotland. [London] 1792. Folio.

'Boards, uncut.' Not in MC.

SH SALE, v.212 (with Dudin and Frederick II), to Strong, £1.15.0; offered in Strong's Catalogue for 1843, lot 49, for £1.8.0.

☞ Also issued as part of the Society of Antiquaries' 'Vetusta Monumenta.'

3397 BALTIMORE, FREDERICK CALVERT, 6th Baron

Trial . . . for a rape on the body of Sarah Woodcock. London, 1768. Folio.

'Calf.' Press-mark D.2 in MC; moved with other books in Press D to the Library in the Offices.

SH SALE, v.231 (with Brettingham and Knight), to Thorpe, 10/–; offered in Rodd's Catalogue for 1846, Part 2 (Law), lot 2589, for 6/–.

☞ According to Rodd, HW had inserted portraits of Lord Baltimore and Miss Woodcock.

3398 BARTOLOZZI, FRANCESCO

Prints engraved after Guercino, and other masters, published by J. and J. Boydell. London, [1764?] Folio.

'Sewed, uncut.' Not in MC.

SH SALE, v.213, to Strong, £1.1.0; offered in Strong's Catalogue for 1843, lot 72, for £2.12.6.

☞ In the sale catalogue, these are described as 'A folio volume of prints, by Bartolozzi, after Guercino, and No. 1 of prints, by ditto, after

the old masters.' In Strong's Catalogue the volume is said to contain 42 prints, but No. 1 [of the second volume] does not seem to be listed.

Some of the original drawings of Guercino are in the Royal Collection at Windsor.

BEAUJOYEULX, BALTAZARINI, called   3399

Balet comique de la Royne, faict aux nopces de Monsieur le duc de Joyeuse & de Mademoyselle de Vaudemont sa soeur. With 27 engravings by Jacques Patin. Paris, 1582. 4to.

Rebound. BP² early state. No press-mark preserved. Press-mark F.9.43 in MC, entered by HW. Apparently moved with a few other books of plates, and then sold in 1842 in this supplementary group at the end of the Fifth Day.

SH SALE, v.239 (with Giaccone and Spanheim), to Thorpe, 5/–; offered in Strong's Catalogue for 1843, lot 64, for 10/6; now in the New York Public Library.

☞ Another copy was in the Glass Closet, No. 2334 *above*; the copy now in the New York Public Library may be either of these two. According to Strong's Catalogue the copy sold v.239 was bound in vellum; the copy now in New York was rebound in green leather in 1937, and came to the New York Public Library's predecessor, the Lenox Library, in the Drexel Collection in 1888; it was probably the copy in vellum, not identified as HW's, that was sold at Sotheby's, 2 August 1877 (Rimbault Sale), lot 1011, for £14.10.0.

This copy has on the title-page both HW's BP and the book-stamp of Sir Henry Brooke Cobham, Knight, who was the English ambassador resident in Paris in 1582. Also on the title-page are the motto and signature of Ben Jonson, both partially obliterated by hand but apparently quite genuine. This copy was therefore of distinguished provenance before it came to SH.

[BRAY, WILLIAM]   3400

Sketch of a tour into Derbyshire and Yorkshire. London, 1778. 8vo.

'Uncut, with several very interesting notes by HW.' Not in MC.

SH SALE, v.244 (with Amsterdam, Catalogues, Cumberland, Dyde, Mensaert, Strange, and Wyndham), to Rodd, £1.4.0; offered in Thorpe's Supplement for 1842, lot 13278, for £2.2.0; also offered by Thorpe in 1845 and 1846.

☞ Probably this copy, rebound in russia by Clarke, was sold at Sotheby's, 19 July 1855 (Charles Meigh Sale), lot 134, to Sampson, 12/–. Another copy, in the Glass Closet, No. 2345 *above*, is recorded as purchased

by Thorpe. But the other items in that lot do not appear in Thorpe's Supplement, whereas nearly all in v.244 do; and the copy in the Glass Closet was presumably bound by or for HW, whereas the books shelved in the Library in the Offices were generally in boards. This is probably the copy in Edward Hailstone's Yorkshire collection, now in the York Minster Library. It has numerous characteristic notes by HW on archaeological and other matters.

3401 BRETTINGHAM, MATTHEW

The plans, elevations, and sections of Holkham Hall, in Norfolk. London, 1761. Folio.

Press-mark C.2.15 in MC; apparently moved with a few other folios to the Library in the Offices.

SH SALE, v.231 (with Baltimore and Knight), to Thorpe, 10/–.

3402 BUONANNI, FILIPPO

Recreatio mentis et oculi in observatione animalium testaceorum. Rome, 1684. 4to.

'Vellum, with HW's BP.' Press-mark C.5.12 (altered from C.4?) in MC; apparently moved with a few other books to the Library in the Offices.

SH SALE, v.237 (with Manfredi), to Rodd, 8/–; offered in Thorpe's Supplement for 1842, lot 12025, for £2.2.0.

3403 BYNG, Hon. JOHN, Admiral

A bundle of tracts relative to the case of Admiral Byng. [London, 1756–7.] Various sizes.

Not in MC.

SH SALE, v.221, to Thorpe, 5/–.

☞ His letters of 1756–7 show HW's immediate concern with the government's willingness to condemn Byng for political reasons. Of special interest is the Hon. David Erskine's discovery among Augustus Lord Hervey's papers of the MS of HW's *Queries*, printed 10 February 1757 in the *London Chronicle*.

Included was probably *A Letter to a Member of Parliament in the country from his friend in London, relative to the case of Admiral Byng*, 1758, 8vo. This was offered, but not identified as HW's, in Thorpe's Supplement for 1842, lot 12088, 'sewed.' There is unfortunately no record of what else was in this bundle.

CATALOGUES   3404

A large bundle of Catalogues, most of them of the period of 1760, with memoranda by HW.

Not in MC.

SH SALE, V.222, to Thorpe, £1.6.6. Rodd offered in his *Catalogue* [1842]: Collection of 40 catalogues of sales of books, prints, pictures, coins, &c., 1758–90, most of them marked by HW. Thorpe sold 23 art catalogues, 14 June 1845, to the British Museum. But some were destroyed by a bomb in the second World War; others have no annotation by HW. Those identifiable by HW's notes are Dr. Bragge (1757), Mrs. Dunch (1761), Joseph Goupy (1765), (Sir) William Hamilton (1761, 1765), and Lord Waldegrave (1763). *See also* Introduction, p. xxxviii.

☞ Surely HW owned such collections as Joseph Ames, 1760; Smart Lethieullier, 1761; Bishop Thomas Hayter, 1762; and Ralph Thoresby, 1764. And Baron von Stosch's Catalogue for 1759 was important to him.

On 6 May 1770 HW wrote to Mann about the recent auction of stuffed birds, at which prices seemed to him ridiculously high. Even if he did not buy anything, he may have owned the catalogue: the sale was conducted by Langford & Son, 25 April 1770 and four following days (Collection of the late James Leman), and the catalogues were priced at six-pence.

CATALOGUES   3405

Two volumes, 8vo.

Not in MC.

SH SALE, V.244 (with Amsterdam, Bray, Cumberland, Dyde, Mensaert, Strange, and Wyndham), to Rodd, £1.4.0.

☞ The sale catalogue has only 'two catalogues, one priced, by Horace Walpole.' Very probably these are two of the Catalogues offered in Thorpe's Supplement:

(1) BOISSET, PAUL RANDON DE. *Catalogue des tableaux et desseins précieux.* Paris, 1777.

(2) CONTI, LOUIS FRANÇOIS DE BOURBON, Prince de. *Catalogue des tableaux, desseins* [etc.] Paris, 1777.

Both are offered in Thorpe's Supplement for 1842, lots 12906–7; but although both are probably equally rare and both have identical descriptions 'with the prices and purchasers' names, from HW's collection, with his autograph and note by him,' Boisset is priced at 18/– and Conti at 10/6. (Boisset is also described as interleaved.) Possibly the description was copied carelessly for the second entry in Thorpe's Catalogue; the sale

catalogue's differentiation, 'one priced,' seems to fit Thorpe's differing prices.

Mme. du Deffand offered to have these catalogues sent to HW, in her letter of 1 December 1776.

The Boisset Catalogue is now in the Bibliothèque Municipale at Nantes; HW's note reads: 'A present from Monsr. de Presle of Paris, a collector & judge. One cannot know the real purchasers from this catalogue, as most purchasers employ others to bid & buy for them. But the prices paid are here specified. H. Walpole. 1777.'

3406 CAVALLIER, JEAN

Memoirs of the wars of the Cevennes. Dublin, 1726. 8vo.

Press-mark I.4.18 in MC; apparently moved with a few other volumes to the Library in the Offices.

SH SALE, v.242 (with Coke, Europe, Manning, Marchant, Milward, and Thucydides), to Kerslake, 10/–.

☞ Entered in the sale catalogue as 'Memoirs by Cavallier, 4.' Very probably the other 3 volumes included Vertot's *Sweden* (I.4) and Jebb (I.6) not found in the sale catalogue: other volumes in lot 242 came from I.4 and I.6 of the Main Library.

3407 CHARLES VI, Emperor of Germany

Relation de l'inauguration solemnelle de . . . Charles VI. Ghent, 1719. Folio.

'Calf.' Not in MC.

SH SALE, v.235 (with Nicetas, Raspono, and Vries), to Rodd, £1; offered in Strong's Catalogue for 1843, lot 1409, for 10/6.

3408 CHATTERTON, THOMAS

Miscellanies in prose and verse. Edited by John Broughton. London, 1778. Five copies, 8vo.

Not in MC.

SH SALE, v.209 (with 8 copies of Whitworth), to Thorpe, £1.10.0.

☞ Entered as 'Chatterton's Miscellanies.' Since these were sold with the SH Press Remainders, one is tempted to count them as copies of HW's *Letter on Chatterton.* But one copy of the *Miscellanies,* 'russia with notes by HW,' was sold at Sotheby's, 19 July 1855 (Charles Meigh Sale), lot 355, to Toovey, £1.1.0; and if this was correctly described, it is only identifiable in v.209. The copy that HW bound with his 'Chattertoniana,' now WSL, was sold in Press M of the Round Tower.

Known only from a note preserved in a volume in the British Museum are the MSS of Chatterton's three Eclogues and other poems, 'HW's copy with numerous notes in his handwriting.' Perhaps these were the samples submitted by Chatterton to HW in March 1769.

COKE, ROGER   3409

A detection of the Court and state of England during the four last reigns. The 3d edition. London, 1697. Two volumes in one, 8vo.

Press-mark I.6.33 in MC; apparently moved with a few other volumes to the Library in the Offices.

SH SALE, v.242 (with Cavallier, Europe, Manning, Marchant, Milward, and Thucydides), to Kerslake, 10/–.

COOKE, WILLIAM   3410

Civil liberty, a sermon. Cambridge, 1780. 4to.

Not in MC.

SH SALE, v.207 (with Pennant and SH Remainders), to Thorpe, £1.15.0.

☞ Cooke published three sermons in 1780, but this is probably the one HW had: *see* Cole's letter to HW, 14 May 1780.

CUMBERLAND, RICHARD   3411

Anecdotes of eminent painters in Spain during the sixteenth and seventeenth centuries. London, 1782. Two volumes, 8vo.

'Uncut, but imperfect, with HW's BP and a few interesting MS notes by him.' Press-mark B.7 in MC; apparently moved after HW's death with a few other volumes to the Library in the Offices.

SH SALE, v.244 (with Amsterdam, Bray, Catalogues, Dyde, Mensaert, Strange, and Wyndham), to Rodd, £1.4.0; offered in Thorpe's Supplement for 1842, lot 12251, for 5/–.

☞ In his letter to Mason, 13 April 1782, HW wrote scornfully of the book.

DRAWINGS   3412

Eight masterly sketches in oil, from the antique.

Not in MC.

SH SALE, v.230, to Strong, £1.10.0.

3413 Dudin, ——

L'art du relieur doreur de livres. Paris, 1772. Folio.

'Half-bound.' Not in MC.

SH SALE, v.212 (with Astle and Frederick II), to Strong, £1.15.0; offered in Strong's Catalogue for 1843, lot 461, for £1.1.0; Fletcher, 8 April 1846 (Britton Sale, Part 4), lot 724, to Pickering, 8/–.

☞ Sponsored by the Académie des Sciences at Paris, in its series, 'Descriptions des arts et métiers.' This volume seems first to have been included in vii.26, the closet in the Round Tower, but moved to the Fifth Day in the revised catalogue.

3414 Dutens, Louis

L'ami des étrangers qui voyagent en Angleterre. London, 1787. 8vo.

Rebound *ca.* 1850 in half calf, with other York tracts, for Robert Davies (1793–1875), with his bookplate. Press-mark B.9 in MC; apparently moved after HW's death with a few other volumes to the Library in the Offices.

SH SALE, v.243 (with England, German, Johnson, Mason, Montenoy, Rigacci, and Wilkinson), to Rodd, 7/–; offered in Strong's Catalogue for 1843, lot 475, 'boards, with HW's BP,' for 6/–; Fletcher, 7 April 1846 (Britton Sale, Part 4), lot 315, to R. Smith, 1/–; given by Mrs. Davies, October 1875, to the York Minister Library.

☞ Notes and identifications by HW on eleven pages; e.g., an exclamation point opposite 'les profondes connoissances de Lord Bute dans la botanique'; and 'mediocre' opposite the mention of the Duke of Bedford's 'beaux appartemens.'

3415 [Dyde, William]

The history and antiquities of Tewkesbury. Tewkesbury, 1790. 8vo.

Press-mark B.9 in MC; apparently moved after HW's death with a few other volumes to the Library in the Offices.

SH SALE, v.244 (with Amsterdam, Bray, Catalogues, Cumberland, Mensaert, Strange, and Wyndham), to Rodd, £1.4.0; probably the copy offered, but not identified as HW's, in Thorpe's Supplement for 1842, lot 12456, for 5/–.

3416 England. Army

Regulations. 8vo.

Not in MC.

SH SALE, v.243 (with Dutens, German, Johnson, Mason, Montenoy, Rigacci, and Wilkinson), to Rodd, 7/–.

☞ Almost any one of the numerous handbooks of the time is possible. A volume containing regulations for Field Exercises was published in 1792, and one for the West Indies troops in 1795.

ENGRAVINGS   3417

Two private plates, large folio.

SH SALE, v.211, to Thorpe, £3.3.0; offered in Thorpe's Supplement for 1842, lots 13355 and 13355*, for 10/6 each.

☞ The sale catalogue identifies them as large copper plates: one 'the genealogical table of the Walpole family,' and the other a 'View of Twickenham, engraved by Muntz'; but doubtless the prints were so described, not the copper. A copy of the Twickenham engraving (actually engraved by John Green from Müntz's painting of 1756) is in HW's extra-illustrated *Description of SH*, and Bull likewise inserted the engraving in *his* extra-illustrated *Description*: Bull marked it 'Engraved from a private plate of Mr. Walpole's.' The genealogical table is the plate that HW had engraved in 1776, 'A pedigree of Walpole to explain the portraits and coats of arms at Strawberry Hill'; prints from this plate are preserved in the Storer Collection at Eton, in Lord Rothschild's collection, in Bull's *Description*, and in HW's *Description* (with his MS additions). An early draft of this pedigree in MS (by Kirgate with HW's additions) was sold at Sotheby's, 4 June 1907 (Miscellaneous Sale), lot 333, to B. F. Stevens; later owned by Francis Gaskill; bought in the Gaskill Collection, 1939, by WSL.

ESSEX   3418

Antiquities in Essex. Folio.

Not in MC.

SH SALE, v.217 (with 14 other volumes), to Thorpe, £1.15.0. The other items in the lot are very miscellaneous; but this may have been a second copy of Salmon's *History and antiquities of Essex*. Or perhaps it was a part of Morant's new edition, which was published in parts. (Earlier copies of Salmon and Morant were in A.1, No. 7 *above*, and in A.2, No. 22 *above*.)

EUROPE   3419

Compleat history of Europe, for the year 1709. London, 1710. 8vo.

Press-mark I.4.45 in MC; apparently moved with a few other volumes to the Library in the Offices.

SH SALE, V.242 (with Cavallier, Coke, Manning, Marchant, Milward, and Thucydides), to Kerslake, 10/–.

☞ There seems to have been at SH just one volume of this serial compilation by David Jones.

3420 FOOTE, SAMUEL
Dramatic works. London, 1766. Two volumes, 8vo.

Not in MC.

SH SALE, V.241 (with Gorges, Oldcastle, Pearch, Vertot, and Whear), to Slatter, £2.2.0.

☞ The sale catalogue records only 'Foote's Works, 2 vols.' It may have been this collection of separate plays issued with a new title-page.

3421 FOWLER, WILLIAM
Engravings of mosaic pavements. Winterton, 1796. Folio.

Not in MC.

SH SALE, V.217 (with 13 other volumes), to Thorpe, £1.15.0.

☞ Probably this is what is entered in the sale catalogue as 'Mosaics, 2.' The work, completed in 26 plates in 1818, was dedicated to Sir Joseph Banks. But HW may have had only the first two plates.

3422 FREDERICK II, the Great, King of Prussia
Antiquités dans la collection de sa Majesté le Roi de Prusse à Sans Souci. Berlin, 1769. Royal folio.

'Boards, uncut.' Not in MC.

SH SALE, V.212 (with Astle and Dudin), to Strong, £1.15.0; offered in Strong's Catalogue for 1843, lot 34, for 18/–.

☞ Twenty-four plates of antique busts.

3423 GEOGRAPHY
Two volumes, folio.

Not in MC.

SH SALE, V.229 (with odd numbers of other works), to Thorpe, 10/6.

☞ Entered in the sale catalogue as 'Two folio books of Geography, and 15 numbers of different works, among them . . . portraits of the Walpole family.' The Walpole family portraits were offered in Thorpe's Supplement for 1842, lot 13379, where they were identified as 'twenty-one portraits engraved for Coxe's *Memoirs of Sir Robert Walpole,* 1802, and presented to the representative [Mrs. Damer?] of the Walpole family.'

Thorpe confused the two works by Coxe; these portraits were for the *Memoirs of Horatio, Lord Walpole.*

The Geography was very possibly George Bickham's engraved work in folio, *The British Monarchy; or a new chorographical description of all the dominions of the King of Great Britain* (and the British colonies in America), 1749. This work is customarily in a single volume; but a copy in two volumes, not identified as HW's, was offered in Thorpe's Supplement for 1842, lot 12002, for 18/–.

George III, King of England   3424
Print of the Procession to St. Paul's in 1789.

> Not in MC.

> SH SALE, v.227 (with Herculaneum and Pitt), to Strong, 10/–.

☞ Not recorded in the sale are two tracts on the coronation of George III, offered in Rodd's *Catalogue of Books recently added* [1842] as HW's copies with some identifications by him. They are:
(1) *An account of the ceremonies observed at the coronation* [of George III], 1761. 4to.
(2) England. Office of Earl Marshal. *The form of the proceeding to the Royal Coronation* [of George III], 1761. Folio.

German Lessons   3425
Two volumes, 8vo.

> Not in MC.

> SH SALE, v.243 (with Dutens, England, Johnson, Mason, Montenoy, Rigacci, and Wilkinson), to Rodd, 7/–.

☞ Not identifiable, and they may have been Mrs. Damer's.

Giaccone, Alfonso   3426
Istoria . . . dell'anima di Trajano. Siena, 1595. 4to.

> 'Boards, with HW's bookplate.' Press-mark L.3.29 in MC; apparently moved with a few other large books to the Library in the Offices.

> SH SALE, v.239 (with Beaujoyeulx and Spanheim), to Thorpe, 5/–; offered in Strong's Catalogue for 1843, lot 594, for 7/6.

Gorges, Ferdinando   3427
America painted to the life. London, 1658–9. Four parts in one volume, 4to.

> Press-mark I.8.41 in MC, entered by HW; apparently moved with a few other volumes to the Library in the Offices.

sh sale, v.241 (with Foote, Oldcastle, Pearch, Vertot, and Whear), to Slatter, £2.2.0.

☞ Presumably this is the copy in the Peter Force collection, purchased in 1867 by the Library of Congress: it was rebound by J. C. McGuire of Washington. The pamphlets are in poor condition, the general title-page is in facsimile, and the plates are wanting; but BP² early state is appropriate for a volume acquired 1763–6.

Included as Part 3 of the volume is the *Wonder working Providence of Sions Saviour*, by Captain Edward Johnson.

3428 HARRISON, STEPHEN

The arches of triumph erected in honor of James the First at his entrance . . . through London. Engraved by William Kip. London, 1604. Folio.

Press-mark C.5.2 in MC; apparently moved with some other folios to the Library in the Offices.

sh sale, v.226, to Thorpe, £8; probably the copy offered, but not identified as HW's, in Thorpe's Supplement for 1842, lot 12620, for £12.12.0.

☞ A newspaper account of the sale records six other copies, and adds: 'Whence Walpole obtained this set is not known.' Lord Derby marked opposite this lot in his copy of the SH Catalogue: 'imperfect.'

The volume is mentioned by HW in a note on Kip in his *Engravers*. Under Harrison in the second volume of his *Anecdotes*, he says he never saw the book except in the library at Chatsworth [in 1760]; he therefore secured his copy *ca.* 1761–3.

3429 HEARNE, THOMAS

Antiquities of Great Britain, illustrated in views of monasteries, castles, and churches now existing. Engraved by William Byrne from Hearne's drawings. London, 1786. Oblong folio.

Not in MC.

sh sale, v.217 (with 14 other volumes), to Thorpe, £1.15.0.

☞ Another copy was sold with the books in the Round Tower. It is conceivable that the book sold here in Press Y was a duplicate of the edition of 1737, sold in E.2 in the Main Library.

3430 HERCULANEUM

Four prints, from pictures discovered at Herculaneum.

Not in MC.

sh sale, v.227 (with George III and Pitt), to Strong, 10/–.

☞ These may possibly have been duplicate prints of the set recorded in Press D of the Round Tower, No. 3590 *below*.

Johnson, Henry   3431

An introduction to logography. London, 1783. 8vo.

Not in MC.

SH SALE, v.243 (with Dutens, England, German, Mason, Montenoy, Rigacci, and Wilkinson), to Rodd, 7/–; very probably the copy offered, but not identified as HW's, in Strong's Catalogue for 1843, lot 1800, 'sewed,' for 3/–. A copy bound in half calf, with BP² later state, was offered by Colin Richardson, Catalogue 116 (February 1961), lot 48, for £45.

Knight, Richard Payne   3432

The progress of civil society. A didactic poem in six books. London, 1796. 4to.

Not in MC.

SH SALE, v.231 (with Baltimore and Brettingham), to Thorpe, 10/–.

☞ For HW's vigorous denunciation of this poem, *see* his letter to Mason, 22 March 1796, in reply to Mason's letter of 15 March.

Le Rouge, George Louis   3433

Détails des nouveaux jardins à la mode. Paris, 1770–87. Twenty-one parts containing 480 plates, oblong folio.

Not in MC.

SH SALE, v.216, to H. G. Bohn, 15/–.

☞ Entered in the sale catalogue as 'A French work on Gardening, in 22 parts, fine plates.' Le Rouge seems probable, if one assumes that '22' is an error for twenty-one. Bohn perhaps relied on the catalogue's description, since he wrote to Beckford, 4 May 1842: 'The only book of my own purchases at Strawberry Hill (but I bought very little) is a set of books in 22 parts oblong folio containing several hundred plates of old French and English gardens, which was unappropriately called *Jardins Anglo Chinois à la Mode*. . . . There is nothing in the execution of the plates, but the subject is just now so much sought after that I am very glad of the book.' (Letters now WSL)

Gardens at Chiswick, Richmond, Kew, and Claremont were included, as well as French and German gardens.

3434 Lysons, Samuel

An account of the Roman antiquities discovered at Woodchester in the County of Gloucester. London, 1797. Folio.

Not in MC.

SH SALE, v.234 (with Topham), to Strong, £1.18.0.

☞ *See* HW to Mary Berry, 29 July 1796: 'Sir Joseph Banks has carried Lysons to Kew with drawings of all his discoveries at Woodchester. They made great impression, and he is to send patterns of the mosaics for the Queen and Princesses to work.'

3435 Lysons, Samuel

Views and antiquities in the County of Gloucester. London, 1791–   . Sixteen numbers, folio.

Not in MC.

SH SALE, v.218, to Strong, £2.

☞ The sale catalogue lists 'Sixteen nos. of prints illustrating the History of Gloucestershire.' This surely means Lysons, but HW may have had duplicates of some numbers, unless the final numbers were sent to SH after he died.

When these were re-offered, in a clipping from an unidentified catalogue, they were listed as '75 plates in 13 numbers, folio, sewed, uncut,' and inscribed 'Hon. H. Walpole, from the Author.' To Lysons, 17 September 1789, HW wrote: 'Your *Gloucestershire* will I am persuaded be the most perfect body of county history existing.' On 28 June 1790, he wrote of some Gloucester drawings 'which may be to your purpose.' To Mary Berry he wrote, 11 November 1793: 'Lysons has been drawing churches in Gloucestershire.'

3436 Magazines

Various magazines, 8vo.

Not in MC. The sale catalogue's description is 'A large bundle of magazines, reviews, &c.'

SH SALE, v.247, to Rodd, 8/–.

☞ These may have been magazines published later than 1797.

3437 Malton, Thomas

A picturesque tour through the cities of London and Westminster. London, 1792. In 12 parts, folio.

Not in MC.

SH SALE, v.214, to Davis, Coleman Street, £1.18.0.

MANFREDI, GIROLAMO DI   3438

Liber de homine; . . . de conservatione sanitatis [Libro del Perchè].
   Bologna, 1474. Folio.

'With HW's BP.' Not in MC.

SH SALE, v.237 (with Buonanni), to Rodd, 8/–; offered in Thorpe's Supplement for 1842, lot 12478, for £5.5.0.

☞ The sale catalogue reads: 'Il Perche, very curious, old Italian.' Another copy or edition was in the Glass Closet, No. 2413 *above*.

[MANNING, ROBERT]   3439

The rise and fall of the heresy of the iconoclasts. London, 1731. 8vo.

Press-mark I.5.20 in MC, altered by Mrs. Damer to I.4.44 (cf. Birch, I.5 *above*); apparently moved with some other volumes after 1797 to the Library in the Offices.

SH SALE, v.242 (with Cavallier, Coke, Europe, Marchant, Milward, and Thucydides), to Kerslake, 10/–.

MARCHANT, JOHN   3440

The history of the present rebellion. London, 1746. 8vo.

Press-mark I.6.41 in MC; apparently moved with a few other volumes to the Library in the Offices.

SH SALE, v.242 (with Cavallier, Coke, Europe, Manning, Milward, and Thucydides), to Kerslake, 10/–.

MARLOW, WILLIAM   3441

Views in Italy drawn and etched by William Marlow [London?
   post-1780?] Oblong 4to.

Original blue boards. With BP of HW as Lord Orford, type 1. No pressmark, and not in MC. Title in MS by HW. Notes by J. H. Anderdon, 1845, who marked it 'Gift of a valued brother.' Bookplate of Edward Jackson Barron. A collation note by a bookseller, 1881.

SH SALE, v.238 (with Walpole), to Thorpe, £3.15.0; offered in Thorpe's Supplement for 1842, lot 12758, for 18/–; Sotheby's, 2 June 1935 (Heseltine Sale), lot 136, to Colnaghi, £1.15.0; given by Sir Kenneth Clark, July 1937, to WSL.

☞ This book, acquired after 1780, with no press-mark, seems likely to have been shelved in the little library in the Cottage until 1797; but the hypothesis cannot be proved.

3442 Mason, William

Essays, historical and critical, on English church music. York, 1795.
8vo.

Press-mark K.8.76, entered by Mrs. Damer, in MC; apparently moved
after 1797 with a few other volumes to the Library in the Offices.

SH SALE, v.243 (with Dutens, England, German, Johnson, Montenoy,
Rigacci, and Wilkinson), to Rodd, 7/–; probably the copy offered, but
not identified as HW's, in Strong's Catalogue for 1843, lot 2115, 'sewed,
uncut,' for 3/6.

3443 Mensaert, Guillaume Pierre

*Le peintre amateur et curieux, ou description générale des tableaux
des plus habiles maîtres . . . dans l'étendue des Pays-Bas autrichiens.*
Brussels, 1763. Two parts in one volume, 8vo.

'Sewed, uncut.' Not in MC.

SH SALE, v.244 (with Amsterdam, Bray, Catalogues, Cumberland, Dyde,
Strange, and Wyndham), to Rodd, £1.4.0; offered in Thorpe's Supplement
for 1842, lot 12787, for 5/–.

☞ Another copy was sold in B.7, No. 345 *above*.

3444 Milward, Edward

Trallianus reviviscens; or, an account of Alexander Trallian. London,
1734. 8vo.

Press-mark K.9.11, altered to K.5, in MC; apparently moved with other
volumes, mostly from Press I, to the Library in the Offices. The change to
K.5 is in Kirgate's hand.

SH SALE, v.242 (with Cavallier, Coke, Europe, Manning, Marchant, and
Thucydides), to Kerslake, 10/–.

3445 Miscellaneous

Five odd volumes, 4to, and a large bundle of magazines and pamphlets, of modern date.

Not in MC.

SH SALE, v.233, to Thorpe, 18/–.

☞ These may have been *non*-Walpolian oddments.

MISCELLANEOUS   3446

Thirty odd volumes of books, principally bound. 8vo.

Not in MC.
SH SALE, v.246, to Rodd, 16/–.

☞ Such lots as this, if the books were Walpolian, may have been the books moved by Mrs. Damer from the little library in the Cottage.

[MONTENOY, CHARLES PALISSOT DE]   3447

L'homme dangereux, comédie. Amsterdam, 1770. 8vo.

'Sewed.' Not in MC.
SH SALE, v.243 (with Dutens, England, German, Johnson, Mason, Rigacci, and Wilkinson), to Rodd, 7/–; offered in Strong's Catalogue for 1843, lot 906, for 2/6.

MUSIC   3448

A large bundle of manuscript music, tracts, &c.

Not in MC.
SH SALE, v.249, to Thorpe, 16/–.

☞ Some or all of these may have been *non*-Walpolian. But in some such lot there must have been odd pieces of music. For example, HW wrote to Mann, 14 May 1761: 'I wish you would send me the music of your present [burletta],' apparently Goldoni's *Gli Uccellatori* with music by Gassman. (He thanked Mann on 4 January 1762 for two burlettas that Mann had had copied to send him.)

Similarly he wrote to Lady Ossory, 16 December 1787, that he had 'bought the book to read at home' of the new opera about King Theodore, of which he said 'the words are ten times stupider than our operas generally are.' The work was G. B. Casti's *Il Re Teodoro in Venezia. A new comic opera.* The music by Paisiello. London, 1787.

Still another piece that does not appear in the SH records is the satirical opera, *Il Conclave dell'anno MDCCLXXIV*, attributed to Gaetano Sertor. It was based on material taken from Metastasio; printed surreptitiously in Florence with a Rome imprint, in two editions of a thousand copies each. Mann wrote to HW about it, 13 December 1774, and sent it on 27 December: 'I must send you one enclosed, however angry they may be for swelling the packet [to Lord Rochford].' On 25 January 1775, HW thanked Mann for it.

3449 NICETAS, the Physician

Graecorum chyrurgici libri. Edited by Antonio Cocchi. Florence, 1754. Folio.

Press-mark M.1.5 in MC. Apparently moved to the Library in the Offices. SH SALE, v.235 (with Charles VI, Raspono, and Vries), to Rodd, £1.

☞ *See* HW to Mann, 4 March 1749: 'Pray tell Dr. Cocchi that I shall be extremely ready to do him any service in his intended edition of the old physicians. . . .' When the work was published, Dr. Cocchi sent five copies to HW, as presents for HW and four friends: *see* Mann to HW, 14 June 1754. Then HW replied, 5 July 1754: 'Thank Dr. Cocchi for the book . . . though I scarce understand anything less than Greek and physic; the little I knew of the first I have almost forgot, and the other, thank God, I never had any occasion to know.'

3450 OLDCASTLE, Sir JOHN, Baron Cobham

A brefe chronycle concernynge the examynacyon and death of . . . Syr Johan Oldecastell. Written originally by John Bale, and republished by Bishop John Blackbourne, the non-juror. London, 1729. 8vo.

Press-mark I.8.38 in MC, entered by HW; apparently moved with other volumes to the Library in the Offices. SH SALE, v.241 (with Foote, Gorges, Pearch, Vertot, and Whear), to Slatter, £2.2.0.

3451 PATCH, THOMAS

Engravings from Fra Bartolommeo and Giotto, with notes on their lives. Florence, 1772. Two parts in one volume, folio.

Not in MC.

SH SALE, v.215 (with Patch's Caricatures), to E. D. Davenport, Esq., £5.

☞ When Mann sent Patch's Masaccio to HW, in 1771, HW urged that Patch prepare a series from Fra Bartolommeo, and he acknowledged to Mann the receipt of the first series, 28 December 1771. So it was appropriate for the completed Fra Bartolommeo to be dedicated by Patch to HW, after HW granted him permission to do so in a letter to Mann, 12 February 1772. On 12 March 1773, HW asked Mann to thank Patch for the dedication: he praised the prints from both Fra Bartolommeo and Giotto as very well executed, but felt Fra Bartolommeo was not so striking as Masaccio. Mann replied, 30 March 1773, that Patch considered HW's criticism of the Fra Bartolommeo series a just one.

PATCH, THOMAS   3452
A series of 24 caricatures. [Florence], 1770. Folio.

Not in MC.

SH SALE, V.215 (with Patch's Fra Bartolommeo), to E. D. Davenport, Esq., £5.

☞ In a letter to Mann, 23 July 1772, HW asked for the series; and
Mann replied, 11 August 1772: 'I will send you Patch's *caricaturas.*' Mann
sent Patch's engraving of Death coming to Sterne to HW, 15 March 1768;
purchased in a collection in 1932 by WSL; an identifying note by HW.

PEARCH, GEORGE, Editor   3453
A collection of poems. London, 1768. Two volumes, 8vo.

Press-mark I.8 in MC; apparently moved after 1797 with other volumes
to the Library in the Offices.

SH SALE, V.241 (with Foote, Gorges, Oldcastle, Vertot, and Whear), to
Slatter, £2.2.0.

PENNANT, THOMAS   3454
Miscellanies. [1788?] 4to.

'Uncut.' Not in MC.

SH SALE, V.207 (with Cooke and SH Remainders), to Thorpe, £1.15.0;
offered in Thorpe's Supplement for 1842, lot 13360, for £1.8.0.

☞ Thirty copies were printed at George Allan's Darlington Press;
Thorpe's Catalogue asserts this was printed at Strawberry Hill.

PERCY, THOMAS   3455
Reliques of ancient English poetry. The 2d edition. London, 1767.
    Three volumes, 8vo.

Rebound by F. Bedford in mottled calf. Press-mark I.8 in MC; apparently
moved with other books after 1797 from I to the Library in the Offices.

SH SALE, V.240, to Thorpe, £1.5.0; offered in Thorpe's Supplement for
1842, lot 12942, 'old calf,' for £3.3.0; Sotheby's, 12 April 1875 (John Young
Sale), lot 273; Sotheby's, 4 July 1932 ('Property of a gentleman'), lot 26, to
Elkin Mathews, £12.10.0; Elkin Mathews, November 1932, to WSL,
£12.10.0.

☞ On the fly-leaf is Percy's presentation inscription: 'To the Honourable Horace Walpole, these volumes, containing specimens of the composition of some of his Royal and Noble Authors, are presented with great
respect by the Editor.' A copy of the fourth edition was in Press O, No.
2919 *above.*

3456 PITT, WILLIAM, Earl of Chatham

The death of Lord Chatham. Print engraved by Bartolozzi from the painting by Copley, 1780.

Not in MC.

SH SALE, v.227 (with George III and Herculaneum), to Strong, 10/–.

3457 PLAYS

Miscellaneous Plays. One volume, 4to.

The sale catalogue describes this volume as 'old English plays, with list [by HW], date 1700.'

SH SALE, v.236 (with Printing), to Thorpe, £2.2.0.

3458 PORTFOLIO

A large oblong portfolio for prints and drawings.

Not in MC.

SH SALE, v.232, to Rev. Richard J. St. Aubyn, 16/–.

☞ The Earl of Derby, in his copy of the sale catalogue, marked this: 'dirty old vellum portfolio.'

3459 PRINTING

Eighteen tracts, 4to.

Press-mark C.5.21 (altered from C.4) in MC; apparently moved to the Library in the Offices.

SH SALE, v.236 (with Plays), to Thorpe, £2.2.0; offered in Rodd's *Catalogue of Books recently added* [1842], for £4.4.0.

☞ According to MC, there were 19 various tracts. The sale catalogue calls them 'rare and curious tracts relative to early printing, date about 1640, with a list of the tracts, in fly-leaf, by HW.' Rodd's catalogue lists eighteen, including the first edition of Milton's *Areopagitica*, 1637; Middleton's *On the origin of printing*, 1735; and the *Trial of Zenger*, 1738. The lot cost HW 18/6 at Joseph Ames's sale in 1760.

3460 PRINTS

A portfolio of prints after Claude, Zoffany, Müntz, Wilson, &c. Folio.

Not in MC.

SH SALE, v.228, to Strong, £1.

☞ Very probably dispersed. The Earl of Derby, in his copy of the sale catalogue, marked this lot 'dirty rubbish.'

PRINTS   3461

A portfolio containing a large quantity of prints and drawings. Folio.

Press-mark C.3.28 in MC; perhaps moved to the Round Tower in 1790, and then apparently moved with a few other folios to the Library in the Offices.

SH SALE, v.223, to Thorpe, £1.10.0.

☞ Entered in MC as 'Collection of Prints, Galle, Van de Velde, Goltzius, &c.' This resembles other portfolios in the London sale, but it does not quite match the description of any volume there, and so is probably a different collection.

RASPONO, CESARE   3462

De basilica et patriarchio Lateranensi, libri quattuor. Rome, 1656.
    Folio.

'Vellum.' Not in MC.

SH SALE, v.235 (with Charles VI, Nicetas, and Vries), to Rodd, £1; offered in Strong's Catalogue for 1843, lot 1248, for 16/–.

RIGACCI, GIUSEPPE   3463

Raccolta di varie canzoni . . . A sua Eccellenza Myledy Walpole
    [Margaret Rolle]. Florence, 1739. 12mo.

Original flowered paper wrapper. BP[1]. No press-mark and not in MC. Note in cover probably by William, 8th Earl Waldegrave. Bookplates of Lord Carlingford and of William Frederick, 9th Earl Waldegrave (Lord Carlingford's wife was Frances, Countess Waldegrave).

SH SALE, v.243 (with Dutens, England, German, Johnson, Mason, Montenoy, and Wilkinson), to Rodd, 7/–; offered in Strong's Catalogue for 1843, lot 1238, for 6/6; included in the Waldegrave Collection purchased in 1948 by WSL.

☞ The first copy of Rigacci was in L.6, No. 2111 *above*. This second copy has no press-mark, but the note on the title, 'Margaret Rolle Countess of Orford who died at Pisa in 1781' is certainly by HW. The BP was present when Strong offered the volume in 1843, and it must be original, wherever the book was shelved during HW's lifetime. I think it may well be one of the books moved from the little library in the Cottage by Mrs. Damer. A third copy in the Glass Closet, No. 2462 *above*, is in an identical binding and BP[1] is in the same position above the engraving at the front of the volume.

3464 Rossi, Giovanni Giacomo de

Le fontane di Roma. Engraved by G. B. Falda. Rome, 1691. Folio.

Not in MC.

SH SALE, v.219 (with his *Fabriche*), to Thorpe, £1.

3465 Rossi, Giovanni Giacomo de

Il nuovo teatro delle fabriche et edificii in prospettiva di Roma moderna. Engraved by G. B. Falda. Rome, 1665. Folio.

Press-mark C.3.22 in MC; *see* note *below.*

SH SALE, v.219 (with his *Fontane*), to Thorpe, £1.

☞ It seems probable that these two volumes by Rossi were shelved in the Round Tower after 1790, but moved with Rubens and a few others to the Fifth Day's Sale during the cataloguing. The two volumes recorded here are listed in the sale catalogue as 'Rossi's Views in Rome, 2 vols.' Another copy of the *Fontane* was sold in the Round Tower Closet, No. 3515 *below.*

Or it may be that 'Rossi's *Views in Rome,* 2 vols.' was Pietro Ferrerio's *Palazzi di Roma,* Rome [1655], with engravings by Falda, published by Rossi in two volumes, folio. This was entered in MC as C.3.7, and is not otherwise traceable in the sale.

3466 Rubens, Peter Paul

Palazzi di Genova. [Antwerp], 1622. Two volumes, folio.

'Calf, with HW's BP.' Press-mark C.3.5 in MC.

SH SALE, v.220, to Thorpe, £2.18.0; offered in Thorpe's Supplement for 1842, lot 13095, for £4.14.6; Sotheby's, 30 November 1927 (Sneyd Sale), lot 650.

☞ These volumes seem to have been listed in vii.26, in the Closet of the Round Tower, in the first edition of the Catalogue; they were there counted as '3 vols.' Very probably the third was Domenico de Rossi's *Romanae magnitudinis monumenta,* Rome, 1699, which has the press-mark C.3.23 in MC (next to G. G. Rossi's books): it is not otherwise listed in the SH catalogue, but is lot 982 in the London Sale, to Lilly, 19/–.

3467 [Spanheim, Friedrich]

Mémoires sur la vie et la mort de . . . Loyse Juliane, Electrice Palatine. Leyden, 1645. 4to.

'Old calf, Richard Bentley's copy with his autograph and notes.' Not in MC.

SH SALE, v.239 (with Beaujoyeulx and Giaccone), to Thorpe, 5/–; offered in Strong's Catalogue for 1843, lot 1114, not priced.

☞ Strong's note does not say this was HW's copy, but since he offers the other two items in this lot, there seems little doubt of the identification.

STRANGE, Sir ROBERT   3468

An inquiry into the rise and establishment of the Royal Academy of Arts. London, 1775. 8vo.

Press-mark B.9 in MC; apparently moved after 1797 with other volumes to the Library in the Offices.

SH SALE, v.244 (with Amsterdam, Bray, Catalogues, Cumberland, Dyde, Mensaert, and Wyndham), to Rodd, £1.4.0; probably the copy offered, but not identified as HW's, in Thorpe's Supplement for 1842, lot 13209, 'uncut,' for 10/6.

☞ In his 'Book of Materials,' HW noted that this pamphlet was published in May.

STRAWBERRY HILL PRESS REMAINDERS   3469

Many if not all of these books seem to have been unbound, in sheets. Most uncut copies that have appeared in the market since 1842 are probably from these lots.

(1) EDWARD VI, King of England. *Copies of seven original letters,* 1772. Eight copies, 4to. SH SALE, v.207 (with 2 other volumes), to Thorpe, £1.15.0; offered in Thorpe's Supplement for 1842, lot 12332, for 15/–. One of these is perhaps the copy sold at Puttick's, 13 November 1852, and now in the Edward J. Sage Bequest (1906) to the Stoke Newington Public Library, London; on the wrapper is HW's note, 'My own copy.'

(2) FLOYD, PHILIP. *Prosperity to Houghton.* This is listed together with *Houghton Hare-Hunting* as about 80 copies in all. SH SALE, v.200 (with *Magpie*), to Thorpe, £1.1.0; copies were offered in Lilly's Catalogue for 1866, for 2/6. A copy of each is now at Farmington with HW's annotations. Also at Farmington is HW's copy of Sir William Yonge's *Norfolk Garland*, printed or reprinted at the same time. The three broadsides were preserved by HW in his MS of *Aedes Walpolianae* (viii.12), now at the Metropolitan Museum, but were removed from it and sent to WSL in 1925. Although these three pieces were not printed at SH, they were sold in this group in 1842.

(3) HERBERT, EDWARD, Baron Herbert of Cherbury. *Life.* Edited by HW, 1764. 4to. SH SALE, v.208, to Thorpe, £1.15.0; probably the copy offered in Thorpe's Supplement for 1842, lot 13356, for £6.6.0. Perhaps this

3469   was the copy, now bound in calf, with BP of HW as Lord Orford and bookplate of George Ormerod: Sotheby's, 16 August 1875 (Ormerod Sale), lot 967; offered by Quaritch, Catalogue 282 (1909), for £4.4.0; Goodspeed, *ca.* 1920, to Mr. William Zimmerman, Jr., of Washington. It has a pencilled note, '5th Day, #208,' but this may be a recent bookseller's note.

A copy, now at Farmington, of the edition of 1770 in contemporary calf is inscribed: 'This copy I purchased at Walpole's sale. J. [or T?] B.' It was possibly concealed in some miscellaneous lot; owned in 1874 by Charles H. H. Parry (later Sir Charles) and his wife, Elizabeth Maude Herbert.

(4) JONES, Sir WILLIAM. *The muse recalled,* 1781. Fifty-nine copies, 4to. SH SALE, v.199, to Thorpe, £1.1.0; offered in Thorpe's Supplement for 1842, lot 12644, for 12/–, and lot 13369 for 15/–.

(5) LUCANUS, MARCUS ANNAEUS. *Pharsalia,* with notes by Richard Bentley, the Elder, 1760. 4to. SH SALE, v.205, to Thorpe, 10/–; offered in Thorpe's Supplement for 1842, lot 13354, for £6.6.0; reduced to £5.5.0 in 1845 and 1846, to £4.4.0 in 1849.

(6) *The Magpie and her brood,* from the French of Des Periers, 1764. Forty-five copies, 4to. SH SALE, v.200 (with others), to Thorpe, £1.1.0. An uncut copy was offered in Thorpe's Supplement for 1842, lot 13218, for 7/6.

(7) [MILLER, CHARLES] *To Lady Horatia Waldegrave, on the death of the Duke of Ancaster,* [1780]. Eighteen copies, 4to. SH SALE, v.210 (with 'sundry parts of waste'), to Thorpe, £1.5.0; copies were offered in Thorpe's Supplement for 1842, lots 12798 and 13366, for 7/6.

(8) MORE, HANNAH. *Bishop Bonner's ghost,* 1789. Twenty-six copies, 4to. SH SALE, v.203, to Thorpe, £1.10.0. A copy, uncut, was offered in Thorpe's Supplement for 1842, lot 13215, for 10/6, and also in lot 13374.

(9) SPENCE, JOSEPH. *A parallel in the manner of Plutarch,* 1758. Three copies, 8vo. SH SALE, v.201 (with 3 other volumes), to Thorpe, £1.2.0. Thorpe offered three copies in his Supplement for 1842, and two of them (lots 13192 and 13210) were no doubt his offer of these copies. A copy acquired by the Library of Congress in 1871, old panelled calf, rebacked, with bookplate of J. Knight, has a bookseller's note: 'Walpole's copy with bookplate'; but it is BP² early state, and seems likely to have been a *post*-1842 insertion. The binding may date from about 1759, but it is not a Walpolian binding; and BP¹ would be expected if it was placed in the volume by HW in 1758 or 1759.

(10) WALPOLE, HORACE. *Description of the villa at SH*, 1774. Seventeen copies, 4to. SH SALE, v.196–8, to Forster, £8.18.6. Described as 'no cuts' and so presumably from the early edition. One copy, in boards uncut, was offered by Thorpe, lot 13212. In a letter (now WSL) Forster writes of finding 12 (not 17) copies in a cupboard in HW's bedroom, with other MSS and papers. One of those copies (now WSL) is the edition printed in 1774.

(11) WALPOLE, HORACE. *Essay on modern gardening*, 1785. Three copies, 4to. SH SALE, v.204, to Thorpe, 14/–; a copy was offered in Thorpe's Supplement for 1842, lot 13367, for 18/–. In 1846 Thorpe still had one, 'the author's own copy, uncut,' at £1.1.0.

(12) WALPOLE, HORACE. *Fugitive pieces*, 1758. 8vo. SH SALE, v.201 (with 5 other volumes), to Thorpe, £1.2.0; offered in Thorpe's Supplement for 1842, lot 13349, for £2.2.0.

(13) WALPOLE, HORACE. *Letter on Chatterton*, 1779. 8vo. SH SALE, v.201 (with 5 other volumes), to Thorpe, £1.2.0; offered in Thorpe's Supplement for 1842, lot 12169, for 7/6. This is perhaps the copy, with numerous notes, corrections, and identifications by HW, that was sold at Sotheby's, 28 June 1912 (A. C. Drummond Sale), lot 404, to Sabin, £5; it is now in the Berg Collection in the New York Public Library. Although unbound in 1842, it was closely trimmed and bound in red morocco by Riviere *ca.* 1850.

(14) WALPOLE, HORACE, Editor. *Miscellaneous antiquities*, 1772. Twelve parts, 4to. SH SALE, v.206, to Thorpe, £1.1.0; a copy was offered in Thorpe's Supplement for 1842, lot 13362, for 15/–.

(15) WALPOLE, HORACE. *The mysterious mother*, 1768. 8vo. SH SALE, v.201 (with 5 other volumes), to Thorpe, £1.2.0.

(16) WALPOLE, HORACE. *The mysterious mother*. London, Dodsley, 1781. Fourteen copies, 8vo. SH SALE, v.202, to Thorpe, 10/–; a copy was offered in Thorpe's Supplement for 1842, lot 13368, for 12/–; and in 1846 for 7/–.

(17) WHITWORTH, CHARLES, Baron Whitworth. *Account of Russia*, 1758. Eight copies, 8vo. SH SALE, v.209 (with 5 other volumes), to Thorpe, £1.10.0; offered as if one copy in Thorpe's Supplement for 1842, lot 13211, 'uncut,' for 10/6.

THUCYDIDES   3470

History of the Grecian war. Translated by Thomas Hobbes. The 3d edition. London, 1723. Two volumes, 8vo.

Press-mark H.4.39 in MC; perhaps misplaced in I.4, and then moved with other volumes to the Library in the Offices.

SH SALE, v.242 (with Cavallier, Coke, Europe, Manning, Marchant, and Milward), to Kerslake, 10/–.

3471 TOMKINS, PELTRO WILLIAM

The birth and triumph of Cupid. London, 1795. Oblong 4to.

Not in MC.

SH SALE, v.217 (with 14 other volumes), to Thorpe, £1.15.0; offered in Thorpe's Supplement for 1842, lot 12335, for £1.11.6.

☞ Engraved by Tomkins from designs by Princess Elizabeth; re-issued with a poem by Sir James Bland Burges in 1796.

Thorpe quotes HW's MS note: 'The cuttings were really designed and executed by her Royal Highness the Princess Elizabeth, . . . though published under the name of her friend, Lady Dashwood, wife of Sir Henry Dashwood.'

3472 TOPHAM, JOHN

Some account of the Collegiate Chapel of Saint Stephen, Westminster. London, 1795. Folio.

Not in MC.

SH SALE, v.234 (with Lysons), to Strong, £1.18.0.

☞ Engraved by James Basire from drawings by John Carter, and published by the Society of Antiquaries.

3473 VERTOT, RENÉ AUBERT DE

Miscellanies. London, 1723. 8vo.

Press-mark I.4.36 in MC; apparently moved with other volumes to the Library in the Offices.

SH SALE, v.241 (with Foote, Gorges, Oldcastle, Pearch, and Whear), to Slatter, £2.2.0.

3474 VRIES, JAN VREDEMAN DE

Hortorum viridariorumque elegantes . . . formae. Engraved by Philippus Gallaeus. Antwerp, 1583. Oblong folio.

Not in MC.

SH SALE, v.235 (with Charles VI, Nicetas, and Raspono), to Rodd, £1.

☞ This seems to be another of the few books that the auctioneer moved from the Round Tower: it is catalogued at viii.128 (Press I of Round Tower), and again in the London Sale, 895, and in the printed price list it is assigned to Captain Leckie, being described as Galle on

Gardening and then Galle on Horticulture. But it does not reappear in Captain Leckie's sale, and one suspects it was merely copied out from the SH SALE and bid on without any glimpse of the volume itself, because H. G. Bohn wrote to Beckford, 16 June 1842: '895 is not to be found, and either lost or catalogued in some other part under a different title.' (Letter owned by WSL)

WALDEGRAVE FAMILY 3475

Two prints.

Not in MC.

SH SALE, v.224, to Thorpe, £1.18.0; copies are offered in Thorpe's Supplement for 1842, lots 13332–3, for £1.1.0 each; reduced to 10/6 each in his Catalogue for 1846.

☞ The sale catalogue lists ten copies of James, 2d Earl [McArdell after Reynolds, 1762], and ten copies of George, 4th Earl [Earlom after Rigaud, ca. 1785]. These engravings were prepared as private prints for presents and seem not to have been offered for sale by HW. Copies of the prints (one a proof before letters) are preserved in Bull's extra-illustrated *Description of SH*. Under his copy of the 4th Earl, Bull pasted a slip in HW's hand: 'Lord Orford is extremely obliged to Mr. Bull for the two prints. He has not the plate of Lord Waldegrave, but he believes Lady Waldegrave has. . . .' A copy of James, 2d Earl, was preserved by HW in his own extra-illustrated *Description of SH*; the print of George, 4th Earl, was sold at SH, xix.10. The Reynolds painting of James, the 4th Earl, was in the Gallery at SH.

WALPOLE, HORACE, Editor 3476

Miscellaneous antiquities. Strawberry Hill, 1772. Two parts, 4to.

Rebound in 19th-century half calf, and press-mark not preserved. BP² early state. Not in MC.

SH SALE, v.238 (with Marlow), to Thorpe, £3.15.0; offered in Thorpe's Supplement for 1842, lot 13363, for £2.2.0; offered again by Thorpe in 1848. Now in Gonville & Caius College, Cambridge.

☞ This is one of several books gathered at the end of the fifth day in the revised cataloguing: it was first listed in the Round Tower, vii.31, but the printed price list notes that it was sold v.238. Bound with the *Miscellaneous Antiquities* are:

(1) *Copies of letters of Edward VI.* SH, 1772.

(2) IVES, JOHN. *Select papers chiefly relating to English antiquities.* Lon-

don, 1773. This book, dedicated to HW, was presumably the dedication copy.

There are some 14 MS notes by HW, on antiquarian matters, chiefly in Ives. All three tracts are untrimmed; the volume was in boards in 1842.

3477 WARBURTON, WILLIAM, Bishop

A supplemental volume of Bishop Warburton's works. Edited by Richard Hurd. London, 1788. 8vo.

Not in MC.

SH SALE, V.245 (with one *non*-Walpolian volume), to Webb & Co., Leeds, 14/–.

☞ Another copy was in Press T, No. 3266 *above.*

3478 WHEAR, DIGGORY

The method and order of reading both civil and ecclesiastical histories. . . . To which is added an appendix . . . by Nicholas Horseman. The 2d edition. London, 1694. 8vo.

Press-mark I.4.15 in MC; apparently moved with other volumes to the Library in the Offices.

SH SALE, V.241 (with Foote, Gorges, Oldcastle, Pearch, and Vertot), to Slatter, £2.2.0.

☞ Entered in the sale catalogue as 'Horseman's Method.'

3479 WILKINSON, TATE

Memoirs. York, 1790. Four volumes, 12mo.

Press-mark B.9 in MC; apparently moved after 1797 with other volumes to the Library in the Offices.

SH SALE, V.243 (with Dutens, England, German, Johnson, Mason, Montenoy, and Rigacci), to Rodd, 7/–.

☞ The list of subscribers includes HW's name.

3480 WINSTANLEY, HENRY

. . . Ground-platts, general and particular prospects of . . . Audley End. Littlebury, [1676–88]. Folio.

Not in MC, presumably because it was in the Glass Closet in 1763.

SH SALE, V.225, to Thorpe, £7.7.0.

☞ The first attempt by HW to secure a copy, at Dr. Mead's sale, is described in his letter to Bentley, 13 December 1754: '. . . What an escape

I had. . . . In the Catalogue I saw Winstanley's views of Audley Inn, which I concluded was, as it really was, a thin, dirty folio, worth about fifteen shillings. As I thought it might be scarce, it might run to two or three guineas: however, I bid Graham *certainly* buy it for me. He came the next morning in a great fright, said he did not know whether he had done very right or very wrong, that he had gone as far as *nine-and-forty guineas*—I started in such a fright! Another bookseller had luckily had as unlimited a commission, and bid fifty—when my Graham begged it might be adjourned, till they could consult their principals.' (The copy in Dr. Mead's Sale was lot 440, 3 December 1754, £50. The successful bidder at that price, according to HW's note in his own copy of Gough's *British Topography* in the Huntington Library, was Thomas Barrett of Lee in Kent.)

The SH catalogue describes HW's set as 'a very fine set.' A newspaper account of the SH SALE says that HW appears to have obtained his set later from 'the heirs of the last Earl of Suffolk, who were in possession of the original plates.' But this was a misunderstanding of a note in the book, or else of HW's explanation in his *Catalogue of Engravers*, where he had said 'the plates are reserved by the descendants of the Earls of Suffolk.'

It appears that HW secured his copy from the sale of Vertue's prints and drawings, 16 March 1757, lot 70, for the reasonable price of £3.10.0. (Information from HW's MS list of his purchases, formerly in the Penzance Library, sold at Sotheby's, 26 May 1964, to K. V. Hostick for £40; Hamill & Barker, April 1968, to WSL, $650.)

The set was dedicated to James Howard, Earl of Suffolk, who died in 1688. Lowndes reports under Kip a rumor that the original copper-plates were sold to a brazier in Cambridge as old copper, and destroyed; Gough in 1780 had printed essentially the same report.

[WYNDHAM, HENRY PENRUDDOCKE]   3481
A gentleman's tour through Monmouthshire and Wales. London, 1775. 8vo.

Press-mark B.9 in MC; apparently moved after 1797 with other volumes to the Library in the Offices.

SH SALE, v.244 (with Amsterdam, Bray, Catalogues, Cumberland, Dyde, Mensaert, and Strange), to Rodd, £1.4.0; probably the copy offered, but not identified as HW's, in Thorpe's Supplement for 1842, lot 13337, 'sewed, uncut,' for 5/–.

☞ The SH copy of the enlarged edition of 1781 was in Press S, No. 3221 *above*.

THE ROUND TOWER

THE ROUND TOWER

The room on the second floor in the Round Tower was fitted out with shelves in 1790, and it then became the library of prints and drawings, the Print Room. To this library were removed most of the large books of prints that in 1763 had been placed in Presses B, C, and D of the Main Library. (This removal permitted certain newly acquired books to be assigned to those presses in the Main Library; it likewise made possible the shifting of certain books from overcrowded Presses A, K, and L.)

The books in the Round Tower were catalogued in 1842 to be sold on the seventh and eighth days. But Robins the auctioneer announced at the first day's sale, according to a contemporary newspaper, that he had catalogued all the books exactly as they appeared on the shelves, and that he wanted to sell the books of prints in the Round Tower just as they had been catalogued in the seventh and eighth days; and he explained that Lord Waldegrave had been persuaded to order those books recatalogued and arranged by subject in the hope of realizing better prices. The arrangement planned by HW and recorded by the original cataloguing in 1842 is here preserved, since it was HW's arrangement, but with the addition of such pertinent information as can be gleaned from the London Sale.

The bookcases in the Round Tower were sold in the Nineteenth Day: the one in the Closet, with six shelves, in lot 5; and the others in lots 16–19. They had surrounded the room, to form 22 presses marked A to Y; their dimensions are recorded in the sale catalogue. (The presses in the Main Library were offered in the Twenty-fourth Day, lot 75, but were not sold, and they are still in the room at SH.)

THE CLOSET

The Closet in the Round Tower, with six shelves, contained books of special interest to HW (somewhat like those in the Glass Closet in the Main Library). Since four of these that have been recovered have the press-mark K, they were moved again at some time, after having been

shelved in Press K of the Round Tower in 1790. The auctioneer seems
also to have made some changes at the last minute: at least four books
that were catalogued in the Closet in the first edition of the catalogue
were actually sold in what I have marked Press Y above, the supplementary lots sold with the Library in the Offices.

Besides the books of special interest, the Closet also contained
in 1842 various unbound prints, especially separate numbers of incomplete sets. Some of these pieces will be found collected under
'Antiquities' (No. 3485); others are Angus, Bonafons, Grose, Halfpenny, Holbein, Middiman, Milton, Raphael, Schnebbelie, Smith,
and Thoroton. Most if not all of these unbound prints I judge to have
been referred to in HW's Codicil to his will, 27 December 1796: 'The
large red Exchequer trunk in the back room on the ground floor in
Berkeley Square containing prints, books of prints, and incomplete
numbers of prints should be removed to SH and deposited either
in the Round Library of Prints in the Round Tower or in the Ward-
robe in the new Offices' to complete the various books of prints as they
should be published. (This Exchequer trunk had been Sir Robert's:
see HW's letter to Mann, 22 March 1771.)

3482 ANDERSON, JAMES (1739–1808)

Observations on the means of exciting a spirit of national industry [in
　　Scotland]. Edinburgh, 1777. 4to.

'Calf.' Not in MC.

Not in the sale catalogue, but perhaps in a miscellaneous lot like 920 in
the London Sale. Puttick, 14 January 1867 (Leckie Sale), lot 260, to
Murray, 1/–.

3483 ANDROUET DU CERCEAU, JACQUES

Livre des grotesques. Paris, [1566?] Folio.

'Vellum, with HW's BP.' Press-mark B.1.14 in MC; moved to the Round
Tower.

SH SALE, vii.16, to Strong [London, 954]; Hodgson, 8 April 1872 (Rev.
Robert Willis Sale), lot 857.

☞ Entered in SH SALE as 'Designs for Ceilings,' and in MC as 'Collection of French Designs of Ornaments, Gardens, &c.' There are 35 plates.

ANGUS, WILLIAM   3484
The seats of the nobility and gentry. Islington, 1787. Nos. 1–7 and
No. 11, oblong 4to.

Not in MC.
SH SALE, vii.2 (with Middiman, Milton, and Antiquities), to Evans.
[London, 916].

ANTIQUITIES   3485
Numerous engraved views and serial parts, many incomplete.

Not in MC.
The sale catalogue identifies a few items, and adds '20 others on Antiquities' (vii.2), '27 nos. on Antiquities' (vii.4), '200 loose prints' (vii.24),
and 'a large quantity of prints in the roll' (vii.27).

☞ From the London Sale, these can be partly identified as follows:

(1) CUMBERLAND. 'Hassel's [Views] of the Lakes in Cumberland, Nos.
1–3.' London 916, to Evans. These were plates engraved from paintings
of John Rathbone by John Hassell, in 4to, 1795.

(2) HEREFORD. 'Antiquities of Hereford, No. 1.' London, 915, to Captain
Leckie; listed in Leckie Sale, lot 296, as 'Kennion's Antiquities of the
Counties of Hereford, etc., No. 1.' This was published by Edward Ken-
nion in 4to in 1784.

(3) MEDLAND, THOMAS. *Collection of select views of London and Westminster*, Nos. 1 and 2. London, 915, to Captain Leckie; listed in Leckie
Sale, lot 296.

(4) *Copper Plate Magazine*, edited by John Walker. Nos. 51 and 52, 1796.
London, 915, to Captain Leckie; not named in the Leckie Sale. (Called
the *New Copper Plate Magazine* in the London sale catalogue.)

(5) ESSEX, JAMES. *Some observations on Lincoln Cathedral.* London, 1776.
4to. London, 917, to Adamson. This was an off-print from the 4th volume of *Archaeologia.*

(6) *Antiquarian Repertory*, three numbers, 4to. London, 914, to Lilly.
A complete set was in Press T in the Round Tower, No. 3850 *below.*

(7) SIMCO, JOHN. 'Monuments in Fulham Church, Nos. 1 and 2.' London,
914, to Lilly. Simco published these engravings in 1794; several are reproduced, from the originals in the Guildhall Library, in C. J. Fèret's
Fulham Old and New, 1900.

(8) STRUTT, JOSEPH. *Complete view of the dress and habits of the people of
England.* London, 1796– . Nos. 1–20. 4to. London, 1071, with 'sundry
odd prints of a similar nature,' to Adamson, £2.10.0.

3485   (9) The Marble eagle found at Rome in 1742; two engravings of it made for HW in 1755 (*see* his letter to Mann, 16 July 1755) by Grignion after Wale. A total of 26 impressions and the original plates. London, 902, to Evans. Copies of the engravings were preserved by HW in his own extra-illustrated *Description of SH*, now WSL; the eagle itself, sold SH xxiii.86, is now owned by the Earl of Wemyss, Longnidry, East Lothian. In a note in his own copy of Ireland's *Picturesque Views* (now at Newnham College), HW corrected Ireland to say that Chute, not Mann, purchased the eagle for him in Rome in 1747.

(10) TWICKENHAM. Seven views of seats in and near Twickenham. London, 902, to Evans.

(11) SANDBY, PAUL. Thirty-nine views in aquatint, of North and South Wales. London, 903, to Captain Leckie, £1.3.0; Puttick, 14 January 1867 (Leckie Sale), lot 297, to J. R. Smith, 5/–.

(12) SANDBY, PAUL. Ten views in aquatint, of Windsor Castle and Warwick Castle. London, 904, to Captain Leckie, 11/–; Puttick, 14 January 1867 (Leckie Sale), lot 306, to Noseda, 11/–. Two views of SH by Sandby, perhaps in this or a similar lot, were purchased in 1962 by WSL.

(13) LONDON. Twenty views of various buildings, in aquatint by Jukes and Malton. London, 905, to Captain Leckie, 16/–; Puttick, 14 January 1867 (Leckie Sale), lots 298–304, to Noseda, £2.12.6. Two of these, Marlow's views of Blackfriars Bridge and Westminster Bridge, engraved by Green and Jukes, were sold by Sabin, August 1960, to WSL, $75.

(14) CATHEDRALS. Twenty-two views, including Bath, Eton College, Norwich, and Salisbury, in aquatint by various artists. London, 906, to Captain Leckie, 11/–; probably Puttick, 14 January 1867 (Leckie Sale), lots 305, 307, 308, for 19/6.

(15) Miscellaneous views by Rooker, Basire, etc. (19), Westall's illustrations to Boydell's edition of *Paradise Lost*, etc. (32). These engravings, identifiable from the Leckie Sale, lots 294 and 309, may have been in one of these lots, or possibly in the unnamed lot 1017 of the London Sale, for which Captain Leckie paid 5/–.

No doubt other miscellaneous prints, if portraits, were sorted into the chronological series in the first days of the London Sale. From among these lots, also, or from an unnamed lot like 1017, were perhaps gathered the prints of Buck's *Antiquities*, 1774: a set newly bound in russia by Aitken, from HW's collection, was offered in Bohn's Catalogue for 1847 (Prints), p. 78, for £21. A second portfolio perhaps made up from these lots was offered in Bohn's Catalogue, p. 105, for £6.16.6: 'Oblong portfolio in vellum containing 103 views of English seats, palaces, churches, public buildings, gardens, &c., including three original drawings.' A third portfolio was

offered by Bohn, p. 194, for £3.3.0: 'sixteen views of Stowe, 1752, by Chatelain, and 39 views of scenes in London.'

One of the drawings in some such portfolio (except that it seems to have
been given to Richard Bull) may have been the original drawing by Nathaniel and Samuel Buck for their *Long View of London*; this is now in the
British Museum, with HW's note: 'Buck's original drawing of Modern London, finished in the reign of George II. Mem: Buck's widow had refused
£70 for it—I bought it afterwards at a sale at Baker's in Covent Garden.'

BARTOLI, PIETRO SANTI   3486

Parerga atque ornamenta ex Raphaelis Sanctii prototypis. Rome,
    n.d. Oblong folio.

Press-mark C.3.25 in MC, 'Raphael's Friezes in the Vatican, by Bartoli';
moved to the Round Tower.

SH SALE, vii.11, to Colnaghi, £1.11.6. [London, 1169]

BENEDICT XIV, Pope   3487

*Benedetto XIV ultimi ufizj renduti alla memoria di dall' Card.
    Antonio Sersale*. Naples, 1758. Folio.

'For the Hon. Horace Walpole from Sir Horace Mann.' Not in MC.

Not in the sale catalogue, but perhaps in a miscellaneous lot like 920 in
the London Sale. Puttick, 14 January 1867 (Leckie Sale), lot 273, to
'Money,' 1/–.

BONAFONS, LOUIS ABEL DE   3488

*Galerie du Palais Royal, gravée d'après les tableaux des différentes
    écoles*. Paris, 1786. Thirty-two numbers, folio.

Not in MC.

SH SALE, vii.22, to Adamson, £3.10.0. [London, 1170]

☞ At Farmington, among the Walpole papers acquired from Mrs.
Bentley in 1937, there is a receipt, dated 10 April 1787, for 16/– in payment for the fifth number.

BURGOYNE, General JOHN   3489

*A state of the expedition from Canada, as laid before the House of
    Commons*. London, 1780. 4to.

SH SALE, vii.4, a lot dispersed in the London Sale; not separately
identifiable in the London Sale, but perhaps in a lot like 1059, 'and 2
others' on History.

☞ Described as the 'Expedition to Canada.' But HW wrote with interest of Burgoyne's defence in Parliament; the book was perhaps placed in the Round Tower because it contained engraved plates.

3490 CHUTE, JOHN

Original drawings and sketches. MS. Oblong folio.

Original marbled boards. Second SH fleuron used as BP. Press-mark K.13, but moved to the Closet. Not in MC; probably kept in the Glass Closet until 1790. Inscribed on the fly-leaf: 'Lady Waldegrave from W. V. Harcourt, July 6, 1867.' Bookplate of Lord Carlingford, who married Lady Waldegrave in 1863.

SH SALE, vii.25, to H. G. Bohn, £2.17.6 [London, 1256]; offered in Bohn's Catalogue for 1847 (Architecture), p. 223, for £5.5.0; Lord Waldegrave, 1948, in a collection to WSL.

☞ Title by HW in MS on the fly-leaf: 'Slight Sketches of Architecture.' Identifying notes by HW throughout. This most important volume includes a sketch for the Gallery and Round Tower at SH, and one inspired by a doorcase in Dugdale's *St. Paul's* for the presses in the Library. Chute's design for the Library, HW wrote to Bentley in 1753, had 'a conventual look' that Bentley's lacked. Not surprisingly, HW included this volume in his list of 'Curious books in the Glass Closet' in his *Description of SH,* 1774.

3491 CLEMENTINA MARIA SOBIESKI, Princess

Parentalia Mariae Clementinae. Rome, 1736. Folio.

Press-mark D.3.10 in MC; moved to the Round Tower.
SH SALE, vii.14, to H. G. Bohn, 9/–. [London, 1085]

☞ Princess Clementina, the wife of the Old Pretender, entered a nunnery in 1724; her funeral in 1735 was elaborate.

3492 EDWARDS, JOHN

The British Herbal. London, 1770. Folio.

Not in MC.
SH SALE, vii.16, to Lilly, 10/–. [London, 1140]

3493 EISENBERG, Baron d'

Description du manège moderne, dans sa perfection. [Amsterdam?], 1727. Oblong folio.

Press-mark C.3.9 in MC; moved to the Round Tower.
SH SALE, vii.6 (with Sandford), to H. G. Bohn, £3.3.0. [London, 1143]

☞ A copy in old calf was offered, but not identified as HW's, in Bohn's Catalogue for 1847 (Prints), p. 127, for £1.5.0.

GERBIER, Sir BALTHAZAR 3494

Genealogie de Messire Balthazar Gerbier. Coats of arms and documents, 17th century. MS. Folio.

Black morocco, rebacked, with Gerbier arms on sides. BP². Not in MC. Later bookplate of Charles John Shoppee.
SH SALE, vii.13 to Rodd, £2.10.0 [London, 1109]; Sotheby's, 20 June 1885 (Crossley Sale), lot 2990, to T. Noble, £5.15.0; bequeathed by H. J. B. Clements to the Victoria and Albert Museum in 1940.

☞ Note by HW on the fly-leaf: 'For a full account of Sir Balthazar Gerbier see the second volume of Walpole's *Anecdotes of Painting in England*. Some of Gerbier's dispatches are printed in the two volumes of miscellaneous *State Papers* published by Philip Earl of Hardwicke in quarto 1778.'

GIOVANNOLI, ALO 3495

Roma antica. Rome, 1619. Oblong folio.

'Vellum.' Press-mark C.3.24 in MC; moved to the Round Tower.
SH SALE, vii.20, to Captain Leckie, 17/– [London, 983]; Puttick, 14 January 1867 (Leckie Sale), lot 265, to Glaisher, 8/–.

☞ Entered in the sale catalogue as 'Vientanus' Roman Antiquities' ('Vienture' in first edition of the catalogue).

GROSE, FRANCIS 3496

Antiquities of Ireland, 1791. Five numbers, 4to.

Not in MC.
SH SALE, vii.1 (with Schnebbelie and Thoroton), to Lilly, £1.2.0. [London, 914]

☞ This work, edited with the help of Edward Ledwich, is probably what was sold. It is not listed in vii.1 at all, where Schnebbelie's *Antiquaries Museum* is wrongly credited with 15 numbers; but in the London Sale, Schnebbelie is reduced to 10 numbers, and a new entry is made for 'Antiquities of Ireland, Nos. 1 to 5.'

3497 Halfpenny, Joseph

Gothic ornaments in the Cathedral Church of York. [York], 1795.
Eight numbers, 4to.

Not in MC.

SH SALE, vii.3 (with Martin and Smith), to Adamson, £1.12.0. [London, 917]

Derek Nightingale
£40.00.
1988

3498 Hamilton, Sir William

*Collection of engravings from ancient vases discovered in the sep-
ulchres in the Kingdom of the Two Sicilies.* Naples, 1791–5. Two
volumes, folio.

Not in MC.

SH SALE, vii.19, to Lilly, 12/–. [London, 1000]

3499 Heraldry

The English Baronage from William I to James I. MS. Folio.

Not in MC.

SH SALE, vii.8, to Thorpe, £3.15. [London, 1105]

☞ This contained 514 colored drawings of arms of the Barons.

3500 Holbein, Hans

*Imitations of original drawings by Hans Holbein in the collection of
His Majesty for the portraits of illustrious persons of the Court
of Henry VIII.* Engraved by Bartolozzi, with biographical notices
by Edmund Lodge, and published by John Chamberlaine, Keeper
of the King's Drawings. London, 1792. Nos. 1–9 and an extra copy
of No. 1, folio.

Not in MC.

SH SALE, vii.5, to Colnaghi, £3. [London, 593]

☞ The work was completed in 14 numbers in 1800.

3501 Kit-Cat Club

*The Kit-Cat Club, done from the original paintings of Sir Godfrey
Kneller.* Engraved by John Faber, Junior, and published by Faber
and Jacob Tonson. London, 1735. Portraits mounted in a portfolio.

Half-calf, with the sides covered by decorated paper. BP[1]. Press-mark
C.3.3, altered by Kirgate in book (not in MC) to K.1 (Round Tower), but
finally sold with books in the Closet.

SH SALE, vii.7, to Lilly, £1.8.0 [London, 591]; Sotheby's, 21 December 1853 (J. H. S. Pigott Sale), lot 1025, to Lilly, £4.7.0 (catalogued for sale in 1848 with Pigott's library, but apparently bought in); offered by Quaritch in several catalogues, 1909–14, for £42; presented to the Virginia Historical Society with the Conway Robinson collection in 1923; Virginia Historical Society, March 1955, by exchange through the Yale Library, for the Lewis Walpole Collection.

☞ The original paintings are preserved in the National Portrait Gallery in London. The Kit-Cat portraits are mentioned by HW in his *Anecdotes*: 'The Kit-Cat Club, generally mentioned as a set of wits, in reality the patriots that saved Britain, were Kneller's . . . last public work.' Since Faber's engraved trade card is pasted above HW's BP, this copy is described in a 19th-century MS note on the fly-leaf as a presentation copy.

LENS, BERNARD   3502
Drawings of scenes in and near London. MS. Oblong folio.
  Not in MC.
  SH SALE, vii.25, to 'Money,' £2. [London, 1257]

LETHIEULLIER, SMART   3503
Drawings of ancient buildings in England, and of classical antiquities.
  Three volumes, folio.
  Rebound in half blue morocco. BP² early state. Not in MC, being kept in the Glass Closet until 1790.
  SH SALE, vii.12, to H. G. Bohn, £20.10.0 [London, 1260]; offered in Bohn's Catalogue for 1847 (Prints), p. 99, for £31.10.0; sold by Bohn, May 1866, to the British Museum; now BM Add. MSS 27348–50.

☞ Some of the drawings are by Charles Frederick. Note by HW in the first volume that he bought the set for £60 in 1761, after the death of Mr. Lethieullier. He made a few notes from these volumes in his 'Book of Materials,' *ca.* 1761, and he wrote to Cole, 20 May 1762, concerning a drawing of a tomb. (In his marked copy of the *Description of SH*, HW recorded the price as £63, i.e. sixty guineas.)

Gough wrote in his *British Topography*, 1780, p. x, that HW had thought the price too high and that the volumes now belonged to the Earl of Bute; but HW marked in his copy of Gough: 'This account is totally erroneous. Mr. Walpole did by Bp. Lyttelton's intervention purchase of Mr. Lethieullier's sister for £60 the three volumes of drawings.' In his letter to Cole, 11 November 1780, HW recounted the details even more circumstantially. Not surprisingly, ·HW included these volumes in his list of 'Curious books in the Glass Closet' in the *Description of SH*, 1774.

3504 LORT, MICHAEL

Observations on celts. [London, 1778] 4to.

> Not in MC.
> Not named in SH SALE, but perhaps among the miscellaneous lots of antiquities in the Closet. London Sale, lot 920, to Lilly.
>
> ☞ An off-print from *Archaeologia*, Volume 5. Lort sent it to HW on 20 June 1778.

3505 LYDGATE, JOHN

Copies of Limnings in the Harleian MS of his *Life of King Edmund*, and others on vellum from a MS of Froissart's *Chronicle*. MS. Folio.

> Now mounted on leaves in an old vellum binding. BP^1. Not in MC.
> SH SALE, vii.13 to Rodd, £2 [London, 1122]; offered in Strong's Catalogue for 1843, lot 935, for £3.10.0; Fletcher, 13 April 1846 (J. Britton Sale, Part 4), lot 1522, to Smither, £1.19.0; Sotheby's, 4 February 1847 (Strong Sale), lot 1338, to Miller, 12/–; Sotheby's, 3 June 1946 (Miscellaneous Sale), lot 128, to Maggs for WSL, £11.
>
> ☞ In his copy of the *Harleian Catalogue* now at Farmington, HW marked the Lydgate MS, No. 2278. According to a note by Sir Frederic Madden, this SH volume was really part of Strong's stock when catalogued in the Britton Sale in 1846.

3506 MARTIN, ELIAS

Prints from his collection of drawings. 47 colored plates in three brochures. London [1779]. 4to.

> Not in MC.
> SH SALE, vii.3, to Captain Leckie [London, 891]; Puttick, 14 January 1867 (Leckie Sale), lot 295, to Harvey, £1.15.0. This was owned in 1937 by the art dealer Heinrich Tiedemann of Berlin.
>
> ☞ The SH catalogue lists this as 'Prints from Elias Martin's Drawings, 2.' as if they were only two of the separate engravings; but the London sale appears to record the same item when it lists 'twenty-seven [error for 47] prints in three brochures.'

3507 MIDDIMAN, SAMUEL

Select views in Great Britain. London, 1784. Nos. 1–8, oblong 4to.

> Not in MC.
> SH SALE, vii.2 (with Angus, Antiquities, and Milton), to Captain Leckie

[London, 915]; Puttick, 14 January 1867 (Leckie Sale), lot 296, to J. R. Smith.

MILTON, THOMAS   3508
A collection of select views from the different seats of the nobility and
    gentry in Ireland. [London, 1794] Nos. 1–6, oblong 4to.
    Not in MC.
    SH SALE, vii.2 (with Angus, Antiquities, and Middiman), to Evans.
[London, 916]

NAPLES. Reale Accademia delle Scienze e Belle Lettere   3509
Istoria de' fenomeni del tremoto avvenuto nelle Calabrie. With an
    atlas volume. Published by the Royal Academy of Science. Naples,
    1784. Two volumes, folio.
    Not in MC.
    SH SALE, vii.18, to Strong, £1.18.0. [London, 972]

NUNDOCOMAR BAHADER   3510
Trial of Maha Rajah Nundocomar Bahader . . . for forgery. London,
    1776. 4to.
    Not in MC.
    Not in the sale catalogue, but perhaps in a miscellaneous lot like 920
in the London Sale. Puttick, 14 January 1867 (Leckie Sale), lot 261, to
Westell.

Oxford Almanack. Volumes for 1674, 1677, 1679, 1681, 1700–1768, 3511
    1770, 1771, 1773, 1779, 1781–1789, 1791, 1792. 88 volumes, folio.
    Not in MC.
    SH SALE, vii.27, to Thorpe, £10. [London, 951]

PAINE, JAMES   3512
Plans, elevations, and sections of noblemen and gentlemen's houses.
    London, 1767. Folio.
    Not in MC.
    SH SALE, vii.23, to Captain Leckie, 6/– [London, 924]; not found in the
Leckie Sale.
    ☞ Paine issued a second part in 1783, but HW seems to have owned only
the first part.

Catalogued with this in vii.23 were '11 Nos. [17 in 1st edition] of Pinkerton's Portraits, &c.' These were doubtless scattered, but they included part of lot 592 in the London Sale: 'Pinkerton's Scottish Portraits, Nos. 1 and 2, and Herbert's Portraits of Illustrious Persons of Scotland, Nos. 1 and 2.' (The final revision of the SH catalogue, Edition V, lists 10 numbers 'of Pinkerton's Portraits, and 2 Illustrious Persons in Scotland.')

3513 PIGAGE, NICOLAS DE

La Galerie Électorale de Dusseldorff, ou catalogue raisonné de ses tableaux. Engraved by Chrétien de Méchel. Basel, 1778. Two volumes, oblong 4to.

Not in MC.

SH SALE, vii.10, to H. G. Bohn, £2.

☞ A copy was offered, but not identified as HW's, in Bohn's Catalogue for 1847 (Prints), p. 113, for £4.4.0, in boards.

3514 RAPHAEL of Urbino

Essays of character, after the cartoons of Raffaele at Windsor by J. Ruyssen, engraved by Anthony Cardon. [London, 1797?] Thirteen plates in two numbers, folio.

Not in MC.

SH SALE, vii.28, to Lilly, £1.1.0. [London, 1168]

☞ Entered in the SH catalogue as 'Raphael's Heads, 6 nos.' (corrected to 2 nos. in revised catalogue). The set when completed in 1802 comprised 15 plates.

3515 ROSSI, GIOVANNI GIACOMO DE

Le fontane di Roma. Engraved by G. B. Falda. Rome, 1691. Folio.

Original vellum. BP[1]. Press-mark C.3.21; altered in book to K.14 (Round Tower), and later moved to the Closet.

SH SALE, vii.11, to Evans, 16/– [London, 981]; acquired at some time by Mr. George Fox Steedman for $100, and given in 1929 with the Steedman Collection to the St. Louis Public Library.

☞ Another copy seems to have been sold with the supplementary books, Press Y in the Library in the Offices, No. 3464 *above*—unless this book was listed a second time in error. Either copy may have been the copy now in St. Louis, but at least three other books in K were sold with the books in the Closet.

ROSSI, LORENZO FILIPPO DE   3516

*Raccolta di vasi diversi formati da illustri artefici antichi, e di varie
  targhe sopraposte.* Rome, 1713. Folio.

'Old vellum.' Press-mark C.3.20 in MC; moved to the Round Tower.
SH SALE, vii.19, to H. G. Bohn, £1.2.0 [London, 1001]; offered in
Bohn's Catalogue for 1847 (Prints), p. 183, for £1.16.0.

☞ Engraved by Aquila, from the collections of Pope Clement.

SANDFORD, FRANCIS   3517

The history of the coronation of James II and of Queen Mary. London, 1687. Folio.

'Original calf.' Press-mark B.1.5 in MC; moved to the Round Tower.
SH SALE, vii.6 (with Eisenberg), to H. G. Bohn, £3.3.0 [London, 1070];
offered in Bohn's Catalogue for 1847 (Prints), p. 186, for £3.5.0.

SCHENK, PETER   3518

Roma aeterna. [Amsterdam? 1705]. Oblong folio.

'Half bound.' Press-mark C.6.6 in MC; altered probably from C.5 (the
numbers are blurred), but moved to the Round Tower.
SH SALE, vii.20, to Captain Leckie, 17/– [London, 974]; Puttick, 14
January 1867 (Leckie Sale), lot 257, to Westell, 4/–.

☞ Called 'Antiquities of Ancient Rome' in the SH catalogue. William
Beckford wrote to Bohn that he already had a fine copy of this work.

SCHNEBBELIE, JACOB   3519

The Antiquaries Museum. London, 1791. Ten numbers, 4to.

Not in MC.
SH SALE, vii.1 (with Grose and Thoroton), to Lilly, £1.2.0. [London,
914]

☞ Listed as 'The Antiquarian Museum, 15 numbers,' in the SH SALE
catalogue but corrected to 10 numbers in the London Sale, where other
pieces are itemized.

SGRILLI, BERNARDO SANSONE   3520

Descrizione e studi dell' insigne fabbrica di S. Maria del Fiore. Florence, 1733. Folio.

Not in MC.
SH SALE, vii.17, to H. G. Bohn, 7/–. [London, 973]

☞ William Beckford had two copies, one of which may have been HW's, but no provenance is indicated in the Beckford catalogue.

3521 SMITH, JOHN THOMAS

Antiquities of London and its environs. London, 1791. Eight numbers, 4to.

Not in MC.

SH SALE, vii.3 (with Halfpenny and Martin), to Adamson, £1.12.0. [London, 917]

☞ Described in the SH catalogue as 'Views to Pennant's London.'

3522 SWORDFEAGER, MARTHA SOPHIA

The case of the unfortunate Martha Sophia Swordfeager. Privately printed, 1771. 4to.

Not in MC.

Not in either sale catalogue by name. Perhaps in a lot like '18 other tracts' in the London Sale, lot 920.

☞ We know only that HW bought this pamphlet in Dr. Lort's sale, April 1791, lot 286, for 6/–.

3523 THOROTON, ROBERT

History of Nottinghamshire. London, 1790. Twenty numbers, 4to.

Not in MC.

SH SALE, vii.1 (with Grose and Schnebbelie), to Lilly, £1.2.0. [London, 914]

☞ This revised edition, compiled by John Throsby, was completed in three volumes in 1797.

3524 THULDEN, THEODOR VAN

Les travaux d'Ulysse. Engraved from the paintings by Francesco Primaticcio. Paris, 1640. Folio.

Press-mark D.4.19 in MC; moved to the Round Tower.

SH SALE, vii.16, to Lilly, 10/–. [London, 1172]

3525 VALDOR, JEAN

Les triomphes de Louis XIII . . . representées en figures . . . par un poëme héroique de Charles de Beys. Latin and French. With portraits, plans of battles, etc. Paris, 1649. Folio.

Not in MC.

SH SALE, vii.15, to Dodd, 9/–. [London, 1084]

VAN DER DORT, ABRAHAM   3526

*Catalogue of paintings and other rarities belonging to King Charles
I, 1639.* MS. Folio.

Arms of King Charles stamped on the sides. Third SH fleuron used as
BP. Press-mark K.17. Not in MC.

SH SALE, vii.21, to Rev. Henry Wellesley, £22 [London, 1116]; Sotheby's,
3 August 1866 (Wellesley Sale), lot 45, to Sir William Tite, £50; purchased
from the Tite collection, 4 June 1874, for the Royal Library; now in the
Royal Library at Windsor. (A letter from Baron James de Rothschild of
Waddesdon Manor, 3 June 1874, stating that he was withdrawing his bid,
is laid in the volume.)

☞ Note by HW: 'This is the fair copy made [by a scribe] for King
Charles the first of Vanderdort's catalogue. . . . The blank leaves have been
stuffed with nonsense by some late possessor, who seems to have used it as a
commonplace-book. I bought it in November 1786, for two guineas.' A
transcript by Vertue, probably not from this MS but from the Ashmolean
MSS, is also in the Royal Library: *see* No. 3704 *below*.

Pinkerton told HW about this MS in October 1786. It has been published
in the Walpole Society's 37th volume (1960), with the other MSS by Van der
Dort.

Villa Pamphilia ejusque Palatium cum suis prospectibus, statuae,   3527
fontes, [etc.] Rome, [*ca.* 1690] Folio.

Not in MC.

SH SALE, vii.14, to H. G. Bohn, 12/–. [London, 978]

☞ The plates are by Dominique Barrière, *d.* 1678.

Bohn reported to William Beckford, 16 June 1842, that this was 'fair,
not fine—some folding plates at the end which I don't remember. Not I
think a desirable book. About £2.10.0.' Beckford replied: 'I don't want
Villa Pamphilia—having two superior copies already.' (Letters now
WSL)

WATTS, WILLIAM, Engraver   3528

Views of Bath and Bristol. [London, *ca.* 1795] 4to.

Not in MC.

Not named in the SH SALE but perhaps among the miscellaneous views in
the Closet. London Sale, lot 920, to Lilly.

3529 WILLIAM III, King of England

Relation du voyage de sa Majesté Britannique en Holland et de la réception qui luy a faite. Engravings by Romeyn de Hooghe. The Hague, 1692. Folio.

Old calf, rebacked. BP² later state. Press-mark O.7, apparently moved from Press O to the Closet. Not in MC. Signature of Cosmo Gordon (librarian of the Institute of Chartered Accountants).

SH SALE, vii.15, to Strong, 16/– [London, 967]; offered in Strong's Catalogue for 1843, lot 1558 and again in lot 1648, for £1.4.0; John Hodgson, September 1942, to WSL, £10.10.0.

☞The French translation is attributed to Jean Tronchin du Breuil. A copy of the Dutch original was in Press Q, No. 3800 *below*.

3530 ZOCCHI, GIUSEPPE

Vedute delle ville et d'altri luoghi della Toscana. Florence, 1744. Folio.

'Vellum.' Press-mark C.2.8 in MC; moved to the Round Tower.
SH SALE, vii.17, to Evans, £1.12.0. [London, 971]

PRESS A

Press A in the Round Tower was entirely devoted to architectural works and architectural antiquities in folio.

Many of the books of drawings and prints in Presses A to L were in atlas folio or mounted in portfolios, but these have been recorded simply as in folio.

3531 ADAM, ROBERT

Ruins of the palace of the Emperor Diocletian at Spalatro. London, 1763. Folio.

'Vellum, with HW's arms on sides.' Press-mark C.2.16 in MC, entered by HW. (He assigned the number that had already been given to the first volume of Félibien's *Cabinet du Roi*; but he had trouble with this number, which he also assigned to Stuart's *Athens*.) Moved to the Round Tower.

SH SALE, viii.8, to Lilly, £1.13.0 [London, 987]; offered by Rodd in an undated catalogue, *ca.* 1843, and also in his Catalogue for 1847, Part 3

(Arts and Sciences), lot 1878, for £3; Sotheby's, 10 June 1895 (Orford Sale), lot 1, to Quaritch, £2.4.0.

☞ The list of subscribers includes HW's name.

CHAMBERS, Sir WILLIAM   3532

Plans, elevations, sections, and views of the gardens and buildings at Kew in Surrey. London, 1763. Folio.

'Vellum.' Press-mark C.2.15 in MC, entered by HW; moved to the Round Tower.

SH SALE, viii.4, to the Earl of Buckinghamshire, 19/–. [London, 945]

CHAMBERS, Sir WILLIAM   3533

Treatise on civil architecture. London, 1759. Folio.

'Vellum.' Press-mark C.2.13 in MC; moved to the Round Tower.

SH SALE, viii.3, to the Earl of Buckinghamshire, £1.10.0. [London, 944]

☞ This work was praised by HW in the Preface to his *Anecdotes of Painting*; he made one note from it in his 'Book of Materials,' *ca.* 1759, and a few more *ca.* 1762.

CHANDLER, RICHARD, and REVETT, NICHOLAS   3534

Ionian antiquities. London, 1769. Folio.

'Vellum, with HW's arms on sides.' Not in MC.

SH SALE, viii.2, to Captain Leckie, £1.1.0 [London, 990]; Puttick, 14 January 1867 (Leckie Sale), lot 266, to Bezzi, 8/–.

☞ Published by the Society of Dilettanti; the drawings were by William Pars, and the preface by Robert Wood.

GIBBS, JAMES   3535

A book of architecture, containing designs of buildings and orna-ments. London, 1728. Folio.

Press-mark D.1.18 in MC; moved to the Round Tower.

SH SALE, viii.11, to H. G. Bohn, £1.7.0 [London, 943]; probably one of two copies offered in Bohn's Catalogue for 1847 (Architecture), p. 225.

☞ On 4 August 1753, HW wrote to Chute from Stowe: 'In the heretical corner of my heart I adore the Gothic building, which by some unusual inspiration Gibbs has made pure and beautiful and venerable.'

3536 HAMILTON, Sir WILLIAM

Collection of Etruscan, Greek, and Roman antiquities. Text by P. F. Hugues, *called* D'Hancarville. Naples, 1766–7. Four volumes, folio.

'Green morocco.' Not in MC.
SH SALE, viii.15, to H. G. Bohn, £15.15.0. [London, 1007]

☞ There are several references in the letters between Mann and HW to the difficulties that D'Hancarville had in the next decade with his plates for his *Antiquités étrusques*. D'Hancarville's *Recherches sur l'origine . . . des arts de la Grèce*, 1785, was called by HW one of the three worst-written books (among important ones) ever produced (his 'Book of Materials,' *ca.* 1787), and he seems not to have purchased a set.

Bohn wrote on 17 June 1842 to Beckford (letters now WSL) that these volumes were fine and might fetch £35; but Beckford replied that he already owned a set.

3537 HAMPDEN, ROBERT TREVOR, 1st Viscount

Britannia, Lathmon, Villa Bromhamensis, Poematia. Parma, Bodoni, 1792. Folio.

'Green morocco.' Not in MC.
SH SALE, viii.16, to the Earl of Buckinghamshire, £1.18.0. [London, 918]

☞ Copies were not offered for sale; HW wrote to Lady Diana Beauclerk, 2 December 1793, to ask her to beg a copy for him from John Trevor who had had his father's poems printed.

3538 JONES, INIGO

Designs of Inigo Jones, consisting of plans and elevations for buildings, published by William Kent. London, 1727. Two parts in one volume, folio.

'Calf.' Press-mark D.1.19 in MC; moved to the Round Tower.
SH SALE, viii.14, to H. G. Bohn, 14/–. Not found in the London Sale.

☞ The work includes several designs by Lord Burlington, who arranged for its preparation and publication by Kent. Sir Robert Walpole subscribed to two sets.

KIRBY, JOHN JOSHUA   3539

*The perspective of architecture deduced from the principles of Dr.
    Brook Taylor.* London, 1761. Folio.

> 'Vellum.' Press-mark C.2.12 in MC; moved to the Round Tower.
> SH SALE, viii.10, to J. R. Smith, £1.11.0. [London, 942]

LASTRI, MARCO   3540

L'Etruria pittrice, ovvero storia della pittura Toscana. Florence,
    1791. Folio.

> 'Russia.' Not in MC.
> SH SALE, viii.17, to Adamson, £6. [London, 1207]
>
> ☞ The work was edited by Niccolo Pagni and Giuseppe Bardi; the
> parallel French text was by Barthélémi Renan.

LE ROY, DAVID   3541

Les ruines des plus beaux monuments de la Grèce. Paris, 1758. Two
    volumes in one, folio.

> 'Vellum.' Press-mark C.2.9 in MC; moved to the Round Tower.
> SH SALE, viii.9, to H. G. Bohn, £1.19.0 [London, 988]; offered in Bohn's
> Catalogue for 1847 (Prints), p. 184, for £3.3.0.

MAJOR, THOMAS   3542

The ruins of Paestum, otherwise Posidonia, in Magna Graecia. Lon-
    don, 1768. Folio.

> 'Vellum, with arms on the sides.' Not in MC.
> SH SALE, viii.1, to Lilly, 14/– [London, 989]; offered in Strong's Cata-
> logue for 1843, lot 953, for £1.10.0.
>
> ☞ Strong describes this as a subscription copy.

PIRANESI, GIOVANNI BATTISTA   3543

Le Antichità Romane. Rome, 1756. Four volumes, folio.

> 'Calf.' Press-mark D.4.1 in MC; moved to the Round Tower.
> SH SALE, viii.18, to Lilly, £7.10.0 [London, 1008]; Christie's, 20 October
> 1938 (Savile of Rufford Abbey Sale), £13.13.0.

3544 STUART, JAMES, and REVETT, NICHOLAS

The antiquities of Athens measured and delineated. London, 1762–
94. Three volumes, folio.

'Vellum.' Press-mark (of Volume I) C.2.27 in MC. (Entered under Stuart
by HW, who also entered it under Athens with an erroneous number.)
Moved to the Round Tower.

SH SALE, viii.7, to Graves, £12. [London, 993]

☞ The third volume was prepared by Willey Reveley; and William
Newton, the architect, completed the second volume, in 1787.

3545 VENUTI, RIDOLFINO

Collectanea antiquitatum Romanarum. Rome, 1736. Folio.

Italian vellum, with HW's signature dated 1740. BP[1]. Press-mark B.1.15 in
MC; moved to the Round Tower. Press-mark altered in the book to L.20;
in the Round Tower Presses A and L were both devoted to architectural
works. Bookstamp of Howard C. Levis.

SH SALE, viii.13, to H. G. Bohn, £1.1.0 [London, 1006]; offered in Bohn's
Catalogue for 1847 (Prints), p. 203, for £1.10.0; Christie's, 29 April 1965
(Miscellaneous Sale), lot 214, to Pickering & Chatto for WSL, £50.

☞ Published by Antonio Borioni.

The BP was uncovered when the new end-paper was lifted at Farmington
in 1965.

3546 WALPOLE, HORACE

*Aedes Walpolianae, or, a description of the collection of pictures at
Houghton Hall.* Original MS by HW, with 120 drawings and prints,
and Ripley's original drawings of buildings. Folio.

Original marbled boards. BP[1]. Press-mark D.1.3 in MC, altered to
C.20 in book; perhaps misplaced in A because of the architectural drawings.

SH SALE, viii.12, to Lilly, £14.3.6 [London, 1124]; offered in Strong's
Catalogue for 1843, lot 1881; offered in April 1925 by Spurr & Swift for
£135; purchased in 1925 by the Metropolitan Museum of Art in New York.

☞ Note added to the MC by HW: 'These are the drawings from whence
the prints were taken.' And he listed this volume among the rare books in
his library in the *Description of SH,* 1774. By an arrangement between
WSL and the Metropolitan Museum in 1925, Houston's mezzotint (1761)
from Reynolds's portrait of Lady Waldegrave and her daughter, as well as
three broadsides (*Houghton Hare-Hunting, Prosperity to Houghton,* and

the *Norfolk Garland*) were removed from the volume and sent to WSL for $50; the broadsides are mentioned under No. 3469:2 *above*.

William Beckford wrote to Bohn that books like this and the *Description of SH* (in Press C, No. 3582 *below*) were too heavy for him.

WOOD, ROBERT   3547

The ruins of Balbec, otherwise Heliopolis, in Coelosyria. London, 1757. Folio.

'Vellum.' Press-mark C.2.10 in MC; moved to the Round Tower.

SH SALE, viii.6, to H. G. Bohn, £2.2.0 [London, 992]; the two volumes (Balbec and Palmyra) offered in Bohn's Catalogue for 1847 (Prints), p. 216, for £6.16.6.

WOOD, ROBERT   3548

The ruins of Palmyra, otherwise Tedmor, in the desert. London, 1753. Folio.

'Vellum.' Press-mark C.2.11 in MC; moved to the Round Tower.

SH SALE, viii.5, to H. G. Bohn, £2.10.0. [London, 991]

☞ Wood was assisted on his journey to Balbec and Palmyra by James Dawkins. *See* HW to Bentley, 19 December 1753: '*Palmyra* is come forth, and is a noble book; the prints finely engraved, and an admirable dissertation before it.' In the Preface to his *Anecdotes*, HW wrote: 'Of all the works that distinguish this age, none perhaps excel those beautiful edions of Balbec and Palmyra—not published at the command of a Louis Quatorze . . . but undertaken by private curiosity and good sense, and trusted to the taste of a polished nation. When I endeavor to do justice to the editions of Palmyra and Balbec, I would not confine the encomium to the sculptures; the books have far higher merit. The modest descriptions prefixed are standards of writing: the exact measure of what should and should not be said . . . was never comprehended in more clear diction, or more elegant style.'

PRESS B

Press B in the Round Tower contained books of prints, especially historical works, in large folio. The most impressive appearance was perhaps made by the set of Thuanus in fourteen volumes, but Pine's *Tapestry hangings in the House of Lords* was, I think, the most beautiful volume.

3549 ANDERSON, JAMES

Selectus diplomatum & numismatum Scotiae thesaurus. Completed
   by Thomas Ruddiman. Edinburgh, 1739. Royal folio.

Original vellum. BP[1]. Press-mark D.1.27; altered in book to B.1 (the
Round Tower). Later bookplates of I. A. Maconochie and Edward Ellice.
Signature of I. A. Maconochie, 1842.

SH SALE, viii.20, to Rob. Maconochie, Esq., £7 [London, 1079]; Maggs,
September 1949, to WSL, £10.10.0.

☞ In his 'Book of Materials,' *ca.* 1760, HW entered one reference
to a seal of Mary Queen of Scots, from the index at the end of the book.

3550 CROZAT, JOSEPH ANTOINE

*Recueil d'estampes d'après les plus beaux tableaux qui sont en
   France.* Paris, 1729–42. Two volumes, folio.

Press-mark C.1.2 in MC; moved to the Round Tower.

SH SALE, viii.29, to Lilly, £12.12.0. [London, 1187]

☞ From paintings 'dans le Cabinet du Roy, dans celuy de Monseigneur le Duc d'Orléans, et dans autres cabinets.' It was perhaps this
set that Mann sent to HW in 1743: *see* Mann's letter, 12 March 1743, and
HW's acknowledgment, 14 August 1743.

3551 GARTER, ORDER OF THE

Procession of the Order of the Garter in 1577. Thirteen drawings in
   water-color by Vertue, copied from the original engravings by
   Gheeraerts. MS. Oblong folio.

Press-mark C.3.27 in MC; moved to the Round Tower.

SH SALE, viii.25, to Graves, £13.13.0. [London, 599]

☞ This is listed among the rare books in the library in the *Description of SH*, 1774. In his *Anecdotes*, HW dates the engravings of Gheeraerts
in 1584, and says that he bought Vertue's drawings at the Vertue sale. The
catalogue of the London Sale in 1842 mentions a note by HW in the
book.

Hollar copied the same Gheeraerts engravings for Ashmole's *Institution
of the Order of the Garter, 1693.*

3552 PINE, JOHN, Engraver

The tapestry hangings of the House of Lords [representing the defeat
   of the Spanish Armada]. Engraved in two colors by Pine, with
   historical text by Philip Morant. London, 1739. Folio.

Original red morocco, gilt, with gilded floral end-papers. BP[1]. Press-mark C.2.20; altered in book to B.25 (the Round Tower). Label of Scottowe Hall Library.

SH SALE, viii.24, to Colonel Durrant, £9.9.0 [London, 1075]; Sotheby's, 3 November 1952, lot 105, to Maggs for WSL, £40.

☞ Inserted by HW is an engraved portrait of Henry Cornelius Vroom, and HW wrote under the name 'who designed the tapestry.' Among the subscribers were HW's father and his brother Edward.

Bohn wrote on 17 June 1842 to William Beckford (letters now WSL) that this volume was 'very fine in old red morocco, perhaps £6.6.0 or more.' But Beckford replied that he already owned a copy.

POST, PIETER   3553

*Begraeffenisse van syne Hoogheyt Frederick Henrick, Prince van
   Orange.* Amsterdam, 1651. Folio.

Press-mark D.4.7 in MC; moved to the Round Tower.

SH SALE, viii.21, to Lilly, £1.18.0. [London, 1094]

☞ Engraved by Pieter Nolpe.

REGENFUSS, FRANZ MICHAEL   3554

Choix de coquillages, de limaçons, et de crustaces. Colored plates.
   Copenhagen, 1758. Folio.

'Calf, with red morocco back.' Not in MC.

SH SALE, viii.28, to H. G. Bohn, £3.5.0 [London, 1138]; Sotheby's, 22 June 1887 (Crawford Sale, Part 1), lot 1706, to B. F. Stevens, £2.15.0.

☞ On 26 October 1778 HW wrote to Thomas Walpole to thank him for 'a most magnificent and beautiful book,' but failed to name the book; on 26 June 1792 he wrote Thomas Walpole, Jr., that a Dane [i.e. Thorkelin in 1788] had asked for a set of SH editions in the name of his Prince and had offered in return 'their splendid book of shells (which, by the way, your father, dear Sir, gave me many years ago).'

This work was published at the expense of Frederic V, King of Denmark.

RYMSDYK, JAN and ANDREAS VAN   3555

Museum Britannicum. London, 1778. Folio.

Not in MC.

SH SALE, viii.22, to Captain Leckie [not found in London Sale]; Puttick, 14 January 1867 (Leckie Sale), lot 269, to Westell, 1/–.

3556 THOU, JACQUES AUGUSTE DE

Historia sui temporis. Edited by Thomas Carte and published by
Samuel Buckley with Dr. Mead's encouragement. London, 1733.
Seven volumes in fourteen, folio.

'Calf.' Press-mark L.8.1 in MC; moved to the Round Tower.
SH SALE, viii.19, to Tiffin, £40. [London, 1099]

☞ In MC, HW entered the set with this note: 'This magnificent
set of books belonged to Sr. Clement Cotterel Dormer, & is adorned
with a great variety of the finest & most scarce prints of the principal
personages. When Sr. Charles Cotterel sold his father's library by auction
in 1764 [lot 2590], Mr. Walpole bought this edition of Thuanus there,
& gave fifty guineas for it.' He also listed this set of Thuanus among his rare
books in his *Description of SH,* 1774. In the MC Kirgate added a note,
probably in 1797: 'now in the Round Library.'

Shelf L.8 in the Main Library seems to have been installed in 1764
to hold these fourteen volumes, plus Braun's two volumes, No. 3675
below.

The SH set of the French translation of 1734 was in Press Q of the
Library in the Offices, No. 3152 *above.*

3557 VULSON, MARC DE

*Les portraits des hommes illustres françois, qui sont peints dans
la Galerie du Palais du Cardinal de Richelieu.* Engraved by Zacharie
Heince and François Bignon. Paris, 1650. Folio.

Press-mark D.1.23 in MC; moved to the Round Tower.
SH SALE, viii.23, to Evans, 12/–. [London, 574]

☞ Although it does not appear in the SH records, HW bought a copy of
Vulson's *Vray théâtre d'honneur et de chevalerie,* Paris 1648, folio, at Dr.
Lort's sale, 5 May 1791, lot 4474.

3558 WILLYAMS, COOPER

The history of Sudeley Castle, in Gloucestershire. London, 1791.
Folio.

Not in MC.
SH SALE, viii.22, to Evans. [London, 912]

ZANETTI, ANTONIO MARIA   3559

*Delle antiche statue Greche e Romane che nell' antisala della Libreria
    di San Marco.* Venice, 1740. Folio.

'Half-bound, uncut.' Press-mark C.2.6 in MC; moved to the Round
Tower.

SH SALE, viii.26, to H. G. Bohn, £1.12.0 [London, 1009]; offered in
Bohn's Catalogue for 1847 (Prints), p. 218, for 18/–.

☞ Two more volumes were published later. Bohn's reduced price
may indicate that, after he purchased it, he discovered it to be incomplete.

ZUCCARO, TADDEO and FEDERIGO   3560

Illustri fatti Farnesiani coloriti nel Real Palazzo di Caprarola. En-
    graved by Giorgio Gasparo Prenner. Rome, 1748. Folio.

Not in MC.

SH SALE, viii.27, to Evans, £1.16.0. [London, 600]

☞ The letters to and from Mann contain numerous references to this
volume after HW asked for it, 8 May 1783, until he received it in the
summer of 1784. He asked for two copies and received them, one presumably to give away.

PRESS C

Press C contained portfolios of prints and of original drawings. Notable among these were HW's Bunbury collection, the Müntz and
Vertue drawings, and an extra-illustrated copy of the *Description of
SH*, as well as the large collections of original drawings by foreign
artists.

BOYDELL, JOHN   3561

*A collection of prints engraved after the most capital paintings in
    England.* London, 1769–72. Two volumes, folio.

'Morocco.' Not in MC.

SH SALE, viii.49, to Evans, £8. [London, 1204]

☞ Boydell continued to publish prints for many years, and this set is
usually counted complete in nine volumes; HW's two volumes contained
115 prints by the best engravers of the time.

The London sale catalogue describes this as a subscription copy; and HW
was perhaps even a projector, since Tyson wrote to Gough, 1 February

1772: 'Walpole was last year on a treaty with Boydell, who was to undertake the new Illustrious Heads under Walpole's direction, who was to point out the subjects, and Boydell was to find engravers.' (Quoted in Nichols, *Lit. Anecdotes*, viii.580.) Earlier, 20 December 1770, HW wrote to Cole: 'Boydell is going to recommence a suite of illustrious heads, and I am to give him a list of indubitable portraits of remarkable persons that have never been engraved.'

3562 BOYER, JEAN BAPTISTE, Marquis d'Aguilles

Recueil d'estampes, d'après les tableaux . . . qui composoient le cabinet de M. Boyer d'Aguilles. Paris [1744?] Folio.

Not in MC.

SH SALE, viii.44, to H. G. Bohn, £5.10.0 [London, 1186]; perhaps one of two copies offered in Bohn's Catalogue for 1847 (Prints), p. 79.

☞ Engraved by Coelmans, with descriptions by Mariette.

3563 BUNBURY, HENRY WILLIAM

Collection of 280 etchings, prints, and drawings. Two volumes, folio.

Original marbled boards with calf backs. BP² early state. (Later state in the second volume). Press-mark C.19. Not in MC.

SH SALE, viii.50, to H. G. Bohn, £7.7.0 [London, 733]; from an undergraduate at King's College, through Scribner's, May 1952, to WSL, $225.

☞ These two volumes were prepared by HW *ca.* 1776–82. Each has the special title-page printed by Kirgate: 'Etchings by Henry William Bunbury, Esq., and after his Designs.' (These titles were not recorded in the *Bibliography of SH.*) He wrote to Lady Ossory, 13 July 1776: 'I am obeying the Gospel, and putting my house in order, am ranging my prints and papers, am *composing* books, in the literal sense, and in the only sense I will compose books any more. I am pasting Henry Bunbury's prints in a volume.' The two volumes are listed as among the rare books in the Glass Closet, in his second *Description of SH*, 1784, but he continued to add later plates. An account of Bunbury's own collection of his drawings, printed in the *World* for 18 September 1789, adds: 'From these Mr. Horace Walpole had his facsimile copies.'

Notes or identifications by HW on a few prints. In the final volume of his *Anecdotes*, HW compared Bunbury favorably to Hogarth. The original drawing of Bunbury's 'Richmond Hill,' 1782, was sold at SH, xxi.23.

Two other volumes of satirical prints may be recorded here, inasmuch 3563
as neither one was listed in the SH SALE:

(1) *Satiric prints on politics*, 1770–84. Portfolio of 137 prints, 1770–84;
MS title by HW: 'Here follows a few of the best prints, selected from a
vast number, that were published on the Changes of Administration in
1782, 1783, & 1784, on the Coalition between Mr. Fox & Lord North, on
Mr. Fox's East India bill in 1783, and on the Westminster Election in
1784.' Special MS title by HW to the last few prints: 'Satiric prints on
Factions and Dress.' London Sale, lot 729, to H. G. Bohn, £4; in the
Tilden Collection, 1895; now in the Print Room of the New York
Public Library. The portfolio is now bound in buckram; no BP or press-
mark; most of the prints contain identifications or notes by HW.

(2) GILLRAY, JAMES. Portfolio of 120 political and other caricatures, many
in colors, by Gillray, Collet, Cruikshank, Dighton, Heath, Rowlandson,
Sayer, and others. London Sale, lot 730, to Strong, £4.8.0; offered in
Strong's Catalogue for 1843, lot 3364, for £4.14.6; Sotheby's, 13 July
1867 (George Smith Sale), lot 1641, to Harvey, £6. 'Identifications and
notes by HW.' The prints are counted as about 120 in the London Sale,
but Strong says 230 and the Smith Catalogue 215; apparently the cataloguer for the London Sale miscounted by 100.

Three caricatures in Gillray's manner, with identifications by HW,
were formerly in the Dyson Perrins collection, and sold by the Old Print
Shop to WSL in 1961; they may have been in this collection in 1842. Two
caricatures published by Darly, also with identifications by HW, are in the
Morgan Library, in the collection formed by T. Haviland Burke and
owned by Sir Robert Peel; also in the Peel-Morgan collection is a print of
Mrs. Siddons in the *Grecian Daughter*, from a drawing by H. Repton,
with HW's note 'done at Dublin.'

(3) A single political print, 'The Motion' February 1741, was doubtless
removed from one of HW's portfolios in the eighth day's sale, and sold
London, 518, to Strong; offered in Strong's Catalogue for 1843, lot 3372,
for 15/–. It had all the names filled out by HW. He wrote from Florence
to Conway, 25 March 1741: 'I have received a print by this post that
diverts me extremely, *the Motion*. Tell me, dear now, who made the
design, and who took the likenesses; they are admirable: the lines are as
good as one sees on such occasions. I wrote last post to Sir Robert, to wish
him joy.'

(4) A print of Elizabeth Chudleigh as Iphigenia at a masked ball in 1749
(*see* HW to Mann, 3 May 1749) in the Print Room of the British Museum
has a note wrongly ascribed to HW (*Catalogue of Prints and Drawings*,
No. 3032).

3564 CARTER, JOHN

Specimens of the ancient sculpture and painting now remaining in this Kingdom. London, 1780–7. Two volumes, folio.

'Red morocco, with HW's arms on the sides.' Not in MC.

SH SALE, viii.30, to H. G. Bohn for William Beckford, £9 [London, 1128]; Sotheby's, 6 July 1882 (Beckford Sale, Part 1), lot 1629, to Samuel, £8.10.0.

☞ Beckford inquired of Bohn about this on 13 June 1842 (letters now WSL); Bohn replied on 16 June: 'Carter is a fine copy of the original edition, in old red morocco binding—perhaps by Kalthoeber, or earlier; one of the sides somewhat bleached either by damp or the sun. Value £10.10.0 or £12.12.0. (I published a new edition of this work, and had the plates colored more expensively.)' To this Beckford replied on 18 June: 'Carter—only if reasonable, but as to a colored copy—God forbid.'

3565 CASTEELS, PETER

Twelve months of flowers. Designed by Casteels from the gardens of Robert Furber, Gardener at Kensington, and engraved by Henry Fletcher. London, 1730. Folio.

Press-mark D.1.11 in MC; moved to the Round Tower.

SH SALE, viii.52, to H. G. Bohn. [Not found in London Sale]

☞ In his 'Book of Materials,' *ca.* 1761, in a series of notes from Vertue concerning artists, HW wrote down 'Casteels painted flowers.' Perhaps he acquired his copy of this book soon afterwards. He devoted a short paragraph, chiefly from Vertue, to Casteels in the last volume of his *Anecdotes,* 1771.

3566 [COMBE, WILLIAM]

History of the River Thames. Colored aquatints engraved by Stadler from drawings by Farington, published by the Boydells. London, 1794–6. Two volumes, folio.

Not in MC.

SH SALE, viii.39, to H. G. Bohn, £3. [London, 946]

☞ Dedicated to HW; this was planned as part of a series, 'History of the principal rivers of Great Britain,' and copies usually contain that added title-page. The binding is said to be morocco in the catalogue of the London Sale, but 'elegantly bound in russia' in the SH catalogue. The first plate in the 2d volume is a view of SH.

DRAWINGS   3567

Portfolio of about 150 original drawings by various masters, ancient and modern. Folio.

Not in MC.

SH SALE, viii.38, to Graves, £53.11.0. [London, 1266]

☞ Since this collection is entered in his Appendix (1781) to the *Description of SH*, 1774, HW must have formed it between 1774 and 1781.

The artists named in the sale catalogue include: Asselijn, Backhuysen, Boucher, Chatelain, Cignani, Cooper, Dürer, Gillot, Hollar, Janet, Kent, La Fosse, La Guerre, Le Nain, Le Paon, Luti, Maratti, Marchetti, Nanni, Oliver, Poussin, Restout, Ricci, Richardson, Riley, Romano, Schellincks, Storck, Talman, Tillemans, Van der Meulen, Van Dyck, Varotari, Leonardo da Vinci, Vroom, Watteau, Wootton, Wyck, and Zuccaro.

This collection was broken up: Jonathan Richardson's 40 drawings were owned in 1902 by E. Parsons & Sons, and soon afterwards sold (by Colnaghi) to the British Museum; two of the nine by Watteau are in the Metropolitan Museum in New York. One group of twelve drawings by Leonardo da Vinci and others, almost certainly from this collection, was sold at Sotheby's, 21 January 1854 (Edward Martin Sale), lot 193, to Lilly, £1.2.0; offered in Lilly's Catalogue, [1868], for £12.12.0. Lilly described them as 'from the library of HW, who has written upon them, "From Richardson's Collection." '

Four other drawings (three of Pope and one of Milton) by Richardson, now at Windsor Castle, are probably from this or a similar portfolio. They were owned by C. S. Bale and sold at Christie's in 1881, when they were bought by the Queen's Librarian.

DRAWINGS   3568

Portfolio of 56 original drawings by various Italian masters. Folio.

Press-mark D.3.16 in MC; moved to the Round Tower.

SH SALE, viii.34, to Tiffin, £18.18.0. [London, 1264]

☞ Artists named in the sale catalogue are: Caliari, Caravaggio, Carracci, Castiglione, Cortese, Mantegna, Maratti, Mascherino, Mazzuoli, Romano, Rubens, Sarto, Vasari, Zampieri, and Zuccaro.

In his letter of 31 July 1743 OS, HW asked Mann to try to buy for him a few selected drawings by Florentine masters: 'I have begun to collect drawings.'

Two other portfolios of drawings may be mentioned here; neither is identifiable in the SH records:

(1) Formerly in the library of Lord Beauchamp, Madresfield Court, Great Malvern, was a portfolio containing 169 drawings by Tiepolo; it had HW's BP[1] but no press-mark. This portfolio was sold at Christie's, 15 June 1965.

(2) A portfolio containing HW's BP was sold at Sotheby's, 1 December 1964, lot 139: it contained on 22 leaves various studies of architectural designs, grotesques, &c., identified as Italian drawings of the 16th century. It was in an 18th-century binding, but it lacked HW's press-mark.

3569 DRAWINGS

Portfolio of 101 original drawings by various Italian masters, from the library of the King of Spain. Folio.

'Red morocco, with Spanish royal arms on the sides.' Press-mark D.1.24 in MC; moved to the Round Tower.

SH SALE, viii.35, to Robert Holford, Esq., £126. [London, 1265]

☞ Included with this in MC were two similar portfolios in similar bindings, as follows:

(1) Portfolio of 109 original drawings; SH SALE, viii.45, to Tiffin, £21. [London, 1262]

(2) Portfolio of 107 original drawings; SH SALE, viii.46, to Tiffin, £42. [London, 1263]

Artists named in the sale catalogue are: Fra Bartolommeo, Biscaino, Bril, Callot, Cambiaso, Caravaggio, Carracci, Castiglione, Cortona, Franco, Grimaldi, Guercino, Claude Lorrain, Mantegna, Maratti, Poussin, Rosa, Rubens, Sacchi, Tempesta, Van Dyck, Tiziano Vecelli, Leonardo da Vinci, and Zampieri.

The three volumes are recorded as among the rare books in the library in the *Description of SH*, 1774.

3570 FLORENCE. UFFIZI GALLERY

Portfolio of original drawings of antiquities, sculpture, and other works of art in the Gallery of the Grand Duke, executed in Florence in 1741–2. Folio.

Press-mark D.1.2 in MC; moved to the Round Tower.

SH SALE, viii.51, to H. G. Bohn, £2. [London, 1129]

☞ These were executed at HW's request by a 'little man' (Mann to HW, 3 June 1741); neither HW nor Mann liked the results: *see* HW to Mann, 14 August 1743, and Mann to HW, 17 September 1743. But HW listed this portfolio among the rare books in his library in the *Description of SH*, 1774.

Possibly this is the portfolio that is offered in Bohn's Catalogue for 1847 (Prints), p. 112, for £10.10.0: 'A series of 77 drawings, finely executed in Indian ink, elegantly half bound, red morocco.' But no SH provenance is indicated. Instead, Bohn lists as HW's a copy in original vellum of *Disegni originali d'eccelenti pittori esistenti nella Galleria di Firenze*, tinted imitations of drawings published by Scacciati and Mulinari at Florence in 1766; this volume is now in the Ashmolean Museum, Oxford: it has an inserted BP, but no other evidence of SH provenance.

In a letter to Mann, 30 September 1784, HW wrote that Sir William Hamilton had given him a copy of Lanzi's *La reale Galleria di Firenze*, Florence 1782, 12mo. This was perhaps sold in some miscellaneous group such as No. 288 in 1842, without being specified by name. In his letter he also asked Mann to send him if it should be published the 'ampler account' that Lanzi said was in preparation. Presumably the work in question was the *Description de la Galerie Royale* by Francesco Zacchiroli, 1783; but perhaps Mann never sent this.

HAMILTON, GAVIN   3571

Schola Italica picturae. Rome, 1773. Folio.

Not in MC.
SH SALE, viii.47, to P. and Dom. Colnaghi, £2.15.0. [London, 1208]

HOUGHTON GALLERY   3572

A set of prints engraved after the most capital paintings in the collection of . . . the Empress of Russia, lately in the possession of the Earl of Orford at Houghton in Norfolk. With plans, and descriptions of the paintings from *Aedes Walpolianae.* London, Boydell, 1788. Two volumes, folio.

'Russia.' Not in MC.
SH SALE, viii.48, to James Baker, Esq., £47.5.0. [London, 1125]

☞ As early as 1 September 1773, HW wrote to Lady Ossory: '. . . painters are making drawings from the whole collection [at Houghton] which Boydell is going to engrave.' To Cole, 14 December 1775, he wrote: 'Boydell brought me this morning another number of the prints from the pictures at Houghton. . . . Alas, it will be twenty years before the set is completed.' The prints were published serially beginning in 1774.

3573 KIP, JOHN

*Britannia illustrata, or views of royal palaces and seats of the nobility
and gentry.* London, n.d. Folio.

'Half-bound.' Press-mark C.3.26 in MC; moved to the Round Tower.
SH SALE, viii.43 to H. G. Bohn for William Beckford, £2.7.6 [London,
948]; Sotheby's, 16 December 1882 (Beckford Sale, Part 2), lot 1349, to
Robson & Kerslake, £7.7.0.

☞ Engraved from designs by Leonard Knyff. In the Avery Library at
Columbia a copy of the edition of 1727 is marked Walpole's copy; but it is
the wrong edition and the MS notes in an 18th-century hand are not by HW.
The SH copy had 77 plates. In his *Essay on Modern Gardening*, HW comments on the uniformity of the landscaped approaches to English country
seats, as portrayed by Kip.

Beckford inquired about this volume in a letter to Bohn, 13 June 1842
(letters now WSL); Bohn replied, 16 June, with an estimate of eight or ten
guineas for the lot: 'Some of the scarcer ones and fine; they are apparently
earlier impressions than what occur in the complete sets, and they have
not been folded.' Beckford then authorized Bohn to bid as high as £14
or £15 or £16 'if we cannot help it. Size is no longer objectionable, as I
am concocting a new gallery with very deep shelves.' This last explanation
was a response to Bohn's warning that it was a large folio.

3574 LOUIS XIV, King of France

Two prints after paintings by Le Brun, 1731. Two sheets.

Not in MC.

Not in SH SALE. London, 1093, to Strong, 5/–; offered in Strong's Catalogue for 1843, lot 3370, for 12/–.

☞ The subjects were (1) 'Entrevuë de Louis XIV et de Philippe IV en
1660' and (2) 'Mariage de Louis XIV avec Marie Thérèse en 1660.' Possibly these plates were included in one of HW's portfolios in the eighth day's
sale.

3575 MÜNTZ, JOHN HENRY

Portfolio of views in and around Twickenham, and other drawings,
by Müntz, Scott, Edwards, Leave, and Rysbrack, 33 in all. Folio.

Press-mark C.1.22 in MC; moved to the Round Tower.
SH SALE, viii.31 to William Knight, Esq., £1.14.0. [London, 1259]

☞ This portfolio is recorded by HW in his *Description of SH*, 1774, as
among the rare books of prints and drawings in the Library. It was broken

up at some time after 1842: a considerable number of drawings from it were sold at Sotheby's, 30 July 1919 (Col. Fellows Sale), and have since been acquired by WSL. On many of the drawings are notes by HW.

OVERBEKE, BONAVENTURA VAN   3576
Stampe degli avanzi dell'antica Roma. London, 1739. Folio.
   Press-mark C.2.7 in MC; moved to the Round Tower.
   SH SALE, viii.40, to Captain Leckie, 12/– [London, 979]; Puttick, 14 January 1867 (Leckie Sale), lot 267, to Bezzi, 8/6.
   ☞ The text to accompany these plates, in octavo, was in B.4, No. 306 *above.*
   In his Catalogue for 1847 (Prints), p. 158, for £2.8.0, H. G. Bohn offered the SH copy of Overbeke's *Reliquiae antiquae urbis Romae*, Amsterdam 1708, 'old gilt calf,' in three volumes, imperial folio. This work does not appear in the SH records at all, and it seems too large to be concealed in any miscellaneous lot; perhaps Bohn's cataloguing was in error.

PALLADIO, ANDREA   3577
Fabbriche antiche. Published by Lord Burlington. London, 1730. Folio.
   'Half-russia, with HW's BP.' Press-mark D.3.19 in MC; moved to the Round Tower.
   SH SALE, viii.41, to H. G. Bohn for William Beckford, £2.10.0 [London, 947]; Sotheby's, 29 November 1883 (Beckford Sale, Part 4), lot 810, to Quaritch, 15/–; Sotheby's, 12 May 1902 (Ford Sale), lot 227, to Thorp, £3.
   ☞ Included in this volume were some plates of Lord Burlington's Villa at Chiswick, so that the sale catalogue called it 'Views of Lord Burlington's Villa.' A note by HW recorded that this volume had been given to him by Lord Burlington.
   Beckford inquired about this volume in his letter to Bohn, 13 June 1842 (letters now WSL); Bohn replied, 16 June: 'Burlington's Villa has three additional plates, one scarce but patched; a quotation by Walpole from his *R&NA*; perhaps £3.3.0. It is merely half bound.' Beckford then authorized Bohn to go as high as £6 'if necessary.'

PARIS   3578
Le plan en perspective de la Ville de Paris. Designed by Louis Bretez and engraved by Claude Lucas. 20 plates. [Paris, 1739] Folio.
   'Morocco.' Not in MC.

SH SALE, viii.42, to H. G. Bohn, £1 [London, 969]; perhaps the copy offered, but not identified as HW's, in Bohn's Catalogue for 1847 (Prints), p. 68, for £1.11.6.

3579 REYNST, GERARD

Variarum imaginum a celeberrimis artificibus pictarum caelaturae elegantissimis tabulis representae. Amsterdam, n.d. Folio.

Rebound in calf. BP[2] early state. Press-mark C.2 in MC. (Entered by HW in MC, where it stood for shelf C.2 in the Main Library.) Bookplate of Lord Derby.

SH SALE, viii.36, to Boone for Lord Derby, £7.10.0 [London, 1185]; Christie's, 20 October 1953 (Knowsley Hall Sale), lot 256, bought by the Surveyor of the Queen's Pictures, St. James's Palace, £30.

☞ Engraved by Cornelis Visscher. The volume is sometimes called 'Cabinet du Bourgmestre Reynst.' Reynst was mentioned by HW in his *Anecdotes*, when he recorded that some of the royal pictures sold 1645–53 went into Reynst's cabinet and were later restored to Charles II. He also mentioned the same fact in a MS note in the Preface to Vertue's *Catalogue of Charles I's pictures*, in the copy he presented to the King in 1760. But he learned this from Vertue's notes, now published by the Walpole Society; the entry in MC indicates that HW acquired his own copy of Reynst after 1763.

Bohn wrote on 17 June 1842 to William Beckford (letters now WSL) that the Reynst Gallery was a fine copy, worth perhaps eight or ten guineas. But Beckford replied that he already had a copy.

3580 VAN HULLE, ANSELM

Portraicts des hommes illustres . . . qui ont negocié les célèbres traités de Munster et Osnabrug. Amsterdam, 1706. Folio.

Press-mark B.1.17 in MC; moved to the Round Tower.
SH SALE, viii.37, to Adamson, £2.12.6. [London, 576]
☞ A collection of 84 portraits.

3581 VERTUE, GEORGE

Portfolio of original drawings of Heads, Antiquities, Monuments, Views, &c., by Vertue and others, 120 in all. Folio.

Some of these, about fifty, are now mounted and rebound in red morocco, with HW's MS title-page preserved. BP[1]. Press-mark D.3.13 in MC; moved to the Round Tower. Bookplate of William Frederick, 9th Earl Waldegrave.

SH SALE, viii.32, to Smith, £31.10.0 [London, 1268]; Lord Waldegrave, July 1948, to WSL, in a collection.

☞ This large portfolio was made up by HW from various lots he acquired at Vertue's sale, 16 March 1757; and one or two drawings were added later. This portfolio was recorded by HW in his *Description of SH*, 1774, as among the rare books of prints and drawings in the Library. In his *Catalogue of Engravers* he mentioned particularly that he had purchased Vertue's Holbein drawings in 1757 at Vertue's sale.

Probably from this portfolio were taken eight portrait-drawings sold at Christie's, 20 October 1953 (Knowsley Hall Sale), lot 306, to Maggs for WSL, £80.

WALPOLE, HORACE   3582

Description of the Villa. Inlaid to folio, illustrated with 32 original drawings, 100 engraved portraits, and other prints. Strawberry Hill, 1784. Folio.

    Russia, rebacked, with arms of HW on the sides. Not in MC.

    SH SALE, viii.33, to William Knight, £22.11.6 [London, 1123]; Sotheby's, 30 July 1919 (Col. Fellows Sale), lot 159, to Sabin, £1,650; Sabin, August 1927, to WSL, £600.

☞ Included are drawings by Barrow, Carter, Edwards, and Müntz. One rare print, of Henry VIII and his family by William Rogers, was removed and sold separately in the London Sale, lot 18, to the British Museum, £22.1.0, and is now in the Dept. of Prints and Drawings. The engraving of HW's nieces after Reynolds was removed by Sabin and in 1939 sold for £100 to WSL. Some drawings which were loose have been framed by WSL. The volume is HW's chief collection of memorabilia about SH; it was made up about 1792, and many of the notes are in Kirgate's hand. At least one error that had remained undetected from the edition of 1774, 'Pope Benedict 13th' instead of 14th, was corrected by HW in this copy (p. 24). Carter's *Drawings and sketches of . . . Strawberry Hill*, 1788, containing more than one hundred original drawings, is in the Huntington Library; it is recorded in the *Bibliography of SH*, pp. 129, 262.

To illustrate this volume, HW cut up a volume listed among the rare books of prints and drawings in his *Description of SH*: it was listed in MC as 'Prints from Pictures, Antiquities, and Curiosities in the Collection of Horace Walpole,' D.1.10. Opposite this entry Kirgate noted: 'Cut up for the Illustration of Strawberry.'

William Beckford wrote to Bohn that books like this were too heavy for him.

3583 Zocchi, Giuseppe

Scelta di XXIV vedute delle principali contrade, piazze, chiese e palazzi della Citta di Firenze. Florence, [1744]. Folio.

Old calf, rebacked, with HW's BP. Press-mark C.1.21 in MC; moved to the Round Tower.

SH SALE, viii.52 to H. G. Bohn, £2.10.0 [London, 970]; Sotheby's, 29 November 1883 (Beckford Sale, Part 4), lot 652, to Bain, £3.3.0; now in the library of the Earl of Rosebery, Barnbougle Castle.

☞ The work was sponsored by Zocchi's patron, Gerini. Mann sent specimens to HW in 1743, together with Gerini's request to have one or more London booksellers subscribe for extra copies: *see* Mann's letter to HW, 12 March 1743.

Press D

Press D contained collections of historical and archaeological prints, and some portfolios of drawings. To HW the show pieces in Press D must have been the Bentley drawings, the portfolio of etchings by his friends, and eight volumes of the Cabinet du Roi; but the Bentley drawings belonged in Press C.

3584 Allegrini, Francesco

Chronologica series simulacrorum Regiae Familiae Mediceae centum expressa toreumis. Florence, 1761. Folio.

Press-mark B.1.4 in MC; moved to the Round Tower.

SH SALE, viii.61, to J. T. Simes, Esq., £4. [London, 580]

☞ Mann sent these engravings to HW in September 1761; as late as 28 December 1781 HW wrote to Mann of having looked up a print of Camilla Martelli in the volume.

William Beckford inquired of Bohn, 13 June and 17 June 1842, concerning the volume of 'Portraits and genealogical tree of the House of Medici,' but he seems to have had no report on it from Bohn. (Letters now WSL)

3585 Bentley, Richard, the Younger

Drawings and designs. Drawings for SH, and other designs, 75 in all, in a portfolio. Folio.

Mottled calf, gilt. BP² later state, possibly inserted in 1790. Press-mark D.3.14; moved to the Round Tower and altered in the book to C.1.

SH SALE, viii.57, to William Knight, Esq., £4.2.0 [London, 1255—the lot number still preserved on spine]; Spencer, May 1926, to WSL, £210.

☞ A special title-page was printed at SH, *ca.* 1760. This portfolio was recorded by HW in his *Description of SH*, 1774, as among the rare books of prints and drawings in the library: 'bound in marble and gilt,' the word 'marble' being used for what is now more commonly called 'mottled calf.' Though now broken and badly worn, the volume with its gilt design must have been handsome in 1760.

The drawings elucidate numerous points in the growth of SH, including the first plans for the Main Library. They contain various notes by HW and by Bentley. Besides the designs for SH, there are plans for other buildings, views of Jersey, sketches for Gray's poems, etc.

CHOISEUL-GOUFFIER, MARIE GABRIEL AUGUSTE FLORENS, 3586 Comte de

Voyage pittoresque de la Grèce. Paris, 1782. Folio.

'Morocco.' Not in MC.

SH SALE, viii.55, to Lilly, £1.1.0. [London, 966]

☞ The work was published in parts and various letters make reference to it: Mme. du Deffand to HW, 28 April and 4 May 1780; HW to Thomas Walpole, 8 October 1780; HW to Thomas Walpole, Jr., 6 September 1782 and 25 October 1786. Two more volumes appeared after HW died, in 1809 and 1822.

DRAWINGS 3587

Portfolio of original drawings by Dutch masters, on sixty leaves. Folio.

Press-mark D.3.15 in MC; moved to the Round Tower.

SH SALE, viii.63, to Graves, £10.10.0. [London, 1261]

☞ Artists named in the catalogue are: Eccardt, Ehret, Genoels, Glauber, van Huysum, Rademaker, and Rembrandt (13 pen sketches).

ETCHINGS BY AMATEURS 3588

A Collection of Prints engraved by various persons of quality. 142 prints in a portfolio. Folio.

Red morocco, gilt, with HW's arms on the sides. Not in MC. Bookplate of John Waldie, Hendersyde.

SH SALE, viii.56, to Pickering, £16.10.0 [London, 1126]; offered in Strong's Catalogue for 1843, lot 1867, and sold at Sotheby's in 1851; Sotheby's, 28 October 1942 (Miscellaneous Sale), to Maggs for WSL, £92.

☞ Some sixty separate prints included with this lot in 1842 were mounted and bound before 1851 into a matching portfolio (half red morocco) and are now with the collection.

The first volume was organized by HW in 1775, when he wrote to Mason, 7 May 1775: 'I have just made a *new book*. . . . It is a volume of etchings by *noble authors*. They are bound in robes of crimson and gold; the titles are printed at my own press, and the pasting is *by my own hand*.' The volume is listed in HW's Appendix (1781) to his *Description of SH, 1774*.

Numerous notes by HW, and presentation notes from several people. Four special title-pages were printed at SH (this is a correction to the *Bibliography of SH*): *A Collection of Prints engraved by various persons of quality; Etchings by Isabella Byron, daughter of William Lord Byron, and second wife of Henry Howard, fourth Earl of Carlisle; Etchings by Lady Louisa Augusta Greville, eldest daughter of Francis Earl of Brooke and Warwick; Etchings by George Simon Harcourt Viscount Nuneham, eldest son of Simon Earl of Harcourt*. Also included in the two volumes are drawings or engravings by C. W. Bampfylde, Lady Beaumont, Miss C. S. Blake, the Earl of Buchan, the Countess of Burlington, Hon. Richard Byron, Emma Crewe, Lady Cunynghame, the Countess of Drogheda, Lord Grantham, Eliza Gulston, E. Haistwell, Sir William Hamilton, Mary Hartley, Georgiana Keate, Ellis Cornelia Knight, Lady Elizabeth Montagu, the Duchess of Newcastle, Viscountess Polwarth, Sir Thomas Reeve (*see* HW to Montagu, 3 October 1763), Catherine St. Aubyn, the Earl of Sunderland, J. Tobin, Caroline Yorke (engravings from drawings by her mother, Mrs. Agneta Yorke), and others; and engravings after Lavinia Countess Spencer and Lady Diana Beauclerk. Many of these amateurs are mentioned by HW in his 'Books of Materials,' gathered in Chapter VIII of the Hilles-Daghlian fifth volume of *Anecdotes of Painting*, 1937.

3589 GIRARDON, FRANÇOIS

Cabinet. Engravings of statues in his collection and of Richelieu's tomb. Paris, n.d. Folio.

Not in MC.

SH SALE, viii.62, to William Beckford, £2.15.0 [London, 1127]; a copy not identified as HW's was sold at Sotheby's, 11 December 1882 (Beckford Sale, Part 2), lot 200, to Quaritch, £3.

☞ Beckford wrote to William Smith, the dealer (letters now WSL), on 13 April: '[Girardon] I *must* have. The imp[ressions] are good particularly the port[rait]; it is scarce. *Miss it not*.' No doubt Smith purchased this in June for Beckford, since he replied on 14 April: 'I will take care not to

neglect . . . the Cabinet de Girardon.' Beckford mentioned it to Smith again on 18 April; and on 13 June he wrote to Bohn: 'Girardon I have long since desired Smith to buy for me, so don't contest that lot.'

HERCULANEUM   3590

Catalogo degli antichi monumenti, 1754, by O. A. Bayardi; and *Le antichita di Ercolano esposte*. Edited by O. A. Bayardi. Naples, 1757–92. Nine volumes, folio.

Press-marks D.1.20 and 21 (Volume I of *Antichita*) in MC; moved to the Round Tower. In MC, HW noted that these volumes were very scarce.

    SH SALE, viii.60, to H. G. Bohn, £6.12.6. [London, 999]

    ☞ On 3 September 1757 HW wrote to Mann: 'There is a book . . . which I wish I could by your means procure. It is the account, with plates, of what has been found at Herculaneum. You may promise the King of Naples in return all my editions.' (On 25 December 1758, he offered the SH and Baskerville editions in exchange.) He wrote of it again to Mann, 10 May 1759: '[I have] just seen the Neapolitan book of Herculaneum. . . . Though it is far from being finely engraved, yet there are bits in it, that make me wish much to have it, and if you could procure it for me, I own I should be pleased.' Finally, 3 February 1760, he wrote: 'Herculaneum is arrived; Caserta is arrived: what magnificence you send me! . . . You must take care to send me the subsequent volumes of Herculaneum as they appear, if ever they do appear.' Other letters to and from Mann record the difficulties of procuring this and subsequent volumes. For the engravings of Caserta, *see* Vanvitelli, No. 3596 *below*.

    The later volumes of this set were prepared not by Bayardi but by Pasquale Carcani.

LOUIS XIV, King of France   3591

Cabinet du Roi. Engravings (*ca.* 1664–1685) of pictures and buildings associated with or commemorative of Louis XIV. [Paris, 1664, &c.] Eight volumes, folio.

Old red morocco, gilt, with arms of France on the sides. The bindings have been attributed both to Ruette and to Padeloup, the royal binders. Entered separately in MC, as listed below. Three volumes are now at Farmington.

    SH SALE, viii.65–72, to Bohn, Lilly, and Strong, as listed below. [London, 1189–96]

3591   ☞ Eight volumes, as follows:

(1) [Plans and views of royal palaces, by Le Clerc and others] BP¹. Press-mark C.2.19 in MC, altered to D.9 in book. Lot 65, to H. G. Bohn, £5.10.0. Probably the copy sold at Sotheby's, 2 May 1884 (Hamilton Sale), lot 424, to Quaritch, £14; now at Waddesdon Manor.

(2) [Plans and views of the gardens, fountains, and grotto at Versailles, by Le Pautre and Silvestre] BP¹. Press-mark C.2.21; moved to the Round Tower. Lot 66, to H. G. Bohn, £3.10.0; Sotheby's, 9 May 1884 (Hamilton Sale), lot 2042, to Bain, £17.5.0; now in the collection of the Earl of Rosebery, Barnbougle Castle.

(3) [Battles and sieges of Louis XIV, after paintings by Van der Meulen] BP¹. Press-mark C.2.17, altered to D.10 in book. Lot 67, to Strong, £4.10.0; Sotheby's, 22 January 1873 (Miscellaneous Sale), lot 19, to Moffatt, £4.18.0; Hodgson's, 11 July 1946 (Goodrich Court Library), lot 192, to Eisemann, £195; Maggs, May 1951, to WSL, £225.

(4) [Engravings of paintings, and of statues and busts, in the royal collection] BP¹. Press-mark C.2.18, altered to D.11 in book. Bookplate of the Duke of Hamilton. Lot 68, to H. G. Bohn, £7.7.0; Sotheby's, 2 May 1884 (Hamilton Sale), lot 425, to Quaritch, £20; in the George Lothrop Bradley Collection at the Library of Congress; Library of Congress, February 1952, to Yale for the Lewis Walpole Collection, by exchange.

(5) [Engravings of the ceilings at Versailles, &c., after Le Brun] BP¹. Press-mark D.1.8 in MC; moved to the Round Tower. Lot 69, to H. G. Bohn, £2.2.0. Probably the copy sold at Sotheby's, 6 May 1884 (Hamilton Sale), lot 1165, to Quaritch, £10.15.0; given to the library of the University of California (Berkeley) in 1899 by Mrs. Phoebe Apperson Hearst. The original press-mark, D.1.8, has been marked over to make it D.6 in the Round Tower.

(6) [Engravings of the Battles of Alexander, in five plates, after Le Brun] 'With HW's BP.' Press-mark D.1.4 in MC; moved to the Round Tower. Lot 70, to H. G. Bohn, £6.6.0; Sotheby's, 2 May 1884 (Hamilton Sale), lot 422, to Quaritch, £5; Sotheby's, 15 March 1894 (Garrett Sale), lot 579, to Hiscock £1.14.0.

(7) [Engravings from tapestries illustrating the conquests of Louis XIV, by Le Clerc and others after Le Brun] BP¹. Press-mark C.2.22, altered to D.12 in book; moved to the Round Tower. Lot 71, to H. G. Bohn, £2.18.0. Probably the copy sold at Sotheby's, 2 May 1884 (Hamilton Sale), lot 423, to Quaritch, £5; later owned by Laurence Currie, with his bookplate; Christie's, 8 December 1958 (Capt. Bertram Currie Sale), lot 73, to Maggs for WSL, £145.

(8) [Engravings of Tilts and Tournaments during the reign of Louis XIV]
Press-mark C.2.16 in MC; moved to the Round Tower. Lot 72, to
Lilly, £1.10.0.

The SH SALE catalogue asserts that these were a present from Louis XVI.
But this is surely an error, perhaps suggested by the bindings. For one
thing, HW owned these eight volumes in 1763, when the MC was drawn up.
Years later HW wrote to Thomas Walpole, Jr., 26 June 1792: 'In 1766 the
royal librarians desired to have my editions for the Bibliothèque du Roi.
. . . I did imagine they might have given me a set of the Louvre prints of
Louis Quatorze's victories, palaces, &c., a common present for contributions
to their library.'

Several of these volumes seem to have been combined by Bohn with other
volumes, to offer a set of fifteen volumes, red morocco bound at various
times, mostly with royal arms on sides, 'from HW's library,' in his Catalogue
for 1847 (Prints), p. 79, for £63. This set or most of it was then purchased
by the Duke of Hamilton.

MARIETTE, PIERRE JEAN   3592
*Description des travaux qui ont précédé, accompagné, et suivi la fonte
en bronze d'un seul jet de la statue équestre de Louis XV. Dressée
sur les Mémoires de M. Lempereur. Plates. Paris, 1768. Folio.*
Not in MC.
SH SALE, viii.59, to Lilly, 6/–. [London, 1152]

☞ Perhaps HW also owned the volume of plates depicting the coronation of Louis XV, *Le Sacre de Louis XV*, edited by Antoine Danchet [1722],
in folio; Mme. du Deffand twice offered to send it to him if he wished it,
and then wrote that since he had not replied she would send it when she
had an opportunity.

PALLADIO, ANDREA   3593
*The architecture of Andrea Palladio. . . . Revis'd by Giacomo Leoni.
With notes and remarks by Inigo Jones. London, 1742. Two vol-
umes, folio.*
Press-mark C.3.1 in MC; moved to the Round Tower.
SH SALE, viii.58, to H. G. Bohn, £1.9.0. [London, 957]

PATCH, THOMAS   3594
A series of 26 engravings after Masaccio, with his life, dedicated to Sir
Horace Mann; also caricatures and 3 plates of Ghiberti's bronze
doors. [Florence, 1770] Folio.
Not in MC.

SH SALE, viii.64, to Smith, £3.15.0. [London, 581]

☞ Other works by Patch were sold in Press Y of the Library in the Offices. When he thanked Mann for this book, 20 January 1771, HW wrote with the greatest enthusiasm.

William Beckford asked Bohn about this volume on 15 and 17 June; but Bohn seems not to have commented on it or to have bought it. (Letters now WSL)

3595 RUBENS, PETER PAUL

La gallerie du Palais du Luxembourg peinte par Rubens. Engraved
by various artists. Paris, 1710. Folio.

Press-mark D.1.9 in MC; moved to the Round Tower.

SH SALE, viii.54, to Strong, £3.18.0 [London, 1188]; offered in Strong's
Catalogue for 1843, lot 583, for £7.17.6.

☞ Strong catalogued it as 'newly bound in russia.'

3596 VANVITELLI, LUIGI

Dichiarazione dei disegni del Reale Palazzo di Caserta. Naples, 1756.
Folio.

Press-mark D.1.5 in MC; moved to the Round Tower.

SH SALE, viii.53, to H. G. Bohn, £1.10.0. [London, 956]

☞ The palace was built for Don Carlos, King of the Two Sicilies, later Charles III of Spain. In a letter to Mann, 3 February 1760, HW exclaimed: 'Herculaneum is arrived; Caserta is arrived. . . . Mr. Chute and I admire Caserta, and he is at least no villainous judge of architecture.' Mann replied, 8 March 1760: 'I am glad . . . that Herculaneum and Caserta were arrived, and that you like them. . . . I will do all in my power to send you the subsequent volumes as they appear. . . .'

A copy of Vanvitelli's *Caserta* is at Farmington, in original Italian calf, with BP[2] early state. This can hardly be the copy originally shelved in D.1. But in 1766 HW asked Mann to try to secure the new Herculaneum volumes, with no mention of Caserta. Mann replied, 8 August 1767, to report 'my complete success . . . in the acquisition of the volumes of Caserta and Herculaneum that are published, and a surety of having the others as they come out. These you will receive from the king, being in the royal list, and they will be sent to me for you. . . . I send you a bill of lading for a case containing all those that are extant. But I must beg that you will not mention the means by which you have obtained them. It would . . . create a jealousy in Mr. Hamilton.' Mann again mentioned the bill of lading for the case containing the volumes of Herculaneum and

Caserta on 9 October and sent a duplicate bill on 17 October 1767; HW acknowledged receipt of this second bill on 29 October. It therefore seems certain that Mann (through oversight) sent a second copy of Vanvitelli in 1767; unless the BP is a later insertion, this may be the volume now at Farmington, perhaps given away by HW before 1797.

PRESS E

Press E was almost entirely filled with a collection of portfolios of prints after paintings by various artists. They were moved in 1790 from Press C in the Main Library; all were uniformly bound in vellum. Many of these portfolios were perhaps broken up by the print dealers soon after the sale.

ADAM, ROBERT and JAMES   3597
Works in Architecture. London, 1773. Two volumes, folio.

> Not in MC.
> SH SALE, viii.73, to Adamson and Lilly, 15/–. [London, 921 and 922]
> ☞ Each part was published with its own preface and list of plates. The SH catalogue reads 'Adams' Architecture of Sion House, 2 vols.'
> From the London Sale, in which lot 921 is described as Luton House, and lot 922 as Sion House, Caen Wood, &c., it would appear that HW owned the first few parts only: Part 1 was Sion House; Part 2 Kenwood or Caen Wood; Part 3 Luton House. He wrote to Mason, 29 July 1773: 'Mr. Adam has published the first number of his *Architecture*. In it is a magnificent gateway and screen . . . at Sion. . . . From Kent's mahogany we are dwindled to Adam's filigree. Grandeur and simplicity are not yet in fashion. . . .'

BARTOLI, PIETRO SANTI   3598
Portfolio of 620 engravings from the works of Bartoli, views in Rome, antiquities, lamps, &c. Two volumes, folio.

> Vellum. BP¹. Press-marks C.2.4, 5; altered in books to E.21, 22.
> SH SALE, viii.89, to H. G. Bohn, £3.10.0 [London, 1002]; offered in Bohn's Catalogue for 1847 (Prints), p. 70, for £7.7.0; Sotheby's, 15 February 1856 (Miscellaneous Sale), lot 21, to Lilly, £2.19.0; Blackwell, July 1931, to WSL, £9.
> ☞ Mounted copies of various works edited by Bellori, with plates by Bartoli: *Veteres Arcus Augustorum triumphis insignes* (1690), *Columna*

Cochlis M. Aurelio Antonino Augusto dicata (1704), *Colonna Traiana*
(1673), *Admiranda Romanarum antiquitatum . . . vestigia* (1693), *Pitture
antiche del sepolcro de' Nasonii* (1702) of which another copy was in
Press P in the Round Tower, *Notae in numismata . . . Apibus insignita*
(1658), and *Antiche Lucerne sepolcrali* (1704); also Menestrier's
Symbolica Dianae Ephesiae statua (1688), and Bartoli's plates for Virgil
(1677) and his *Antichi Sepolcri* (1704).

3599 CARRACCI, ANNIBALE

Portfolio of 245 engravings after the works of the Carracci family, by
various artists. Two volumes, folio.

> Old vellum. Press-mark C.1.15 in MC; moved to the Round Tower.
> SH SALE, viii.77, to H. G. Bohn, £7.17.6 [London, 1221]; offered in
> Bohn's Catalogue for 1847 (Prints), p. 82, for £12.12.0; Sotheby's, 15 February 1856 (Miscellaneous Sale), lot 33, to Quaritch, £11.

3600 DE VOS, MARTEN

Portfolio of 641 engravings after De Vos, by Jan Galle, Crispin de
Passe, Jan Sadeler, and the brothers Wierix. Three volumes, folio.

> 'Vellum.' Press-mark C.1.12 in MC; moved to the Round Tower.
> SH SALE, viii.88, to Adamson, £15. [London, 1218]

☞ These portfolios were certainly broken up, since J. H. Anderdon
noted in his copy of the catalogue (now WSL): 'These were not by any
means fine or in good condition, but I had the opportunity of selecting
several'; and also in reference to this lot: 'The works of the Passes
were soon in the print shops where I purchased several fine ones, and my
brother also added to his collection. In 1868 I gave the chief of mine to
the Print Room of the British Museum.'

3601 DÜRER, ALBRECHT

Portfolio of 296 engravings by and after Dürer. Folio.

> 'Vellum.' Press-mark C.1.5 in MC; moved to the Round Tower.
> SH SALE, viii.80, to Adamson, £21. [London, 1223]

☞ The London Sale specifies 'engravings and some few of his wood
cuts.' The only other engravers named are Raimondi and Wierix.

FREY, JOHANN JACOB, Engraver   3602
Portfolio of engravings after Sebastian Conca, Guido, Zampieri, and
  others. [Rome, *ca.* 1725] Folio.
  Press-mark D.1.1 in MC; moved to the Round Tower.
  SH SALE, viii.73, to Colnaghi, £1.10.0. [London, 1210]

LE PAUTRE, JEAN   3603
Portfolio of 195 engravings, designs in architecture, cabinets, vases,
  and arabesques. Folio.
  'Vellum.' Press-mark C.2.3 in MC; moved to the Round Tower.
  SH SALE, viii.83, to H. G. Bohn, £3.7.6. [London, 1213]

PERELLE, GABRIEL   3604
Portfolio of 225 engravings, of views, landscapes, historical subjects,
  palaces, gardens, &c. Folio.
  'Vellum, with HW's BP.' Press-mark C.2.1 in MC; moved to the Round
Tower.
  SH SALE, viii.82, to H. G. Bohn, £2.6.0 [London, 1212]; offered in
Bohn's Catalogue for 1847 (Prints), p. 163, for £3.13.6; offered by Soth-
eran, 1883–5, for £4.10.0.
  ☞ A somewhat similar volume, 'Views of famous cities, castles, towers,
monasteries, passes, palaces, waterfalls, &c. in all parts of Europe,' by
Bodenehr, 288 plates, Augsburg 1704, &c., in old calf, was offered in Bohn's
Catalogue for 1847 (Prints), p. 206, for £2.10.0; Bohn described it as
'from the library of Perceval, Earl of Egmont, and since from HW's.' This
does not seem to be identifiable in the SH catalogues.

PRINTS   3605
Portfolio of 110 engravings, by Crispin de Passe, and by Sadeler after
  Bloemaert and Marten de Vos. Folio.
  Not in MC.
  Not in SH SALE. London Sale, lot 1164, to Adamson, £4.

PRINTS   3606
Portfolio of 123 engravings, after various artists. Folio.
  'Vellum.' Press-mark C.1.19 in MC; moved to the Round Tower.
  SH SALE, viii.86, to Lilly, £4.4.0 [London, 1216]; offered by Lilly
(Library of Robert Glendening), *ca.* 1865, for £3.13.6.

☞ Artists named are Bloemaert, Goltzius, and Spranger. The Lilly Catalogue names as other engravers Collaert, J. Müller, Maetham, Sadeler, and Saneredam.

3607 PRINTS

Portfolio of 214 engravings by various artists. Folio.

'Vellum.' Press-mark C.1.4 in MC; moved to the Round Tower.

SH SALE, viii.81. [Separated in the London Sale into lots 1224–46, and sold to various dealers for about £86]

☞ These engravings were by or after Israel van Mecheln, Mantegna, and Schongauer.

3608 PRINTS

Portfolio of 519 engravings by Dutch and German artists. Folio.

'Vellum.' Press-mark C.1.6 in MC; moved to the Round Tower.

SH SALE, viii.79, to Evans, £7.15.0. [London, 1222]

☞ The London Sale specifies the following artists: Lucas van Leyden (160), Aldegrever (169), Pencz (74), and Beham (110).

3609 RAPHAEL, of Urbino

Portfolio of 460 engravings after Raphael, by various artists. Three volumes, folio.

'Vellum.' Press-mark C.1.7 in MC; moved to the Round Tower.

SH SALE, viii.75, to P. and Dom. Colnaghi, £21. [London, 1219]

☞ In his Catalogue for 1847 (Prints), p. 178, H. G. Bohn offered HW's copy of Raphael's *Teste scelte di personaggi illustri . . . dipinte nel Vaticano*, engraved by Fidanza, Rome, 1757–62, 4 volumes bound in two, half-bound, russia. (The complete set comprises six volumes.) This, not identifiable in SH catalogue, may be recorded here: one would expect those prints to be in HW's collection.

3610 RENI, GUIDO

Portfolio of 160 engravings after Guido Reni, by various artists. Folio.

'Vellum.' Press-mark C.1.17 in MC; moved to the Round Tower.

SH SALE, viii.78, to Lilly, £2.11.0. [London, 1211]

☞ Some prints were then removed, but 131 were catalogued by English & Son, 16 October 1849 (J. H. S. Pigott Sale), lot 305.

SILVESTRE, ISRAEL   3611

Portfolio of 410 engravings, views of royal palaces and seats of the nobility of France and other parts of Europe. Folio.

'Vellum.' Press-mark C.2.2 in MC; moved to the Round Tower.
SH SALE, viii.84, to P. and Dom. Colnaghi, £5. [London, 1214]

TENIERS, DAVID   3612

Portfolio of engravings from his pictures, by himself, Le Bas, and others. Folio.

Press-mark D.1.14 in MC; moved to the Round Tower.
SH SALE, viii.74, to Evans, £19. [London, 1198]

☞ In the SH catalogue 263 prints are counted; but some were removed in the London catalogue, which describes this lot as 'about 200.' The rest (57) were sold in lots 1199–1203, where some of the subjects are specified, to Brown of Richmond, Evans, and Lilly.

TESTA, PIETRO   3613

Portfolio of 79 engravings of pictures. Folio.

'Vellum, with HW's BP.' Press-mark C.1.18 in MC; moved to the Round Tower.
SH SALE, viii.85, to Lilly, 19/– [London, 1215]; offered in Lilly's Catalogue for 1863, for £4.14.6. (Another Lilly catalogue, probably earlier, offered it for £6.6.0.)

VECELLI, TIZIANO   3614

Portfolio of 165 engravings after Titian, by various artists. Two volumes, folio.

'Vellum.' Press-mark C.1.10 in MC; moved to the Round Tower.
SH SALE, viii.76, to P. and Dom. Colnaghi, £9. [London, 1220]

ZUCCARO, TADDEO   3615

Portfolio of 119 engravings, by or after Taddeo and Federigo Zuccaro and Tempesta. Folio.

'Vellum.' Press-mark C.1.20 in MC; moved to the Round Tower.
SH SALE, viii.87, to Parker, Hampton Wick, £2. [London, 1217]

PRESS F

Press F contained various collections of engravings, in portfolios or in published volumes. Most impressive, perhaps, were HW's three portfolios of engravings by Wenceslaus Hollar.

3616 BELLORI, GIOVANNI PIETRO

Veteres Arcus Augustorum triumphis insignes. Engraved by Bartoli. Rome, 1690. Folio.

Press-mark D.3.8 in MC; moved to the Round Tower.

SH SALE, viii.108, to 'Money,' £1. [London, 980]

☞ In addition to this separate volume, HW had the plates in his Bartoli portfolio, sold in Press E of the Round Tower.

3617 CATESBY, MARK

The natural history of Carolina, Florida, and the Bahama Islands. Colored plates. London, 1731–43. Two volumes, folio. Published in parts.

Original vellum, blind panelled, with the spines labelled 'Catesby's History of Birds.' The bookplates have been removed. Press-marks D.3.11–12, altered in the books to F.15–16.

SH SALE, viii.103, to H. G. Bohn, £3.5.0 [London, 1141]; offered in Bohn's Catalogue for 1847 (Natural History), p. 50, for £8.8.0. The set was purchased by Dr. Thomas B. Wilson, who gave it in November 1847 to the Academy of Natural Sciences of Philadelphia.

☞ Opposite the entry in MC, Kirgate wrote: 'Catesby is not in the Collection'; against this is a note by Mrs. Damer: 'In the Round Tower'; and underneath Kirgate then wrote: 'Letter'd the History of Birds.' All three notes were presumably entered in 1797.

The list of subscribers includes 'The Right Hon. the Lady Walpole,' i.e. the wife of HW's brother Robert.

3618 CONTINI, FRANCESCO

Pompa introitus honori . . . Ferdinandi Austriaci. Antwerp, [1641]. Folio.

Not in MC.

SH SALE, viii.99, to Rodd. [London, 965 and 984]

☞ In a letter to Mann, 8 June 1771, HW wrote: 'We . . . have as pure architecture and as classic taste as there was in Adrian's or Pliny's villas.'

FARNESE GALLERY   3619

Portfolio of engravings after paintings by Carracci and Raphael, in
the Farnese Gallery; and from Albani's *Picturae in aede Verospia*,
engraved at Rome in 1704 by Frezza. Folio.

Press-mark D.3.17 in MC; moved to the Round Tower.
SH SALE, viii.102, to Strong, £2.18.0. [London, 1174]

GEVARTIUS, JOANNES CASPARUS   3620

Pompa introitus honori . . . Ferdinandi Austriaci. Antwerp, [1641].
Folio.

Original vellum. BP[1]. Press-mark C.1.1 in MC (erased in book); moved to
the Round Tower. Bookplate of the Hon. Percy Ashburnham (1799–
1881).

SH SALE, viii.100, to Lilly, £2.10.0 [London, 1090]; Maggs, July 1951,
to WSL, £35.

☞ Engravings after Rubens by Van Thulden. Note by HW inside the
cover: 'Bought at Lord Oxford's sale, 1746, £1.10.0'; and a note on the title-
page by HW: 'Most of the original designs by Rubens for the arches are
in Lord Orford's Collection of Pictures.' (*See Aedes Walpolianae*, 1747,
p. 65, where HW listed them and added: 'They are printed with a Description.')

GUALTIERI, NICCOLÒ   3621

Index testarum conchyliorum. Engraved by P. A. Pazzi and others.
Florence, 1742. Royal folio.

Vellum. BP[1]. Press-mark D.1.22; altered in book to F.12.

SH SALE, viii.107, to H. G. Bohn, 17/– [London, 1142]; offered in
Bohn's Catalogue for 1847 (Natural History), p. 21, for £2.5.0; Sotheby's,
29 July 1938 (Miscellaneous Sale), lot 724, to Maggs for WSL, £9.

☞ A letter tipped in, dated 13 October 1868, shows that the volume was then given by C. W. Standidge to Henry Lee (1826–1888) of
Blackfriars, the naturalist. Mann sent the Proposals to HW, 30 October
1742; HW asked for the book in his letter of 15 November, and Mann
promised, 1 January 1743, to procure a copy for HW.

HOLLAR, WENCESLAUS   3622

Portfolios of 934 engravings by Hollar, arranged by classes. Three volumes, folio.

'Vellum.' Press-mark D.1.15 in MC; moved to the Round Tower.
SH SALE, viii.91, to various purchasers, £94.15.6.

☞ In the London Sale, this collection was broken up, and sold in lots 807–880; the three empty portfolios were sold in lot 899. A collection of 131 engravings, representing his purchases in lots 807–880, was offered by Strong in his Catalogue for 1843, lot 746, for £6.6.0.

3623 LONDON

Portfolio of 140 views of London, Westminster, Cambridge, and Oxford, published by Henry Overton in *Britannia Illustrata*, &c. Folio. Not in MC.

SH SALE, viii.104, to H. G. Bohn, £3.10.0. [London, 913]

☞ Possibly this was similar to the volume that is listed as No. 3818, in Press R *below*, since each lot is recorded as sold to Bohn for £3.10.0, and the other volume is not separately recorded in the London Sale. Only 92 views are now bound in that volume, but the Oxford and Cambridge views could have been separated from it after 1842.

Bohn seems to have combined these volumes in some way, because his Catalogue for 1847 (Prints), p. 131, offers for £10.10.0 three volumes of Kip's *Britannia illustrata*, 225 plates including royal palaces, houses, cathedrals, and the colleges at Oxford and Cambridge, 'broken binding, not uniform, from SH,' 1709–12–17. On 17 June 1842, Bohn wrote to Beckford (letters now WSL) that lot 913 was 'rather good, £6.6.0'; but Beckford made no response to this note, and Bohn seems to have purchased the portfolio for stock.

3624 MALVASIA, CARLO CESARE

Descrizione del Claustro di San Michele in Bosco dipinto da Lodovico Carracci, ed intagliato da Giacopo Giovannini. Bologna, 1694. Folio.

Press-mark B.1.20 in MC; moved to the Round Tower.

SH SALE, viii.109, to Lilly, 9/–. [London, 1176]

3625 MARLBOROUGH, GEORGE SPENCER CHURCHILL, 4th Duke of

Gemmarum antiquarum delectus. (The Marlborough Gems, engraved by Bartolozzi.) London, 1781–90. Two volumes, folio.

Green morocco, probably by Kalthoeber, with HW's arms on sides and his Orford BP, type 1, on each title-page. Press-marks R.3 and R.4; perhaps misplaced in 1842. Not in MC. With bookplates of William Henry Watts and of C. A. and V. Baldwin.

SH SALE, viii.90, to Lilly, £59.6.6 [London, 1028]; Sotheby's, 16 April 1896 (Adrian Hope Sale), lot 3530, to Howell, £4.4.0; William P. Wreden, of Palo Alto, California, September 1959, to WSL, $650.

☞ Most of these gems came from the Arundel collection bequeathed through Lady Elizabeth Germain to the Duke's brother, who gave them to the Duke. The Duke then purchased for £5000 Lord Bessborough's collection of gems; also additional gems from Zanetti of Venice. An extended note in the book by HW concerning the history of this collection is in Kirgate's hand. In a marginal note in *L'Ami des étrangers* by Dutens, 1787, HW objected to the phrase that Marlborough added to the Arundel Collection 'qu'il avait acquise,' and wrote: 'Lady Betty Germain lui en fit present.' And in a marginal note in Bray's *Tour*, 1778, he wrote emphatically: 'The gems were not sold, but given by Lady Eliz. Germain to the present Duke of Marlborough, on the marriage of his brother Lord Charles to her Ladyship's great niece.'

PRINTS   3626

Portfolio of 123 portraits of foreigners, engraved by various artists. Folio.

Not in MC.

SH SALE, viii.94, to Adamson, £2.12.6. [London 594]

☞ Engravers named are: De Leeuw, Drevet, Gaultier, Houbraken, Moncornet, Suyderhoef, and Van Schuppen.

It seems likely that the price given for this portfolio includes the volume by Van Hulle in Press C in the Round Tower, because the price list of the London sale, lot 594, reads 'sold before, no. 576,' and lot 576 was the Van Hulle. Perhaps they were put together in the sale merely because their subjects were somewhat similar.

ROGERS, CHARLES   3627

A collection of prints in imitation of drawings. London, 1778. Two volumes, folio.

Not in MC.

SH SALE, viii.92, to Lilly, £3.10.0. [Not found in the London Sale, but possibly lot 1016 which is not identified but which went to Lilly for £3.10.0.] When sold at Hodgson's, 8 February 1928 (Miscellaneous Sale), lot 410, the set was described as 'uncut, binding broken, one plate wanting.'

☞ The engravings were by Bartolozzi and others.

3628 ROSSI, DOMENICO DE, Engraver

Raccolta di statue antiche e moderne. Notes by P. A. Maffei. Rome, 1704. Folio.

'Vellum, with HW's arms.' Press-mark C.2.24 in MC; moved to the Round Tower.

SH SALE, viii.106, to H. G. Bohn, £2 [London, 1010]; offered in Kerslake's Catalogue for 1848, lot 3406, for £2.2.0.

3629 SACCHI, ANDREA

Portfolio of 20 engravings after Andrea Sacchi by Smith, Picart, J. Frey, and others. Folio.

'Vellum.' Press-mark D.1.13 in MC; moved to the Round Tower.

SH SALE, viii.101, to Strong, £1.17.0. [London, 1175]

☞ The entry in MC reads 'Andrea Sacchi, Carlo Maratti, and his scholars,' perhaps more correctly. In the printed price list, this portfolio seems to have been confused with Frey's prints sold viii.73, in Press E, so that the purchaser of viii.101 is wrongly given as Colnaghi.

3630 SANDRART, JOACHIM VON

Academia nobilissimae artis pictoriae. Nuremberg, 1683. Folio.

Press-mark D.4.18 in MC; moved to the Round Tower.

SH SALE, viii.96, to H. G. Bohn, £1.13.0. [London, 1158]

☞ Dated 1683 in MC, but 1679 in the London Sale. The German original was published in two volumes, 1675–79. Sandrart is frequently cited in the first two volumes of HW's *Anecdotes*.

3631 SÉVIGNÉ, MARIE DE RABUTIN-CHANTAL, Marquise de

Portfolio of 144 portraits of Mme. de Sévigné and of persons in her circle. Folio.

Not in MC.

SH SALE, viii.93, to Smith, £16.16.0. [London, 577]

☞ In a letter to Mann, 30 September 1783, HW wrote: 'I have lately been putting together into a large volume a collection of portrait-prints of all the persons mentioned in the Letters of Mme. de Sévigné; of whom for many years I have been amassing engravings. . . .' He recorded this volume among the rare books of prints and drawings in the library, in his *Description of SH*, 1784. A special title-page, *Sevigniana, or a collection of portraits*, was prepared at the SH Press.

SIGISMUND, Emperor of Germany   3632

Sigismundi Augusti Mantuam adeuntis profectio ac triumphus . . .
   anno 1432. Engraved by Bartoli in 26 plates with notes by Bellori.
   Rome [1680]. Folio.

   Vellum. BP¹. Press-mark D.3.21, altered in book to F.10. Bookplates
of the Hon. Percy Ashburnham (1799–1881), and Michel C. Ralli.

   SH SALE, viii.98 to Strong, £1.4.0 [London, 1091]; F. H. Swift, April
1947, to WSL, £25.

   ☞ Bound with it is: *C. Julii Caesaris Dictatoris triumphi*, ten plates by
Audenaerd after Mantegna. Rome, 1692.

TENIERS, DAVID   3633

Theatrum pictorum, in quo exhibentur . . . picturae archetypae
   Italicae quas Archidux Leopold . . . collegit. Antwerp, 1658. Folio.

   'Calf.' Press-mark C.3.4 in MC; moved to the Round Tower.

   SH SALE, viii.97, to Capt. Leckie, £4.17.0 [London, 1209]; Puttick, 14
January 1867 (Leckie Sale), lot 264, to Bezzi, £6.6.0.

   ☞ A copy of the edition of 1684, owned in 1958 by Mr. Laurence
Witten of New Haven, has HW's BP¹ inserted.

VAN DYCK, Sir ANTHONY   3634

Portfolio of 150 engravings, after portraits and other paintings by Van
   Dyck, with several of his own etchings.

   Press-mark D.1.12 in MC; moved to the Round Tower.

   SH SALE, viii.105, to Tiffin, £8. [London, 597]

   ☞ The sale catalogue records that the collection was 'interspersed
with MS notes by HW.' When Eccardt painted Bentley, Gray, and Montagu
for the SH collection, he imitated the attitudes and costumes in Van Dyck's
engravings.

WATTEAU, ANTOINE   3635

Collection of 595 engravings by or after Watteau, published by
   Julienne. [Paris, 1734–40] Four volumes bound in three, folio.

   'Red morocco.' Not in MC.

   SH SALE, viii.95, to Sir H. Campbell, Bt., £49 [London, 1197]; Christie,
4 May 1866 (W. Curling Sale), lots 353–4, to Boone, £111.6.0.

   ☞ Included were *Oeuvre de Watteau gravé d'après ses tableaux et
desseins originaux* [1734] and *Figures de différents caractères, de paysages,*

et d'études (with a life of Watteau) [*ca.* 1740]. J. H. Anderdon wrote in his copy of the SH catalogue (now WSL): 'Altogether the finest collection I ever saw. These volumes of Watteau's works contain only fine impressions—many rare things, some I never saw. I have no doubt it will bring 100 guineas.'

PRESSES G AND H

In Presses G and H were shelved HW's major collections of British portraits, in 19 portfolios. These were too much to be absorbed in a lot or two by the market, and it was perhaps sets like these that induced Lord Waldegrave to insist on recataloguing all the books of prints.

3636 PRINTS

English Portraits. Nineteen portfolios of English portraits, eighteen of them arranged in chronological order and the last volume not arranged. Folio.

Press-marks D.1.29–40 in MC; moved to the Round Tower. Six volumes of prints of the Reign of George the 3d are not in MC. The last volume, containing prints not arranged, was C.3.30 in MC.

SH SALE, viii.110–11, sold for a total of £1217.8.0.

☞ These 19 volumes containing over 5000 prints, many with HW's notes, were broken up in the London Sale, and offered in lots 1–570, 601–728, containing one to forty or more prints each. Purchasers included the leading dealers and numerous private collectors; more than a thousand were re-offered in Strong's Catalogue for 1843, lots 2182–3363. Some 50 prints from this collection are now in the British Museum; more than a score are at Farmington. Three prints probably from this collection are in the Detroit Institute of Arts, two in the New York Public Library, four in the Morgan Library; others are scattered and unidentified.

The last volume, called 'a supplementary volume of portraits, not arranged,' was entered in MC as 'Heads by Hollar, &c.' The twelve earlier portfolios, 'Prints from the earliest times to the Reign of George the 2d,' are described as bound in vellum in the list printed in the *Description of SH*, 1774; to this in the edition of 1784 HW added 'Five larger folios of prints of the Reign of George 3d, and an additional volume of heads of different reigns collected since [i.e., since the original 12 volumes were compiled?].' For the index to the original 12 volumes, compiled

in 1774, *see* Press M in the Main Library, No. 2163 *above*. For the six volumes containing 'Portraits in the Reign of George the 3d' and the supplementary volume, special titles were prepared at the SH Press. (*Bibliography of SH Press*, pp. 259–60.)

A good many prints were purchased by HW at Vertue's sale in 1757, but of course he continued to collect English portraits all his life, both before and after Granger. His letters are filled with references to prints: for example, to Cole, 23 February 1764 and 15 July 1769.

PRESS I

In Press I were shelved numerous miscellaneous books of historical, antiquarian, and architectural prints. Notable also were the portfolios in which HW collected the engravings of Faithorne, Hogarth, and Vertue.

BIRCH, THOMAS   3637

The heads of illustrious persons of Great Britain. Engraved by Houbraken and Vertue, with lives by Birch. London, 1743–51. Two volumes in one, on large paper, folio.

Original mottled calf. BP¹. Press-mark C.2.23 in MC; altered in book to G.1 when moved to the Round Tower.

SH SALE, viii.139, to Lilly, £6 [London, 595]; Marks & Co. (from the collection of Mrs. Van Der Elst), January 1960, to WSL, £20.

☞ In a letter to Cole concerning Boydell's continuation of this collection, 20 December 1770, HW protested against including as illustrious persons 'any old head of a family' and 'spurious or doubtful heads; both sorts apt to be sent in by families who wish to crowd their own names into the work; as was the case more than once in Houbraken's set, and of which honest Vertue often complained to me.'

Included among the subscribers are the names of HW's father, his uncle, and his brother Edward. The work was published in monthly parts from 1737; in the Lewis Walpole collection is Vertue's set of proofs of the engravings, with many of the monthly wrappers.

BOISSARD, JEAN JACQUES   3638

[*Bibliotheca chalcographica.* Additional volume or part of] *Iconum virorum illustrium.* Engraved (and published) by Clemens Ammonius. Frankfurt, 1652. 4to.

'Vellum, with HW's BP.' Not in MC.

SH SALE, viii.134, to Lilly, £1.1.0 [London, 573]; offered in Strong's Catalogue for 1843, lot 10, for £2.6.0.

☞ Entered in SH catalogue only as 'Collection of Portraits' (revised to 'English and Foreign Portraits'), but the London catalogue identifies it as the volume published at Frankfurt in 1652 by Clement Ammon; Strong's Catalogue makes the identification certain.

William Beckford inquired about this volume in his letters to Bohn, 13 June and 17 June 1842 (letters now WSL); but Bohn made no comment on it and evidently failed to buy it.

3639 CHAMBERS, Sir WILLIAM

Designs of Chinese buildings. London, 1757. Folio.

Press-mark C.2.14 in MC; moved to the Round Tower.

SH SALE, viii.121, to Lilly, 12/–. [London, 960]

3640 CHINESE DRAWING

A roll, about 20 x 1½ feet, on stout Chinese paper, with a painting of an extensive procession. Roll.

Not in MC.

SH SALE, viii.136, to H. G. Bohn, £4.15.0. [London, 1267]

3641 DRAWINGS

Portfolio containing 50 drawings by Lady Diana Beauclerk and her daughter Mary, Miss Sebright, Miss Knight, Mrs. Damer, John Gooch, Samuel Lysons, Sir Edward Walpole, and Thomas Walpole. Folio.

Not in MC.

SH SALE, viii.127, to Graves, Pall-Mall, £1.5.0. [London, 1258]

☞ These drawings are now preserved in HW's copy of the *Description of SH*, 1774 (sold in the Glass Closet, iv.152), where they were inserted when the volume was rebound soon after 1844.

A group of four small drawings (three in pencil and one in ink) in the Dartmouth College Library may derive from this or a similar lot: on one of them HW has written 'Corner of the wood at Strawberry Hill.'

3642 EUROPE

Green's Map of Europe, in a case.

Not in MC.

SH SALE, viii.132, to J. R. Smith. [London, 938]

FAITHORNE, WILLIAM   3643

Portfolio of 280 engravings by William Faithorne. Folio.

Press-mark D.1.28 in MC; moved to the Round Tower.
SH SALE, viii.114, to various purchasers, £204.1.6.

☞ The collection was broken up for the London Sale, and offered in
lots 737 to 808; twenty prints were secured by the British Museum, but
the others were widely dispersed among dealers and collectors.

GOUGH, RICHARD   3644

Sepulchral monuments in Great Britain. London, 1786–96. Two volumes, imperial folio.

'Boards, uncut.' Not in MC.
SH SALE, viii.123, to H. G. Bohn, £10.5.0. [London, 950] A set bound
in five parts, 'red russia by Clarke & Bedford with HW's BP,' was sold at
Sotheby's, 21 July 1855 (Charles Meigh Sale), lot 813, to Toovey, £59; this
may have been the same set, rebound.

☞ Gough received important help from HW on this work: *see* HW's
letters to Gough, 21 June 1786 and 5 December 1796, and the *Bibliography of HW*, p. 143. He showed the second volume to Farington, 10
January 1797. Although HW promised Gough (5 December 1796) that
he would as soon as it was complete 'have the whole work bound in the
most superb manner that can be,' it was not completed until 1799; and
HW's set, still in boards in 1842, may have lacked the Introduction published in 1799.

HEARNE, THOMAS   3645

*Antiquities of Great Britain, illustrated in views of monasteries,
castles, and churches now existing.* Engraved by William Byrne
from Hearne's drawings. London, 1786. Oblong folio.

'Green morocco.' Not in MC.
SH SALE, viii.125, to H. G. Bohn, £2.4.0 [London, 925]; Sotheby's, 22
July 1855 (Charles Meigh Sale), lot 1056, to Grundy, £5.

☞ 'Notes by HW.' What was apparently a second copy was in Press Y,
in the Library in the Offices, No. 3429 *above*. But added to this copy in the
Round Tower were six engravings of seats in Twickenham after drawings
by James Spyers; HW's notes were written concerning these six plates.

3646 HOGARTH, WILLIAM

Portfolio containing 365 original drawings by, or prints engraved by and after, Hogarth. Folio.

Press-mark D.3.18 in MC; moved to the Round Tower. Added to the entry in MC is a note by HW: 'the most complete collection of his works.'
SH SALE, viii.124, to various purchasers, £378.16.0.

☞ The collection was broken up for the London Sale, and offered in lots 1272–1331: some 45 pieces are now in the British Museum, four at Farmington, one at Windsor, one in the Fitzwilliam Museum. Complete descriptions of the prints and drawings are in the catalogue of the London Sale. J. H. Anderdon, in his copy of the catalogue now WSL, copied out various notes by HW and made comments on many pieces. He added that when the last Hogarths were sold, the auctioneer said 'This is the end of the treasures of Strawberry Hill.' From this collection of Hogarth HW drew up the Catalogue in the fourth volume of his *Anecdotes*. He records in his preliminary note that he had added to the collection that was originally formed by Arthur Pond.

3647 HUET, CHRISTOPHE

Singeries ou différentes actions de la vie humaine représentées par des singes. Twelve plates engraved after Huet by J. B. Guelard. [Paris, 1742]

Not in MC.

SH SALE, viii.131, to Strong [London, 736]; offered in Strong's Catalogue for 1843, lot 1383, for £2.2.0.

3648 LE BRUN, CHARLES

La Galerie de Monsr. le président Lambert représentant l'Apothéose d'Hercule. Paris, [1740?] Royal folio.

Not in MC.

SH SALE, viii.120, to H. G. Bohn, 19/– [London, 1173]; perhaps the copy offered, but not identified as HW's, in Bohn's Catalogue for 1847 (Prints), p. 113, for £1.16.0.

☞ Engraved by Bernard Picart. The Lambert Gallery was visited by HW in August 1771.

Beckford wrote to Bohn on 13 June to inquire whether this was the first edition (letters now WSL); Bohn replied on 16 June that it contained 'only the one portion by Le Brun, viz. 14 plates. (The part which should accompany it is by Le Sueur 22 plates.) I have a finer copy. . . . [both parts] for £4.14.6. If you prefer Walpole's, perhaps three or four guineas.' Beck-

ford wrote on 18 June: 'The Galerie Lambert I *wish to have* and should also wish to look at your copy with the additions by Le Sueur.' But the copy in the Beckford Sale (now Lord Rosebery) is not HW's.

MEYSSENS, JOANNES   3649

True effigies of the most eminent painters and other famous artists ... in Europe. Engravings of 120 painters by Meyssens and Theodor Galle, with descriptions by Sebastiano Resta. London [i.e. Antwerp?], 1694. Folio.

Press-mark B.1.25 in MC; moved to the Round Tower.

SH SALE, viii.138, to Lilly, 16/−. [London, 579]

MURPHY, JAMES CAVANAH   3650

Plans, elevations, sections, and views of the Church of Batalha in Portugal. London, 1795. Imperial folio.

Not in MC.

SH SALE, viii.119, to Rodd, £1.1.0. [London, 963]

☞ In part translated from Manoel de Sousa Coutinho. The list of subscribers includes HW's name.

PENMANSHIP   3651

Specimens of penmanship.

Not in MC.

SH SALE, viii.132, to Graves, Pall-Mall. [London, 894]

☞ This is entered merely as 'Specimens of penmanship' in both catalogues. If it was an engraved copybook, it may have been one of Joseph Champion's works, or any one of numerous other copybooks.

PINE, JOHN   3652

The procession and ceremonies observed at the time of the installation of the Knights Companions of the ... Order of the Bath. London, 1730. Folio.

Old mottled calf. BP[1]. Press-mark D.4.6, altered in book to I.15.

SH SALE, viii.117, to Lilly, £1.10.0 [London, 1076]; Hodgson, 13 December 1946 (Miscellaneous Sale), lot 548, to Maggs for WSL, £15.

☞ Note by J. Lilly on the fly-leaf: 'This copy cost me £2.5.0.' Sir Robert Walpole subscribed for four copies, one of which very probably came to SH.

3653 Prints

Portfolio containing 37 engravings by F. Mazot, including Charles I and his Queen, Oliver Cromwell, and Sir Thomas Fairfax. 4to.

'Calf.' Not in MC.

SH SALE, viii.137, to — Newton, Esq. [London, 572]; Sotheby's, 5 July 1889 (Buckinghamshire Sale), lot 709.

3654 Prints

Portfolio of 80 engravings by Galle and Collaert. Folio.

Not in MC.

SH SALE, viii.128, to Lilly, £1.19.0. [London, 896; and listed a second time in lot 1165]

☞ One other book listed in viii.128, 'Galle on Gardening,' i.e. Galle's engravings after De Vries, seems to have been moved: *see* note under De Vries, Press Y in the Library in the Offices, 3474 *above*.

William Beckford wrote of this lot to William Smith, the dealer (letters now WSL), 'A strange omnium gatherum: Wilton Gardens, Galle, Collaert.' Smith replied on 14 April that he had not yet seen lot 128. Then when these books were recatalogued, Beckford wrote to Bohn to ask about '896 Galle &c. a lot separated from Wilton Gardens in the old catalogue.' But he seems finally to have decided against it.

3655 Prints

Portfolio containing 180 engravings of illustrious persons in France. Folio.

'With HW's BP.' Not in MC.

SH SALE, viii.129, to — Newton, Esq., £2.5.0 [London, 578]; Sotheby's, 5 July 1889 (Buckinghamshire Sale), lot 708.

☞ This volume, from Brantôme's collection with his notes, was doubtless purchased at Mariette's sale in 1775. Engravers named in the catalogue of the London Sale are L'Armessin, Daret, Frosne, and Moncornet.

William Beckford asked William Smith, the dealer (letters now WSL), about this collection; but Smith replied that it was 'a quantity of villainously bad portraits in the most wretched condition, and . . . not a single print worth having in it.'

The volume of Janet's drawings reputedly from Brantôme's collection was sold in the Glass Closet, No. 2358 *above*.

PRINTS 3656

Volume containing 32 portraits of plenipotentiaries. 4to.

'Vellum, with HW's BP.' Press-mark C.5.10 (altered from C.4) in MC; moved to the Round Tower.

SH SALE, viii.137, to — Newton, Esq. [London, 572]; Sotheby's, 5 July 1889 (Buckinghamshire Sale), lot 620.

☞ The description in the SH catalogue, 'a small volume containing portraits of illustrious men,' is vague; but the London sale says '32 portraits of plenipotentiaries,' and this is confirmed by the Buckinghamshire sale: the work was F. Bignon's *Portraictz au naturel avec les armoires et blazons . . . des plenipotentiaires assemblez à Munster et Osnaburg*, Paris 1648, 4to. Actually 33 plates.

It is possible that some such lot as this contained a partial set of Hans Burgmaier's prints of the events of the time of Maximilian I, since a complete set of 237 woodcuts (Augsburg, *ca.* 1520), laid in a royal folio volume, 'from the SH collection,' was offered in Bohn's Catalogue for 1847 (Prints), p. 78, for £4.4.0. But the Burgmaier prints are not identified in the SH catalogue.

In Bohn's Catalogue also, p. 172, was offered HW's copy of Pieter Schrijver's *Principes Hollandiae, Zelandiae, et Frisiae*, 38 plates, Harlem, 1650, imperial folio, bound in vellum. This volume is likewise not identified in the SH catalogue.

SCHENK, PETER 3657

Paradisus oculorum. [Amsterdam? 1695?] Oblong 4to.

Original boards with calf back. BP[1]. Press-mark C.6.4 (altered from C.5?); moved to the Round Tower. Bookplate of the 5th Earl of Rosebery.

SH SALE, viii.133, to H. G. Bohn for William Beckford, 16/– [London, 975]; Sotheby's, 10 July 1883 (Beckford Sale, Part 3), lot 1806, to Bain, £2; now in the library of the Earl of Rosebery, Barnbougle Castle.

☞ One hundred views of palaces, after drawings by Jacob Romans.

Beckford inquired of Bohn about this volume, 13 June 1842 (letters now WSL); Bohn replied on 16 June: 'I don't think much of [Schenk] either as to condition or impressions, and believe I have had it finer. About 30/–.' Beckford responded on 18 June: 'If you have any doubts of 975, don't think of it; nothing second rate enters here.' But at 16/– Bohn seems to have believed it worth buying.

3658 SOCIETY OF ANTIQUARIES

Vetusta Monumenta. London, 1747–89. Two volumes, imperial folio.

The first volume is entered in MC, 'Prints by the Society of Antiquaries,' as D.3.20; moved to the Round Tower.

SH SALE, viii.122, to Strong, £5.12.6. [London, 949]

☞ Engraved by Vertue and Basire. There are references to two or three of these prints in HW's *Anecdotes.*

3659 STRADANUS, JOHANNES

Portfolio of 62 engravings after Stradanus by Philipp Galle and Adrian Collaert. Oblong 4to.

Not in MC.

SH SALE, viii.126, to Lilly, £2. [London, 897]

☞ When this volume was listed a second time in the London Sale, lot 1166, it was described as having at the end three prints of 'Cries of London' in 120 figures.

3660 VAN DYCK, SIR ANTHONY

Portfolio of 59 prints, engraved after paintings by Van Dyck. Folio.

Press-mark C.1.23 in MC; moved to the Round Tower.

SH SALE, viii.113, to Lilly, £2.12.6. [London, 596]; offered in Strong's Catalogue for 1843, lot 3258, for £4.14.6.

☞ Perhaps two or three prints were removed: the SH catalogue counts 62 prints, the London catalogue 61, and Strong's catalogue 59.

3661 VAN HULLE, ANSELM

Portraicts des hommes illustres qui ont vécu dans le XVIIe siècle, les . . . ambassadeurs, et plenipotentiaires . . . aux conférences de Munster. 4to.

Not in MC. Press-mark C.5.10 (altered from C.4) in MC; moved to the Round Tower.

SH SALE, viii.135, to W. Stevenson Fitch, Esq., 16/–. [London, 575]

☞ First printed in 87 plates in 1648. Since the sale catalogue records 131 plates, it would seem that HW owned a later edition of these engravings; the edition of 1706 was in Press C *above,* No. 3580.

VENICE   3662

Teatro delle fabbriche più cospicue in prospettiva della Citta di
   Venezia. Engravings by F. Zucchi and G. Filosi. [Venice, 1760?]
   Oblong 4to.

   Press-mark C.6.6 (altered from C.5?) in MC, 'Perspective views in
Venice'; moved to the Round Tower.

   SH SALE, viii.130, to Graves [London, 894]; Christie, 12 December 1884
(William Russell Sale), lot 554, to Breun, 9/–.

   ☞ The Christie catalogue describes the volume as having HW's BP.

   Both the SH catalogue and the London catalogue add to this lot 'and 2
others.' Almost any unidentified book of plates may have been sold here,
but there seems at present no way to determine which two they were.
Indeed, Robins's cataloguer had trouble with the lot: the first edition of the
sale catalogue lists 'Views in Venice and Views in Rome'; this was revised to
'Views in Venice and 2 others' (as in the London Sale), and then to 'Views
in Venice, Views of the Chinese, and 1 other.' (The Views of the Chinese
and the Views in Rome, if they existed, have not been identified.)

   Some such lot (but one finally sold at SH in April, not deferred until
June) contained a rare volume perhaps originally shelved in the Glass
Closet, and not identified in the sale: Johann Agricola's *Warhaffte Bildnis
etlicher hochlöblicher Fürsten und Herren*, Wittenberg 1562, 4to. This was
purchased from Rodd, 6 June 1842, by the British Museum, for £8.18.6.
Printed on vellum, and bound in leather with the arms of Pierre de Villars,
Archbishop of Vienne. BP[1]. Not in MC. With HW's note: 'Bought at Lord
Oxford's sale, 1746, £1.3.0.'

VERTUE, GEORGE   3663

The heads of the Kings of England proper for Mr. Rapin's History and
   Monuments of the Kings of England. London, 1736. Royal folio.

   Rebound in red morocco. BP[1]. Press-mark D.1.29 in MC (not preserved
in volume).

   SH SALE, viii.115, to Lilly, £3.10.0 [London, 571]; Sotheby's, 25 May
1875 (Benzon Sale), lot 271, to Harvey, £13.10.0; note inserted of purchase from Harvey in 1877 for £20; Sotheby's, 28 May 1946 (Cunliffe Sale),
lot 877, to Maggs for WSL, £14.

   ☞ Long note in pencil by HW on the last plate.

   In his own copy of Gough's *British Topography* (now in the Huntington
Library), HW wrote opposite Gough's admission that he had found no drawings of churches and antiquities by Gravelot: 'Mr. Walpole has a few of the
original drawings which Gravelot made of the Monuments of the Kings of

England, whence Vertue engraved his prints, and which were purchased at Vertue's sale.' Probably these were the drawings purchased for £2.3.0 by HW at Vertue's sale, 17 March 1757, lot 46: 'Seven curious drawings of Henry the Seventh's Chapel, and others of English monuments.'

3664 VERTUE, GEORGE

Portfolios containing 470 prints and drawings of English artists, from which engravings were made for HW's *Anecdotes*. Two volumes, folio.

Not in MC, but recorded in the *Description of SH*, 1774, among the rare books of prints and drawings in the library.

SH SALE, viii.112, to Evans, £61.19.0. [London, 1270]

☞ The note by HW in the first volume is quoted in the SH catalogue; he bought these from Vertue's widow, but then perhaps added to them. Important or rare prints in the collection are named in the London Sale.

For this collection special titles were prepared (*Bibliography of SH Press*, p. 258). Although Robins declined to break up these portfolios in 1842, they seem to have been broken up some years later: the British Museum owns three of the drawings and more than one hundred prints (purchased from Evans in February 1852), as well as the original of HW's note and at least one of the special titles.

The original drawings were principally 70 by Vertue, with a few by other artists; 34 of Vertue's drawings were sold by Drake, December 1949, to WSL, for $1,000.

3665 VERTUE, GEORGE

Portfolios containing 585 engravings by Vertue: portraits, views, monuments, coins, medals, and historical subjects. Two volumes, folio.

Entered in MC, without a press-mark.

SH SALE, viii.116, to Smith, £44.2.0. [London, 1269, where the price is recorded by error as £3.15.0]

☞ At Farmington is a MS list prepared by Vertue of a *Collection of his Engraved Prints*. It seems likely to have been prepared to accompany a portfolio such as he arranged for several people; but the list does not appear to derive from SH.

3666 WATTEAU, ANTOINE

Figures de modes, &c. [Paris, *ca.* 1710] Two volumes, 4to.

Press-mark C.6.13 (altered from C.5?) in MC; moved to the Round Tower.

SH SALE, viii.131, to Strong. [London, 736]

☞ Since the London catalogue reads 'Figures de monde, &c.' the two volumes were probably *Figures de modes* [*ca.* 1710] and *Figures françoises et comiques* [*ca.* 1715]. The MC reads 'Watteau's Dresses, &c.'

WILTON   3667

Hortus Pembrochianus. Le jardin de Wilton. Engraved by Isaac de
    Caus. [London, *ca.* 1645?] Oblong 4to.

'Old calf, with HW's BP.' Press-mark C.6.5 (altered from C.5?) in MC;
moved to the Round Tower.

SH SALE, viii.128, to Graves [London, 894]; Sotheby's, 11 June 1895
(Orford Sale), lot 338, to Quaritch, £19.

☞ William Beckford inquired of William Smith about this lot on 13
April, and of Bohn on 13 June. When it was finally catalogued, Beckford
wrote, 18 June: 'There were views of Wilton Gardens I saw in the Round
Tower, but where they lurk at present I cannot tell.' [The description in
the London Sale is not at all precise.] Then Beckford wrote on 21 June: 'I
see by the *Morning Post* of yesterday that the book I so much wanted,
viz. lot 894 Wilton Gardens, was purchased by Graves for £3.17.6—dear
enough but I would willingly give more for it. The foolish ill-judged trans-
fer of the sale from the Round Tower to Covent Garden has turned all
my commissions topsey-turvey and deprived me of the book I most wanted
and would have given more for than any other person.' (Letters now
WSL)

WINSTANLEY, HAMLET   3668

Portfolio of 20 engravings after pictures at Knowsley Hall, the Derby
    Gallery. London, 1728–9. Folio.

Not in MC.

SH SALE, viii.118, to Lilly, £1. [London, 1177]

PRESS K

Press K seems oddly small, with its single folio of Claude Lorrain.
But also sold in this press were five large volumes of Playfair's *British
Family Antiquities*, 1809, perhaps brought to SH by Mrs. Damer. And
at least four folios that HW and Kirgate had assigned to Press K were
actually sold in the Closet of the Round Tower: *see above* in Closet
under Chute, Kit-Cat Club, Rossi, and Van Der Dort.

3669 LORRAIN, CLAUDE

Liber Veritatis or a collection of two hundred prints. Engraved by
Richard Earlom from the original drawings owned by the Duke of
Devonshire. London, 1777. Folio.

'Half-bound, uncut.' Not in MC.

SH SALE, viii.141, to Charles S. Bale, Esq., £18.7.6. [London, 1180]

☞ This volume may have been broken up: at Farmington, given to WSL
by Miss Elizabeth Manwaring in 1947, is Boydell's portrait frontispiece of
Claude Lorrain, with HW's BP² later state.

PRESS L

Press L contained principally large foreign books of architectural and
historical prints. In 1763 these had been shelved variously in Presses
B, C, and D of the Main Library.

3670 AESOP

The fables of Aesop paraphras'd in verse. By John Ogilby, with 150
prints by Hollar, Barlow, and others. London, 1665–8. Folio.

Press-mark B.2.1 in MC; moved to the Round Tower.

SH SALE, viii.146, to Lilly, 12/– [London, 892]; Sotheby's, 19 December
1853 (Pigott Sale), lot 333, to Aladdin, £4.

3671 ANDROUET DU CERCEAU, JACQUES

*Le premier (–second) volume des plus excellents bastiments de
France.* Paris, 1576–9. Two volumes, folio.

Press-mark C.2.25 in MC; moved to the Round Tower.

SH SALE, viii.144, to Evans, £4.6.0. [London, 962]

☞ Opposite these two volumes in MC, HW marked: 'scarce, the two
volumes are seldom to be found together.'

3672 ANDROUET DU CERCEAU, JACQUES

De architectura opus. Paris, 1559–61. Two volumes in one, folio.

'Old calf.' Press-mark D.4.22, entered by HW, in MC; moved to the Round
Tower.

SH SALE, viii.144 (with his *Livre d'Architecture*), to H. G. Bohn, £2.12.6
[London, 961]; offered in Bohn's Catalogue for 1847 (Architecture), p. 219,
for £2.2.0.

☞ It is tempting to think that this and the succeeding French edition, both entered in MC by HW and hence acquired shortly after 1763, were purchased by him at the Cottrell sale, 23 February 1764, lots 585–6.

ANDROUET DU CERCEAU, JACQUES   3673

Livre d'architecture. Paris, 1582. Folio.

'Old calf.' Press-mark D.4.23, entered by HW, in MC; moved to the Round Tower.

SH SALE, viii.144 (with his *De Architectura*), to H. G. Bohn, £2.12.6 [London, 961]; offered in Bohn's Catalogue for 1847 (Architecture), p. 219, for £1.8.0.

BANDURI, ANSELMUS   3674

Imperium orientale, sive antiquitates Constantinopolitanae. Paris, 1711. Two volumes, folio.

Press-mark D.4.13 in MC; moved to the Round Tower.
SH SALE, viii.143, to Lilly, £1.13.0. [London, 1013]

BRAUN, GEORG   3675

Civitates orbis terrarum. Plates by Franz Hogenberg and others. Cologne, 1572–1618. Six parts in two volumes, folio.

Old vellum, gilt. BP² early state. Press-mark L.8.15, entered by HW, in MC; moved to the Round Tower and press-mark altered to L.1 in the book. (Its reappearance in Press L of the Round Tower is merely coincidence.) Bookplates of William Stirling.

SH SALE, viii.148, to H. G. Bohn, £4 [London, 1181]; offered in Bohn's Catalogue for 1847 (Prints), p. 76, for £6.16.6; Sotheby's, 15 February 1856 (Miscellaneous Sale), lot 27, to Quaritch, £2.13.0; Christie's, 20 May 1958 (Stirling-Maxwell Sale), lot 44, to Meyer Elte, The Hague, £520; Meyer Elte, June 1958, to WSL, £680.

☞ Shelf L.8 in the Main Library seems to have been installed in 1764 to hold the fourteen volumes of Thuanus (No. 3556 *above*) and these two volumes of Braun.

The SH press-marks were revealed at Farmington by removing the new end-papers.

3676 CASTELLAMONTE, AMEDEO DI

La venaria reale, palazzo di piacere e di caccia ideato . . . da Carlo Emmanuele II. Plates of hunting parties and of architectural designs engraved after Jan Miel by Tasnière, published by Zapata. Turin, 1674. Folio.

'Russia, gilt, with HW's BP.' Press-mark B.2.25 in MC; moved to the Round Tower.

SH SALE, viii.146, to Strong, 18/– [London, 893]; offered in Strong's Catalogue for 1843, lot 777, for £3.3.0; Sotheby's, 25 May 1925 (Miscellaneous Sale), lot 343, to B. F. Stevens, £9.10.0.

☞ Described in the SH catalogue as 'Zapata's Book on Hunting.'

3677 DESGODETZ, ANTOINE BABUTY

Les édifices antiques de Rome. Paris, 1682. Folio.

Press-mark B.1.6 in MC; moved to the Round Tower.

SH SALE, viii.151, to H. G. Bohn, 12/–. [Not found in the London Sale, but lot 1015 in which no book is specified was bought by Bohn for 12/–]

☞ Two copies were offered in Bohn's Catalogue for 1847 (Architecture), p.223.

3678 DRAWINGS

Portfolio containing 120 drawings and prints, including views of Strawberry Hill by Barrow. Folio.

Not in MC.

SH SALE, viii.154, dispersed.

☞ This collection was dispersed, but it can be partially identified in the London Sale, probably all of lots 1247–54. Artists named include: Adam, Barrow, Bentley, Carter, Maria Cosway, Gillot, Heckel, Laroon, Sharpe, Strange, Watteau, and Woollett. Several of the drawings are now at Farmington, including a group from Lord Waldegrave's collection in 1948.

Either in this portfolio or in his own copy of the *Description of SH* (No. 3582 *above*) were probably the originals of the plates used by HW to illustrate the *Description*.

3679 DU MOLINET, CLAUDE

Le cabinet de la Bibliothèque de Sainte-Geneviève. Paris, 1692. Folio.

Press-mark B.1.7 in MC; moved to the Round Tower.

SH SALE, viii.149, to Fuller, 15/–. [London, 1178]

FRANCIS, Duke of Anjou, and of Alençon   3680

La joyeuse et magnifique entrée de Monseigneur Françoys fils de France . . . Duc de Brabant en sa très-renommée ville d'Anvers. Antwerp, 1582. Folio.

Press-mark D.4.20 in MC; moved to the Round Tower.

SH SALE, viii.152, to Adamson, 5/–. [London, 1078]

☞ Another copy was in Press P of the Round Tower, No. 3741 *below*.

LE PAUTRE, JEAN   3681

Portfolio of architectural designs and ornaments by Le Pautre and Berain. Folio.

Press-mark B.2.18 in MC; moved to the Round Tower.

SH SALE, viii.147, to Adamson. [London, 955]

MARTINI, JOSEPHUS   3682

Theatrum Basilicae Pisanae. Rome, 1705. Folio.

'Red morocco, with arms of Grand Duke of Tuscany, and HW's BP.' Press-mark B.1.11 in MC; moved to the Round Tower.

SH SALE, viii.150, to H. G. Bohn, £4.7.0 [London, 1011]; Sotheby's, 21 December 1882 (Beckford Sale, Part 2), lot 2267, to Robson & Kerslake, £2.17.6.

☞ Bohn wrote to Beckford on 17 June 1842 (letters now WSL) that this was 'in beautiful old morocco, red, & a very nice book—perhaps £10.10.0.' Beckford replied that he already owned a copy, but Bohn seems to have persuaded Beckford to take HW's copy, perhaps after the sale.

MONTFAUCON, BERNARD DE   3683

Royal and ecclesiastical antiquities of France. London, 1750. Two volumes in three, folio.

Press-mark B.1.8 in MC; moved to the Round Tower.

SH SALE, viii.142, to Strong, £3.10.0 [London, 1012]; rebound in half blue morocco in two volumes, sold at Sotheby's, 27 April 1857 (Library of an antiquary), lot 591, to Saye, £3.13.0.

☞ Somewhat reduced from Montfaucon's *Monumens de la monarchie françoise*, 5 volumes, 1729–33. In the first volume of his *Anecdotes*, HW wrote (p. 30): 'I find by Montfaucon that the use of crayons was known in this age in France.'

3684 PALAZZI, GIOVANNI

Monarchia imperii occidentalis. Venice, 1671. Folio.

Press-mark D.4.15 in MC; moved to the Round Tower.
SH SALE, viii.153, to Wilcox, Warwick, 11/–. [London, 1179]

☞ Completed in 1679 in eight parts: the SH catalogue gives only the title of the first part, 'Aquila inter lilia,' but HW presumably had all parts.
William Smith, the dealer, called this to William Beckford's attention on 14 April 1842 (letters now WSL); Beckford then asked Bohn about it when he saw it in the London catalogue, on 13 June, and Bohn replied that it was a poor copy of a common book.

3685 PICART, BERNARD

Cérémonies et coutumes religieuses de tous les peuples du monde. Volume I. Amsterdam, 1723. Folio.

Press-mark D.4.12 in MC; moved to the Round Tower.
SH SALE, viii.143, to Lilly, 7/–. [London, 1083]

☞ Edited by J. F. Bernard and others.

3686 [VAN NIDECK, A.]

Antiquitates sacrae et civiles Romanorum explicatae. Latin and French. The Hague, 1726. Folio.

'Calf, with HW's BP.' Press-mark B.1.18 in MC; moved to the Round Tower.
SH SALE, viii.145, to Lilly, 15/– [London, 1014]; offered in Strong's Catalogue for 1843, lot 33, for £1.4.0; offered in Lilly's Catalogue for 1865, for £1.4.0; sold with Part 2 of Lilly stock at Sotheby's, 19 June 1871.

☞ Also ascribed to one André van Nartow.

3687 WRIGHT, JOHN MICHAEL

An account of Roger Earl of Castlemaine's embassy from James II to Innocent XI. London, 1688. Folio.

Press-mark B.1.24 in MC; moved to the Round Tower.
SH SALE, viii.147, to Adamson. [London, 1078]

☞ First published in Italian in 1687; the plates are by Arnold van Westerhout. In his *R&NA*, HW recorded this as a splendid book, with cuts.

PRESS M

Press M seems to have been used chiefly to shelve large volumes acquired shortly before 1790 or afterwards. But it likewise held Gray's *Poems* in which HW had pasted the original drawings by Bentley, and the important collection of Chattertoniana.

[BLACKBURNE, FRANCIS]   3688
Memoirs of Thomas Hollis, Esq. London, 1780. Two volumes, royal 4to.

Green morocco, with HW's BP. Not in MC. With bookplate of the Earl of Gosford.

SH SALE, vii.58, to Payne & Foss, £5.5.0 [London, 1053]; Puttick, 21 April 1884 (Gosford Sale), lot 1498, to Lord Rosebery; now in Lord Rosebery's collection at Barnbougle Castle.

☞ To Mann, 7 April 1780, HW wrote: 'I am diverted at present to . . . the memoirs of that singular being Thomas Hollis . . . as simple a poor soul as ever existed, except his editor, who has given extracts from the good creature's diary, that are very near as anile as Ashmole's. . . .' He added further comments to Mason on 17 April.

BONDE, GULIELMUS   3689
De Julii Clovii . . . operibus libri tres. [London] 1733. Folio.

Bound in calf in the manner of Kalthoeber about 1793. Seal of HW as Lord Orford, type 1. Press-mark M. Not in MC. Armorial stamp and bookplate of William Stirling.

SH SALE, vii.62, to Graves, Pall-Mall, £3.3.0 [London, 1148]; Christie's, 20 May 1958 (Stirling-Maxwell Sale), lot 38, to Maggs for WSL, £88.

☞ Mounted at the front is a page of notes concerning the volume by HW, dated 28 February 1793, at Strawberry Hill.

CHATTERTON, THOMAS   3690
Collection of pieces by and about him. One volume, 4to, and 17 volumes, 8vo.

One volume in original calf, rebacked, with HW's arms on the sides, and the title in MS by HW. Press-mark M.2. Not in MC.

SH SALE, vii.49, to Strong, £4.10.0 [London, 1040*–1042*]; Edwards, 1 November 1848 (Pigott Sale), lot 1609. The volume in 4to, the *Poems*

3690 edited by Milles, is now in the British Museum. The other pieces were gathered into four volumes about 1860: one of these was left in original calf as described above, while the other 16 pieces were bound in three volumes for A. A. Smets. These four volumes were sold by Leavitt, 25 May 1868 (Smets Sale), lot 446; then owned by George T. Strong of New York; acquired by the Clinton Hall association of New York for the New York Mercantile Library; sold by the library in 1934 to WSL.

☞ Full transcripts of HW's notes are in Appendix 1 to Volume 16 of the Yale Walpole, the *Correspondence with Chatterton*. Pieces included are:

(1) *Poems . . . by Thomas Rowley*, edited by Milles, in 4to, 1782. Now in the British Museum. Although HW sent this to Mason, he asked Mason to return it. (*See* Mason's letter to HW, 14 July 1782.)

(2) *Poems . . . by Thomas Rowley*, edited by Tyrwhitt, 1777.

(3) Chatterton's *Miscellanies*, edited by John Broughton, 1778.

(4) Walpole's *Letter to the Editor of the Miscellanies of Thomas Chatterton*, printed at SH, 1779.

(5, 6) BRYANT, JACOB. *Observations upon the Poems of Thomas Rowley*, 1781. Two parts; the Yale editors counted this as only one piece.

(7) Tyrwhitt's *Appendix*, [1778].

(8) GREGORY, GEORGE. *Life of Thomas Chatterton*, 1789.

(9) Tyrwhitt's *Vindication of the Appendix*, 1782.

(10) Warton's *Inquiry into the authenticity of the Poems*, 1782.

(11) HICKFORD, RAYNER. *Observations on the Poems*, with John Fell's *Remarks* on Tyrwhitt's *Appendix*, [1781].

(12) MATHIAS, THOMAS JAMES. *Essay on the evidence . . . relating to the Poems*, 1783.

(13) *The Genuine copy of a letter found . . . near SH*, 1783.

(14) *A Supplement to the Miscellanies*, edited by John Broughton, 1784.

(15) *The Ode, Songs, Chorusses, etc. for the concert in commemoration of Chatterton*, by Richard Jenkins, [1784].

(16) MALONE, EDMOND. *Cursory observations on the Poems*, 2d edition, 1782.

(17) GREENE, EDWARD BURNABY. *Strictures* [upon Malone's *Cursory Observations* and Warton's *Inquiry*], 1782.

(18) *The Monthly Review* for March 1782 (containing the review of Dean Milles's edition of the *Poems*), with clippings from other magazines.

Mr. Roger Senhouse of London owns a copy of the *Poems*, 1777, rebound, with HW's BP. It is conceivable, as suggested by the Yale editors, that this volume was originally in HW's collection, a duplicate. But the

collection as described above seems to be complete, 17 volumes in 8vo; the description of lot 1041 in London Sale as '2 vols.' means only that the volume now in original calf contained both Tyrwhitt's and Broughton's collections, and Bryant's *Observations* filled two volumes with continuous pagination. The bookplate is more probably an insertion in the Senhouse copy. (An added count against the volume is that it was in 1886 in the collection of Richard C. Jackson, an eccentric collector who did not always exclude items of dubious provenance.) Still another copy of this edition with HW's BP, sold at the Parke-Bernet Galleries, 29 April 1953, showed clearly that the bookplate was an insertion. Probably this same copy was sold again at Sotheby's, 14 April 1959.

COMBE, CHARLES   3691

Nummorum veterum populorum et urbium qui in Museo Gulielmi Hunter asservantur descriptio. London, 1782. 4to.

'Old red morocco, with HW's arms on sides.' Not in MC.

SH SALE, vii.52, to H. G. Bohn for William Beckford, £3.15.0 [London, 1018]; Sotheby's, 8 July 1882 (Beckford Sale, Part 1), lot 2068, to Sotheran, £2.15.0; offered in Sotheran catalogues, 1883–5, for £3.15.0.

☞ In the Preface, HW's help is acknowledged, for permitting engravings to be made of Greek coins in his collection. On 26 November 1780, HW wrote to Lady Ossory that Dr. Hunter 'came to talk to me about Greek medals.'

Beckford asked Bohn to look at this volume in a letter of 13 June (letters now WSL): 'Hunter's Coins—a fine copy in morocco if I recollect right.' Bohn replied: 'Hunter is good, but nothing superlative, plain red morocco (Kalthoeber?) not lettered; arms on sides; portraits of Dr. Hunter and Queen Charlotte inserted, but clumsily. As the book seldom occurs in morocco, perhaps £7.7.0 or £8.8.0.' Beckford wrote back: 'Hunter I should like *extremely*—but if you are run up—drop.'

DALLAWAY, JAMES   3692

Inquiries into the origin and progress of the science of heraldry in England. Gloucester, 1793. 4to.

Green morocco, in the manner of Kalthoeber, with Orford arms on sides. Press-mark M. Not in MC. Bookplate of Laurence Currie.

SH SALE, vii.53, to Lilly, £2.10.0 [London, 1098]; Puttick, 21 April 1884 (Gosford Sale), lot 889, to Bain, £4.12.6; B. Halliday, October 1925, to the Columbia University Library; Columbia, February 1960, to Yale for the Lewis Walpole collection, by exchange.

☞ Perhaps Samuel Lysons presented the book, on behalf of Dallaway; HW wrote to Lysons, 19 March 1794: 'Since I left you, I have done nothing but examine Mr. Dallaway's book, and am delighted with it; . . . I lose no time to ask you whether it would be possible to induce him to let me have duplicates of *five* of the plates; I would willingly pay any price he would value them at.'

3693 DUBUY, PIERRE ANCHER TOBIÉSEN

Recueil général des pièces obsidionales et de nécessité. Paris, 1786. Imperial 4to.

'Red morocco.' Not in MC.

SH SALE, vii.57 (with his *Traité*), to H. G. Bohn, £4 [London, 1021]; Sotheby's, 14 July 1883 (Beckford Sale, Part 3), lot 2632 (with his *Traité*), to Rimell, £2.2.0.

☞ A second copy, in boards, was first catalogued in vii.71, but sold with this one in the London Sale, 1021: it is unreported since 1842.

3694 DUBUY, PIERRE ANCHER TOBIÉSEN

Traité des monnoies des barons. Paris, 1786. Two volumes, imperial 4to.

Straight-grained red morocco, attributed to Kalthoeber. BP² later state. Press-mark M. Not in MC.

SH SALE, vii.57 (with his *Recueil général*), to H. G. Bohn, £4 [London, 1021]; Sotheby's, 14 July 1883 (Beckford Sale, Part 3), lot 2632 (with his *Recueil général*), to Rimell, £2.2.0; Sotheran, December 1931, to WSL, £6.6.0.

☞ Bohn wrote on 17 June 1842 to Beckford (letters now WSL) that the Dubuy volumes in lot 1021 were fine, worth perhaps £6.6.0. Beckford replied on 18 June that he had not 'the slightest wish' for lot 1021, but Bohn seems to have persuaded him to take the volumes.

3695 ECKHEL, JOSEPH HILARIUS VON

Choix des pierres gravées du Cabinet Impérial des Antiques. Vienna, 1788. Folio.

'Green morocco, with HW's arms on sides.' Not in MC.

SH SALE, vii.56, to Strong, £4 [London, 1026]; offered in Strong's Catalogue for 1843, lot 478, for £5.15.6.

☞ Bohn wrote to William Beckford on 17 June 1842 (letters now WSL) that this volume was pretty, worth perhaps £4.4.0; but Beckford replied that he already had a copy.

GORI, ANTONIO FRANCESCO   3696

Dactyliotheca Smithiana. Venice, 1767. Two volumes, folio.

'Russia.' Not in MC.

SH SALE, vii.59, to Strong, £3.10.0 [London, 1027]; English, 15 October 1849 (Pigott Sale), lot 119.

GOSTLING, GEORGE   3697

*Extracts from the treaties between Great Britain and other kingdoms
and states.* London, 1792. 4to.

'Red morocco, by Kalthoeber.' Not in MC.

SH SALE, vii.55, to Strong, £1.11.6 [London, 1069]; offered in Strong's
Catalogue for 1843, lot 621, for £2.12.6; Fletcher, 8 April 1846 (Britton
Sale, Part 4), lot 653, to Palmer, 14/–; offered in Lasbury's Catalogues in
1848 and 1849, for 18/–.

☞ Inserted was a letter of presentation from the author.

GRAY, THOMAS   3698

Designs by Mr. R. Bentley, for six poems by Mr. T. Gray. London,
1753. Folio.

Original red morocco. No BP. Press-mark M. Not in MC. Bookplate of
Laurence Currie.

SH SALE, vii.54, to H. G. Bohn for William Beckford, £8.8.0 [London,
1044]; Sotheby's, 3 July 1882 (Beckford Sale, Part 1), lot 802, to Ellis &
White, £20; offered by Ellis & White, Catalogue 50, *ca.* 1882, for £65;
Maggs, November 1933, to WSL, £230.

☞ Inserted are all the original drawings by Bentley in place of the engravings; also Gray's original sketch of Stoke House. With HW's note on
the fly-leaf: 'These are the original drawings by Mr. Bentley from whence
Grignion and Müller engraved the plates for this edition.' Before 1790 HW
kept this among his 'curious books in the Glass Closet,' and it is the first
book listed in his *Description of SH*, 1774. Details concerning the preparation of this book and a record of other copies may be found in the
Bibliography of HW, 1948. In his letter to Gray, 20 February 1753, HW
speaks disparagingly of people 'who have seen Mr. Bentley's drawings, and
think to compliment him by mistaking them for prints.'

Beckford inquired about this volume in a letter to Bohn, 13 June 1842
(letters now WSL); Bohn replied on 16 June: '[It is] beautiful old morocco.
The drawings are in pen and ink, so exactly like the engravings that I
had to look pretty closely to satisfy myself. No doubt they will fetch

£10.10.0, but perhaps it will fetch more than double as there is no fixing its value.' Beckford replied that he would think the Gray dear at £15.15.0, and instructed Bohn to let it drop should it be run up.

3699 GRAY, THOMAS

Elegia Inglese sopra un Cimitero Campestre. Translated by G. Torelli. Parma, Bodoni, 1793. 4to.

Red morocco. BP of HW as Lord Orford. Press-mark M. Not in MC.
SH SALE, vii.51 (with his *Poems*), to Lilly, £3 [London, 1043]; Pickering, July 1844, to the British Museum.

☞ Note on the fly-leaf: 'From Strawberry Hill Sale, 2–2–0.'

3700 GRAY, THOMAS

Poems. Parma, Bodoni, 1793. 4to.

'Morocco.' Not in MC.
SH SALE, vii.51 (with his *Elegy* in Italian), to Lilly, £3. [London, 1043]

3701 LAVATER, JOHANN CASPAR

Essais sur la physiognomonie. The Hague, 1781–7. Three volumes, 4to.

Not in MC.
SH SALE, vii.61, to Lilly, £1.11.6. [London, 1080]

☞ The work was completed by a fourth volume published in 1803.

3702 [PINKERTON, JOHN]

Medallic history of England to the Revolution. London, 1790. Imperial 4to.

Etruscan calf, rebacked. BP² later state. Press-mark M. Not in MC.
SH SALE, vii.60, to H. G. Bohn, £3.5.0 [London, 1020]; presumably the copy sold at Sotheby's, 5 July 1883 (Beckford Sale, Part 3), lot 782, to Nattali & Bond, £2.12.0; Dulau, August 1935, to WSL, £9.10.0.

☞ Pinkerton's work was based on Snelling's *English Medals*, 1776.
Bohn wrote to Beckford on 17 March 1842 (letters now WSL) that this copy was 'fine paper, Etruscan calf, by Edwards of Halifax, perhaps £3.3.0.' He seems to have persuaded Beckford to take it, although Beckford replied on 18 June that he had not 'the slightest wish' for it.

ROSCOE, WILLIAM   3703

Life of Lorenzo de' Medici, called the Magnificent. Liverpool, 1795.
    Two volumes, 4to.

Bound in calf, Etruscan style, by Edwards, with HW's arms as Lord
Orford on sides. Press-mark M in both volumes. Bookplate of Horatio Walpole, 4th Earl of Orford of the new creation.

    SH SALE, vii.50, to Thorpe, £5.10.0 [London, 1054]; owned by Mrs. Colin
Davy, Heckfield Place, Basingstoke. Christie's, 17 December 1957 (Mrs.
Davy's Sale), lot 69, to Maggs for WSL, £75.

    ☞ A note by Kirgate says 'Bound under the direction of Mr. Edwards,
Pallmall.' Bound in the 2d volume is Roscoe's presentation letter, 9 February 1796; HW thanked Roscoe for the first volume 4 April 1795, but
Roscoe had sent sample sheets to HW somewhat earlier (he began printing
it in 1793).

PRESS N

VERTUE, GEORGE   3704

Collection of Notebooks. MS. 38 volumes, folio, 4to, and 8vo.

    Now rebound in brown morocco, with HW's BP and his notes of pur-
chase from Vertue's widow, 22 August 1758. (Most were originally in
vellum or in boards.) Not in MC.

    SH SALE, vii.63, to Thorpe, £26.10.0. [By error, the printed price list
assigns this to Rodd, corrected in the London Sale, 1110.]

    ☞ Of these, 36 volumes were offered in Thorpe's Catalogue of MSS for
1842–3, lots 388, 524–48, 564, and 567; Thorpe offered 31 volumes in one
lot in 1844 and 1848, for £130; these 31 volumes were sold at Puttick's, 9
June 1859 (Dawson Turner Sale), lot 517, to Boone for the British Museum, £45. Other volumes acquired separately by the British Museum are:
Thorpe's lot 528, sold at Sotheby's, 26 July 1855 (Charles Meigh Sale),
lot 1807, to Boone for the B.M., £4.12.0; lot 535, sold at Puttick's, 14 May
1857 (Miscellaneous Sale), lot 765, to Boone for the B.M., £1.1.0; lot
526, sold at Sotheby's, 19 March 1852 (Thorpe Sale), lot 226, to the
B.M. One volume not found in Thorpe, containing lists of paintings and
tapestries, and a list of pictures at Windsor written by the Prince of Wales,
was sold at Puttick's, 9 November 1852 (Hillier Sale), lot 212, to the
B.M.; and one volume listed in the London Sale was missing at that time,
according to Sir Frederic Madden's note, to make a total of 38.

    Thorpe's lots 530 and 533 are at Nostell Priory, and have been printed in
the Walpole Society's 30th volume.

Not listed in the London Sale but offered in Thorpe's Catalogue for 1844, lot 57, is a *Catalogue of the pictures and rarities which were kept at St. James's . . . removed by His Majesty's command to Whitehall . . . as also other pictures, medals, aggats . . . ; a second book, or Catalogue of the King's statues . . . limn'd pieces and pictures*, in folio. Although the transcriber was not named by Thorpe, this MS was probably Vertue's transcript of Van Der Dort's original; it is probably the transcript now in the Royal Library at Windsor.

Thorpe offered a few other Vertue MSS, perhaps the 'several MS books collected and marked by G. Vertue' in lot 1110, and these presumably explain why vii.63 counts 52 volumes instead of 38. Thorpe may also have sold some before he prepared his SH Catalogue. Of the MSS now in the British Museum from this collection, 32 are listed in the Walpole Society's 18th volume, and three omitted there are listed in the Walpole Society's 3d volume.

One MS perhaps sold with this collection, HW's *Catalogue of Sir Robert Walpole's Pictures*, 1736, is in the Morgan Library. Hilliard's *Arte of Limning*, 1624, now at the University of Edinburgh, was sold in the Glass Closet, vi.122, not in this collection.

Not sold with the Vertue MSS, but in the portfolio of materials concerning the *Anecdotes*, listed under No. 2534 *above*, are some miscellaneous notes by Vertue; these are printed in the Walpole Society's 30th volume.

PRESS O

In Press O were shelved some rather miscellaneous books of prints and historical MSS, in small folio or in quarto, books of wood-cuts, and several books about painting and engraving (Basan, De Caus, Heineken, Papillon). Another group in Press O included books presented to HW and several editions of his own *Castle of Otranto*.

3705 BASAN, PIERRE FRANÇOIS

Dictionnaire des graveurs anciens et modernes. The 2d edition. Paris, 1789. Two volumes, 8vo.

Red morocco, attributed to Roger Payne. BP of HW as Lord Orford, type 1. Press-mark O. Not in MC. Book-label of Charles Butler of Warren Wood, Hatfield.

SH SALE, vii.78, to Smith, £1.19.0 [London, 1145]; Sotheby's, 5 April

1911 (Charles Butler Sale), lot 123, to Rimell, £4; Maggs, December 1954 (from the Rauch Sale at Geneva, 1 December, lot 7), to WSL, £12.

☞ A few notes by HW, with short lists of passages interesting to him. A copy of the 1st edition was in Press B.4 in the Main Library, No. 290 *above*.

BELOE, WILLIAM   3706

The Attic nights of Aulus Gellius. London, 1795. Three volumes, 8vo.

'Red morocco.' Not in MC.
SH SALE, vii.77, to H. G. Bohn for William Beckford, £4.10.0 [London, 1031]; Sotheby's, 1 July 1882 (Beckford Sale, Part 1), lot 477, to Quaritch, £6.6.0.

☞ Bohn reported to Beckford, 16 June 1842 (letters now WSL): 'Beloe's Aulus Gellius, Kalthoeber, *very good*; £3.3.0 or more.'

[BOOTHBY, Sir BROOKE]   3707

Sorrows sacred to the memory of Penelope. London, Bulmer, 1796. Folio.

'Blue morocco by Hayday, with BP.' Not in MC.
SH SALE, vii.70, to Rodd, 13/– [London, 1035]; Sotheby's, 16 May 1848 (Eyton Sale), lot 277, to Pickering, 19/–; Sotheby's, 23 March 1868 (B. G. Windus Sale), lot 262.

CAUS, SALOMON DE   3708

La Perspective, avec la raison des ombres et miroirs. London, 1612. Folio.

Not in MC.
SH SALE, vii.67, to Evans, 11/–. [London, 958]

☞ Although HW seems not to have acquired his copy until after 1763, he described the volume accurately in his *Anecdotes*, from Vertue's note-book. (*See* the Walpole Society's 26th volume, p. 80.)
William Beckford inquired of Bohn about lot 958, on 13 June and again on 18 June (letters now WSL); but he seems to have elicited no response from Bohn.

3709 FERDINAND IV, King of the Two Sicilies

Interprétation des peintures dessinées sur un service de table, travaillé d'après la Cosse, dans la Royal Fabrique de Porcellaine, par ordre de Sa Majesté le Roi des Deux Siciles. Naples, 1787. 4to.

Not in MC.

SH SALE, vii.72, to Strong, £1.7.0. [London, 1130]

3710 FERRERO DI LAVRIANO, FRANCESCO MARIA

Augustae regiaeque Sabaudiae domus arbor gentilitia. Turin, 1702. Folio.

Not in MC.

SH SALE, vii.66, to E. W. Martin, Esq., 16/–. [London, 590]

☞ Perhaps too late to reach Bohn, William Beckford wrote on 17 June 1842 that this was a book he wanted. (Letters now WSL)

3711 GOLDSMITH, OLIVER

Poems by Goldsmith and Parnell. Wood-cuts by Bewick. London, Bulmer, 1795. 4to.

'Green morocco by Hayday, with BP.' Not in MC.

SH SALE, vii.70 (with Somerville), to Rodd, 18/– [London, 1036]; Sotheby's, 17 May 1848 (Eyton Sale), lot 647, to Sotheran, £1.8.0.

3712 [HEINEKEN, CARL HEINRICH VON]

Idée générale d'une collection complette d'estampes. Leipzig and Vienna, 1771. 8vo.

Not in MC.

SH SALE, vii.78, to Lilly, £1.5.0. [London, 1146]

☞ Other copies were in B.4, No. 299 *above,* and in Press Q in the Library in the Offices, No. 3105 *above.*

3713 HENRY VII, King of England

Description of the coronation of Henry VII and his Queen, with other regulations and ceremonies. MS, early 16th century. Folio.

'Calf.' Not in MC.

SH SALE, vii.73, to Rodd, £3.7.6 [London, 1118]; offered in Thorpe's Catalogue of MSS for 1842, lot 210, for £15.15.0.

☞ 'Notes by HW.' He purchased this at the sale of John Ives's library, 5 March 1777, lot 465, for £3.3.0. At some later date he wrote a note in his

own copy of his *Historic Doubts* (1771), now WSL: 'I have an account of the Coronation of Henry VII's Queen which I bought at the sale of Mr. Ives in 1777. . . .'

HODGES, WILLIAM, Painter   3714

Travels in India during the years 1780–3. London, 1793. 4to.

'Uncut.' Not in MC.

SH SALE, vii.71, to Captain Leckie [London, 968]; Puttick, 14 January 1867 (Leckie Sale), lot 261, to Westell.

HOLBEIN, HANS   3715

The Dances of Death, through the various stages of human life. Engraved by David Deuchar. Edinburgh, 1788. Small 4to.

Old mottled calf, rebacked. With BP as Lord Orford, type 2. (BP² later state, also inserted.) Bookplate of William Henry Fosdick.

SH SALE, vii.79, to Cribb, King Street, 11/– [London, 1182]; Mrs. K. T. Riggs, daughter of Mr. Fosdick, of Athens, Georgia, October 1947, to WSL, $50.

☞ Presentation inscription to HW, 31 March 1796, by Sir James Colquhoun, Bart. His covering letter, tipped in by HW, was removed by WSL; in it, Sir James explained that the book was an admirable specimen of Scots engraving and binding; he did not praise the rather dull printing, but instead enclosed MacNeill's *Scotland's Skaith* as a specimen of Scots printing. (MacNeill was in Press H.2, No. 1357 *above*.) When HW wrote to thank Sir James, 3 May 1796, he excused his delay by a dangerous fit of the gout.

HOLBEIN, HANS   3716

Oeuvre de Jean Holbein, ou recueil de gravures. Edited by Chrétien de Méchel. Basel, 1780. Three parts in one volume, small folio.

Not in MC.

SH SALE, vii.68, to Lilly, £1.11.0. [London, 1184]

☞ Apparently HW's set lacked the fourth part: his copy is recorded as 'the three parts complete.'

HOLBEIN, HANS   3717

Todten-tanz. Engraved by Matthew Merian. Frankfurt, [1633?] 4to.

Not in MC.

SH SALE, vii.79, to H. G. Bohn, 14/– [London, 1183]; offered in Bohn's Catalogue for 1847 (Prints), p. 125, for £1.10.0.

☞ According to Bohn's description, this volume had several leaves of MS notes by Vertue, and a note by HW.

3718 KNIGHT, ELLIS CORNELIA

Marcus Flaminius. London, 1792. Two volumes, 8vo.

'Red morocco.' Not in MC.

SH SALE, vii.77, to Strong, £1.1.0 [London, 1032]; offered in Strong's Catalogue for 1843, lot 868, for £1.8.0.

☞ This historical novel told in letters was dedicated to HW.

3719 LAVENHAM CHURCH

Specimens of Gothic ornaments selected from the Parish Church of Lavenham, in Suffolk. Forty plates by Isaac Taylor. London, 1796. 4to.

Not in MC.

SH SALE, vii.71, to Strong, 8/–. [London, 959]

3720 MEDICI FAMILY

Secret history of the House of Medici. MS. Folio.

'Vellum.' Not in MC.

SH SALE, vii.65, to Pickering, £1.1.0. [London, 1100]

☞ The catalogue of the London Sale says this was in French, and adds: '*Vide* Lord Orford's note on this production at p. 150.'

3721 MILLIN, AUBIN LOUIS

Antiquités nationales . . . de l'empire français. Paris, 1790. Four volumes, 4to.

Not in MC.

SH SALE, vii.75, to George Corner, Esq., £1.11.6. [London, 996]

☞ A fifth volume was published in 1799. In his 'Book of Materials,' in 1792, HW made a note of an epitaph, on a subject like that of his *Mysterious Mother,* in Millin's 2d volume.

3722 PAPILLON, JEAN BAPTISTE MICHEL

Traité historique et pratique de la gravure en bois. Paris, 1766. Three parts in two volumes, 8vo.

Original mottled calf, rebacked. BP² later state. Press-mark O.

SH SALE, vii.78, to Smith, 15/– [London, 1144]; Hodgson, 26 March 1929

(Miscellaneous Sale), lot 122, to Maggs, £11.10.0; Maggs, September 1931, to WSL, £11.7.0.

☞ Monogram initials inked in by HW inside the cover, and he made several notes and markings in the text. He noted the interest of the book for Holbein's engravings in his 'Book of Materials,' *ca.* 1776; this was perhaps the date of acquisition, with the BP inserted after 1780. In his own Holbein (sold in the Glass Closet, No. 2398 *above*), he wrote a reference to Papillon, and in Papillon (where editions of the Holbein are dated 1539 and 1543), he noted from his own copy that another edition is dated 1547.

PARKINSON, JOHN · 3723

Paradisi in sole, Paradisus terrestris, or a Garden of . . . flowers. London, 1629. Folio.

Not in MC.

SH SALE, vii.67, to Thorne. [London, 1139]

☞ There is a later issue, and a 2d edition, but the original edition seems likely to be what HW had. The work contains 110 full-page wood-cuts.

SOMERVILLE, WILLIAM · 3724

The Chase, a poem. Wood-cuts by Bewick. London, Bulmer, 1796. 4to.

Not in MC.

SH SALE, vii.70 (with Goldsmith), to Rodd, 18/–. [London, 1036]

☞ Possibly this copy, green morocco by Hayday, was in the Eyton Sale in 1848, lot 1401, to Pickering, £1.7.0.

TETIUS, HIERONYMUS · 3725

Aedes Barberinae ad Quirinalem . . . descriptae. Rome, 1642. Folio.

'Vellum.' Not in MC.

SH SALE, vii.69, to H. G. Bohn, 9/– [London, 1005]; offered in Bohn's Catalogue for 1847 (Prints), p. 70, for 18/–.

☞ In his Introduction to his *Aedes Walpolianae,* HW mentions this work as one of his models; if he owned a copy as early as 1747, it was perhaps kept in the Glass Closet in 1763 and so not catalogued.

THYNNE, FRANCIS · 3726

The plea betweene the advocate and the ant'advocate, concerning the Bathe and Bacheler Knights, 1605. MS. Folio.

Morocco, with arms of James I on the sides, rebacked. BP² early state.

Press-mark O.8 (revealed when the end-paper was lifted in 1948). Not in MC.

SH SALE, vii.64, to the British Museum, £12.12.0 [London, 1108]; now Add. MS. 12530.

☞ Note by HW: 'A present from Sir Joseph Banks, President of the Royal Society, 1786.' By a misprint the author was catalogued in 1842 as Francis Heyme.

Sir Frederic Madden in his Diary wrote of this work that he 'attended the sale of Walpole's MSS (included with his prints) at Robins's rooms and bought Thynne's account of the privileges of the Knights of the Bath, the presentation copy to King James I, to whom the book is dedicated.' He added: 'The Vertue papers and other MSS fell into the hands of the book-sellers.'

3727 VERHEIDEN, JACOBUS

Praestantium aliquot theologorum, qui Rom. Antichristum praecipuè oppugnarunt, Effigies. Engravings by Hondius. The Hague, 1602. Small folio.

Old blind-stamped calf with clasps, rebacked, with initials G K and M over a coronet stamped in gold. BP² later state. Press-mark O.14 above press-mark of an earlier owner. Not in MC. Signatures of A. Cant and Philip Bliss. Bookplate of James P. R. Lyell.

SH SALE, vii.74, to Smith, Lisle-Street, 10/– [London, 587]; note by Philip Bliss: 'Purchased for H. J. B. at the SH SALE, given me by H. J. B. Esq. F. R. S. &c. &c. March 15, 1847'; Sotheby's, 14 July 1858 (Bliss Sale, Part 1), lot 4511, to Boone, £3.5.0; Sotheby's, 1 May 1884 (Gosford Sale), lot 3029, to Stibbs, £1.10.0; Sotheby's, 14 July 1915 (Ginsburg Sale), lot 924, 13/–; Swift, July 1945, to WSL, £36.

☞ The earliest mark of ownership, early 17th century, is an inscription 'Ex libris A. Cant dono M. Gilberti Keith,' i.e. Gilbert Keith, son of George Keith, fourth Earl Marischal, gave the book to Andrew Cant (1590?–1663), the Aberdeen reformer; and the stamp on the binding is presumably that of the Earl Marischal. The purchaser in 1842, H. J. B., was Henry James Brooke (1771–1857), the mineralogist.

Another copy of Verheiden was bound with Holland's *Herωologia* in Press Q in the Round Tower, No. 3783 *below*.

3728 WALPOLE, HORACE

Il Castello di Otranto. Translated by Jean Sivrac. London, 1795. Large paper copy, royal 8vo.

Original straight-grained red morocco by Charles Hering. With BP of

HW as Lord Orford, type 2. Press-mark O.21. Not in MC. Inserted inside cover is HW's BP² early state. Anonymous bookplate (motto: Festina lente).

SH SALE, vii.76 (with Bodoni edition), to Payne & Foss, £1.11.6 [London, 1030]; probably the copy offered by Payne & Foss in 1845 for £2.2.0; American Art–Anderson, 14 October 1931 (Miscellaneous Sale), lot 201, $12; James F. Drake, May 1951, to WSL, $75.

☞ The plates are colored. At the end is pasted a slip in Kirgate's hand: 'Miss Clark, niece of Sir Charles Ratcliffe, made the drawings for the prints to the Castle of Otranto.' The binding ticket, C. Hering, 10 St. Martin Street, is of interest: this volume was bound probably in 1795 and not later than 1796, and is therefore one of the earliest identifiable bindings by Hering.

WALPOLE, HORACE   3729

The Castle of Otranto. The 6th edition. Parma, Bodoni, 1791. 4to.

Rebound in red morocco by C. Lewis, with crest of Lord Gosford on the sides. With BP of HW as Lord Orford, type 1, on half-title. Not in MC. Bookplates of Robert Hoe, and of the Earl of Cromer, 1912.

SH SALE, vii.76 (with Italian translation of 1795), to Payne & Foss, £1.11.6 [London, 1030]; Puttick, 1 May 1884 (Gosford Sale), lot 3071, to Harvey, £7; Christie's, 1 April 1897 (Reginald Cholmondeley Sale), lot 114, to Quaritch, £11.5.0; thence to John W. Ford, who owned this copy in 1905; Sotheby's, 21 May 1909 (Miscellaneous Sale), lot 362, to B. F. Stevens, £15.5.0; Anderson, 19 January 1912 (Hoe Sale, Part 2), lot 3420, $60; Sotheby's, 10 December 1913 (Hoe Books), lot 173, to Edwards, £7; thence to the Earl of Cromer; Edwards, March 1937, to WSL, £20.

☞ Bound in are four drawings by Bertie Greatheed, a letter by HW (in Kirgate's hand, with signature 'Orford'), and a letter from Edwards, the publisher. There are also some notes and extracts in the hand of J. W. Ford.

WALPOLE, HORACE   3730

The Castle of Otranto. Four different editions. 8vo.

Not in MC.

SH SALE, vii.80, to H. G. Bohn. [London, 1029]

☞ This lot may have included a copy of the Berlin edition of 1794, described in Press X, No. 3391 *above*; the edition of 1782, bound in green morocco with Jephson's *Count of Narbonne*, described in *Bibliography of HW*, p. 56, now owned by Mrs. Davy of Heckfield; and possibly a copy of the 2d edition, calf with HW's BP, now owned by Mr. Roger Senhouse. And a copy, rebound in blue morocco for George Daniel, of Jeffery's edition of 1796, now at Heckfield, was no doubt in this lot.

Included in this lot were 'Histoire de Gil Blas, tome premier, fine plates,' perhaps the first volume of a fine edition published in Paris in 1796; one *non*-Walpolian book; and 'a small vol. in manuscript,' possibly the small quarto sold London, 1119: 'A small volume on religious topics, in the hand-writing of Sir Kenelm Digby, ... 1636.'

PRESS P

Press P contained miscellaneous books of prints in quarto and folio. They were chiefly historical and almost all were foreign works. These books were originally shelved in Press B in the Main Library.

3731 BACCO, ENRICO

Effigie di tutti i re che han dominato il reame di Napoli. Naples, 1602. Folio.

Not in MC.

SH SALE, vii.94, to Rodd [London, 586]; probably the copy offered, but not identified as HW's, in Rodd's Catalogue for 1847, Part 3 (Arts and Sciences), lot 2547, for 16/–.

☞ Dated 1698 in the sale catalogue, but the description seems to fit only this book: 'Effigies of the Kings of Naples, commencing with Roger the Norman, wood cuts of masterly execution.'

William Beckford wrote to Bohn on 17 June 1842 that this was a book he wanted; but his letter perhaps did not reach Bohn in time. (Letter now WSL)

3732 BARBUO, SCIPIO

Sommario delle vite de' Duchi di Milano. Venice, 1574. Small folio.

Bound in 18th-century calf. BP¹. Press-mark B.2.27, altered in book to P.26.

SH SALE, vii.88, to H. G. Bohn [London, 1089]; Sotheby's, 1 July 1882 (Beckford Sale, Part 1), lot 569, to Rimell, £1.18.0; Blackwell, October 1941, to WSL, 15/–.

3733 BARTOLI, PIETRO SANTI

Le antiche lucerne sepolcrali figurate, raccolta dalle cave e grotte di Roma. Edited by Bellori. Rome, 1729. Folio.

'Vellum.' Press-mark B.2.14 in MC; moved to the Round Tower.

SH SALE, vii.81 (with his *Pitture Antiche*), to Strong, £1.1.0 [London, 997]; offered in Strong's Catalogue for 1843, lot 73, for £1.8.0.

BARTOLI, PIETRO SANTI   3734

Le pitture antiche del sepolcro de' Nasonii. Edited by Bellori, with
engravings by Bartoli. Rome, 1702. Folio.

Vellum. BP[1]. Press-mark B.2.15, altered in book to O.9 and then to P.9.
Signature of J. A. Symonds.

SH SALE, vii.81 (with his *Antiche Lucerne*), to Strong, £1.1.0 [London,
997]; owned by Mr. William von Metz, of Oakland, California. David
Magee, March 1968, to WSL, $228.

BIE, JACQUES DE   3735

Les vrais portraits des Rois de France. Paris, 1634. Folio.

Press-mark B.2.7 in MC; moved to the Round Tower.

SH SALE, vii.83, to Lilly. [London, 589]

☞ William Beckford must have expressed interest in this volume,
because William Smith, the dealer (letters now WSL), listed it on 14 April
as one of the items he would watch for.

BOXHORN, MARCUS ZUERIUS   3736

Monumenta illustrium virorum, et elogia. Amsterdam, 1638. Folio.

'Vellum.' Press-mark B.2.38 in MC; moved to the Round Tower.

SH SALE, vii.91, to Captain Leckie, 5/– [London, 1003]; Puttick, 14
January 1867 (Leckie Sale), to Parsons, 5/–.

BRY, JOHANN THEODOR DE   3737

Florilegium novum. Eighty-four plates. [Oppenheim] 1612. Folio.

Rebound in half calf in the late 19th century. BP[1]. Press-mark B.2.22 in
MC; moved to the Round Tower. Press-mark in the Round Tower, P.20,
recorded in pencil on the new end-paper. Collation note by H. B. C.

SH SALE, vii.91, to Thorne [London, 1139]; Sotheby's, 23 November
1908 (Miscellaneous Sale), lot 289, to Stow, £2.4.0; since 1908 in the Wellcome Historical Medical Library.

CANINI, GIOVANNI ANGELO   3738

Iconografia. Paris, 1669. Folio.

'Calf.' Press-mark B.2.13 in MC; moved to the Round Tower.

SH SALE, vii.83, to Captain Leckie, 6/– [London, 588]; Puttick, 14
January 1867 (Leckie Sale), to Westell, 6/6.

☞ Engravings of ancient philosophers and poets by Étienne Picart.

3739 CAOURSIN, GULIELMUS

Obsidionis Rhodie urbis descriptio. Ulm, 1496. Folio.

Old red morocco, with HW's BP² early state. Press-mark B.2.29, altered in the book to P.25. Bookplate and notes of George Dunn.

SH SALE, vii.92, to Evans, £2.5.0 [London, 986]; offered in Lilly's Catalogue for 1863, for £4.14.6; Sotheby's, 13 June 1887 (Crawford Sale, Part 1), lot 614, to Jones, £21.10.0; Sotheby's, 28 March 1895 (Gennadius Sale), lot 716, to Quaritch, £30; offered by Quaritch in Catalogue 159 (1896), lot 39, for £36; Sotheby's, 6 December 1898 (William Morris Sale), lot 340, to Hazlitt, £31.10.0; Sotheby's, 3 February 1914 (George Dunn Sale, Part 2), lot 914, to Leighton, £70; Sotheby's, 14 November 1918 (Leighton stock), lot 199, to Quaritch, £61; now in the Earl of Crawford's library, having been bought by his father, the 27th Earl. He noted that the book was 'feliciter redemptus, 1918.'

3740 FIRMANUS, HANNIBAL ADAMUS

Seminarii Romani Pallas purpurata. Rome, 1659. Folio.

'Calf.' Press-mark B.2.9 in MC; moved to the Round Tower.

SH SALE, vii.82, to Lilly [London, 589]; offered in Bohn's Catalogue for 1847 (Prints), p. 174, for 18/–.

☞ Engravings of the Cardinals. To a note in his *Aedes Walpolianae*, HW added in the 2d edition (p. 57) a reference to Firmanus.

3741 FRANCIS, Duke of Anjou, and of Alençon

La joyeuse et magnifique entrée de Monseigneur Françoys fils de France . . . Duc de Brabant en sa très-renommée ville d'Anvers. Antwerp, 1582. Folio.

'Vellum, with HW's BP.' Not in MC.

SH SALE, vii.94, to H. G. Bohn [London, 1092]; Sotheby's, 12 July 1882 (Beckford Sale, Part 1), lot 2824, to Quaritch, £7.15.0; offered by Quaritch in January 1885, when it was described as lacking one plate, for £2.10.0.

☞ Another copy was in Press L in the Round Tower, No. 3680 *above*.

3742 GODEFROY, FRANÇOIS

Recueil d'estampes représentant les différents évènemens de la Guerre qui a procuré l'Indépendance aux États-Unis de l'Amerique. Paris [1783]. 4to.

'With HW's BP.' Not in MC.

SH SALE, vii.95, to Evans [London, 1088]; offered in Rodd's Catalogue
[1843?], for £1.1.0.

☞ Sixteen plates engraved by Nicolas Ponce and Godefroy.

GORI, ANTONIO FRANCESCO   3743
*Monumentum sive Columbarium libertorum et servorum Liviae
Augustae et Caesarum.* Florence, 1727. Folio.
   'Vellum, with HW's BP and signature, 1741.' Press-mark B.2.11 in MC;
moved to the Round Tower.
   SH SALE, vii.81, to H. G. Bohn, 13/– [London, 998]; offered in Bohn's
Catalogue for 1847 (Prints), p. 118, for £1.8.0.

GRAZIOLI, PIETRO   3744
De praeclaris Mediolani aedificiis . . . dissertatio. Milan, 1735. 4to.
   Press-mark B.3.21 in MC; moved to the Round Tower.
   SH SALE, vii.90 (with Orsini Rosenberg and Suarès), to H. G. Bohn, £1
[London, 985]; a copy in old calf gilt, not identified as HW's, was sold
Sotheby's, 12 December 1882 (Beckford Sale, Part 2), lot 350, to Quaritch,
£1.2.0.

[GRIGNETTE, BENIGNE]   3745
*Les armes triomphantes de Son Altesse, Monseigneur, le duc d'Esper-
non.* Dijon, 1656. Folio.
   Red morocco by Clarke & Bedford. BP¹. Press-mark B.2.23 in MC; moved
to the Round Tower.
   SH SALE, vii.91, to H. G. Bohn for Beckford [London, 1092]; Sotheby's,
30 November 1883 (Beckford Sale, Part 4), lot 1041, to Quaritch, £9.12.0;
Davis & Orioli, July 1953, to WSL, £65.

HELMAN, ISIDORE STANISLAUS   3746
Abrégé historique des principaux traits de la vie de Confucius. [Paris,
1785?] 4to.
   'French calf.' Not in MC.
   SH SALE, vii.84, to H. G. Bohn. [London, 1087]

HELMAN, ISIDORE STANISLAUS   3747
Faits mémorables des Empereurs de la Chine. Paris, 1788. 4to.
   'French calf.' Not in MC.

SH SALE, vii.84, to H. G. Bohn [London, 1087]; the two volumes offered in Bohn's Catalogue for 1847 (Prints), p. 84, for £1.10.0.

3748 LA CHAUSSE, MICHEL ANGE DE

Le gemme antiche. Rome, 1700. 4to.

Vellum. BP[1]. Signature: Hor. Walpole 1740. Press-mark B.3.13, altered to P.31. Name on the fly-leaf: T. Jones, 1873.

SH SALE, vii.86, to Strong [London, 1022]; English, 18 October 1849 (Brockley Hall Sale), lot 666; Goodspeed, July 1940, to WSL, $35.

☞ A few markings and a pencilled sketch may be by HW.

3749 LA CHAUSSE, MICHEL ANGE DE

Romanum Museum, sive thesaurus eruditae antiquitatis. Rome, 1690. Folio.

Press-mark B.2.17 in MC; moved to the Round Tower.

SH SALE, vii.86, to Strong. [London, 1022]

3750 LYONNET, PIERRE

Traité anatomique de la Chenille. The Hague, 1760. 4to.

Original calf, rebacked. BP[2] early state. Press-mark B.4.27 (entered by HW), altered in book by Kirgate to P.24. Bookplate of George Livingston Nichols.

SH SALE, vii.88, to Thorne [London, 1139]; Carnegie Book Shop, July 1951, to WSL, $125.

☞ Note by HW on the fly-leaf: 'This book was given to me by my brother Sr Edward Walpole. It is said that the author, not being content with any artists as capable of executing so laborious and nice a work, applied himself to the art, and arrived at that unparalleled perfection, of which the following plates are samples.'

3751 MAROT, JEAN

Recueil des plans, profiles, et élévations des plusieurs palais, chasteaux, églises, sépultures, grotes, et hostels bâtis dans Paris. [Paris, n.d.] 4to.

'Old calf, with HW's BP.' Press-mark B.3.11 in MC; moved to the Round Tower.

SH SALE, vii.84, to Strong [London, 954]; Sotheby's, 16 December 1903 (Walter Sneyd Sale), lot 488, to Belin, £3.3.0.

MORRIS, ROBERT   3752

Rural architecture. London, 1750. 4to.

Press-mark B.3.3 in MC; moved to the Round Tower.

SH SALE, vii.95, to Evans. [London, 955]

☞ The name of HW is listed among the subscribers, 'Horace Walpole, Esq.'

ORSINI ROSENBERG, JUSTINE, Countess   3753

Alticchiero, par Made. J. W. C. D. R. Padua, 1787. 4to.

Calf by Clarke & Bedford, rebacked. BP² later state. Not in MC.

SH SALE, vii.90 (with Grazioli and Suarès), to H. G. Bohn, £1 [London, 985]; Sotheby's, 9 July 1883 (Beckford Sale, Part 3), lot 1494, to Rimell, 7/–; in the Avery Library at Columbia University. By exchange to Yale for the Lewis Walpole Collection, May 1967.

☞ The writer is identified on the title-page by HW. The initials stand for Justine Wynne Comtesse de Rosenberg.

PALAZZI, GIOVANNI   3754

Fasti ducales. Venice, 1696. 4to.

Press-mark B.3.8 in MC; moved to the Round Tower.

SH SALE, vii.88, to H. G. Bohn [London, 1089]; offered in Bohn's Catalogue for 1847 (Prints), p. 98, for 15/–.

PASSERI, GIOVANNI BATTISTA   3755

Lucernae fictiles Musei Passerii. Pisa, 1739. Folio.

Vellum. BP¹. Press-mark B.2.8, altered in the book to O.8 and then to P.8. Bookplates of R. S. Williams and John Camp Williams.

SH SALE, vii.93, to H. G. Bohn, 19/– [London, 1004]; offered in Bohn's Catalogue for 1847 (Prints), p. 163, for £1.5.0; American Art–Anderson, 8 November 1929 (Williams Sale, Part 2), lot 992; Dawson's, December 1932, to WSL, $20.

☞ Two additional volumes were published, 1743–51, after HW had returned to England.

Persepolis illustrata: or, an account of the ancient and royal palace 3756
of Persepolis in Persia. London, 1739. Folio.

Press-mark B.2.3 in MC; moved to the Round Tower.

SH SALE, vii.82, to Captain Leckie, 8/– [London, 964]; Puttick, 14 January 1867 (Leckie Sale), lot 270, to Westell, 2/–.

☞ With 21 plates; published by Harding.

3757 Piccolomini Museum

Engravings of ancient gems, &c. in the Museo Piccolomini. [Rome, 1710?] 4to.

'Vellum.' Press-mark B.3.15 in MC; moved to the Round Tower.

SH SALE, vii.86, to Strong. [Not listed separately in London Sale but perhaps included in lot 1022.] Offered in Strong's Catalogue for 1843, lot 1076, for 10/6.

3758 Pompadour, Jeanne Antoinette Poisson Le Normand d'Etioles, Marquise de

Suite d'estampes gravées, par Madame la Marquise de Pompadour, d'après les pierres gravées de Guay, graveur du Roy. Paris, 1782. 4to.

Original mottled calf. BP² later state. Not in MC. Press-mark P.19.

SH SALE, vii.85, to Lilly [London, 1024]; G. Salet, Paris, May 1956, to WSL, 150,000 fr.

☞ A pencilled note, partially erased, seems to indicate that the book was purchased from Lilly in March 1844.

As early as 13 May 1758 Mann wrote to HW: 'Mme. Pompadour who engraves herself has put this branch of virtù into fashion.'

3759 Santos, Francisco de los

Descripcion breve del Monasterio de San Lorenzo del Escorial. Madrid, 1681. Folio.

Press-mark B.2.28 in MC; moved to the Round Tower.

SH SALE, vii.93, to Rodd. [London, 965]

☞ A copy of the English translation by George Thompson of York, *A Description of the Royal Palace and Monastery of St. Laurence called the Escurial,* London, 1760, 4to, bound in calf with HW's arms on sides, is now at Farmington. The binding is certainly original, although the book has been rebacked and the present end-papers are perhaps later. Mr. John K. Egan of Lake Elmo, Minnesota, bought it many years ago from Stevens & Brown; Mr. Egan, March 1955, to WSL, by exchange. There is now no press-mark; it was perhaps in the Glass Closet, but it does not appear in the catalogues of the sale unless it was in one of the unidentified lots. The likeliest explanation may be that HW lent or gave it to a friend.

The long list of subscribers includes Garrick, Hanway, Horace Mann, Sterne, Voltaire, and Lord Walpole, but not HW.

SGRILLI, BERNARDO SANSONE   3760

Descrizione della regia villa, fontane, e fabbriche di Pratolino. Engravings by Stefano della Bella. Florence, 1742. Folio.

> Press-mark B.2.19 in MC; moved to the Round Tower.
> SH SALE, vii.94, to Adamson. Not found in the London Sale.

SPILSBURY, JOHN   3761

A collection of fifty prints from antique gems. London, 1785. 4to.

> Not in MC.
> SH SALE, vii.85, to Lilly. [London, 1024]

STOSCH, PHILIPP VON, Baron   3762

*Pierres antiques gravées sur lesquelles les graveurs ont mis leurs
noms, dessinées et gravées par Bernard Picart.* Amsterdam, 1724.
Folio.

> Bound in vellum, with new end-papers. BP[1]. Signature on the fly-leaf:
> H. Walpole. Press-mark B.2.2 in MC; moved to the Round Tower.
> SH SALE, vii.89, to Evans, Great Queen Street, 16/– [London, 1025];
> offered in Strong's Catalogue for 1843, lot 1437, for £2.10.0; offered in
> Kerslake's Catalogue for 1848, lot 3344, for £1.16.0; Spurr & Swift,
> August 1934, to WSL, £1.1.0.
>
> ☞ In French and Latin throughout. In his *Description of SH*, 1784, p.
> 67, HW cited the work.

SUARÈS, JOSEPH MARIE   3763

Praenestes antiquae libri duo. Rome, 1655. 4to.

> 'Rebound in half morocco, uncut, with HW's signature, 1740, and BP.'
> Press-mark B.3.22 in MC; moved to the Round Tower.
> SH SALE, vii.90 (with Grazioli and Orsini Rosenberg), to H. G. Bohn, £1
> [London, 985]; offered in Bohn's Catalogue for 1847 (Prints), p. 196, for
> 12/–; Sotheby's, 28 July 1903 (Miscellaneous Sale), lot 259, to E. J. Allen,
> 16/–.

VIGNOLA, GIACOMO BAROZZI DA   3764

Regla de las cinco orderes de Architectura. Madrid, 1651.

> 'Vellum.' Not in MC.
> SH SALE, vii.93, to Evans [London, 955]; Puttick, 14 January 1867
> (Captain Leckie Sale), lot 272, to Parsons, 2/–.

3765 VINCI, LEONARDO DA

Recueil de testes de caractère et de charges, dessinées par Léonard de Vinci et gravées par M. le Cte. de Caylus. Paris, 1730. 4to.

'Calf, with HW's BP.' Press-mark B.3.6 in MC; moved to the Round Tower.

SH SALE, vii.84, to H. G. Bohn [London, 1167]; Sotheby's, 10 July 1882 (Beckford Sale, Part 1), lot 2379, but not identified as HW's, to Quaritch, £2.10.0; offered in Quaritch's General Catalogue, Part VI (1883), lot 10342, for £4; Puttick, 2 April 1891 (Miscellaneous Sale), lot 256, to Salisbury, £1.2.0.

☞ Engraved title, and 60 portraits; published by Mariette.

3766 WEYERMAN, JACOB CAMPO

De levens-beschryvingen der Nederlandsche konst-schilders. The Hague, 1729. 4to.

Press-mark B.3.16 in MC; moved to the Round Tower.

SH SALE, vii.87, to Lilly, £1.15.0. [London, 1151]

☞ With engravings by Houbraken. This work is cited once in HW's *Anecdotes*.

3767 WINCKELMANN, JOHANN JOACHIM

Description des pierres gravées du feu Baron de Stosch. Florence, 1760. 4to.

Press-mark B.3.26 in MC; moved to the Round Tower.

SH SALE, vii.85, to Lilly, £1.18.0. [London, 1023]

PRESS Q

The books shelved in Press Q seem somewhat miscellaneous. They were books of prints, of course, but the unifying principle in Press Q was perhaps only that books of prints and books important to art history were shelved here if they did not seem closely related to the books in any of the other presses.

3768 AMES, JOSEPH

A Collection of initial letters from the beginning of printing. Collected by Ames, and begun in 1733. Folio.

Russia, with SH lot label preserved on spine and largely covered by the lot number of the London Sale. BP² early state. Press-mark D.4.22, altered

in book to Q.7. Bookplates of Joseph Ames and of Ames's friend, T. Barber of Norfolk. Note inside cover: 'J. Hume Campbell from H. Bought at Strawberry Hill sale.'

SH SALE, vii.101, to Sir H. Campbell, Bart., £7.10.0 [London, 1150]; owned by Mrs. Harold Warrender, Gerrard's Cross, Bucks; sold by her through Peter Murray Hill, November 1957, to WSL, £280.

☞ Note by HW on the fly-leaf: 'Bought at Mr. Ames's sale May 13, 1760. 2–12–6. HW.' No other notes by HW, but in his 'Book of Materials,' *ca.* 1760, he noted one error in Ames's 'Collection of initial letters in my possession.' Among many sets of initials, one set was engaved by George Vertue and given by him to Ames in 1737.

AMMAN, JOST   3769

Eygentliche Beschreibung aller Stände auff Erden . . . in Teutsche Reimen gefasset. With woodcuts by Amman. Frankfurt, 1568. 4to.

'Old calf, with royal arms on sides.' Not in MC.

SH SALE, vii.113 (with his *Kunstbüchlin*), to H. G. Bohn, £2.8.0 [London, 1149]; offered in Bohn's Catalogue for 1847 (Prints), p. 185, for £3.3.0; offered in Quaritch's General Catalogue for 1868, lot 11363, for £4.4.0.

☞ Identified in the sale only as a volume 'of Handicraft Operations' by Amman, Frankfurt 1568, but described in Bohn's Catalogue. The verses are by Hans Sachs.

AMMAN, JOST   3770

Kunstbüchlin. Frankfurt, 1599. 4to.

'Red morocco.' Not in MC.

SH SALE, vii.113 (with the preceding volume), to H. G. Bohn, £2.8.0 [London, 1149]; Sotheby's, 29 November 1883 (Beckford Sale, Part 4), lot 695, to B. F. Stevens, £15.

BARLOW, FRANCIS   3771

Severall wayes of hunting, hawking, and fishing, according to the English manner. Twelve plates engraved by Hollar. London, 1671. Oblong 4to.

Not in MC.

SH SALE, vii.110, to Lilly. [Not listed in the London Sale, but perhaps combined with other works of Hollar, lots 807–880]

☞ In his *Anecdotes*, HW mentioned other works by Barlow, but was silent about this volume; doubtless he acquired it later than 1763.

3772 BERNES, Dame JULIANA

The Gentlemans Academie. Or, the Booke of St. Albans. Edited by
    Gervase Markham. London, 1595. 4to.

Not in MC.

SH SALE, vii.109, to Lilly. [London, 1061]

3773 BONARELLI DELLA ROVERE, PROSPERO

Il Solimano, tragedia. Engravings by Callot. Florence, 1619. 4to.

'Calf.' Not in MC.

SH SALE, vii.105, to H. G. Bohn [London, 1147]; offered in Bohn's
Catalogue for 1847 (Prints), p. 80, for 9/–.

3774 BOSSE, ABRAHAM

Traicté des manières de graver en taille-douce. Paris, 1645. 8vo.

Vellum. BP² early state. Press-mark B.4.34, entered in MC by HW ca.
1766; altered in book to Q.28.

SH SALE, vii.113, to H. G. Bohn [London, 1147]; offered in Bohn's
Catalogue for 1847 (Prints), p. 75, for 5/–; sold from the U.S. Patent
Office Library; purchased in a second-hand store in Washington, ca. 1920–
5, by the late Newton M. Perrins of Rochester, New York.

☞ It is tempting to think that HW purchased this at the Cottrell sale,
29 February 1764, lot 1308.

3775 CAESAR, Sir JULIUS

Travelling library of classical authors. Leyden [&c.] 1591–1619. Forty-
    four volumes, 16mo.

Vellum, in a box covered with olive morocco; the names of the authors
engrossed inside the cover. No BP or press-mark in the box. Press-mark
B.7 in MC, the only item above B.6 in 1763; moved to the Round Tower.

SH SALE, vii.98, to Lilly, £11 [London, 1081]; Pickering, September
1842, to the British Museum, £16; now in British Museum.

☞ Purchased by HW at the sale of Sir Julius Caesar's library, December
1757, lot 120.

The collection is divided into three shelves of authors by subject:
(1) Theology and Philosophy; (2) History; (3) Poetry. The volumes are
the small Plantin editions printed about 1600. Pictures of the library may
be seen in W. Y. Fletcher's *English Bookbindings in the British Museum*
(1895), Plates 43–5.

CARLETON, GEORGE, Bishop   3776

A thankful remembrance of Gods mercie. Engravings by Hulsius.
  London, 1630. 4to.

  Not in MC.

  SH SALE, vii.109, to Lilly, 15/– [London, 1064]; perhaps the copy in
vellum, not identified as HW's, offered in Thorpe's Supplement for 1842,
lot 12103, for £1.11.6.

CAUS, SALOMON DE   3777

*Hortus Palatinus a Friderico Rege Boemiae Electore Palatino Heidel-
  bergae exstructus.* Frankfurt, 1620. Folio.

  Old vellum, rebacked. BP² later state. Press-mark Q.8. Not in MC.

  SH SALE, vii.99 [Not recorded in London sale, unless perhaps it is 'one
other' in lot 1139]; Hodgson's, 31 March 1933 (Miscellaneous Sale), lot
576, to Maggs for WSL, £15.10.0.

  ☞ On the fly-leaf is the signature, 'Thomas Carlyle, Esq.' and beneath
is a note in Carlyle's hand in blue crayon: 'Kind gift to me (at Seaforth
Lodge, Augt. 1872) by W. E. Nesfield [architect, 1835–88];—had been
picked up by him at a stall on the Quai d'Orsay, Paris, sevl years before;
—and is now, with many best regards, my poor gift to Louisa Lady Ashburton, who desires farther to possess a *second* bookplate for appending
to the notable first one, wh. appears to have bn *Horace Walpole's.*'

  This book was purchased by HW at Dr. Lort's sale in May 1791, lot 4747,
for 1/–.

CRESSWELL, JOSEPH   3778

Histoire de la vie et ferme constance du Père Henri Valpole. Translated from Spanish. Arras, 1597. 12mo.

  Not in MC.

  SH SALE, vii.112, to Lilly. [London, 1047]

  ☞ The sale catalogue adds to this book a tantalizing 'and 4 other scarce
volumes,' presumably the same as 'and 4 others' in the London Sale, lot
1047. One of them was very probably:

CORNAZANO, ANTONIO. *Sonetti e Canzone.* [Venice, 1502] Small 8vo. Bound
with this is Ludovico Gandini's *Lettione . . . sopra un dubbio, come il
Petrarca non lodasse Laura espressamente dal Naso.* Venice, 1581. This
volume was in the Pinelli Sale, 17 March 1789, lot 2933, sold for 4/6; note
by HW on the fly-leaf: 'From the Pinelli Library 1790. The second tract is
curious!' Bound in early 18th-century vellum; BP² later state; press-

mark Q.36. Bookplates of Edward Cheney, J. Maitland Thomson, and Arthur Kay, and Cheney book-stamp on the cover. Sotheby's, 27 May 1930 (Arthur Kay Sale), lot 200; Davis & Orioli, November 1932, to WSL, £5.13.6.

3779 GAUTIER, SOLOMON

Collection des vues et monumens anciens des sept Provinces Unies. Part I. Engraved by Rademaker. Amsterdam, 1725. 4to.

'Half calf.' Not in MC.

SH SALE, vii.105, to Captain Leckie [London, 968]; Puttick, 14 January 1867 (Leckie Sale), lot 259, to E. Parsons, 1/–.

3780 GOEREE, WILLEM

Inleydingh tot de practijck der algemeene schilder-konst. Amsterdam, 1704. 8vo.

Press-mark B.4.18 in MC; moved to the Round Tower.
SH SALE, vii.107, to H. G. Bohn.

☞ Not listed in the London Sale, but perhaps it was '1 other' with Bosse's *Traité* in lot 1147.

3781 GUALTEROTTI, RAFFAELLO

Feste nelle nozze del serenissimo Don Francesco Medici, Gran Duca di Toscana, et della sereniss. sua Consorte la Sig. Bianca Cappello. Florence, 1579. Two parts in one volume, 4to.

Original vellum, rebacked with leather. BP² later state. Not in MC. Book label of Jacob Manzoni.

SH SALE, vii.105, to Thorpe, 18/– [London, 1086]; H. P. Kraus, May 1958, to WSL, $940.

☞ The engraved plates are printed in red and green. The SH press-mark, partially defaced, was perhaps Q.5.

3782 HERALDRY

Arms of the nobility from William the Conqueror to James I, in color. MS, 17th century. 4to.

Old sheep, rebacked. BP² early state. Press-mark Q.22. Not in MC.
SH SALE, vii.103, to H. G. Bohn, £8.8.0 [London, 1106]; offered in Bohn's Catalogue for 1847 (Heraldry), p. 289, for £11.11.0; Sotheby's, 1872, to Francis Haury? whose note says he sold it to Arthur Potts in October 1877; Sotheby's, 29 April 1937 (Potts Sale), lot 756, to Maggs for WSL, £13.

HOLLAND, HENRY

Herωologia Anglica. Engravings by Crispin de Passe. [London, 1620]
Folio.

Press-mark B.2.26 in MC; moved to the Round Tower.

SH SALE, vii.102, to Lilly, £3.12.6. [London, 583]

☞ Bound with it, according to the sale catalogue, was Jacobus Verheiden's *Lives of the Foreign Reformers,* i.e., *Praestantium aliquot
theologorum qui Rom. Antichristum praecipuè oppugnarunt Effigies,*
1602; HW's other copy of Verheiden was in Press O in the Round Tower,
No. 3727 *above.* In his *R&NA* HW referred to Holland twice; in his *Anecdotes* he mentioned a copy with MS notes in Lord Oxford's library. But
then HW acquired a second copy of Holland from Thoresby's collection in
1764: this copy, not in MC, was sold vii.100, to Lilly, £3.3.0 [London, 582]

William Beckford inquired of William Smith, the dealer (letters now
WSL), whether the Herωologias were reasonably fine; to this Smith replied:
'The two Herωologias are remarkably bad, and I think the worst copies
I ever saw.'

JONES, INIGO   3784

*Some designs of Mr. Inigo Jones and Mr. Wm. Kent. Published by
John Vardy according to Act of Parliament.* [London] 1744. Folio.
Vellum. BP[1]. Press-mark D.3.9, altered in book to Q.3.

SH SALE, vii.104, to H. G. Bohn, 14/– [London, 923]; offered in Bohn's
Catalogue for 1847 (Architecture), p. 227, for £1.4.0; Sotheby's, 28 March
1895 (Gennadius Sale), £1.18.0; Sotheby's, 12 May 1902 (Ford Sale),
lot 340, to W. Brown, £4.12.6; given by Louis Butler McCagg of Newport,
Rhode Island, to WSL, August 1928.

☞ Fifty-three plates. A later owner, J. W. Ford, titled the plates in pencil from the printed Table.

In the SH catalogue this lot also included the following pieces (they are
not named in the London sale but may have been in some lot like 920, '18
other tracts'):

(1) [BLIZARD, Sir WILLIAM] *Stanzas on viewing Strawberry Hill.* Privately
printed, 1793.

(2) *Specimens of printing types.* 4to. Possibly identifiable with two specimens offered, but not identified as HW's, in Rodd's Catalogue for 1845,
Part 4 (Literature), lots 13501 and 13567: Caslon of 1763 and Fry of
1785. In addition, Baskerville sent a specimen to HW, 2 November 1762,
presumably his folio specimen dated 1762.

(3) 'And 1 other.'

3785 MEAD, RICHARD

Museum Meadianum, sive Catalogus Nummorum. Sold by Langford.
London, 1755. 8vo.

'Old calf.' Not in MC.

SH SALE, vii.107, to H. G. Bohn [London, 1019]; Sotheby's, 22 December
1882 (Beckford Sale, Part 2), lot 2353, to Robson & Kerslake, £2.13.0.

☞ Bound in the volume were two supplementary catalogues of the
Mead collections:

(1) *Catalogue of the . . . collection of prints and drawings*, 1755.

(2) *Catalogue of the . . . collection of valuable gems, bronzes, marble and
other busts and antiquities*, 1755. Some items were purchased by HW at
these sales as well as at the sales of the books. He paid 13/– for this
volume of Mead catalogues at Dr. Lort's sale in 1791, lot 2641.

Also listed in lot 1019 of the London Sale were two copies of [Richard
Gough's] *Catalogue of the coins of Canute.* London, 1777. 4to.

3786 MISSAL

Book of Hours. Heures à l'usage de Rome. Printed on vellum, with
wood-cut borders. 8vo.

Not in MC.

SH SALE, vii.108, to Lilly, £2.17.6. [London, 1082]

☞ William Beckford must have expressed interest in this Missal, because William Smith, the dealer (letters now WSL), listed it on 14 April
as an item he would watch for.

Two other Missals, not sold with the books, may be recorded here:

(1) MISSAL. MS on vellum, executed at Rome, 1532. With miniatures of the
School of Raphael, believed by HW to have been executed for Queen
Claude, wife of Francis I of France; in Italian Renaissance binding, with
rubies and turquoises set in the covers. Note by HW on the fly-leaf; he
purchased it at Dr. Mead's sale (Collection of Valuable Gems, 14 March
1755, lot 42), for £42, and Dr. Mead is said to have paid £100 for it. SH
SALE, xv.77, to Forster for Lord Waldegrave, £115.10.0; later in Alfred
de Rothschild's collection; Christie's, 20 May 1925 (Countess of Carnarvon Sale), lot 141, to S. J. Phillips for Lord Rothermere, £2100;
Sotheby's, 26 March 1942 (Rothermere Sale), to Phillips, £2500. The
binding and four pages of text were illustrated in Sotheby's catalogue in
1942.

(2) MISSAL. *Psalter.* MS on vellum, 1537, illuminated by Julio Clovio;
bound in leather, richly ornamented. In the Arundel and Oxford col-

lections; inserted is a description of it by George Vertue, dated 1748; sold with the Duchess of Portland's Museum, 24 May 1786, lot 2952, to HW, £169.1.0; SH SALE, xv.90, to Lord Waldegrave, £441; now in the John Carter Brown Library at Providence. On the fly-leaves HW wrote two notes about the history of the MS, and he later inserted his book-plate as Lord Orford.

Sir Frederic Madden in his Diary noted that these two MSS had been bought in by Lord Waldegrave, and he listed the prices as £110 and £450, not the £115 and £441 reported by Robins, by some confusion of pounds and guineas.

PASSE, CRISPIN DE   3787

Della luce del dipingere e disegnare. Amsterdam, 1643. Five parts in one volume, folio.

'Calf, with HW's BP.' Press-mark C.1 in MC, entered by HW; later moved to the Round Tower.

SH SALE, vii.99, to H. G. Bohn for William Beckford, £2.6.0 [London, 1161]; Sotheby's, 4 July 1883 (Beckford Sale, Part 3), lot 492, to Ellis & White, £3.15.0.

☞ The preface to this book was quoted by HW in his comments on De Passe in his *Engravers*, but he said he had never seen the book and so quoted from Vertue; in his second edition (1765) he was able to make corrections from his own copy of the book.

William Beckford inquired of Bohn about lot 1161 on 13 June (letters now WSL); Bohn replied on 16 June that the Drawing book had fine impressions and was 'rather a nice book in old binding, £5.5.0.' Beckford wrote on 18 June: 'C. de Passe's drawing book, being fine in point of impressions, should find its way hither unless most madly contested à la Thorpe.'

PASSE, CRISPIN DE   3788

Metamorphoseon Ovidiarum figurae . . . laminis aeneis incisae. [Cologne?] 1602. Oblong 4to.

'Morocco, with HW's BP.' Not in MC.

SH SALE, vii.106, to Lilly, £1.13.0 [London, 1162]; Edwards, 24 October 1849 (Smith Pigott Sale), lot 933; Sotheby's, 2 August 1928 (Miscellaneous Sale), lot 214, to Dobell, £7.5.0.

3789 PASSE, CRISPIN DE

*Les vrais pourtraits de quelques unes des plus grandes dames de la
Chrestienté desguisées en bergères.* Amsterdam, 1640. Oblong 4to.
Not in MC.
SH SALE, vii.106, to Lilly, £2.7.6. [London, 585]

3790 PEACHAM, HENRY

Minerva Britanna, or a garden of heroical devises. London, 1612. 4to.
'Red morocco.' Press-mark B.4.35 in MC, added by HW and hence ac-
quired *ca.* 1763–6; moved later to the Round Tower.
SH SALE, vii.113, to Lilly [London, 1060]; offered in Lilly's Catalogue for
1863, for £6.16.6.
☞ Another copy was in H.1 of the Main Library, No. 1342 *above.*

3791 PEACHAM, HENRY

The truth of our times. London, 1638. 12mo.
Not in MC.
SH SALE, vii.111, to Lilly. [London, 1060]
☞ Another copy was in the Main Library, Press M.7, No. 2251 *above.*

3792 PERRAULT, CHARLES

Les hommes illustres qui ont paru en France pendant ce siècle. Paris,
1696–1700. Two volumes, folio.
Not in MC.
SH SALE, vii.96, to P. and Dom. Colnaghi, £3.3.0. [London, 584]
☞ In his 'Book of Materials,' *ca.* 1759, HW made a few notes from
Perrault.

3793 PLATT, Sir HUGH

*The garden of Eden: or, an accurate description of all the flowers and
fruits now growing in England.* London, 1675. 8vo.
Not in MC.
SH SALE, vii.111, to Lilly. [London, 1062]
☞ Another edition was in Press O of the Library in the Offices, No.
2928 *above.* In his little bibliography of Platt in his 'Book of Materials,'
ca. 1786, HW recorded that edition; at some later time, presumably from
a newly acquired copy, he added a note of an edition of 1675.

Pluvinel, Antoine de   3794

Instruction du Roy en l'exercice de monter à cheval. Paris, 1629. Folio.

Press-mark D.1 in MC, entered by HW; later moved to the Round Tower.
SH SALE, vii.97, to — Wood, Esq., £1.11.0. [London, 1153]

☞ Engravings by Crispin de Passe. From the entry in MC, one can guess
that HW acquired the book soon after 1763; and in the second edition, 1765,
of his *Catalogue of Engravers*, he inserted a paragraph in praise of the engravings: 'this valuable book is little known, though not very scarce.'

Topographical miscellanies. Edited by Sir Samuel Egerton Brydges.   3795
      Volume I. London, 1792. 4to.

Not in MC.
SH SALE, vii.110, to Lilly. [London, 933]

☞ This was a continuation of the *Topographer*. It is described in the
London Sale as 'English Topographical Antiquities, 1.'

Tracts   3796

A volume of very rare and curious tracts. 4to.

Not in MC.
SH SALE, vii.107, to Lilly.

☞ Probably, not certainly, this was lot 1065 in the London Sale. It
included:

(1) *The Counter-Scuffle; whereunto is added, the Counter-Rat.* London,
      1635. Attributed to R. Speed.

(2) Taylor, John, the Water Poet. *A swarme of sectaries and schisma-
      tiques.* London, 1641.

(3) *The Most Wonderful Wonder . . . Being an account of the travels of
      Mynheer Veteranus . . . with an account of his taking a most monstrous
      She Bear, who had nurs'd up the Wild Boy. . . . Written by the Copper-
      Farthing Dean.* London, 1726.

Tracts   3797

      Several volumes not clearly identifiable are here listed.
      SH SALE, vii.109 '3 curious old tracts.' Items that may have been among
these three are:

(1) Peacham, Henry. *The Period of Mourning, disposed into six visions.*
      London, 1613. On Henry, Prince of Wales. London Sale, lot 1061, to
      Lilly.

3797   (2) GERBIER, Sir BALTHAZAR. *A sommary description . . . off America.* Rotterdam, 1660. London Sale, lot 1063, to Lilly.

(3) GEDDE, WALTER. *A booke of sundry draughtes principaly serving for glaziers . . . whereunto is annexed the manner how to anniel in glas.* London, 1615. 4to. Not found in the SH records, but offered in Lilly's Catalogue for 1860, 'morocco, from the SH collection,' for £6.16.6. The book, which contains patterns for Gothic windows, may have attracted HW, and its appearance in Lilly's collection suggests that it was perhaps concealed in some miscellaneous lot like vii.109.

SH SALE, vii.110 'a volume of curious old tracts.' This may be lot 1063 in the London Sale, 'a volume of tracts, *vide* contents on fly-leaf,' to Lilly, £3.5.0. This volume was perhaps a quarto that is now at Farmington; it is bound in old mottled calf of the late 17th century, now rebacked; BP¹; no press-mark; contents on the fly-leaf in a 17th century hand. There is a collation note, September 1914, by Messrs. Quaritch; formerly in the Spedding Collection; purchased by the 17th Earl of Derby, *ca.* 1914; two different bookplates of the 17th Earl of Derby; Christie's, 20 October 1953, (Knowsley Hall Sale), lot 263, to Maggs for WSL, £58.

Contents:

(1) SALTERN, GEORGE. *Of the ancient lawes of Great Britaine,* 1605. Numerous markings in HW's manner, and some notes by an earlier owner. Old name, W. Walter, on title.

(2) COKE, Sir EDWARD. *The Lord Coke his speech and charge,* 1607. Old name, W. Walter, on title.

(3) ELLESMERE, Sir THOMAS EGERTON, Baron. *The speech of the Lord Chancellor of England, in the Eschequer chamber, touching the Post-Nati,* 1609.

(4) JAMES I, King of England. *His Maiesties speach in the Starre-Chamber,* 1616. Old name, Richard Kimbe, on title.

(5) *Star-Chamber cases,* 1641. Collected from the work of Richard Crompton.

(6) CHARLES I, King of England. *Orders and directions, together with a commission for the better administration of justice . . . how, and by whom the lawes and statutes tending to the reliefe of the poore . . . are executed,* 1630.

(7) [PARKER, HENRY] *The Case of ship mony briefly discoursed, . . . and most humbly presented to . . . the High Court of Parliament,* 1640. Name, Fabian Phillips, at end.

(8) [PRYNNE, WILLIAM] *An humble remonstrance to his Maiesty, against the tax of ship-money,* 1641.

(9) HUTTON, Sir RICHARD. *The arguments of Sir Richard Hutton . . . and Sir George Croke . . . upon a Scire facias brought . . . against John Hampden*, 1641.

URQUHART, Sir THOMAS 3798

The discovery of a most exquisite jewel. London, 1652. Pot 8vo.

Old sheep. BP² early state. Press-mark Q.41. Not in MC.

SH SALE, vii.111, to Lilly [London, 1062]; Sotheby's, 19 June 1885 (James Crossley Sale), lot 2671, to Rimell, £1.12.0; Sotheby's, 21 June 1948 (Foley Sale), to Raphael King, £23; King, July 1948, to WSL, £38.

☞ Note by HW on the fly-leaf: 'Of this wonderfully absurd and rare book, the 129th page is perhaps the most extraordinary for its amazing bombast indecency. The title, the motto with the cases of the words specified, and the pedigrees, are not less singular in their kinds.'

Granger, in the Supplement to his *Biographical History*, noted that Urquhart gives a long account of Crichton. On this HW wrote in his own copy of Granger: 'That strange book is a greater curiosity than Crichton was: the language more bombast than the marvels attributed to his hero. The account of his intrigue & death is a compound of gravity & obscenity.'

VEEN, OTTO VAN 3799

Amorum Emblemata. Antwerp, 1608. Oblong 4to.

Old vellum. BP¹. Press-mark B.4.25, altered in the book to Q.34. Bookplate of Dr. S. Elliott Hoskins (1799–1888).

SH SALE, vii.106, to Dr. Hoskins, Guernsey, 10/– [London, 1163]; Swift, November 1937, to WSL, £1.15.0.

WILLIAM III, King of England 3800

Komste van Zyne Majesteit Willem III . . . in Holland. Engravings by Romeyn de Hooghe. The Hague, 1691. Folio.

Press-mark D.4.11 in MC; moved to the Round Tower.

SH SALE, vii.97, to H. G. Bohn, £2.8.0. [London, 1074]

☞ The catalogue of the London Sale notes that this volume had the Hogarthian bookplate and signature of John Holland, the heraldic painter. The text is by Govard Bidloo. A copy of the French translation was in the Closet of the Round Tower, No. 3529 *above*.

ZANETTI, ANTONIO MARIA 3801

XII Teste e Figure. Published by Gribelin. London, n.d. 4to.

'Red morocco.' Press-mark C.4.5 in MC; moved to the Round Tower.

SH SALE, vii.105, to H. G. Bohn [London, 1167]; almost certainly the

copy, not identified as HW's, sold Sotheby's, 29 November 1883 (Beckford Sale, Part 4), lot 631, to B. F. Stevens, £6.10.0.

PRESS R

Press R was somewhat miscellaneous; it included a number of literary and historical works that are unexpected in the Print Room. There were also a number of seventeenth-century books, books by Pinkerton and Mrs. Piozzi, books on art history, and miscellaneous volumes acquired at different times.

3802 ANACREON

Carmina.

> Not in MC.
> SH SALE, vii.118, to Thorpe. [London, 1051]

☞ Listed in the London Sale as 'Odes of Anacreon,' and probably among '3 others' in vii.118. The edition can hardly be ascertained; but Pinkerton who proposed that HW print Anacreon at the SH Press (*see* his *Walpoliana,* i.104, note on HW's letter of 27 July 1785) may have sent an edition to him.

In 1947 Myers & Co. offered a copy, Saumur 1680, old calf, with BP¹ inserted on the verso of the title-page; but there is little likelihood that this can have been HW's.

3803 *The Arno Miscellany.* Florence, 1784. 8vo.

> Not in MC.
> SH SALE, vii.123, to Thorpe. [London, 1052]

☞ Contributors include Bertie Greatheed, Robert Merry, William Parsons, and Mrs. Piozzi. To Mann, 16 March 1786, HW wrote that the painter Allan Ramsay, another contributor, sent this volume to him; he said the same thing in a note on his copy of his letter to Mann, 9 August 1784. He supposed at first (letter to Mann, 8 July 1784) that the poems were the work of the younger William Beckford.

Also in this lot were '4 others': these seem unidentifiable, since lot 1052, 'various,' is similarly vague. But one was presumably Mrs. Piozzi's *Anecdotes, below.*

BARBARY STATES   3804

Late newes out of Barbary. In a letter . . . from a merchant there.
   (Signed: R.S.) London, 1613. 4to.

Not in MC.
SH SALE, vii.121, to Lilly. [London, 1068]

☞ The London Sale lists 'the History of Barbary,' probably this
tract, and it was probably among 'and 3 others' in lot 121.

BIDDULPH, WILLIAM   3805

*The travels of certaine Englishmen into Africa, Asia, Troy, Bythinia,
   Thracia, and to the Black Sea.* Edited by Theophilus Lavender.
   London, 1609. Pot 4to.

Mottled calf of 18th century, rebacked. BP² later state. No press-mark
and not in MC.
Not found in SH SALE. Perhaps sold in some miscellaneous lot; but
it might well have been shelved with the old books of travels by Sherley
sold in vii.121. Offered in Lilly's Catalogue (Library of Robert Glendening), *ca.* 1865, for £2.12.6; Sotheby's, 13 December 1937 (MacDonald
Sale), lot 37, to Maggs, £4.15.0; Sotheby's, 26 July 1938 (Miscellaneous
Sale), lot 280, to Maggs for WSL, £10.

☞ Perhaps this volume was not in the sale at all. But it certainly belonged to HW, since it has his note: 'Bought at Dr. Monro's sale, [23 April]
1792.' Dr. John Monro had attended HW's nephew, George, 3d Earl of Orford, who died in December 1791.
Or it may have been included in lot 19 in the Sixth Day with Mandeville,
inasmuch as Panizzi added the title in the margin of his copy of the sale
catalogue at that lot. The Biddulph might well have been placed in the
Glass Closet in 1792.

BRAND, JOHN   3806

Observations on popular antiquities. (Including Henry Bourne's
   Antiquitates vulgares). Newcastle, 1777. 8vo.

Not in MC.
SH SALE, vii.119, to Thorpe. [London, 933]

☞ Both the SH and London sales add 'and 1 other' to this lot.

3807 BROMLEY, HENRY

Catalogue of engraved British portraits, from Egbert to the present time. London, 1793. 4to.

Not in MC.

SH SALE, vii.115, to Thorpe. [London, 1095]

3808 COCHIN, CHARLES NICOLAS

Collection de vignettes, fleurons, et culs-de-lampe, ou suite chronologique de faits relatifs à l'histoire de France. Paris, 1767. 4to.

Not in MC.

SH SALE, vii.117, to Lilly, £1.16.0. [London, 1096]

☞ These were the illustrations prepared for a new edition of Hénault's *Abrégé chronologique.* Cochin's engraving of Mme. du Deffand's cats, preserved by HW in his own copy of the *Description of SH*, is reproduced in the Yale Walpole to illustrate Mme. du Deffand's letter of 17 September 1776.

3809 DARWIN, ERASMUS

The Botanic Garden, a poem. London, 1791. 4to.

Not in MC.

SH SALE, vii.115, to Lilly. [London, 1066]

☞ The second part, published two years earlier, may have been bound in: HW gave or lent a copy of Part II to the Misses Berry on 28 November 1789, when he called it 'the most delicious poem on earth'; he also lent a copy to Hannah More, 22 April 1789.

3810 *The Florence Miscellany.* Florence, 1785. 8vo.

'Half bound, uncut.' Not in MC.

SH SALE, vii.120, to Thorpe [London, 1058]; probably the copy offered, but not identified as HW's, in Thorpe's Supplement for 1842, lot 12389, for £2.2.0; identified as HW's copy in Thorpe's Catalogue for 1844, lot 2621, £2.2.0; Puttick, 2 April 1852 (Miscellaneous Sale), lot 191, to Bumstead, 9/6.

☞ Contributions by Bertie Greatheed, Robert Merry, William Parsons, and Mrs. Piozzi; edited by Parsons, with a preface by Mrs. Piozzi. Of it HW wrote to Mann, 16 March 1786: 'I have very lately been lent a volume of poems, composed and printed at Florence, in which . . . Mrs. Piozzi has a considerable share. . . . If you have not sent me a copy by your nephew, I should be glad if you could get one for me: not for the merit of the verses . . . but for a short and sensible and genteel preface

by la Piozza. . . . Though I ask for that volume, it made me very indignant.
. . . I turned over the whole set of verses (though I did not read a quarter),
and could not find the only name I expected to see—yours. What
stocks and stones! . . . If you send me the book, I think I will burn all
but the preface.'

Mann had already sent a copy, the receipt of which HW acknowledged
28 March 1786. Thorpe in 1844 described the volume as having a presentation note from Robert Merry to Francessi Gianfigliazzi, in 1785, and
HW's note that the book was sent to him by Sir Horace Mann.

GERBIER, Sir BALTHAZAR   3811

Lectures on Fortification. London, 1649–50. 4to.

Not in MC.
SH SALE, vii.121, to Lilly. [London, 1068]

☞ This is listed in the London Sale, and was probably among 'and 3
others' in lot 121. Just what parts of Gerbier's lectures were included
in the volume cannot be identified; but HW added to his *Anecdotes* in
1786 a note concerning the fifth lecture, on Military Architecture, 1650,
'with which I have lately met.'

GOUGH, RICHARD   3812

*An account of a rich illuminated Missal, executed for John Duke of
Bedford.* London, 1794. 4to.

Bound in half morocco, *ca.* 1850. Orford seal, type 1. No press-mark preserved. Not in MC.
SH SALE, vii.124, with six other tracts not named, but sold with
other lots in the London Sale. [Possibly among 18 tracts in London, 920.]
Sotheby's, 6 June 1844 (Miscellaneous Sale), lot 134, to Thorpe, 3/6;
Sotheby's, 17 May 1848 (Eyton Sale), lot 657, to Longman, 13/–; T. & L.
Hannas of Bromley, Kent, purchased it from a private library in Sussex;
sold it in November 1957 to Professor E. L. McAdam, Jr.; given by Professor McAdam, December 1957, to WSL.

☞ A note in Kirgate's hand concerning the auction is pasted on p. 82.
The Missal was in the Harleian Collection, and lot 2951 in the Portland
Sale in 1786, bought by Edwards, the bookseller, for £213.3.0, in competi-
tion with the King's agent; it is now in the British Museum.

3813 GRANGER, JAMES

Biographical history of England, from Egbert the Great to the Revolution. London, 1769. Two volumes in four, with leaves printed on one side, 4to.

Original calf, with HW's arms on the sides; rebacked and press-mark not preserved. No BP. Not in MC.

SH SALE, vii.116, to Thorpe [London, 1095]; given to Princeton in April 1905 by Junius S. Morgan; now in the Morgan Collection in the Princeton University Library.

☞ Notes by HW on a few pages. The copy that he annotated more extensively was in the Main Library, Press D.5, No. 541 *above*. Full information about the preparation and publication of the work is gathered in the *Bibliography of SH*.

3814 HARINGTON, HENRY, Editor

Nugae Antiquae. London, 1779. Three volumes, 12mo.

'Red morocco with HW's BP.' Not in MC.

SH SALE, vii.120, to H. G. Bohn for William Beckford, £2.2.0 [London, 955]; Sotheby's, 13 December 1882 (Beckford Sale, Part 2), lot 566, to A. R. Smith, £6; Sotheby's, 26 May 1910 (Ford Sale), lot 505, to Quaritch, £5; offered in Quaritch Catalogues, 1910–15, for £7.7.0.

☞ Another set was in B.9 in the Main Library, No. 411 *above*.

The bookseller Bohn reported to Beckford, 16 June 1842 (letters now WSL): 'Nugae, good, Kalthoeber, £2.2.0 or £3.3.0.' Beckford replied: 'The Nugae and Beloe [Press O, No. 3706 *above*] will suit us well unless Mr. Thorpe should fancy them.'

3815 HERODOTUS

Historiarum libri IX. Edited by Jacobus Gronovius. Leyden, 1715. Folio.

Press-mark M.2.4 in MC; moved to the Round Tower.

SH SALE, vii.114, to H. G. Bohn, 3/–. [London, 1097]

3816 KING, EDWARD

Remarks concerning stones said to have fallen from the clouds. London, 1796. 4to.

Not in MC.

Not found in the SH SALE. London Sale, lot 932, to Thorpe.

☞ Conceivably this was among the 'six others' in the SH SALE, vii.122.

KYNASTON, SIR FRANCIS   3817

The Constitutions of the Musaeum Minervae. London, 1636. 4to.

    Not in MC.

    SH SALE, vii.121, to Lilly. [London, 1068]

    ☞ This is listed in the London Sale, and was perhaps among 'and 3 others' in lot 121. In the Bliss Sale in 1858, lot 2578, a single volume contained this and Gerbier's *Lectures on fortification* (No. 3811 *above*); one is tempted to think that they may have been HW's copies.

LONDON   3818

Prospects of the most remarkable places in and about the Citty of London, neatly engraved. [London] Published by Henry Overton [1723?] Oblong 4to.

    Rebound in green morocco, with bookplate of Archibald Philip, 5th Earl of Rosebery. Not in MC.

    SH SALE, vii.117, to H. G. Bohn [Not listed in London Sale]; Sotheby's, 29 June 1933 (Rosebery Sale), lot 847, to Maggs for WSL, £12.10.0.

    ☞ This volume, which now includes 92 plates from various sources, numbered by hand, is listed only as 'A collection of Views of London and its environs, oblong 4to, very curious, from the Library of A. C. Ducarel'; it has no sign of HW's ownership except that on plate 73, Houghton, it carries an unmistakable note in HW's hand: 'This was designed by Campbell, but it was much altered in building, particularly in the Turrets, which are round not square.' Included in the volume are some plates by John Kip and part of Henry Overton's *Britannia Illustrata*, 1724.

    This was very probably the book listed at vii.117; but *see also* the book of London views listed in Press F of the Round Tower, No. 3623 *above*. Beckford must have inquired about vii.117, because William Smith the dealer wrote to Beckford, 14 April 1842: 'The views of London (7–117) contain nothing but comparatively modern rubbish, and have no pretensions to be curious.' (Letters now WSL)

[MARSHALL, —]   3819

Catalogue of five hundred authors of Great Britain, now living. London, 1788. 8vo.

    Not in MC.

    SH SALE, vii.118, to Thorpe. [London, 1051]

    ☞ In his 'Book of Materials,' *ca.* 1788, HW copied from this volume an anecdote concerning Fanny Burney.

3820 MASTERS, ROBERT

Memoirs of the life and writings of Thomas Baker, from the papers of Zachary Grey. Cambridge, 1784. 8vo.

Not in MC.

SH SALE, vii.118, to Thorpe. [London, 1051]

☞ Since HW had himself written a memoir of Baker, he was interested in this volume and made several notes from it in his 'Book of Materials.' In his own copy of Gough's *British Topography* (now in the Huntington Library), HW wrote at i.220: 'Mr. Masters has since published a life of Mr. Baker, & proved how insufficient his materials or he himself were.'

3821 MEDICI, LORENZO DE'

Poesie. Published by William Roscoe. [Liverpool, 1791]. 8vo.

Rebound by Hayday in an elaborate inlaid morocco. BP of HW as Lord Orford, type 2. Not in MC.

SH SALE, vii.123, to Thorpe [London, 1052]; Sotheby's, 19 May 1848 (Eyton Sale), lot 1060, to Darby, £9; Christie's, 5 April 1917 (Red Cross Sale), lot 1901, to Maggs, £7.10.0; Sotheby's, 5 March 1937 (Moss Sale), lot 993, to Maggs for WSL, £25.

☞ Beneath the BP, on the verso of the title-page, is a note by Kirgate: 'Of this edition of the Sonnets of Lorenzo de' Medici, published by Mr. William Roscoe of Liverpool, author of the Life of that great man in 1795, only twelve copies were printed; this, which was one of them, was given by that gentleman to Horace Earl of Orford.'

3822 MOUNTMORRES, HERVEY REDMOND MORRES, Viscount

The letters of Themistocles. London, 1795. 8vo.

Old calf. Orford BP. Press-mark R.27. Not in MC.

SH SALE, vii.122, to Thorpe [London, 1052]; purchased from Thorpe, 17 December 1846, by the British Museum.

☞ The presentation inscription is dated 18 February 1795.

3823 PINKERTON, JOHN

An essay on medals. The 2d edition. London, 1789. Two volumes, 8vo.

Green morocco, the dedication copy. Press-marks R.21 & 22. Not in MC. Note on the fly-leaf by C. R. Taylor of Montague Street, Russell Square.

SH SALE, vii.122, to Adamson [London, 592]; Sotheby's, 27 February 1893 (Buckley Sale, Part 1), lot 2326, to Reader, £1.8.0; acquired in April 1895 by the British Museum.

☞ Three notes by HW. Another copy was in B.3 in the Main Library, No. 279 *above*.

PINKERTON, JOHN   3824

Iconographia Scotica; or portraits of illustrious persons of Scotland. London, 1797. 8vo.

Not in MC.

SH SALE, vii.118, to Thorpe. [Not named in the London Sale, but perhaps included in lot 1051]

☞ The work is listed only as 'Pinkerton's Scotch Portraits' in the catalogue. The letter to Pinkerton, 25 January 1795, shows that HW had taken an interest in the engravings before publication.

[PINKERTON, JOHN]   3825

Letters of literature. By Robert Heron, Esq. [*pseud.*] London, 1785. 8vo.

Bound in half red morocco by E. Rau of Philadelphia, for Mr. Barton. BP² later state. Press-mark not preserved. Not in MC.

SH SALE, vii.118, to Thorpe [London, 1051]. In the Barton Collection of the Boston Public Library since 1873.

☞ *See* HW's letters to Pinkerton, 22 June, 26 June, and 27 July 1785, for some comments on this work; he was generally pleased by it. By some people HW was himself suspected of being the author: *see* his letter to Lady Ossory, 29 August 1785. He had urged her to buy it, in his letter of 30 June.

The volume preserves the presentation inscription: 'To the Honorable Horace Walpole Esqr. from the author'; to which HW added 'J. Pinkerton.' He also inserted a newspaper advertisement concerning the book, with his date 'Decr. 15, 1785.' There are pencilled markings throughout, and a few notes, by HW. He noticed Pinkerton's praise of Akenside on p. 21, and wrote: 'How could this author, who is so severe on Virgil for want of originality, admire Akenside who has nothing original & was not even a poet?'

PIOZZI, HESTER LYNCH (THRALE)   3826

Anecdotes of the late Samuel Johnson. London, 1786. 8vo.

Original boards. BP² later state. Press-mark R.33. Not in MC. Bookplate of William Frederick, 9th Earl Waldegrave.

Not named in the SH SALE, but probably among '4 others' sold with the *Arno Miscellany* in vii.123, to Thorpe [and among 'various' in London, 1052]; Lord Waldegrave, 1948, to WSL, in a collection.

☞ Marginal markings and exclamation points by HW throughout, and numerous notes and identifications. He read the book promptly, and wrote to Mann, 28 March 1786: 'Two days ago appeared Madam Piozzi's *Anecdotes of Dr. Johnson.* I am lamentably disappointed—in her, I mean, not in him. I had conceived a favourable opinion of her capacity. But this new book is wretched—a high-varnished preface to a heap of rubbish, in a very vulgar style....'

A copy of the third edition was sold at Sotheby's, 28 April 1947, with an old note on the end-paper: 'Horace Walpole's copy.' But WSL examined the volume, found the marginal notes not HW's, and found no other evidence of SH provenance. The same volume was offered again at Hodgson's, 26 May 1966.

3827 SHERLEY, Sir ANTHONY
Relation of his travels into Persia. London, 1613. 4to.
> Not in MC.
> SH SALE, vii.121, to Lilly. [London, 1068]
> ☞ Dr. Lort gave this work to HW in 1778: *see* his letter, 20 July 1778. It is marked in the SH catalogue as 'from the library of Mr. Lort.' But HW had seen the narrative earlier in Green's *Collection of Voyages,* 1745, as he noted in his 'Book of Materials,' *ca.* 1759. He also refers to this narrative (presumably as printed in Green) in a MS note in his own copy of Vertue's *Catalogue of Charles I's pictures.*

3828 [SHERLEY, Sir ANTHONY]
A true historical discourse of Muley Hamets rising to the three King-domes.... The adventures of Sir Anthony Sherley. By Ro. C. London, 1609. 4to.
> Not in MC.
> SH SALE, vii.121, to Lilly. [London, 1068]
> ☞ The compiler was perhaps Robert Cottington. This was perhaps a gift from Dr. Lort, since it is combined in the SH catalogue as 'Shirley's Travels, 2 vols., from the Library of Mr. Lort.'

3829 [SULIVAN, RICHARD J.]
Observations made during a tour through parts of England, Scotland, and Wales. London, 1780. 4to.
> Original grey boards. BP² early state. Press-mark R.6. Not in MC.

SH SALE, vii.115, to Lilly [London, 1066]; now in the Dyce Collection in the Victoria and Albert Museum.

☞ Numerous notes by HW. On verso of the title-page: 'This is one of the worst of our many modern books of Travels. It is silly, pert, vulgar, ignorant; aims at florid diction, which is no merit unless absolutely necessary to description of prospects; it is larded with affectation of tenderness & sentiment. The blunders & false spellings are numerous, & the whole betrays total want of taste.' Another sample is HW's objection on p. 118, where Sulivan called the inside of Gloucester Cathedral 'clumsy to a degree'; HW wrote: 'The author here betrays his utter want of taste; nothing in Gothic architecture is lighter or more beautiful than many parts of Gloucester Cathedral.'

TAYLOR, BROOK 3830

Contemplatio philosophica. Ed. by Sir William Young. London. Privately printed, 1793. 8vo.

'Red morocco by Hayday, with Orford BP.' Not in MC.

Not listed separately in SH SALE. London, 1058, to Thorpe; Sotheby's, 22 May 1848 (Eyton Sale), lot 1514, to Lilly, 6/–; English, 17 October 1849 (J. H. S. Pigott Sale), lot 486; in the collection of the late Marquess of Crewe.

☞ Laid in is a draft of a letter from HW to William Seward, 15 February 1793, thanking him for the gift of the book.

The Topographer . . . illustrative of the local history and antiquities 3831
of England. Edited by Sir Samuel Egerton Brydges. London, 1789–91. Four volumes, 8vo.

Not in MC.

SH SALE, vii.119, to Thorpe. [London, 933]

TRACTS 3832

One volume, folio.

Not in MC.

SH SALE, vii.116, to Lilly, 12/– [London, 1067]; the volume was broken up, and some pieces offered by Thorpe, as described.

☞ Four pamphlets are listed in the London Sale, which adds: '*Vide* general contents, written by Lord Orford, within cover.'

(1) TAUBMAN, MATTHEW. *London's Triumph, or the Goldsmith's Jubilee.* London, 1687. In honor of Sir John Shorter. Offered in Thorpe's Gen-

eral Catalogue for 1844, lot 1646, for £3.3.0. Purchased of Thorpe, 13 March 1847, by the British Museum. One note by HW. Sir John Shorter was HW's great-grandfather.

(2) *The London Belles: or, a description of the most celebrated beauties in the Metropolis.* London, 1707. Offered in Thorpe's Catalogue for 1846, lot 1031, for £2.2.0.

(3) SACHEVERELL, HENRY. *An impartial account of what pass'd most remarkable in the last Session of Parliament relating to . . . Dr. Sacheverell.* London, 1710.

(4) BLOOD, THOMAS. *Narrative . . . concerning the design . . . against . . . George Duke of Buckingham.* London, 1680. Offered in Thorpe's General Catalogue for 1844, lot 1531, for £1.11.6; offered again by Thorpe in 1847.

3833 TRACTS
'A bundle of tracts and catalogues relative to the arts.'

SH SALE, vii.126, dispersed. [London, 1155, in part, sold with the Royal Academy Catalogues in Press V; and London, 1065, included 'Catalogues of early Picture Sales.']

☞ The first edition of the SH catalogue reads 'Three bundles.' J. H. Anderdon in his copy of the catalogue wrote: 'I saw only one bundle.' He also noted that there were 25–30 pieces, including 'Early Catalogues of the Royal Academy, M. de Calonne, Reynolds, Cosway; Memoir of Gainsboro, Thicknesse; Dundas 1794; Orleans one part.' So far as identifiable, these included:

(1) CALONNE, CHARLES ALEXANDRE DE. *Catalogue of paintings,* &c. London, 1795.

(2) COSWAY, RICHARD. *Catalogue of paintings.* London, 1792.

(3) DUNDAS, Sir LAWRENCE. *Catalogue of paintings.* London, 1794. Christie's, 24 November 1965 (Miscellaneous Sale), lot 202, to Pickering & Chatto for WSL, £130 (with Jennings, Halifax, and two other catalogues). Priced by Kirgate and some notes by HW. The two other catalogues, 1795 and 1800, are priced by Kirgate; they may well have been in the collection as sold in 1842. All five catalogues seem to have been in the library of Lord Northwick, perhaps since 1842.

(4) ORLÉANS, LOUIS PHILIPPE JOSEPH, Duc d'. *The Orleans Gallery.* London, 1793. Notes on the pictures by HW.

(5) PEARSON, Mr. and Mrs., of Highgate. *Catalogue of Stained Glass.* London, 1800. (This was hardly HW's, but it seems to be what is mentioned in London, 1155.)

(6) REYNOLDS, SIR JOSHUA. *Catalogue of Ralph's exhibition of Reynolds's paintings.* London, 1791. Note by HW that Ralph [Kirkley] was Sir Joshua's servant.

(7) THICKNESSE, PHILIP. *Sketch of . . . Thomas Gainsborough.* [London] 1788. Possibly included in some such lot as this was Thicknesse's *Memoirs and Anecdotes*, London, 1788, in two volumes; HW's name is in the list of subscribers.

(8) JENNINGS, HENRY CONSTANTINE. *Catalogue of Paintings*, sold at Christie's, 1778. Not mentioned by Anderdon, but a collection of catalogues offered by Rodd in 1847, lot 2397, includes Jennings. This doubtless came from some such bundle at SH. Christie's, 24 November 1965, with Dundas, &c. to WSL. The prices are in Kirgate's hand.

(9) REYNOLDS, SIR JOSHUA. *Catalogue of pictures*, March 1795. Mr. Anderdon's note identifies Ralph's exhibition of 1791 (*see* No. 6 *above*) as in this bundle. But HW wrote on 17 March [1795?] to an unidentified correspondent: 'I . . . had sent my secretary to attend the sale of Sir Joshua Reynolds's pictures, and had nobody to write for me.' (Letter in Toynbee, Supplement II, p. 72.) So this important sale of Reynolds's collection of old masters was doubtless in some such bundle.

(10) SIRIÈS, LOUIS. *Catalogue des pierres gravées*, Florence, 1757. 4to. Not mentioned by Anderdon, but HW bought this catalogue at the Lort Sale, April 1791, lot 4129, for sixpence; it was doubtless included in some lot like vii.126 in the SH SALE. Siriès had been Goldsmith to the King of France, and in 1757 he was 'Directeur des ouvrages en pierre dure' at the Palazzo Vecchio in Florence; HW who knew him in Florence in 1740 refers to him three times in his letters.

(11) CHÉRON, ELISABETH SOPHIE. *Pierres gravées* [52 engravings from antique gems, Paris, 1711–14], 4to. A copy described as HW's, in old red morocco, was offered in Bohn's Catalogue for 1847 (Prints), p. 84, for £2.2.0. It may have been in some such miscellaneous lot.

(12) HALIFAX, GEORGE MONTAGU DUNK, 2d Earl of. *Catalogue of pictures*, sold at Christie's, 1782. Christie's, 24 November 1965, with Dundas, &c., to WSL. Priced by Kirgate, and some notes by HW.

VYNER, ROBERT, *pseud.*   3834
A very long, curious, and extraordinary sermon preached . . . at a noted chapel in Westminster, 14 March 1732/3. London, 1733. 4to.
'Sewed.' Not in MC.

sh sale, vii.125, to Lilly [London, 1068]; offered in Thorpe's Supplement for 1842, lot 13342, for 10/6; offered again by Thorpe in 1843.

☞ A satirical tract against Walpole's Excise Bill, printed in white on a black background; in other editions the pseudonym is spelled Winer and Wyner.

This lot also included '3 tracts in 4to, scarce prints.' One of them, no doubt, was sold London, 1068, 'The Times newspaper of 25 January 1793, with a black border [for] the execution of Louis XVI.' Another was probably London, 1059, 'Elegiac Monody on the Death of Louis XVI': this was offered, but not identified as hw's, in Thorpe, lot 12105, for 7/6, [Frederick Earl of Carlisle's] Funeral oration for Louis XVI, 1794, 4to.

3835 WALKER, GEORGE, Painter

Select views of picturesque scenery in Scotland, engraved from original drawings. No. I. London, 1796. Folio.

Not in mc.
sh sale, vii.122, to Thorpe. [London, 932, 'a volume of views in Scotland']

☞ The sh catalogue lists only 'Select Views in Scotland, and 6 others.' The engravings from Walker seem probable. The six others are not identifiable, but see King, No. 3816, and Wilkins, No. 3836.

3836 WILKINS, WILLIAM

Essay towards a history of the Venta Icenorum of the Romans, and of Norwich Castle. [London, 1795]. 4to.

Not in mc.
Not found in the sh sale. London Sale, lot 932, to Thorpe.

☞ Conceivably this was among the 'six others' in the sh sale, vii.122. It was an off-print from the 12th volume of Archaeologia.

PRESS S

Press S must have presented a handsome appearance: thirty large volumes in green morocco, gilt. The collection was entirely devoted to volumes of topographic views. Into this press Mason's Gray surely intruded at some time only because of its similar binding.

BIRCH, WILLIAM   3837

Delices de la Grande Bretagne. London, 1791. 4to.

'Green morocco, with Orford arms on the sides.' Not in MC.

SH SALE, vii.132, to H. G. Bohn, £1.7.0 [London, 931]; offered in Bohn's
Catalogue for 1847 (Prints), p. 74, for £2.5.0; Sotheby's, 23 March 1868
(B. G. Windus Sale), lot 214.

☞ The list of subscribers included the name of HW.

The Copper Plate Magazine, or monthly cabinet of picturesque prints. 3838
Edited by John Walker. London, 1792–6. Two volumes, oblong
4to.

'Green morocco, with Orford arms on the sides.' Not in MC.

SH SALE, vii.132, to H. G. Bohn, £2.1.0 [London, 930]; offered in
Bohn's Catalogue for 1847 (Prints), p. 87, for £2.8.0; Sotheby's, 23 March
1868 (B. G. Windus Sale), lot 239 (with three added volumes to complete
the set), to Harvey, £5.5.0; Sotheby's, 21 June 1880 (Cecil Dunn Gardner
Sale), lot 449.

The Copper Plate Magazine; or monthly treasure for the admirers of 3839
the imitative arts. Landscapes and country seats after Sandby, &c.
London, Kearsley, 1774–8. 4to.

Green morocco, with HW's arms on sides. Press-mark S.20. Not in MC.

SH SALE, vii.133, to H. G. Bohn, £1.7.0 [London, 929]; purchased from
Bohn by a member of the Bartol family of Boston, Massachusetts, and bequeathed by Miss Elizabeth Bartol to the Boston Public Library.

☞ In his 'Book of Materials' in 1774, HW noted that Rooker's last
published plate was his engraving of Sandby's view of SH in the *Copper
Plate Magazine*, November 1774. William Watts and Rooker's son did
most of the engraving thereafter.

The bookseller Bohn wrote on 17 June 1842 to William Beckford
(letters now WSL) that the volume contained some MS notes by HW and
might fetch £5.5.0. But Beckford replied the next day that he would not
take the *Copper Plate Magazine* as a present. Bohn seems to have purchased it for stock.

The volume has a number of extra plates (1786–91), one correction, one
identification, and two rather long notes by HW. The original drawing of
SH by Sandby, from which the plate was made for this work, is now at Farmington.

The spine of HW's copy is labelled 'Views'; he did not include the portraits after Houbraken and the mythological scenes usually included in a
complete set.

3840 CORDINER, CHARLES

Remarkable ruins and romantic prospects of North Britain. Engraved
by Mazell. London, 1795. 4to.

Green morocco, with Orford arms on the sides. Press-mark S.14. Not
in MC. Bookplate of Charles W. G. Howard, the gift of Sir David Dundas,
1877.

 SH SALE, vii.129, to Payne & Foss, £2.2.0 [London, 935]; Pickering
& Chatto, April 1950, to WSL, £8.10.0.

3841 GRAY, THOMAS

*Poems. To which are prefixed Memoirs of his life and writings by
William Mason.* York, 1775. Large paper, royal 4to.

Green morocco, gilt, with HW's arms on the sides; marbled end-papers.
Press-mark X.1, apparently misplaced in S. Not in MC. Bookplate of
George Soaper.

 SH SALE, vii.128, to George Soaper, £20.10.0 [London, 1045]; Sotheby's,
10 April 1902 (Hibbert Sale), lot 354, to Quaritch for Amy Lowell,
£197; bequeathed by Amy Lowell in 1925 to Harvard.

 ☞ Note by HW on title: 'Enriched with prints and notes by Horace
Walpole.' A few of the notes were written long after 1775, but most
were doubtless entered when he first read the completed book. In addition to numerous engravings, HW inserted a sketch for the 'Bard' by
Bentley.

 The SH copy of the new edition in four volumes, 8vo, York 1778,
is in Lord Waldegrave's library. This does not appear in the SH SALE records; but it is in a characteristic Walpolian calf binding, and it contains a
few notes by HW. It was perhaps kept in town, and hence bequeathed to
Elizabeth Laura, Dowager Countess Waldegrave, in 1797.

3842 GROSE, FRANCIS

Collection of his works. Thirteen volumes, 4to.

'Green morocco, with arms of HW as Lord Orford on the sides.'
Not in MC.

 SH SALE, vii.127, to H. G. Bohn, £13. [London, 936]

 ☞ Included in this set were:

(1) *Antiquities of England and Wales* (6 vols.); *of Scotland* (2 vols.);
of Ireland (2 vols.); 1773–91.

(2) *Military Antiquities respecting a history of the English army*; two
volumes, 1786–8.

(3) *A Treatise on ancient armour and weapons*, 1786–9.

In his 'Book of Materials,' *ca.* 1775, HW made a note from Grose, and there are scattered references in his correspondence with Cole.

A set of the *Antiquities*, ten volumes, bound in calf, with notes believed to be by HW, was among Mrs. Damer's books, sold at Hodgson's, 30 April 1902, lot 221.

MOORE, JAMES   3843

Monastic remains and ancient castles in England and Wales. Aquatints by G. I. Parkyns. London, 1792. 8vo.

'Green morocco, with Orford arms on sides.' Not in MC.

SH SALE, vii.131, to Lilly, 16/– [London, 910]; offered in Strong's Catalogue for 1843, lot 1058, for £1.16.0.

SANDBY, PAUL   3844

The Virtuosi's Museum, containing select views. Engraved by Watts and others. London, Kearsley, 1778. Oblong 4to.

'Green morocco, with HW's arms on the sides; with his BP and MS notes.' Not in MC.

SH SALE, vii.133, to Lilly £1.18.0 [London, 928]; Sotheby's, 11 May 1908 (Miscellaneous Sale), lot 161, to Bloomfield, £4.

☞ *See* HW to Cole, 24 November 1780: 'I endeavored to give our antiquaries a little wrench towards taste—but in vain. Sandby and our engravers of views have lent them a great deal, but there it stops.'

STRUTT, JOSEPH   3845

The Chronicle of England from the arrival of Julius Caesar to the Norman Conquest. London, 1777–8. Two volumes, 4to.

'Green morocco, with Orford arms on the sides.' Not in MC.

SH SALE, vii.130 (with his *Regal Antiquities*), to Payne & Foss, £7.17.6. [London, 1072]

STRUTT, JOSEPH   3846

Complete view of the manners, customs, arms, habits, etc. of the inhabitants of England. London, 1775–6. Three volumes in two, 4to.

'Green morocco, with Orford arms on the sides.' Not in MC.

SH SALE, vii.130, to H. G. Bohn, £15.10.0. [London, 1073]

3847 STRUTT, JOSEPH

The regal and ecclesiastical antiquities of England. London, 1773.
4to.

'Green morocco, with Orford arms on the sides.' Not in MC.

SH SALE, vii.130 (with his *Chronicle*), to Payne & Foss, £7.17.6. [London,
1072]

3848 TOMKINS, CHARLES

Tour to the Isle of Wight. London, 1796. Two volumes, 8vo.

Green morocco, with Orford arms on the sides. Press-marks S.21 and S.22.
Initials of later owner stamped on title-page, 'C. F.' Not in MC.

SH SALE, vii.131, to Evans [London, 912]; Sotheby's, 29 July 1864 (S.
Palmer Sale), lot 137, to Nattali, £1.1.0; Sotheby's, 5 November 1934 (Miscellaneous Sale), lot 586, to Ellis, £2.5.0; Christie's, 29 June 1959 (Books
consigned by Mrs. I. L. Lenton, from the library of the late P. H. Padwick),
lot 271, to Maggs for WSL, £24.

3849 WATTS, WILLIAM, Engraver

Seats of the nobility and gentry in a collection of the most in-
teresting views. London, 1779–86. Oblong 4to.

'Green morocco, with HW's arms on the sides.' Not in MC.

SH SALE, vii.134, to P. and Dom. Colnaghi, £7.4.0 [London, 926–7];
American Art Association, 2 March 1923 (Bement Sale), lot 1141.

☞ Included with the Watts was a similarly bound copy of Harrison
& Co.'s *Picturesque Views of the principal seats of the nobility and gentry*
in England and Wales. London, 1786–8. Oblong 4to.

In the Watts was HW's note: 'This set of views is the best that has been
executed; the trees are engraved with singular lightness & delicacy.' Numerous other annotations by HW.

PRESS T

Press T contained various topographic works, not unlike those in
Press S. But the books in Press T were generally smaller, and they
were not uniformly bound.

3850 *The Antiquarian Repertory, a miscellany.* Edited by Grose, Astle,
and others. London, 1775–84. Four volumes, 4to.

'Boards.' Not in MC.

SH SALE, vii.136, to Strong, 19/–. [London, 934]

☞ Perhaps this set, rebound in half russia, 4 volumes in 2, 'from the sh collection,' was offered by John Russell Smith in 1849 for £3.

BROWNE, ALEXANDER   3851
Ars pictoria: or an academy treating of drawing, painting, limning, etching. London, 1675. Folio.
Press-mark B.2.24 in MC; moved to the Round Tower, but perhaps misplaced in Press T.
SH SALE, vii.142, to Graves, Pall-Mall. [London, 1157]
☞ In his account of Hilliard in the *Anecdotes*, HW mentioned that Browne had printed an extract from Hilliard's treatise.

[CLARKE, EDWARD DANIEL]   3852
Tour through the South of England, Wales, and part of Ireland. London, 1793. 8vo.
Not in MC.
SH SALE, vii.141, to Lilly. [London, 907]

[COGAN, THOMAS]   3853
The Rhine: or a journey from Utrecht to Francfort. London, 1793. Two volumes, 8vo.
Not in MC.
SH SALE, vii.141, to Lilly. [London, 907]

GILPIN, WILLIAM   3854
Collection of works. London, 1782–92. Eight volumes, 8vo.
'Seven elegantly bound and one in boards.' Not in MC.
SH SALE, vii.138, to — Wood, Esq., £2.9.0. [London, 909]
☞ The separate works, presumably all first editions, were:
(1) *Remarks on forest scenery, and other woodland views,* 1791. Two volumes. *See* HW to Mason, 10 January 1782: 'Mrs. Delany has lent me another most pleasing work of Mr. Gilpin—his *Essay on Forest Trees* considered in a picturesque light. It is perfectly new, truly ingenious, full of good sense in an agreeable style, and void of all affectation—sad recommendations to such times. Consequently, I suppose, it will not be published.'
(2) *Observations relative chiefly to picturesque beauty . . . particularly the mountains and lakes of Cumberland and Westmoreland,* 1786. Two volumes.

(3) *Observations relative chiefly to picturesque beauty . . . particularly the High-lands of Scotland, 1789. Two volumes.*

(4) *Observations on the River Wye, and several parts of South Wales . . . relative chiefly to picturesque beauty, 1782.*

(5) *Three Essays: on picturesque beauty, on picturesque travel, and on sketching landscape, 1792.*

3855 GREEN, VALENTINE

The history and antiquities of the city and suburbs of Worcester. London, 1796. Two volumes, 4to.

'Boards.' Not in MC.

SH SALE, vii.137, to Dodd, 11/–. [London, 937]

3856 HASSELL, JOHN

Tour of the Isle of Wight. With aquatint engravings. London, 1790. Two volumes. 8vo.

Now bound in one volume, in half calf of the 19th century. No BP and no press-mark. Not in MC.

SH SALE, vii.140, to Lilly [London, 907]; Maggs, July 1934, to WSL, £7.15.0.

☞ Several notes and corrections by HW; most interesting is perhaps his general criticism: 'The style of this work is extravagantly poetic; but may be excused in a young painter, especially as it may assist in coloring landscapes. The prints have more force than Mr. Gilpin's, tho often too hard: the clouds are generally too much broken, & are the worst parts. The encomiums on some modern artists are pushed to hyperbole.' This was presumably HW's subscriber's copy.

3857 IRELAND, SAMUEL

Collection of works. London, 1790–94. Six volumes, 4to.

'Boards.' Not in MC.

SH SALE, vii.139. [London, 908 and 1331]

☞ The separate works, presumably all first editions, were:

(1) *Graphic illustrations of Hogarth,* 1794. London, 1331, to R. D'A. Newton, Esq.

(2) *A Picturesque Tour through Holland, Brabant, and part of France,* 1790. Two volumes. London, 908, to Lilly.

(3) *Picturesque Views on the River Medway,* 1793. London, 908, to Lilly.

(4) *Picturesque Views on the River Thames*, 1792. Two volumes. London, 908, to Lilly. Offered in Thorpe's General Catalogue for 1844, lot 2886, for £2.2.0; offered again by Thorpe in 1846, for £1.11.6; offered by G. Willis, August 1854, lot 342, for £1.4.0; in the Harold Edgar Young bequest now in the library of Newnham College, Cambridge. (Young was the son of Henry Young, the Liverpool bookseller. His catalogue of his library shows that he purchased the Ireland for £18.18.0.) The volume is now rebound in half-morocco by Mackenzie, with BP². Press-marks not preserved. Numerous interesting notes and corrections by HW in both volumes; his comments are often genealogical, but he corrects Ireland's use of the word 'apartment' as follows: 'It is a small closet, not an apartment, which properly means a set of chambers, but is now often used by auctioneers & vulgar writers affecting elegance, for a single room.'

KIRBY, JOHN JOSHUA   3858

An historical account of the twelve prints of monasteries, castles, antient churches, and monuments in Suffolk. Engraved by John Wood. Ipswich, 1748. 4to.

Listed in MC but without press-mark; moved to the Round Tower. SH SALE, vii.142, to J. R. Smith. [London, 940]

LYSONS, DANIEL   3859

The environs of London. Dedicated to HW. London, 1792–6. Four volumes, royal 4to.

Red morocco, with Orford arms on the sides; the fourth volume, in boards in 1842, now in matching red morocco. Press-marks T.4 to T.6 in the three volumes not rebound. Not in MC. Bookplate of Henry Labouchere, whose grandson was E. A. V. Stanley.

SH SALE, vii.135, to H. G. Bohn, £6.16.6 [London, 939]; sold (with the fifth volume to complete the set) Sotheby's, 3 December 1920 (Stanley Sale), lot 457, to Michelmore, £6; offered in Michelmore's Catalogue 2, for £150; offered in Michelmore's Catalogue, February 1922, lot 200, for £75; Anderson, 23 January 1924 (Miscellaneous Sale), lot 380, $125; Brick Row, October 1927, to WSL, $350.

☞ A few plates inserted by HW, a few scattered notes, and four pages of notes inserted by him in each of the first three volumes; a short note by Lysons (not to HW) now inserted in fourth volume. Laid in by WSL is a hand-colored copy of the dedication leaf to HW: from the Phillipps Collection, 10 July 1928, to Spencer, and thence to WSL, September 1932, for £3.

3860 NICHOLS, JOHN

Biographical anecdotes of William Hogarth. The 2d edition. London, 1782. 8vo.

Not in MC.

SH SALE, vii.141, to R. D'A. Newton, Esq. [London, 1331]

☞ A copy of the first edition, in the Glass Closet, No. 2435 *above*, is now at Farmington. William Cole gave Nichols some help towards the second edition, and HW sent his own corrections to Nichols in a long letter, 31 October 1781.

3861 REPTON, HUMPHRY

Sketches and hints on landscape gardening. London, 1794. Oblong 4to.

Not in MC.

SH SALE, vii.137, to Evans, £1. [London, 941]

3862 ROBERTSON, ARCHIBALD

Topographical survey of the Great Road from London to Bath and Bristol. London, 1792. Two volumes, 8vo.

Rebound in half green morocco in 1937. BP² later state (in the 1st volume only). Press-marks T.20 and T.21 were present before the volumes were rebound in 1937. Not in MC.

SH SALE, vii.140, to Evans [London, 911]; offered in Thorpe's Catalogue for 1845, lot 6461, for £1.11.6; purchased in 1893 by the British Museum.

☞ Extended notes and corrections by HW in the first part. The set was in boards, uncut, in 1842.

3863 ROBERTSON, DAVID

A tour through the Isle of Man. London, 1794. 8vo.

'Boards.' Not in MC.

SH SALE, vii.140, to Evans. [London, 911]

PRESS V

In Press V were books of natural history, many with colored plates, a few books of music, and books on the arts.

ALBIN, ELEAZAR   3864

A natural history of birds. Volume I. London, 1731. 4to.

'Old calf, with HW's BP.' Press-mark B.2.35 in MC; moved to the Round Tower.

SH SALE, vii.144, to Lilly, 13/– [London, 1132]; Hodgson, 28 March 1928 (Miscellaneous Sale), lot 535, to Marks, £3.14.0.

☞ Two more volumes completed the set in 1738, but HW seems to have had only the first volume. The plates were colored in HW's volume.

ALBIN, ELEAZAR   3865

A natural history of English insects. London, 1720. 4to.

Old panelled calf, rebacked. BP¹. Press-mark B.2.36, altered in book to V.8.

SH SALE, vii.144, to Thorne, Richmond, 15/– [London, 1133]; Sawyer, August 1933, to WSL, £5.5.0.

☞ The plates are colored.

BASAN, PIERRE FRANÇOIS   3866

Catalogue d'une belle collection de dessins Italiens, Flamands, Hollandais, et Francais qui composaient le cabinet de Neyman. Paris, 1776. 8vo.

'Sewed; presentation copy to HW.' Not in MC.

SH SALE, vii.148, to Strong.

☞ No doubt in the London Sale, lot 1154, which lists Mariette's catalogue as in two volumes.

BASAN, PIERRE FRANÇOIS   3867

Catalogue raisonné des differens objets de curiosités . . . qui composaient le cabinet de feu M. Mariette. Paris, 1775. 8vo.

'Sewed.' Not in MC.

SH SALE, vii.148, to Strong [London, 1154]; offered in Strong's Catalogue for 1843, lot 237, for 7/6.

☞ When he was in Paris, in September 1775, HW attended the exhibition but he returned to London before the sale; among his purchases was the Petitot miniature sold in SH SALE, xiv.53.

3868 BEWICK, THOMAS

A general history of quadrupeds. Newcastle, 1790. 8vo.

Original green morocco. BP² later state. Press-mark V.25. Not in MC.

SH SALE, vii.147, to Thorne, Richmond [London, 1131]; Sotheby's, 5 May 1904 (Ford Sale), lot 17, to Tregaskis, £1.13.0; given by Mrs. John Frederick Lewis in 1934 to the Free Library of Philadelphia.

3869 BROWN, PETER

New illustrations of zoology. In English and French, with colored plates. London, 1776. 4to.

Not in MC.

SH SALE, vii.144, to H. G. Bohn, 19/–. [London, 1134]

3870 BURKITT, WILLIAM

Expository notes with practical observations on the New Testament, with plates. London, 1752. Folio.

Not in MC.

SH SALE, vii.147, to Lilly. [London, 1083]

☞ This work, frequently reprinted after 1700, seems out of place among the books on art and natural history; if it was HW's, he perhaps kept it for the plates in this fine edition: the catalogue records only 'Burkitt's Notes on the New Testament.'

3871 CERVETTO, GIACOBBE

Six solos for the violoncello. Dedicated to Sir Edward Walpole. London, [*ca.* 1750]. Oblong 4to.

'Splendidly bound in morocco.' Not in MC.

SH SALE, vii.151, to Payne & Foss. [London, 1057]

☞ The SH catalogue lists only one volume for lot 151, but names Cervetto and adds 'and 2 other books of music.' One of these, identified in lot 1057 of the London Sale, was Heighington, No. 3878 *below.*

3872 EDWARDS, GEORGE

Gleanings of natural history. With colored plates. London, 1758–60. Two volumes, 4to.

Not in MC.

SH SALE, vii.146, to Nattali. [London, 1137]

☞ *See* HW to Montagu, 14 January 1760: 'I was much diverted t'other morning with another volume on birds by Edwards, who has published four or five. . . . What struck me most were his dedications; the last was to God, this to Lord Bute, as if he was determined to make his fortune in one world or t'other.'

EDWARDS, GEORGE 3873

A natural history of uncommon birds and . . . animals. With colored
plates. London, 1743–51. Four volumes, 4to.

In boards in 1842. Press-mark B.2.31 in MC; moved to the Round
Tower.

SH SALE, vii.146, to Nattali. [London, 1136]

☞ A set, completed in eight volumes (including the *Gleanings* and
Brown's *New Illustrations*) and handsomely bound in the middle of the
19th century in red morocco, now in the Dowse Collection at the Massachusetts Historical Society, is described in the printed catalogue of the
collection as having belonged to Horatio Walpole. There is no evidence
to support this in the books themselves; but the catalogue's description
seems likely to be correct. *See* note under Capell, No. 2003 *above.*

A correspondent of the *Times Literary Supplement,* 23 November 1940,
wrote that HW's subscription set was at Houghton, but Lord Cholmondeley
reported that the set at Houghton exhibited no trace of HW.

EDWARDS, GEORGE 3874

Some memoirs of the life and works of George Edwards. London,
1776. 4to.

Not in MC.

SH SALE, vii.143, to Nattali. [London, 1137]

GRIBELIN, SIMON 3875

*Livre de petite estampes gravée sur plusieurs ouvrage, fait relié à
Londre,* 1722. Scrap book on 89 leaves. 4to.

Calf. Press-mark B.3.20 in MC; altered in book to V.23.

SH SALE, vii.150, to Pickering, £9.10.0 [London, 598]; bought by Hugh
Hume Campbell, and given to Juliana Hume Campbell, 18 June 1842;
now at St. Mary's College, Strawberry Hill.

☞ Of this, HW wrote in his *Engravers:* 'I have a thick quarto collected
by himself [Gribelin], of all his small plates, which was sold by his son
after his decease.'

3876 GULSTON, JOSEPH

Catalogue of [his] *collection of prints.* Sold by Mr. Greenwood. London, 1786. Two parts, 8vo.

Old three-quarter calf. BP² later state. Not in MC.

SH SALE, vii.148, to Strong [London, 1154]; offered in Strong's Catalogue for 1843, lot 649, for 16/–; since 1930 in the Huntington Library.

☞ Partially priced by HW, who wrote in it: 'This collection containing particularly the largest number of English portraits ever assembled, and even exceeding that made by Richard Bull, Esq., which he sold to Lord Mount Stewart, was formed by Joseph Gulston, Esq., of Ealing, at the expense, as was said and generally believed, of £16,000. The collection was sold to pay his debts contracted with print and booksellers, and produced but £4500, though most extravagant and ridiculous prices were given for some prints. . . .' The collection also contained the portrait of Gulston by his daughter.

At this sale HW bought a number of prints, but he seems to have been especially interested in the erratic prices produced at the sale.

Rodd, in his Catalogue for 1847, Part 3 (Arts and Sciences), lot 2850, offered Kirgate's copy of Gulston's Catalogue, 'filled with notes by Lord Orford.'

3877 GWYNN, JOHN

London and Westminster improved. London, 1766. 4to.

Press-mark B.4 in MC, entered by HW; moved to the Round Tower. SH SALE, vii.148, to J. R. Smith. [London, 938]

☞ In his 'Book of Materials,' *ca.* 1766, HW made one note from Gwynn.

3878 HEIGHINGTON, MUSGRAVE

Six select odes of Anacreon in Greek and six of Horace in Latin, set to music. London [1736?]. Oblong folio.

Not in MC.
SH SALE, vii.151, to Payne & Foss. [London, 1057]

☞ Only the Odes of Horace are specified in the sale catalogue; it is therefore conceivable that this volume was divided, and that the Anacreon is what has been entered in Press R of the Round Tower, No. 3802 *above*, but the other books in that lot were all in octavo.

HERALDRY   3879

A Collection of the coats of arms of the nobility and gentry of Gloucester. 4to.

Not in MC.

SH SALE, vii.143, to H. G. Bohn.

☞ This does not appear in the London Sale. It consisted of 62 plates, collected by Sir George Nayler; published at Gloucester in 1786, and some copies are dated London 1792. But lot 1107 in the London Sale was a folio MS not listed in SH SALE:

NORFOLK. *Visitation of Norfolk with pedigrees and arms.* MS in several hands, 17th century. Old calf, rebacked. BP² early state. No press-mark. Note by HW: 'Bought at the sale of Mr. Ives, 1777' (5 March 1777, lot 423, £3.3.0); London, 1107, to Rodd, £6.12.6; Phillipps MS 13829; Robinson, from the Phillipps Collection, April 1950, to WSL, £50. One note by HW on the Walpole entry.

HOGARTH, WILLIAM   3880

The analysis of beauty. London, 1753. 4to.

Original mottled calf, rebacked. BP¹. Press-mark B.3.28, altered to V.24 in book.

SH SALE, vii.148, to R. D'A. Newton, Esq. [London, 1331]; T. Thorp, March 1929, to R. W. Chapman, £2.2.0; given by Dr. Chapman to WSL.

☞ A few notes and markings by HW. He wrote to Bentley, 19 December 1753: 'You have not been much more diverted, I fear, with Hogarth's book—'tis very silly.'

JONES, EDWARD   3881

Musical and poetical relicks of the Welsh Bards. London, 1784. 4to.

Press-mark D.3 in MC; apparently moved to the Round Tower.

SH SALE, vii.143, to H. G. Bohn [Not listed separately in the London Sale]; offered in Lilly's Catalogue for 1863, for 18/–.

KATE, LAMBERT TEN   3882

The Beau Ideal. Translated by Le Blon. London, 1732. 4to.

Not in MC.

SH SALE, vii.143, to H. G. Bohn. [Not listed separately in London Sale; possibly '1 other' in lot 1147.]

☞ Le Blon dedicated his translation to Lady Walpole. An imperfect copy of this book in red morocco, with HW's BP, was in the Stirling-Maxwell

Sale at Christie's, 21 May 1958, lot 254; it was purchased by Hertzberger, The Hague, for £70, and resold to a private collector in the Netherlands.

3883 Le Blon, Jacques Christophe

Coloritto, or the harmony of colouring in painting, reduced to mechanical practice. In English and French, with colored plates. London [1730]. 4to.

Press-mark B.3.7 in MC; moved to the Round Tower.
SH SALE, vii.145, to Graves, Pall Mall. [London, 1157]

3884 Monkeys

A volume on natural history, in German. 4to.

Not in MC.
SH SALE, vii.147, to Thorne, Richmond. [London, 1131]

☞ In the London Sale this was described as a German work on Monkeys. There seems to be no other clue. One such book is Petrus Camper's *Naturgeschichte des Orang-Utang.* Translated from Dutch; 8 plates. Düsseldorf, 1791. Or perhaps HW had one part of Johann Schreber's *Die Säugthiere*, published in parts with colored plates, Erlangen, 1775 ff., in 4to. The first volume contains some hundred fine colored plates of simians, after Edwards, Huet, and other artists.

3885 Royal Academy of Arts, London

Collection of Catalogues, 1769–96. Twenty-eight numbers, 4to.

Not in MC.
SH SALE, vii.149, to Smith, Lisle Street, £52.10.0 [London, 1160]; bound in two volumes by Riviere in half green morocco *ca.* 1850, apparently for John Sheepshanks whose bookplate is in them. Sotheby's, 2 March 1891 (Miscellaneous Sale), lot 826, to Harvey; now in the library of the Earl of Rosebery.

☞ Numerous notes by HW, selections from which were printed by Cunningham, Graves, and Whitley.

Included with the Royal Academy set were the following:

(1) Society of Artists of Great Britain (later called the Incorporated Society or the Royal Incorporated Society). Collection of Catalogues, 1760–91.

(2) Society of Artists of Great Britain. *Copy of the Royal Charter. . . . With a list of the present Directors and Fellows,* 1767.

(3) FREE SOCIETY OF ARTISTS, sometimes called confusingly the SOCIETY OF ARTISTS. Collection of Catalogues, 1760–83. This exhibition was sponsored until 1765 by the Society for the Encouragement of Arts, Manufactures, and Commerce, now known as the Royal Society of Arts.

(4) *A Letter to the Members of the Society for the Encouragement of Arts, Manufactures, and Commerce.* The 2d edition. London 1761.

(5) *Catalogue of pictures, sculptures, &c. the works of artists who have exhibited at the Great Room in Spring Garden, Charing Cross, which will be sold by auction by Mr. Langford,* 1763.

(6) *A Critical review of the pictures . . . exhibited . . . in Spring Gardens.* By I. N. 1765.

(7) *A Critical review of the pictures . . . exhibited . . . in Spring Gardens,* 1766.

(8) *The Exhibition: or, a candid display of the genius and merits of the . . . works . . . at Spring Gardens,* [1766].

(9) *A Critical examination of the pictures . . . exhibited . . . in Spring Gardens,* 1767.

(10) *Le Pour et le Contre. Being a poetical display of the merit and demerit . . . exhibited at Spring Gardens,* 1767.

(11) *Critical observations on the pictures . . . exhibiting at the Great Room, Spring Garden,* 1768.

(12) *Candid observations on the principal performances now exhibiting at the New Room of the Society of Artists,* 1772.

(13) *Historical and critical review of the paintings . . . of the Society instituted for the Encouragement of Arts,* 1762.

(14) *Catalogue of the paintings . . . now exhibiting by the Free and Independent Artists of Great Britain,* 1768. This was an attempt to imitate the exhibition of the Free Society.

These catalogues and pamphlets (here numbered 1–14) were bound into four volumes by Riviere in half green morocco *ca.* 1850, apparently for John Sheepshanks, whose bookplate is in them; they were sold at Sotheby's, 2 March 1891 (Miscellaneous Sale), lots 818–20, to Grego; sold by Maggs, in 1925, to WSL, £20. This set was fully recorded and its notes transcribed by Mr. Hugh Gatty in the 27th volume of the Walpole Society, 1939; W. T. Whitley transcribed some of the notes and published them in 1928 in his *Artists and their Friends in England.*

The late Algernon Graves owned a somewhat similar set, into which he had transcribed many notes; this set is now also at Farmington (from Reginald Grundy to Rimell to WSL, 1939). Comparison shows that he tran-

scribed from notes in the set in the British Museum, which he thought (wrongly) to have notes in HW's hand.

Also included in the Royal Academy set (vii.149) was a set of presidential *Discourses* by Reynolds and West, with presentation inscriptions to HW. The fifteen *Discourses* by Reynolds, 1769–1791, bound in half calf, were sold at the American Art Association, 11 December 1918, and again (separated and unbound) at the Walpole Galleries, 29 July 1919. On the *Discourse* of December 1782, HW wrote: 'This discourse is a tacit avowal of his own object in painting, which was general effect:—but ought not to be a general rule, for he neglected the other parts: his flesh does not, like Titian's, represent the various tints of flesh; nor his draperies, like Van Dyck's, represent velvet satin silk &c; his hands are generally as ill drawn as colored; and even in effect his pictures that were not striking in the first year were commonly faded in the next.' A very similar criticism of this *Discourse* is in HW's letter to Mason, 10 February 1783.

This whole collection in 1842 was half-bound in three thick volumes; it was also described as including 'sale catalogues of magnificent collections.' But the three largest groups seem to have been: (1) the Royal Academy Catalogues, (2) the Society of Artists and the Free Society Catalogues, (3) the Reynolds *Discourses*.

3886 WILKES, BENJAMIN

The English moths and butterflies. With colored plates. London [1749]. 4to.

Press-mark B.2.30 in MC; moved to the Round Tower.

SH SALE, vii.145, to Thorne, Richmond, £2. [London, 1135]

PRESS X

Press X in the Round Tower was somewhat miscellaneous. Instead of books of prints, these were all books that had some personal association: books by or about the Walpoles, books by Mason and Gray, and books presented to HW. In the Main Library these would all have been kept in the Glass Closet, and one may guess that some or all of them were moved from the Glass Closet in 1790.

3887 [BAKER, THOMAS]

Reflections upon learning. London, 1714. 8vo.

Rebound in calf. No BP or press-mark. Not in MC. Bookplates of John Mitford (with his signature) and Lord Orford (1813–94).

SH SALE, vii.37 (with Luxborough and Pope), to Payne & Foss, £2.8.0 [London, 1055]; Sotheby's, 24 April 1860 (Mitford Sale), lot 137, to Bumstead, 6/–; now in Lord Walpole's collection at Wolterton Park.

☞ Many derogatory notes by HW.

COLLINS, ARTHUR 3888

History of the noble and ancient family of Walpole. [London, 1756] 8vo.

Bound in decorated boards with HW's signature. Press-mark X.14. Not in MC.

SH SALE, vii.30, to Lilly [London, 1046]; in Lord Waldegrave's Library, with the 9th Earl's bookplate; given by Lord Waldegrave, November 1964, to WSL.

☞ Several extended notes by HW, some of which were entered many years later. This is an off-print, with special MS title, of the article on the Walpole family in Collins's *Peerage* of 1756; the MS title was prepared by Collins who also prepared off-prints of several other important families. His MS *Genealogy of the Family of Walpole*, presumably compiled *ca.* 1727, is now WSL; it is on folio sheets. At the College of Arms, in Sir Isaac Heard's pedigree of Walpole in the collection of Peers' Pedigrees, there are two notes made in January 1792 by HW.

The sale catalogue is confusing about the books sold in vii.30. The first printing names Collins, Gardening Miscellanies, Mason, and Richard Walpole; the revised printing repeats Mason, adds Waller, and then says '8 others.' The London Sale is not always easy to match up, but one can guess that the ten volumes also included Rigby, Thicknesse, and HW's *Modern Gardening.* Two books out of ten are therefore not identified.

But because of the Gray and Mason books in lots 29 and 30, two other pamphlets by Mason may be included here: HW surely had copies even if they do not appear in the catalogues.

(1) MASON, WILLIAM. *An occasional discourse preached in the Cathedral . . . in York . . . on the subject of the African Slave-trade.* York, 1788. 4to. A copy was offered, but not identified as HW's, in Thorpe's Supplement for 1842, lot 12772, for 2/–, 'sewed.'

(2) MASON, WILLIAM. *Secular Ode in commemoration of the Glorious Revolution.* London, 1788. 4to. A letter from Harcourt to Mason, 20 November 1788, makes clear that Mason had sent a copy of his *Ode* to HW: *see* Appendix to the Yale Walpole, Volume 29.

3889 CONGREVE, WILLIAM

Works. Birmingham. Printed by John Baskerville, 1761. Three volumes, royal 8vo.

Original calf. BP² early state. Press-mark M.3.17; moved to the Round Tower. Bookplate of E. W. B[urroughs?].

SH SALE, vii.38, to James Baker, Esq., £4.10.0 [London, 1039]; Carnegie Book Shop, January 1949, through Stonehill, to WSL, $82.50.

3890 DU FRESNOY, CHARLES ALPHONSE

The art of painting, translated into English verse by William Mason. With annotations by Sir Joshua Reynolds. York, 1783. 4to.

'Green morocco, with HW's arms on sides.' Not in MC.

SH SALE, vii.32, to George Soaper, £2.15.0 [London, 1040]; Sotheby's, 16 April 1894 (Buckley Sale, Part 2), lot 1336, to B. F. Stevens, £3.5.0; Anderson, 26 April 1911 (Hoe Sale, Part 1), lot 1176, $125.

☞ A note by HW at beginning, and several plates inserted by him. He wrote to Mason, 10 February 1783: 'I have at last received your Fresnoy from Sir Joshua. You have made it a very handsome book. . . .'

3891 GARDENING

Two volumes, 8vo.

Not in MC. 'Various tracts on Gardening, by Mr. Walpole, &c., 2 vols.' in the sale catalogue.

SH SALE, vii.30, to H. G. Bohn. [London, 1038]

☞ Since the first edition of the sale catalogue specified 'Miscellanies on Gardening, from Mr. Lort's collection,' one volume can be identified from the Lort Catalogue, April 1791, lot 265, bought by Walpole for 1/–; it contained:

(1) *Elements of modern gardening.* London, 1785. Attributed doubtfully to John Trusler. The preface acknowledges the use of material from HW's *Essay.*

(2) *An historical view of the taste for gardening . . . among the nations of antiquity,* by William Falconer. London, 1783.

(3) *Miscellanies on ancient and modern gardening,* by Samuel Felton. London, 1785.

This volume of three tracts was offered in Bohn's Catalogue for 1847 (Architecture), p. 228, for 4/–.

The second volume was perhaps a copy of HW's 'Modern Gardening' in the fourth volume of his *Anecdotes*; lot vii.45 included a single volume of the *Anecdotes*, and this lot was dispersed in the London Sale.

GRAY, THOMAS   3892

The Latin Odes of Mr. Gray, in English verse, with an Ode on the death of a favourite spaniel. By Edward Burnaby Greene. London, 1775. 8vo.

Not in MC.

SH SALE, vii.29, to Strong. [London, 1037]

☞ The spaniel of the poem was HW's Tory. But Greene appended only his initials to the volume, so that HW had to inquire of Cole, 10 December 1775, who the author was.

Two other pamphlets not specified in lot 1037 were doubtless included in vii.29 (and perhaps sold London 1034, '5 others'); the sale catalogue totals six volumes for vii.29.

On 19 July 1774, HW sent to Mason a copy with MS additions of Gray's *Catalogue of the antiquities, houses, parks . . . in England and Wales*, printed for private distribution in 1773 by Mason. This copy has not been traced, and no copy of the later edition of 1787 is identifiable in the SH records.

GRAY, THOMAS   3893

Elegy written in a country church-yard, translated into Italian verse by J. Giannini. London, 1782. 8vo.

Not in MC.

SH SALE, vii.29, to Strong. [London, 1037]

[GRAY, THOMAS]   3894

Ode on the death of Mr. Gray. MS. 8vo.

Not in MC.

SH SALE, vii.29, to Strong. [London, 1037]

☞ This was apparently a MS of the verses first published in Gray's *Poetical Works*, 1799.

GRAY, THOMAS   3895

Poems. Edited by Gilbert Wakefield. London, 1786. 8vo.

Original boards, uncut. BP[1], inserted perhaps in 1842, and no press-mark. Not in MC. Bookplate of George Soaper.

SH SALE, vii.29 (with other Gray items), to Strong, 9/– [London, 1037]; Sotheby's, 19 April 1844 (Eyton Sale), lot 468, to Thorpe, 1/–; Traylen, from the F. A. Barrett collection, November 1954, to WSL, £15.

☞ There are no notes, save 'From Strawberry Hill,' in George Soaper's hand. The lettering on the spine, 'Wakefield's Notes on Gray's Poems, 1786,' is by HW. Despite the inserted bookplate and the absence of a press-mark, the volume must have been at SH: *see* No. 2827 *above*.

3896 LUXBOROUGH, HENRIETTA KNIGHT, Baroness
Letters . . . to William Shenstone, Esq. Edited by J. Hodgetts. London, 1775. 8vo.

Contemporary calf. BP². Press-mark X.12. Not in MC. Signature of John Mitford, 1844.

SH SALE, vii.37 (with Baker and Pope), to Payne & Foss, £2.8.0 [London, 1055]; Sotheby's, 24 April 1860 (Mitford Sale), lot 2128, to Booth, 16/–; owned by Bolton Corney; Sotheby's, 24 April 1903 (John Taylor Brown Sale), lot 1716, to B. F. Stevens, £26; Parke-Bernet, 5 May 1939 (Spoor Sale), lot 1108, to Rosenbach, $145; purchased in 1946 by Lord Rothschild. (No. 1338 in the Catalogue of his Library)

☞ Some 40 notes and comments by HW: he noted satirically that Lady Luxborough admired the *Scribleriad* and Shenstone but liked Gray 'only *well*.' He wrote to Mason, 27 November 1775: 'We have had nothing at all this winter but Sterne's *Letters*, and what are almost as nothingly—Lady Luxborough's. She does not write ill, or, as I expected, affectedly, like a woman, but talks of *scrawls*, and of her letters being *stupid*. She had no spirit, no wit, knew no events; she idolizes poor Shenstone, who was scarce above her, and flatters him, to be flattered. A stronger proof of her having no taste is that she says coldly, she likes Gray's Churchyard *well*.'

On 24 January 1778, HW wrote to Mason: 'I have got two more volumes of Shenstone's correspondence, and they are like all the rest, insipidity itself.' These two volumes were *Select letters between the late Duchess of Somerset, Lady Luxborough, . . . William Shenstone, Esq., and others*, ed. by Thomas Hull, London 1778; two volumes, 8vo. They do not appear in the records of the sale.

3897 MASON, WILLIAM
The English Garden: a poem. In four books. Edited by William Burgh. York and London, 1783. 8vo.

Not in MC.

SH SALE, vii.30, to H. G. Bohn. [London, 1038]

☞ *See* HW to Mason, 14 March 1782: 'I rejoice on Mr. Burgh's intended Commentary on your *Garden*: such things will survive, whatever perishes.'

On 18 May 1775, Mason wrote to HW to look at the 2d edition of Burgh's *Scriptural confutation of . . . Mr. Lindsey*, published in 1775, but HW seems not to have owned a copy.

MORE, HANNAH   3898

Florio: a tale . . . and the Bas Bleu. London, 1786. 4to.

> Not in MC.
>
> SH SALE, vii.32, to H. G. Bohn. [London, 1038]
>
> ☞ The poems were dedicated to HW, apparently as a surprise; he thanked the authoress for the volume 9 February 1786. Another copy is in his 'Poems of the Reign of George the 3d' at Harvard.
>
> On 6 March 1784, HW thanked Hannah More for a copy of her *Bas Bleu* in MS.

PISAN, CHRISTINE DE   3899

Le trésor de la cité des dames. Paris, 1536. 8vo.

> Not in MC.
>
> SH SALE, vii.39 (with Pomfret), to Lilly, £1.10.0. [London, 1050]
>
> ☞ The catalogue adds at vii.39 'and 7 others'; but while in the first edition, the total is entered as nine, this is changed to two in the corrected edition. Other volumes were perhaps dispersed (to end of Fifth Day, &c.) before the sale began.

POMFRET, THOMAS   3900

The life of . . . Lady Christian late Countess Dowager of Devonshire. London, 1685. 8vo.

> Rebound in calf in the late 18th century. BP² later state. Press-mark X.19. Not in MC. Bookplate of Charles George Milnes Gaskell.
>
> SH SALE, vii.39 (with Pisan), to Lilly, £1.10.0 [London, 1050]; Hodgson's, 29 February 1924 (Milnes Gaskell Sale), lot 98, to Bain, £8.15.0; Sotheby's, 29 June 1938 (Miscellaneous Sale), lot 247, to Maggs for WSL, £11.
>
> ☞ Signature of Ralph Thoresby, who paid 16 pence for the volume. Note by HW: 'Bought at Mr. [Thomas] Crofts' Sale 1783.' Several notes by HW, in addition to a biographical notice of the Countess, and two notes in a 17th century hand. On p. 80, HW was struck by the assertion that the Countess of Carlisle was imprisoned in the Tower; he wrote

'I have nowhere else met with an account of her imprisonment,' and in his 'Book of Materials,' *ca.* 1786, he made a note to himself: 'To inquire when or why the famous Countess of Carlisle was committed to the Tower before the Restoration, as it is said she was, in the *Life of Christian Countess of Devonshire*. I have nowhere else met with that event.'

3901 POPE, ALEXANDER

Additions to the works of Alexander Pope. Edited by Warburton. London, 1776. Two volumes in one, 8vo.

Now bound in half red morocco. BP² early state. No press-mark preserved. Not in MC.

SH SALE, vii.37 (with Baker and Luxborough), to Payne & Foss, £2.8.0 [London, 1055]; Sotheby's, 24 April 1860 (Mitford Sale), lot 2800, to Pickering, £2.10.0; now in British Museum.

☞ Numerous notes by HW. Another copy was in the Glass Closet, No. 2452 *above*.

3902 PORTLAND, MARGARET CAVENDISH (HARLEY) BENTINCK, Duchess of

A catalogue of the Portland Museum. . . . Sold by auction by Mr. Skinner and Co. The sale lasted 38 days, beginning 24 April 1786. (Catalogue of cameos, sold 8 June 1786, bound in; the printed catalogue of prices, present in 1842, has since been removed.) [London 1786.] 4to.

Original marbled boards with calf back, now rebacked. Large SH fleuron used as BP, and fleuron from *Anecdotes* at end. Press-mark X.7. Not in MC.

SH SALE, vii.32, to H. G. Bohn for William Beckford, £1.6.0 [London, 1156]; Sotheby's, 6 July 1882 (Beckford Sale, Part 1), lot 1675, to Jefferies for Spencer George Perceval, £5.5.0; Hodgson's, 27 October 1927 (Miscellaneous Sale), to Maggs; offered by Maggs in Catalogues 505 and 536 (1928–30) for £125; Maggs, August 1931, to WSL, £60.

☞ The catalogue was profusely annotated by HW: he identified the executrix as Lady Weymouth; he noted that 2000 catalogues were distributed before the sale (his copy was No. 753); he identified the Vase, the Jupiter Serapis, and the Carp of Chelsea porcelain in the frontispiece; he made notes on items he bought and on others that interested him; he noted that two bronze horses were from Lady Elizabeth Germain's Sale; he noted of a specimen of the hair of Mary Queen of France 'I have some of the

same hair'; of a portrait said to be of the Duchess de la Vallière, he wrote: 'This is not the Duchess. . . . It was offered to me for about 12 guineas, and I wd not buy it, nor was it then named. The possessor then christened it and sold it to the Duchess of Portland, I don't know for how much, but I know it is not worth five guineas [it fetched £84]'; of a miniature of Milton, he wrote: 'I do not believe it Milton'; he noted that Queen Elizabeth's Prayer Book was from West's Sale; he noted that the King failed to get a Missal because he limited his bid; he totalled the proceeds of the whole sale at the end; and he wrote a four-page history of the Duchess's collection. (This last was printed in 1936 by WSL in his 'Miscellaneous Antiquities' No. 11.) Perhaps HW's most interesting purchases were the Missal by Julio Clovio and the Barberini head of Jupiter Serapis in green basalt.

See HW to Conway, 18 June 1786: 'Do you know that I have bought the Jupiter Serapis as well as the Julio Clovio. . . . I am glad Sir Joshua Reynolds saw no more excellence in the Jupiter than in the Clovio. . . . I told Sir William Hamilton and the late Duchess, when I never thought it would be mine, that I had rather have the head than the vase. I shall long for Mrs. Damer to make a bust to it. . . . I have deposited both the illumination and the Jupiter in Lady Di's cabinet, which is worthy of them. And here my collection winds up; I will not purchase trumpery after such jewels.' Lady Diana Beauclerk's cabinet, sold in the Sixteenth Day, is now at Farmington.

In response to Beckford's inquiry, Bohn wrote on 16 June 1842: 'Portland Cat. Scrubby outside, but clean within. The notes are scarcely discoverable, but there is a long character of Robert Harley extracted by himself from his Royal and Noble Authors. Perhaps £2.2.0.' Beckford responded: 'I should not grudge 3 or 4 [guineas] . . . notwithstanding its exterior scrubbiness.' (Letters now WSL)

RIGBY, RICHARD   3903

Authentic memoirs and a sketch of the real character of . . . Richard Rigby. London, 1788. 8vo.

Not in MC.

SH SALE, vii.30, to Lilly. [London, 1046]

☞ At Farmington a fragment only survives: the title and fly-title, in which HW inserted a print of Rigby (1782) and wrote in the name; BP² later state; a note signed GV says: 'This was bought at SH SALE—should be inserted in my autograph book.' Spencer, through Spurr & Swift, June 1932, to WSL.

3904 SHAKESPEARE, WILLIAM

A Collection of prints from pictures painted for . . . the dramatic works. London, 1790– . Eleven parts, with 55 plates, folio.

Not in MC.

SH SALE, vii.34, to Michael, £2.2.0. [London, 1205]

☞ This grandiose project was completed by John Boydell in 1805 in two volumes. In the London Sale, lot 1206 is a similar set of 55 plates, subscriber's copy, to Wilcox, £3.3.0. Both sets were apparently included as one in vii.34.

3905 SHAKESPEARE, WILLIAM

A Series of prints illustrative . . . of Shakespeare. Engraved by Bartolozzi from drawings by Bunbury. London, 1792–6. Twenty plates in five numbers, oblong folio.

Not in MC.

SH SALE, vii.35, to H. G. Bohn, £1.3.0. [London, 734]

☞ The SH set of Silvester and Edward Harding's *Shakespeare illustrated by an assemblage of portraits and views,* 150 plates in 31 numbers in original wrappers, 1789–93, was not in the SH SALE. Instead, Mrs. Damer kept it; it was sold at Sotheby's, 5 August 1886 (Miscellaneous Sale), lot 72, to Johnston for £5.5.0, and is now in the Folger Shakespeare Library.

3906 [THICKNESSE, PHILIP]

Sketches and characters of the most eminent . . . persons now living. Bristol, 1770. 12mo.

'Sewed, uncut, with blanks filled in by HW.' Not in MC.

SH SALE, vii.30, to Lilly [London, 1046]; offered in Lilly's Catalogue for 1861, for £6.6.0.

☞ *See* HW to Mason, 19 September 1772: 'Mr. Granger lent me a book called *Sketches and Characters* . . . , printed a year or two ago. My brother is mentioned and said to be the only *surviving* son of a late great minister.'

3907 WALLER, Sir WILLIAM

A vindication of the character and conduct of Sir William Waller explanatory of his conduct in taking up arms against King Charles the First. London, 1793. 8vo.

'Morocco.' Not in MC.

SH SALE, vii.30, to Payne & Foss, 14/–. [London, 1048]

WALPOLE, HORACE   3908

Le Chateau d'Otrante. Translated by Marc Antoine Eidous. Amsterdam and Paris, 1767. Two volumes in one, 12mo.

Old calf. BP² later state. Press-mark X.18. Not in MC.

SH SALE, vii.33, to Holloway [not named in London Sale]; offered in Thorpe's General Catalogue for 1845, Part 2, lot 5132, for 5/–; purchased from Thorpe, 13 March 1847, by the British Museum.

☞ In his 'Short Notes' for March 1767, HW wrote: 'A bad translation of *The Castle of Otranto* into French was published at Paris this month.'

WALPOLE, HORACE   3909

Historic doubts on the life and reign of King Richard the Third. Printed at SH, 1771. 4to.

Old mottled calf. BP² later state. Press-mark X.3. Not in MC.

SH SALE, vii.33, to Holloway [London, 1049]; signature of Edward Herries (1821?–1911); David C. Herries, through John Hodgson, September 1942, to WSL, £31.10.0.

☞ Several notes and corrections by HW, at least one of which was written after 1777; and his 'Postscript' written in 1793, in his autograph.

The copy of HW's *Miscellaneous Antiquities* and other tracts that was first catalogued in Press X (Round Tower) was moved in the revised catalogue to Press Y, the added books catalogued at the end of the books in the Library in the Offices, No. 3476 *above*.

WALPOLE, RICHARD, Jesuit   3910

Authentic memoirs of . . . Father Richard Walpole . . . by a gentleman. London, 1733. 8vo.

Not in MC.

SH SALE, vii.30 (in 1st edition of catalogue only), to Lilly. [London, 1046]

☞ Another copy was with the Tracts in L.1, No. 2050 *above*.

WALTON, PETER   3911

List of the pictures belonging to the Crown at the time of Queen Anne. MS. 4to.

Rebound in brown morocco by C. Lewis, with crest of the Earl of Clare on the sides. BP². Not in MC.

SH SALE, vii.36, to Rodwell, Bond-Street, £21 [London, 1117]; Sotheby's,

31 January 1881 (Earl of Clare Sale), lot 146, to Quaritch, £17; now in the Office of the Surveyor of the Queen's Pictures at St. James's Palace.

☞ Some notes by HW. This MS was previously in the collection of Richard Topham of Windsor, whose heir Topham Beauclerk presented it to HW in 1775. It was added in MS to the printed list of rarities in the Glass Closet by HW in his own copy of the *Description of SH*, 1774, and then listed in the Appendix (printed *ca.* 1781).

Bound with this is *The Principal pictures arras hangings and statues of King Charles the First with the prices for which they were sold*, 1649, with one note by HW. This was printed by Bathoe in 1757 (from another MS) to accompany the *Catalogue of Charles I's Pictures*.

PRESS Y

Press Y contained books somewhat similar to those in Press X, miscellaneous books presented to HW and copies of some of his own writings. It also contained a number of guides to theatrical history.

3912 BAKER, DAVID ERSKINE

Biographia dramatica, or, a companion to the playhouse. New edition, revised by Isaac Reed. London, 1782. Two volumes, 8vo.

Rebound in half calf, now rebacked. BP² later state. Not in MC, and no press-mark preserved. Bookplate of Edward Cheney and note by him that the book was bought at the SH SALE.

SH SALE, vii.46, to Lilly [London, 1038*]; Maggs, February 1939, to WSL, £52.

☞ Each volume is signed 'Hor. Walpole 1782,' and he made comments or markings occasionally throughout both volumes. When Baker praised Shakespeare's *Merry Wives* as a comic masterpiece, HW wrote: 'It is very inferior to the comic parts of *Henry IV*.' It is of some interest that among numerous cancels in this work, two were made to introduce a completely different essay on HW's *Mysterious Mother*, revised at his request.

3913 [BUNBURY, HENRY WILLIAM]

An academy for grown horsemen. By Geoffrey Gambado, *pseud.* London, 1787. Royal 4to.

'Boards, with HW's BP.' Not in MC.

SH SALE, vii.44 (with his *Annals of Horsemanship*), to H. G. Bohn, 7/-
[London, 735]

☞ Twelve plates. Another set was preserved by HW in his collection of
Bunbury's etchings, in Press C of the Round Tower, No. 3563 *above*.
Francis Grose is sometimes said to have been Geoffrey Gambado.

[BUNBURY, HENRY WILLIAM]   3914

Annals of horsemanship. By Geoffrey Gambado, *pseud.* Sixteen plates.
    London, 1791. Royal 4to.

'Boards, with HW's BP.' Not in MC.

SH SALE, vii.44 (with his *Academy for grown horsemen*), to H. G. Bohn,
7/- [London, 735]; the two volumes offered in Bohn's Catalogue for 1847
(Prints), p. 116, for 18/-. The two bound together by Hodge of Exeter are
in the library of the Earl of Morley at Saltram in Devon, now part of the
National Trust; HW's BP's but press-marks not kept.

CHESTERFIELD, PHILIP DORMER STANHOPE, 4th Earl of   3915

Miscellaneous works. (With Maty's *Memoirs.*) London, 1777. Two
    volumes, 4to.

Rebound in half blue morocco by F. Bedford. BP² early state. Press-
mark not preserved. Not in MC.

SH SALE, vii.40, to H. G. Bohn, £4 [London, 1056]; owned by R. S.
Turner; Sotheby's, 11 June 1895 (Lord Orford Sale), lot 332, to Sabin,
£15.15.0; acquired in May 1899 by the British Museum, on Paget Toynbee's recommendation.

☞ Numerous notes and comments by HW, published by Turner in
1867: HW wrote about these two volumes to Mason, 13 March 1777.

The sale catalogue (vii.40) says 'and 3 tracts relative to Lord Chesterfield'; in the London Sale (1056) the books are described as 'Miscellaneous
Works, 2 vols. and Memoirs of his Lordship's Life, by Dr. Maty, with
supplement, 2.' Although the counting is inconsistent, one may guess that
these represent the following supplementary volumes:

(1) *Characters by Lord Chesterfield . . . also Letters . . . intended as an
Appendix to his Lordship's Miscellaneous Works.* London, 1778. 4to.
Both the *Characters* and the *Letters* were published separately in 1777,
and HW may have had the separate editions, since he wrote to Mason,
18 April 1777: 'Lord Chesterfield's *Characters* are published, and are
not even prettily written. . . . My father's is tolerably impartial, and in
some parts just. . . .' But Turner's Sale in 1888 lists the *Miscellaneous*

Works, 3 vols. (*see* next item) and *Characters*, four volumes in quarto, and these are almost certainly from SH though not so identified.

(2) *Miscellaneous works . . . Volume the Third*. London, 1778. 4to.

3916 CHESTERFIELD, PHILIP DORMER STANHOPE, 4th Earl of

Works in verse and prose. MS. Folio.

Not in MC.

SH SALE, vii.43, to Evans, Great Queen Street, £10. [The list of purchasers at the London Sale, 1120, assigns the same volume to Sir George Chetwynd for £5.10.0.]

☞ 'Numerous notes by HW.' In his own copy of the *Description of SH*, 1774, HW added this to the printed list of MSS in the Glass Closet, but he failed to print it in the revised *Description* of 1784; one can assume that he acquired the volume between 1774 and 1784.

3917 COWLEY, ABRAHAM

Select works in verse and prose. Edited by Richard Hurd. The 2d edition. London, 1772. Two volumes, 8vo.

Original calf. BP² early state. No press-mark. Not in MC. Inscribed on the fly-leaf: 'From the Author.'

SH SALE, vii.47 (with Downes and *Theatrical Records*), to Thorpe, 17/– [London, 1037*]; given by Charles Gwinn to his brother-in-law, Thomas H. Morris, from whom it was inherited by his grandson, Professor Clayton M. Hall of Rutgers University; given by Professor Hall, June 1968, to Yale University for the Lewis Walpole collection.

☞ At Farmington is the copy of the first edition that HW gave to Cole, April 1773; Cole's note reads (a somewhat similar note is in the 2d volume): 'Dr. Hurd sent this copy as a present to Mr. Walpole, who before had purchased it; so he gave it to me.' More properly, it seems, HW gave this copy to Cole because Hurd had sent him the new edition.

The portrait engraved on the title was done from the original picture by Zincke, owned by HW, a fact noted by HW in his *Description of SH*, 1774.

3918 DAVIES, THOMAS

Dramatic miscellanies, consisting of critical observations on several plays of Shakespeare. London, 1784. Three volumes, 8vo.

Rebound in red morocco by Riviere. BP¹ inserted in the 1st volume. Not in MC and no press-mark preserved. Note by George Daniel dated 1842. Bookplate of Sir William Augustus Fraser. In the 1st volume, the

black leather book-label of Horace, Earl of Orford, i.e., Horatio William
(1813–94), 4th Earl of the new creation, is inserted.

SH SALE, vii.46, to Lilly, 9/– [London, 1039*]; Sotheby's, 26 July
1864 (George Daniel Sale), lot 1476, to Lilly, £3.12.0; offered in Lilly's
Catalogue, [1864], for £5.5.0; Sotheby's, 22 April 1901 (Fraser Sale),
lot 495, to W. Brown, £41; offered by Brown in Catalogue 151, 1904;
Sotheby's, 3 December 1929 (Dundas Sale), lot 207, to Maggs for WSL,
£98.

☞ More than 40 notes, some long, by HW, plus other markings. He
wrote of the whole work: 'The criticisms in general are poor & trifling,
& all that is curious in the three volumes might have been contained in
one; & would make a good supplement to the lives of Cibber & Garrick,
as comprising the history of our stage.' Of Hume, he wrote: 'Mr. Hume
had no taste, especially for poetry, as few Scots have. When Hume afterwards went to France, & was idolized there for his sceptical writings, he
preferred French authors to Shakespeare!' On Davies's criticism that the
Groom's speech in *Richard II*, V.v, about the horse Barbary disgraced the
tragedy, HW wrote: 'Yet this is one of those exquisite & affecting touches of
nature, in which Shakespeare excelled all mankind. To criticize it is being
as tasteless as Voltaire.'

[DOWNES, JOHN]   3919

Roscius Anglicanus, or an historical review of the stage. Revised by
   Thomas Davies. London, 1789. 8vo.

Not in MC.

SH SALE, vii.47 (with Cowley and *Theatrical Records*), to Thorpe, 17/–
[London, 1037*]

☞ Edited by F. G. Waldron. The SH catalogue adds to this lot 'and 5
others,' but they are not readily identifiable; they seem to reappear in
the London Sale, lot 1034, again described as 'and 5 others.' They
may have included Drumgold and Egerton, immediately below.

Possibly in some such miscellaneous lot, since it does not appear in the
sale records, was HW's copy (perhaps presented by its author?) of an anonymous and extravagant pseudo-Chinese tale, *The Bonze, or Chinese anchorite, an oriental epic novel. Translated from the Mandarin language of
Hoamchi-van, a Tartarian proselite, by Monsr. d'Alenzon.* London 1768.
Two volumes, 8vo. A copy of the second volume only, bound in calf with
HW's arms on the sides, without press-mark, was purchased in 1957 from a
bookseller in Bristol by Mr. William Rees-Mogg. The lack of a press-mark
suggests that HW shelved the set in 1768, with other presentation books, in

the Glass Closet. A name on the fly-leaf, 'Henry James, his book, 1791,' may mean that the volumes departed from SH at about that time; there is another name, 'John Scott.'

3920 [DRUMGOLD, JOHN]

La gaieté, poëme. Amsterdam [i.e. Paris], 1772. 8vo.

Brown calf. BP² early state. Press-mark Y.30. Not in MC.

Not identified in SH SALE. But it seems very likely to have been among the 'five others' sold in vii.47, to Rodd [London, 1034]. It was sold by Thorpe, November 1846, to the British Museum.

☞ Three notes by HW. Bound with it are:

(1) [DRUMGOLD, JOHN] *Avis aux vivants.* Amsterdam [i.e. Paris], 1772. Three identifications by HW.

(2) [DRUMGOLD, JOHN] *Charles et Vilcourt.* Amsterdam [i.e. Paris], 1772. The author is identified by HW. Drumgold was one of HW's Parisian friends, and an occasional correspondent.

(3) BOUFFLERS, STANISLAS JEAN DE, Chevalier de Boufflers. *Lettres . . . pendant son voyage en Suisse.* [Geneva?], 1771. Several notes by HW. This was sent to HW by the Duchesse d'Aiguillon: *see* Mme. du Deffand to HW, 23 September 1771.

3921 EGERTON, JOHN

Theatrical remembrancer. London, 1788. 12mo.

Untrimmed, but now rebound in modern library buckram. No BP and no press-mark. Not in MC.

Not identified in SH SALE. But it seems very likely to have been among the 'five others' sold with other stage histories in vii.47, to Rodd [London, 1034]. Purchased in 1914 by the Yale Library; Yale, February 1941, to WSL for the Walpole Collection, by exchange.

☞ Signature, 'Horace Walpole 1788,' and brief identifications and comments throughout, with a few notes on the last fly-leaf.

An Apology for the life of George Anne Bellamy, London 1785, six volumes in 12mo, does not appear in the SH records, and HW perhaps never owned a set, but he wrote Lady Ossory, 9 July 1785: 'I read such books [D'Hancarville] as I do Mrs. Bellamy's, and believe in them no more.'

3922 [FELTON, SAMUEL]

Imperfect hints towards a new edition of Shakespeare. London, The Logographic Press, 1787–8. 4to.

Not in MC.

SH SALE, vii.40, to Payne & Foss. [London, 1057]

☞ The two parts were dedicated to HW and Sir Joshua Reynolds. In his letter to Lady Ossory, 22 July 1788, HW mentions the dedication from his new but anonymous admirer.

George Steevens probably gave HW a copy of his *Account of the Felton portrait of Shakespeare*, privately printed, 1794. This does not appear in the SH records, but a copy not identified as HW's is in Thorpe's Supplement for 1842, lot 13140, for 10/6.

GROSE, FRANCIS   3923
The Olio, being a collection of essays, dialogues, letters. London, 1792. 12mo.

Bound in 19th-century half calf. BP of HW as Lord Orford, type 1. Not in MC. Bookplate of Christopher Harrison.

SH SALE, vii.45, to Rodd [London, 1034]; Sotheby's, 21 July 1965 (Miscellaneous Sale), lot 664, to Seven Gables for WSL, $168.

☞ Lot 45 was dispersed, but the *Olio* is specifically listed in the London Sale in lot 1034, which was sold to Rodd. In his 'Book of Materials,' HW noted that Grose included accounts of several artists.

In the volume are several annotations by HW. A pencilled note on the title reads: 'Bt. sale Strawberry Hill, in boards.'

HARDWICKE, PHILIP YORKE, 2d Earl of   3924
Walpoliana. London, Privately printed, 1781. 4to.

Half calf. BP[2] later state. Press-mark X.5, perhaps merely misplaced in Y. Not in MC. Bookplates of Lord Rosebery and Hugh Walpole.

SH SALE, vii.41 (with HW's *Aedes Walpolianae*), to Lilly, £3.19.0 [London, 1159]; Sotheby's, 4 August 1847 (William Knight Sale), lot 573; Sotheby's, 14 July 1916 (Van de Weyer Sale), lot 1466, to Bain, £35; Sotheby's, 30 June 1933 (Lord Rosebery Sale), lot 1310, to Bain for Hugh Walpole, £82; given by Hugh Walpole in 1938 to the King's School, Canterbury.

☞ Extensive notes and corrections by HW.

LETTERS   3925
Letters concerning the present state of England, particularly respecting the politics, arts, manners, and literature of the times. London, 1772. 8vo.

Not in MC.

SH SALE, vii.46, to Rodd. [London, 1034]

☞ Not identified with complete certainty, but the SH SALE lists 'Letters on England' and this seems to be what was called in the London Sale 'Letters on Politics and the Fine Arts.' *See* HW to Cole, 28 January 1772, for a considerable comment on the volume; HW did not know who the author was.

3926 [LYTTELTON, GEORGE, Baron Lyttelton]

Letters from a Persian in England, to his friend at Ispahan. The 3d edition. London, 1735. 12mo.

Original panelled calf. BP¹. Press-mark Y.33. Not in MC. Signature: 'J. Mitford 1844'; and the date July 1842 and notes in his hand.

SH SALE, vii.48, to Payne & Foss [London, 1033]; Sotheby's, 24 April 1860 (Mitford Sale, Part 2), lot 2238, to Booth, 11/–; Sotheby's, 1 December 1888 (R. S. Turner Sale, Part 2), lot 2436; Sotheby's, 27 June 1903 (Bools Sale), lot 1672, to Dobell, 9/–; American Art Association, 14 October 1931, lot 292; Brick Row, November 1931, to WSL, $40.

☞ Numerous markings and a few notes by HW, who collated this and the edition of 1747 with some care. He mentioned the changes in his discussion of the authorship of the *Letter to the Tories* in *Old England*, 23 April 1748.

3927 LYTTELTON, GEORGE, Baron Lyttelton

Letters from a Persian in England, to his friend at Ispahan. The 5th edition, altered by the author. London, 1747. 12mo.

Original mottled calf. BP¹. Press-mark Y.32. Not in MC. Signature, dates, and notes of John Mitford as in the 3d edition.

SH SALE, vii.48, to Payne & Foss [London, 1033]; Sotheby's, 24 April 1860 (Mitford Sale, Part 2), lot 2239, to Booth, 5/–; Sotheby's, 1 December 1888 (R. S. Turner Sale, Part 2), lot 2436; Sotheby's, 27 June 1903 (Bools Sale), lot 1673, to Dobell, 5/–; offered by Tregaskis in 1915–17, for £3.15.0; Sotheby's, 28 July 1933 (Lady Mount-Stephen Sale), lot 596, to Maggs for WSL (with 4 other books), £34.

☞ Passages added to this edition are marked by HW. These two editions of the *Persian Letters*, presumably kept in the Glass Closet in 1763, are not named in vii.48, but they are doubtless part of '4 others' there listed. The other two items seem to be unidentified in the London Sale.

Bibliographically, this edition of 1747 is a re-issue of the sheets of 1744, with the altered date on the engraved title-page and one cancel leaf to insert an omitted phrase.

PENNANT, THOMAS   3928

Of London. London, 1790. 4to.   (1743) PH

'Green morocco, with HW's arms on sides.' Not in MC.

SH SALE, vii.42, to 'Money,' £3.13.6 [the record of purchasers at the London Sale, 919, lists it as sold to the Earl of Buckinghamshire, perhaps in error]; Sotheby's, 29 July 1905 (Miscellaneous Sale), lot 345, to Sabin, £36.10.0.

☞ Numerous notes and additions by HW; views of SH and other plates inserted; printed additions, 1791, laid in. Some of HW's additions were quoted in John Miller's *Fly-Leaves*, 1854.

H. G. Bohn wrote on 17 June 1842 to Beckford (letters now WSL): 'Pennant's *London* is a nice volume, with MS notes at end of volume. The additions however are separate and unbound. £4.4.0.' But Beckford made no response and Bohn did not purchase the volume.

Claude Cox
£55.00
25. Aug 1988
1743 edition
'though title is
tipped in to
what is prob.
the 1740 printing
Cat 65 # 87

Theatrical records; or, an account of the English dramatic authors and   3929
*   their works.* London, 1756. 12mo.

Press-mark K.7.41 in MC; presumably moved to be shelved with other similar books in the Round Tower.

SH SALE, vii.47 (with Cowley and Downes), to Thorpe, 17/– [London, 1037*]; Sotheby's, 24 April 1860 (Mitford Sale, Part 2), lot 3471, to Skeffington, 10/–.

☞ 'A few notes by HW.' The book is a routine compilation published by Dodsley and sometimes attributed to him. In his *R&NA*, HW cited this work twice.

VICTOR, BENJAMIN   3930

Original letters, dramatic pieces, and poems. London, 1776. Three volumes, 8vo.

Not in MC.

SH SALE, vii.46 to Lilly. [London, 1038*]

WALPOLE, HORACE   3931

Aedes Walpolianae, or, a description of the collection of pictures at
*   Houghton Hall.* The 2d edition. London, 1752. 4to.

Now rebound in red morocco by F. Bedford. No BP or press-mark. Not in MC.

SH SALE, vii.45, to Holloway [London, 1049]; Sotheby's, July 1855 (Charles Meigh Sale), lot 1812, to Willis, £4.5.0; offered by Willis in 1855

for £7.10.0; Sotheby's, 7 May 1904 (Ford Sale), lot 642, to Harvey, £15.15.0; now in the Morgan Library.

☞ This must have been HW's own copy of the 2d edition, although the SH catalogue does not identify the volume at all; it is omitted entirely in the revised catalogue, and the lot was dispersed in the London Sale. Bound in it is HW's MS catalogue (with additions by Sir Robert) of Sir Robert's pictures at Houghton, &c., 1736, the MS offered separately by Thorpe in his Catalogue of MSS for 1842, lot 564, for £2.2.0; this was no doubt inserted soon after 1842, and it was recorded as in the volume in 1855.

Some plates inserted by HW, who also added numerous interesting notes in MS. (These are unprinted because the third edition, 1767, was merely reprinted *verbatim* from the second.) References to numerous books, some published many years after 1752, show that HW continued to annotate this copy for many years.

Another copy of the edition of 1752, now in the library of the Earl of Rosebery, has a note that it was purchased at the SH SALE.

3932 WALPOLE, HORACE

Aedes Walpolianae, or, a description of the collection of pictures at Houghton Hall. The 3d edition. London, 1767. 4to.

Original calf, rebacked. With BP as Lord Orford, type 1, dated 1792. Press-mark Y.9. Not in MC. Bookplate of William Frederick, 9th Earl Waldegrave.

SH SALE, vii.41 (with Hardwicke), to Lilly, £3.19.0 [London, 1159]; Lord Waldegrave in a collection, 1948, to WSL.

☞ Bound with it is Walpole's *Description of SH*, 1784.

A few notes by HW in each piece; he also inserted a MS title-page: 'Descriptions of Houghton-hall and Strawberry hill by Horace Walpole.'

3933 [WALPOLE, HORACE]

A letter to the Whigs. London, 1747. 8vo.

Original mottled calf. BP¹. Press-mark Y.27. Not in MC. Signature: 'J. Mitford 1842.'

SH SALE, vii.48, to Payne & Foss [London, 1033, not named but probably one of 'and 3 others']; Sotheby's, 24 April 1860 (Mitford Sale, Part 2), lot 3676, to Booth, £1.8.0; Sotheby's, 24 November 1937 (Newcastle Sale), lot 911, to Maggs for WSL, £11.

☞ Numerous notes and identifications by HW. Bound with it are:

(1) [WALPOLE, HORACE] *A second and third letter to the Whigs.* London, 1748. Numerous notes by HW.

(2) *A Letter to the Tories*. The 2d edition. London, 1748. This was
believed by HW (when he wrote his *Letter to the Whigs*) to be by Lord
Lyttelton; in the margin of his *Second Letter* HW noted that the *Letter
to the Tories* had also been attributed to Thirlby.

[YOUNG, EDWARD] 3934

Love of fame, the universal passion. The 2d edition. London, 1728.
8vo.

Now rebound in 19th century calf. BP¹. No press-mark preserved. Not
in MC.

SH SALE, vii.48, to Payne & Foss [London, 1033]; Sotheby's, 24 April 1860
(Mitford Sale, Part 2), lot 3802, to Pickering, £2.5.0; now in the British
Museum (acquired in March 1861).

☞ Numerous notes by HW. In his own copy of his *Description of SH*,
1774, HW added this book in MS to the printed list of 'curious books in
the Glass Closet'; so perhaps he acquired it after 1774, despite the presence
of the early bookplate.

[YOUNG, EDWARD] 3935

Love of fame, the universal passion. The 3d edition. London, 1730.
8vo.

Not in MC.

SH SALE, vii.48, to Payne & Foss [London, 1033]; Sotheby's, 24 April
1860 (Mitford Sale, Part 2), lot 3803, to Waller, £2.

☞ According to the Mitford catalogue, this had MS notes on the
margins, and HW's note that he had bought it at auction in 1785.

APPENDIX 1

FALSE ATTRIBUTIONS

Included in this Appendix are books that for one reason or another have been recorded as from sh. Many such books have been entered, more appropriately, in the main catalogue in connection with the sh copy or edition; the reader will thus find falsely attributed books recorded at such places. This Appendix includes, therefore, only such books as do not readily fit into notes in the main catalogue.

The reasoning that leads to the rejection of these items is varied, and seldom absolute: lack of press-mark, absence from the sale records, suspicious appearance of the bookplate, confusion with another Walpole, &c. Smaller pamphlets may well have been in bound volumes, so that the provenance has been obscured by the breaking up of the volume, and numerous small volumes or pamphlets were sold together without individual identification in 1842; hence almost any item may conceivably have been at sh. But the weight of evidence seems to rule against each of the following items.

Books from the collection of Horatio William (1813–94), 4th Earl of Orford of the new creation, are included only when they have been described in the twentieth century as from hw's library; all his books contained his close imitation of hw's seal as Lord Orford, type 1.

AINSWORTH, ROBERT   3936
An abridgement of Ainsworth's Dictionary. By Nathanael Thomas.
    London, 1758. Two volumes, 8vo.
    A copy with the signature 'Horace Walpole' in a childish hand and a note 'Given to him by his father in London' has been reported in a cottage in Puddletown, near Dorchester, Dorset. This is presumably the hand of hw's cousin, born in 1752, later Lord Walpole and (in 1809) Earl of Orford; one of Lord Walpole's seats was at Puddletown.

AKENSIDE, MARK   3937
The pleasures of imagination. London, 1744. 4to.
    A copy has been sold in New York several times, always described as

having extensive notes in HW's hand. The handwriting is contemporary, but it exhibits no particular resemblance to HW's.

3938 [ALLESTREE, RICHARD, attributed author]

The gentleman's calling. London, 1677. 8vo.

A copy 'from the Earl of Orford's library' was sold at Sotheby's, 3 June 1929. It seems safe to assume that this book came from the library of Horatio William (1813–94), 4th Earl of the new creation. (The authorship of the *Gentleman's Calling* has also been attributed to Lady Pakington and to Archbishop Richard Sterne.)

3939 [ALLESTREE, RICHARD, attributed author]

The government of the tongue. Oxford, 1667 [i.e. 1675?] 8vo.

A copy 'with the Earl of Orford's bookplate' was sold at Sotheby's, 3 June 1929. It seems safe to assume that this book, like the previous one, came from the library of Horatio William (1813–94), 4th Earl of the new creation. (The authorship of the *Government of the tongue* has also been attributed to Lady Pakington and to Archbishop Richard Sterne.)

3940 *Amusemens serieux et comiques.* Luxemburg, 1731. 8vo.

Compiled by Charles Rivière du Fresny. An uncut copy in original red paper boards, with HW's BP[1], was offered by the Seven Gables Bookshop in 1954. But the bookplate was a later insertion, and there was no other evidence of SH provenance.

3941 ARIOSTO, LODOVICO

Orlando Furioso. Translated by Sir John Harington. London, 1634. Folio.

Professor J. H. Whitfield of Birmingham has a copy with an old pencil note: 'Walpole's Sale—18s.' There is no evidence of SH provenance, although HW did purchase many seventeenth-century books after 1763.

3942 [ARNAUD, ANTOINE]

The art of speaking. London, 1696. 12mo.

A copy in old panelled calf, with HW's BP[1] inserted, is now WSL. There is no evidence of SH provenance.

BECKFORD, WILLIAM 3943
Vathek. London, 1786. 8vo.

A copy in original boards was bequeathed in the Amy Lowell Collection in 1925 to Harvard; a note on the fly-leaf has been attributed to HW, but it is certainly not in his hand. The book does not appear in the SH records.

BAPHIUS, BARTHOLOMAEUS 3944
Oratio habita in oecumenico Concilio Tridentino. Brescia, 1562. 4to.

A copy formerly in the Harmsworth collection and now at Farmington was marked on the wrapper, probably by Sir Leicester Harmsworth's librarian: 'Sotheby's, March 13, 1922 (Horace Walpole item), lot 584.' But lot 584 in Sotheby's sale contained 77 unbound tracts in Italian; and although the 88 volumes of Tracts bound in calf (No. 1608 *above*) from Windsor Castle were in lots 555–95 of that sale, few if any of the hundreds of unbound tracts can have come from SH.

This tract is in the same category as Pratt and Shebbeare *below*, and other tracts that have been called HW's because of their presence in the Windsor Castle Sale.

BIBLE 3945
The Bible, printed in Greek. Venice, [1498?]

The copy now at Yale has the Orford seal, imitated by Horatio William (1813–94), 4th Earl of the new creation; it was sold with other books from his library at Sotheby's in 1895. It has no association with SH.

In the Huntington Library is a copy of the Latin Bible edited by Tremellius and Junius, Amsterdam 1669, in 12mo. It is in a handsome vellum binding ascribed to Samuel Mearne: formerly in the Henry W. Poor collection; sold at the Anderson Galleries in 1908 (Poor), 1917 (Learmont), and 1919 (Halsey). It has HW's BP^1 but no press-mark, and the bookplate is probably an insertion.

BICKERTON, G. 3946
Accurate disquisitions in physick. Translated from the Latin. London, 1719. 12mo.

Old English red morocco, with HW's BP. Sold at Sotheby's in 1922, and offered by Maggs in 1926 and 1930. Since this book does not appear in the SH records, the bookplate was perhaps an insertion; it has not been reported since 1930.

3947 BICKHAM, GEORGE

Deliciae Britannicae. London, 1742. 8vo.

In a copy at Farmington, in original calf, HW's BP¹ has been inserted. The book does not appear in the SH records, although it is a book such as HW might have owned.

3948 BOCCACCIO, GIOVANNI

Ameto (with other pieces). Venice, 1524. 8vo.

A copy sold at Sotheby's, 17 March 1952, was described as having HW's BP as Earl of Orford. But the plate was the imitation prepared for Horatio William (1813–94), 4th Earl of the new creation, and this volume was sold with other books from his library in 1895.

3949 [BOLTON, ROBERT]

On the employment of time. The 2d edition. 1751. 8vo.

In a copy at Farmington, in original mottled calf, HW's BP¹ has been inserted. A copy with HW's identification of the author is bound in the Tracts, No. 1608, volume 62.

3950 BOYLE, ROBERT

Disquisitions about the final causes of natural things. London, 1688. 8vo.

A copy in original calf with HW's BP¹ was offered by Maggs in 1936. Since there was no other evidence of SH provenance, WSL returned the book.

3951 CHAPMAN, THOMAS

An essay on the Roman Senate. Cambridge, 1750. 8vo.

A copy in original mottled calf, with Lord Orrery's signature (Dublin, 6 July 1750) and his armorial bookplate as Earl of Cork and Orrery, was sold by the Seven Gables Book Shop, November 1955, to WSL, for $10. In it has been inserted, presumably since the Orrery books were dispersed, HW's BP¹.

3952 CHILLINGWORTH, WILLIAM

Works. The 10th edition. London, 1742. Folio.

The late Professor Edward N. Hooker of the University of California at Los Angeles had a copy formerly owned by W. S. B. Brassington, with

his MS note: 'This copy belonged to Horace Walpole and had his book-plate.' The work, a weighty folio, does not appear in the MC or in the sale catalogue, so that the MS note may be erroneous.

CHURCHILL, CHARLES   3953

Poems. London, 1763–4. Two volumes, 4to.

The copy in original calf owned by Admiral Dennis Hoare of Wraysbury, Buckinghamshire, has BP¹ inserted in each volume. But there is no other evidence of SH provenance, and BP¹ (especially a washed specimen) could not normally be used so late as 1763.

COLLINS, WILLIAM   3954

Poetical works. Edited by John Langhorne. London, 1765. 8vo.

A copy in contemporary calf, with HW's BP, was sold at Sotheby's, 3 June 1935 (Miscellaneous Sale), lot 37, to Tregaskis, for £1.10.0. Since this does not appear in the SH records, the bookplate was probably an insertion. I think there is no mention of Collins in HW's correspondence.

DRAYTON, MICHAEL   3955

The historie of the life and death of the Lord Cromwell. London, 1609. 4to.

A copy now in the Huntington Library, rebound in the last century by C. Lewis, was formerly in the Bright and Miller collections. It was not marked as HW's in the Britwell Sale in 1923, and there is no indication of SH provenance in the volume; but Miller marked Bright's Catalogue 'Good copy, Strawberry Hill,' and the volume is marked in the Britwell *Handlist* as having been HW's. Miller may have made an error, although it is possible that this volume was in some quarto volume of tracts or poems at SH in 1842.

ENGLAND   3956

A Free conference touching the present state of England. London, 1668. 8vo.

A copy in old red morocco, with a recent pencilled attribution to John Evelyn, recently presented to Christ Church, Oxford, has HW's BP inserted. Such a pamphlet may have been in HW's library, but there seems no evidence save for the bookplate that this one was at SH.

[271]

3957 EVELYN, JOHN

Silva. York, 1776. 4to.

A copy was offered in 1935 and again in 1956 by booksellers as from HW's library; it is bound in old calf with vellum spine. This work does not appear in any SH records: there is no bookplate or press-mark, and the supposed Walpolian association is derived from a misreading of the cypher on the spine. It is now in the Burndy Library, Norwalk, Connecticut.

3958 FÉNELON, FRANÇOIS DE SALIGNAC DE LA MOTHE

Avantures de Télémaque. Amsterdam, 1734. Folio.

A copy was sold at Sotheby's, 23 November 1891 (Library of a Collector), lot 234, described as 'russia, gilt, with HW's BP.' Since the work does not appear in any SH records and since the volume has not reappeared since 1891, the book is doubtful; the plate was perhaps an insertion.

3959 FLORUS, LUCIUS ANNAEUS

[*Opera*] Amsterdam, Elzevier, 1664. 12mo.

Messrs. Lowe of Birmingham offered a copy in September 1955, in original brown calf with the signature of H. Walpole, dated 1744. But WSL examined the book and rejected the signature as not HW's; furthermore, we do not know that HW owned this edition. The signature, apparently genuine, is probably that of HW's cousin Horace (1723–1809), 1st Earl of Orford of the new creation.

The volume was offered again in a miscellaneous sale at Sotheby's, 4 February 1963, lot 269.

3960 FREDERICK II, the Great, King of Prussia

Matinées royales. [Berlin? 1766?] 16mo.

Of this collection of essays, pretended to be by Frederick the Great, the author is still unknown; but some scholars believe the essays to be by Frederick. A copy is catalogued under Walpole in the Grenville Catalogue, 2d Part (compiled by Payne & Foss, 1848); now in the British Museum, G.16393. But although HW might well have owned a copy, it does not appear in the SH records and the Grenville copy has no visible trace of Walpolian provenance.

3961 HAKEWILL, GEORGE

A comparison between the dayes of Purim. Oxford, 1626. 4to.

This pamphlet, now in the Folger Library from the Harmsworth collection, is in a red wrapper with no trace of Walpolian association. It is

marked on the cover as having been purchased in the Windsor Castle Sale at Sotheby's, 14 March 1922, lot 535. Like several other pamphlets, therefore, this was an unbound pamphlet in the sale at which Sir Leicester Harmsworth purchased HW's collection of Tracts. It is unlikely to have been at SH.

HENRY, Prince of Wales 3962

True accompt . . . of the baptism, 1594. Edinburgh, reprinted, 1687.
A MS copy made in the 18th century. Foolscap 8vo.

In this MS, now at Farmington, HW's BP^1 has been inserted. Perhaps because of the bookplate, the MS was described at Sotheby's in 1930 as in HW's autograph. But the hand is not HW's, and this MS does not appear in the SH records.

HENSBERGH, VINCENT 3963

Viridarium Marianum septemplici rosario. Antwerp, 1615. 12mo.

A copy in old green morocco, with the Marquess of Crewe's bookplate, contains a washed copy of HW's BP^2. There is no press-mark, and the book does not appear in any SH records.

HOMER 3964

Iliad and Odyssey. Translated by Pope and others. London, 1760.
Eleven volumes, 8vo.

An imperfect copy of this edition, owned in 1938 by Mr. Carl de Gersdorff of New York, had the Orford seal (perhaps the imitation used by Horatio William, 4th Earl of the new creation) in the first volume only. There was no other evidence of SH provenance.

The House of Peeresses: or, female oratory. London, 1779. 4to. 3965

A copy of this satire on the Bishop of Llandaff's bill to discourage adultery is in the Folger Library, with notes said to be by HW. But the notes are not in his hand, and the pamphlet cannot be traced to SH.

KEMBLE, JOHN PHILIP 3966

Fugitive pieces. York, 1780. 8vo.

A copy in tree calf, with an original MS by Mrs. Kemble bound in, with HW's BP, was in the Bement Sale, American Art Association, 28 February 1923. It is true that HW knew Kemble, and this volume may have been included in some 'bundle of tracts' in 1842. But the sale catalogue in

1923 mentioned no MS notes by HW or any evidence other than the book-plate for SH provenance. Since the volume has not reappeared since 1923, it cannot be examined.

The long list of subscribers to the 5th edition of Charlotte Smith's *Elegiac Sonnets*, 1789, includes 'Hon. Horace Walpole.' But since the book does not appear in the SH records, the subscriber was perhaps HW's cousin Horace (1752–1822), later 2d Earl of the new creation.

3967 LACTANTIUS, LUCIUS CAECILIUS FIRMIANUS

Traité de la mort des persecuteurs de l'église. Paris, 1680. 12mo.

This volume was described as having the BP of Horace, Earl of Orford. But it was in the sale of books from the library of Horatio William (1813–94), 4th Earl of Orford of the new creation, in 1895, lot 169. There was at SH a Latin edition of 1692, recorded in M.4 *above*.

3968 LELAND, JOHN

Itinerary. Edited by Thomas Hearne. The 2d edition. Oxford, 1744. Nine volumes, royal 8vo.

A copy was sold at Sotheby's, 26 May 1910 (J. W. Ford Sale), lot 669, 'half bound, uncut,' with a MS note doubtfully attributed to HW. Since this multi-volumed work could scarcely be concealed in the SH records, its absence from the records seems sufficient evidence that the note was not HW's.

3969 MORE, HANNAH

Remarks on the speech of M. Dupont. London, 1793. 8vo.

In a copy at Farmington, uncut in original wrappers, HW's BP[1] has been inserted. Although HW knew of this pamphlet (*see* his letter to Hannah More, 23 March 1793) and may have owned a copy, the BP in this copy is certainly an insertion.

3970 NEANDER, JOANNES

Tabacologia. Leyden, 1626. 4to.

A copy now at Farmington was described as having the bookplate of Horace Walpole as Earl of Orford. But the plate is the imitation prepared by Horatio William (1813–94), 4th Earl of the new creation; the work does not appear in either of the two sales of selections from his library.

A New collection of poems relating to state affairs. London, 1705. 3971
8vo.

A copy of this pirated reprint from the *Poems on affairs of state* was
offered in Raphael King's catalogue in 1952 as having the signature of Mary
Berry, and additions and corrections by HW. But WSL examined the volume,
and found that the notes were not in HW's hand. It was offered in 1961 and
1962 by Messrs. Dawson, priced at £60.

PLAYS   3972

Three plays in one volume. 8vo.

A collection of three plays (Italian and French) was offered in 1955 by
John Rothwell; purchased by the Folger Library, and then sold to WSL in
1956. Each play has the signature 'Hor. Walpole' on the title-page, in a
youthful hand. The owner seems likely to have been HW's young cousin,
Horace (1752–1822), 2d Earl of Orford of the new creation.

The three plays are: *Alfonso*, 1744, by Paolo Rolli; *Germondo*, 1776, by
Goldoni, translated by F. Bottarelli; and *La Belle Arsene*, Paris 1781, by
Favart.

[PRATT, SAMUEL JACKSON]   3973

The tears of genius. Occasioned by the death of Dr. Goldsmith. By
Courtney Melmoth, *pseud.* London, 1774. 4to.

A copy of the second edition, certainly HW's, is in Volume 14 of the
'Poems of George the 3d,' No. 3222 *above.* But at Farmington there is
an unbound copy of the first edition in modern wrapper, from the Harmsworth collection: it was sold to WSL in 1952 as a Walpolian item. (Sir
Leicester Harmsworth purchased it in a large collection of unbound pamphlets in the Windsor Castle Sale at Sotheby's, 14 March 1922, lot 582.) Mr.
Lewis agrees that the pencilled notes which seem to suggest Walpolian
provenance were made by Quaritch or by Sir Leicester Harmsworth's librarian in the belief that all these unbound pamphlets derived from SH.

PSALMS   3974

The Whole Book of Psalms. London, 1630 [i.e. 1632]. 24mo.

In a copy at Farmington, in original calf, HW's BP[1] has been inserted.
The book does not appear in the SH records.

3975 ROBERT, the Devil

A transcript, probably from Wynkyn de Worde's edition, with 14 colored drawings. MS. Small 4to.

This MS in the British Museum is bound in 18th-century calf, with HW's BP[1]. It was in John Ratcliffe's Sale in 1776; owned later by John Brand, Richard Heber, and Sir Thomas Phillipps; Hodgson, 13 June 1934 (H. T. Butler Sale), lot 1; now Egerton MS 3132A in the British Museum. The MS could only be Walpolian if HW sold it or gave it away, before 1776; but his BP is inserted above John Brand's, an unlikely position for HW to have put the plate before Brand owned the MS. Since in the Heber Sale, Part 11 (10 February 1836) there is no mention of Walpolian provenance whereas HW's BP is mentioned in the Phillipps Sale (27 April 1903), there is a reasonable presumption that the plate was inserted between 1836 and 1903, probably soon after 1842.

In the Morgan Library is a MS of *Roman de la Rose*, ca. 1400, with HW's BP[1] inserted. This MS was in the Galitzin Collection, 1816–25, and cannot have been HW's.

3976 *The Sale of the House of Peers, Spiritual and Temporal.* London, 1782. 4to.

A copy of this satire, with numerous identifications said to be in HW's hand, has been catalogued as his at various times since 1842. When first traceable, in Strong's Catalogue for 1843, it was described only as having MS notes, with no mention of HW. It was recently in the library of the late Marquess of Crewe; sold by Maggs, November 1950, to WSL, £2.2.0. The notes are not HW's, and the pamphlet cannot be traced to SH.

3977 *Scriptores rei rustici.* Reggio, 1482. Folio.

A copy in old pigskin over wooden boards was sold at Sotheby's in 1936 and later offered in December 1936 by Quaritch, from the Mensing library, as 'from HW's library, with the circular Orford seal.' But this was the close imitation prepared by Horatio William (1813–94), 4th Earl of the new creation; the volume was in the sale of books from his library in 1895, lot 275.

3978 [SHEBBEARE, JOHN]

A fourth letter to the people of England. London, 1756. 8vo.

The first three of Shebbeare's *Letters* and an anonymous reply called the *Fourth Letter* are in Volume 82 of Tracts, No. 1608 *above*. The present *Fourth Letter*, by Shebbeare, unbound in a modern wrapper, was sold by

Quaritch to WSL in 1942 as HW's because Mr. F. S. Ferguson believed it came from Windsor Castle in 1922: a pencilled note on the title-page refers to Volume 82 of the Tracts.

But although this tract doubtless came from Windsor Castle, the pencilled note seems to refer only to the presence of the other Shebbeare *Letters* in Volume 82: the notation was perhaps made by the librarian at Windsor Castle (or by Quaritch) for reference only, not to suggest Walpolian provenance.

SHENSTONE, WILLIAM   3979

Poems upon various occasions. Oxford, 1737. 8vo.

This volume, now in the Bodleian Library, has HW's BP and a MS note ascribed (in the Harmsworth Sale in 1939) to HW. But the note is not by HW, and the BP is certainly a late insertion.

A somewhat similar volume, John Philips's *Whole Works*, 1720, in 8vo, has a washed copy of BP² inserted on the verso of the title-page. The volume is not in the SH records; it was offered to WSL by Mr. I. Kyrle Fletcher in 1939, and is now in the library of the University of Colorado.

And a copy of John Philips's Latin *Ode to Henry St. John*, 1707, folio, rebound *ca.* 1900 with the spine lettered 'Pope and Walpole copy,' was owned in 1959 by Professor E. Maurice Bloch of the University of California at Los Angeles (from American Book Auction, 10 May 1946). It is inscribed 'A. Pope, Twitenham' and 'Hor. Walpole, Florence Feb. 1741.' But Professor George Sherburn doubted the authenticity of Pope's signature, and Mr. Lewis doubts Walpole's; and the poem is unrecorded in any Walpolian record. This careful simulation, if that is what it is, of HW's signature seems to be one of few recorded attempts to imitate HW's writing.

STRAPAROLA, GIOVANNI FRANCESCO   3980

Le tredici piacevolissime notte. Venice, 1608. 8vo.

A copy in old red morocco, with HW's BP, was offered in 1946 by Robinson. Since it does not appear in any SH records, the plate was probably an insertion.

STRAUCH, AEGIDIUS   3981

Breviarum chronologicum. London, 1699. 8vo.

A copy with the signature of Horatio Walpole was offered by I. K. Fletcher, Catalogue 152 (1952), lot 136. Since the book does not appear in any SH records, the signature may be assumed to be that of HW's uncle, Horatio Walpole, later Lord Walpole of Wolterton.

3982 SWIFT, JONATHAN

A letter to the whole people of Ireland. The 2d edition. Dublin, 1724. 8vo.

A copy was offered by Maggs in 1913, with signature on the title-page: 'Hor. Walpole, Gift.' This was probably HW's uncle, Horatio Walpole, later Lord Walpole of Wolterton.

3983 [SWIFT, JONATHAN]

A short character of Thomas Earl of Wharton. London, 1711. 8vo.

A copy in modern blue morocco, with the name 'Horace Walpole' on the title-page, was sold at the Parke-Bernet Galleries, 13 October 1947. But WSL examined it and found the signature certainly not HW's. The signature if not a forgery was probably that of HW's uncle, Horatio Walpole, later Lord Walpole of Wolterton.

3984 SWIFT, JONATHAN

Some observations upon a paper call'd the Report of the Committee of the most honourable the Privy Council in England, relating to Wood's half-pence. Dublin, 1724. 8vo.

A copy was offered by Maggs in 1922 and 1931, with signature on the title-page: 'Hor. Walpole, Gift.' This, like the *Letter* just above, must surely have been given to HW's uncle, Horatio Walpole, later Lord Walpole of Wolterton.

3985 *Le Temple des Muses, orné de LX tableaux.* Engraved by Bernard Picart; the text by La Barre de Beaumarchais. Amsterdam, 1733. Folio.

Both the text and plates are based upon Michel de Marolles's *Tableaux du Temple des Muses*, first published in 1655. A copy of the edition of 1733 at Farmington, the gift of Mr. Aubrey J. Toppin, York Herald, is bound in original mottled calf but rebacked; in it is HW's BP¹. This work does not appear in any SH records.

A similar large folio at Farmington, Blair's *Chronology*, 1768, has BP¹ inserted. It was purchased by WSL in 1925.

3986 TRACTS

Two early tracts in one volume, small 4to.

This volume, with the signature of John Burns dated 1922, was sold at Sotheby's, 26 April 1944 (Burns Sale), lot 324, to Maggs for WSL, £2.5.0. The two items are:

FALSE ATTRIBUTIONS

(1) SCALIGER, JOSEPH JUSTUS. *Epistola de vetustate et splendore gentis Scaligerae.* (With a memoir of J. C. Scaliger.) Leyden, 1594. 4to.

(2) NICHOLAS I, Pope. *Antiqua et insignis epistola. . . . Fragmenta quarundam Tho. Mori epistolarum ad Erasmum Rot. & ad Joannem Coc*[hleum]. Leipzig, 1536. 4to.

The volume is in 18th-century calf, similar but not identical to HW's customary binding, with BP[1]. There is no other evidence of ownership, and although the volume might have been at SH, it is not one that was likely to interest HW; the plate is probably an insertion.

VENICE 3987
Habiti d'huomeni et donne Venetiane. By Giacomo Franco. [Venice, 1610] Folio.

A copy rebound in vellum in the 19th century, with a mutilated copy of BP[1] inserted, is in the Folger Library. The volume has been sophisticated, the title-page being supplied from another copy. It was included in the Orford Sale at Sotheby's, 14 March 1902, although it does not contain Lord Orford's bookplate.

VERDIZOTTI, GIOVANNI MARIO 3988
Cento favole morali. Venice, 1570. Small 4to.

A copy sold at Hodgson's, 10 May 1933 (Miscellaneous Sale), lot 541, was described as 'bound at Strawberry Hill in crimson crushed morocco.' This does not seem to have had any association with HW; it was merely bound at SH, probably in the 19th century.

VERSTEGAN, RICHARD 3989
Theatre des cruautez des heretiques. Antwerp, 1607. 4to.

A copy in the Chapin Library at Williamstown, Massachusetts, has the seal of Horatio William (1813–94), 4th Earl of Orford of the new creation, the close imitation of HW's Orford seal; the book was in the Orford Sale in 1895, lot 315.

VOLTAIRE, FRANÇOIS MARIE AROUET DE 3990
Mémoires. London, 1784. 8vo.

In a copy at Farmington, original calf rebacked, HW's BP[1] has been inserted. The book does not appear in the SH records, although HW at least saw a copy; he wrote to Lady Ailesbury, 8 June 1784: 'Mr. Conway wonders I do not talk of Voltaire's *Mémoirs.* Lord bless me! I saw it two

months ago; the Lucans brought it from Paris and lent it to me. . . .' He also mentioned the book in a conversation of 30 May 1784, recorded in Mary Hamilton's journal.

3991 WALPOLE, HORACE

Memorandum book containing omissions in the *Memoirs of Count Grammont*, written in French. 8vo.

This MS was described as being written in HW's hand, in a miscellaneous sale at Sotheby's, 17 April 1946. It was purchased by WSL, but returned because it was not written by HW.

3992 WOUWERMAN, PHILIPS

Oeuvres. Engraved by Moyreau, Le Bas, and others. 114 plates. [Paris] 1737–57. Folio.

A copy of this work, in old calf with HW's BP, was sold at Hodgson's, 15 June 1916 (Miscellaneous Sale), lot 627, for £22. Since the book does not appear identifiably in any SH record and since it has not reappeared since 1916, the bookplate must be presumed to be an insertion.

A volume of costume plates by Moreau le jeune was offered in September 1967 for $3,000 by the firm of Dr. Helmut Tenner, Heidelberg, Catalogue 340. It is *Monument du costume physique et moral de la fin du dix-huitième siècle, ou tableaux de la vie*, Neuwied, 1789, large folio, with 24 plates by Moreau le jeune. Bound in green morocco of the 19th century, stamped with the arms of Horace Walpole. This was presumably HW's cousin Horace (1752–1822), 2d Earl of the new creation, who was a vigorous collector.

3993 ZOUCH, RICHARD

Elementa jurisprudentiae. Oxford, 1636. 4to.

Messrs. Quaritch included this work, in a letter to WSL in 1938, as a Walpolian item already sold (to the Folger Library). But there is now no evidence to support the attribution, and the work does not appear in any SH records. It was published in three parts with continuous signatures: the three parts have been separated, and two of them in modern red wrappers are marked as having been in the sale of the Walpole Collection at Sotheby's, 14 March 1922 [the Windsor Castle Sale]. The supposed association with Walpole therefore derives from that sale record only, the assumption being that unbound pamphlets in the sale as well as the 88 volumes of bound tracts had been HW's.

A somewhat similar example of false association is a volume now in the

FALSE ATTRIBUTIONS

Music Library at Yale, *Descrizione delle feste fatte in Firenze per le reali nozze de serenissimi sposi Ferdinando II, gran duca di Toscana, e Vittoria, principessa d'Urbino*, printed in Florence in 1637. A bookseller's note asserts that the volume was formerly owned by HW, and cites the Windsor Castle Sale, lot 531. Although HW might have liked the book, he did not own it, and the supposed association is derived only from its presence in the Windsor Castle Sale.

APPENDIX 2

BOOKS GIVEN AWAY

In the Introduction I have commented on the essential completeness of HW's library in 1842. The following short list of books given away by him may be of some interest. These are the miscellaneous books only, not books written or printed by HW. Not listed either are the many new books and tracts he sent to Mann, Conway, and others.

AGINCOURT, JEAN BAPTISTE LOUIS GEORGES SEROUX D'   3994
Recherches relative à l'origine de l'ogive. MS. 4to.

This volume, not in the SH SALE, is now in Sir John Soane's Museum. It is an essay on the *arco acuto* or pointed arch, in the handwriting of a secretary or scribe but apparently the work of Seroux d'Agincourt. At the end HW made a few notations, perhaps to guide him in his acknowledgment to d'Agincourt. The volume is bound in marbled boards with calf spine, 4to. It has a cypher bookplate (G. T.) and Sir John Soane's bookplate, with a note by Sir John that the book had once been at SH; it was perhaps given away by HW between 1784 and 1797, and later purchased by Soane.

Bound in is a letter from d'Agincourt to HW, 29 June 1784, asking for some drawings of SH to be used in his *Histoire de l'art*; also bound in is the MS of his *Recherches sur l'ancien style de l'architecture en Angleterre*, which is marked 'Envoyé le 4 juin 1783 à Mr. Walpole par M. Byres.' D'Agincourt had visited SH in 1777; he sent numerous comments on HW's *Anecdotes* in his letter of 20 July 1783.

ARRIAN   3995
History of Alexander's expedition. Translated into English by John Rooke. London, 1729. Two volumes, 8vo.

A copy in old blue morocco, having a signature on the fly-leaf, 'H. Walpole, 1731,' was sold at Sotheby's, 15 January 1896 (Rev. Alleyne Fitz-Herbert Sale of books formerly owned by William Mason), lot 200. Since no copy was catalogued in 1763, it seems likely that HW gave this to Mason in the early days of their friendship. It was purchased by John Gennadius in December 1902, from Sotheran, for £2.2.0, and is now in the Gennadeion Library at Athens.

3996 BERRY, AGNES

Sketches of Italian peasants. Drawings in water color. 1791.

This volume, with HW's title-page in MS and BP² later state, is owned by Mr. Arthur Monro Ferguson, Raith House, Fife. It was entered in MS by HW among the 'More Additions' at the end of his own copy of his *Description of SH*, 1774. Since it was not in the sale in 1842, the volume was probably taken back after HW's death by Miss Berry: a similar drawing by Miss Berry, listed in the printed *Description*, was marked 'Returned' by Mrs. Damer in the margin of her copy.

3997 BIBLE

The Holy Bible. Bath and London, 1785. Three volumes, 4to.

A copy in blue morocco at Farmington is inscribed by HW: 'To his excellent friend Miss Hannah More this book . . . is offered, as a mark of his esteem and gratitude, by her sincere and obliged humble servant, Horace Earl of Orford, 1795.' Hannah More in turn presented it in 1828 to Lord Teignmouth.

3998 BOILEAU-DESPRÉAUX, NICOLAS

Oeuvres. The Hague, 1722. Four volumes, 12mo.

The copy in the Dyce Collection at the Victoria and Albert Museum has a partly obliterated note: 'E libris Thomae Gray ex dono — Walpole.' Since HW owned the new edition of 1729, he perhaps gave this set to Gray.

3999 CERVANTES SAAVEDRA, MIGUEL DE

Don Quixote. Translated by T. Shelton. With cuts after Coypel. London, 1725. Four volumes, 12mo.

Original panelled calf, rebacked. Three of the volumes contain HW's signature, one of which is dated September 1726. Bookplate of Thomas Gaisford.

Since the signatures seem certainly genuine, the set seems to have been given away before 1763. It was owned by the late Charles Scribner; Seven Gables Book Shop, September 1956, to WSL, $185.

4000 CLARENDON, EDWARD HYDE, 1st Earl of

Life of Edward, Earl of Clarendon. Oxford, 1759. Folio.

A copy in old calf at Farmington is inscribed: 'This book is the gift of the Honble. Mr. Walpole to the Honble. Mrs. Harriot Seymour Con-

way, May 3d, 1760.' Henrietta Seymour Conway asked HW for a copy on 11 April, and thanked him for it on 6 May 1760.

COWLEY, ABRAHAM   4001
Select works. London, 1772. Two volumes, 8vo.

Bishop Hurd, the editor, gave HW a copy of the second (revised) edition (*see* No. 3917 *above*). Although HW had already put his bookplate in this first edition, he gave it to William Cole in April 1773; it is now at Farmington.

DALRYMPLE, Sir JOHN   4002
Memoirs of Great Britain. Volume 2. London, 1773. 4to.

On 2 March 1773 HW promised to send a copy to Mason; one may assume that he purchased an extra copy to send to Mason.

[DESAINLIENS, CLAUDE]   4003
The pretie and wittie historie of Arnalt and Lucenda. London, 1575. 16mo.

This book is in the British Museum, rebound in calf, with HW's signature: 'H. Walpole 1731.' It likewise has Cole's bookplate and signature: 'Wm. Cole, Coll. Regal. A. B. June 17, 1738.' On the fly-leaf is the name 'W. Bayntun, Gray's Inn,' presumably William Bayntun, F. S. A., who died in 1785. The book was purchased from Rodd by the British Museum in 1839.

There seems little doubt that this was a book acquired by HW when he was at Eton, and then given or lent to Cole in 1738 when they were at Cambridge. Since it does not seem to be in the Cole sale in 1784, it perhaps passed to Bayntun before Cole's death. Such books, illustrative of HW's early love for old romances, were likely not to survive in his library as he outgrew this unsophisticated early passion.

ÉON DE BEAUMONT, CHARLES, Chevalier d'   4004
Lettres, mémoirs, & negotiations particulières. London, 1764. 4to.

Of this work, which interested him greatly, HW kept one copy in his Glass Closet; he sent one copy to Lord Hertford and two to Mason.

GARTH, Sir SAMUEL   4005
The dispensary. London, 1741. 12mo.

In the sale of books from Kirgate's library, 4 December 1810, lot 294 was a copy of Garth 'with MS notes by Lord Orford.'

4006 GIANETTI, MICHEL ANGELO

Elogio del Capitano Cook. With an English translation by Robert Merry. Florence, 1785. 4to.

Mann sent four copies of this to HW. We know that he gave one of them to Richard Gough (HW to Mann, 28 March 1786; and to Gough, 21 June 1786).

4007 HERVEY, THOMAS

Letter to the Reverend Sir William Bunbury. London, [1753]. 8vo.

On 16 August 1753, HW wrote to Montagu that he was sending him a copy of this letter.

4008 HUME, DAVID

Supplement to the life of David Hume containing genuine anecdotes. Perhaps compiled by S. J. Pratt. London, 1777. 8vo.

Because of the attack on Mason included in this, HW sent a copy to Mason, 16 May 1777, but he seems not to have kept a copy himself.

4009 JEPHSON, ROBERT

Braganza. London, 1775. 8vo.

On 7 March 1775, HW sent a copy to Mason, but it was of course an extra copy.

4010 LINE, FRANCIS, *alias* HALL

An explication of the diall sett up in the King's garden at London, an. 1669. Liège, 1673. 4to.

Richard Bull's copy, sold in 1926 and now WSL, has Bull's note: 'This book, printed at Liège, was given to me by Mr. Horace Walpole.' The dial is mentioned in the *Anecdotes,* ii.55, but only from Vertue's notes.

4011 MARMONTEL, JEAN FRANÇOIS

Les Incas. Paris, 1777. Two volumes, 12mo.

Mason asked about this in his letter to HW, 14 April 1777; although HW did not like the book, he was glad to send a copy to Mason, 2 May 1777. Mason thanked him and promised to return the work, but on 16 May 1777 HW replied: 'Do not return me the *Incas*; I shall never read it.' Mason likewise found the work heavy reading.

MONTPENSIER, ANNE MARIE LOUISA D'ORLÉANS, Duchesse de 4012
Divers portraits.

In his letter to Lady Hervey, 20 February 1759, HW offered to lend her a little book of characters of the French court. This volume, which does not seem to be in the SH records, was perhaps an edition of Mademoiselle de Montpensier's *Divers portraits*, first published in 1659 in 4to, and reprinted in smaller format as *Recueil de portraits* or *Portraits de la cour.*

SANSON, NICOLAS 4013
Table alphabétique de toutes les villes . . . de l'Italie. Paris, 1648.
Folio.

A copy with the bookplates of HW and Agnes Berry, bound in russia by Hayday, was in the Twopenny Sale at Sotheby's in May 1902; sold to Sotheran for £44. Notes on the fly-leaf read: 'Agnes Berry, the gift of Lord Orford. The legacy of Agnes Berry to W. Twopenny, 1852.'

SCOTT, JOHN 4014
The foundation of the Universitie of Cambridge. MS. 1621. Folio.

This MS is at Pembroke College, in a fine Cambridge binding, now rebacked. It has HW's BP; he gave it to Pembroke College, Cambridge, *ca.* 1772.

STUART, ANDREW 4015
Letters to Lord Mansfield. London, 1773. 4to.

On 27 March 1773 HW sent a copy to Mason; but he told Mason it was one of two copies that had been given to him.

THOMAS, WILLIAM 4016
The historie of Italie. London, 1549. 4to.

This work, supposed to have been suppressed and hence extremely rare, seems to have appealed to HW. He kept two copies and a later edition, and in addition he gave a copy to Samuel Lysons; it is now in the Chapin Library, Williamstown, Massachusetts.

VOLTAIRE, FRANÇOIS MARIE AROUET DE 4017
One or more volumes.

On 11 December 1755 Conway thanked HW for sending some Voltaire and other books to him in Dublin.

In 1773 Mme. du Deffand sent to HW a copy of Voltaire's *Les Lois de Minos*. When HW had received it, he condemned it totally in his letter to Mme. du Deffand, 25 January 1773. He then sent it to Lady Ossory, expressing the hope on 11 March 1773 that she had not liked it.

4018 BRUCE, JAMES

Travels to discover the source of the Nile. Edinburgh, 1790. Five volumes, 4to.

Although Conway praised Bruce's work, HW wrote to Conway: 'I am sick of his vanity, and (I believe) of his want of veracity; I am sure, of his want of method and of his obscurity.' (25 June 1790) On 7 (?) July 1790 he added: 'It is the most absurd, obscure, and tiresome book I know. . . .' So we know he read at least some of Bruce; but he did not keep the set, and Pinkerton in his *Walpoliana* (ii.2) recorded an informal book-club arrangement as HW had described it: 'Bruce's book is both dull and dear [published at £5.5.0]. We join in clubs of five, each pays a guinea, draw lots who shall have it first, and the last to keep it for his patience.' Whether HW used such a method to gain access to other large works I do not know.

4019 CHARLES LOUIS, Elector Palatine

La vie et les amours de Charles Louis Electeur Palatin. Amsterdam, 1697.

Not a gift but a borrowing is recorded in this final item. In his 'Book of Materials,' January 1787, HW noted several details from this book, which Sir William Musgrave had lent him.

BOOKS OWNED BY WALPOLE
AT ETON AND CAMBRIDGE

Because of the interest attaching to a young man's reading, all books known to have been owned by Walpole before 1739 when he left Cambridge are here listed. One can guess that he owned many others, especially some of the titles recorded in K.7 and Press M, but this list is limited to those that can be certainly identified as in his collection before 1739. They were owned and probably used by him at Eton, 1727–34, or at Cambridge, 1735–38. Since all these books are entered in the main text of this *Catalogue*, they are not numbered here, and not indexed.

When Walpole was only about nine, he wrote to his mother: 'I want yearl of assax and Jan Shore,' possibly two chap-books. But more important intellectually is a letter from Conway, 18 April 1745, that emphasizes one aspect of Walpole's early reading, his love of romances. This would not be clear in any study of the whole library, partly because he failed to keep all his boyhood books; it helps to define the adult habit of mind that has been described in the Introduction. Conway wrote from Dover:

> I have been vastly obliged to your Abelard, and with that melancholy companion have visited all the cliffs upon the coast, till I was ready to take a lover's leap from some of 'em in errant despair. . . . It's a long time since you were romantic. I remember you buried in romances and novels; I really believe you could have said all the Grand Cyrus's, the Cleopatra's, and Amadis's in the world by heart; nay, you carried your taste for it so far that not a Fairy Tale escaped you. *Quantum mutatus*. But one thing I comfort myself with, you have laid up a vast stock of romance.

Earlier, 25 October 1743, Conway had also alluded to Walpole's love of romances. In a later letter, 10 August 1745, he added further details:

> You might for ought I know have some pleasure in the stories of Agincourt and Cressi in your infancy as you say [a reply to Wal-

pole's letter of July 1st]; if ever you were heroically inclined, it was in those very early days, but you soon fell from your taste for those substantial honors to the imaginary glories of *Amadis* and *Cassandra*, from whence it dwindled gradually into *Zaide* and the *Princess of Cleves* and lost itself entirely in the *Egaremens* and *History of Marianne*.

The list follows,[1] with the date of acquisition (not publication) whenever it is ascertainable:

Addison and Steele, *Spectator* and other works. Twenty-one volumes. 1729.
Arrian, *History*. Two volumes. 1731.
Bible. Given to him by his father when he was at Eton.
Bramston, *Art of Politicks*, and other tracts. 1731.
Brathwait, *Drunken Barnaby's four journeys*. 1732.
Cervantes, *Don Quixote*. Four volumes. 1726.
Classics, in red morocco. A set of seventy-six volumes. *Ca.* 1730.
Congreve, *Works*. Two volumes. 1728.
Desainliens, *Arnalt and Lucenda*. 1731.
Du Halde, *Description de la Chine*. Four volumes. 1735.
Echard, *Roman history*. Five volumes. Probably before 1733.
Euclid, *Elements*. 1735.
Gay, *Poems*. Two volumes. 1732.
Glover, *Leonidas*. 1738.
Hederich, *Lexicon Graecum*. Probably before 1733.
Heylyn, *Cosmographie*. 1730.
History of England. Two volumes. 1731.
Horace, *Opera*. 1733.
Jonson, *Three plays*. Probably before 1733.
Limborch, *History of the Inquisition*. Two volumes. 1732.
Littleton, *Latin Dictionary*. *Ca.* 1735.
Milton, *Poems*. Two volumes. 1731.
Moll, *Geographia*. 1731.
New Testament. 1730.
Nichols, *British Compendium*. 1730.
Ovid, *Epistles*. 1731.
Ovid, *Metamorphoses*. Two volumes. 1730.

1. A list preserved at Houghton but not dated preserves a record of the books 'taken out by your son at his going to Cambridge.' Since none of these books, largely standard editions of the classics, can be identified in the SH records and since none were at Houghton in 1956, the list is probably the record of books taken by Edward Walpole, who entered Cambridge in 1725.

BOOKS OWNED AT ETON AND CAMBRIDGE

Ovid, *Opera*. Three volumes. 1733.

Palairet, *French grammar*. 1730.

Petronius, *Satyricon*. 1730.

Pill to purge state-melancholy. 1730.

Plutarch, *Lives*. Eight volumes. Probably before 1733.

Pomfret, *Poems*. 1730.

Prior, *Poems*. Three volumes. 1730.

Ramsay, *Travels of Cyrus*. Two volumes. 1728.

Thomson, *Seasons*. 1731.

Trapp, *Praelectiones poeticae*. 1733.

Wake, *Principles of the Christian religion*. 1732.

Waller, *Works*. 1729.

Webster, *Practical mathematics*. Three volumes. 1730.

Wycherley, *Plays*. Two volumes. 1734.

School books, grammars, &c. Fifty volumes. Recorded as No. 3175 of this *Catalogue*.

School exercises, a note-book. 1733.

French grammars. Four volumes, itemized on shelf G.6, were surely acquired 1730–35.

INDEX OF BINDERS

Although Walpole's collection is not of special interest to students of the history of bookbinding, most of the books being in unsigned contemporary calf or original boards, such binders as can be identified are listed here as a potentially useful record.

Aitken 3485

Bateman, Thomas 834
Baumgarten, John (d. 1782) p. xi
Bayntun, George, Bath 1339
Bedford, Francis (1800–84) 58, 122, 186, 189, 191, 199, 204, 214, 658, 1079, 1126, 1315, 1318, 1335, 1657, 2029, 2331, 2724, 3455, 3915, 3931
Bevan, Charles Stanley 2507:4, 2516
Brindley, John (d. 1758) 323

Cambridge binding 4014
Campbell, James (d. 1784) 32, 3097
Clarke, John 3400
Clarke & Bedford 141, 2523, 3163, 3644, 3745, 3753
Club Bindery, New York 2032

Dublin binding 2263
Du Seuil, Augustin, Paris (1673–1746) 896

Edwards, of Halifax 262, 2482, 2515, 3702, 3703
Edwards, James. See Edwards, of Halifax
Edwards, William. See Edwards, of Halifax

Hathaway 1810:29
Hayday, James 371, 2011, 3707, 3711, 3724, 3821, 3830, 4013
Hering, Charles (fl. 1795–1812?) 3728
Hodge, of Exeter 3914
Hodgson, of Liverpool 1143, 2371, 2760
Hollis binding 2647, 2730, 2775, 3172, 3176

Jenkins & Cecil 2528
Johnson (fl. 1765–80) p. xi
Jugge, Richard 2601

Kalthoeber, Christian Samuel (fl. 1782–1813) 3564, 3625, 3689, 3691–2, 3694, 3697, 3706, 3814
Keeley, Messrs., Maidstone 3

Le Gascon 1055
Leighton, John 197
Lewis, Charles (1786–1836; the firm continued until 1854) 212, 3729, 3911, 3955
Low, Peter 2003

McGuire, J. C., Washington, D.C. 3427
Mackenzie, John 100:4, 3286, 3857:4
Mathews. See Matthews
Matthewman, John 3172
Matthews, Alfred, New York 2387:2, 4, 6
Matthews, William, New York (1822–96) 376
Mearne, Samuel (d. 1683) 3945
Murton, Charles 1893

Padeloup, Antoine Michel, Paris (1685–1758) 2207, 3591
Payne, Roger (1738–97) 1876, 3705
Pingo, Thomas 3172
Pratt, William 193, 2410

Rau, Edward H., Philadelphia (d. 1895?) 3825
Riviere, Robert (later Riviere & Sons) 92, 1788, 1810:12, 18, 19, 33; 2453, 2456:2, 2724, 3119, 3469:13, 3885, 3918

INDEX OF BINDERS

Robiquet, John (*fl.* 1740–62) 2368
Ruette, Antoine, Paris (1609–64?) 2343, 3591

S., J. 34
Sampson, J., of York 162
Sanford, P. B. 1810:14, 35

Sangorski & Sutcliffe 2616
Smith, Charles 2456:3
Stamper, H. 2625
Stikeman & Co. (successor to Alfred Matthews) 1810:20, 25

Zaehnsdorf & Co. 271

INDEX OF OWNERS

Indexed here are all records of ownership or association, both institutions and private collectors, whether known from catalogues or identifiable from the volumes themselves. Booksellers, who have so much influence in the distribution of antiquarian volumes, have been included, but not auctioneers. Institutions are recorded by their familiar names, e.g., the Folger Library and the Huntington Library, not by their complete corporate titles. All references are to the numbers assigned in this *Catalogue*.

Identifying dates have been included, whenever possible, with the names of private collectors, except for those still living. Sometimes, when the surname only appears in a sale record, the collector cannot be identified or differentiated with certainty; but the names have been completed when a reasonable probability exists.

Surnames only, without attempted identification, are usually to be interpreted as fictitious names announced by the auctioneer to protect a consignor's anonymity when the lot was bought in because the bid was below the consignor's reserve.

Abbott 2555

Acheson, Archibald. *See* Gosford

Adam, Robert Borthwick (1863–1940) 1810:5, 2494, 2616

Adams 412

Adams, Frederick A. (d. 1941) 2196

Adams, Frederick Baldwin, Jr. 1793

Adams, Joseph Quincy (1881–1946) 1810:33

Adamson, Charles, London, bookseller (purchaser in 1842) 3485:8, 3488, 3497, 3521, 3540, 3580, 3597, 3600–1, 3605, 3626, 3680–1, 3687, 3760, 3823

Addams, Richard 2421

Advocates' Library. *See* National Library of Scotland

Aiguillon, Anne Charlotte de Crussol de Florensac, Duchesse d' (1700–72) 2424, 3058, 3089, 3920

Aikman, Thomas (owner in 1688?) 1608:8

Ailesbury, Charles Bruce, Earl of (1682–1747, 1441

Aladdin 3670

Alcorn, Paul 469

Aldenham, Henry Hucks Gibbs, Baron (1819–1907) 501, 1331, 1615

Aldington 626

Aldridge, Colonel John (1832–88) 2528

Allatt, John (owner 1656?) 1979

Allbutt, Sir Thomas Clifford (1836–1925) 1285

(?) Allen, C. 1768

Allen, Edward George, & Son, London, booksellers 3763

Allington, Charles (Fellow of Queens' College, Cambridge, 1671–80) 150

Allis, William Watson (1849–1918) 1884

American Antiquarian Society 1386, 2046, 2680

American School of Classical Studies at Athens. Gennadeion Library 3995

Ames, Joseph (1689–1759) 515, 780, 2598, 3459, 3768

Anderdon, James Hughes (d. 1879) 3441, 3600, 3646, 3833

Andrews 1104

Andrews, William, Bristol, bookseller 108

Andrews, William Loring (1837–1920) 676, 2387, 2400, 2526, 2597

Anne, Queen of England (1665–1714) 2613

Anstis, John (1669–1744) 2537, 2558, 2583, 2607

Apple, Maxwell Alexander 872

Appleton, Daniel Fuller (1826–1904) 1639

Appleton, William Sumner (1874–1947) 1872

Arbuthnot, William (1833–96) 2689

Armes, William Dallam (b. 1860) 2131

Armour, George Allison (d. 1936) 1860

Armstrong 1955

Arnold, Augustus A. 3

Arnold, William Harris (1854–1923) 1233, 2286

Art Institute of Chicago 482

Art Union of London 2595

Arthur, Thomas, Holywell Street, London, bookseller 2575, 3180

Arundel, Thomas Howard, Earl of (1585–1646) 3786:2

Ashburnham, Bertram, Earl of Ashburnham (1797–1878) 118, 1209, 1617, 2628

Ashburnham, Hon. Percy (1799–1881) 3620, 3632

Ashburton, Louisa Caroline, Lady (1827–1903) 3777

Ashford, William Ker, of Twickenham (1806?–63) 1825, 1833, 1838, 2459

Ashmolean Museum 3570

Atherley, Arthur (ca. 1772–1844) 1841

Atkins, Penelope, Baroness Rivers. See Rivers

Atkinson, Fred Washington (1865–1941) 1810:14

Atkinson, Nicolas 101

Atlee, John (owner 1677?) 2055

Attwill, Theodore (fl. 1880) 1832

Augustus Frederick, Duke of Sussex. See Sussex

Avery, Samuel Putnam (1822–1904) 2523

Avery Library, Columbia University. See Columbia University

B., F. C. 644

B., H. J., Esq., F. R. S. See Brooke

B., J. 3469:3

Baikie, William Balfour (1825–64) 1584

Bailey, John Eglinton (1840–88) 1109

Bain, James, Ltd., London, booksellers 37, 507, 722, 741, 1657, 2387:5, 2487, 2498, 2525, 3019, 3123, 3591:2, 3657, 3692, 3900, 3924

Baker, Mrs. Ernest E. 734

Baker, James, Esq. (purchaser in 1842) 3572, 3889

Baker, Thomas (1656–1740) 201

Baldwin, C. A. and V. 3625

Bale, Charles Sackville (purchaser in 1842) 3567, 3669

Balliol College, Oxford. See Oxford University

Bandinel, Bulkeley, Bodley's librarian (1781–1861) 1615

Banks 2374

Banks, Sir Joseph (1743–1820) 2404, 3726

Barber, Thomas, of Norfolk (d. 1785) 3768

Barchard, Robert Wildman (1793?–1848) 2325, 2406

Barlow, Charles (entered Emmanuel College in 1733) 2423, 2427

Barnard, Henry Gee (1789–1858) 2207:22

Barnard, W., Esq. (purchaser in 1842) 2470, 3165, 3223

Barnbougle Castle. See Rosebery, Earl of

Barnes, Mabel F. 1832

Barnes, Orson, London, bookseller 331, 340, 3027

Barrett, Frank Ashley (1878–1954) 1810:13, 3895

Barrett, Thomas (1698?–1757) 3480

Barrett-Lennard, Thomas, Baron Dacre. See Dacre

Barron, Edward Jackson, F. S. A. (d. 1918) 3441

Bartlett, Edward T. 1332

Bartlett, George G. 1332

Bartol, Elizabeth 3839

Barton, Thomas Pennant (1803–69) 3825

Bateman, Thomas (1821–61) 358

Bates, H. 790

Bateson, Frederick Wilse 106

Bathoe, William, London, bookseller (d. 1768) 1609:13; 1810:9; 2479

Batty, W. Rayner 518

Baylis, Thomas (1786?–1853) 19, 563, 573–4, 610–11, 632, 641, 775, 781, 790–1, 798, 809, 811–13, 2490, 2630, 2656, 2669, 2742, 2749–50, 2752, 2754, 2957

Bayntun, George, Bath, bookseller 1339

Bayntun, H. (owner *ca.* 1700?) 3385

Bayntun, William (*d.* 1785) 4003

Beam, Mrs. Fay K. 2102

Beauchamp, William Lygon, 8th Earl (1872–1938) 2888, 3568

Beauclerk, Lady Diana (Spencer) (1734–1808) 3537

Beauclerk, Topham (1739–80) 390, 402, 1872, 3019, 3911

Beaufoy, Henry Benjamin Hanbury (1786–1851) 3119

Beckford, William (1760–1844) 263–4, 273, 277, 506–7, 510, 587, 589, 722, 726, 741, 757, 769, 836, 842, 848–9, 855, 864, 980, 982, 987, 992, 994, 998, 1006, 1055, 1139, 1606, 2207: 37, 2328–9, 2339, 2343–4, 2349, 2351–2, 2359, 2365, 2368–9, 2378, 2380, 2387, 2398, 2400, 2404, 2408, 2411, 2415, 2436, 2469, 2487, 2498, 2522, 2525–6, 2628, 3391, 3433, 3474, 3518, 3520, 3527, 3536, 3546, 3552, 3564, 3573, 3577, 3579, 3582–4, 3589, 3594, 3623, 3638, 3648, 3654–5, 3657, 3667, 3682, 3684, 3691, 3693–5, 3698, 3702, 3706, 3708, 3710, 3731–2, 3735, 3741, 3744–5, 3753, 3765, 3770, 3783, 3785–7, 3801, 3814, 3818, 3839, 3902, 3928

Bedford, Francis Russell, Duke of (1765–1802) 2619

Bedford, Gertrude Leveson-Gower, Duchess of (1715–94) 2471

Beet, Thomas, London, bookseller 3053–4

Belfast. *See* Queen's University

Belin, Théophile, Paris, bookseller 3751

Bell, James (1813?–1902) 2068, 2071–3, 2075

Bell, Thomas (1785–1860) 1897

Bellchambers, Jonathan, Strand, London, bookseller 313

Bement, Clarence Sweet (1843–1923) 2029, 2446, 2528, 3849, 3966

Benn, Arthur Shirley, later Baron Glenravel (1858–1937) 2475

Benn, Thomas, Vicar of Millom (*fl.* 1724) 1681

Bennett, M. L. (purchaser in 1888) 1449

Benson, Mrs. William Arthur Smith (library sold 1940) 2001, 2069, 2079

Bentley, H. H. 178

Bentley, Rev. Horatio (1833–91) 178

Bentley, Richard (1708–82) 2344, 2549, 3467

Bentley, Richard (1794–1871) 44, 54, 57–8, 84, 149, 159, 170, 178, 181, 436, 439–40, 445, 713–15, 720, 724, 730, 745, 747, 749, 753–4, 763, 766, 768, 773, 831, 934, 939–40, 949, 2576, 2710, 3254

Bentley, Richard (1853–1936) 2576

Bentley, Mrs. Richard (collection sold 1937) 1619, 1621, 2489, 3084, 3488

Benzon, Ernest Leopold S. (*d.* 1873) 2029, 3663

Berès, Pierre, Paris, bookseller 2545

Berg Collection, Henry W. and Albert A. *See* New York Public Library

Berry, Agnes (1764–1852) 3996, 4013

Berry, Donald A., London, bookseller 1285

Berry, Mary (1763–1852) 2489, 3971

Berwick, Thomas Henry Noel-Hill, Baron (1877–1947) 1255, 1280, 2528

Bessborough, Vere Brabazon Ponsonby, Earl of (1880–1956) 49

Beyer, Barnet J., New York, bookseller (*d.* 1947) 2517

Bezzi 3534, 3576, 3633

Bibliothèque Nationale, Paris 2545

Bidwell, Charles, of Ely (1863–1922) 541

Bindley, James (1737–1818) 2251, 2383

Birch, Thomas (1705–66) 120

Birrell & Garnett, London, bookseller 3249

Bishop, Cortlandt Field (1870–1935) 101, 1075, 1521, 2424

Blackton, James Stuart (1875–1941) 2617

Blackwell, Basil H., Ltd., Oxford, bookseller 21, 631, 1782, 3159, 3227, 3598, 3732

Blickling Hall, Aylsham, Norfolk 1782

Bliss, Philip (1787–1857) 23, 92, 125, 155, 207, 479, 688, 759, 904, 1441, 1572–3, 1743, 1898, 1936, 1984, 2009, 2131, 2338, 2347, 2362, 2469, 2472, 2575, 3180, 3319, 3727, 3811, 3817

Bloch, E. Maurice 3979

Bloomfield 3844

Blunt, Christopher 162

Boddy, of Woolwich, bookseller? (purchaser in 1842) 422, 427, 429–30, 433

Bodleian Library. *See* Oxford University

Bohn, Henry George, London, bookseller (1796–1884) 72, 90, 94, 96, 99, 103, 111, 231, 244, 263–4, 273, 277–9, 315–16, 464, 467, 497, 506–7, 510, 527, 531, 561, 575, 587, 589, 616, 636, 645, 674, 708, 722, 726, 741, 757,

Bohn, Henry George (*cont.*)

769, 836, 841–2, 848–9, 855, 864, 913, 980, 982, 987, 992, 994, 998, 1006, 1092, 1095, 1141, 1952, 1966, 1972, 1983, 1985, 2054, 2059, 2063, 2078, 2207, 2328–9, 2339, 2341, 2343–4, 2349, 2352, 2359, 2368–9, 2378, 2380, 2385, 2387, 2398, 2400, 2408, 2411, 2415, 2420, 2434, 2436, 2460, 2469, 2487, 2498, 2521–2, 2525–6, 2594, 2603, 2714, 3119–20, 3163, 3270, 3281–2, 3433, 3474, 3485, 3490–1, 3493, 3503, 3513, 3516–17, 3520, 3527, 3535–6, 3538, 3541, 3545, 3547–8, 3554, 3559, 3562–6, 3570, 3573, 3576–8, 3583–4, 3590–1, 3593–4, 3596, 3598–9, 3603–4, 3609, 3617, 3621, 3623, 3628, 3630, 3638, 3640, 3644–5, 3648, 3654, 3656–7, 3667, 3672–3, 3675, 3677, 3682, 3684, 3691, 3693–5, 3698, 3702, 3706, 3708, 3710, 3717, 3725, 3730–2, 3740–1, 3743–7, 3753–5, 3763, 3765, 3769–70, 3773–4, 3780, 3782, 3784–5, 3787, 3800–1, 3814–15, 3818, 3833:11, 3837–9, 3842, 3846, 3859, 3869, 3879, 3881–2, 3891, 3897–8, 3902, 3905, 3913–15, 3928

Bohn, James Stuart Burgess, London, bookseller (1803–80) 2176, 2184, 2848, 2884, 2920, 2968:4

Boileau family. *See* Ketteringham Hall

Bools, William Edward, of Enderby House, Clapham (1837?–1902) 195, 1572, 1897, 1905, 2472, 3926–7

Boone, Thomas & William, London, booksellers 12, 19, 45, 49–50, 53, 56, 91, 243, 246, 255, 259, 287–9, 291, 295–6, 298–300, 303, 308–12, 324–6, 328–30, 332, 335, 338–9, 343–5, 347, 349–51, 353–4, 356–7, 359–62, 367, 370–1, 378, 381, 387, 397, 399, 532, 538, 568, 594, 613, 626, 647–9, 651, 654, 663–4, 668–9, 671, 677, 689, 706–7, 873–4, 884, 889, 891, 895, 914–15, 930, 1104, 1122, 1126, 1140, 1143, 1322, 1341, 1773, 1818, 1900–2, 1917, 1984, 2011, 2044, 2047–50, 2156, 2160, 2207, 2328, 2338, 2347, 2357, 2371, 2401, 2421, 2478, 2486, 2515, 2519, 2535, 2538, 2546, 2551, 2559, 2578, 2581–3, 2596, 2600–1, 2604, 2606, 2608, 2610, 2618, 2620–1, 2637, 2649, 2653, 2703, 2712, 2727–8, 2748, 2760, 2767, 2786–9, 2830, 2832–3, 2862, 2864, 2872, 2874, 2877, 2892–4, 2896, 2899, 2907, 2919, 2939–40, 2956, 2974,

Boone, Thomas & William (*cont.*)

2977, 3286, 3296, 3309, 3317–18, 3320, 3331, 3333, 3336, 3340, 3365–7, 3370, 3373, 3385–6, 3579, 3635, 3704, 3727

Booth, Lionel, Duke Street, London, bookseller 92, 143, 182, 184, 486, 697, 2977–8, 3019, 3896, 3926–7, 3933

Bordes, Henri, of Bordeaux (1842–1912) 2415

Boston Public Library 2724, 3839

Boston Public Library. Barton Collection 3825

Bourke, Myles (owner *ca.* 1700?) 1825

Bowes & Bowes, Cambridge, bookseller 541

Bowles, William, of Trinity College, Oxford, (*b. ca.* 1720) 1587

Bradley, George Lothrop (1846–1906) 3591:4

Braithwaite, Joseph Bevan (1818–1905) 906

Brand, John (1744–1806) 3975

Brander, Gustavus (1720–87) 1609:41

Brantôme, Pierre de Bourdeille, Seigneur de (1535–1614) 2358, 3655

Brassington, W. S. B. 3952

Brereton, Thomas (owner 1720) 2008

Brett, Oliver, Viscount Esher. *See* Esher

Breun, John Needham, London, printseller 3662

Brick Row Book Shop, Inc., New Haven and New York, booksellers 110, 310, 321, 323, 359, 412, 435–6, 834, 1075, 1325, 1367, 1507, 1561, 1806, 1810 (74 plays), 1860, 1881, 1890, 1897, 1905, 2029, 2033, 2120:7, 2184, 2206, 2326, 2424, 2453, 2521, 2597, 3123, 3393, 3859, 3926

Bridges, Victor 581

Brienne, Louis Henri de Loménie, Comte de (1636–98) 896

Bright 3257

Bright, Benjamin Heywood (1788?–1843) 204, 1680, 2628, 3955

Brimmer, Martin (1829–96) 199

Bristol, Augustus John Hervey, 3d Earl of (1724–79) 3403

Bristol Baptist College 2627

British Museum 88, 100:4, 141, 309, 475, 500, 509, 565, 582, 615, 787, 840, 857–8, 881, 1082, 1087, 1109, 1166, 1252, 1306, 1478, 1606, 1751, 1904, 1915, 1922, 1941, 1986, 2050:5, 22, 24; 2135, 2146:7, 2338, 2347, 2356, 2358, 2368, 2370, 2401, 2418, 2448, 2467, 2469, 2479, 2486, 2531, 2533, 2535–7, 2539–41,

British Museum (*cont.*)
2543-4, 2546, 2557-8, 2562, 2569, 2576 (Lort & Pole), 2577, 2584-6, 2589-92, 2595-6, 2598, 2607-8, 2613, 2626, 2628, 2642, 2650, 2658, 2670, 2685, 2719, 2927, 3097, 3113, 3131, 3172, 3267, 3309, 3381, 3404, 3408, 3485, 3503, 3563:4, 3567, 3582, 3600, 3636, 3643, 3646, 3662, 3664, 3690, 3699, 3704, 3726, 3775, 3822-3, 3832:1, 3862, 3885, 3901, 3908, 3915, 3920, 3934, 3960, 3975, 4003

British Museum. Grenville Collection 141, 2467, 2658, 3172, 3960

Briton, Thomas (owner *ca.* 1600?) 1606

Britton, John (1771-1857) 61, 77, 85, 124, 144, 314, 377, 390, 453, 497, 1032, 1037, 1214, 1273, 1316, 1343, 1346, 1396, 1668, 1670, 1746, 1763, 1814, 1820, 2010, 2076, 2172, 2190, 2555, 2570, 2622, 2710, 2878-9, 2950, 2971, 3053, 3230, 3232, 3239, 3254, 3257, 3351, 3354-5, 3382, 3413-14, 3505, 3697

Britwell Court 104, 113, 116, 119, 122, 163, 186, 189, 191, 193, 204, 208, 214-15, 435, 780, 1111, 1113, 1315, 1318, 1326, 1335, 1608:90, 1619, 1625, 1633, 1779, 1787-9, 1800, 1806, 1810, 1933, 2021-2, 2037, 2174, 2179-81, 2386, 2399, 2410, 2452, 2504-5, 2724, 2731, 2757, 2802, 3955

Broadbent, N. M., London, bookseller 2162

Brocklehurst, Geoffrey Mark Dent 2576 (Catherine Parr)

Brockley Hall. *See* Pigott

Brodick Castle 2380

Brodie, John Clerk (1811-88) 1840

Brooke, Francis Greville, Earl; later Earl of Warwick (1719-73) 1478

Brooke, Henry James (1771-1857) 3727

Brooke, Sir John Arthur (1844-1920) 1955

Brooke, Sir Thomas (1830-1908) 1955

Brown, of Richmond. *See* Browne

Brown, Elvered M. 1833

Brown, John Carter (1797-1874) 3786:2

Brown, Dr. John Taylor (1811-1901) 61, 3253, 3896

Brown, William, Edinburgh, bookseller 3784, 3918

Brown University. John Carter Brown Library 3786:2

Browne, Edward, Ivy House, Marsh Gate, Richmond, bookseller (purchaser in 1842) 808, 822, 1103, 2353, 2407, 3098, 3612

Browne, Michael (owner *ca.* 1700?) 2499

Bruce, Charles, Viscount Bruce, Earl of Ailesbury. *See* Ailesbury

Bruce, R. T. Hamilton (library sold 1900) 271

Brunswick, Augustus William, Duke of (*d.* 1731) 2207

Brunton, of Edinburgh, bookseller 2207:9

Bryant, John, London, bookseller 441, 569, 572, 577, 588, 615, 638, 642, 655, 676, 686, 694, 710, 801-3, 806, 815-16, 820, 824, 856, 862, 865, 917-18, 924-5, 958, 965, 968-9, 1055, 1074, 1085-6, 1352-4, 1357, 1359, 1362-3, 1509, 1513, 1516, 1524, 1535, 1538, 1540, 1544, 1547, 1549, 1551, 1554, 1559, 1583, 1586, 1608, 2084-5, 2090-2

Buchan, David Stewart Erskine, 11th Earl of (1742-1829) 1609:42

Buchanan, Thomas Ryburn (1846-1911) 2249

Buckingham Palace Library. *See* Windsor Castle

Buckinghamshire, Augustus Edward Hobart, Earl of (1793-1885) 1786, 1798-9, 3653, 3655-6

Buckinghamshire, George Robert Hobart-Hampden, Earl of (1789-1849) 2361, 2574, 3532-3, 3537, 3928

Buckinghamshire, John Hobart, 2d Earl of (1722-93) 2576 (Peter the Third)

Buckler, Riggin 289

Buckler, William Hepburn (1867-1952) 2374

Buckley, Rev. William Edward (1817?-92) 2207:9, 3823, 3890

Buddy, Lewis, III (*d.* 1941) 2077

Bull, Richard (1725-1806) 2515, 2521, 2978, 3417, 3475, 3485, 4010

Bulwer, Henry A. 3224

Bumstead, George, London, bookseller 23, 98, 688, 995, 997, 1200, 1291, 1343, 1572, 1762, 1935, 1984, 2009, 2362, 2457, 2472, 3810, 3887

Burdett-Coutts, Angela Georgina, Baroness (1814-1906) 2344

Burke, Father Redmond 261

Burke, Thomas Haviland (1795-1852) 3563:2

Burlington, Richard Boyle, Earl of (1694-1753) 3577

Burmann, Thomas (*d.* 1675) 150

Burndy Library 3957

Burnet, Gilbert, Bishop (1643–1715) 101

Burns, John (1858–1943) 752, 3986

Burra, James S. (1838–1911) 584

Burra, John S. (1876–1913) 584

Burroughs, E. W. 3889

Burton, C. L. (owner 1645) 1342

Burton, William Evans (1802–1860) 1009, 1835

Burwell, Mary (*d.* 1711) 3165

Busfeild, Rev. Johnson Atkinson (1775?–1849) 2945

Bute, John Patrick Crichton-Stuart, 3d Marquess of (1847–1900) 3372

Bute, John Stuart, 3d Earl of (1713–92) 3503

Butler, Charles, of Warren Wood, Hatfield (1821–1910) 773, 3705

Butler, Charles H. A. 773

Butler, Herbert Trevanon (*d.* 1933) 3975

Butler, Louis Fatier (1871–1929) 2202

Butler, Sydney Courtauld (Mrs. R. A.) (1902–54) 2528

Bygrave, Robert (owner 1743) 2547

C., E. 1864

C., H. B. 3727

C., H. M. 1864

C., J. M. 2253

Cadwalader, Capt. John 2055

Cadwalader, Sophia 2055

Caesar, Sir Julius (1558–1636) 2535, 3775

California, University of 3591:5

Calthorpe, James (1604–52) 1625

Cambridge University 109, 1449, 1810:14

Cambridge University. Fitzwilliam Museum 2427, 2527, 3646

Cambridge University. Gonville & Caius College 3476

Cambridge University. King's College 2050:21

Cambridge University. Newnham College 3857:4

Cambridge University. Pembroke College 4014

Cambridge University. St. John's College 3352

Cambridge University. Trinity College 3152

Cameron, Arnold Guyot (1864–1947) 695

Cameron, John M. (1867–1939) 2029

Campbell, Alexander, later Earl of Marchmont (1675–1740) 2400

Campbell, Lord Frederick (1729–1816) 1109

Campbell, Sir Hugh Purves Hume (1812–94) 3635, 3768, 3875

Campbell, Juliana Hume (*d.* 1886) 3768, 3875

Canham, Anthony John (1814?–53) 571

Cant, Andrew (1590?–1663) 3727

Cape Town, University of 2576 (Bowle)

Carbery, John Vaughan, Earl of (1639–1713) 187, 1113

Cardiff Castle. *See* Bute, Marquess of

Cardonnel, Philip de (*d.* 1667) 1893

Carew Hunt, Basil 278

Carlingford, Chichester Samuel Parkinson-Fortescue, Baron (1823–98) 296, 448, 450, 916, 1021, 1464, 1471, 2421, 2462, 2528, 3463, 3490

Carlyle, Thomas (1795–1881) 3777

Carnarvon, Anne Catherine Tredick, Countess of; now Mrs. Grenfell 3786:1

Carnegie Book Shop, New York, booksellers 2160, 3750, 3889

Caroline Wilhelmina, Queen Consort of George II of England (1683–1737) 1148

Carter, Albert Charles Robinson (1864–1957) 501

Carter, John (owner *ca.* 1600?) 787

Carter, John, London, bookseller 2506

Castletown, Bernard Fitz-Patrick, Baron 1900

Castletown, John Wilson Fitz-Patrick, 1st Baron (1811–83) 1900

Catherine of Braganza, Queen of England (1638–1705) 2329

Catherine Parr, Queen of England (1512–48) 834

Caulfield, William, London, bookseller 2190

Cavendish, Lord George (*d.* 1794) 258

Cazenove 2411

Century Association, New York 1793

Chaloner, Margaret Bruce 195

Chaloner, Thomas, Baron Gisborough. *See* Gisborough

Chandler 543

Chandon de Briailles, Comte 2425

Chapin, Alfred Clark (1848–1936). *See* Williams College

Chapin Library, Williams College. *See* Williams College

Chapman, John Jay (1862–1933) 1461

Chapman, Robert William (1881–1960) 472, 2436, 2520, 3137, 3880

Charlemont, James Caulfield, Earl of (1728–99) 2933

Charles I, King of England (1600–49) 846, 2551, 3526

Charlett, Arthur (1655–1722) 1608:3

Charlotte Sophia, Queen of England (1744–1818) 2356

Charlton, Joseph (owner *ca.* 1700?) 19

Chatto, William John Potts, barrister 2423

Chaucer Head Book Shop, Inc., New York, booksellers 101, 695

Cheney, Edward (*d.* 1884) 195, 1860, 1873, 1993, 2433, 3309, 3778, 3912

Chetham's Library 154

Chetwynd, Sir George (1783–1850) 3916

Chew, Beverley (1850–1924) 1871, 2453, 3377

Chicago, University of 1810:14, 3223

Chicago Art Institute 482

Chichester, John Hopton Russell, F. S. A. (library sold 1863) 296

Cholmondeley, George Horatio Charles, 5th Marquess of Cholmondeley 3873

Cholmondeley, Harriet, Baroness Delamere. *See* Delamere

Cholmondeley, Reginald, of Condover Hall (1826–96) 3729

Chouler, Christopher 2945

Christ Church, Oxford. *See* Oxford University

Christie, Richard Copley (1830–1901) 2292–3

Christie-Miller, Samuel. *See* Britwell Court

Christie-Miller, Major Samuel Vandeleur 2399

Chute, Sir Charles (1879–1956) 591

Chute, John (1701–76) 630, 3485:9

Cincinnati Public Library 2526

Clancarty, Donough MacCarthy, 4th Earl of (1668–1734) 2731

Clare, Richard Hobart FitzGibbon, Earl of (1793–1864) 2479, 3911

Claretie, Jules (1840–1913) 3001

Clark, Charles Walker (1871–1933) 1906

Clark, Sir Kenneth McKenzie 2344, 3441

Clarke, George, Wickham, bookseller 3290, 3297, 3360

Claude, Consort of Francis I, King of France (*d.* 1524) 3786:1

Clawson, John Lewis (1865–1933) 1617

Clearwater, Alphonzo Trumpbour (1848–1933) 1393

Clearwater, Thomas H. 1393

Clements, Henry John Beresford (1869–1940) 589, 1810:18, 3494

Clements, Col. Henry Theophilus Wickham 589, 2381

Clifton, Ann (*b. ca.* 1662) 3165

Clinton Hall Association, New York. *See* New York Mercantile Library

Clumber Sale. *See* Newcastle

Cobham, Sir Henry Brooke (1538–1605?) 3399

Coke, Thomas (*d.* 1727) 2411

Colbert, Jules Armand, Marquis d'Ormoy (1663–1704) 2408

Colburn, Henry, London, publisher (*d.* 1855) 2576

Colby House. *See* Baylis

Cole 3069

Cole, William (1714–82) 304, 636, 645, 2322, 2432, 2444, 2690, 3054, 3222:9, 3917, 4001, 4003

Colesworthy's Book Store, Inc., Boston, booksellers 237

Colgate, William G. 2905

Collins, Arthur (1682–1760) 17, 2543

Collins, Robert, London, bookseller (*d.* 1786) 389, 2251

Colnaghi, Paul and Dominic, & Co., London, booksellers 2351, 2377, 2433, 2622, 3441, 3486, 3500, 3567, 3571, 3602, 3609, 3611, 3614, 3629, 3792, 3849

Colorado, University of 3979

Colquhoun, Sir James (1741–1805) 1357, 3715

Columbia University 3692

Columbia University. Avery Library 3573, 3753

Comerford, James, F. S. A. (*d.* 1880) 636

Commin, Horace G., Bournemouth, bookseller 2994

Commin, James G., Exeter, bookseller 1674

Conant, John (*d.* 1723) 703

Constable, David 1990

Conway, Henrietta Seymour (1706–71) 2, 4000

Conway, Henry Seymour (1719?–95) 4016

Cook, Robert (*d.* 1593) 2583

Cooke, Edward, Esq. 1810:30

Coombs, of Worcester, bookseller 261

Cooper 1993

Cooper, Charles Henry (1808–66) 637

Cooper, E. (owner *ca.* 1700?) 1893

Cope, Sir Anthony (1632–75) 834

Cope, Mary (*fl.* 1694) 834

Cork and Orrery, John Boyle, Earl of (1707–62) 3951

Corner, George Richard (*d.* 1863) 3721

Corney, Bolton (1784–1870) 1378, 1666, 1871, 2512, 2709, 3896

Cornish, William, Birmingham, bookseller 790

Corser, Thomas (1793–1876) 1984, 2011, 2486, 2575

Cosmo III (Medici), Grand Duke of Tuscany (1642–1723) 3682

Cotton, Lynch (library sold 1856) 557, 2163

Cottrell, Sir Charles (*d.* 1779) 3556

Cottrell, Sir Clement (*d.* 1758) 801, 803, 1076–7, 1929–30, 1949, 1990, 2445, 2599, 3556, 3672–3, 3774

Coulton, David Trevena (1810–57) 13, 20, 271, 280, 319–20, 322–3, 406–7, 414, 418, 420–1, 447–8, 450–1

Courtauld, Mrs. Augustine 2528

Courtauld, Samuel Augustine (1865–1953) 2528

Coutts, Baroness Burdett. *See* Burdett-Coutts

Coventry, Roy 2091

Cowles, Mrs. W. Sheffield 1867

Coxeter, Thomas (1689–1747) p. xviii

Cozens, Frederick William (library sold 1890) 2528

Craig, J. T. Gibson. *See* Gibson-Craig

Craig, John 1810:4

Cranch, John (1751–1821) 2388

Craufurd, Rev. Charles Henry. *See* Crawford

Crawford, Rev. Charles Henry (1803?–76) 3186

Crawford, David Robert Alexander Lindsay, Earl of 3739

Crawford, Francis Marion (1854–1909) 2286

Crawford, James Ludovic Lindsay, Earl of (1847–1913) 2050, 3554, 3739

Creswick, Harry Richardson 2576 (Sévigné)

Crewe, Margaret (Primrose) Crewe-Milnes, Marchioness of 2506

Crewe, Robert Offley Ashburton Crewe-Milnes, Marquess of (1858–1945) 673, 2506, 2549, 2556, 3830, 3963, 3976

Cribb, William, King Street, London (purchaser in 1842) 3715

Crichton, David, Esq. 1180

Criddle 263

Crocker, Templeton (1884–1948) 2517

Crofts, Rev. Thomas (1722–81) 3900

Croker, Thomas Crofton (1798–1854) 2490

Croker, Thomas Francis Dillon, F. S. A. (1831–1912) 2490

Cromer, Evelyn Baring, Earl of (1841–1917) 917, 2349, 3007, 3729

Crosse 2879, 3053

Crossley, James (1800–83) 1501, 1724, 1897, 2146:2, 2292–3, 2383, 3340, 3494, 3798

Crouter, Gordon 1363

Crowninshield, Edward Augustus (1817–59) 2401, 2513

Cunliffe, Henry (1826–94) 1342

Cunliffe, Rolf, Baron Cunliffe 1342, 3663

Cunningham, Peter (1816–69) 98, 1670, 1881, 2511, 2514

Curling, William, of Maesmawr Hall (1808–65?) 3635

Currie, Barton Wood (1878–1962) 2474

Currie, Captain Bertram Francis George 2368, 3591:7

Currie, Bertram Wodehouse (1827–96) 2359, 2487, 2522

Currie, Laurence (1867–1934) 2359, 2522, 3591:7, 3692, 3698

Curt, Joseph, Leicester Square, London, dealer in ancient coins 1138, 1142

Curtis, Mrs. Edith Fanny (Onslow), of Langford Hall, Newark (*d.* 1944) 1807

Dacre, Thomas Barrett-Lennard, Baron (1717–86) 2559

Damer, Anne Seymour (Conway) (1749–1828) 1585, 1619, 2164, 2506, 2517, 2520, 2559, 2576, 2622, 3842, 3905

Damer, Col. George Lionel Dawson (1788–1856) 2528

Dana, Dr. Charles Loomis (1852–1935) 2088

Daniel, George (1789–1864) 1150, 1810:30, 1938, 1942, 1956, 1971, 1980, 2368, 2494, 3069, 3363, 3730, 3918

Danlos fils et Delisle, Paris, booksellers 864

Darby, Charles, London, stationer 3821

Dartmouth College Library 3641

Dauber & Pine, New York, booksellers 1007

Davenport, Edward Davies (1778–1847) 3451–2

Davies, Robert (1793–1875) 3414

Davis, Charles, Coleman Street, London, bookseller 216, 2477, 3437

Davis, J. T. (owner in 1842) 917, 3007

Davis & Orioli, London, booksellers 1865, 2344, 3745, 3778

Davy, Mrs. Colin (Dorothy Walpole Scott-Murray) 818, 1440, 1996, 2527, 2622, 3703, 3730

Dawson, William, & Sons, Ltd., London, booksellers 458, 1538, 3971

Dawson-Damer, Colonel. *See* Damer

Dawson's Bookshop, Los Angeles, booksellers 3755

Days (Booksellers), Ltd., Oxford 1876

Deacon, Henry 361:2

Deane 1037, 1273, 1820

De Beer, Esmond Samuel 2179

De Gersdorff, Carl 3964

Delafield, Mrs. Guy 713

Delamere, Harriet Cholmondeley, Baroness (1786–1852) 2351

Delany, Mrs. Mary Granville (1700–88) 3854:1

De la Warr, George John Sackville-West, Earl (1791–1869) 1148

Dempster, George (1836–75) 1476

Denham, Alexander, & Co., London, booksellers 2374, 2389, 2415

Dennett, Vaughan 2240

Dent 2470

Dent, John (1795–1845) 2576 (Catherine Parr)

Derby, Edward George Villiers Stanley, 18th Earl of (1865–1948). *See* Derby, Edward, 13th Earl of

Derby, Edward Smith-Stanley, 13th Earl of (1775–1851) 78, 538, 594, 613, 648–9, 651, 654, 663–4, 668–9, 671, 677, 689, 706–7, 889, 891, 895, 1143, 1322, 1818, 2047–8, 2328, 2357, 2371, 2478, 2519, 2538, 2546, 2551, 2578, 2581–3, 2601, 2604, 2608, 2610, 2618, 2620–1, 2637, 2696, 2703, 2712, 2760, 2872, 2919, 2977, 3579, 3581

Derby, Frederick Arthur Stanley, 17th Earl of (1841–1908) 3797

De Ricci, Seymour (1881–1942) 705, 2494

Desportes, Philippe (1546–1606) 435

Detroit Institute of Arts 3636

Deutsches Museum, Munich 1538

Devonshire, William George Cavendish, Duke of (1790–1858) 2628

Dibdin, Thomas Frognall (1776–1847) 2363, 2384, 2421, 2431, 2622

Dicey, Thomas (*fl.* 1745–51) 1608:7

Dickenson, Mary (Hamilton) (1756–1816) 2311

Dickinson, Henry A. 1794

Diffo, William A. 1501, 3734

Digby, Sir Kenelm (1603–65) 2091

Dillon, John (library sold 1869) 790, 2735

Dimsdale, Sir Joseph Cockfield (1849–1912) 2470

Dobell, Bertram, London, bookseller (*d.* 1914) 61, 1572, 1897, 2091, 2429, 3253, 3926–7

Dobell, P. J. and A. E., London, booksellers 371, 1331, 1625, 1850, 1864, 1893, 1930, 1933, 1952, 1955, 2021, 2179, 2504, 3137, 3379, 3788

Dockray, Hannah (owner in 1857) 2001, 2069, 2079

Dodd, Thomas, auctioneer (1771–1850) 2163, 3525, 3855

Dodge, Mrs. Frank F. (*d.* 1963) 2240

Dolling 633

Donnelley, R. R., & Sons, Chicago, printers 2088

Dorman, Sir Arthur 195

Dormer, Sir Clement Cottrell. *See* Cottrell

Downes, J. (owner in 1727) 211

Downing 434

Downing, William, Birmingham, bookseller 434

Dowse, Thomas (1772–1856) 2003, 2388, 3873

Dowse Collection. *See* Massachusetts Historical Society

Doyle, Mrs. M. Dorland 324

Drake, James F., Inc., New York, booksellers 1810:28, 1893, 2387:4, 6; 3664, 3728

Drexel, Joseph William (1833–88) 3399

Drexel Collection. *See* New York Public Library

Dring, Edmund Hunt (1864–1928) 1608:91

Dring, E. M. 1608:91

Driscoll, Emily, New York, bookseller 1608:96

Drummond, Andrew Cecil (1865–1913) 3469: 13

Drummond, Henry, of Albury Park, Surrey (1786–1860) 642

Dublin Public Library. John T. Gilbert Collection. *See* Jephson 1810:30

Ducarel, Andrew Coltee (1713–85) 266, 3222: 5, 3818

Duckworth, Samuel (1786–1847) 1156, 1158–9, 1163, 1167

Du Deffand, Marie de Vichy, Madame (1696–1780) 952, 1168, 1680, 2050:6, 25; 2285, 2295, 2323, 2335, 2394, 2545, 2597, 2614, 2999, 3003, 3013, 3017, 3020, 3023, 3026, 3036, 3042, 3055, 3058, 3060, 3066, 3068, 3075, 3082, 3088, 3096, 3124–5, 3130, 3133, 3137, 3143, 3147, 3150–1, 3388, 3405, 3586, 3592

Duff, John, of Greenock 1449

Dugdale, Sir William (1605–86) 2558

Dukes, W. B. (library sold 1942) 1448

Dulau & Company, Ltd., London, booksellers 1348, 3702

Dundas, Sir David (1803–77) 2372, 3840

Dundas, Robert W. (library sold 1929) 3918

Dunn, George (1865?–1912) 3739

Du Pont, Pierre Samuel (1870–1954) 1270

Durrant, Col. William (1779–1846) 3552

Dutton, Joan 2091

Dyce, Alexander (1798–1869). *See* Victoria and Albert Museum

Dyce-Sombre, David Ochterlony (1808–51) 2545

Dyson, Humphrey (*d.* 1632) 174

Eaton, Peter, London, bookseller 751

Edinburgh, University of 2560

Edinburgh, University of. Dugald Stewart Collection 253

Edwardes, Sir Henry Hope (1829–1900) 2374

Edwards, Francis, Ltd., London, booksellers 119, 195, 722, 761, 1507, 1633, 2791, 3007, 3053, 3729

Edwards, H. W., Ltd., Newbury, bookseller 665, 2627, 3047

Egan, John K. 999, 3759

Egmont, John Perceval, Earl of (1683–1748) 2328, 3604

Eicks, Clement S. 2047

Eisemann, Heinrich, London, bookseller 3591:3

Eleutherian Mills Historical Library 1270

Eliot, Sir John. *See* Elliott

Elizabeth I, Queen of England (1533–1603) 2551, 2596

Elizabeth II, Queen of England 3579, 3911

Elkin Mathews. *See* Mathews

Elkins, William Henry, London, bookseller 1342, 2527

Elkins, William McIntire (1882–1947) 1810:18

Ellacombe, Rev. Henry Thomas, F. S. A. (1790–1885) 1674

Ellice 1129

Ellice, Edward, of Glenquoich 3549

Elliot, Sir Gilbert (1751–1814) 3130

Elliott, Sir John (1736–86) 3006

Elliott, Thomas (*fl.* 1695) 1123

Ellis, Frederick Startridge, London, bookseller (successor to Boone) (1830–1901) 589, 2398, 2494

Ellis, Sir Richard (1688?–1742) 2225, 2249

Ellis & Co., London, booksellers 101, 140, 1120, 2472, 2731, 3848

Ellis and Elvey, London, booksellers 984, 1955, 2163–4, 2368

Ellis & White, London, booksellers 589, 2365, 2398, 3698, 3787

Ellsworth, James William (1849–1925) 57, 151, 2387

Ellys, Sir Richard. *See* Ellis

Elmsley, Peter, London, bookseller (1735?–1802) 37

Elte, Meyer, The Hague, bookseller 3675

Elton, Mrs. Charles (1838–1914) 2585

Elyott. *See* Elliott

Embleton, H. C. 1126

Emerson, Mrs. William 2456:1

Emery, agent? 2325

Emmott, George Henry 906

Erskine, John Elphinstone (1806–87) 999

Erving, Henry Wood (1851–1941) 2202

Erving, Selma 2202, 2462

Esher, Oliver Sylvain Baliol Brett, 3d Viscount 2599

Essex 2331

Essex Institute Library 2254

Eton College 2096, 2521, 2547, 2619, 3417

Evans, D. D. 1876

Evans, Edward David, Great Queen Street, London, bookseller (1818–60) 220, 222, 225,

Evans, Edward David (*cont.*)
227, 237–8, 252, 2534, 3484, 3485:1, 10;
3508, 3515, 3530, 3557–8, 3560–1, 3608,
3612, 3664, 3671, 3708, 3739, 3742, 3752,
3762, 3764, 3848, 3861–3, 3916
Evans, Herbert McLean 769
Eyton, Joseph Walter King (1820?–72) 424,
2050:7, 2330, 2419, 2430, 2507:4, 2511, 2528,
2619, 2845, 2921, 3220, 3261, 3323, 3347,
3707, 3711, 3724, 3812, 3821, 3830, 3895

F., C. 2768, 3848
Fairfax, Henry (1634–1702) 2628
Fairfax, John (*b.* 1634) 3377
Fairfax, Thomas, Baron Fairfax (1612–71)
202, 2627
Fauconberg, Thomas Belasyse, Earl (1627–
1700) 1484
Fearing, Daniel Butler (1859–1918) 1842
Feilde, Henry (*fl.* 1641) 118
Feisenberger, H. A., London, bookseller 3282
Feiss, Carl 2423
Feiss, Paul Louis 2423
Fellows, Col. Robert Bruce (1830–1922) 3575,
3582
Ferguson, Arthur Monro 3996
Ferguson, Frederic Sutherland (*d.* 1967) 3978
Ferguson, Milton James (1879–1954) 1744
Ferrand, Louis (1645–99) 898
Field, John (1768?–1849) 242, 248, 259, 266–7,
282, 2480
Field, William Bradhurst Osgood (1870?–
1949) 1508
Findlay, Mrs. Frank, of Auchtermuchty (library sold 1930) 3188
Fisher, Harold (library sold 1941) 1806
Fisher, Dr. O. O. 1608:96
Fitch, William Stevenson (1793–1859) 3661
FitzHerbert, Rev. Alleyne (1815–60) 3995
Fitz-Patrick, John Wilson, Baron Castletown.
See Castletown
Fitzwilliam Museum, Cambridge. *See* Cambridge University
Fletcher, H. M., Enfield and London, bookseller 542
Fletcher, Ifan Kyrle, London, bookseller 760,
2120:9, 3255, 3979, 3981
Foley, Major Henry Thomas Hamilton (library sold 1948) 3798

Folger, Henry Clay (1857–1930). *See* Folger
Library
Folger Library 64–5, 122, 186, 189, 191, 204,
214, 1315, 1554, 1608:95, 1810 (42 plays),
2037, 2429, 2470, 2615, 3286, 3905, 3961,
3965, 3972, 3987, 3993
Folkes, Martin (1690–1754) 49
Force, Peter (1790–1868) 3427
Ford, John Walker (1838–1921) 2162–4, 2389,
2521, 3577, 3729, 3784, 3814, 3868, 3931,
3968
Fordham, Alfred Stanley, C. M. G. 2768
Forster, John (1812–76). *See* Victoria and Albert Museum
Forster, William, picture dealer, and assistant
to Robins, auctioneer 55, 60, 147, 166, 168,
172, 178, 318, 363, 366, 382, 386, 388, 392,
439, 449, 452, 456, 1056, 1172, 1176–7, 1181,
1187, 1206, 1210, 1212–13, 1215–16, 1219,
1221, 1229–30, 1233, 1236, 1238, 1323, 1620,
1627, 1868, 3009–10, 3021, 3023, 3044, 3046,
3056, 3065, 3078, 3087, 3091, 3099, 3102,
3114, 3117, 3129, 3144, 3153, 3469:10,
3786:1
Fortescue, Chichester S. P., Baron Carlingford. *See* Carlingford
Fortescue, Sir John William (1859–1933) 1608
Fosdick, William Henry 3715
Foulkes, William Wynn (*d.* 1903) 547
Fox, Henry Edward, 4th Baron Holland. *See*
Holland
Fraiser, Sir Alexander (1610?–81) 1933
France 717, 2507:5
Franks, Sir Augustus Wollaston (1826–97)
2591
Fraser 1718
Fraser, Sir William Augustus (1826–98) 1378,
2453, 3918
Frederickson, Charles William (1823–97)
2044, 2692
Freer, Major William Jesse, F. S. A. (1853–
1932) 3349
Frego, Thomas, Charlotte Street, London,
bookseller 3084
French & Company, New York, art dealers
2050
Fuller, Samuel and Joseph, London, printsellers 3679
Furbush, Mrs. C. C. 2415

Gaisford, Thomas (1779–1855) 3999

Gale, Samuel (1682–1754) 683

Galitzin, Prince Dmitry Vladimirovich (1771–1844) 3975

Gardner, Cecil Dunn (library sold 1880) 1508, 2472, 3163, 3838

Gardner, John Dunn (1811–1903) 169, 1906

Garfield, Harry Augustus (1863–1942) 1860

Garner, Professor Frederick Horace (1893–1964) 1109

Garrett, John (library sold 1894) 3591:6

Garth, William 371

Gaselee, Sir Stephen (1882–1943) 1810:14

Gaskell, Charles George Milnes (1842–1919) 2432, 2492, 2528, 3900

Gaskill, C. Francis (sold collection to WSL 1939) 3417

Gaskill, George A. 1810:29

Gaskill Collection 1233, 1810:29, 3417

Gay, Ernest Lewis (1874–1916) 1810:10, 20, 32

Gay, George Henry 1810:10

Gay, John (1685–1732) 2474:2

Gay Collection (E. L. Gay). See Harvard University

Gay Collection (John Gay). See Harvard University

Geddes, Sir William Duguid (1828–1900) 518

Gem, Dr. Richard (ca. 1706–1800) 3026

Gennadeion Library. See American School of Classical Studies at Athens

Gennadius, John (1844–1932) 2411, 3739, 3784

George, George B. 1523

George, Henry, Westerham, Kent, bookseller 114, 123, 128, 134–5, 426, 432, 496, 501, 518, 570, 620, 629, 688, 721, 765, 770, 833, 837, 847, 851, 854, 868, 879–80, 893, 900, 903, 905, 912, 916, 922–3, 927, 933, 972, 979, 989, 991, 996, 1007–11, 1013, 1017–18, 1020, 1023, 1025, 1029–31, 1033–5, 1039, 1041, 1043–52, 1093–4, 1097, 1105–6, 1269, 1272, 1274, 1278, 1285–7, 1502–3, 1546, 1596, 1612, 1701, 1707–8, 1710, 1712, 1714, 1720, 1722–3, 1731, 1740, 1744, 1748, 1750, 1766, 1999, 2001, 2009, 2024, 2033–4, 2038, 2050, 2055, 2057, 2062, 2064, 2069, 2077, 2079, 2082, 2097–100, 2102–3, 2106, 2108–16, 2168–9, 2172, 2182, 2230, 2232, 2234–6, 2238–42, 2244–8, 2250–4, 2256, 2265, 2379

Germain, Lady Elizabeth (1680–1769) 1109

Getz, Mrs. Milton E. (library sold 1936) 2597

Gianfigliazzi, Francessi 3810

Gibbs, Henry Hucks, Baron Aldenham. See Aldenham

Gibbs, James Ethan Allen (1829–1902) 3290, 3360

Gibson, Francis, of Saffron Walden (owner in 1842) 2765

Gibson-Craig, James Thomson (1799–1886) 423, 2368

Gifford, John A. 301

Gilbert, Sir John Thomas (1829–98). See Dublin Public Library

Ginsburg, Dr. Christian David (1831–1914) 3727

Gisborough, Thomas Chaloner, 3d Baron 195

Glaisher, William, Ltd., London, bookseller 3495

Glascook, Robert 858

Glendening, Robert 3606, 3805

Glenravel, Arthur Shirley Benn, Baron. See Benn

Godolphin, W. (owner in 17th century) 2008

Goelet, Ogden (1846–97) 136

Goldschmidt, E. P., & Co., Ltd., London, booksellers 752, 769, 2051

Goldschmidt, Ernst Philip, London, bookseller (1887–1954). See Goldschmidt & Co.

Goldschmidt, Lucien, New York, bookseller 3309

Gonville & Caius College, Cambridge. See Cambridge University

Gooch, Sir Robert 1609:23

Goode, Edward 2685

Goodrich Court Library 3591:3

Goodspeed's Book Shop, Boston, bookseller 1810:29, 1872, 2389, 3002, 3253, 3469:3, 3748

Gordon, Cosmo (d. 1965) 3529

Gosford, Archibald Brabazon Sparrow Acheson, Earl of (1841–1922) 37, 1521, 1694, 1987, 2527, 2647, 2730, 2775, 3123, 3688, 3692, 3727, 3729

Gosse, Sir Edmund William (1849–1928) 1512

Gott, William (1797–1863) 1850

Gottschalk, Paul, New York, bookseller 136

Gough, Richard (1735–1809) 424, 2655, 4006

Gould, Frank E. 1905

Grace, John Gregory (library sold 1890) 633

Graham, James Lorimer (d. 1876) 1793

Graham, Josiah, London, bookseller (*fl.* 1737–57) 3480

Granger, James (1723–76) 3906

Grant, John, Edinburgh, bookseller 518

Grantstown Manor 1900

Granville, John Carteret, Earl (1690–1763) 1325

Graves, Algernon (1845–1922) 3885

Graves, Frances Marjorie (purchaser in 1915) 546

Graves, Henry, & Co., Pall-Mall, London, printsellers 3544, 3551, 3567, 3587, 3641, 3651, 3662, 3667, 3689, 3851, 3883

Gray, George (1652–1711) 1606

Gray, Thomas (1716–71) 2620, 3054, 3998

Gray, William, Canon of Ripon (1785–1863) 3188–9, 3329, 3379–80

Greathead, Samuel Stephenson 2968:8

Green, John, London, bookseller 3088, 3094, 3140, 3155

Greenwood, Isaac John (1833–1911) 1638

Grego, Joseph, London, bookseller 3885

Gregory, Robert (*b.* 1819?) 1123

Grenfell, Mrs. Geoffrey. *See* Carnarvon

Grenville, Thomas (1755–1846) 2350–1

Grenville Collection. *See* British Museum

Grinke, Paul, London, bookseller 751

Grose, William, London, bookseller 757, 1572, 1897

Grundy, Cecil Reginald (1870–1944) 3885

Grundy, Robert Hindmarsh, Liverpool, bookseller (1816?–65) 3645

Guild, Dana 237

Guise, Sir William Vernon (1816–87) 2530

Gurney, Hudson (1775–1864) 3244

Gwinn, Charles 39

Gwynn, Edward (*d.* 1645?) 93

Haber, Louis I. (library sold 1909) 2088

Hack, Roy Kenneth 2089

Hailstone, Edward (1818–90) 2599, 3400

Hale, Mrs. G. B., of Torquay (library sold 1916) 2427

Hall, Bryan 699, 3055

Hall, Clayton M. 3917

Hall, R. 210

Halliday, Bernard, Leicester, bookseller 577, 2520, 3349, 3692

Halliwell-Phillipps, James Orchard (1820–89) 1315

Halsey, Frederick Robert (1847–1918) 3945

Hamill, Frances. *See* Hamill and Barker

Hamill and Barker, Chicago, booksellers 261, 2950, 3480

Hamilton 848, 998

Hamilton, Joseph (owner 1749) 1872

Hamilton, Mary. *See* Dickenson

Hamilton, William Alexander Louis Stephen Douglas, 12th Duke of (1845–95) 2380, 3591

Hamilton Bruce, R. T. *See* Bruce

Hamilton Palace. *See* Beckford

Hammelmann, H. A. 2464

Hammond, Frank, Birmingham, bookseller 722, 981

Hamond, Anthony 684

Hamond, Philip (1815–86) 684, 3165

Hamond family 3165

Hampden, John Trevor, Viscount Hampden (1749–1824) 3537

Hankinson, Rev. Robert (1769–1863) 2194, 2202, 2205

Hannah, John (1818–88) 472

Hannas, T. & L., Bromley, Kent, booksellers 3812

Harcourt, William Vernon (1789–1871) 3490

Harding, Samuel, London, bookseller 605

Hare 153

Hare, Sholto Vere (library sold 1904) 1642, 2576 (Albemarle, Cromwell)

Harington, Sir John (1561–1612) 523

Harleian Collection. *See* Oxford, Earl of

Harmsworth, Sir Robert Leicester (1870–1937) 122, 186, 189, 191, 204, 214, 1113, 1608–9, 1625, 1955, 2037, 2146:2, 2724, 3188, 3286, 3363:2, 3; 3944, 3961, 3973, 3979

Harper, Lathrop C., Inc., New York, bookseller 169, 1617, 2331

Harris, Robert (name in volume) 201

Harrison, Christopher 3923

Harrod, Henry (1817–71) 2422

Hart, Gerald Ephraim, of Montreal (library sold 1890) 2352

Hartshorne, Robert (library sold 1945) 436

Harvard University 58, 150, 199, 439, 1021, 1078, 1326, 1508, 1619, 1766, 1777, 1810 (32 plays), 1938, 1984, 2021, 2512, 2518, 2616, 3222, 3363, 3841, 3943

Harvard University. Ernest L. Gay Collection 1810 (14 plays)

Harvard University. John Gay Collection 1810:32

Harvard University. Merritt Collection 150, 1078, 1810 (7 plays), 2512, 2518, 2616

Harvard University. Sumner Collection 58

Harvey, Francis, London, bookseller 2029, 2146:2, 2527–8, 2978, 3506, 3563:2, 3663, 3729, 3838, 3885, 3931

Haury, Francis (owner in 1872) 3782

Hauser, Lionel (library sold 1934) 866

Hawkins, Major-General Edward Brian Barkley (library sold 1961) 2317

Hawkins, Sir John (1719–89) 2690

Hawkins, Phillip (owner in 1662) 1332

Hawtrey, Edward Craven (1789–1862) 1508, 2527

Hay, Robert (1799–1863) 1506

Hayward, John (1905–1965) 2506

Hazlitt, William Carew (1834–1913) 118, 3739

Hearne, Thomas (1678–1735) 201, 1608:3, 22

Hearst, Mrs. Phoebe Apperson (1842–1919) 3591:5

Heartman, Charles F., New York, bookseller 393

Heber, Richard (1773–1833) 3975

Heffer, W., & Sons, Ltd., Cambridge, booksellers 266, 2120:11

Henderson, John (1747–85) 2451

Henry IV, King of France (1553–1610) 435, 2546

Herbert, Mary, Countess of Pembroke. See Pembroke

Herbert, William, Earl of Pembroke. See Pembroke

Herbert, William (1718–95) 189

Herries, David C. 3909

Herries, Edward (1821?–1911) 3909

Hertford, Francis Seymour-Conway, Marquess of (1718–94) 4004

Hertzberger, Menno, The Hague and Amsterdam, bookseller 3882

Hervey, Augustus John, Earl of Bristol. See Bristol

Hervey, John, Baron Hervey (1696–1743) 874

Hervey, Mary Lepell, Lady (1700–68) 4012

Heseltine, John Postle (library sold 1935) 3441

Heugh, John 630

Heygate, Sir William (1782–1844) 2576

Hibbert, Edward George (d. 1901) 2517, 3841

Hibbethwaite, J. H., Esq., (purchaser in 1842) 457, 559, 567, 599, 612

Higgins (purchaser in 1842) 218

Higgs, William (corrections in volume, 1717) 1608:15

Hildyard, Robert Charles, Q. C., M. P. (1800–57) 2777

Hill, Heywood, London, bookseller 258

Hill, Peter Murray, London, bookseller 542, 2372, 3768

Hill, Walter M., Chicago, bookseller 412, 827, 1810:12, 19, 33; 2088, 3236

Hillier, W. C. (1789?–1851) 3704

Hillingdon, Arthur Robert Mills, 3d Baron (1891–1952) 984

Hiscock 3591:6

Hitchcock, Ethan Allen (1798–1870) 1509

Hoare, Admiral Dennis 3953

Hobart, George Robert, Earl of Buckinghamshire. See Buckinghamshire

Hobart, John, Earl of Buckinghamshire. See Buckinghamshire

Hodgson, John, London, bookseller 3529, 3909

Hoe, Robert (1839–1909) 37, 1939, 1987, 2032, 2456, 3729, 3890

Hogan, Francis Joseph (1877–1944) 412

Hogg, Thomas Jefferson (1792–1862) 3137

Holden, Edwin Babcock (1861–1906) 393, 1325

Holford, Robert Stayner (1809–92) 34, 1920, 2351, 3569

Holgate, William (library sold 1846) 2814

Holland, Henry Edward Fox, Baron (1802–59). See Holland House

Holland, Henry Richard Vassall Fox, Baron (1773–1840) 2837

Holland, John, heraldic painter 3282, 3800

Holland House 873, 1244, 1835, 2050:22, 2433, 3385

Holles, Denzil, Baron Holles (1599–1680) 2167

Hollis, Thomas (1720–74) 2647, 2730, 2775, 3172, 3176

Holloway, Marseille, London, printseller 3908–9, 3931

Holmden, Richard (purchaser in 1940) 2366

Hooker, Edward Niles (1902–57) 3952

Hope, Adrian John (1811–63) 3625

Hornby, Charles (library sold 1739) 2182

Horner, Rev. John Stuart Hippisley (1811?–74) 614

Hoskins, Dr. Samuel Elliott (1799–1888) 3799

Hosmer, Zelotes, of Cambridge, Mass. (library sold 1861) 1893

Hostick, King V., Chicago, bookseller 2576 (Amelia), 3480

Houghton, Arthur Amory Jr. 3069

Houghton, Richard Monckton Milnes, Baron. See Milnes

Howard, Charles Wentworth George (1814–79) 2372, 3840

Howe, George 713

Howe, Leonard, and Co., Boston 3169

Howell, Edward, Liverpool, bookseller 3625

Howell, John, San Francisco, bookseller 2131

Howell, Warren R., San Francisco, bookseller 2131

Hoym, Charles Henri, Comte d' (d. 1736) 2225

Hudson, Elizabeth 2434

Hughes, John Newington (purchaser in 1842) 3, 492

Hunnewell, James Melville (1879–1954) 1766

Hunstanton Hall 2902

Hunt, Basil Carew. See Carew Hunt

Hunt, W., Norwich, bookseller 2902

Hunter, William (1718–83) 3691

Huntington, Henry Edwards (1850–1927). See Huntington Library

Huntington Library 33, 37, 174, 207–8, 761, 1318, 1335, 1619, 1810:25, 45; 1871, 2032, 2410, 2452, 2456, 3377, 3581, 3876, 3945, 3958

Hurleston, Charles, of Picton (d. 1734) 598

Hurst 358

Huth, Henry (1815–78) 1906, 2331, 2494

Hyde, Savile (owner in 1719) 2037

Ilchester, Giles Stephen Holland Fox-Strangways, Earl of (1874–1929). See Holland House

Iliffe, Samuel (owner ca. 1700) 2016

Iliffe, William 2016

Illinois, University of 441, 1810:16, 25

Indiana University. Lilly Collection 1920

Inglis, John Bellingham (1780–1870) 1090

Irwin, John E. 482

Isaacson, Rev. Stephen (1798–1849) 2534, 2535:7, 2619:3

Isham, Ralph Heyward (1890–1955) 1810:16, 3069

Ives, John (1751–76) 2577–8, 3713, 3879

Jackson, G., Esq. (purchaser in 1842) 3183

Jackson, Richard C. 3690

Jackson, Stuart W. 1740

Jackson, William Alexander (1905–64) 1832

James I, King of England (1566–1625) 834, 3726

James 2339

James, Mr., (?) agent for John Dent 2576 (Catherine Parr)

James, Henry (owner 1791) 3919

James, Macgill 289

Jefferies, Charles T., Bristol, bookseller 3902

Jeffery, Charles T. (1876?–1935) 2044

Jekyll, Sir Herbert (1846–1932) 531

Jenks, Dr. William (owner in 1852) 2680

Jessel, Frederic Henry (1859–1934) 1572

Jesuits College, Paris 435

John Carter Brown Library 3786:2

Johnson, Crompton T., Farmington, Conn., bookseller 1512, 1810:29

Johnson, J. (owner ca. 1700) 2102

Johnson, John (1882–1956). See Walpole 2622

Johnson, Manuel John (1805–59) 626

Johnson, Samuel (1709–84) 2904

Johnston 3905

Jolley, Thomas, F. S. A. (1782?–1854) 1336

Jones 3739

Jones, Herschel Vespasian (1861–1928) 1906

Jones, T. (owner in 1873) 3748

Jones, Thomas, Blackman Street, London, straw and Leghorn hat merchant 1718, 3011, 3072, 3126, 3128, 3130, 3146, 3177, 3279, 3283, 3335, 3338:2, 3, 6, 7

Jonson, Ben (1573?–1637) 3399

Joyce, David G. (library sold 1923) 2400, 2526

Joye, Jacob 1920

Juckes, George T., Co., London, booksellers 2349

Juel-Jensen, Bent E. 1876, 2014

Kalbfleisch, Charles C. (library sold 1944) 2206

Kay, Arthur (*d.* 1939) 3778

Keats, Edwin, Esq. (purchaser in 1842) 2554, 2614, 2836, 2910, 2972

Keats Bookshop, Stamford, Conn., booksellers 1884

Keith, George, Earl Marischal (1553?–1623) 3727

Keith, Gilbert 3727

Kennet, White, Bishop (1660–1728) 1454, 1608:8, 2298

Kern, Jerome (1885–1945) 412, 3069

Kerr & Richardson, Glasgow, booksellers 849, 992, 1990

Kershaw, John 2317

Kerslake, Thomas, Bristol, bookseller (1812–91) 217, 250, 485, 535, 539, 544, 815, 820, 898, 921, 926, 928–9, 1246, 1252, 1257–8, 1260, 1262, 1266, 1270, 1277, 1281, 1284, 1361, 1390, 1642, 2067, 2070, 2074, 2083, 2119, 2129, 2131–2, 2155, 2158, 2185–6, 2189, 2192, 2195, 2198, 2201, 2203, 2536, 2763, 3013, 3019, 3024, 3028–9, 3038, 3055, 3066, 3068, 3070, 3080, 3085–6, 3100, 3103, 3136–7, 3141, 3406, 3409, 3419, 3439–40, 3444, 3470, 3628, 3762

Ketteringham Hall 2207:2

Ketton-Cremer, Robert Wyndham 699, 1911

Keynes, Sir Geoffrey Langdon 1933, 1955, 3065

Kimbe, Richard 3797:4

Kimpton, Benjamin, London, bookseller 3338:1

King, Raphael, London, bookseller 984, 1681, 1718, 2053, 3798, 3971

King's College, Cambridge. *See* Cambridge University

King's School, Canterbury 450, 3924

Kingsbury, George 994

Kingsley, George 2102

Kinsale, Gerald de Courcy, Lord (1700–59) 2569–70

Kirgate, Thomas (1734–1810) 347, 2050, 2619, 2978, 3833:3, 3876, 4005

Knight, J. (library sold 1860) 2091, 3469:9

Knight, Joseph, F. S. A. (1829–1907) 1078

Knight, William, F. S. A. (*d.* 1847) 1810, 1918, 2418, 3575, 3582, 3585, 3924

Knowsley Hall. *See* Derby, Earl of

Kraus, Hans P., New York, bookseller 101, 2422, 3781

Krech, Alvin W. (1858–1928) 1867

Labouchere, Henry, Baron Taunton (1798–1869) 33, 1255, 1280, 1609, 1810:59, 3222, 3859

Laing, David (1793–1878) 8, 252, 1990, 2560

Lakeside Press, Chicago 2088

Lambe, Richard Capel, London, printseller (*d.* 1856) 2576 (Walpole)

Lane, Rev. Charles (*d.* 1879) 581

Larocque, Joseph (library sold 1940) 1890

Lasbury, Olive, assistant to W. Strong, Bristol 3206, 3697

Laski, Harold Joseph (1893–1950) 1526

Lathbury, Thomas (1798–1865) 2050:13

Lawrence, Abbott (1792–1855) 1905

Lawson, E. M., Sutton Coldfield, bookseller 3065

Lazare, Edward 1744

Leader, Mrs. Miriam 2207:17

Leard, W. J., Walpole, Mass., bookseller 2415

Learmont, Joseph Bowles, of Montreal (library sold 1917) 860, 3945

Leather, John Towlerton (1804–85) 1890

Leckie, Captain James Henry (1792?–1866) 463, 543, 609, 672, 678, 690, 699, 975, 978, 986, 993, 995, 997, 1000, 1003, 1014, 1078, 1088, 1190–2, 1195, 1198, 1205, 1291, 1303–4, 1618, 1622, 1626, 1631, 1638, 1640, 1652–3, 1655, 1661–2, 1845–7, 1853, 1855, 1878, 2795, 2824, 2855, 2895, 2904, 2941–3, 2967, 3010, 3012, 3021, 3046, 3056, 3474, 3482, 3485, 3487, 3495, 3506–7, 3510, 3512, 3518, 3534, 3555, 3576, 3633, 3714, 3736, 3738, 3756, 3764, 3779

Lee, Henry (1826–88) 3621

Lee, John (owner *ca.* 1720) 610

Lefroy, Edward Heathcote (1859–1945) 3165

Lefroy, Langlois Massy (1885–1957) 3165

Leicester, Thomas Coke, Earl of (1697–1759) 2549

Leigh, Peter (*fl.* 1749) 1608:69, 1726

Leighton, Messrs. J. & J., London, booksellers 1065, 1651, 2253, 2486, 2509, 2599, 2710, 2765, 3739

Leighton, Walter James, London, bookseller (1850?–1917). *See* J. and J. Leighton

Leman, James 3404

Le Neve, Peter (1661–1729) 2540

Lenox Library. *See* New York Public Library
Lenton, Mrs. I. L. 3848
Leo, Edgar F. (library sold 1921) 1810:20,25
Leo, Rita Wellman (library sold 1921) 1810:20,25
Leslie, George Dunlop, of Compton House, Lindfield (1835–1928) 64
Le Strange, Bernard, of Hunstanton Hall, Norfolk 2902
Le Strange, Hamon (1840–1918) 2902
Letton, Robert (owner? in 1864) 19
Le Vasseur, Crespinne 2424
Levassor, Joseph 889
Levinson, Harry A., Los Angeles, bookseller 2765
Levis, Howard Coppuck (*b.* 1859) 3545
Lewis, John Frederick (1860–1932) 3868
Lewis, Lewis Alpha, Fleet Street, London, auctioneer and bookseller 777, 779, 793, 795
Lewis, Samuel (1813–90) 1514
Lewis, Wilmarth Sheldon 2–3, 10, 16, 21, 29, 34, 49, 52, 57, 59, 61, 64–5, 73–4, 78, 80, 89, 91–2, 106, 110, 112–13, 118–19, 127, 136, 140, 151, 153, 160, 162, 178, 193, 196–7, 211, 218, 224, 237, 245, 254, 256, 261–2, 266, 289, 296, 300–1, 310, 317, 320–1, 323–4, 359, 361:2, 5; 371, 412, 435–6, 448, 458, 466–7, 469, 472, 482, 487, 501, 507, 522–3, 538, 541–2, 561, 577, 581, 584, 589, 592, 594, 610, 613, 624, 630–1, 633, 636–7, 642, 644, 648–9, 651–2, 654, 658, 663–5, 668–9, 671, 673, 677, 689, 695, 699, 703, 706–7, 713, 717, 731, 748, 751–2, 755–6, 760, 767, 769, 773, 784, 790, 813–14, 827, 834, 866, 872–4, 876, 879, 889, 895–6, 906, 914, 916–17, 921, 937, 981, 984, 994, 997–9, 1007, 1019, 1021, 1027, 1058, 1063, 1065, 1075, 1079, 1093, 1101, 1109, 1111, 1113, 1120, 1123, 1126, 1129, 1139, 1143, 1165, 1175, 1180, 1221, 1233, 1244, 1247, 1255, 1270, 1280, 1285, 1289, 1322, 1331–32, 1342, 1348, 1360, 1363, 1367, 1370, 1378, 1386, 1393, 1433, 1438, 1448, 1461, 1464, 1471, 1473, 1476, 1486, 1501, 1507, 1509, 1512, 1523, 1554, 1561, 1587, 1593, 1608–9, 1615, 1617–19, 1625–6, 1633, 1636, 1638, 1642, 1651, 1674, 1681, 1689, 1693, 1717–18, 1724–6, 1740, 1744, 1766, 1768, 1782, 1785, 1788, 1792–4, 1806–7, 1810 (390

Lewis, Wilmarth Sheldon (*cont.*)
plays), 1810:59, 1814–15, 1818, 1822, 1825, 1829, 1832, 1835, 1840, 1850, 1860, 1864–5, 1867, 1872–3, 1876, 1881, 1884, 1886, 1890, 1897, 1900, 1905, 1912, 1930, 1933, 1952, 1989–90, 1993, 2001, 2008, 2010, 2013–14, 2016, 2029, 2033, 2039, 2044, 2046–8, 2050–1, 2053, 2056, 2061, 2066, 2069, 2072, 2077, 2079, 2088–9, 2091, 2102, 2120, 2122, 2131, 2146, 2150, 2160, 2180, 2184, 2196–7, 2202, 2206–8, 2211, 2215, 2217, 2235, 2240, 2253–4, 2263, 2266, 2286, 2317, 2325–6, 2328, 2332, 2349, 2351, 2359, 2366, 2371, 2374, 2378, 2384, 2387, 2389, 2395, 2400, 2402, 2404, 2415, 2417, 2420–5, 2428, 2432–6, 2446, 2453, 2456, 2459, 2462, 2466, 2470, 2474–5, 2478–80, 2482, 2489, 2492, 2499, 2506, 2509–11, 2514–15, 2517–23, 2525, 2528, 2530, 2535:7, 2538, 2545, 2551, 2556, 2572, 2576, 2578, 2581–3, 2597, 2599, 2601, 2604, 2610–11, 2615–18, 2619:3, 4; 2620–2, 2624–5, 2631, 2637, 2647, 2680, 2689, 2702–3, 2705, 2710, 2712, 2731, 2760, 2765, 2768, 2777, 2791, 2796, 2814, 2821, 2827, 2837, 2857, 2872, 2888, 2902, 2905, 2913, 2919, 2945, 2950, 2978, 2994, 3001–3, 3006–7, 3015, 3043, 3047, 3053, 3055, 3065, 3069–70, 3084, 3123, 3137, 3159, 3165, 3167, 3222:12, 3223–4, 3227, 3236, 3244, 3249, 3253, 3255, 3282, 3309–10, 3333, 3349, 3355, 3363, 3372, 3374, 3379–80, 3385–6, 3393, 3417, 3441, 3452, 3455, 3463, 3469:2, 3475, 3480, 3485:12, 13; 3490, 3501, 3505, 3529, 3545–6, 3549, 3552, 3563, 3575, 3581–2, 3585, 3588, 3591, 3596, 3598, 3620–1, 3625, 3632, 3636–7, 3646, 3652, 3663–5, 3669, 3675, 3678, 3689–90, 3692, 3694, 3698, 3702–3, 3705, 3715, 3722, 3727–9, 3732, 3734, 3745, 3748, 3750, 3753, 3755, 3758–9, 3762, 3768, 3777–8, 3781–2, 3784, 3797–9, 3805, 3812, 3818, 3821, 3826, 3833, 3839–40, 3848, 3856, 3859, 3865, 3879–80, 3885, 3888–9, 3895, 3900, 3902–3, 3909, 3912, 3917–18, 3921, 3923, 3926–7, 3932–3, 3942, 3944, 3947, 3949–51, 3959, 3962, 3969–74, 3976, 3978–9, 3985–6, 3990–1, 3997, 3999, 4000
Leyton. *See* Leighton
Library Company of Philadelphia. *See* Philadelphia

Library of Congress 80, 127, 202, 218, 256, 1509, 1810:13, 34, 54; 2217, 2266, 3427, 3469:9, 3591:4

Libri, Conte Guglielmo (1803–69) 2304

Lilly, Joseph, London, bookseller (1804–70) 92, 199, 207, 242, 252, 259, 266–7, 675, 698, 772, 984, 1061, 1315, 1356, 1360, 1657, 1743, 1938, 2182, 2208, 2215, 2330–1, 2384, 2386, 2456:4, 2480, 2493, 2496, 2514, 2528, 2549, 2585, 2598, 2619, 2845, 2879, 3236, 3363, 3466, 3469:2, 3485:6, 7; 3492, 3496, 3498, 3501, 3504, 3514, 3519, 3523–4, 3528, 3531, 3542–3, 3546, 3550, 3553, 3567, 3586, 3591–2, 3597–8, 3606, 3610, 3612–13, 3620, 3624–5, 3627, 3637–9, 3649, 3652, 3654, 3659–60, 3663, 3668, 3670, 3674, 3685–6, 3692, 3699–3701, 3712, 3716, 3735, 3739–40, 3758, 3761, 3766–7, 3771–2, 3775–6, 3778, 3783, 3786, 3788–91, 3793, 3795–8, 3804–5, 3808–9, 3811, 3817, 3827–30, 3832, 3834, 3843–4, 3852–3, 3856–7, 3864, 3870, 3881, 3888, 3899, 3900, 3903, 3906, 3910, 3912, 3918, 3924, 3930, 3932

Lilly, Josiah Kirby, Jr. (1893–1966) 1920

Lilly Collection, Indiana University. See Indiana University

Lindsay, Mrs. (owner in 1951) 1927

Linfield, H. S. 2197

Lissauer, Arthur W. 101

Little, Brown, & Co., Boston, bookseller 1893

Liverpool, University of 2872

Lloyd, J. W., of Kington, Herefordshire (owner ca. 1890) 3227

Locker-Lampson, Frederick (1821–95) 1938

Lockyer, James (1796?–1875) 226, 228–9, 245, 256, 260, 268, 275–6, 285, 431

Lockyer, James Morant, F. R. I. B. A. (1823?–65) 256

Logan, Robert R. (d. 1956) 487

Lomas, R. W. 3047

Loménie de Brienne. See Brienne

Londesborough, William Henry Forester Denison, Earl of (1834–1900) 1109

London, University of 2508

Longepierre, Hilaire Bernard de Roqueleyne, Baron de (1659–1721) 154, 1209

Longman & Co., London, booksellers 4, 66, 376, 423, 2041, 2198, 2483, 3187, 3193, 3213, 3217, 3812

Longueville, Henry Yelverton, Viscount de (1664?–1704) 2347

Longwood Library. See Eleutherian Mills Historical Library

Lonsdale 390

Lonsdale, Hugh Cecil Lowther, Earl of (1857–1944) 1148

Lort, Michael (1725–90) 252, 295, 359:4, 366, 379–81, 385–8, 391, 393–4, 397–8, 729, 760, 1361, 1601, 1608:28, 90; 2050:5, 17, 18; 2217, 2251, 2319, 2332–3, 2383, 2387:4, 2390, 2414, 2457, 2752, 2966–7, 3067, 3285, 3307, 3312, 3344, 3395, 3522, 3557, 3777, 3785:2, 3827–8, 3833:10, 3891

Louis XIV, King of France (1638–1715) 301, 497, 876, 3591

Louis XVI, King of France (1754–93) 3591

Lovelace, Anne Wentworth, Baroness (1623?–97) 2692

Lovell, Arthur, Chicago, bookseller 2821

Low, David, London, bookseller 3352

Lowe Bros., Ltd., Birmingham, booksellers 755, 3959

Lowell, Amy (1874–1925) 3841, 3943

Lucy, Sir Berkeley (1672?–1759) 2326

Ludlow, Alice Sedgwick (Mankiewicz) Lopes, Baroness (d. 1945) 2366

Luttrell, Narcissus (1657–1732) 3281

Lyell, James Patrick Ronaldson (1871–1949) 2180, 3727

Lysons, Daniel (1762–1834) 2867

Lysons, Samuel (1763–1819) 1090, 2456:4, 3692, 4016

Lyttelton, Charles Bishop (1714–68) 2454, 3503

Mabbott, Thomas Ollive (1905–1968) 522

McAdam, Edward Lippincott, Jr. 2050, 3812

Macalister, Anne 1360

MacAlister, Frances Dorothy Seaton, Lady 2263

McAlpin Collection, Union Theological Seminary. See Union Theological Seminary

MacBean, William Munro (1852–1924) 1890

McCagg, Louis Butler 3784

MacDonald, Major Eric William (d. 1937) 3805

Macdonell, William John 2240

MacGeorge, Bernard Buchanan (1845?–1924) 2044

McGill University 2905

Mackenzie, John Whitefoord, W. S. (1794–1884) 1370

McKesson, John 713

McLaren, Martin 531

McLeish & Sons, London, booksellers 317, 467, 472, 1101, 1175

McNalty, Bruce 1900

Maconochie, I. A. (owner in 1842) 3549

Maconochie, Robert (1778?–1858) 3549

MacVeagh, Charles (1860–1931) 1860

Madden, Sir Frederic (1801–73) 2535, 2544, 2576 (Lort), 2628

Magee, David, San Francisco, bookseller 1501, 3734

Maggs Brothers, Ltd., London, booksellers 29, 49, 59, 92, 160, 196–7, 262, 320, 417, 501, 507, 523, 538, 592, 594, 613, 636, 648–9, 651, 654, 663–5, 668–9, 671, 673, 677, 689, 706–7, 717, 731, 748, 752, 767, 814, 866, 873–4, 876, 889, 895–6, 917, 973, 998, 1079, 1113, 1126, 1129, 1139, 1143, 1244, 1322, 1342, 1433, 1471, 1473, 1486, 1608, 1615, 1619, 1626, 1810:9, 12, 19, 33, 40; 1818, 1822, 1829, 1835, 2001, 2010, 2016, 2021, 2044, 2048, 2069, 2079, 2091, 2110:2, 2150, 2162, 2180, 2207: 17, 30; 2208, 2219, 2317, 2325, 2328–9, 2332, 2349, 2351, 2359, 2366, 2371, 2378, 2384, 2433, 2435, 2458, 2475, 2478, 2519, 2522, 2528, 2538, 2551, 2556, 2576 (Peter III), 2578, 2581–3, 2601, 2604, 2610, 2615–16, 2618, 2620–1, 2625, 2637, 2703, 2705, 2708, 2712, 2724, 2760, 2765, 2768, 2902, 2913, 2919, 3003, 3123, 3244, 3374, 3385, 3505, 3549, 3552, 3581, 3588, 3591:3, 7; 3620–1, 3652, 3663, 3689, 3698, 3703, 3705, 3722, 3777, 3782, 3797, 3805, 3818, 3821, 3849, 3856, 3885, 3900, 3902, 3912, 3918, 3927, 3833, 3946, 3950, 3976, 3984, 3986

Malcomson, Mrs. Rosalie 1825, 2459

Malmesbury, James Edward Harris, Earl of (1872–1950) 665

Malone, Edmond (1741–1812) 466, 2451

Manchester, University of 2292–3

Mandel, Leon, II 1810:33

Manley, M. C. 3065

Mann, Sir Horace (1701–86) 2285, 2588, 2921, 3097, 3207, 3448, 3451–2, 3487, 3550, 3560, 3568, 3570, 3583–4, 3590, 3594, 3596, 3621, 3810

Manwaring, Elizabeth Wheeler (1879–1949) 3669

Manzoni, Jacob 3781

Marchmont, Alexander Hume-Campbell, Earl of. See Campbell

Marden, Rev. Owen (1793?–1869?) 2207:11

Mariette, Pierre Jean (1694–1774) 2357, 3655

Marjoribanks, Edward. See Tweedmouth, Baron

Markham, Thomas R. 1007

Markham Memorial Library 1007

Markland, James Heywood (1788–1864) 1815, 1890

Marks & Co., London, booksellers 1111, 3637, 3864

Marlay, Charles Brinsley (d. 1912) 2527

Marshall, Harold 2765

Marshall, Julian (1836?–1903) 1126, 1886

Martin, Edward Wenman, Esq. (1780?–1853) 3567, 3710

Martin, Thomas (1697–1771) 2578, 2655

Maskell, Rev. William (1814?–90) 160

Mason, William (1724–97) 3995, 4002, 4004, 4008–9, 4011, 4015

Massachusetts Historical Society. Dowse Collection 2003, 2388, 3873

Massey, Charles. See Pickering & Chatto

Massey, Dudley. See Pickering & Chatto

Massigli, René, French Ambassador to England 1148

Mathews, Alister, Bournemouth, bookseller 1063

Mathews, Elkin, Ltd., London, bookseller 162, 469, 1289, 1815, 2013, 2050, 2814, 3053, 3455

Mathieson 412

Mawdesley, Frederick Leyland (library sold 1910) 546

Maxwell, Philip, East Sullivan, New Hampshire, bookseller 994

Mayer, Mrs. Robert 1626

Mead, Richard (1673–1754) 2343, 2398, 2415, 3480, 3786:1

Meigh, Charles, J. P., of Grove Lodge, Shelton 313, 557, 1805, 2523, 2534, 2565, 2567, 3400, 3408, 3644–5, 3704, 3931

Melbourne, F. F. (owner ca. 1850) 2056

Mendoza, Isaac, Book Co., New York, bookseller 2066

Mensing, Ant. W. M. (library sold 1936) 3977

Mentmore. *See* Rosebery, Earl of

Mercantile Library. *See* New York Mercantile Library

Merivale, Herman (1806–1874) 2120:7

Merriam, Olin Lane (library sold 1920) 2362, 2462, 2518

Merridan 3261

Merritt, Edward Percival (1860–1932) 1810: 58

Merritt Collection. *See* Harvard University

Merry, Robert (1755–98) 3810

Mersey, Edward Clive Bigham, Viscount 317, 2133

Messenger, Maria Gerard (library sold 1938) 2120:7

Metcalf, Keyes DeWitt 1832

Metropolitan Museum of Art, New York 3469:2, 3546, 3567

Mexborough, John Charles George Savile, 4th Earl of (1810–99) 545–6, 548, 592, 598, 717, 731, 750–2, 758, 761, 764, 767, 771, 896, 1129, 1139

Michael (purchaser in 1842) 3904

Michelmore, George, London, bookseller 33, 466, 1593, 1608:90, 1810:59, 3859

Michigan, University of 1810 (36 plays)

Mien 1853

Miller, Mrs. Elizabeth Clark Tyler (library sold 1940) 110, 359

Miller, John, London, bookseller 3505, 3928

Miller, Samuel Christie (d. 1889). *See* Britwell Court

Miller, William Henry (1789–1848). *See* Britwell Court

Miller, William Wilson (1870–1940) 310

Mills, Richard L., Bennington, Vermont and New Haven, Conn., bookseller 254, 1794

Milnes, Richard Monckton, Baron Houghton (1809–85) 479, 1805, 2506, 2549

Mingay, John 1933

Mitchell, Silas Weir (1829–1914) 1438

Mitford, John (1781–1859) 486, 697, 1872, 1912, 2050:1, 2215, 2370, 2435, 2446, 2527, 2609, 2735, 2978, 3019, 3267, 3887, 3896, 3901, 3926–7, 3929, 3933–5

Moeller, Chester S., New Haven, bookseller 2387, 3161

Moffatt, George, of Goodrich Court (1806–78). *See* Goodrich Court Library

Molini, Charles Frederick, Strand, London, bookseller 1178, 2609, 3069

Molyneux, William (1656–98) 609

Monro, Dr. John (1715–91) 3805

Montagu, George (1713?–80) 313, 2263, 4007

Montagu, Lady Mary Wortley (1689–1762) 2399, 2421

Montrose, Marie Louise Douglas, Duchess of (1884–1957). *See* Brodick Castle

Morant, George (1791–1875) 187–8, 192, 209, 269

More, Hannah (1754–1833) 3997

Morgan, Alexander Perry 2482

Morgan, John Pierpont (1837–1913) 2482, 2501, 2647, 2730, 2775, 3172, 3176

Morgan, Junius Spencer (1866–1932) 2482, 3813

Morgan, Thomas, London, china and print-seller 2050

Morgan Library 780, 1694, 2146:4, 2331, 2501, 2528, 2623, 2647, 2730, 2775, 3172, 3176, 3377, 3563:2, 3636, 3704, 3931, 3975

Morley, Edmund Parker, Earl of (1772–1864) 3914

Morrice, John Walter, barrister 2197

Morrice, Lewis Edward (1862–1933) 2197

Morris, Harry K. 695

Morris, John 1872

Morris, Richard Brandon 1638

Morris, Thomas Hollingsworth 3917

Morris, William (1834–96) 3739

Morrow, Dwight Whitney, Jr. 2432

Morton 155, 1898

Moss, Lt.-Col. William E. (library sold 1937) 3821

Mott, Howard S., Sheffield, Mass., bookseller 994, 1843

Mount-Stephen, Georgina Mary (Tufnell) Stephen, Baroness (1863?–1933) 95, 998, 1810:40, 2435, 3003, 3927

Mowbray, Segrave, and Stourton, William Marmaduke Stourton, Baron (1895–1965) 3006

Munby, Alan Noel Latimer 610, 1876, 2207:9, 3333, 3349, 3372

Munich. Deutsches Museum 1538

Müntz, John Henry (1727–98) 2549

Murdock, Harold (1862–1934) 1810:14, 22, 29; 3393

Murphy, Fred Towsley (1872–1948) 2515

INDEX OF OWNERS

Murray, Alexander Henry Hallam (1854–1934) 2576 (Sévigné)

Murray, Charles Fairfax (1849–1919) 2425

Murray, Lady Charlotte, of Richmond (purchaser in 1842) 1153, 1157, 1164, 1173, 2792, 2801, 2810, 2822, 2906, 2960–1, 3073–4, 3077, 3093, 3095, 3101, 3150

Murray, John, London, bookseller 453, 1316, 1618, 2795, 3482

Musgrave, Sir William (1735–1800) 4019

Mussell, Ebenezer (d. 1764) 2765

Myers, Winifred, London, bookseller 2215

Myers & Co., London, bookseller 813, 876, 1726, 2235, 3802

Nantes 2122

Nantes. Bibliothèque Municipale 3405

National Gallery of Art, Washington 2351, 3119

National Library of Scotland 2050:3

National Trust. See Blickling Hall; Saltram; Waddesdon Manor

National Trust for Scotland. See Brodick Castle

Nattali, Henry Combe, London, bookseller (1831?–1917). See Nattali & Bond

Nattali, Michael Angelo, London, bookseller (d. 1848) 3872–4

Nattali & Bond, London, booksellers 1487, 2419, 2485, 3320, 3323, 3702, 3848

Nesfield, William Eden (1835–88) 3777

Nevill, Lady Dorothy Fanny (Walpole) (1826–1913) 2384

New York Mercantile Library 3690

New York Public Library 2523, 3399, 3469: 13, 3563, 3636

New York Public Library. Henry W. and Albert A. Berg Collection 3469:13

New York Public Library. Drexel Collection 3399

New York Public Library. Spencer Collection 2523

New York Public Library. Tilden Collection 3563:1

Newarke, Thomas (owner ca. 1700) 2604

Newberry Library 101, 1810:18, 19; 1864, 1886, 1906

Newcastle, Henry Francis Hope, Duke of (1866–1941) 92, 2150, 2625, 3933

Newman, Harry Shaw, New York, printseller. See Old Print Shop

Newman, James, Holborn, London, bookseller (1804–77) 247, 533, 621, 2595, 2631, 2654, 2664, 2697, 2726, 2737, 2741, 2753, 2758, 3182, 3195, 3197, 3205, 3215, 3220, 3273, 3276, 3280

Newnham College, Cambridge. See Cambridge University

Newton 1989

Newton, Alfred Edward (1863–1940) 834, 1912, 3393

Newton, Raymond D'Arcy (purchaser in 1842) 1821–2, 1829, 3653, 3655–6, 3857, 3860, 3880

Nicholls, Mrs. A. R. 1509

Nichols, Charles Lemuel (1851–1929) 1810:29

Nichols, George Livingston (d. 1932) 3750

Nichols, James (owner in 1848) 140

Nichols, John (1745–1826) 2385

Nicol, George, London, bookseller (ca. 1741–1828) 435

Nightingale 2430

Nightingale, of Wilton, bookseller? 122

Nivernois, Louis Jules Barbon Mancini-Mazarini, Duc de (1716–98) 2617

Noailles, Louis de, Duc de Noailles (1713–93) 3130

Noble, Humphrey 300

Noble, T. (purchaser in 1885) 3494

Norgate, Col. 501

Norman, Francis, London, bookseller 2466

Norman, Hubert James (d. 1948) 1865

Northumberland, Helen Magdalen Gordon-Lennox, Duchess of (d. 1965) 642

Northwestern University 871

Northwick, John Rushout, Baron (1770–1859) 2417, 3833:3

Norton, Charles Eliot (1827–1908) 439

Noseda, John, London, printseller 3485:12, 13

Nostell Priory 2050, 2534, 3704

Notre Dame, University of 101

Old Print Shop, Inc., New York, bookseller 3563:2

Oldmixon, Esq. (purchaser in 1842) 39–40, 46, 52, 364, 369, 373, 379–80, 398, 403, 542, 778, 786, 788, 838–9, 844–5, 859, 863, 867, 876, 931, 938, 946, 951, 954, 956–7, 959–64,

Oldmixon, Esq. (*cont.*)
966–7, 970–1, 1004, 1012, 1016, 1021, 1026, 1038, 1042, 1053, 1057, 1075, 1077, 1365–6, 1368, 1371, 1380, 1383, 1387–9, 1407–8, 1410, 1412–14, 1419, 1421, 1459, 1461, 1466, 1471–2, 1480, 1486, 1488, 1552, 1562, 1571, 2000, 2012, 2016, 2019, 2031, 2035–6, 2375, 2439

Oldys, William (1696–1761) 2585

Oliver 2921

Orford, Earls of. *See* Walpole

Orford, Horatio William, 4th Earl of (1813–94) 37, 169, 818, 1021, 1365, 1680, 1996, 2050, 2091, 2096, 2266, 2269, 2273–4, 2278, 2280, 2284, 2289, 2446, 2527, 2622, 3019, 3069, 3342, 3531, 3667, 3703, 3887, 3915, 3918, 3938–9, 3945, 3948, 3964, 3967, 3970, 3977, 3987, 3989

Orford, Margaret (Rolle) Walpole, Countess of (1709–81) 3617

Oriental Institute, Luxor. *See* Chicago, University of

Ormerod, George (1786–1873) 3469:3

Ormerod, Herbert Eliot (1831–1911) 65

Osborne 3340

Osborne, John 2579

Osborne, Thomas, London, bookseller (*d.* 1767) p. xviii, 91, 683:2, 2146:4, 2474:2

Ossory, Anne, Lady. *See* Upper Ossory

Oxford, Edward Harley, Earl of (1689–1741) 917, 1608:15, 2146:4, 2474:2, 2772, 3620, 3662, 3783, 3786:2

Oxford University. Balliol College 40

Oxford University. Bodleian Library 121, 210, 212, 520, 938, 1174, 1337, 1379, 1441, 1483, 1572–3, 1597, 1605, 1979, 2249, 2397, 2545, 2614, 3019, 3979

Oxford University. Christ Church 3955

Oxford University. Worcester College 894, 1146

Oxford University Press. *See* Walpole 2622

Padwick, P. H. (*d.* 1959?) 3848

Paine 1461

Paine, Cornelius (library sold 1891) 275, 1936

Paine, Henry 1993

Paine, Richard C., Jr. 2389

Paine, Wyatt 1109

Palmer 77, 314, 3697

Palmer, C. 2253

Palmer, George Herbert (1842–1933) 2060

Palmer, Harold (library sold 1941) 1806

Palmer, Samuel, London, bookseller 3848

Papantonio, Michael. *See* Seven Gables Bookshop

Parker, of Hampton Wick, bookseller? 3615

Parker, Augustin Hamilton (1875?–1951) 1810:14, 3222

Parker, George Phillips (*d.* 1856) 1639

Parker-Jervis, William Robert (1841–1919) 2545

Parkes, Joseph (1796–1865) 2215, 2475

Parr, Catherine, Queen of England. *See* Catherine

Parry, Sir Charles Hubert Hastings (1848–1918) 3469:3

Parsons, Edwin, & Sons, London, booksellers 1652, 1661–2, 1878, 3012, 3119, 3567, 3736, 3764, 3779

Patenôtre, Mme. Jules 1786

Payne, T. (owner in 1770) 1521

Payne & Foss, London, booksellers 33, 37–8, 42, 48, 59, 108, 118, 141, 146, 150, 152, 154, 161, 163, 173–4, 179, 240, 253, 313–14, 321, 375, 384, 395–6, 400–2, 424, 476, 536, 540, 547, 549, 551, 553, 556–7, 590–1, 596, 600, 604, 618, 631, 635, 650, 657, 666, 711, 834, 850, 886, 888, 1091, 1098, 1101, 1243, 1245, 1247–8, 1251, 1253–6, 1259, 1264–5, 1275–6, 1280, 1301–2, 1608, 1778, 1796, 1828, 1832, 1841, 2158, 2196, 2206, 2208, 2211, 2216, 2220, 2227–9, 2297–9, 2301–2, 2307–8, 2312, 2318–19, 2324, 2360, 2370, 2396, 2446, 2482, 2576, 3199, 3274, 3277, 3688, 3728–9, 3840, 3845, 3847, 3871, 3878, 3887, 3896, 3901, 3907, 3922, 3926–7, 3933–5, 3960

Peacock, Thomas Love (1785–1866) 1178, 1200

Pearson, John, & Co., London, booksellers 436, 982, 1507, 2374

Peel, Sir Robert (1788–1850) 2576 (Cromwell)

Peel, Sir Robert (1822–95) 3563:2

Pellett, Thomas (1671–1744) 2399

Pembroke, Mary Herbert, Countess of (1561–1621) 2347

Pembroke, Philip Herbert, Earl of (1584?–1650) 2429

Pembroke, William Herbert, 3d Earl of (1580–1630) 1615

Pembroke College, Cambridge. *See* Cambridge University

Penn, Granville (1761–1844) 2208

Penn, William (1644–1718) 1113

Pennypacker, Gov. Samuel Whitaker (1843–1916) 2077

Penrice, Charles Berners (1828–1913) 2424

Penrice, John (1787–1844) 2424

Penzance Library 2576 (Amelia), 3480

Perceval, Spencer George (1838–1922) 769, 3902

Percy, Thomas, Bishop (1729–1811) 2436

Perkins, E. 501

Perkins, Hugh, of Liverpool (library sold 1916) 1893

Perrins, Charles William Dyson (1864–1958) 3563:2

Perrins, Newton M. (*d.* 1956) 3774

Peterborough Collection 1109

Petre, Charlotte Elizabeth (*d.* 1903) 2576 (Eglisham and Petre)

Pettingill, B. D. 1363

Philadelphia Academy of Natural Sciences 3617

Philadelphia College of Physicians 1514

Philadelphia Free Library 1810:18, 3868

Philadelphia. Library Company 487, 1221, 2055

Philip V, King of Spain (1683–1746) 3569

Philipot, John (1589?–1645) 2051

Philipps, Sir John (*d.* 1764) 2624

Phillipps, Sir Thomas (1792–1872) 74, 78, 81, 87, 89, 102, 211, 756, 2162–4, 2389, 2404, 2420, 2480, 2499, 2511, 2535:7, 2572, 2582, 2611, 2619:3, 2622, 3310, 3386, 3879, 3975

Phillips, Fabian 3797:7

Phillips, S. J., New Bond Street, London, silversmith 3786

Phillips, Thomas (1760–1851) 320

Phillips, General William Cornwallis (*d.* 1887) 2490

Pickering, Basil Montagu, Piccadilly, London, bookseller (1836–78) 160, 881, 1980, 2370, 3267, 3901, 3934

Pickering, William, London, bookseller (1796–1854) 28–9, 32, 64–5, 83, 88, 92, 95, 97, 254, 262, 270, 290, 292, 302, 304–5, 424, 442–3, 565, 582, 605, 609, 615, 623, 630, 640, 644, 646, 683, 872, 877, 887, 892, 904, 906, 910, 932, 1252, 1319, 1351, 1356, 1358, 1428,

Pickering, William (*cont.*)
1811, 1815–16, 1848–50, 1862, 1864, 1906, 1915, 1955, 1957, 1959, 1965, 1982, 1986, 2013, 2152, 2336–7, 2374, 2481, 2596, 2603, 2648, 2650, 2658–9, 2662, 2667, 2672–3, 2675, 2685, 2689, 2691, 2698, 2709, 2715, 2717, 2721, 2732, 2734, 2740, 2744, 2762, 2772, 2785, 2790, 2814, 2819, 2827, 2849, 2875, 2897, 2905, 2913, 2917, 2945, 2958, 2964, 2981, 3156–7, 3159, 3169, 3173, 3179, 3181, 3190–1, 3198–9, 3224–6, 3229–30, 3232, 3234, 3236–8, 3240–50, 3252, 3254–5, 3257, 3260–1, 3263–6, 3268–9, 3285, 3288, 3291–2, 3294–5, 3298–9, 3303–4, 3307–8, 3311–12, 3314–16, 3323, 3326–8, 3332, 3334, 3337, 3338:4, 5; 3339, 3343–6, 3353, 3355, 3357–9, 3368–9, 3371–2, 3374, 3378, 3381, 3383–4, 3386–93, 3413, 3588, 3699, 3707, 3720, 3724, 3775, 3875

Pickering & Chatto, Ltd., London, booksellers 16, 89, 169, 589, 756, 773, 831, 842, 1090, 1109, 1291, 1378, 1448, 1461, 1674, 1725, 1810, 1815, 1886, 1906, 1936, 1990, 1993, 2420, 2433, 2474, 2490, 2528, 2827, 3167, 3222, 3363:1, 2, 3; 3545, 3840

Pigott, John Hugh Smyth, F. S. A. (*d.* 1853) 98, 108, 151, 482, 600, 628, 693, 1058, 1109, 1342, 1384, 1566, 1593, 1881, 1887, 1970, 1991–2, 2018, 2507:5, 2511, 2514, 2556, 2561, 2599, 2714, 3249, 3253, 3501, 3610, 3670, 3690, 3696, 3748, 3788, 3830

Pinelli, Maffei, of Venice (library sold 1789–90) 3778

Pinkerton, John (1758–1826) 2347, 3802

Pitcher 547, 2163

Pitt, Penelope Atkins. *See* Rivers

Pittar, Parke Mayhew (1856?–1918) 412, 2616

Pocock, Lewis (1808–82) 2595

Pollard 2436

Pollard, Alfred William (1859–1944) 29

Pollington, Viscount. *See* Mexborough

Pollock, A. Russell, of Greenhill 482

Pompadour, Jeanne Antoinette Poisson, Marquise de (1721–64) 1021

Pond, Arthur (1705?–58) 3646

Ponsonby, Catherine, later Duchess of St. Albans (1742–89) 276

Poor, Henry William (1844–1915) 324, 3945

Pope, Alexander (1688–1744) 280:14, 1938, 2399, 3979

Pope-Hennessy, Sir John (1834–91) 2211

Porteous, William Wade 3

Portland, Margaret Cavendish (Harley) Bentinck, Duchess of (1715–85) 3786:2

Pottinger, Henry Allison (1824–1911) 894, 1146

Potts, Arthur, of Hoole Hall, Cheshire (1814–88) 3782

Potts, Robert A. 106

Pountney, Ro. (*fl.* 1734) 469

Povey, Kenneth (1898–1965) 1608:43, 2872

Powell, David Thomas (1763–1848) 756

Powis, Edward Clive, 2d Earl of (1785–1848) 174

Powis, George Charles Herbert, Earl of (1862–1952) 174, 2226, 3167

Poynder, Rev. Frederick (owner in 1844) 1360

Pratley, H. W., Tunbridge Wells, bookseller 3, 3355

Presle, M. de 3405

Preston, Richard Rushton, Q. C. (1811?–45) 41

Prideaux, Col. William Francis (1840–1914) 1500

Princeton University 2576 (Amelia), 3813

Prior, Harris 296

Proctor, Robert (1868–1903) 29

Public Record Office 2576 (Cromwell)

Purdy, Jacob Harsen (*d.* 1916) 169

Putnam, Mrs. Mary Lowell (1810–98) 2089

Pym, Roland 3081

Quaritch, Bernard, Ltd., London, booksellers 37, 113, 122, 153, 186, 189, 191, 204, 220, 256, 264, 271, 276, 558–9, 598, 644, 673, 697, 703, 705, 768, 831, 836, 855, 879, 1126, 1219, 1325, 1608–9, 1625, 1724, 1788, 1806, 1814, 1889, 2037, 2050–1, 2146:1, 2149, 2162–4, 2181, 2263, 2329, 2332, 2344, 2359, 2368, 2378, 2408, 2446, 2456:1, 2479, 2487, 2517, 2522, 2585, 2702, 2724, 2757, 2802, 3069, 3188, 3391, 3469:3, 3501, 3531, 3577, 3589, 3591, 3599, 3667, 3675, 3706, 3729, 3739, 3741, 3744–5, 3765, 3769, 3797, 3814, 3841, 3911, 3973, 3977–8, 3993

Queen's University of Belfast 2207:22

Radford, Mrs., of Lested Lodge, Well Walk, Hampstead (*d.* 1943) 1850

Radstock, William Waldegrave, Baron. *See* Waldegrave

Ralli, Michel Constantine (1871–1929) 3632

Ramsay, Allan (1713–84) 3803

Rappoport 2350

Ratcliffe, John (*d.* 1776) 201, 3975

Rau, Arthur, Paris, bookseller 1786, 2425

Rauch, Nicolas, Geneva, bookseller (1897?–1962) 3705

Rawlinson, Richard (1690–1755) 679, 1322, 1336, 1782, 1979, 2355

Rawlinson, Thomas (1681–1725) 208, 761, 1318

Read, Sarah Elizabeth (*ca.* 1710) 2016

Reade, Henry (*d.* 1762) 118, 1911

Reader, Arthur, Red Lion Square, London, bookseller 3823

Reager, Sir Benjamin (*fl.* 1644) 2536

Red Cross Sale (1917) 2616

Redmond, Roland Livingston 3377

Reece, Richard, M. D., F. S. A. (1772?–1850) 760

Reed, Isaac (1742–1807) 2419

Reed, Talbot Baines (1852–93) 275, 515

Rees-Mogg, William 1608:27, 2372, 3919

Reid, Hugh Galbraith, F. S. A. (*d.* 1899) 371, 1889, 2402

Reighard, Paul 2428

Rice, Susan 3003

Rich, Obadiah, London, bookseller (1783–1850) 1061

Richardson, Colin, London, bookseller 3431

Richardson, Jonathan (1665–1745) 3567

Richmond, Carleton Rubira 948

Ridge 2060

Ridler, William, Strand, London, bookseller 8, 277, 1090, 1114, 2383

Riggs, Mrs. K. T. 3715

Rimbault, Edward Francis (1816–76) 487, 2381, 3399

Rimell, James, & Son, Ltd., London, booksellers 34, 637, 2207:37, 2411, 3693–4, 3705, 3732, 3753, 3798, 3885

Rivers, Penelope Atkins Pitt, Baroness (*d.* 1795) 2576 (Sévigné)

Roberts 2162, 2389

Robertson, Walter, Mayor of King's Lynn 2551

Robins, Edmund L., London, auctioneer 2518

Robinson 2971

Robinson, Charles Leonard Frost (*d.* 1916) 2374

Robinson, Conway (1805–84). *See* Virginia Historical Society

Robinson, Mark P. (library sold 1918) 1561

Robinson, William H., Ltd., Newcastle and London, booksellers (1881–1956) 73–4, 78, 89, 112, 211, 642, 1180, 1255, 1280, 2008, 2404, 2480, 2499, 2530, 2535:7, 2572, 2622, 3188, 3310, 3386, 3879

Robson & Kerslake (later Robson & Co.), London, booksellers 510, 587, 987, 994, 1501, 2352, 2387:1, 3; 3573, 3682, 3785

Rodd, Thomas, London, bookseller (1796–1849) 2, 5, 14–15, 24–5, 27, 34, 67–70, 77, 79–80, 82, 85, 93, 98, 109, 136–7, 139, 190, 196, 198, 200, 202, 211, 213–14, 235–6, 239, 250–1, 258, 348, 368, 374, 377, 383, 385, 390, 393–4, 410, 415, 417, 460, 475, 477–80, 485, 494–5, 497, 499, 500, 502–4, 508–9, 511–14, 517, 519–25, 552, 554–5, 576, 614, 682, 692–3, 697–8, 704, 716, 728, 734, 740, 746, 755–6, 762, 787, 825, 828–9, 840, 843, 852, 857–8, 861, 871, 881–2, 885, 897–8, 901, 907–8, 935, 944, 1054, 1059–60, 1063, 1072, 1079, 1082, 1087, 1144, 1146–7, 1171, 1175, 1179, 1185, 1188, 1193, 1196–7, 1199, 1289–90, 1292, 1296, 1298–9, 1305–6, 1308, 1311, 1314, 1317, 1330, 1333, 1337, 1339, 1343, 1346, 1348–9, 1355, 1361, 1364, 1379, 1392, 1394, 1397–8, 1400–3, 1422, 1428–9, 1432, 1434–6, 1440, 1442, 1444–5, 1451–2, 1454–6, 1593, 1597, 1605–6, 1615, 1643–8, 1651, 1654, 1656–9, 1698, 1700, 1704, 1706, 1711, 1715–16, 1721, 1726, 1728, 1730, 1732, 1745, 1751, 1755, 1888, 1904–6, 1918, 1922, 1926, 1928–9, 1932, 1936–7, 1939, 1943–4, 1947, 1950–1, 1953–4, 1961–4, 1968, 1970, 1973–5, 1978–9, 1982, 1986–8, 1991–6, 2002–4, 2006, 2010–11, 2015, 2023, 2026, 2030, 2050, 2053, 2058, 2060, 2080–1, 2215, 2267, 2271, 2276, 2282–3, 2286, 2288–9, 2291, 2293–5, 2342, 2355, 2358, 2365, 2376, 2381–2, 2413–14, 2418, 2429, 2440–1, 2444, 2451, 2454, 2462, 2465–6, 2468, 2476, 2484, 2488–9, 2497, 2535, 2544, 2548, 2552, 2561, 2563, 2566, 2570, 2576, 2593, 2603, 2605, 2613, 2623–5, 2628, 2775, 2998–9, 3008, 3031, 3036, 3040, 3048–51, 3058–62, 3075, 3079, 3089–90,

Rodd, Thomas (*cont.*)
3096, 3113, 3115–16, 3124, 3133, 3135, 3143, 3149, 3152, 3158, 3166, 3171, 3175, 3363, 3395, 3397, 3400, 3404–5, 3407, 3411, 3414–16, 3425, 3431, 3436, 3438, 3442–3, 3446–7, 3449, 3459, 3462–3, 3468, 3474, 3479, 3481, 3494, 3505, 3531, 3618, 3650, 3662, 3704, 3707, 3711, 3713, 3724, 3731, 3742, 3759, 3833:8, 3876, 3879, 3920–1, 3923, 3925, 4003

Rodwell, John, Bond Street, London, bookseller (*d.* 1852) 1115, 1121, 2165, 2170, 2479, 3911

Rogers, Arthur, Newcastle, bookseller (*d.* 1961) 1840

Rogers, Mrs. Mary Benjamin (*d.* 1956) 3309

Rolle, Margaret. *See* Orford

Roscoe, William (1753–1831) 237

Rose, Robert Selden (1887–1964) 713

Rosebery, Archibald Philip Primrose, Earl of (1847–1929) 17, 232, 347, 507, 722, 1786, 2005, 2387, 2487, 2507:3, 4; 2516, 2525, 3123, 3236, 3583, 3591:2, 3648, 3657, 3688, 3818, 3885, 3924, 3931

Rosenbach, Abraham Simon Wolf, Philadelphia, bookseller (1876–1952) 57, 118, 151, 174, 193, 208, 412, 1318, 1335, 1619, 1920, 1989, 2044, 2351, 2446, 2452–3, 2474, 2616, 3119, 3896

Rosenbach Company, Philadelphia and New York, booksellers. *See* Rosenbach, A. S. W.

Rosenthal, Bernard M., New York, bookseller 3258

Rosenwald, Lessing Julius 2351

Rostenberg, Leona, New York, bookseller 2466

Rothermere, Harold Sidney Harmsworth, Viscount (1868–1940) 3786:1

Rothschild, Alfred de (1842–1918) 3786:1

Rothschild, Ferdinand James de, Baron Rothschild (1839–98). *See* Waddesdon Manor

Rothschild, James Armand de (*d.* 1957). *See* Waddesdon Manor

Rothschild, Nathaniel Mayer Victor, Baron Rothschild 2517, 2837, 3188, 3417, 3896

Rothwell, John, London, bookseller 467, 3972

Rowell 1989

Royal Institute of British Architects 536

Rufford Abbey 3543

Russell, Anthony, Manchester, bookseller 933

Russell, John Fuller (1814–84) 673

Russell, Rev. Thomas (1781?–1846) 186, 2628

Russell, William (d. 1884) 3662

Rutgers University 2113

Ryley, Clara Vowell (owner in 1844) 1448

S., J. H. 2326

Sabin, Frank T., London, bookseller 435, 1378, 2029, 2453, 3469:13, 3485:13, 3582, 3915, 3928

Sacheverell, William (owner in 1576) 2472

Sadleir, Michael (1888–1957) 1636, 1810:36, 38

Sage, Edward J. (1828–1905) 1172, 1416, 1506, 1608:70, 2529, 2701, 3469:1

St. Asaph Cathedral 2576 (Garrick)

St. Aubyn, Rev. Richard John (1805?–49) 3067, 3071, 3092, 3107, 3110, 3121, 3134, 3148, 3458

St. Bride Printing Library 275, 515

St. David's College 320

St. Dominic's Priory, London 2705

St. James's Palace 2479

St. John's College, Cambridge. See Cambridge University

St. Louis Public Library 3515

St. Mary's College, Strawberry Hill 3875

St. Oswald, Rowland Denys Guy Winn, Baron. See Nostell Priory

Salet, G., Paris, bookseller 3758

Salisbury 3765

Salt, William (1805–63) 2579, 2602

Salt, William, Library, Stafford 2579, 2602

Saltram 3914

Sampson 3400

Samuel 3564

Sandars, Samuel (1837–94) 1449

Savile, George Halifax Lumley-Savile, Baron. See Rufford Abbey

Savile, John Charles George, Earl of Mexborough. See Mexborough

Sawyer, Charles J., Ltd., London, booksellers 722, 921, 2796, 3865

Saye 3683

Schiff, Mortimer Leo (1877–1931) 2332

Schreiner, T. W. 2428

Schuhmann, Robert (library sold 1920) 3119

Schweizer, Raymond J. (library sold 1929) 1810:5

Scopes, of Albany, bookseller 3070

Scott, John 3919

Scott, Mrs. John 2356

Scott, Mrs. Samuel (d. 1781) 2576 (Walpole)

Scott-Murray, Dorothy (Walpole), now Mrs. Colin Davy. See Davy

Scottowe Hall 3552

Scribner, Charles (1890–1952) 3999

Scribner's Book Shop, New York, booksellers 359, 436, 2332, 2402, 2456:1, 2474, 3563

Seabury-Western Theological Seminary. See Society for the Home Study of Holy Scripture and Church History

Seaforth, Kenneth Mackenzie, Earl of (1661–1701) 3385

Seasongood, Murray 2526

Seaton, Thomas (owner in 1844) 2263

Seeley, Leonard & George, London, booksellers 31

Seligmann, Ernest, London, bookseller 624

Senhouse, Roger 973, 3690, 3730

Seven Gables Bookshop, New York 91, 773, 1717, 1768, 1810:9, 2415, 2611, 2625, 3069, 3923, 3940, 3951, 3999

Seward, William (1747–99) 3830

Sexton, Eric 658

Shaw, Esq., of Richmond (purchaser in 1842) 2803, 2838

Sheepshanks, John (1787–1863) 3885

Shepard, Amos (owner in 1703) 2400

Sherring, Richard, of Bristol 2627

Shipperdson, Edward (1780–1855) 2050

Shirley, Evelyn Charles (1889–1956) 636, 2010

Shirley, Evelyn Philip (1812–82) 196, 636, 755, 2010

Shivers, Francis 2089

Shoppee, Charles John 3494

Shorter, Catherine, Lady Walpole. See Walpole

Shute, Thomas Deane (1792?–1854) 1930

Sidney, Mary, later Mary Herbert, Countess of Pembroke. See Pembroke

Silver, Louis H. (1902–63) 101, 1906

Simes, John Thomas, of Camberwell, Surrey (purchaser in 1842) 3584

Skeat, ——, Strand, London, bookseller 313

Skeffington, William, Piccadilly, London, bookseller 3929

Skerrett, Maria (*ca.* 1702–38) 1428, 1503, 1626, 1825, 2411, 2421, 2619:2

Skippon, Jane (owner in 1664) 2470

Skippon, Luke 2470

Skippon, Susanna 2470

Slade, Felix (1790–1868) 2207:28, 2528

Slatter, Henry, Oxford, bookseller 6, 16, 18, 88, 106–7, 115, 117, 125–6, 131–3, 138, 140, 145, 151, 153, 164, 171, 233, 257, 293–4, 297, 301, 306–7, 425, 428, 434, 455, 465, 470, 472, 526, 528, 530, 534, 564, 578, 584, 625, 633, 643, 732–3, 735–6, 744, 759, 772, 774, 782–5, 823, 830, 832, 835, 866, 883, 1064, 1067, 1069–70, 1073, 1081, 1089, 1112, 1116–17, 1123, 1127–8, 1131–3, 1145, 1149, 1313, 1331–2, 1336, 1338, 1344–5, 1347, 1350, 1391, 1399, 1404, 1409, 1411, 1417, 1424–5, 1433, 1437, 1441, 1443, 1453, 1463–4, 1476–7, 1483, 1492, 1497, 1504, 1510–12, 1514, 1517–20, 1522, 1525, 1527–8, 1530–1, 1533–4, 1536–7, 1539, 1542–3, 1548, 1550, 1553, 1555–7, 1561, 1564–6, 1572–4, 1577, 1584–5, 1589, 1621, 1699, 1702–3, 1705, 1713, 1717, 1719, 1725, 1727, 1729, 1743, 1752, 1759, 1768–9, 1809, 1814, 1852, 1854, 1856–9, 1887, 1889–94, 1897–9, 1911, 1914, 1919, 1921, 1923, 2050–2, 2056, 2065–6, 2166, 2171, 2173, 2175, 2180, 2188, 2193, 2200, 2204, 2213, 2218–19, 2222, 2224, 2268, 2270, 2272, 2275, 2277, 2279, 2281, 2285, 2287, 2290, 2292, 2296, 2423, 2425–7, 2429, 2455, 2543, 2808, 2815, 2839, 2861, 2873, 2928, 2950, 3081, 3118, 3164, 3302, 3313, 3321, 3325, 3342, 3348, 3420, 3427, 3450, 3453, 3473, 3478

Slevin, James 80

Sligo, Denis Edward Browne, 10th Marquess of 1079

Smets, Alexander A. (library sold 1868) 928, 976, 1767, 3690

Smith, Albert E. (1875?–1958) 2617

Smith, Alfred Russell, London, bookseller 3814

Smith, Algernon Emmerick Clementi (owner in 1847) 2120:8

Smith, Austin D., of Southport (library sold 1950) 1148

Smith, David Nichol (1875–1962) 1476

Smith, George, of Russell Square (*d.* 1867?) 125, 904, 1956, 1971, 1980, 2884, 3019, 3053, 3563:2

Smith, George D., New York, bookseller (1870–1920) 37, 324, 412, 2374, 2387:2, 2523, 2616

Smith, Harry Bache (1860–1936) 2453

Smith, John 1904

Smith, John Russell, London, bookseller (1810–94) 124, 144, 377, 439, 445, 672, 678, 690, 699, 1032, 1214, 1346, 1593, 2010, 2050:7, 2614, 3232, 3414, 3485:11, 3507, 3539, 3581, 3594, 3642, 3850, 3858, 3877

Smith, R. *See* Smith, John Russell

Smith, Solomon Charles Kaines (1876–1958) 2120:2

Smith, Thomas 2499

Smith, William, Lisle Street, London, printseller (retired 1848) 2351, 2628, 2631, 3654–5, 3665, 3667, 3684, 3705, 3722, 3727, 3735, 3783, 3786, 3818, 3885

Smither 3505

Smith's Book Store, Baltimore 289

Smithsonian Institution, Washington 2217

Smyth-Pigott, John Hugh. *See* Pigott

Sneyd, Ralph (1793–1870) 101, 566, 577, 703, 705, 814, 2436, 2520

Sneyd, Ralph (1863–1949). *See* Sneyd, Rev. Walter

Sneyd, Rev. Walter (1809–88) 101, 566, 577, 604, 703, 705, 814, 874, 2014, 2436, 2520, 2576 (Peter III), 3305, 3466, 3751

Soane Museum, London 3994

Soaper, George (*d.* 1848) 973, 999, 2827, 2905, 2994, 3841, 3890, 3895

Society for the Home Study of Holy Scripture and Church History 1123

Society of Antiquaries 569

Society of Dilettanti, London 2404

Solly, Edward (1819–86) 578

Soltykoff, Prince Alexis 1109

Sombre, David Ochterlony Dyce. *See* Dyce-Sombre

Sotheran, Henry, & Co., London, booksellers (active from 1866) 93, 263, 506, 2349, 2456:3, 2511, 3604, 3691, 3694, 3711, 3995, 4013

South, Thomas 3070

Southey, Robert (1774–1843) 1641, 2963, 3169

Sowers, Roy Vernon, San Francisco, bookseller 784

Spain, King of. *See* Philip V

Sparrow, John 2120:8

Spear, William 2240

Speck, William Alfred (1864–1928). *See* Yale University. Speck Collection

Spedding, James (1808–81) 3797

Spence, Ruth 140

Spencer, Walter Thomas, London, bookseller 827, 2519, 3043, 3585, 3859, 3903

Spencer, William Augustus (*d.* 1912). *See* New York Public Library. Spencer Collection

Spoor, John Alden (1851–1926) 1881, 1897, 2521, 3069, 3896

Spurr & Swift, London, booksellers 584, 984, 1618, 1693, 2146:1, 2492, 3055, 3546, 3762, 3903

Standidge, C. W. (library sold 1877) 3621

Stanhope, Charles, Baron Stanhope (1595–1675) 17, 2429

Stanhope, James Richard, 7th Earl Stanhope, and Earl of Chesterfield 2576 (Holland)

Stanley, Edward Arthur Vesey (1879–1941) 33, 1609, 1810:59, 3222, 3286, 3859

Stanley, Edward James (1826–1907) 1989

Stannard, Rt. Rev. Robert William 1109

Stechert-Hafner, New York, booksellers 1744

Steedman, George Fox (1871–1940) 3515

Steevens, George (1736–1800) 2463

Sterling, Sir Louis Saul (1883?–1958) 2508

Stevens, Benjamin Franklin, London, bookseller 273, 1871, 1881, 1987, 2050:13, 2387: 2, 4, 6; 2400, 2434, 2521, 2526, 3417, 3554, 3676, 3729, 3770, 3801, 3890, 3896

Stevens, B. F. & Brown, Ltd. (successor to B. F. Stevens), London, booksellers 871, 999, 1886, 2528, 3759

Stevens, Henry, Son and Stiles, London, booksellers 2968:8

Stevens, Robert B. 937

Stewart. *See also* Stuart

Stewart, Charles James, London, bookseller (1798–1883) 1006, 1384, 1441, 1573, 2131, 3319

Stewart, Cosmo Gordon (1869–1948) 921

Stewart, Dugald (1753–1828) 253

Stewart, Col. Matthew (*d.* 1851) 253

Stibbs, Edward C., Holy-well Street, London, bookseller 607, 660, 1262, 1464, 1820, 2564, 3727

Stillingfleet, R. W. 245

Stirling. *See* Stirling-Maxwell

Stirling-Maxwell, Sir John (1866–1956) 197, 3675, 3689, 3882

Stirling-Maxwell, Sir William (1818–78) 197, 3675, 3689

Stoddard, Richard Henry (1825–1903) 2286

Stoke Newington Public Library 1172, 1416, 1506, 1608:70, 2529, 2701, 3469:1

Stonehill, Charles A., London and New Haven, bookseller 1058, 1788, 2160, 2619:3, 3889

Storer, Anthony Morris (1746–99) 2521, 3417

Stow 3737

Strachey, Giles Lytton (1880–1932) 973

Strachey, Richard (1781–1847) 1726

Strachie, Edward Strachey, Baron 296, 448, 1021, 1464

Streatfield, Rev. Thomas (1777–1848) 280, 2429

Street 3351

Strong, George Templeton (1829–75) 376, 3690

Strong, William, Bristol, bookseller 4, 8, 21, 23, 26, 30, 35, 61, 77, 79–80, 85, 105, 116, 118, 120, 124, 127, 130, 142, 144, 155, 157, 160, 162, 186, 189, 204–5, 224, 230, 232, 241, 249, 254, 261, 265, 272, 274, 281, 283–4, 286, 313–14, 321, 327, 334, 341–2, 346, 352, 368, 372, 377, 383, 385, 389–91, 393, 404, 408, 411, 419, 423, 437, 444, 446, 453, 474, 476, 481–4, 486–91, 493, 505, 515–17, 572, 580, 617, 619, 630, 646, 675, 679–81, 687, 696, 703, 705, 709, 712, 718, 725, 727, 729, 739, 742, 760, 776, 789, 794, 796, 842, 921, 926, 1022, 1024, 1027–8, 1032, 1037, 1040, 1058, 1061–2, 1065–6, 1068, 1071, 1076, 1080, 1083–4, 1090–1, 1098–1100, 1108, 1114, 1117, 1124–5, 1135, 1137, 1182, 1184, 1189, 1204, 1209, 1214, 1218, 1226–7, 1267–8, 1271, 1273, 1279, 1283, 1309–10, 1316, 1327, 1329–30, 1333, 1343, 1346, 1369–70, 1373–4, 1376, 1378, 1381, 1386, 1396, 1415–16, 1448–50, 1500–1, 1505, 1508, 1521, 1599–1600, 1613, 1616–17, 1632, 1656, 1668, 1670, 1677, 1692, 1697, 1739, 1746, 1749, 1760, 1763–5, 1767, 1770–1, 1775, 1812–14, 1820, 1826, 1831, 1837, 1839, 1866, 1871–2, 1881–3, 1924–5, 1932–3, 1936, 1940, 1951, 1968–9, 1973, 1989, 2003, 2006, 2008, 2010, 2013–15, 2017, 2020, 2023, 2025, 2027, 2076, 2104–5, 2107, 2119–20, 2122–3, 2126, 2128–34,

Strong, William (*cont.*)
2137–8, 2146, 2168, 2172, 2182, 2187, 2190–1, 2197, 2331, 2388, 2401, 2403, 2412, 2416–17, 2422, 2438, 2443, 2463, 2511, 2514, 2528, 2534, 2536, 2542, 2555, 2570, 2599, 2612, 2622, 2627, 2632–6, 2638–41, 2643, 2646, 2650, 2652, 2655, 2660–1, 2665–6, 2668, 2670–1, 2676–84, 2686–8, 2693–6, 2700–1, 2704, 2706, 2710, 2713, 2716, 2719, 2723, 2725, 2729, 2735–6, 2738, 2743, 2745–7, 2751, 2755–6, 2759, 2761, 2763–6, 2770–1, 2773–4, 2776–7, 2779–84, 2791, 2793, 2797, 2807, 2812–13, 2817–18, 2821, 2829, 2837, 2841, 2845, 2847, 2850, 2854, 2857, 2860, 2863, 2878–9, 2882–3, 2885, 2903, 2911, 2915, 2917, 2926, 2946, 2950, 2952, 2966, 2969, 2971, 2978, 2983, 2987, 2991, 2995–7, 3001, 3007, 3027, 3037, 3041, 3053, 3069, 3082–3, 3097, 3106, 3108, 3123, 3127, 3131, 3138–9, 3147, 3154, 3161, 3178, 3185–6, 3200, 3202, 3206, 3210, 3212, 3218, 3220–1, 3227–8, 3230–3, 3235, 3239, 3243, 3250, 3253–4, 3256–9, 3262, 3265, 3267, 3287, 3350–1, 3354–5, 3382, 3396, 3398–9, 3412–14, 3422, 3424, 3426, 3430–1, 3434–5, 3442, 3447, 3456, 3460, 3462–3, 3467, 3472, 3483, 3505, 3509, 3529, 3542, 3546, 3563:2, 3; 3574, 3588, 3591, 3595, 3619, 3622, 3629, 3632, 3636, 3638, 3647, 3658, 3660, 3666, 3676, 3683, 3686, 3690, 3695–7, 3709, 3718–19, 3733–4, 3748–9, 3751, 3757, 3762, 3843, 3850, 3866–7, 3876, 3892–5, 3976
Stuart. *See also* Stewart
Stuart, William, of Aldenham Abbey (1825–93) 2507:3, 4; 2516
Sturges, Henry Cady (1846–1922) 2428
Suckling & Co., London, booksellers 578, 2619:3
Sumenon, G., of Woodmansey (owner in 1853) 16
Sumner, Charles (1811–74) 3363
Sumner Collection. *See* Harvard University
Surveyor of the Queen's Pictures 3579, 3911
Sussex, Augustus Frederick, Duke of (1773–1843) 1641
Sutherland, George Granville, Duke of (1786–1861) 2357
Suzannet, Comte de 2351
Swan, Joseph Rockwell (1878–1965) 2511
Swift, F. H., London, bookseller 224, 1019,

Swift, F. H. (*cont.*)
1093, 1370, 1689, 2007:2, 2056, 2777, 2945, 3015, 3632, 3727, 3799
Sydenham, Sir Philip (1676?–1739) 1599, 2052
Sylvester, Thomas (owner in 1643) 518
Symonds, John Addington (1840–93) 3734

Tabor, Charles J. 2466
Taintor, Charles M. 2821
Talbot, James, Jr. 2332
Tasker, Joseph, of Middleton Hall, Essex (1796?–1861) 1822
Taunton, Henry Labouchere, Baron. *See* Labouchere
Taylor, Charles Richard (library sold 1874) 3823
Taylor, Francis, of York 2627
Taylor, Tom (1817–80) 2519
Téchener, Léon, Paris, bookseller (1833–88) 1055, 2415
Teignmouth, John Shore, Baron (1751–1834) 3997
Tenner, Helmut, Heidelberg, bookseller. *See* Wouwerman 3992
Terry, Dr. Roderick (1849–1933) 1810:12, 19
Thackeray, William Makepeace (1811–63) 1438
Thibaudeau, Alphonse Wyatt 726
Thieme, Hugo Paul (1870–1940) 3001
Thomas, Abel Cary (1883–1945) 1561
Thomas, Louis A. 1438
Thomas, William 751
Thompson, Henry Yates (1838–1928) 2827
Thompson's Book Shop, San Francisco 633
Thomson, John Maitland (1847–1923) 3778
Thomson, Mark Alméras (1903–62) 1608:43
Thoresby, Ralph (1658–1725) 2537, 2539, 2544, 2575, 2585, 2589, 2602–3, 2627–8, 3783, 3900
Thorkelin, Grimur Jonsson (1752–1829) 3554
Thorn-Drury, George (1860–1931) 2016
Thorne, of Richmond, bookseller 3723, 3737, 3750, 3865, 3868, 3884, 3886
Thorne, Samuel Edmund 1860
Thorp, Thomas, Guildford, bookseller 3, 64, 546, 561, 1833, 2122, 2464, 2528, 3577, 3880
Thorpe, Thomas, London, bookseller (1791–1851) 1, 10–11, 17, 22, 47, 62–3, 67–70, 76, 86, 94, 98, 100–1, 148, 150, 154, 156, 161,

Thorpe, Thomas (*cont.*)

167, 169, 179, 185, 190, 194–6, 200–2, 206–7, 210–15, 217, 219, 221, 223, 230, 253, 280, 288, 314, 358, 365, 372, 375–6, 384, 389, 391, 395–6, 400–2, 404, 408, 419, 424, 435, 438–9, 454, 469, 471, 473, 475, 529, 535, 537, 541, 552, 554–5, 558, 560, 562, 565, 576, 579, 581–3, 585, 592–3, 596–8, 601–3, 606, 608, 628, 652, 656, 659, 665, 670, 673, 683–4, 691, 695–6, 700–2, 718, 725, 727–8, 734, 739, 746, 755–6, 760, 762, 787, 797, 799–800, 804–5, 810, 814, 817–19, 821, 827, 834, 846, 853, 860, 882, 896, 909, 919–20, 932, 973–4, 976–7, 981, 983–5, 990, 999, 1001–2, 1004–5, 1060, 1107, 1110–11, 1113, 1129–30, 1139, 1150–2, 1154–5, 1160–2, 1165–6, 1168–70, 1180, 1183, 1194, 1201–2, 1207–8, 1211, 1217, 1222–5, 1228, 1231–2, 1234, 1237, 1240–2, 1244, 1249–50, 1261, 1267–8, 1271, 1273, 1279, 1282–3, 1288, 1293–4, 1297, 1309–10, 1312, 1315–16, 1318, 1320–1, 1324–9, 1334–5, 1340, 1342, 1351, 1356, 1358, 1360, 1372, 1377–8, 1382, 1384, 1390, 1393, 1395–6, 1405–6, 1415–16, 1418, 1420, 1423, 1426–8, 1430–1, 1434, 1438–40, 1444, 1446–52, 1454–8, 1460, 1462, 1465, 1467–70, 1473–5, 1478–9, 1482, 1484–5, 1487, 1489–91, 1494, 1496, 1498–9, 1506–7, 1515, 1523, 1526, 1532, 1541, 1545, 1560, 1563, 1567–8, 1575, 1579–80, 1587, 1590–2, 1594–5, 1598–9, 1601–4, 1607–11, 1614, 1619, 1623–5, 1628–30, 1633–7, 1639, 1641–5, 1648–50, 1657, 1660, 1665–7, 1669, 1672–6, 1678–91, 1693–6, 1728, 1730, 1732–3, 1745, 1749, 1751, 1755, 1760, 1762–3, 1771, 1775, 1777, 1779–83, 1785, 1787–9, 1791, 1793, 1795, 1800, 1802, 1804–7, 1810:59, 1819, 1823–4, 1827–8, 1830, 1832, 1834, 1836, 1840–2, 1860, 1866, 1871, 1873, 1876, 1881–3, 1885–6, 1888, 1895–6, 1904–5, 1907–10, 1912–13, 1915–16, 1918, 1920, 1922, 1927, 1930–1, 1934–5, 1941, 1945–6, 1948–9, 1958, 1967, 1977, 1981, 1984, 1990, 1996–8, 2005, 2007, 2014, 2017–18, 2021–2, 2027–9, 2032, 2037, 2039, 2041–6, 2049–50, 2061, 2076, 2086–9, 2093–4, 2096, 2118, 2121, 2124–5, 2127, 2135–6, 2146–7, 2151, 2153–4, 2157, 2159, 2161, 2164, 2182, 2190–1, 2199, 2207–10, 2212, 2214–15, 2217, 2221, 2223, 2225–6, 2267, 2271, 2276,

Thorpe, Thomas (*cont.*)

2282–3, 2286, 2288–9, 2291, 2293–5, 2297–314, 2316–23, 2326–7, 2330, 2332–5, 2340, 2345–6, 2348, 2351, 2354–6, 2364, 2366–7, 2372–3, 2379, 2383, 2386, 2390–5, 2397, 2402, 2405, 2409–10, 2413, 2419, 2428, 2430, 2432, 2435, 2437, 2442, 2444–5, 2447–51, 2453, 2457–8, 2461, 2464, 2467, 2469, 2471, 2473–5, 2481, 2483, 2485–6, 2488, 2492–3, 2495–6, 2500–10, 2512–13, 2516–17, 2523, 2527–32, 2534–5, 2544–5, 2550, 2552–3, 2556, 2560, 2563–7, 2571, 2575–6, 2580, 2586–8, 2593, 2597, 2602, 2619, 2625–6, 2629, 2639, 2641–7, 2651–2, 2655, 2657–8, 2663, 2665, 2670, 2674–7, 2680–3, 2690, 2692–3, 2702, 2705, 2707–9, 2711, 2714, 2717–20, 2722, 2724, 2729–31, 2733, 2735–6, 2739, 2745–6, 2757, 2761, 2764, 2769, 2772, 2775, 2778, 2780, 2784, 2791, 2793–4, 2796–800, 2802, 2804–7, 2809, 2811, 2813–14, 2816–18, 2820–1, 2823, 2826–9, 2831, 2834–5, 2837, 2840–3, 2846–7, 2849–54, 2856–9, 2863, 2865–71, 2875–6, 2878–80, 2882–3, 2885–9, 2897–8, 2900–3, 2905, 2908–9, 2912–16, 2918, 2921–2, 2924–5, 2927, 2929–38, 2944–51, 2953, 2959, 2962–6, 2968–71, 2973, 2976, 2979–80, 2982–6, 2988–90, 2992–5, 3000, 3005–6, 3012–16, 3018–20, 3024–5, 3028–30, 3032–4, 3038–9, 3042–3, 3045, 3052–5, 3063, 3069, 3083, 3104–5, 3108, 3131–2, 3142, 3152, 3154, 3156–7, 3160–2, 3167–70, 3172, 3174–6, 3180, 3184, 3192, 3194, 3196, 3200–1, 3203–4, 3206–9, 3211–12, 3214, 3216, 3218–19, 3221–2, 3224–6, 3231, 3233–4, 3236, 3241, 3245–6, 3251–2, 3255–6, 3258, 3264, 3268–9, 3271–2, 3274–5, 3277–8, 3284, 3287, 3289, 3292–3, 3295, 3299–301, 3305, 3307, 3310, 3312, 3322–4, 3330, 3332, 3338:4, 3341, 3347, 3354–6, 3361–4, 3372, 3375–8, 3388–9, 3394–5, 3397, 3399–405, 3408, 3410–11, 3415, 3417–18, 3421, 3423, 3426, 3428–9, 3432, 3438, 3441, 3443, 3445, 3448, 3454–5, 3457, 3459, 3461, 3464–9, 3471, 3475–6, 3480–1, 3499, 3511, 3703–4, 3713, 3776, 3781, 3802–3, 3806–7, 3810, 3812–13, 3816, 3819–22, 3824–6, 3830–2, 3834–6, 3857, 3862, 3888:1, 3895, 3908, 3917, 3919–20, 3922, 3929, 3931

Thorpe, Thomas, the younger (librarian at Britwell Court) 122, 204, 2724

Thynne, Francis (1545?–1608) 2558

Tieck, Johann Ludwig (1773–1853) 1755

Tiedemann, Heinrich, Berlin, bookseller 3506

Tiffin, Walter B., London, printseller 3556, 3568, 3569:1, 2; 3634

Tilden Collection. *See* New York Public Library

Times Book Club, London 610

Tinker, Chauncey Brewster (1876–1963) 1810: 35

Tite, Sir William (1798–1873) 199, 207, 768, 1657, 3526

Tomkinson, Michael (1841–1921) 263

Toms 1993

Toovey, Charles James, son of James Toovey. *See* Toovey, James

Toovey, James, London, bookseller (1814?–93) 98, 207, 834, 1670, 1694, 1881, 1955, 2207:28, 2368, 2482, 2511, 2523, 2647, 2730, 2775, 3172, 3176, 3408, 3644

Topham, Richard (1671?–1730) 3911

Toppin, Aubrey John 3985

Toynbee, Paget Jackson (1855–1932) 2120:6, 2545, 3019, 3915

Trahman, Carl 2089

Traylen, Charles W., Guildford, bookseller 1165, 3895

Treat 1779, 1789

Tregaskis, James, London, bookseller 218, 300, 546, 1233, 2505, 2511, 2576 (Carter), 3019, 3868, 3927, 3954

Trelawny, Charles Trelawny Collins (1793?–1878) 1674

Trevor, John, Viscount Hampden. *See* Hampden

Trinity College, Cambridge. *See* Cambridge University

Trotter 2616

Tunstall, William Cuthbert Brian 10

Turner, Dawson (1775–1858) 2622, 3704

Turner, Robert Samuel (1819–87) 151, 287, 834, 911, 984, 1175, 1178, 1572, 1871, 1955, 2033, 2456, 2597, 2609, 2970, 2982, 3915, 3926–7

Turnor, Christopher (1809–86) 262

Tuscany, Cosmo III (Medici), Grand Duke of. *See* Cosmo III

Tutet, Mark Cephas (d. 1785) 198, 2397, 3012

Tuttle, Charles E., Co., Rutland, Vt., bookseller 245

Tweedmouth, Edward Marjoribanks, 2d Baron (1849–1909) 697

Twopenny, William, of Woodstock Park, Sittingbourne (library sold 1902) 1104, 4013

Twysden, Sir William (1635–97) 722

Tyler 1104

Tyler, Elizabeth Clark. *See* Miller

Tytler, Patrick Francis (1791–1849) 2560

Udny, Robert Fullarton (1722–1802) 2162

Umphreville, Edward (1670–1739) 2579, 2608

Union Theological Seminary. McAlpin Collection 201

United Service Club, London 253

United States Patent Office 3774

Upcott, William (1779–1845) 2050, 2576 (Walpole)

Upham & Beet, London, booksellers 254, 3186

Upper Ossory, Anne (Liddell) Fitzroy Fitzpatrick, Countess of (*ca.* 1738–1804) 2619

Urquhart, Francis Fortescue (d. 1934) 40, 1471

Utterson, Edward Vernon (1776?–1856) 169, 1356, 1428, 1906, 1982, 2011, 2481, 2485–6, 2506, 2509

Vade-Walpole, Henry Spencer (1837–1913) 1503

Vail, Theodore Newton (1845–1920) 3069

Vale 85, 3239

Vancouver Public Library 3224

Van de Weyer, Victor, of Windsor (library sold 1916) 3924

Van Der Elst, Mrs. V. 3637

Van der Gucht, Gerard, London, printseller (1696–1776) 1681

Van Harlingen, Dr. Arthur (1845–1936) 1221

Vaughan, John, Earl of Carbery. *See* Carbery

Vernon, Francis William Lawrence Venables-Vernon, Baron (1889–1963) 59, 658, 3374

Vernon, George John Venables-Vernon, Baron (1803–66) 1920

Vertue, George (1684–1756) 324, 361:2, 596, 1606, 2359, 2378, 2540, 2560, 2595, 2610, 2619:1, 3480, 3526, 3551, 3581, 3637, 3663–4, 3704, 3717, 3768, 3786:2

Victoria, Queen of England (1819–1901) 1608

Victoria and Albert Museum 19, 53, 348, 390, 498, 514, 1813, 1841, 1845, 1853, 1911–12, 1918, 1942, 1954, 1984, 2050:1, 2052, 2221, 2447, 2483, 2507:5, 2513, 2576 (Cole), 2942, 3294, 3494, 3829, 3998

Victoria and Albert Museum. Alexander Dyce Collection 19, 53, 348, 390, 498, 514, 1813, 1841, 1845, 1853, 1911, 1918, 1942, 1954, 2052, 2221, 2447, 2483, 2507:5, 2513, 2942, 3294, 3829, 3998

Victoria and Albert Museum. John Forster Collection 1912, 1984, 2050:1, 2576 (Cole)

Villars, Pierre de, Archbishop of Vienne (1543–1613) 3662

Virginia, University of 872

Virginia Historical Society. Conway Robinson Collection 3501

Von Metz, William (formerly William A. Diffo) 1501, 3734

Waddesdon Manor 2050:23, 2408, 3526, 3591:1

Waite, Arthur Edward (d. 1942) 1109, 1199

Wagner, Henry Raup (1862–1957) 1638

Waldegrave, Lady Elizabeth (d. 1867) 2509

Waldegrave, Elizabeth Laura, Countess Waldegrave (1760–1816) 308, 652, 707, 916, 1785, 3841

Waldegrave, Frances (Braham), Countess Waldegrave (1821–79) 296, 308, 652, 707, 916, 1785, 2211, 2421, 2509, 2622, 3490

Waldegrave, Geoffrey, 12th Earl Waldegrave 308, 652, 707, 916, 1785, 2211, 2395, 2421, 2509, 2518, 2524, 2576 (Lincoln), 2616, 2968:7, 3363, 3463, 3490, 3581, 3678, 3786:1, 2; 3826, 3841, 3888, 3932

Waldegrave, George Edward, 7th Earl Waldegrave (1816–46) p. xxviii, 1360, 2152, 3786

Waldegrave, William, later Baron Radstock (1753–1825) 2576 (Hassan)

Waldegrave, William Frederick, 9th Earl Waldegrave (1851–1930) 52, 2211, 2395, 2509, 3463, 3581, 3826, 3888, 3932

Waldie, John, of Hendersyde (1781–1865?) 3588

Walford, Robert, & Sons, London, booksellers 199, 235, 423

Walker, Sir Edward (1612–77) 2558

Walker, Joseph Cooper (1761–1810) 2490

Wallace 2076

Wallace, Walter Thomas (library sold 1920) 1810:18

Waller, Sir Jonathan Wathen (1769–1853) 2506, 2622

Waller, Sir Wathen Arthur (1881–1947) 1619, 2039, 2511, 2559, 2576, 2615–16, 2622

Waller, William, & Son, Fleet St., London, booksellers 276, 284, 557, 719, 723, 737–8, 743, 748, 826, 875, 878, 937, 941–2, 947–8, 953, 955, 1569–70, 1576, 1578, 1581, 2565, 2567, 3935

Walmer Castle. See Beauchamp

Walpole, Catherine Shorter, Lady (ca. 1682–1737) 1461, 2047

Walpole, Dorothy (Mrs. Colin Davy). See Davy

Walpole, Sir Edward (1706–84) 2547, 2565, 3750

Walpole, Harriet Bettina Frances (Pellew), later Countess of Orford (d. 1886) 2266

Walpole, Horatio, 1st Baron Walpole (1678–1757) 1456, 2225, 2249, 3981–4

Walpole, Horatio, 1st Earl of Orford of the new creation (1723–1809) 3959

Walpole, Horatio, 2d Earl of Orford of the new creation (1752–1822) 2827, 3147, 3258, 3936, 3966, 3972

Walpole, Horatio William, 4th Earl of Orford. See Orford

Walpole, Sir Hugh Seymour (1884–1941) 450, 1471, 2208, 3924

Walpole, Margaret Rolle, Countess of Orford. See Orford

Walpole, Robert (1650–1700) 2622

Walpole, Sir Robert, later Earl of Orford (1676–1745) 65, 652, 1503, 2555–6, 2580, 2622, 3538, 3552, 3652, 3931

Walpole, Robert, 2d Earl of Orford (1701–51) 2351, 2623–4

Walpole, Robert, 7th Baron Walpole of Wolterton 69, 124, 280, 698, 1330, 1336, 1503, 1877, 2077, 2162, 2164, 2373, 2493–4, 2515, 2622, 3887

Walpole, Thomas (1727–1803) 2801, 2997, 3035, 3554, 3586

Walpole, Thomas, Jr. (1755–1840) 2801, 3586

Walrond, Theodore (1824–87) 2066

Walter, W. 3797:1, 2

Walters, Mrs. Henry (d. 1943) 2398

Warburton, John (1682–1759) 359, 2048

Warrender, Mrs. Harold 3768

Warwick, Francis Greville, Earl of. *See* Brooke, Francis Greville, Earl

Warwick, George Guy Greville, 4th Earl of (1818–93) 1315

Washington Cathedral 1123

Waterhouse, Ellis 2050

Watney, Oliver Vernon (1902–66) 756, 1725, 2433

Watney, Vernon James, of Cornbury Park (1860–1928) 756, 1725, 2433

Watson, James, London, bookseller 317, 459, 461–2, 468, 622, 624, 627, 634, 637, 639, 894, 899, 902

Watson, Wenman Langham 2060

Watts, William Henry (1850?–1902) 3625

Way, Albert (library sold 1907) 235

Webb 1346, 1668

Webb, Philip Carteret (1700–70) 2329

Webb & Co., Leeds, booksellers 3306, 3319, 3349, 3352, 3477

Webster 2435

Webster, J. 2343

Webster, John, LL. D. (d. 1891) 1657

Weddell, Edward, London, bookseller 2122

Weinreb, B., London, bookseller 2417

Welby, Sir Oliver Charles Earle 3282

Welland, James, clerk to George Robins (d. 1845) 1120, 1869, 1875, 1880

Wellcome Historical Medical Library 1199, 3737

Wellesley, Rev. Henry (1791–1866) 818, 1440, 2051, 2139–45, 2147, 2582, 3526

Wellesley College 2060

Wells, Edgar H., & Co., New York, bookseller 301, 3069

Wells, Gabriel, New York, bookseller (1862–1946) 1810:59, 2286, 2400

Wemyss and March, Francis David Charteris, Earl of 3485:9

Wentworth, Anne, Baroness Lovelace. *See* Lovelace

Wertheim, Maurice (1886–1950) 1884

Wesleyan University 61

West, Esq. (perhaps James Roberts West, 1811–82) 661–2, 667, 869–70

Westell, James, New Bond Street, London, bookseller 463, 609, 975, 1000, 1003, 1078, 1088, 1303, 1622, 1626, 1631, 1638, 1655, 1845–6, 1855, 2402, 2895, 2904, 2941–3, 2967, 3021, 3510, 3518, 3555, 3714, 3738, 3756

Weyhe, Ernst, New York, bookseller 324, 630

Wharton, Philip, Duke of Wharton (1698–1731) 2421

Wharton, Thomas, Marquess of Wharton (1648–1715) 2421

Whatman, James (1813–87) 523

Wheatley, Benjamin Robert (1819–84) 1746

Wheatley, Henry Benjamin (1838–1917) 1936, 2435

Wheeler, Charles Van Cise (library sold 1919) 3393

Wheeler, Nell Rose (library sold 1919) 3393

Whiston, John, London, bookseller (1711–80) 187

White, Alfred Tredway (1846–1921) 2326

White, Algernon Holt (purchaser in 1842) 7, 9, 458, 466

White, Joseph, Holborn, London, bookseller 3335

White, Richard 872

White, William Augustus (1843–1927) 118, 1938, 2456

Whitelaw, David 2207:9

Whitfield, John Humphreys 3941

Whitney, John Hay 2387:4

Whitney, Mrs. Payne 2387:4

Widener, Joseph Early (d. 1943) 3119

Wilcox, of Warwick, bookseller? 3684, 3904

Wilkes, Robert, Craven-Street, London, bookseller 2844, 2881, 2890–1, 2954–5, 2975, 3004, 3017, 3026, 3035, 3057, 3064, 3076, 3109, 3111–12, 3122, 3125, 3145, 3151, 3230

Williams, of Richmond, bookseller? 1734, 1736–8, 1741–2, 1747, 1753–4, 1758, 1761

Williams, John Camp (1859?–1929) 1617, 3755

Williams, John Hughes (b. ca. 1796) 1561

Williams, Robert Stanton (1828–99) 3755

Williams, Thomas Goddard, barrister 866

Williams College. Chapin Library 169, 1090, 1810:28, 1893, 3989, 4016

Willis, Mrs. (purchaser in 1842) 1367, 1375, 1385

Willis, George, London, bookseller (1813–95) 276, 431, 874, 1396, 1763, 1936, 3347, 3857:4, 3931

Willis, Rev. Robert, F. R. S. (1800–75) 3483

Willis & Sotheran, London, booksellers (active 1856–66) 389, 1872, 1912, 2082, 2446, 3168, 3186

Wills, Howell (library sold 1894) 1057

Wills, William Henry (1810–80) 2475

Wilmerding, Lucius (1879–1949) 435, 1507, 2091

Wilson, Dr. Thomas Bellerby (1807–65) 3617

Winchilsea, Heneage Finch, Earl of (ca. 1620–89) 2497

Windsor Castle 1249, 1608, 2146:2, 2329, 2479, 3398, 3526, 3567, 3646, 3704, 3944, 3961, 3973, 3978, 3993

Windus, Benjamin Godfrey (library sold 1868) 984, 2208, 2368, 2384, 2402, 2457, 3707, 3837–8

Winn, Rowland Denys Guy, Baron St. Oswald. See Nostell Priory

Witkower's, Hartford, Conn., booksellers 2631

Witten, Laurence, New Haven, bookseller 3633

Wolsey, Thomas, Cardinal (1475?–1530) 2430

Wolverton, Frederic Glyn, Baron (1864–1932) 813

Wood, Esq. (purchaser in 1842) 3794, 3854

Wood, Don C. 1339

Wood, Miss H. F. (owner in 1917) 2616

Wood, Melvin S. 1339

Wood, Mrs. Robert (fl. 1775) 37

Woodburn, Henry, St. Martin's Lane, London (purchaser in 1842) 71, 75, 110, 112, 121, 129, 197, 199, 203

Woodin, William Hartman (1868–1934) 1367

Woodroffe 986

Woodruffe, John Bratton, London, bookseller 1192, 1304, 3010, 3046, 3056

Worcester College, Oxford. See Oxford University

Wreden, William P., Palo Alto, California, bookseller 3342, 3625

Wright, George (owner in 1844) 3349

Wyckoff, James 1810:20, 2453

Ximenes Book Shop, New York 1007, 2072

Yale University 80, 127, 218, 256, 937, 1509, 1638, 1762, 1810 (12 plays), 2061, 2217, 2266, 2515, 3501, 3591:4, 3917, 3921, 3993

Yale University. Speck Collection 1810:57

Yates, Joseph St. John (1809?–87) 1814

Yelverton, Henry, Viscount de Longueville. See Longueville

York Minster Library 3400, 3414

Young, Harold Edgar (d. 1931) 3857:4

Young, Henry, & Sons, Liverpool, booksellers 29, 1057, 3857:4

Young, John, F. S. A. (d. 1874) 2576 (Peter III and Stanislaus), 3172, 3176, 3455

Young, Thomas Patrick (1724?–78) 1342

Zaehnsdorf, Ltd., London, booksellers 2435

Zimmerman, William, Jr. (d. 1967) 66, 790, 1639, 2362, 3469:3

GENERAL INDEX

This is an index to authors, and to the titles of anonymous works. But the subjects of anonymous works have often been indexed for convenience. In addition, personal subjects have been included, and all topographic subjects in titles have been indexed because the topographic reference is so easily recalled.

All references are to the numbers assigned in this *Catalogue*; a number after a colon indicates either the volume in a multi-volume set (especially of Plays, Poems, or Tracts) or the item within a volume when several pieces are bound together. Since titles are regularly referred to the entry under which they can be found, the name appearing as the reference is not necessarily that of the author.

A., H., Gent. *See* Waring 1990
A. B. C. set forthe by the Kynges maiestie 141
Abbadie, Jacques:
    Traité de la divinité de Notre Seigneur Jésus-Christ 1017
Abbaye Royale de Saint-Denys. *See* Félibien 875
Abbaye Royale de Saint Germain des Prez. *See* Bouillart 868
Abbot, George. *See* Oldys 417
Abdallah. *See* Bignon 2339
Abelard to Eloisa. See Warwick 3222:20
Abercorn, James Hamilton, Lord Paisley, afterwards 7th Earl of:
    Calculations and Tables 142
    One letter. *See* Letters 2576
    See Pepusch 2444
Abguerbe, Quentin Godin d':
    Dictionnaire des théâtres de Paris 775
Abingdon, Thomas:
    Antiquities of the Cathedral Church of Worcester 671
Abingdon, Willoughby Bertie, 4th Earl of:
    Thoughts on the Letter of Edmund Burke 1609:38, 40
Abra-mule. See Trapp 1818:21
Abrégé chronologique de l'histoire et du droit public d'Allemagne. See Pfeffel 1281

Abrégé de la vie des plus fameux peintres avec leur portraits. See Dezallier d'Argenville 265
Abridgement of Geography. See Geography 2174
Abrocomas and Anthia. See Egerton 1677
Absent man. See Bickerstaffe 1810:12
Abyssinia. *See* Bruce 4018; Johnson 1747
Académie des inscriptions et belles lettres:
    Histoire de l'Académie Royale 3062
    See France 410
Académie des Sciences. *See* Dudin 3413
Académie Française:
    Recueil des harangues 912
Académie Royale de Peinture et de Sculpture:
    Conférences de l'Académie . . . pendant l'année 1667 260
    See Arts 288:2
Academy for grown horsemen. See Bunbury 3913
Acajou et Zirphile. See Duclos 3091
Accademia Etrusca. *See* Cortona 2076
Accomplished maid. See Toms 1810:9
Account of a dream at Harwich. See Detection 2677
Account of a late conference on the occurrences in America. See Steele 1609:13

Account of all the manors. See Commissioners 427

Account of John Westcote. See Westcote 1609:9

Account of Livonia. See Blomberg 1467

Account of Mademoiselle Theresa Paradis 1609:47A

Account of Mr. Blunts late book 1608:8

Account of St. Paul's Cross. See Paul's Cross 2587

Account of several new inventions and improvements. See Hale 2701

Account of Sueden. See Robinson 1421

Account of the affairs of Scotland. See Balcarras 105

Account of the burning of the City of London. See Duckett 683

Account of the ceremonies at the coronation. See George III 3424

Account of the conduct of the Dowager Duchess of Marlborough. See Hooke 126

Account of the conduct of the ministers. See Tracts 400:7; 2475:14

Account of the Court of Portugal, under . . . Dom Pedro II. See Colbatch 680

Account of the Earl of Peterborow's conduct in Spain. See Freind 123

Account of the expedition to Sicily. See Corbett 1608:32

Account of the giants lately discovered. See Walpole 1609:15

Account of the late revolution in Denmark. See Caroline Mathilde 1609:29

Account of the life of Mr. Richard Savage. See Johnson 1608:20

Account of the life of Mr. Thomas Betterton. See Betterton 1608:20

Account of the present war between the Venetians and Turks. See Castlemaine 153

Account of the progress of Georgia. See Tracts 2146:6

Account of the Revolution. See Revolution 2593

Account of the sufferings of the persecuted Protestants. See Villars 1550

Account of the trial of the letter Υ alias Y. See Edwards 1608:79

Account of the wonders of Derbyshire 1810:30

Accurate description of the principal beauties . . . in and about Antwerp. See Tracts 2768

Achates Isiacus anularis commentariolo explicatus. See Stukeley 640

Acherley, Roger:
   Free parliaments 1698

Achilles in petticoats. See Colman 1810:21

Act before the first act of Elvira. See Mallet 1810:4

Acta Fratrum Unitatis. See Wesley 1608:19

Actor. See Hill 1522

Ad C. W. Bampfylde, Arm. See Anstey 3222:15

Adair, James:
   Thoughts on the dismission of officers 1609:10

Adair, James Makittrick:
   Methodist and mimick 3222:7

Adam, Robert:
   Ruins of the palace of the Emperor Diocletian 3531
   See Drawings 3678; *Particulars* 1609:58

Adam, Robert and James:
   Works in Architecture 3597

Adams, John:
   Essay concerning self-murther 1458
   See Sermons 1451

Addington. See Haddington

Addison, Joseph:
   Free-Holder 1843
   Maxims 1608:16
   Miscellaneous works 1844
   Old Whig. See Tracts 400:3; Tracts 2475:4
   Remarks on Italy 1844
   See Medleys 1487; *Spectator* 1860; Tracts 1608:5

Additions to the Diaboliad. See Combe 3222:15

Address. See Critical, expatiatory . . . address

Address from the independent freeholders. See Munster 1608:61

Address to both parties 1609:10

Address to Junius 1609:24

Address to the Cocoa-Tree. From a Whig. See Butler 1609:54

Address to the electors of Great Britain 1608:56

Address to the free and independent voters 1609:40

Address to the gentlemen of the Grand-Jury 1608:61
Address to the landed, trading and funded interests. See Rokeby 1609:50
Address to the proprietors of East-India stock 1609:55
Address to the public 1608:19
Address to the public. See Guthrie 1609:8
Address to the public. See Unconnected *Whig's address* 1609:38
Address to the publick on the subject of the East India dividend. See East India Company 1609:18
Address to the remaining members of the coterie 1609:10
Address to the Volunteers of Ireland 1609:45
Address to the Whigs 1608:30
Adelphi lottery. See Particulars 1609:58
Administration of the colonies. See Pownall 1609:7, 11
Adolphus Frederick, King of Sweden. See Sweden
Advantages of the difinitive treaty 1608:58
Adventurer 2148
Adventurers. See Morris 1810:48
Adventures of a night. See Hodson 1810:35
Adventures of Abdallah, son of Hanif. See Bignon 2339
Adventures of David Simple. See Fielding, Sarah 1563
Adventures of Melinda 1608:63
Adventures of Mr. Loveill 1551
Advice to a son. See Osborne 1715
Advice to John Ranby 1609:51; 2493:3
Advice to Mr. Loggan. See Poems 881:25
Advice to the officers of the British army. See Grose 2862
Aelianus, Claudius:
  Varia historia 2207:1
Aeneas and his two sons 1608:91
Aequipoise 1608:84
Aeschines, Socraticus:
  Dialogi tres 2207:2, 3
Aeschines, the Orator. *See* Demosthenes 2153
Aeschines the Third. *See* Mounteney
Aeschylus:
  Tragedies 3156
  Tragoediae septem 2165
Aesculapius. *See Siege* 1810:12

Aesop:
  Fables 2325, 3670
  Fabulae 1728, 2230
  Select fables 2208
Africa. *See* Lambert 3025; Thunberg 3262; Tracts 2146:1
African Company:
  Importance of . . . supporting The Royal African Company. See Tracts 2146:1
  Remarks on a pamphlet 1608:6
  Short view of the dispute . . . concerning the regulation of the African trade. See Tracts 2146:1
Age of wonders. See Black-bird 2646:22
Aggas, Edward. *See* La Noue 2720; Louis XIII 1608:1
Agincourt, Jean Baptiste Louis Georges Seroux d' 3994
Agis. See Home 1818:16
Aglionby, William:
  Painting illustrated 474
Agnan d'Orbessan, Anne Marie d', Marquis. *See* Orbessan
Agneaux, Charles Jean Baptiste d'. *See* Devienne
Agneaux Devienne, Charles Jean Baptiste d'. *See* Devienne 3308
Agostini, Leonardo:
  La Sicilia di Filippo Paruta. See Paruta 244
Agricola, Johann. *See* Venice 3662
Agrippa, Henricus Cornelius:
  De occulta philosophia libri tres 2149
Agrippina. See May 1968
Aguilles, Marquis d'. *See* Boyer, Jean Baptiste
Agujari, Lucrezia. *See* Silver 3222:13
Ah! quel conte. See Crébillon 977
Ahmet al Mansur, Sultan of Morocco. *See* Sherley 3828
Aiguillon, Anne Charlotte de Crussol de Florensac, Duchesse d':
  Verses. See Collection 2508
Aikin, John:
  Essays on song-writing 2786
Aikman, William. *See* Mallet 1876
Ainsworth, Robert:
  Dictionary 3936
Airs and chorusses in the Sirens. See Thompson 1810:25

GENERAL INDEX

Airs and chorusses in the Sylphs 1810:21
Airs, duets, chorusses in the Druids 1810:22
Airs, songs, duetts, trios. See Brooke 1810:45
Aix-la-Chapelle. *See Mysterious Congress* 1608:26, 44
Aix-la-Chapelle, Peace of:
  Definitive treaty 1608:58
  See Dodsley 1818:10; Mounteney and Grand 1608:56; Poems 881:21; *Remarks* and *National,* 1608:59; Tracts 1608:58
Akakia, Dr., pseud. *See* Voltaire 1608:76
Akenside, Mark:
  Epistle to Curio. See Poems 3363:11
  Ode to the late Thomas Edwards 3222:7
  Plaisirs de l'imagination 2266
  Pleasures of imagination 3937
  Poems 3063
  See Museum 2431; Poems 3363
Alaric. See Scudéry 1050
Albani, Alexander, Cardinal. *See* Venuti 229
Albani, Francesco. *See* Farnese 3619
Albanis de Beaumont, Jean François. *See* Beaumont
Albany, Luise Maximiliane Stuart, wife of the Young Pretender, called Countess of:
  One letter. *See* Letters 2576
Albemarle, George Monck, Duke of:
  Observations 10
  One letter. *See* Letters 2576
  Pedigree and descent 1608:8
  See Detection 2677:3; Oxford 2061:1; Sandford 3282; Skinner 1656
Albemarle Street Club. *See* Letter 1609:55
Albergati, Vianesio. *See* Pazzia 2439
Alberoni, Giulio, Cardinal. *See* Hervey 2050:5
Albert, Charles d', Duc de Luynes:
  Recueil des pièces les plus curieuses 713
Alberus, Erasmus. *See* Bartholomaeus 1021
Albin, Eleazar:
  Natural history of birds 3864
  Natural history of English insects 3865
Album in MS 1150
Albumazar. See Garrick 1810:20
Alby, Antoine de Sartine, Comte d'. *See* Sartine
Alcimus and Vannoza. *See* Camus 2816
Alciphron. See Berkeley 1464
Alciphron:
  Epistles 2996

Alcoforado, Marianna:
  Lettres d'amour 1018
Alcoran des Cordeliers. See Bartholomaeus 1021
Alcoran of Mahomet. *See* Koran 1484
Aldegrever, Heinrich. *See* Prints 3608
Alembert, Jean Le Rond d':
  Mélanges de littérature 799
Alençon, Francis, Duke of. *See* Francis
Alenzon, pseud. *See* Bonze
Aleppo. *See* Russell 2948
Alexander the Great. *See* Brindley's Curtius Rufus 2120:3; Curtius Rufus 2207:12; Louis XIV 3591:6
Alexander, Trallianus. *See* Milward 3444
Alexander VI, Pope. *See* Burchard 828
Alexander VII, Pope:
  Philomathi musae juveniles 2118
Alexander, William, Earl of Stirling. *See* Stirling
Alexandro, Alexander ab:
  Genialium dierum libri sex 2207:4
Alexis, of Piedmont, pseud:
  Secrets of Alexis of Piedmont 2629
Alexis Petrovich, Tsarevich of Russia 1608:20
Aleyn, Charles:
  Battailes of Crescey and Poictiers 1924
  Historie of that wise Prince, Henrie the Seventh 1925
Alfieri, Francesco Ferdinando:
  La Scherma 422
Alfonso. See Plays 3972
Alfred the Great, King of England. *See* Spelman 1691; Thomson 1818:8
Alfred. See Home 1810:27; Thomson 1818:8
Alfred: or a narrative of the measures to suppress a pamphlet. See Withers 1609:52
Algarotti, Francesco:
  Letters 2630
Algebra. *See* Kinsale 2570
Ali Abençufian, pseud. *See* Ashley 823
Alison, Archibald:
  Essays on the nature and principles of taste 549
All in the wrong. See Murphy 1810:2
All the world's a stage. See Jackman 1810:27
Allegrini, Francesco:
  Chronologica series 3584
Allen, Rev. Dr.:
  Account of . . . Maclaine 1608:65

Allen, George:
Some occasional thoughts on genius 1608:
29
Allen, William. See Sexby, Edward
Allestree, Richard:
Gentleman's calling 3938
Government of the tongue 3939
Whole duty of man 1389
Works of the . . . author of the Whole duty
of man 867
Alletz, Pons Augustin:
Histoire des singes et autres animaux curi-
eux 3285
Alliance between church and state. See War-
burton 1608:34
Allington family. See Collins 2542
Allot, Robert. See Allott
Allott, Robert:
England's Parnassus 2326
Almanach du diable 1174
Almansor. See Ashley 823
Almeloveen, Theodoor Jansson van:
De vitis Stephanorum 2119
Almida. See Celesia 1810:17
Almon, John:
Appendix to the Review 1609:6
Asylum for fugitive pieces. See Tracts
2050:1
History of the late minority 363; 1609:14
Letter to the Earl of Bute 1609:28
Letter to the Right Hon. George Gren-
ville 1609:54
Review of Lord Bute's administration
1609:6
Review of Mr. Pitt's administration
1609:5
Review of the reign of George the Second
1609:4
Trial of John Almon 1609:28
See Another letter 1609:27; England 1355;
Enquiry 1609:9, 15; Letter 1609:10; Ob-
servations 1609:56; Postscript 1609:10; Sec-
ond postscript 1609:28; Wilkes 1609:24
Alnwick. See Percy 1609:19
Alonzo. See Home 1810:19
Alphabetical catalogue of the pictures at
Strawberry Hill. See Walpole 2162
Alphonse VI, King of Portugal. See South-
well 796
Alps. See Beaumont 2337

Alticchiero. See Orsini 3753
Altieri, Ferdinando:
Dizionario Italiano ed Inglese 2067
Amabella. See Jerningham 3222:8
Amadei, Federigo. See Lioni 274
Amadis de Gaule. See Bibliothèque 2801
Amans malheureux. See Arnaud 2998
Amboise, Georges d', Cardinal. See Louis XII
1227
Ambulator 2327
Amelia Sophia Eleanora, Princess:
One letter. See Letters 2576
Amelia. See Cumberland 1810:12
Amelot de la Houssaie, Abraham Nicolas:
Mémoires 956
America. See College exercise 1609:23; Gorges
3427; Kennedy 1608:48; Lambert 3025;
Letter 1608:80; Paine 1609:37; Pownall
1609:41; Pulteney 1609:38; Reasons 1608:
81; Robertson 2942; Tracts 2050:14; 2146:
6; 3797:2; U.S. 1609:36.
See also 1609:11, 13, 32, 33, 34, 35, 56
America. Natural history. See Catesby 3617
American Continental Congress. See U.S.
Continental Congress
American measures. See Rokeby 1609:34
American paper money. See More 2430
American Revolution. See Godefroy 3742;
Tracts 2966
Americanus. See Evans, Caleb
Ames, Joseph:
Catalogue of English heads 287
Collection of initial letters 3768
Typographical antiquities 261
Typographical antiquities, ed. by William
Herbert 29
See Catalogues 3404; Society of Antiquaries
2598; Wren 1137
Amhurst, Nicholas:
Terrae Filius 1729
See Craftsman 1471, 2140
Amicia. See Mainwaring 751
Aminadab. See Middlesex 1608:69
Aminadab, or the Quaker's vision. See Black-
bird 2646:17
Amman, Jost:
Eigentliche Beschreibung 3769
Kunstbüchlin 3770
Ammianus Marcellinus:
Rerum gestarum libri XVIII 2150

Ammon, Klemens. *See* Boissard 3638

Ammonius, Clemens. *See* Ammon

Amory, Thomas:
Life of John Buncle, Esq. 1636
Memoirs of several ladies of Great Britain 1054

Amour a-la-mode. See Kelly 1810:11

Amours des dames illustres de France 972

Amphitryo. See Plautus 1976

Amphitryon. See Hawkesworth 1818:15

Amsterdam:
Guide ou nouvelle description d'Amsterdam 3395
See Authentic 1608:66

Amusemens d'un Prisonnier. See Amusements 1175

Amusemens serieux 3940

Amusement philosophique. See Bougeant 1178

Amusements:
Amusemens d'un Prisonnier 1175

Amyntor. See Toland 1694

Anacharsis. See Barthélemy 262

Anacreon:
Carmina 2232, 3802
[*Carmina*] ed. by Joshua Barnes 2231
See Heighington 3878

Anatomy of a late negociation 1609:54

Ancaster, Duke of. *See* SH Press 3469:7

Ancient and modern liberty stated. See Hervey 1608:28

Ancient and present state of military law 1608:27

Ancient and present state of the County of Down. See Smith 396

Ancient and present state of the navigation. See Cole 1594

Ancient Scotish poems, never before in print. See Pinkerton 2925

Anderson, Henry. *See* Waring 1990

Anderson, James (1662–1728):
Selectus diplomatum . . . thesaurus 3549

Anderson, James (1680?–1739):
Genealogical history of the House of Yvery 2328
New Book of constitutions . . . of Free and Accepted Masons 2631
Proposals . . . for the genealogical tables of all emperors 615
Royal genealogies 558

Anderson, James (1739–1808):
Observations 3482

Anderton, Thomas:
History of the iconoclasts 1995

Andilly. *See* Arnauld d'Andilly

Andrade, Jacinto Freire de. *See* Freire

Andrews, John:
Inquiry into the manners . . . of the two last centuries in England 2297, 2787

Andrews, Miles Peter:
Better late than never 1810:49
Dissipation 1810:33
Fire and water 1810:32
Mysteries of the castle 1810:56
New musical interlude 1810:22, 32
Reparation 1810:36
Songs, chorusses, &c. in Belphegor 1810:27
Songs in the Enchanted Castle 1810:40

Andro: a new game 1608:29

Androuet du Cerceau, Jacques:
De architectura opus 3672
Livre d'architecture 3673
Livre des grotesques 3483
Premier (-second) volume des plus excellents bastiments de France 3671

Anecdotes de France. See Mémoires 1303

Anecdotes de la cour et du règne d'Edouard II. See Edward II 3010

Anecdotes dramatiques 3064

Anecdotes et recueil de coutumes et de traits caractéristiques particuliers aux différents peuples de la Russie. See Schérer 3146

Anecdotes historiques. See Raynal 1166

Anecdotes littéraires. See Raynal 1165

Anecdotes of British topography. See Gough 3319

Anecdotes of some distinguished persons. See Seward 821

Anecdotes relative to our affairs in Germany 1609:4

Angeloni, Francesco:
Historia augusta da Giulio Cesare infino a Costantino il Magno 231

Anglesey, Arthur Annesley, 1st Earl of:
Memoirs 143
Privileges of the House of Lords and Commons 144

Anglesey. *See* Owen 513; Rowlands 3206

Anglia liberata. See Wotton 103

Anglo-Nativus. *See* Philipps, Sir John

Anglorum speculum. See Sandys 1763
Angola, histoire indienne 1288
Angoulême, Charles de Valois, Duc d'. *See* Collection 3084; Torres 863
Angoulême, Louise de Savoie, Duchesse d'. *See* Savoie
Angus, William:
  Seats of the nobility 3484
Angus family. *See* Hume 2712
Animadversiones in Lamellam Aeneam 2185
Animadversions upon the present laws 1608:2
Anjou, Francis, Duke of. *See* Francis
Anjou. *See* Des Noulis 918
Annales de la Cour et de Paris. See Sandras 1236
Annales of England. See Godwin 17
Annalium 3286
Annals of horsemanship. See Bunbury 3914
Anne, Queen of England:
  Collection of speeches 1608:91
  Tracts. *See Detection* 2677
  See Black-bird 2646:18, 20; Defoe 1608:9; England 1608:94; Kane 1608:50; Peerage 2442; Swift 1693; Walton 3911
Anne, Saint, Mother of the Virgin Mary 1608:8
Anne de Gonzagues de Clèves, Princess. *See* Sénac 3049
Annesley, Arthur, 1st Earl of Anglesey. *See* Anglesey
Annotations by Sam. Johnson. See Ritson 2939
Annual miscellany. See Dryden 1825
Annual Register. See Magazines 3338:1
Another estimate of the manners and principles of the present times 1609:23
Another letter from a proprietor of India-stock. See Bengal 1609:7
Another letter to Mr. Almon 1609:27
Another traveller! See Paterson 1234
Anquetil, Louis Pierre. *See* Villars 3387
Anquetil du Perron, Abraham Hyacinthe. *See* Du Perron
Ansell, Thomas. *See* Francklin 1608:70
Anselme, Antoine. *See* Oraisons 929
Anson, George, Baron Anson:
  Voyage round the world 458
  See Private character 1608:18
Anstey, Christopher:
  Ad C. W. Bampfylde 3222:15

Anstey, Christopher *(cont.)*
  Appendix to the Patriot 3222:9
  Election ball 3222:15
  New Bath guide 1810:59; 3222:7
  On the death of the Marquis of Tavistock 3222:8
  Patriot 3222:8
  Priest dissected 3222:13
  Speculation 3222:17
  See Gray 3222:2
Anstis, John:
  Register of the Order of the Garter 434
  See Heraldry 2558
Answer from a gentleman at The Hague. See Chesterfield 1673
Answer from Lien Chi. See Walpole, *Letter from Xo Ho* 2489
Answer to a late book. See Hoadly 1608:25
Answer to 'A short essay.' See Richmond 1609:47A
Answer to that part of Dr. Middleton's late treatise. See Middleton 1379:4
Answer to the Bishop of Rochester's first [second] *letter. See* Sprat 2760
Answer to The country parson's plea. See Hervey 1608:11
Answer to the Memorial. See Miscellaneous Tracts 89:2
Answer to the Occasional Writer. See Bolingbroke 1608:13
Answer to the Reverend Dr. Middleton's grand objection. See Middleton 1379:11
Answere to certaine scandalous papers. See Salisbury 1169
Anti-Midas 3222:10
Anti-Rosciad 3222:1
Anti-Thespis: or a vindication of the principal performers 3222:7
Anticipation. See Tickell 1609:39; Tracts 2966:6
Antiquarian Repertory 3850
  See Antiquities 3485:6
Antiquaries, Society of. *See* Society of Antiquaries
Antiquaries Museum. See Schnebbelie 3519
Antiquitates sacrae et civiles Romanorum explicatae. See Van Nideck 3686
Antiquitates Sarisburienses. See Salisbury 2949

Antiquités dans la collection [de Frederick II]. *See* Frederick II 3422

Antiquités de la ville de Lyon. See Dominique 1246

Antiquités sacrées. See Van Nideck 3686

Antiquities 3485. *See* Drawings 2371; Lethieullier 3503; Prints 468; Thoresby 2602; Tracts 1348

Antiquities in Essex. See Essex 3418

Antiquities of Hereford. See Antiquities 3485:2

Antonius Musa. *See* Atterbury 1608:16

Antwerp:
  Accurate description. See Tracts 2768:3
  See Francis 3680, 3741

Apollo shroving. See Plays 2451

Apollo turn'd stroller. See Oldmixon 1810:43

Apollonius Tyaneus. *See* Philostratus 249

Apologetic postscript to Ode upon Ode. See Wolcot 3222:21

Apologie pour Jehan Chastel. See Boucher 2343

Apology for a late resignation in a letter from an English gentleman. See Chesterfield 1673

Apology for the business of pawn-broking 1608:53

Apology for the conduct of a late celebrated second-rate minister. See Winnington 1696

Apology for the conduct of Mr. Charles Macklin 1810:21

Apology for the late Mr. Pope. See Spence 1608:13

Apology for the life of Mrs. Shamela Andrews. See Tracts 2474:6

Apology in behalf of the Papists. See Castlemaine 110

Apology of the Earl of Essex. See Essex 81

Appeal to the justice and interests of the people. See Lee 1609:33

Appeal to the landholders 1608:26

Appeal to the public 1608:32
  See Politician 1810:21

Appeal to the public on behalf of Samuel Vaughan. See Vaughan 1609:25

Appearance is against them. See Inchbald 1810:38

Appendix to the Patriot. See Anstey 3222:9

Appendix to the Present state of the nation. See Knox 1609:22

Appendix to the Review of Mr. Pitt's administration. See Almon 1609:6

Appianus, of Alexandria:
  Historia Romana 2207:5

Appius. See Moncreiff 1818:14

Appius and Virginia. See Plays 1623:2

Applebee's Original Weekly Journal 2139

Application of some general political rules 1609:13

Apprius, Prince. *See* Beauchamps 1553

April-Day. See O'Hara 1810:27

Apuleius, Lucius:
  Loves of Cupid and Psyche 1151

Aquila, Francesco. *See* Rossi 3516

Aquino, Carlo d':
  Sacra exequialia, in funere Jacobi II 494, 3270

Arabia. *See* La Roque 1569; Niebuhr 2912; Valle 2181

Arabian Nights. See Cabinet 3074

Arabian Nights' Entertainments 1552

Aranthon, Jean d'. *See* Le Masson 1252

Arblay, Frances Burney, later Mme. d'. *See* Burney

Arbuthnot, John:
  Miscellaneous works 1775
  Of the laws of chance 1608:37
  Table of ancient coins 459
  See Tracts 2474:2

Arcadia; or the Shepherd's Wedding. See Lloyd 1810:2

Archaeologia 3223

Archaeologia Britannica. See Lhuyd 21

Archaeological epistle to the Reverend . . . Jeremiah Milles. See Baynes 3222:18

Arckenholtz, Johann:
  Mémoires concernant Christine, Reine de Suède 913

Arco acuto. *See* Agincourt

Arcot, Nabob of. *See* Muhammad Ali Khan

Aretine, pseud. *See* Mansfield

Aretino, Leonardo Bruni. *See* Bruni

Argens, Jean Baptiste de Boyer, Marquis d':
  Lettres juives 1007

Argenson, René Louis de Voyer de Paulmy, Marquis d':
  Loisirs d'un ministre 2997

Argenville. *See* Dezallier d'Argenville

Argis. *See* Boucher d'Argis

Argonne, Noel Bonaventure d':
  Mélanges d'histoire 1176–7
Argument concerning the militia. See Savile
  1609:54
Argument of the Divine Legation. See Towne
  1379:3
*Arguments against the Pope's supremacy.
  See* Edward VI 160
Argyle, Anne (Cornwallis) Campbell, Count-
  ess of:
  *El Alma del incomparable San Augustin
  sacada del cuerpo de sus Confessions* 2329
Argyle, Archibald Campbell, 1st Marquess of:
  Instructions to a son 185, 2788
Argyle, Archibald Campbell, 3d Duke of:
  Catalogus librorum 2330
Argyle, Elizabeth Gunning, Duchess of. *See
  Mob* 3222:13
Argyle, John Campbell, 4th Duke of:
  Two letters. *See* Letters 2576
Ariosto, Lodovico:
  Orlando Furioso 3941
Aristophanes:
  Comoediae 2151
  Frogs 3222:21
Arithmetic:
  Idea of arithmetic. See Beale 2333
Arlequiniana 1019
Arlington, Henry Bennet, Earl of:
  Letters to Sir William Temple 104
  See Bulstrode 1429
Armagh, Archbishop of. *See* Parr 906
*Arme overo insegne di tutti li nobili . . . di
  Venetia. See* Venice 2051
*Armes triomphantes de Son Altesse, Mon-
  seigneur, le duc d'Espernon. See* Grignette
  3745
Armine and Elvira. See Cartwright 3222:11
Armoires des connestables . . . de France. See
  Le Feron 546
Armorial historique. See La Pointe 545
Armory. *See* Morgan 661; Nisbet 662; Wyrley
  712
Arms and the man. See Poems 881:16
Arms of the Knights of the Garter. See Garter
  2551
Arms of the Nobility. *See* Heraldry 3782
Arms of the nobility of Venice. See Venice
Armstrong, John, engineer:
  History of the island of Minorca 672

Armstrong, John, poet:
  Miscellanies 2789
  Sketches 1608:85
  See Poems 3363
Army and navy lists. *See* Tracts 2050; Tracts
  2146:3
Arnaldus de Villa Nova. *See* Salerno 2289
Arnalt and Lucenda. See Desainliens 4003
Arnaud, Antoine:
  Art of speaking 3942
Arnaud, François. *See* Du Buat 3009; *Gazette*
  3014
Arnaud, François Thomas Marie de Baculard
  d':
  Amans malheureux 2998
Arnauld, Simon. *See* Pomponne
Arnauld d'Andilly, Antoine:
  Mémoires 800
Arnauld d'Andilly, Robert, translator:
  Vies de plusieurs saints illustrés 1264
  Vies de Saints Pères des déserts 1265
Arne, Susannah Marie. *See* Cibber
Arne, Thomas Augustine:
  Artaxerxes 1810:6
  Don Saverio. See Plays 1623:1
  Guardian out-witted 1810:6
  Rose 1810:19
  See Cooper 1810:18; *Whittington's Feast*
  1810:26
Arno Miscellany 3803
Arnold, Samuel James:
  Auld Robin Gray 1810:54
Arnott, Hugo:
  One or more letters. *See* Letters 2576
Arrêts d'amours. See Auvergne 801
Arrian:
  History of Alexander's expedition 3995
Arrived at Portsmouth. See Pearce 1810:54
Arsaces. See Hodson 1810:24
Art d'aimer. See Bernard 3292
Art of governing by partys. See Toland 2766
Art of graveing and etching. See Faithorne
  336
Art of metals. See Barba 145
Art of politicks. See Bramston 1886; Tracts
  2474:1
Art of restoring. See Toland 2677:3
Art of speaking. See Arnaud 3942
Art Union. *See* St. Luke's Club 2595
Arte of English poesie. See Puttenham 2455–6

Artephius. *See* Flamel 737

Artois. *See* Devienne 3308; Tracts 2050:18

Arts. Ten volumes 288

Arts. *See* Tracts 360–1; Tracts 3833

Art's improvement. See Neve 1489

Arundel, Thomas Howard, Earl of:
 True coppy of a letter to Mr. Pym. See Tracts 2769:5
 See Crowne 1061; Norfolk 486

Arundel Castle. *See* Caraccioli 2817

Arundel Collection. *See* Nixon 485; Norfolk 486; Tracts 2050

Arviragus and Philicia. See Carlell 1932

As it should be. See Oulton 1810:47

Ascanius: or, the young adventurer 1500

Ascham, Roger:
 English works 3157

Asgill, John:
 Argument proving that man may be translated into eternal life 1459, 2632
 [De jure divino] *The assertion is that the title . . . is hereditary. See* Miscellaneous tracts 89:2
 Collection of tracts 67
 Complicated question divided. See Tracts 400:8; Tracts 2475:11
 Several assertions proved. See Tracts 100:1

Ashburton, John Dunning, 1st Baron:
 Letter to the proprietors of East-India stock 1609:8
 See Enquiry 1609:9; *Letter* 1609:8

Ashley, Robert:
 Almansor 823

Ashmole, Elias:
 Antiquities of Berkshire 673
 Institution, laws and ceremonies 586
 Memoirs 1501. *See* Tracts 360:1
 Theatrum chemicum Britannicum 1309

Ashton, Thomas:
 Character of the life of the Earl of Orford. See Walpole 2492:2
 Dissertation on II Peter i.19. See Middleton 1379:10
 Sermon. See Sermons 1346
 Sermons 1351, 2790
 Some observations. See Middleton 1379:10

Asia. *See* Lambert 3025; Thunberg 3262

Asiatic Assembly. *See* Debates 1609:17

Askew, Anne:
 First examination 186

Aspinwall, Stanhope:
 Rodogune 1810:7

Asselijn, Jan. *See* Drawings 3567

Assertio . . . adversus Martin Luther. See Henry VIII 84

Assiento Treaty. *See* England 1608:94

Astell, Mary:
 Christian religion 1460
 Serious proposal to the ladies 2633
 See Montagu 814

Astle, Daniel:
 Prospect from Barrow Hill 1609:39

Astle, Thomas:
 Account of the seals of the Kings . . . of Scotland 3396
 One letter. *See* Letters 2576
 Origin and progress of writing 3224
 See Antiquarian 3850; Henry VII 1609:58; Hill 1609:18

Astley, Thomas. *See* Green 542

Aston, Sir Richard. *See* Morris 1609:28

Astronomy 1608:7

Astry, Sir James:
 General charge to all grand juries 2634

Asylum. See Fielding 3222:13

Asylum for fugitive pieces. See Almon 2050:1

Athanasius, Saint. *See* Hermant 1275

Athelstan, King of England. *See* Brown 1818: 14

Athenae Britannicae. See Davies 370

Athenaid. See Glover 2856

Athens. *See* Stuart 3544

Atkins, Richard. *See* Atkyns

Atkinson, Joseph:
 Match for a widow 1810:44
 Mutual deception 1810:38

Atkyns, Richard:
 Original and growth of printing 2331

Atkyns, Sir Robert:
 Ancient and present state of Glostershire 423

Atlas de navigation. See Geography 2174

Atlas historique. See Chatelain 425

Atlas nouveau. See Sanson 533

Atlas topographique 447

Attempt to prove a priori, that Christ Jesus is particularly foretold. See Middleton 1337:7

Atterbury, Francis, Bishop:
 Antonius Musa's character 1608:16

Atterbury, Francis (*cont.*)
  Epistolary correspondence 2791
  Letter 1608:6
  Maxims 1608:16
  Private correspondence 1609:57
  Reasons for not signing the declaration 1608:16
  Rights of an English convocation 1390. *See* Burnet 1608:19
  Sermons and discourses 1365
  See Orrery 1380; *Sermons* 1451; Stackhouse 1608:16
Atterburyana. See Curll 1512
Atticus. See Cooke, Thomas 1608:24
Atticus, pseud. *See Letters* 1609:24
Attiret, Jean Denis:
  Particular account 1608:71
Auberteuil. *See* Hilliard d'Auberteuil
Aubery du Maurier, Louis:
  Mémoires 1008
Aubigné, Françoise d', Marquise de Maintenon. *See* Maintenon
Aubigné, Théodore Agrippa d':
  Avantures du Baron de Foeneste 776
  Histoire universelle 885
  See Scott 2953
Aubin, N. *See* Brandt 891
Aubourg de la Bove, Anne, Comtesse de Miremont. *See* Miremont
Aubrey, John:
  Miscellanies 2298
  Natural history . . . of the County of Surrey 648
Auckland, William Eden, 1st Baron:
  Four letters 1609:40
  See Dagge 3232; *Letters* 1609:48
Auction 3222:10
  See Combe 3222:16
Auction of state pictures. See Black-bird 2646:16
Audenaerd, Robert van. *See* Sigismund 3632
Audinot, Nicolas Médard. *See Cooper* 1810:18
Audley, Henry. *See* Waring 1990
Audley End. *See* Winstanley 3480
Augsburg Confession. *See* Taverner 797
Augusta, Princess of Wales. *See Letter* 1609:5
Augustan history:
  Historia Augustae scriptores sex 2084
Augustine, Saint. *See* Argyle 2329

Aulicus coquinariae. See Sanderson 1585, 1800
Aulnoy, Marie Catherine La Mothe, Comtesse d':
  Comte de Warwick 3065
  Ingenious and diverting letters 364, 1461
  Letters from a lady at Paris 1462
  Memoirs of the Court of England 1391
  Tales of the fairies 1776
Aurelius Victor, Sextus:
  Historia Romana 2207:6
Aussy, Pierre Jean Baptiste Legrand d'. *See* Legrand
Austin, Henry:
  Scourge of Venus. See Hall 2011:1
Austria. *See* Bancks 2637
Austrian Succession, War of. *See General view* 1608:49; *Groans & Enquiry* 1608:56; *Letter* 1608:53; *Netherlands* 1686; *Profit* 1608:38; *Townshend* 1608:32; *Tracts* 1608:26; 1608:44, 46
Auteurs deguisez. See Baillet 714
Authentic, candid, and circumstantial narrative 1609:29
Authentic history of the late Revolution 1608:66
Authentic memoirs of . . . Father Richard Walpole. See Tracts 2050; Walpole 3910
Authentic memoirs of the life of Richard Mead. See Maty 1608:78
Authentic narrative of the late extraordinary proceedings. See Francklin 1608:70
Authentic papers relative to the expedition against the Charibbs 1609:58
Authentick account of the proceedings against John Wilkes 1609:6
Authentick copy of the last will [of Robert, Earl of Orford] 1608:51; 2492:1
Authentick papers 1608:53
Author's farce. See Fielding 1818:2
Auvergne, Henri de la Tour d'. *See* La Tour
Auvergne, Martial d':
  Arrêts d'amours 801
Avaux, Jean Antoine, Comte d':
  Négotiations en Holland 1240
Avignon. *See* Moreau 3034
Avis aux vivants. See Drumgold 3920
Ayliffe, John:
  State of the University of Oxford 674
Aylmer, John, Bishop. *See* Strype 1657

Ayscough, George Edward:
    Semiramis 1810:26
Ayscough, Samuel:
    *Catalogue of the manuscripts preserved in
    the British Museum* 3225

B——, Earl of. *See* Bute, Earl of
B——, Lord. *See Letter* 1609:20
B., A.:
    The happy bride. See Bramston 1886:1
B., A. *See* Tucker 1609:13
B., A. D. *See* James 850
B., I. *See* Beale 2333
B., J. *See* Buckridge, John
B., M. *See* Ruthven 177
B., R.:
    Idea of arithmetic. See Beale 2333:1
B., S. *See Letter* 1608:86
B., T. *See* Masaniello 2019
Baalbec. *See* Wood 3547
Baar, George Louis de:
    Epîtres diverses 802
Baber, Thomas. *See Poems* 881:3
Babington, Zachary:
    Advice to grand jurors 2635
Babuty Desgodetz, Antoine. *See* Desgodetz
Bacallar y Sanna, Vincente, Marquis de San
    Phelippe:
    Mémoires 1266
Bacchini, Benedetto:
    *De sistris, eorumque figuris ac differentia
    dissertatio. See* Stukeley 668:1
Bacco, Enrico:
    Effigie di tutti i re 3731
Bachaumont, Louis Petit de. *See Mémoires*
    3030, 3128
Backhuysen, Ludolf. *See Drawings* 3567
Bacon, Anthony. *See* Birch 1613; Essex 81
Bacon, Francis, Viscount St. Albans:
    Essays 1777
    *Historie of the raigne of King Henry the
    Seventh* 886
    Letters, Speeches 38
    Wisdome of the ancients 1777
    See Mallet 1713
Bacon, Sir Nicholas. *See* Thoresby 2603
Baculard d'Arnaud, François Thomas Marie
    de. *See* Arnaud
Badius, Conrad. *See* Bartholomaeus 1021

Baer, Carl Friedrich:
    Lettre sur l'origine de l'imprimerie. See
    Fournier 3012
Baerle, Kasper van:
    Marie de Medicis entrant dans Amsterdam
    587
Bagdad. *See* Portal 1810:27
Bagley. See Burgess 3222:15
Bahader, Nundocomar. *See* Nundocomar
Baiardi. See Bayardi
Bailey, Nathan:
    Universal etymological English dictionary
    1463
    See Dictionarium rusticum 1353
Baillet, Adrien:
    Auteurs deguisez 714
Baily, Mrs. *See Epistle* 3222:12
Baker, David Erskine:
    Biographia dramatica 3912
    Companion to the play-house 1778
Baker, George:
    Catalogue of SH Books. See Collection 2506
Baker, James:
    *Picturesque guide through Wales and the
    Marches* 3178
Baker, Sir Richard:
    Chronicle of the Kings of England 887
Baker, Thomas, antiquary:
    Reflections upon learning 3887
    See Fisher 685; Masters 3820
Baker, Thomas, dramatist:
    Tunbridge walks. See Plays 1623:2
Balai. *See* Du Laurens 807
Balbec. *See* Wood 3547
Balcarras, Colin Lindsay, Earl of:
    Account of the affairs of Scotland 105
Baldini, Baccio:
    Vita di Cosimo de' Medici 2068
Baldwin, John:
    Liberty invaded 1608:31
Baldwin, William. *See Myrrour* 88
Bale, John:
    Actes of Englysh votaryes 2636
    Scriptorum illustrium Maioris Britanniae
    888
    See Askew 186; Oldcastle 3450
Balet comique. See Beaujoyeulx 2334, 3399
Ballad. See Poems 881:26
Ballads. *See* Collection 2358

Ballard, George:
  Memoirs of several ladies of Great Britain
  1610
Ballard, Henry. *See* Legh 1073
Balliol College, Oxford. *See* Savage 1629
Bally, George. *See* Tracts 2146:5
Balmerino, Arthur Elphinstone, Baron. *See*
  Kilmarnock 2717
Balsam, Briefe discourse of. See Hill 787
Balsamo, Giuseppe. *See* Cagliostro
Baltazarini. *See* Beaujoyeulx
Baltimore, Frederick Calvert, 6th Baron:
  Coelestes et inferi 2332
  Tour to the East 2332
  Trial . . . for a rape . . . of Sarah Woodcock
  3397
  See Letter 1609:20
Balzac, Jean Louis Guez, Sieur de:
  Lettres choisies 1020
Bampfylde, Coplestone Warre. *See* Anstey
  3222:15; Etchings 3588
Banbury, Charles Knowles, Earl of. *See* Stamford 521
Bancks, John, historian:
  *Compendious history of the House of
  Austria and the German Empire* 2637
Bandello, Matteo:
  Novelle 1611
Bandini, Angelo Maria:
  De obelisco Caesaris Augusti 524
Banduri, Anselmus:
  Imperium orientale 3674
  Numismata imperatorum Romanorum 216
Bank of England. *See* Price 1609:49
Banks, John, dramatist:
  Plays. *See* Plays 1907
Banks, John, historian. *See* Bancks
Banks, Jonathan:
  *Life of . . . Edward Rainbow, late Lord
  Bishop of Carlisle* 2638
Banks, Sir Joseph:
  One or more letters. *See* Letters 2576
  See Hawkesworth 2869; Oberea 3222:13;
  Troil 2969; Wolcot 3222:22
Bannatyne, George. *See* Pinkerton 2925
Baphius, Bartholomaeus:
  Oratio 3944
*Baptized Turk, or . . . the happy conversion
  of Rigep Dandulo. See* Warmstry 2776

Bar, George Louis de. *See* Baar
Barba, Alvaro Alonso:
  Art of metals 145
Barbarossa, Dey of Algiers. *See* Brown 1818:
  14
Barbary States:
  Late newes out of Barbary 3804
  See Morgan 1417; Sherley 3828
Barber, Mary. *See* Poems 175
Barber of Seville. See Griffith 1810:26
Barberini, Cardinal Maffeo. *See* Urban 1362
Barberini Palace. *See* Tetius 3725
Barbiellini, Carlo:
  Raccolta di lettere. See Bottari 2342
Barbieri, Giovanni. *See* Guercino
Barbuo, Scipio:
  Sommario delle vite de' Duchi di Milano
  3732
Barclay, John:
  Argenis 2207:7
  Satyricon 2207:8
Bardi, Ferdinand, Grand Duke of Tuscany.
  See Ferdinand II
Bardi, Giuseppe. *See* Lastri 3540
Bardon. *See* Dandré Bardon
Baretti, Giuseppe Marco Antonio:
  Discours sur Shakespeare 1609:38
  Introduction to the Carmen Seculare 1609:
  39
  Journey from London 2792
  Sentimental mother 1810:48
Barleus, Caspar. *See* Baerle
Barlow, Francis:
  Severall wayes of hunting 3771
  See Aesop 3670
Barlow, Thomas, Bishop. *See* Gunpowder
  2700
Barnaby. *See* Brathwait 2235
Barnard, Sir John:
  Defence 1608:47
  Present for an apprentice. See Manual 2414
  See Considerations 1608:21
Barnard, William:
  Serious thoughts on the trial 1608:88
Barnardiston, Sir Samuel. *See* Guilford 3321
Barnes, Joshua:
  Gerania 1730
  See Anacreon 2231; Euripides 2170;
  Homer 2192

Baron, Jules:
  L'Art héraldique 715
Baron, Richard:
  Faithful account 1608:31
  See Gordon 1744; Nedham 2730
Baron, Robert:
  Cyprian academy 2639
  *Baron Mountenay's celebrated dedication of
  . . . Demosthenes. See* Mounteney 1608:66
Baronage. *See* Thoresby 2603
Barozzi, Giacomo, called Il Vignola. *See* Vignola 3764
Barral, Pierre. *See Sévigniana*
Barrett, William:
  History . . . of Bristol 539
Barri, Giacomo:
  Painter's voyage of Italy 324
Barrier Treaty. *See* Swift 1608:13
Barrière, Dominique. *See Villa* 3527
Barrington, Daines:
  Miscellanies 3287
  See Wynn 2785
Barrington, John Shute, 1st Viscount Barrington:
  Essay 106, 1608:19, 22
  Miscellanea sacra 107
Barrington, Shute, Bishop. *See House of Peeresses* 3965
Barrington, William Wildman, 2d Viscount Barrington. *See Considerations* 1608:27; Rich 1609:58
Barrister at law. *See Considerations* 1609:21
Barron, Richard. *See* Baron
Barrow, John:
  Dictionarium polygraphicum 289
Barrow, Joseph Charles. *See* Drawings 3678; Walpole 3582
Barry, Major. *See* Francis 1609:54
Barry, Mrs. Ann Spranger. *See Review* 1810:34
Barry, James:
  Account of a series of pictures 325
  Inquiry into the . . . obstructions to the acquisition of arts in England 2793
Barthélemy, Jean Jacques:
  Entretiens sur l'état de la musique grecque 2999
  Voyage du jeune Anacharsis en Grèce 262
Bartholomaeus, Anglicus
  De proprietatibus rerum 1612

Bartholomaeus, of Pisa
  Alcoran des Cordeliers 1021
Bartholomaeus, a Tuscan. *See* Hill 787
Bartoli, Pietro Santi:
  Antiche lucerne sepolcrali figurate 3733
  Parerga atque ornamenta ex Raphaelis Sanctii prototypis 3486
  Pitture antiche del sepolcro de' Nasonii 3734
  Portfolio of 620 engravings 3598
  See Bellori 3616; Sigismund 3632
Bartolommeo, Fra. *See* Drawings 3569; Patch 3451
Bartolozzi, Francesco:
  Prints engraved after Guercino 3398
  See Holbein 3500; Marlborough 3625; Pitt 3456; Rogers 3627; Shakespeare 3905
Barton, Richard:
  Lectures in natural philosophy 1310
Bary, Jacobus de:
  Catalogus numismatum. See Stukeley 668:7
Basan, Pierre François:
  Catalogue d'une belle collection de dessins 3866
  Catalogue raisonné des curiosités 3867
  Dictionnaire des graveurs anciens et modernes 290, 3705
Basire, James. *See* Antiquities 3485:15; Society 3658; Topham 3472
Baskerville, John:
  Type specimen. *See* Jones 3784
  See Aesop 2208; Book of Common Prayer 1927, 2187; Congreve 3889; Jennings 300; Juvenalis 2196; Milton 2197; Virgilius 2206, 2482
Bassompierre, François de:
  Mémoires. See Miscellaneous 943:1
Bastard child 1810:13
Batalha Monastery. *See* Murphy 3650
Bate, George:
  Elenchus motuum nuperorum in Anglia 2233
Bate, Henry:
  Dramatic puffers 1810:34
  Flitch of bacon 1810:30
  Rival candidates 1810:23
  Travellers in Switzerland 1810:55
  Woodman 1810:49
  See Vauxhall 1609:31

Bate, Julius:
  Hebrew grammar 1608:71
  Use and abuse of prophecy 1379:4
Bateman, Elizabeth, Viscountess:
  One or more letters. *See* Letters 2576
Bath, Thomas Thynne, 1st Marquess of. *See*
  Rudd 1609:34
Bath, William Henry Grenville, Earl of. *See*
  Ode 3222:19
Bath, William Pulteney, Earl of:
  Case of the revival of the salt duty. See
  Political tracts 94:7
  Humble address to the knights 1608:26
  Ode from Paul Foley. See Poems 881:10
  Politicks on both sides 1608:26
  Proper reply to a late scurrilous libel 1608:
  28, 30
  Review of all that hath pass'd 1608:38
  See Craftsman 1471, 2140; *Critical* 1608:38;
  Douglas 1609:2; Kelly 3222:6; *New Year*
  1608:73; Political tracts 94; *Proper* 1608:73
Bath. *See* Bristol 2809; Miller 2420; Watts
  3528; Wood 2784
Bath. Abbey Church. *See* Rawlinson 665
Bath, Order of the. *See* Pine 3652
Bath. See Ellis 3222:15
Batheaston. *See* Miller 2420
Bathoe, William:
  One or more letters. *See* Letters 2576
  See Vertue 2479
Bathurst, Ralph. *See* Warton 1695
Battely, John:
  Opera posthuma 616
Battle of the quills 1609:20
Baudeau, Nicolas:
  Idées d'un citoyen 2640, 3288
Baudelot de Dairval, Charles César:
  Feste d'Athènes. See Tracts 1348:1
Baudier, Michel:
  History of Margaret of Anjou 1608:36
Baudius, Domenicus:
  Epistolae 2234
Baudot de Juilly, Nicolas:
  Histoire et règne de Charles VI 1241
  Histoire de Charles VII 1242
  See Lussan 813, 996
Bavaria. *See* Sandras 3144
Baviad . . . imitation of . . . Persius. See
  Tracts 2050
Bawdin, Sir Charles. *See* Chatterton 3222:12

Bayard, Pierre du Terrail, Seigneur de. *See*
  Collection 3084
Bayardi, Ottavio Antonio. *See* Herculaneum
  3590
Bayle, Pierre:
  General dictionary 2039
  Lettres 957
  Réponse aux questions 934
  See Des Maizeaux 959; Henley 1608:31;
  La Monnoye 990
Baylies, William:
  Narrative of facts. See Tracts 99:1
Bayly, Anselm:
  Antiquity, evidence and certainty of Chris-
  tianity 1379:9
Bayly, Lewis, Bishop:
  Practice of piety. See Manual 2414
Bayly, Thomas:
  Certamen religiosum 146
  See Cartwright 72
Baynes, John:
  Archaeological epistle 3222:18
Beale, John:
  Herefordshire orchards 2333
  See Hartlib 125:6
Bearcroft, Philip:
  Sermon. See Sermons 1346:2
Beard, John:
  Letters . . . between John Beard . . . and
  John Shebbeare 1810:10
Beatae Mariae Virginis Officium. See Missal
  2422
Beattie, James:
  Dissertations moral and critical 3289
  Essays 2794
  Minstrel 3222:11
  Minstrel . . . Second Book 3222:13
Beattie, James Hay:
  Essays and fragments in prose and verse
  404
Beauchamp, Viscount. *See* Hertford, Francis
  Ingram Seymour-Conway, 2d Marquess of
Beauchamps, Pierre François Godart de:
  Histoire du Prince Apprius 1553
  Recherches sur les théâtres de France 1138
Beauchêne, Chevalier de. *See* Le Sage 1300
Beauclerk, Lady Diana. *See* Bürger 2349;
  Drawings 3641; Etchings 3588
Beauclerk, Lord James, Bishop:
  Sermon 1608:6

Beauclerk, Mary. *See* Drawings 3641

Beauclerk, Mary, later Lady Charles Spencer. *See* Spencer

Beauclerk, Topham:
Bibliotheca Beauclerkiana 2795

Beaufort, Henry, Cardinal. *See* Gloucester 2552

Beaufort, Louis de:
Dissertation 1022
Histoire de César Germanicus 1267

Beaufort, Margaret, Countess of Richmond. *See* Richmond

Beaujoyeulx, Baltazarini, called:
Balet comique 2334, 3399

Beaumarchais, Antoine de la Barre de. *See* La Barre de Beaumarchais

Beaumarchais, Pierre Augustin Caron de:
Mémoires 2335
See Griffith 1810:14, 26; Holcroft 1810:37; Voltaire 3057

Beaumont, Anne Louise Élie de. *See* Élie de Beaumont

Beaumont, Chevalier d'Éon de. *See* Éon

Beaumont, Francis:
Maid's tragedy 1818:21
Philaster 1818:21
See Colman 1810:5, 29; Cook 1810:35; *Female duellist* 1810:53; Garrick 1810:20; Plays 1623:2

Beaumont, Francis *and* Fletcher, John:
Fifty comedies and tragedies 2040

Beaumont, Sir Harry, pseud. *See* Spence, Joseph

Beaumont, Jean François Albanis de:
Voyage . . . aux Alpes Pennines 2337
Voyage . . . du Comté de Nice 2336

Beaumont, Sir John:
Bosworth-field 1926

Beaumont, John, geologist:
Considerations on [Dr. Burnet's] *Theory of the earth. See* Derby 79:9
Gleanings of antiquities 675

Beaumont, Margaret Willes, Lady. *See* Etchings 3588

Beauties of England 716

Beavan, Edward:
Box-Hill 3222:15

Beaver, John. *See* Ferrière 1519

Beawillier's Treatise on Comic Masks. See Ficoroni 480

Bec, Abbey. *See* Bourget 2806

Beccaria, Cesare Bonesana, Marchese di:
Traité des délits et des peines 3066

Beck, Cave:
Universal character 2641

Beckett, William:
Free and impartial enquiry into . . . the King's Evil. See Duckett 683:1

Beckford, Peter:
Thoughts on hunting 2796

Beckford, William. *See* Francis 1609:54

Beckford, William, the younger:
Vathek 3943
See Arno Miscellany 3803

Beckingham, Charles. *See* Addison 1608:16

Bedford, Arthur:
Second advertisement 1608:64
Serious advertisement 1608:64

Bedford, Hilkiah. *See* Harbin 1116

Bedford, John of Lancaster, Duke of. *See* Gough 3812

Bedford, John Russell, 4th Duke of. *See* Letter 1608:86

Bedford Level Corporation. *See* Cole 1594

Bedford Missal. *See* Gough 3812

Bedfordshire. *See* Patching 1608:83

Bedingfield, Thomas:
Cardanus Comforte. See Cardano 71

Bedlam, a poem. See Poems 280:9

Bedwell, William:
Mesolabium architectonicum. See Hartlib 125:5

Beef and butt beer. See Poems 881:7

Begum B-rke to Begum Bow 3222:22

Beham, Hans Sebald. *See* Prints 3608

Behn, Aphra:
Love-letters 1428
Plays 1428
See Poems 175

Bekker, Balthasar:
Monde enchanté 1209

Bel-vedere. See Bodenham 1997

Belgium. *See* Netherlands. Southern Provinces

Belhaven, John Hamilton, 2d Baron:
Speech 1609:9

Belisarius. *See* Philips 1818:16

Bell, Henry:
Historical essay on the original of painting 326

Bell, John. *See* Ritson 2939

Bellamont, Charles Coote, Earl of. *See* Bellomont

Bellamy, George Anne:
Apology. See Egerton 3921

Bellamy, Thomas:
Benevolent planters 1810:48

Belle Arsene. See Plays 3972

Belle au crayon d'or. See Contes François 1783:2

Belleforest, F. de. *See* Ruscelli 1086

Belleisle, Charles Louis Auguste de Fouquet, Duc de:
Mémoires sur l'état présent de l'Europe 2531

Belleisle. *See* Smith 1609:2

Bellenden, William. *See* Bellendenus

Bellendenus, Gulielmus:
De statu libri tres 405, 2797
See Parr 2915

Bellers, Fettiplace:
Injur'd innocence 1818:4

Bellicard, Jerome Charles. *See* Cochin 1433

Bellier-Duchesnay, Alexandre Claude. *See* Collection 3084

Bellomont, Charles Coote, Earl of:
Letter 1609:43

Bellori, Giovanni Pietro:
Veteres Arcus Augustorum triumphis insignes 3616
See Bartoli 3598, 3733-4; Sigismund 3632

Belloy, Pierre Laurent Buirette de. *See* Denis 1810:7

Beloe, William:
Attic nights of Aulus Gellius 3706
Miscellanies 2798
Poems and translations 406, 2299
See Alciphron 2996; Bellendenus 2797; *British Critic* 3338:2

Belphegor. See Andrews 1810:27

Benedict III, Pope. *See* Garampi 430

Benedict XI, Pope. *See* Fioravante 481

Benedict XIV, Pope (Prospero Lambertini):
Funeral 3487
Ragionamenti. See Ragionamenti 3366:2

Benevolent epistle to Sylvanus Urban. See Wolcot 3222:22

Bengal:
Another letter from a proprietor of India-stock 1609:7

Bengal (*cont.*)
Memoirs of the revolution in Bengal 1609: 2, 2642
Narrative of what happened in Bengal 1609:7
Supplement to the Narrative 1609:7
See Ashburton 1609:8; Bolts 2803; Coote 1609:55; Holwell 1609:12; *Reflections* 1609:55

Benlowes, Edward:
Theophila 2643

Bennet, H., pseud. *See* Pinkerton 2449

Bennet, Henry, Earl of Arlington. *See* Arlington

Bennet, James. *See* Ascham 3157

Benserade, Isaac. *See* Labyrinte 301

Benson, —:
Britain's glory 1810:56

Benson, William:
Letters 1845
See Tracts 400:2

Bentham, Edward. *See* Burton 1608:70; King 1608:61

Bentham, James:
History and antiquities of Ely 11

Bentinck, Margaret Cavendish Harley, Duchess of Portland. *See* Portland

Bentinck, William Henry Cavendish, Duke of Portland. *See* Portland

Bentivoglio, Guido, Cardinale:
Historicall relations of the United Provinces and Flanders 3290
History of the wars of Flanders 2644
Raccolta di lettere 2096
Relationi 2096

Bentley, Richard, the elder:
Eight sermons 1366
See Cumberland 1609:18; Lucanus 2515, 3469:5; Newton 1608:83; Orrery 1380; Terentius 2201; *Two letters* 1608:11, 15; Wotton 1498

Bentley, Richard, the younger:
Account of the dreadful earthquake 2146:7
Attempt towards an apology 2146:7
Copy of verses. *See* Letters 2576
Drawings and designs 3585
Patriotism 3222:5; 1810:59
Petition to Mr. Pelham 2146:7
Philodamus 3222:8, 19
Reflections on . . . cruelty 2146:7

Bentley, Richard, the younger (*cont.*)
 True account of Manpferdt 2050
 World, No. 190 2146:7
 See Cumberland 1810:2; Drawings 3678;
 Gray 2044; 3698; Hentzner 2395, 2513
Berain, Jean. *See* Le Pautre 3681
Berberich, Baron de:
 Catalogue of pictures 3000
Beresford, Benjamin. *See* Tracts 2050:24
Bergier, Nicolas:
 Histoire des grands chemins de l'Empire
 Romain 914
Berkeley, George, Bishop of Cloyne:
 Alciphron 1464
 Philosophical reflections 1465
 Siris 1608:48
 See Berkeley, George Monck 2799
Berkeley, George, 1st Earl of Berkeley:
 Historical applications 187, 2338
Berkeley, George Monck:
 Literary relics 2799
 Nina 1810:42
Berkeley, Lady Henrietta. *See* Behn
 1428
Berkelius, Abraham. *See* Epictetus 2207:13
Berkenhout, John:
 Biographia literaria 3291
Berkshire. Antiquities. *See* Ashmole 673;
 Stukeley 668
Berlin. *See* Mirabeau 3343
Bernard, Don. *See* Bernardino de Cardenas
Bernard, Sir Francis:
 Letters to the ministry 1609:25
 See Massachusetts 1609:23
Bernard, Jean:
 Discours . . . des Roys . . . d'Angleterre. See
 Bibliothèques 3068
Bernard, Jean Frédéric. *See* Picart 3685
Bernard, Nicholas:
 Life . . . of Dr. James Usher, Archbishop of
 Armagh 1699
Bernard, Pierre Joseph:
 Art d'aimer 3292
Bernard, Sir Thomas:
 One or more letters. *See* Letters 2576
Bernardin de Saint-Pierre, Jacques Henri.
 See Saint-Pierre
Bernardino de Cardenas, Bishop of Paraguay:
 Histoire de la persecution 3067

Berners, John Bourchier, Baron. *See* Frois-
 sart 438, 2043; Guevara 199, 1323; Knyvet
 2573; San Pedro 208, 2467
Bernes, Dame Juliana:
 Gentlemans Academie 3772
Berni, Francesco, Conte:
 Degli eroi della serenissima casa d'Este . . .
 memorie 2069, 2186
Bernis, François Joachim de Pierre de:
 Oeuvres mêlées 1243
Beroalde de Verville, François. *See* Colonna
 2075
Berriman, William:
 Christian doctrines 1590
Berry, Agnes:
 Sketches of Italian peasants 3996
Berthelet, Thomas. *See* Elyot 784
Bertie, Willoughby, 4th Earl of Abingdon.
 See Abingdon
Berton, Thomas:
 Voye de laict ou les chemins des héros 1055
Berton de Crillon, Louis Balbe. *See* Lussan
 1254
Bertram, Charles. *See* Tracts 1348:8
Besly, Jean:
 Histoire des Comtes de Poictou et Ducs de
 Guyenne 889
Bessborough, William Ponsonby, 2d Earl of.
 See Natter 276
Besselius, J. F. *See* Eginhardus 836
Betham, William:
 Genealogical tables of the sovereigns of the
 world 2800
Bethune, Maximilien de, Duc de Sully. *See*
 Sully 1016
Bettenham, James. *See* Marriott 1810:59
Betterton, Thomas 1608:20
Betulius, Xystus. *See* Birck
Bevell, James:
 Authentic narrative 1609:56
Beveridge, William, Bishop. *See* Whitby
 1608:12
Beverly, Robert:
 History of Virginia 1392
Bewick, Thomas:
 General history of quadrupeds 3868
 See Goldsmith 3711; Somerville 3724
Beys, Charles de. *See* Valdor 3525
Bèze, Théodore de. *See* Psalms 1283

Bianchini, Francesco:
    Del palazzo de' Cesari 525
Bible 890, 915, 1502–3, 3945, 3997
    See Holbein 2398; Howell 1375; Lewis
    1415; Simon 1147
Bible. New Testament. *See* New Testament
Bible. Psalms. *See* Psalms
Bibliotheca chalcographica. See Boissard 3638
Bibliotheca literaria. Being a collection of in-scriptions 824, 2645
Bibliothèque du théâtre françois 3001
Bibliothèque Nationale. See France
Bibliothèque universelle des romans 2801
Bibliothèques françoises de la Croix-Dumaine et de Du Verdier 3068
Bickerstaff, Isaac, pseud. *See* Tatler
Bickerstaffe, Isaac:
    Absent man 1810:12
    Captive 1810:14
    Daphne and Amintor 1810:8
    Doctor Last in his chariot 1810:14
    Ephesian matron 1810:14
    Hypocrite 1810:13
    Lionel and Clarissa 1810:12
    Love in a village 1810:3
    Love in the city 1810:10, 38
    Maid of the mill 1810:7
    Padlock 1810:13
    Plain dealer 1810:8
    Recruiting serjeant 1810:16
    Romp 1810:10, 38
    Royal garland 1810:13
    Sultan 1810:42
    Thomas and Sally 1810:1
    'Tis well it's no worse 1810:16
    See Kemble 1810:46, 47
Bickerton, G.:
    Accurate disquisitions 3946
Bickerton, William. *See* Letters 1440
Bickham, George:
    British Monarchy. See Geography 3423
    Deliciae Britannicae 3947
Bicknell, Alexander:
    Patriot king 1810:44
Bicknell, John. *See* Veal 1609:32
Biddulph, William:
    Travels 3805
Bideford. *See* Watkins 2984
Bidloo, Govard. *See* William III 3800

Bie, Jacques de:
    Vrais portraits des Rois de France 3735
Bièvre, J. J. F. Le Conte de. *See* Le Conte de Bièvre
Bigarure. See Nouvelle Bigarure 1202
Biggs, William:
    Military history of Europe 1700
Bigland, Ralph:
    Historical . . . collections relative to the County of Gloucester 526
Bignon, François. *See* Prints 3656; Vulson 3557
Bignon, Jean Paul:
    Adventures of Abdallah 2339
Billon, François de:
    Fort inexpugnable de l'honneur 825
Billy de Prunay, Jacques de. *See* Prunaeus
Bingham, Charles, Earl of Lucan. *See* Lucan
Bingham, Lavinia, Countess Spencer. *See* Spencer
Bingham, Margaret, Countess of Lucan. *See* Lucan
Bingley, William. *See* Fitzgerald 3222:21
Biographia Britannica 217, 2041
Biographical anecdotes of William Hogarth. See Nichols 2435
Biographical Dictionary. See Dictionary 1772
Biographical sketches of eminent persons. See Willis 2990
Biondi, Giovanni Francesco:
    History of the Civill Warres of England 3158
Birch, Busby, pseud. *See* Thornton
Birch, Samuel:
    Adopted child 1810:57
Birch, Thomas:
    Heads of illustrious persons 3637
    Historical view of the negotiations 1637
    History of the Royal Society 1056
    Inquiry 1665
    Life of Henry, Prince of Wales 1666
    Life of Tillotson 1667
    Memoirs of Queen Elizabeth 1613
    See Bacon 38; Bayle 2039; Greaves 1436; Hammond 1609:9; Raleigh 1448; Spenser 323; Thurloe 1104
Birch, William:
    Delices de la Grande Bretagne 3837
Birck, Sixt. *See Sapientia Salomonis* 2596

Birmingham. *See* Hutton 2882

Biron, Charles de Gontaut, Duc de:
True and perfect discourse of . . . treasons.
See Plays 1082:3

Biscaino, Bartolommeo. *See* Drawings
3569

Black, William:
Short view of the trade and taxes of Scotland 1608:8

Blackall, Offspring, Bishop. *See* Hoadly 1608:
19; Sermons 1451

Blackbird's song. See Blackbird's tale 2646

Black-bird's tale 2646

Blackbourne, John, Bishop. *See* Oldcastle
3450

Blackburne, Francis:
Considerations on . . . the controversy between the Protestants and the Papists 2647
Memoirs of Thomas Hollis 3688
Sermon 1608:74

Blackmore, Sir Richard:
Prince Arthur 2052

Blackstone, Sir William:
Great Charter and Charter of the Forest
232
Letter to the author of the Question stated
1609:23
See Dyson 1609:57; *Essay* 1609:25

Blackwell, Thomas:
Enquiry into . . . Homer 1393
Letters concerning mythology 1394
Proofs on the enquiry into Homer's life
1395

Bladen, Martin 1780

Blagden, Sir Charles:
One letter. See Letters 2576

Blagrave, John:
Mathematicall jewell 2648

Blair, John:
Chronology 3985

Blair, Thomas:
Dissertatio physiologica de respiratione
2340

Blake, Miss C. S. *See* Etchings 3588

Blakiston, Mr.:
Pantheon. See Poems 3363

Blakiston, William. *See* Blackstone, Sir William

Blancourt, François Haudicquer de. *See*
Haudicquer de Blancourt 1274

Bland, Humphrey:
Treatise of military discipline 1466

Blane, Sir Gilbert:
Lecture on muscular motion 1591
*Observations on the diseases incident to
seamen* 1591

Blenheim. *See* Guides 2387:2

Blessings of P*** and a Scotch excise 1810:4

Bligh, Thomas. *See* Dodington 1608:87

Bligh, William:
*Narrative of the mutiny on board His
Majesty's Ship Bounty* 2802

Blizard, Sir William. *See* Jones 3784

Bloemaert, Abraham. *See* Prints 3605–6

Bloemaert, Cornelis. *See* Prints 3605–6

Blomberg, Carl Johann von:
Account of Livonia 1467

Blome, Richard:
Britannia 3271

Blomefield, Francis:
Collectanea Cantabrigiensia 649, 3226
*Essay towards a topographical history of
Norfolk* 588

Blondel, David:
Des Sibylles 1057

Blood, Thomas. *See* Tracts 3832:4

Bloomfield, John. *See* Bromfield 2534

Blount, Charles, Earl of Devonshire. *See*
Devonshire

Blount, Charles:
King William and Queen Mary conquerors
1608:1
Reasons humbly offered 1608:1, 7
See Account 1608:8; *Philostratus* 249

Blount, Martha. *See* Pope 1609:22

Blount, Thomas:
Boscobel 1996
*Fragmenta antiquitatis. Ancient tenures of
land* 327
See Estienne 1065

The blow. See Ingram 1609:22

Blunden, Henry. *See* Wit's recreations 2037

Blundering brothers. See Masquerader 2416

Boaden, James:
Fontainville forest 1810:54
Secret tribunal 1810:57

Boadicea, Queen. *See* Glover 1818:13

Boate, Gerard:
Irelands naturall history 147, 188, 1152,
2341

Boccaccio, Giovanni:
Ameto 3948
Contes et nouvelles. See Miscellaneous 943:3
Decamerone 2070, 2097
Boccalini, Trajano:
De' ragguagli di Parnasso 2098
I ragguagli di Parnasso, or advertisements from Parnassus 3293
Bodenehr, Johann Georg. *See* Perelle 3604
Bodenham, John:
Bel-vedere, or the garden of the muses 1997
Bodleian Library, Catalogue of. *See* Wise 230
Boehm, Andrew:
Metaphysica. See Helvétius 552
Boeotia. *See Compliment* 1608:73
Boethius, Anicius Manlius:
Of the consolation of philosophy 148
Bohemia. *See* Mauvillon 1162
Bohun, Edmund. *See* Blount 1608:1; Whear 1664
Boileau, Jacques:
Historia flagellantium 2209
Boileau-Despréaux, Nicolas:
Oeuvres 935, 3998
Boissard, Jean Jacques:
Bibliotheca chalcographica 3638
Topographia Romae 495
See Bry 365
Boissat, Pierre de:
Histoire généalogique de la Maison de Medicis 1244
Boisset, Paul Randon de:
Catalogue des tableaux. See Catalogues 3405:1
Boissy, Louis de. *See* Conway 1810:47
Boivin, François de, Baron du Villars. *See* Du Villars
Bokenham, Katharine (Knyvet). *See* Knyvet
Bolingbroke, Henry St. John, Viscount:
Last will and testament. See Tracts 2146:4
Letters on the spirit of patriotism 3159
Letters on the study of history 3159
Various tracts 1608:13
Works 3159
See Black-bird 2646:15; *Craftsman* 1471; Hill 465; *Memoirs* 52; Political tracts 94; Shenstone 3979; Walpole 59; Warburton 1608:34

Bollan, William:
Mutual interest of Great Britain and the American colonies 1609:56
Bolland, J. *See* Eginhardus 836
Bologna:
Catalogue of pictures 2532
Cloister of San Michele. *See* Malvasia 3624
Bolton, Edmund:
Cities advocate in this case 2649
Bolton, Robert:
On the employment of time 1608:62; 3949
Bolton, Thomas Orde-Powlett, 1st Baron. *See* Pitt 1609:47A
Bolts, William:
Considerations on Indian affairs 2803
Bon ton. See Garrick 1810:25
Bonafons, Louis Abel de:
Galerie du Palais Royal 3488
Bonanno. *See* Buonanni 3402
Bonarelli della Rovere, Prospero:
Il Solimano 3773
Bonasoni, Julio. *See* Cumberland 2367
Bonde, Gulielmus:
De Julii Clovii ... operibus libri tres 3689
Bonducci, Andrea. *See* Pope 2110; Thomson 1608:52
Bonesana, Cesare, Marchese di Beccaria. *See* Beccaria
Boniface VIII, Pope. *See* Rubeus 858
Bonnets, ou Talemik et Zinéra. See Contes François 1783:3
Bonze, or Chinese anchorite. See Downes 3919
Book of Common Prayer 1504, 1927, 2187
Book of Common Prayer: parody. See Lessons for the Day
Book of drawing. See Dürer 502
Book of Hours. See Missal
Book of jewels in the Tower of London. See Caesar 2535:9
Book of St. Albans. See Bernes 3772
Book of the visions of Zabdeel 1608:91
Booke containing the true portraiture of the Kings of England. See Tymme 1606
Books of Materials. See Walpole 2615
Boorde, Andrew. *See* Borde
Booth, George, 2d Earl of Warrington. *See* Warrington 181
Booth, Henry, 1st Earl of Warrington. *See* Warrington 181

Boothby, Sir Brooke:
  Sorrows sacred to the memory of Penelope 3707
  See Rousseau 3369
Borde, Andrew:
  Breviary of healthe 2650
Borde, Charles:
  Prediction 2050:15
  See Hume 1680:2
Bordeaux. *See* Devienne 3089
Borghese. *See* Montelatici 2316
Borioni, Antonio:
  Collectanea. See Venuti 3545
Borlase, William:
  Observations on the antiquities . . . of Cornwall 559
  Observations on the . . . Islands of Scilly 617
Born, Ignaz, Edler von:
  John Physiophilus's specimen of the natural history of monks 1609:45
Borromeo, Charles. *See* Charles Borromeo, Saint 1271
Bosboom, Simon:
  Brief and plain description of the five orders of columns of architecture 233
Boscawen, Mrs. Frances:
  One letter. *See* Letters 2576
Boschereccio, pseud. *See* Foote 3222:16
Boscobel. See Blount 1996
Bosio, Giacomo:
  Dell' Istoria della sacra religione 435
Bosse, Abraham:
  Traicté des manières de graver 3774
Bossewell, John:
  Works of armorie. See Legh 1073
Bossuet, Jacques Bénigne:
  Exposition. See Buckingham 69:2
Boston Massacre:
  Short narrative of the horrid massacre 1609:26
Boswell, James:
  Account of Corsica 3069
  Critical strictures on Elvira 1810:4
  Dorando 1609:19
  Essence of the Douglas Cause 1609:19
  Journal of a tour to the Hebrides 3069
  Letter to the people of Scotland 1609:47
  Life of Samuel Johnson 3294
  No abolition of slavery 3069

Boswell, James (*cont.*)
  See Douglas 1609:19; *Remarks* 1609:48; Scotland 1609:58; Wolcot 3222:20
Bosworth Field. *See* Hutton 2881
Botany Bay. *See* Phillip 2920
Botero, Giovanni:
  Cause of the greatnesse of cities 2804
Bottarelli, F. *See* Plays 3972
Bottari, Giovanni Gaetano, editor:
  Raccolta di lettere 2342
Boucher, François. *See* Drawings 3567
Boucher, Jean:
  Apologie pour Jehan Chastel 2343
Boucher d'Argis, Antoine:
  Variétés historiques 1153
Boucicaut, Jean Le Maingre de. *See* Collection 3084
Boufflers, Stanislas Jean de, Chevalier de Boufflers. *See* Drumgold 3920:3; Du Deffand 2545; Dutens 2306
Bougeant, Guillaume Hyacinthe:
  Amusement philosophique 1178
Bouhours, Dominique:
  Pensées ingénieuses 973, 1179
Bouillart, Jacques:
  Histoire de l'abbaye royale de Saint-Germain des Prez 868
Bouillon, Henri de la Tour d'Auvergne, Duc de. *See* Collection 3084
Boulanger, Nicolas Antoine:
  L'antiquité dévoilé par ses usages 3070
  See Holbach 3018
Boulster lecture. *See* Brathwait 1592
Boulter, Hugh:
  Letters to several ministers of state 2805
Bounce, Benjamin, pseud. *See* Carey, Henry
Bouquet, Henry. *See* Smith 1609:56
Bourbon, Armand de, Prince de Conti. *See* Conti 2670
Bourbon, House of. *See* Desormeaux 3088
Bourchier, John, 2d Baron Berners. *See* Berners
Bourdaloue, Louis:
  Sermons 1180
Bourdeille de Brantôme, Pierre de. *See* Brantôme
Boureau-Deslandes, André François:
  Histoire critique de la philosophie 974
Bourget, Jean:
  History of the Royal Abbey of Bec 2806

Bourlain, Joseph André. *See* Dumaniant

Bourne, Henry. *See* Brand 3806

Bourne, Vincent:
Poems. See Plays 1908:1

Boutet de Monvel, Jacques Marie:
Frédégonde et Brunéhaut 3295

Bow-Street Opera 1810:20

Bowack, John:
Antiquities of Middlesex 560

Bowdler, Thomas:
Letters written in Holland 2807

Bowen, Emanuel. *See* Ogilby 2437; Roads 2287

Bower, Archibald:
History of the Popes 460
See Baron 1608:31

Bowle, John:
One letter. *See* Letters 2576

Bowyer, Robert, Keeper of the Records in the Tower. *See* Cotton 2167

Bowyer, William, Keeper of the Records in the Tower. *See* Cotton 2167

Bowyer, William, printer. *See* Nichols 3349

Boxhorn, Marcus Zuerius:
Monumenta illustrium virorum, et elogia 3736
Theatrum 826

Boy and the wolf. See Black-bird 2646

Boyce, Thomas:
Harold 3222:20

Boyd, William. *See* Kilmarnock

Boydell, J. and J., publishers. *See* Antiquities 3485:15; Bartolozzi 3398

Boydell, John:
Collection of prints. 3561
See Combe 3566; Houghton 3572; Shakespeare 3904

Boyer, Abel:
Dictionnaire royal 916
History of King William III 1668
New French grammar 1210
See Hamilton 1479

Boyer, Jean Baptiste de. *See* Argens 1007

Boyer, Jean Baptiste, Marquis d'Aguilles:
Recueil d'estampes 3562

Boyle, Ann, Countess of Cork and Orrery. *See* Cork and Orrery

Boyle, Charles, 4th Earl of Orrery. *See* Orrery

Boyle, Francis, Viscount Shannon. *See* Shannon

Boyle, John, Earl of Cork and Orrery. *See* Cork and Orrery

Boyle, Mary, Countess of Warwick. *See* Warwick

Boyle, Richard, 3d Earl of Burlington. *See* Burlington

Boyle, Robert:
Disquisitions 3950
Philosophical works 1311
See Bentley 1366

Boyle, Roger, Earl of Orrery. *See* Orrery

Boys, John:
Workes 2651

Boys, William:
Collections for an history of Sandwich 234

Boyse, Samuel:
Historical review of the transactions of Europe 1669

Bozzy and Piozzi. See Wolcot 3222:21

Braamkamp, Gerret. *See* Catalogue 2302

Brabant, Duke of. *See* Francis, Duke of Anjou

Brabant. *See* Descamps 3307; Ireland 3857:2; Sanderus 532

Bracelli, Giovanni Battista:
Bizarie di varie figure 2344

Brackley, Viscount. *See* Ellesmere

Braddock, Edward. *See* Reasons 1608:81; Smith 1608:82

Bradshaw, William. *See* Turkish Spy 1766

Brady, Robert:
Full and clear answer to a book written by William Petyt 2652

Bragge, Dr. Robert:
Catalogue of . . . pictures. See Catalogues 3404

Bramston, James:
Art of Politicks 1886. *See* Tracts 2474:1
Crooked sixpence. See Poems 3363:9
Man of taste. See Poems 881:2

Branch, Thomas:
Thoughts on dreaming 1608:37

Brand, John:
History . . . of Newcastle upon Tyne 3160
Observations on popular antiquities 3806

Brandenburg. *See* Frederick II, the Great, King of Prussia

Brandenburg, House of. *See* Frederick II 1140

Brander, Gustavus. *See* Pegge 1609:41

Brandes, Johann Christian. *See* Holcroft 1810:49

Brandon, Charles and Henry, Dukes of Suffolk. *See* Wilson 402

Brandt, Geeraert:
Vie de Michel de Ruiter 891

Brantôme, Pierre de Bourdeille, Seigneur de:
Mémoires 1211
Spanish rhodomontades 2653
See Clouet 2357; *Collection* 3084; *Prints* 3655

Brathwait, Richard:
Ar't asleep husband? 1592
Drunken Barnaby's four journeys 2235, 2808
English gentleman 1058
English gentlewoman 1312
Natures embassie 1928
Strappado for the divell 1998
Survey of history 1999

Braun, Georg:
Civitates orbis terrarum 3675

Bray, William:
Sketch of a tour into Derbyshire and Yorkshire 2345, 3400

Brecknock, Timothy:
Droit le roy 1609:7

Brefe. See Brief

Bréquigny, Louis George Oudart Feudrix de:
Histoire des révolutions des Gênes 1181

Bretagne. *See* Lobineau 879

Bretez, Louis. *See* Paris 3578

Brett, John:
Conjugal love and duty 1608:88
Tracts 1367

Brettingham, Matthew:
Plans . . . of Holkham Hall 3401

Breval, John Durant:
Compleat key to the Non-Juror 1608:17, 18

Brice, Germain:
Description nouvelle de la ville de Paris 3071

Bridges, John:
History . . . of Northampton 1, 561

Bridges, Noah:
Stenographie and cryptographie 777

Bridges, Sir Samuel Egerton. *See* Brydges

Bridges, Thomas:
Dutch-man 1810:24

Bridgewater, Elizabeth Churchill, Countess of. *See Black-bird* 2646:24

Brief account of Georgia. See Stephens 1608:40

Brief and plesaunte worke. See Hill 787

Brief and short discourse. See Hill 787

Brief for Her Grace the Duchess of Kingston. See Kingston 1609:58

Brief narrative of the late campaigns. See Townshend 1608:32

Brief view of the conduct of Pennsylvania. See Smith 1608:82

Briefe. See Brief

Brienne. *See* Loménie de Brienne

Briggs, William:
Opthalmo-graphia 1731

Brightland, John:
Grammar of the English tongue 2000

Bril, Paulus. *See Drawings* 3569

Brindley's Latin Classics 2120

Brissot de Warville, Jean Pierre. *See* Clavière 3230

Bristol, Augustus John Hervey, 3d Earl of:
Letter 1608:27
See Detection 1608:27; *Objections* 1608:27

Bristol, Elizabeth Chudleigh, Countess of, calling herself Duchess of Kingston. *See* Kingston

Bristol, Frederick Augustus Hervey, 4th Earl of:
One or more letters. See Letters 2576

Bristol, George Digby (1612–1677), 2d Earl of:
Speech in House of Lords 2533
Speech in the House of Lords. See Tracts 2769:7
Speeches 2654
Two speeches. See Tracts 2769:8

Bristol, George William Hervey, 2d Earl of. *See* England 1609:54

Bristol, John Digby (1580–1653), 1st Earl of:
Apologie. See Tracts 2769:9
Speech. See Tracts 2769:6

Bristol:
New history . . . of Bristol 2809
See Barrett 539; *Watts* 3528

Bristol guide. See Bristol 2809

Britain, Jonathan:
History of the life 1609:29

Britannia illustrata. See London 3623
Britannia sancta. See Challoner 619
British bellman 1313
British blood-hounds. See Black-bird 2646:6
British compendium. See Nichols 755
British Critic. See Magazines 3338
British Gazetteer. See Weekly 2147
British Journal. See Weekly 2147
British librarian. See Oldys 700, 2735
British Merlin. See Walpole 2622
British Museum:
    Catalogue of Manuscripts. See Ayscough 3225
    Catalogue of the Harleian collection 218
    See Rymsdyk 3555; Thomson 2965
Britons. *See Evidence* 1609:35
Broad-bottom. See Interest 1608:43
Brodrick, Thomas:
    Compleat history of the late war in the Netherlands 1638
Broglie, Victor François, Duc de:
    Politique de tous les cabinets de l'Europe 3072
Brome, Alexander:
    Covent Garden drolery 1929
    Songs and other poems 1930
Brome, James:
    Account of Mr. Rogers's three years travels over England and Wales 717
Bromfield, John:
    Notes, strictures, and corrections to Walpole's Anecdotes of Painting 2534
    Two letters. See Letters 2576
Bromley, Sir George:
    Collection of letters 3227
Bromley, Henry:
    Catalogue of engraved British portraits 3807
Bromley, J., pseud. *See* Freeman 1818:7
Bromley, William:
    Remarks in the grand tour of France and Italy 291
    Several years travels through Portugal, Spain, Italy, Germany, Prussia, Sweden 1396
Brooke, Frances:
    Airs, songs, duetts 1810:45
    Rosina 1810:35
    Siege of Sinope 1810:32

Brooke, Fulke Greville, Baron:
    Certaine learned and elegant workes 30
    Life of Sidney 1931
    Remains 149
Brooke, Henry, Baron Cobham. *See* Cobham
Brooke, Henry:
    Earl of Essex 1810:1
    See Moore 1834
Brooke, Nathaniel. *See England's glory* 2687
Brooke, Ralph:
    Catalogue . . . of the kings, princes, . . . of this realme 2346
    See Vincent 642
Brooke, Robert Greville, Baron:
    Discourse 68
    Nature of Truth 150
Brooke, Zachary:
    Defensio miraculorum. See Middleton 1337:5
    Examination of Dr. Middleton's Free Inquiry. See Middleton 1379:2
    See Epistle 1379:7
Broome, William. *See* Homer 63
Brother Peter to Brother Tom. See Wolcot 3222:22
Brotherhood of the Holy Ghost. *See* Loggon 696
The brothers. See Cumberland 1810:15
The brothers. See Young 1818:12
Broughton, Hugh:
    Concent of Scripture 2347
Broughton, John. *See* Chatterton 3408, 3690:3, 14
Broughton, Richard:
    Monastichon Britannicum 718
Broughton, Thomas:
    Dictionary of all religions 1091
Broughton, Sir Thomas:
    Speech . . . at . . . Stafford 2966
Brousson, Claude. *See* Louis XIV 1608:23
Brown, John:
    Athelstan 1818:14
    Barbarossa 1818:14
    Cure of Saul 3222:4
    Essay on satire. See Poems 3363
    Honour. See Poems 3363
    Letter to the Rev. Dr. Lowth 1609:12
    Ode to the Legislator Elect of Russia 3222:7

Brown, John, surgeon:
Adenochoiradelogia 2655
Brown, Lady Margaret:
One or more letters. *See* Letters 2576
Brown, Peter:
New illustrations of zoologie 3869
Brown, Thomas (1663–1704). *See* Clifford 1608:1
Brown, W. *See Loves of Mirtil* 381
Browne, Alexander:
Ars pictoria 3851
Browne, Edward:
Account of several travels through . . . Germany 827
Brief account of some travels in Hungary, Servia, Bulgaria [&c.] 827
Browne, Isaac Hawkins:
The fireside. See Poems 280:16
Pipe of tobacco. See Tracts 2474:7
Browne, John. *See* Brown, John
Browne, Joseph. *See* Urban VIII 1362
Browne, Magdalena, Viscountess Montagu. *See* Smith 2294
Browne, Sir Thomas:
Christian morals 2001
Posthumous works 676
Pseudodoxia epidemica 496
Religio medici 1732
True Christian morals 778
Browne, William:
Works 2656
Browne, Sir William:
Ode in imitation of Horace 3222:4
Brownsmith, John:
The rescue 3222:8
Bruce, Charles, Lord Bruce, Earl of Elgin:
One letter. *See* Letters 2576
Bruce, James:
Travels 4018
Bruhier d'Ablaincourt, Jacques Jean:
Caprices d'imagination 1245
Brumoy, Pierre:
Théâtre des Grecs 1268
See Margat 1040
Brunet, Pierre Nicolas:
Abrégé chronologique des grands fiefs de la couronne de France 1289
Bruni Aretino, Leonardo:
Epistolarum libri VIII 2071

Brunswick-Luneburg, Ferdinand, Duke of. *See* Ferdinand 3167
Brunton, Anna Ross:
Cottagers 1810:45
Bruscambille:
Oeuvres 803
Bruslé de Montpleinchamp, Jean Chrysostome:
Histoire des ducs de Bourgogne 1212
Brutus, Marcus. *See* Tunstall 1424
Bruzen de la Martinière, Antoine Augustin:
Nouveau recueil des épigrammatistes françois 1290
Bry, Johann Theodor de:
Florilegium novum 3737
Bry, Theodor de:
Icones 365
Bryan, Sir Francis. *See* Guevara 199
Bryant, Jacob:
Address to Dr. Priestly 1609:41
Farther illustration 1609:39
New system 3161
Observations 3161
See Chatterton 3690:5; Wood 37
Brydges, Grey. *See* Chandos 190
Brydges, Sir Samuel Egerton:
Mary de Clifford 2348
See Topographer 3831; *Topographical Miscellanies* 3795
Brydone, Patrick:
Tour through Sicily and Malta 2810
Brydson, Thomas:
Summary view of heraldry 1314
Buccleugh, Lady Elizabeth Montagu, later Duchess of. *See* Montagu
Buchan, David Stewart Erskine, 11th Earl of:
Discourse at a meeting 1609:42
See Etchings 3588
Buchanan, George:
Poemata quae extant 2236
Buck, Sir George:
History of . . . Richard the Third 475
Buck, Samuel *and* Nathaniel:
Antiquities. See Antiquities 3485
Buckeridge, John. *See* Buckridge
Buckingham, Edward Stafford, 3d Duke of. *See* Hetoum 2397
Buckingham, George Villiers, 1st Duke of. *See* Crowe 2544; Vertue 2479:3

Buckingham, George Villiers, 2d Duke of:
  Rehearsal. See Plays 1910:1
  Short discourse 69, 1608:93
  See Tracts 3832:4
Buckingham, John Sheffield, Duke of:
  Works 448
Buckinghamshire, John Hobart, 2d Earl of:
  One letter. *See* Letters 2576
Buckinghamshire. *See* Kennet 627; Willis 644
Buckridge, John. *See* Burgess, James
Budgell, Eustace:
  Memoirs of the life . . . of the late Earl of Orrery 1670
Budget. See Hartley 1609:55
Buerger. *See* Bürger
Buffier, Claude:
  Grammaire françoise sur un plan nouveau 1213
Buffon, Jean Louis Leclerc, Comte de:
  Histoire naturelle 2152
Buirette de Belloy, Pierre Laurent. *See* Belloy
Bull, John, pseud.:
  Last will and testament. See Detection 2677:9
Bull, Richard:
  Lines sent to Lady Miller's vase 3222:18
  One letter. *See* Letters 2576
Buller, Mrs. Mary:
  One letter. *See* Letters 2576
Bullet, Jean Baptiste:
  Recherches historiques sur les cartes à jouer 3073
Bullot, Maximilien. *See* Helyot 1141
Bulstrode, Sir Richard:
  Memoirs and reflections 1701
  Miscellaneous essays 2002
  Original letters 1429
Bulwer, John:
  Anthropometamorphosis 2657
Bunbury, Henry William:
  Academy for grown horesmen 3913
  Annals of horsemanship 3914
  Collection of 280 etchings 3563
  See Shakespeare 3905
Buncle, John, Esq. *See* Amory 1636
Buonamici, Pietro Giuseppe Maria, Conte:
  Commentariorum de bello Italico 2300
Buonanni, Filippo:
  Recreatio mentis et oculi 3402

Buonarroti, Filippo:
  Osservazioni istoriche 263
Buonarroti, Michel Agnolo, the Younger:
  Il giudizio di Paride. See Cosmo II 2304:1
Burchard, Johann:
  Specimen historiae arcanae 828
Burd, Richard:
  Two sermons. See Derby 79:4
Bure, Guillaume de. *See* La Vallière 3335
Bürger, Gottfried August:
  Leonora 2349
Burges, Sir James Bland. *See* Tomkins 3471
Burgess, Daniel. *See* Miscellaneous tracts 89:1
Burgess, James:
  Lives of the painters 1608:78
  See Piles 308
Burgess, Thomas, Bishop:
  Bagley 3222:15
Burgh, Ulick de. *See* Clanricarde 115
Burgh, William. *See* Mason 3897
Burgher. *See* Bürger
Burghers, Michael:
  Drawings. *See* Walpole 2622
Burghley, William Cecil, Baron. *See* Cecil
Burgmaier, Hans:
  Woodcuts. *See* Prints 3656
Burgoyne, General John:
  Heiress 1810:38
  Letter to his constituents 1609:40
  Lord of the manor 1810:32
  Maid of the oaks 1810:22
  Richard Coeur de Lion 1810:39
  State of the expedition from Canada 3489
  Substance of speeches 1609:39
Burgundy, Dukes of. *See* Bruslé 1212; Des Salles 919
Burgundy. *See* Heuterus 2124
Burgundy, Chronicle of. *See* Vignier 864
Burigny, Jean de:
  Vie de Grotius 1182
Burke, Edmund:
  Letter on the affairs of America 1609:38
  Observations 1609:57
  Reflections on the revolution in France 1609:46
  Speech in Bristol 1609:41
  Speech on American taxation 1609:58
  Speech on Mr. Fox's East India Bill 1609:46

Burke, Edmund (*cont.*)
Speech . . . on moving his resolutions for conciliation 1609:58
Speech on presenting a plan 1609:40
Speeches at his arrival at Bristol 1609:58
Substance of the speech on the Army estimates 1609:53
Thoughts on the cause of the present discontents 1609:57
Two letters 1609:39
See Abington 1609:38; *Begum* 3222:22; England 1609:40; Fox 1609:46; Hastings 1609:49; Knox 1609:22; Macaulay 1609:26; Magazines (*Annual Register*) 3338; Stanhope 1609:53; Tucker 1609:35
Burke, William:
Letters of Valens 1609:38
See Examination 1609:5
Burkitt, William:
Expository notes 3870
Burleigh. See Cecil, William
Burlington, Dorothy Savile, Countess of. See Etchings 3588
Burlington, Richard Boyle, 3d Earl of. See Jones 3538; Palladio 3577
Burman, Charles. See Ashmole 1501; Tracts 360:1
Burmannus, Petrus. See Ovidius 2286; Velleius Paterculus 2207:41
Burn, Richard *and* Nicolson, Joseph:
History . . . of . . . Westmorland and Cumberland 3162
Burnet, Gilbert, Bishop:
Essay on the late Queen 1733
Exposition 830
History of his own time 1092
History of the reformation of the Church of England 1105
Letter on His Majesty's Declaration 1608:8
Life of Sir Mathew Hale 1702
Life of the Earl of Rochester 1703
Reflections 1608:19
Sermon 1608:19
Six papers 829
Burnet, Thomas, D.D.:
Essay upon government 1734
Burnet, Thomas, LL.D.:
Theory of the earth 1106

Burnet, Sir Thomas:
Certain information 1608:9
Second tale of a tub 1779
Some new proofs 1608:9
Summary. See Duckett 683
Verses written on several occasions 3222:15
Burney, Charles:
Account of the musical performances . . . in commemoration of Handel 461
Cunning man 1810:9
General history of music 3163
Memoirs of Metastasio 2811
Present state of music 1368
See Account 1609:47A
Burney, Frances, later Mme. d'Arblay:
Brief reflections relative to the emigrant French clergy 2812
Camilla 2812
Cecilia 2812
Evelina 2812
Burns, Robert:
Poems 2813
Burr, Thomas Benge:
History of Tunbridge-Wells 677
Burrell, Sophia, Lady:
Poems 2814
Thymbriad 1846
Burroughs, Samuel:
Enquiry 1608:21
Burrow, Sir James:
Few anecdotes and observations 1609:6
See Millar 1609:58
Burt, Edward:
Letters 1430
Burton, John, of York:
Monasticon Eboracense 562
Burton, John, D.D.:
Epistola 1608:70
Remarks 1608:70
Burton, William:
Description of Leicestershire 618
Bury, Richard de:
Histoire de la vie de Henri IV 3002
Busbecq, Augerius Gislenius, Sieur de. See Gislenius 2122
Bussières, Jean de:
Parterre historique 1154
Bussy, Comte de. See Rabutin 968, 1002

Butcher, Richard:
Survey . . . of . . . Stamford and Tottenham High-Cross 650. *See* Peck 577
Bute, John Stuart, 3d Earl of. *See* Almon 1609:6, 28; Churchill 3222:4; *Letter* 1609: 56; *Letter* 1609:54; *Letter* 1609:3; *Third Letter* 1609:5; *Triumphs* 3222:11
Buthred 1810:29
Butler, James, Duke of Ormonde. *See* Ormonde
Butler, John, Bishop:
Address to the Cocoa-Tree. 1609:54
Serious considerations 1609:54
Some account of . . . Henry Bilson Legge 1609:56
Butler, Joseph, Bishop:
Analogy of religion 3228
Charge delivered to the clergy 1609:49
Butler, Samuel:
Genuine remains in verse and prose 1821
Hudibras 1822, 1865, 3179
Posthumous works 1887
Buxom Joan. See Willet 1810:29
By-stander. *See* Morris, Corbyn
Byng, George, 1st Viscount Torrington. *See* Torrington
Byng, Hon. John, Admiral:
Bundle of tracts 3403
See Constitution 1608:84; *Tracts* 2146:3
Byres, James. *See* Agincourt
Byrne, William, engraver. *See* Hearne 3429, 3645
Byron, Isabella, Countess of Carlisle. *See* Carlisle
Byron, John:
Narrative of the Honourable John Byron 1609:20
See Voyage 1609:17
Byron, Hon. Richard. *See* Etchings 3588
Byron, William, Baron Byron:
Trial of William Lord Byron 1107
See Circumstantial 1609:56
Bysshe, Edward:
Art of English poetry 1888
See Xenophon 1697

C., G., translator. *See* Weidenfeld 866
C., J. *See* Cleveland 1933
C., Ro. *See* Sherley 3828

C., T. *See* Cibber, Theophilus
C., W. *See* Lyly 2724
Cabal and love 1810:57
Cabala 892
Cabinet des fées 3074
Cabinet du Bourgmestre Reynst. See Reynst 3579
Cabinet du Roi. See Louis XIV 3591
Cabinet Jésuitique 1269
Cabinet of Fancy. See Stevens 1810:35
Cacophron, pseud. *See* Leone, Gabriel
Cadière, Marie Catherine:
Recueil général des pièces concernant la Demoiselle Cadière et le Père Girard 1023
Cadogan, William:
Dissertation on the gout 1609:28
See Shebbeare 1609:31
Cady of Bagdad. See Portal 1810:27
Caen Wood. *See* Adam 3597
Caernarvonshire. See Owen 2914
Caesar, Caius Julius:
Commentaries 1780
Guerre des Suisses 497
Opera 2207:9, 2237
See Brindley 2120:1; Sigismund 3632
Caesar, Charles:
Numerus infaustus 2815
Caesar, Sir Julius:
Travelling library 3775
Various MSS 2535
Caesar Germanicus. *See* Beaufort 1267
Cagliostro, Alessandro, Conte di, assumed name of Giuseppe Balsamo:
Lettre au peuple anglois 1609:48
Cailleau, Charles André. *See* Catalogues 2819
Caimo, Norberto:
Voyage d'Espagne 3075
Calà, Carlo, Duca di Diano:
Memorie historiche dell' apparitione delle Croci prodigiose 2072
Calabria. *See* Naples 3509
Calais. *See* Tencin 3149
Calamy, Edmund:
Compleat collection of farewell sermons. See Sermons 2755
Calculation of the solar eclipses. See Whiston 1608:37
Calculations and tables. See Abercorn 142
Calder, John. *See* Tatler 2963

Calder, Robert. *See* Crockat 1608:24

Calderon de la Barca, Pedro. *See* Bickerstaffe 1810:16; Kemble 1810:46, 47

Calendar of Flora. See Stillingfleet 1609:4

Caliari, Paolo. *See* Drawings 3568

Callimachus:
   Hymni 2207:10

Callistratus. *See* Philostratus 2161

Callot, Jacques:
   Collection of published engravings 2350
   Drawings 2351
   See Bonarelli 3773; Drawings 3569

Calmet, Augustin:
   Dissertation upon the high roads. See Duckett 683:2

Calonne, Charles Alexandre de:
   Catalogue of paintings 3833:1
   See Necker 3035

Calotte:
   Recueil des pièces du Régiment de la Calotte 1270

Calvert, Frederick, 6th Baron Baltimore. *See* Baltimore

Calvin, John. *See* Sadoleto 859

Cambiaso, Luca. *See* Drawings 3569

Cambrai, Archbishop of. *See* Fénelon 1741

Cambrai, Histoire de la Ligue faite à. See Dubos 805

Cambray, Sieur de. *See* Chambray

Cambridge, Richard Owen:
   Account of the war in India 449
   See Poems 3363

Cambridge:
   Cantabrigia depicta. See Guides 2387
   See Blomefield 649, 3226; London 3623

Cambridge University:
   Academiae Cantabrigiensis luctus 12
   Excerptae statutis 1608:18
   Gratulatio academiae Cantabrigiensis 498
   History and antiquities 678
   Pietas academiae Cantabrigiensis in funere ... Wilhelminae Carolinae 2042
   See Scott 4014; Stebbing 1608:70; Thirlby 1608:11

Cambridge University:
   Corpus Christi College. *See* Masters 632; Nasmith 3347; Stanley 583; Tractatus 3383
   Trinity College. *See* Paris 1608:11

Camden, Charles Pratt, 1st Earl:
   Inquiry 1608:87

Camden, Charles Pratt, 1st Earl (*cont.*)
   One letter. *See* Letters 2576
   See Tooke 1609:25

Camden, William:
   Annals 2166
   Britannia 424, 563
   Remaines concerning Britain 1059

Camelford, Thomas Pitt, Baron. *See* Fox 1609:45; *Letter* 1609:42

Cameron, Jenny. *See* Kilmarnock 2717

Camisards:
   Histoire des Camisards 1291

Camoens, Luis de:
   Lusiad 1809

Campagne ... en Allemagne. See Noailles 815

Campanile, Filiberto:
   L'Armi, overo insegne de' nobili 235

Campbell, Anne, Countess of Argyle. *See* Argyle

Campbell, Archibald:
   Lexiphanes 2658
   Sale of authors 366, 2658

Campbell, Archibald, 3d Duke of Argyle. *See* Argyle

Campbell, Archibald, 1st Marquess of Argyle. *See* Argyle

Campbell, Miss Caroline. *See* Conway 3222:22

Campbell, Colin. *See* Stewart 1722

Campbell, George:
   Dissertation on miracles 2659

Campbell, J.:
   Letter ... occasion'd by the case of ... Thomas Winnington 1608:89

Campbell, John (1708–75):
   Character of Pericles 1608:53
   Lives of the admirals 1671
   Political survey of Britain 1397
   Present state of Europe 1397
   See Bengal 1609:2; *Biographia* 2041; Cohausen 1469; Harris 432; *Regulations* 1609:11

Campbell, John (fl. 1736). *See* MacUre 2725

Campbell, John, 4th Duke of Argyle. *See* Argyle

Campbell, Lady Mary. *See* Coke

Campbell, Mungo, defendant:
   Trial of Mungo Campbell 1609:26

Camper, Petrus. *See* Monkeys 3884

Campion, Edmund. *See* Ware 2182

Camus, Jean Pierre:
True tragical history of two illustrious Italian families 2816

Canada. *See Black-bird* 2646:23; Burgoyne 3489; Cockings 1810:8; Meredith 1609:32

Candia. *See* Ceylon

Candid and impartial account 1608:54

Candid observations on the principal performances. See Royal Academy 3885:12

Candide. See Voltaire 1307

Candidus. *See* Smith, William

Candor, pseud. *See Letter* 1609:8

Candour, or an occasional essay. See Poems 280:8

Canini, Giovanni Angelo:
Iconografia 3738

Canning, Elizabeth. *See* Fielding 1608:77; Hill 1608:77; Ramsay 352

Canning, W.:
Gesta Grayorum 108

Canons of criticism. See Edwards 1608:66

Canons of the Church of Scotland. See Scotland 1609:57

Cantelmo, Andreas. *See* Capoa 2073

Cantelupe, Nicholas. *See* Cambridge University 678

Cantelupe, Thomas de, Saint:
Life 1505

Canterbury, George Abbot, Archbishop of. *See* Oldys 417

Canterbury:
Cathedral. *See* Dart 428
Coins. *See* Pegge 246
Court. *See* Mendes 382
See Duncombe 2840; Gostling 2858; Somner 667

Canute, King of England. *See* Mead 3785

Caoursin, Gulielmus:
Obsidionis Rhodie urbis descriptio 3739

Capaccio, Giulio Cesare:
Gli apologi 3296

Capel, Arthur, Baron Capel:
Daily observations 70, 109
Excellent contemplations, divine and moral 151

Capell, Edward:
Prolusions 2003

Capellen, Joan Derk, Baron van der:
Address 1609:43

Capo Ferro da Cagli, Ridolfo:
Gran simulacro dell'arte 499

Capoa, Lionardo di:
Vita di D. Andrea Cantelmo 2073

Cappello, Bianca. *See* Gualterotti 3781

Caprarola Palace. *See* Zuccaro 3560

Capriata, Pietro Giovanni:
History of the wars in Italy 3297

Caprices d'imagination. See Bruhier 1245

Capricious lady. See Cooke 1810:35

The Captive. See Bickerstaffe 1810:14

Captives. See Delap 1810:39

Caracci, Annibale. *See* Carracci

Caraccioli, Charles:
Antiquities of Arundel 2817

Caraccioli, Louis Antoine de:
L'Europe françoise 3076
Vie de Madame de Maintenon 3077
Vie du Pape Clement XIV 3003

*Caractères, par Madame de P****. See* Puisieux 1203

Caractères, pensées, maximes, et sentimens. See Dupuy 1188

Carausius. *See* Stukeley 522

Caravaggio, Michel Angiolo da. *See* Drawings 3568–9

Caravaggio, Polydoro da. *See* Drawings 3568–9

Carcani, Pasquale. *See* Herculaneum 3590

Cardano, Girolamo:
Cardanus comforte 71

Cardenas, Bernardino de. *See* Bernardino de Cardenas

Cardinals of Rome, history of present. See Cogan 722

Cardon, Anthony. *See* Raphael 3514

Cardross, Lord. *See* Buchan

Care, Henry. *See Weekly Pacquet* 865

Carew, Sir George. *See* Stafford 3375

Carew, Richard:
Survey of Cornwall 651

Carew, Thomas:
Poems 1889

Carey, George Saville:
Liberty chastised 1810:13
Magic girdle 3222:10
Noble pedlar 3222:11
Old women weatherwise 1810:16
Shakespeare's jubilee 1810:15
See Momus 3222:8

Carey, Henry, Earl of Monmouth. *See* Monmouth

Carey, Henry:
Chrononhotonthologos 1818:5
Margery 1818:20

Carey, Robert, Earl of Monmouth. *See* Monmouth.

Carib Indians. *See Authentic* 1609:58

Carini, Signor, *See* Carey, Henry

Carion, Johann:
Thre bokes of cronicles 831

Carlell, Lodowick:
Arviragus and Philicia 1932

Carleton, Dudley, Viscount Dorchester. *See* Dorchester

Carleton, George, Bishop:
Thankful remembrance 3776

Carleton, Captain George:
History of the two last wars against France and Spain 1352

Carleton, Lionel. *See* Charlton 3182

Carlisle, Charles Howard, 1st Earl of. *See* Miège 1532

Carlisle, Frederick Howard, 5th Earl of:
Father's revenge 3222:20
Funeral oration for Louis XVI. See Vyner 3834
Poems 3222:12
To Sir Joshua Reynolds 3222:20
See Auckland 40

Carlisle, Isabella (Byron) Howard, Countess of:
Thoughts in the form of maxims 2301
See Etchings 3588

Carlisle, Margaret Caroline Leveson-Gower, Countess of:
One or more letters. *See* Letters 2576

Carlos, Don. *See* Charles VI, Emperor of Germany

Carlos, King of Naples. *See* Charles III, King of Spain

Carlyle, Alexander:
Question relating to a Scots militia 1609:5

Carmarthen, Francis Godolphin Osborne, Marquess of, later 5th Duke of Leeds. *See* Leeds

Carmina novem poetriarum. See Ursinus 2609

Carmontelle, N.:
Théâtre de campagne 3004

Carnarvonshire. *See* Owen 2914

Caroline Mathilde, Queen Consort of Christian VII, King of Denmark:
Account of the late revolution 1609:29

Caroline Wilhelmina, Queen Consort of George II:
Epitaphium Reginae Carolinae. See Tracts 2146:3
See Cambridge University 2042; Clarke 1608:67; Oxford University 2046; Poems 280:3; Sandford 3282

Caron de Beaumarchais, Pierre Augustin. *See* Beaumarchais 2335

Carr, Henry. *See Weekly Pacquet* 865

Carr, William. *See* Tracts 360:3

Carracci, Agostino. *See* Carracci 3599

Carracci, Annibale:
Portfolio of 245 engravings 3599
See Drawings 3568; Farnese 3619

Carracci, Lodovico. *See* Carracci 3599; Malvasia 3624

Carte, Thomas:
Life of James, Duke of Ormonde 1672
See Baudier 1608:36; Morris 1608:41; Squire 1608:61; Thou 3556; Winnington 1696

Carter, Francis:
Journey from Gibraltar to Malaga 2818

Carter, John:
Drawings and Sketches. See Walpole 3582
Specimens of . . . sculpture and painting 3564
See Drawings 3678; Topham 3472

Carter, Mary:
One letter. *See* Letters 2576

Carter, Matthew:
Honor redivivus 719

Carter, William. *See* Cartwright

Carteret, John, Earl Granville. *See* Granville

Carthusian Friar 1810:52

Carthusians, Coins and Medals of. *See Catalogue* 236

Cartier de Saint Philip. *See Passe-Tems* 1046

Cartwright, Christopher:
Certamen religiosum 72

Cartwright, Edmund:
Armine and Elvira 3222:11
Constantia 3222:9
Prince of peace 3222:16

Cartwright, William (*ca.* 1730–99). *See* Tracts 2050:13

Carwitham, John:
Floor-decorations 1608:91

Cary, Grace:
England's Forewarning 2536

Cary, Henry, 1st Viscount Falkland. *See* Falkland

Cary, Lucius, Viscount Falkland. *See* Falkland

Casaubon, Isaac. *See* Augustan 2084

Casaubon, Meric. *See* Dee 1109

Case and memoirs of James Hackman. See Hackman 1609:40

Case between T– D– and W– T– 1608:7

Case of Dunkirk considered. See Political tracts 94:2

Case of His Grace the Duke of Portland. See Portland 1609:20

Case of our present theatrical dispute. See Ralph 1608:45

Case of ship mony. See Tracts 3797:7

Case of the Chief Justice of Gibraltar. See Narrative, Tracts 2049:11

Case of the County of Devon. See Heath 1609:54

Case of the Dissenting ministers. See Mauduit 1609:29

Case of the Dutch ships. See Marriott 1608:87

Case of the Genoese 1608:44

Case of the Hanover forces. See Waller 1608:43, 46

Case of the late election for the County of Middlesex. See Dyson 1609:57

Case of the Opposition. See Political tracts 94:5

Case of the Protestant Dissenters. See Horsley 1609:53

Case of the revival of the salt duty. See Political tracts 94:7

Case of the unfortunate Martha Sophia Swordfeager. See Swordfeager 3522

Caserta. Royal Palace. *See* Vanvitelli 3596

Cash, John. *See* Pool 3255

Casley, David:
Catalogue of the manuscripts of the King's Library 476

Caslon, William:
Specimen of printing types 292
See Jones 3784

Cassandra, pseud.:
Letter to the Bishop of London 1609:50

Cassandra 367

Cassette verte. See Tickell 1609:40

Cassiodorus, Magnus Aurelius. *See* Sainte-Marthe 1207

Castaing, John:
Interest book 1155

Casteels, Peter:
Twelve months of flowers 3565

Castell of love. See San Pedro 208

Castellamonte, Amedeo di:
Venaria reale 3676

Castelnau, Michel de. *See Collection* 3084

Casti, Giovanni Battista. *See* Music 3448

Castiglione, Giovanni Benedetto. *See* Drawings 3568–9

Castlehaven, James Touchet, Earl of:
Earl of Castlehavens Review 152

Castlemaine, Roger Palmer, Earl of:
Account of the late war between the English and Dutch 2660
Account of the war between the Venetians and Turks 153, 2660
Accounts of debts 2537
Apology in behalf of the Papists 110
Catholique apology 154, 2661
Compendium 73
English globe 74
Manifesto 155
Short account of the war between the English and Dutch 156
See Wright 3687

Castres. *See* Sabatier de Castres

Castro, John de. *See* Freire 2172

Casuistical essay. See Webster 1608:60

Caswall, George:
Trifler 3222:7

Cat, Christopher. *See* Kit-Cat Club 3501

Catalogue 2302, 3078

Catalogue:
Complete catalogue of all the English books printed since the year 1700 2662
Catalogue de dessins. See Huquier 339
Catalogue de diamans. See Catalogues 2303:2
Catalogue d'objets rare et curieux . . . de tableaux des écoles d'Italie, de Flandres, de Hollande. See Catalogues 2303
Catalogue d'une collection de tableaux. See Catalogues 2303:1

Catalogue d'une riche collection. See Catalogues 2303

Catalogue historique du cabinet . . . de Monsieur de La Live. See La Live de Jully 3332

Catalogue of curiosities chiefly theatrical 1818:9

Catalogue of five hundred living authors. See Marshall 3819

Catalogue of Greek, Roman and English coins . . . of . . . Edward Earl of Oxford. See Collins 2359:1

Catalogue of paintings . . . by the Free and and Independent Artists. See Royal Academy 3885:14

Catalogue of pictures. See Catalogue 2302; Royal Academy 3885:5

Catalogue of pictures in fourteen palaces at Bologna. See Bologna 2532

Catalogue of plants copyed from nature. See Delany 1609:47, 2369

Catalogue of Strawberry Hill books. See Collection 2506

Catalogue of the chancellors. See Philipot 1608:1

Catalogue of the coins and medals of the Carthusians bought by the Emperor Charles VI 236

Catalogue of the coins of Canute. See Mead 3785

Catalogue of the collection [of paintings and antiquities, prints and a few books of prints] *of . . . Edward Earl of Oxford. See* Collins 2359:2

Catalogue of the Countess of Oxford's miniatures. See Collins 2359:3

Catalogue of the English portraits. See Walpole 2163

Catalogue of the library at Strawberry Hill. See Walpole 2164

Catalogue of the Lords of Session. See Dalrymple 1609:56, 57

Catalogues:
328, 2303, 2819, 3079–80, 3404–5
See Tracts 2050, 3833

Catalogues of the collections of the Duke of Devonshire. See Collection 2507:4; London 697

Catalogus librorum bibliothecae. See Middle Temple 484

Catalogus librorum manuscriptorum. See Nasmith 3347; Stanley 583

Catastrophe Mundi 2352

Catch Club. *See Whittington's Feast* 1810:26

Catches. *See New Collection of catches*

Catesby, Mark:
Natural history of Carolina 3617

Catharine II, Empress of Russia:
Ivan Czarowitz 550
See Houghton 3572

Catharine and Petruchio. See Garrick 1818:14

Cathedrals. Views. *See* Antiquities 3485:14

Catherine, of Braganza, Queen of England. *See* Argyle 2329

Catherine Parr, Queen Consort of King Henry VIII:
One letter. *See* Letters 2576

Catholic Church. *See* Scotland 1609:57

Catholique apology. See Castlemaine 154, 2661

Catilina, Lucius Sergius. *See* Crébillon 1174:1

Catiline's conspiracy 3222:17

Catullus, Caius Valerius:
Catulli, Tibulli, Propertii opera 2120, 2188, 2210, 2238, 2267
See Brindley 2120:2

Caus, Isaac de. *See* Wilton 3667

Caus, Salomon de:
Hortus Palatinus 3777
La Perspective 3708

Causeo, Michel Angelo. *See* La Chausse

Causidicade. See Satires 2319

Cavallier, Jean:
Memoirs of the wars of the Cevennes 3406

Cavan, Richard Lambart, Earl of:
New system of military discipline 3180

Caveat against concluding this session 1608:38

Caveat on the part of public credit 1609:56

Cavendish, Christiana, Countess of Devonshire. *See* Devonshire

Cavendish, Gilbert. *See* Chandos 190

Cavendish, Margaret, Duchess of Newcastle. *See* Newcastle

Cavendish, Sir William (1505?–57). *See* Grove 1521

Cavendish, William, Duke of Devonshire. *See* Devonshire

Cavendish, William, 1st Duke of Newcastle. *See* Newcastle

Cavendish, William, later 2d Earl of Devon-shire. *See* Chandos 190

Cavendish family. *See* Collins 565

Caxton, William. *See* Lewis 273

Cayet, Pierre Victor Palma. *See* Collection 3084

Caylus, Anne Claude Philippe de Tubières, Comte de:
L'Histoire d'Hercule le Thebain 293
Recueil d'antiquités Egyptiennes 477
Tableaux tirés de l'Iliade, de l'Odyssée d'Homère et de l'Énéide de Virgile 294
See Müntz 347; Vinci 3765

Caylus, Marthe Marguerite Hippolyte de Tubières, Marquise de:
Souvenirs 2353

Cebes. *See* Classics 2207:13; Moor 1797

Ceccheregli, Alessandro:
Delle attioni et sentenze del S. Alessandro de' Medici 2121

Cecil, Robert, Earl of Salisbury. *See* Salisbury 1169

Cecil, William, Baron Burghley:
Execution of justice in England 75, 111
Precepts 157, 2820
Sundry foreign arms in trick 2538
See Haynes 441; Mary, Queen of Scots 205; Philopatris 2590

Cecilia. See Burney 2812

Ceilings, Designs for. *See* Androuet 3483

Celesia, Dorothea:
Almida 1810:17

Cellini, Benvenuto:
Life 3181

Centaur not fabulous. See Young 1499

Centlivre, Susanna:
Gamester. See Plays 1908:2
The man's bewitched. See The Ghost 1810:11

Cepari, Virgilio:
Life of Blessed Aloysius Gonzaga 368

Cerceau, Jacques Androuet du. *See* Androuet du Cerceau

Certain information. See Burnet 1608:9

Certaine observations. See Ellesmere 161

Certamen religiosum. See Bayly 146; Cartwright 72

Certeynties and casualties of the revenewe of the Pipe. See Caesar 2535:3

Cervantes Saavedra, Miguel de:
Don Quichotte de la Manche 1024
Don Quixote 3999
Instructive and entertaining novels 1735
Principales avantures de Don Quichotte 3081
See D'Urfey 2270

Cervetto, Giacobbe:
Six solos 3871

Cevennes:
Manifesto of the Cevennois 1608:93
See Cavallier 3406

Ceylon. *See* Castlemaine 153; Knox 2718; Serendip 1237; Wolf 2993

Chabanon, Michel Paul Gui de:
Épitre sur la manie des jardins anglois 3082

Chaigneau, William:
History of Jack Connor 1554

Chain of golden poems. See Cockain 1934

Challoner, Richard:
Britannia Sancta 619

Chalmers, George:
Life of Thomas Ruddiman 2821

Chalmers, James:
Sermon. See Derby 79:5

Chaloner, Sir Thomas:
De Rep. Anglorum instauranda libri decem 112
See Erasmus 195, 2688; Tracts 210

Chaloner, Thomas (1595–1661):
Answer to the Scotch papers 2354
True and exact relation. See Tracts 210

Chalons, Vincent Claude:
Histoire de France 975

Chamber, Anna, Countess Temple. *See* Temple

Chamberlaine, John. *See* Holbein 3500

Chamberlayne, Edward:
Magnae Britanniae notitia 1369

Chamberlen, Paul:
Love in its empire 1736

Chambers, Anne, Countess Temple. *See* Temple

Chambers, Ephraim:
Cyclopaedia 1093

Chambers, Sir William:
Designs of Chinese buildings 3639
Dissertation on Oriental gardening 462; 1609:58

Chambers, Sir William (*cont.*)
Plans of the gardens and buildings at Kew in Surrey 3532
Treatise on civil architecture 3533
See Mason 1619; 3222:12
Chambray, Roland Fréart, Sieur de:
Idea of the perfection of painting. See Tracts 359:1
Chamfort, Sébastien Roch Nicolas:
Eloge de La Fontaine 2050:25
Champagne. *See* Le Pelletier 3117
Champion, Joseph. *See* Penmanship 3651
Champion 1506
Champneys, John:
The harvest is at hand 189
Chances. See Garrick 1810:20
Chandler, Richard:
Travels in Greece 2822
Chandler, Richard, *and* Revett, Nicholas:
Ionian antiquities 3534
Chandler, Samuel:
Vindication 1608:22
See Limborch 1618
Chandos, Grey Brydges, 5th Baron:
Horae subsecivae 190
Chandos, Life and Death of Lord. See Wyrley 712
Chapel Royal. *See* Jeremiah 2564
Chapman, George:
Eastward Hoe. See Lennox 1810:25
Chapman, John, Archdeacon of Sudbury:
Jesuit-Cabal farther opened 1337
Miscellaneous tracts 1398
Popery the bane of true letters 1337
View of the expediency of miraculous powers 832
See Remarks 1379:3
Chapman, Thomas:
Essay 3951
Chappuzeau, Samuel:
History of jewels 779
Character of a trimmer. See Halifax 83
Character of an evil minister. See Political tracts 94:3
Character of Pericles. See Campbell 1608:53
Character of the life and administration of . . . the Earl of Orford. See Walpole 2492:2
Charactères. See Puisieux 1203
Characters 1609:37
Charge to the jury. See Fielding 1608:51

Charity: a poetical essay 3222:13
Charlemagne. *See* Eginhardus 836
Charles le Téméraire, Duc de Burgogne. *See* Des Salles 919
Charles V, Duc de Lorraine. *See* La Brune 1298
Charles IV, Emperor of Germany. *See* Godefroy 1066
Charles V, Emperor of Germany. *See* Leti 2102; Robertson 2943; Saxony 2468; Villegagnon 138
Charles VI, Emperor of Germany:
Reasons humbly offer'd 1608:26
Relation de l'inauguration 3407
See Catalogue 236
Charles I, King of England:
Bibliotheca Regia 113
Catalogue of pictures. See Van Der Dort 3526; Vertue 2478–9, 3704; Walton 3911
Eikon Basilike 1507
Entertainment at Richmond 2355
Orders and directions. See Tracts 3797:6
Reliquiae Sacrae Carolinae 1508
Workes 13
See Bayly 146; Bromley 3227; Bulstrode 1701; Gerbier 2383; Hammond 1609:9; Harris 1643; Havard 1818:6; Herbert 1708; James I 2889; Quarles 2026
Charles II, King of England:
Collection of the most remarkable passages. See Tracts 2146:4
England's triumph 2004
See Bromley 3227; Bulstrode 1701; Caesar 2815; Collection 2358; Halifax 1608:67; Harris 1643; Jones 1749; Lower 603; Miège 1532; Ogilby 575, 3280; Sprat 1132; State tracts 2180; Wyndham 2504
Charles V, King of France. *See* Godefroy 1066
Charles VI, King of France. *See* Baudot 1241; Juvenal des Ursins 901
Charles VII, King of France. *See* Baudot 1242; Chartier 893
Charles, Dauphin, later Charles VIII, King of France. *See* Louis XI 1253
Charles IX, King of France. *See* Varillas 970
Charles II, the Bad, King of Navarre. *See* Secousse 1146
Charles III, King of Spain. *See* Vanvitelli 3596

Charles Borromeo, Saint:
Traitté contre les danses 1271
Charles de Valois, Duc d'Angoulême. *See* Angoulême
Charles Edward Stuart, the Young Pretender:
Manifesto. See Tracts 98:1
Young chevalier 1608:39
See Ascanius 1500; Goldwin 3363:1
Charles Emmanuel II, Duke of Savoy. *See* Castellamonte 3676
Charles Louis, Elector Palatine:
Vie et amours 4019
Charles et Vilcourt. See Drumgold 3920:2
Charleton, Walter. *See* Jones 599
Charlotte, Queen of England:
Poem printed at Buckingham House 2356
See Dublin 313; *Treatise* 1609:2
Charlotte Augusta Matilda, Princess. *See* Windsor 3222:16
Charlotte Elizabeth, of Bavaria, Duchesse d'Orléans:
Fragmens de lettres originales 3298
Charlotte. See Cullum 1810:24
Charlton, —. *See* Sprat 2760
Charlton, Lionel:
History of Whitby 3182
Charnois, Jean Charles Le Vacher de. *See* Le Vacher
Charta de foresta. See Edward I, 1608:8, 2547
Charterhouse, near Smithfield in London. *See* Herne 691
Charters of the following provinces of North America 1609:56
Chartier, Jean:
Histoire de Charles VII 893
Chastel, Jehan. *See* Boucher 2343
Chastelet, Hôtel du. *See* Lambert, Hôtel de
Chatelain, Jean Baptiste Claude. *See* Antiquities 3485; Drawings 3567
Chatelain, Nicolas:
Atlas historique 425
Chatham, William Pitt, Earl of. *See* Pitt
Les Chats. See Moncrif 753
Chatsworth: a poem 3222:21
Chatterton, Thomas:
Collection of pieces 3690
Execution of Sir Charles Bawdin 3222:12
Manuscripts 3408

Chatterton, Thomas *(cont.)*
Miscellanies 3408
See Barrett 539; Bristol 2809; Walpole 1609:39, 3469:13
Chaubert. See Villiers 1810:49
Chaucer, Geoffrey:
Canterbury tales 1431
Legend of good women 2539
Chaucer's Ghoast. See Ovidius 1971
Chauncey, Dr. Charles:
One or more letters. *See* Letters 2576
Chauncy, Sir Henry:
Antiquities of Hertfordshire 564
Chavis, Denis. *See* Cabinet 3074
Chaworth, William. *See* Byron 1107; *Circumstantial* 1609:56
Cheke, Sir John:
True subject to the rebell 1608:1
See Strype 1658
Chelsea Hospital:
Narrative 1608:77
Chelsea pensioner. See Dibdin 1810:30
Chelsum, James. *See* Arts 288:5
Cheltenham. See Williams 1609:51
Chemin des heros au Palais de la Gloire. See Berton 1055
Chénier, Marie Joseph de. *See* Merry 1810:57
Cherbury, Edward Herbert, Baron Herbert of. *See* Herbert
Chéron, Elisabeth Sophie:
Pierres gravées. See Tracts 3833:11
Chéron de Boismorand, Claude Joseph. *See* Lussan 1011
Cheshire. *See* Leicester 601; Leigh 602
Chester:
Concise history of . . . Chester 2663
History of the Cathedral Church 2823
See Doddridge 1062; King 628
Chesterfield, Philip Dormer Stanhope, 4th Earl of:
Apology for a late resignation 1673
Letters to his son 436
Miscellaneous works 3915
Works in verse and prose 3916
See Common Sense 2360; *Compliment* 1608:53; *Graces* 3222:13; Huybert 2146:1; *Interest* 1608:43; Tracts 1608:73; Waller 1608:43, 46; *World* 911, 2501
Chettle, Henry:
Englandes mourning garment 1315

Chetwood, William Rufus:
  General history of the stage 1737
Chevalier, Monsieur Robert. *See* Le Sage
  1300
Chevallier, Clement. *See* Hoadly 1608:85
Chevreau, Urbain:
  Chevraeana 720
Cheyne, George:
  English malady 1468
Chichele, Henry, Archbishop of Canterbury.
  See Duck 1705, 2680; Spencer 2958
Chiffinch, William. *See* Vertue 2479:2
Child, Robert. *See* Hartlib 125
Children of Thespis:
  Part I. *See* Williams 3222:20
  Part II. *See* Williams 3222:21
  Part III. *See* Williams 3222:22
Childrey, Joshua:
  Britannia Baconica 721
Chillingworth, William:
  Works 3952
China. *See* Du Halde 874; Helman 3747;
  Pauw 3134
Chinese, Views of the. *See* Venice 3662
Chinese drawing:
  A roll with a painting of an extensive
  procession 3640
Chiswick. *See* Palladio 3577
Choderlos de Laclos, Pierre Ambroise Fran-
  çois:
  Liaisons dangereuses 3005
*Choice collection of papers relating to state
  affairs* 114
Choiseul, Louise Honorine Crozat du Châtel,
  Duchesse de:
  Two letters. *See* Letters 2576
Choiseul-Gouffier, Marie Gabriel Auguste
  Florens, Comte de:
  Voyage pittoresque de la Grèce 3586
Choiseul-Stainville, Étienne François, Duc de:
  Mémoire historique 1609:54
  Mémoires 3299
  See Treyssac de Vergy 1609:56
Choisnin, Jean. *See* Collection 3084
Choisy, François Timoléon de:
  *Histoire de Madame la Comtesse Des
  Barres* 1292
  *Histoires de Philippe de Valois et du Roi
  Jean* 917

Choisy, François Timoléon de (*cont.*)
  Mémoires ... de Louis XIV 976
Choleric fathers. See Holcroft 1853
Christian VII, King of Denmark. *See Mas-
  querade* 3222:9
Christian religion ... profess'd. See Astell
  1460
Christianisme dévoilé. See Holbach 3018
Christianity not founded on argument. See
  Dodwell 1608:25
Christina, Queen of Sweden:
  Lettres choisies 804
  See Arckenholtz 913
Christine de Pisan. *See* Pisan
Christmas tale. See Garrick 1810:21
Christmas tale, a poetical address 3222:19
Christoforo, Armeno. *See* Serendip 1237
Christ's Church, London. *See* Finch
  1608:1
Chronica Veneta. See Pacifico 2109
Chronicle. See Hetoum 2397
Chronicles of England. See England. Chroni-
  cles
Chrononhotonthologos. See Carey 1818:5
Chrysal. See Johnstone 984
Chrysostom, Saint. *See* Hermant 1276
Chubb, Thomas:
  *Enquiry into the ground and foundation
  of religion* 2664
Chudleigh, Elizabeth, Countess of Bristol,
  calling herself Duchess of Kingston. *See*
  Kingston
Chudleigh, Mary, Lady. *See Poems* 175
Church, Thomas:
  Appeal to the serious 1379:8
  Vindication of the miraculous powers 1370
  See Toll 1379:5
Church of England. *See* Miscellaneous tracts
  89:2; Nelson 1445
Church of England. Convocation. *See* Atter-
  bury 1608:6; Smalridge 1608:6
Churchill, Anne, Countess of Sunderland. *See*
  Sunderland
Churchill, Charles:
  Poems 3953
  Sermons 1609:10
  Various poems 3222:1, 3, 4, 5, 6
  See Lloyd 3222:1; *North Briton* 1576;
  Poems 3363

Churchill, Elizabeth, Countess of Bridge-water. *See* Bridgewater.

Churchill, George Spencer, 4th Duke of Marlborough. *See* Marlborough

Churchill, Henrietta, Duchess of Marlborough. *See* Marlborough

Churchill, James, pseud. *See True Briton* 1609:5

Churchill, John, 1st Duke of Marlborough. *See* Marlborough

Churchill, Louisa Augusta (Greville). *See* Greville

Churchill, Lady Mary. *See Poems* 280:11

Churchill, Mary, Duchess of Montagu. *See* Montagu

Churchill, Sarah, Duchess of Marlborough. *See* Marlborough

Churchill, W.:
Temple of corruption 3222:10

Churchilliad 3222:1

Churchyard, Thomas. *See Mirror* 88

Churlow, Lord. *See* Thurlow, Edward

Chute, John:
Original drawings 3490

Cibber, Colley:
Another occasional letter 1608:90
Apology 450
Caesar in Aegypt. See Plays 1909:1
Character and conduct of Cicero 451
Egotist 1608:90
Lady's lecture 1608:57
Letter to Mr. Pope 1608:90
Love's last shift. See Plays 1910:2
Non-juror. See Breval 1608:17
Of love. See Poems 3363:3
Papal tyranny 1818:20
Plays 936
See Bickerstaffe 1810:13; Dibdin 1810:13

Cibber, Susannah Marie (Arne):
Oracle 1818:10

Cibber, Theophilus:
Dissertations on theatrical subjects 2665
Epistle to David Garrick. See Poems 1835:5
Four original letters 1608:57
Lick at a liar 1608:57
Lives of the poets 2005
Romeo and Juliet 1608:57
See Coffey 1818:5

Cicero, Marcus Tullius:
Cato Major 407, 1399
De finibus bonorum. See Classics 2207:11
De natura deorum. See Classics 2207:11
De officiis. See Classics 2207:11
De oratore. See Classics 2207:11
Epistles to Marcus Brutus 2666
Epistolae ad Atticum. See Classics 2207:11
Epistolae ad familiares. See Classics 2207:11
Letters 1432
Opera. See Classics 2207:11
Orationes. See Classics 2207:11
Orations against Verres 3300
Thre bookes of Tullyes offyces 780
Tusculan disputations. See Review 1608:55
See Cibber 451; Middleton 315; Tunstall 1424

Cicero, Family of. *See* Macé 1279

Cignani, Carlo. *See Drawings* 3567

Cini, Francesco:
Notte d'amore. See Cosmo II 2304:2

Cintio, Giovanni Battista Giraldi. *See* Giraldi

Circumstantial and authentic account of a late unhappy affair 1609:56

Circumstantial narrative 1609:26

Cities advocate in this case. See Bolton 2649

City Latin. See Thornton 1609:2

Clagett, William. *See* Anne, Saint 1608:8

Claim of the colonies to an exemption from internal taxes. See Knox 1609:12

Clamour of the Whigs against the conduct of the Duke of Ormond. See Black-bird 2646:21

Clanricarde, Ulick de Burgh, Marquess of:
Memoirs and letters 115, 437

Clare, John Fitzgibbon, Earl of:
Verses addressed to the Queen 3222:13

Clare, Robert Nugent, Viscount. *See* Nugent

Clarendon, Edward Hyde, 1st Earl of:
Collection of several tracts 14
History of the Rebellion in England 41
History of the Rebellion in Ireland 40
Life 2, 4000
Proceedings touching the impeachment 1738
State papers 426, 3229
See Oldmixon 1651; Thoresby 2602

Clarendon, Henry Hyde, Earl of:
State letters 1060
See Gale 686

Clarendon, John Charles Villiers, later Earl of. *See* Villiers

Clarendon, Thomas Villiers, Earl of. *See* Scotch 3222:16

Clarendon and Whitlock compar'd. See Oldmixon 1651

Claris de Florian, Jean Pierre. See Robson 1810:46

Clark, Hugh:
Concise history of knighthood 3083

Clark, Samuel. *See* Clarke

Clarke, Alured:
Essay 1608:67

Clarke, Edward:
Letters concerning the Spanish nation 3301

Clarke, Edward Daniel:
Tour through the south of England 3852

Clarke, George. *See* Foot 1609:22

Clarke, Richard:
Gospel of the daily-service of the law 2824
Series of letters 2667

Clarke, Samuel (1599–1683):
First part of the marrow of ecclesiastical history 1593
Lives of sundry eminent persons 3302

Clarke, Samuel (1675–1729). *See* Leibnitz 1414; Sermons 1451; Whiston 1727

Classical Dictionary. *See* Dictionary 1515

Classical dictionary of the vulgar tongue. See Grose 2863

Classics 2207

Classics. Latin classics. *See* Brindley 2120

Claude le Lorrain. *See* Lorrain

Claudianus, Claudius:
Claudiani quae exstant 2085
Opera 2239

Claustrum regale reservatum. See Wyndham 2504

Clavière Étienne de, *and* Brissot de Warville, Jean Pierre:
Considerations on . . . France and the United States of America 3230

Clavières, Octavien de Guasco, Comte de. *See* Guasco

Clavis stereometriae 2825

Claybrook. *See* Macaulay 2900

Clayton, Robert, Bishop:
Vindication 1608:34

Cleaveland, Ezra:
Genealogical history of the . . . family of Courtenay 589

Cleaveland, John. *See* Cleveland

Cleland, John. *See* Montagu 814; *Oeconomy* 1608:63

Clement XI, Pope. *See* Rossi 3516

Clement XIV, Pope. *See* Caraccioli 3003

Clément, Jean Marie Bernard. *See Anecdotes* 3064

Clement, Simon:
Discourse of the general notions of money 1608:8

Clementina Maria Sobieski, Princess:
Parentalia Mariae Clementinae 3491
See James Edward Francis Stuart 1608:10; Wogan 1608:5

Clementina. See Kelly 1810:17

Clements, —. *See* Miscellaneous tracts 89:2

Cleopatra, Tragedy of. See May 1968

Cléopatre. See La Calprenède 1224

Clergyman. *See Answer* 1379:11

Clermont, François de. *See Rémonstrance* 1085

Cleveland, John:
Poems by J.C. 1933
Works 1866

Cleveland, Life of Mr. See Prévost d'Exiles 1581

Clifford, Martin:
Notes upon Mr. Dryden's poems 1608:1

Clifford, Mary de. *See* Brydges 2348

Clifton, Ann. *See* Cookery 3165

Clinton, Sir Henry:
Narrative relative to his conduct 1609:44
Observations 1609:44

Clinton, Henry Fiennes, Earl of Lincoln. *See* Lincoln

Clive, Catherine:
One or more letters. *See* Letters 2576
Rehearsal 1818:11

Clive, Robert, Baron Clive:
Letter to the proprietors of the East India stock 1609:7
Lord Clive's speech in the House of Commons 1609:58
See Ashburton 1609:8

Cloacina. See Man 3222:14

Cloister of San Michele in Bosco. *See* Malvasia 3624

Clouet, François, called Janet:
Portraits of Francis I and II of France 2357
See Drawings 3567

Clovio, Julio. *See* Bonde 3689; Missal 3786:2

Clowes, William. *Short and profitable treatise. See* Hill 787

Clubbe, John:
Physiognomy 1609:55

Cluverius, Philippus:
Introductionis in universam geographiam 2189, 2240

Coach drivers 1810:9

Coalition 1609:54

Coats of arms of the King and all the Lords. See Peerage 2442

Coats of arms of the members of the House of Commons 679

Cobb, James:
Doctor and the apothecary 1810:46
English readings 1810:42
First floor 1810:42
Love in the East 1810:44
Strangers at home 1810:38

Cobham, Henry Brooke, Baron. *See* Plays 1082:4

Cobham, Lady. *See* Du Verdier 2683

Cobler of Castlebury. See Stuart 1810:30

Coccaius, Merlinus, pseud. *See* Folengo 2272

Cocchi, Antonio:
Dei bagni di Pisa 2074
Del vitto Pitagorico 1608:52
Lettera critica 1608:52
See Nicetas 3449

Cochin, Charles Nicolas:
Collection de vignettes 3808

Cochin, Charles Nicolas, *and* Bellicard, Jerome Charles:
Observations 1433

Cochlaeus, Johannes. *See* Tracts 3986

Cockain, Sir Aston:
Small poems of divers sorts 1934

Cockburn, Catharine (Trotter):
Revolution of Sweden 1818:21

Cocker, Edward:
Multum in parvo 500

Cockings, George:
Conquest of Canada 1810:8

Cocoa-Tree Club. *See* Butler 1609:54; *Consultation* 1609:54; Francis 1609:54; *Letter* 1609:54

Codicille d'or ou petit recueil. See Joly 1222

Codrus. See Rasbotham 1810:22

Coelmans, Jacob 3562

Coetlogon, Charles Edward de. *See* Wallis 3265

Coetlogon, Dennis de:
Gothic oration 1608:51

Coffey, Charles:
Devil to pay 1818:5

Cogan, Francis. *See Works of celebrated authors* 1864

Cogan, Henry:
Scarlet gown 722

Cogan, Thomas:
The Rhine 3853

Cohausen, Johann Heinrich:
Hermippus redivivus 1469

Coins. *See* Drawings 2371

Coins, List of. *See* Philip IV 488

Cokayne. *See* Cockain

Coke, Sir Edward:
Reports . . . in verse 1847
Speech. See Tracts 3797
See Ellesmere 503

Coke, Lady Mary (Campbell). *See Letter* 1608:73

Coke, Roger:
Detection of the Court 3409

Coker, John:
Survey of Dorsetshire 620

Colbatch, John:
Account of the Court of Portugal 680

Colbert, Jean Baptiste, Marquis de Torcy:
Mémoires 1272

Colchester. *See* Morant 606

Colden, Cadwallader:
History of the five Indian nations of Canada 1400

Cole, Charles Nalson:
Collection of laws 1594

Cole, Christian:
Historical and political memoirs 869

Cole, Thomas, D. D.:
Godly sermon 191

Cole, Thomas, antiquary. *See* Heraldry 2557

Cole, William:
Collection of 186 letters. *See* Letters 2576
See Tyson 1609:57

Coleraine, Henry Hare, 3d Baron. *See* Dyson 2843

Colerus, Jean. *See* Fénelon 1218

Colet, John, Dean of St. Paul's. *See* Knight 1681; St. Paul's School 2751

Coligny, Gaspard de. *See Collection* 3084

Collaert, Adrian. *See* Prints 3606, 3654; Stradanus 3659

Collection des meilleurs ouvrages françois. *See* Kéralio 3021

Collection of all the humorous pieces in the London Journal 1608:24

Collection of all the loose pieces printed at Strawberry Hill 2506

Collection of ballads:
Collection of curious prints 2358

Collection of catches. See Whittington's feast 1810:26

Collection of curious prints. See Collection 2358

Collection of 86 loyal poems 158, 1935

Collection . . . of English prologues and epilogues. See Prologues 2936

Collection of fees and offices of the Crown 2540

Collection of letters addressed to Sir Julius Caesar. *See* Caesar 2535:10–14

Collection of letters and state papers. See Howard 86

Collection of loyal songs 1890

Collection of offices, with the fees of the Crown 2541

Collection of papers. *See Choice collection* 114

Collection of papers pro and con. See Middlesex 1608:69

Collection of pieces printed at Strawberry Hill, 1760–85 2507

Collection of poems. See Pearch 3453

Collection of poems by several hands. See Dodsley 2370

Collection of poems on several occasions. See Egerton 1894

Collection of prints. See Etchings 3588

Collection of proceedings and trials 870

Collection of prologues and epilogues, made by HW 1810:58

Collection of smaller tracts printed at Strawberry Hill 2508

Collection of state trials. *See Collection* 870; Trials 1724

Collection of the letters of Atticus, Lucius, Junius, and others. See Letters 1609:24

Collection of the most remarkable passages in the declarations and speeches by the King. See Tracts 2146:4

Collection of the Spintrian medals. See Spintrian 2599

Collection of tracts. See Asgill 67

Collection of voyages and travels. See Green 542

Collection universelle des mémoires . . . de France 3084

College exercise 1609:23

College Wag. *See Whittington's Feast* 1810:26

Collet, John. *See* Bunbury 3563:2

Collier, Arthur:
Clavis universalis 1781

Collier, Jane:
Essay on . . . tormenting 2190

Collier, Jeremy:
Essays 1401
Great historical dictionary 3272
Short view of the immorality . . . of the English stage 1470

Collier, Joel, pseud. *See* Veal

Collinges, John:
Par nobile 1782

Collins, Anthony:
Discourse concerning ridicule 1509
Discourse of free thinking 1509
Discourse on . . . Christian religion 1402
Philosophical inquiry 1509
Priestcraft in perfection 1608:19
See Letter 1379:11; Sherlock 1422

Collins, Arthur:
Genealogical account of the family of Allington 2542
Genealogical account of the family of Harley 2359
Historical collections 565
History of the family of Walpole 3888
Letters and memorials of state 871

Collins, Arthur (*cont.*)
  Life of Edward, Prince of Wales 1674
  Life of Thomas Cromwell 2543
  Peerage of England 652–3
  See English baronetage 655; Longmate 414
Collins, William:
  Poetical works 3954
Collinson, John:
  Beauties of British antiquity 2668
  History of Somerset 3164
Colls, John Henry:
  Poet: a poem, addressed to Mr. Jerningham
  3222:19
Colman, George, the elder:
  Achilles in petticoats 1810:21
  Bonduca 1810:29
  Clandestine marriage 1810:8
  Comus 1810:19
  Deuce is in him 1810:5
  Dramatic works 1811
  English merchant 1810:10
  Epicoene 1810:25
  Fairy prince 1810:18
  History of King Lear 1810:12
  Jealous wife 1810:2
  Man and wife 1810:15
  Man of business 1810:21
  Manager in distress 1810:31
  Musical lady 1810:3
  Occasional prelude 1810:25
  Oxonian in town. See Garrick 1810:11
  Philaster 1810:5
  Polly Honeycombe 1810:1
  Portrait 1810:16
  Prologue. See Rider 1810:12
  Prose on several occasions 2826
  Spleen 1810:25
  T. Harris dissected 1609:57
  Tit for tat 1810:44
  True state of the differences 1609:56
  See Harris 1609:57; Horatius 3222:19; Kenrick 3222:9; Lillo 1810:36; Linley 1810:43;
  Poems 175
Colman, George, the younger:
  Inkle and Yarico 1810:43
  Ways and means 1810:46
Colomiès, Paul:
  Bibliothèque choisie 1183
  Gallia orientalis 833

Colonia, Dominique de. *See* Dominique 1246
Colonna, Francesco:
  Tableau des riches inventions 2075
Columbine, Peter. *See Cabal* 1810:57
Colvolo, Giambattista dal, Conte. *See* Covolo
Combe, Charles:
  Nummorum veterum populorum et urbium descriptio 3691
Combe, William:
  History of the river Thames 3566
  Various poems 3222:15, 16
  See Lyttelton 2899
Comber, Thomas:
  Examination of a late introductory discourse. See Middleton 1337
Comédie Française. *See Bibliothèque* 3001
Comines, Philip de:
  Memoirs 1639
  See Collection 3084
Commendon, Cardinal Jean François. *See* Fléchier 1156; Graziani 3102
Commines. *See* Comines
Commissioners appointed:
  Account of the manors held by lease from the Crown 427
Committee of London Merchants. *See* London Merchants
Committee of Secrecy. *See* England 1249
Common sense, or the Englishman's Journal 2360
Common sense. See Paine 1609:37
Commons complaint. See Hartlib 125:2
Companion to the Guide. See Guides 2387
Companion to the play-house. See Baker 1778
Company of Merchants of England trading to the Levant. *See* Caesar 2535:7
Company of Royal Adventurers trading to Africa. *See* African Company
Comparison between the Horace of Corneille and the Roman father. See Freeman 1818:7
Compendium:
  Historical compendium 1555
The Compendium: or, a short view of the late tryals. See Castlemaine 73
Complaints of the manufacturers relating to . . . wool. See England. Woollen manufacturers
Compleat collection of all the verses. See Concanen 1608:31

Compleat collection of protests in House of Lords. See England 1740

Compleat collection of the standing orders 1608:2

Compleat country dancing master. See Dancing master 1784

Compleat history of Europe. See Europe 3419

Compleat history of the piratical states of Barbary. See Morgan 1417

Compleat view of the present politicks 1608:44

Complete catalogue of all the English books printed since the year 1700. See Catalogue 2662

Compliment of congratulation 1608:53, 73

Comte de Comminge. See Arnaud 2998

Comus. See Colman 1810:19

Conaught wife 1810:10

Conca, Sebastian. *See* Frey 3602

Concanen, Matthew:
  Compleat collection of all the verses 1608:31
  See Walpole 1608:30

Concise and genuine account of the dispute between Mr. Hume and Mr. Rousseau. See Hume 1609:16

Concise history of . . . Chester. See Chester 2663

Conclave. See Music 3448

Conder, John. *See* Pye 2457

Conduct of a Rt. Hon. gentleman in resigning 1609:3

Conduct of the Allies . . . examined. See Egmont 119:1

Conduct of the Duke of Ormonde 1608:94

Conduct of the government 1608:59

Conduct of the late administration examined. See Lloyd 1609:16

Conduct of the ministry 1609:1

Conduct of the Right Reverend the Lord Bishop of Winchester 1609:26, 2761

Conduct of the two B——RS vindicated. See Egmont 119:2

Confession of the faith of the Germans. See Taverner 797

Confession reciproque. See Le Noble 1200

Confirmation of Dr. Middleton's introductory discourse 1379:3

Confucius. See Helman 3746

Congreve, Thomas:
  Scheme for making a navigable communication 681

Congreve, William:
  Works 1867, 3889

Conjectures on original composition. See Young 1608:85

Conjugal love and duty. See Brett 1367:7; 1608:88

Conjugall counsell. See Hilder 2873

Connaught wife. See Conaught wife

The Connexion. See James I 1746

Connor, Jack. *See* Chaigneau 1554

Conquest of Corsica 1810:18

Consequences of a law for reducing the duties. See Detection 2677:6

Consett, Matthew:
  Tour through Sweden 3303

Considerations concerning the . . . Bill. See Tracts 400:12, 2475:15

Considerations on behalf of the colonists. See Otis 1609:11

Considerations on criminal law. See Dagge 3232

Considerations on proceedings by information and attachment 1609:21

Considerations on several proposals. See Gray 1608:48

Considerations on several proposals lately made for . . . the poor. See Tracts 2049:8

Considerations on the American Stamp Act 1609:12

Considerations on the bill for better government of the Navy 1608:27

Considerations on the definitive treaty 1608:58

Considerations on the Douglas cause. See Douglas 1609:19

Considerations on the establishment of a regency. See Grenville 1609:50

Considerations on the late bill for payment. See Robinson 1608:39

Considerations on the legality of general warrants 1609:10

Considerations on the measures. See Rokeby 1609:32, 33

Considerations on the Peerage Bill. See Tracts 400:13, 2475:7

Considerations on the present coalition of parties. See Tracts 2146:3

Considerations on the present dangerous crisis. See Ruffhead 1609:6

Considerations on the present German war 1609:1

Considerations on the present state of affairs in Europe 1608:43

Considerations on the present state of East-India affairs. See Stuart 1609:46

Considerations on the proposal for reducing the interest 1608:39, 47

Considerations on the propriety of imposing taxes. See Dulany 1609:13

Considerations on the trade and finances of the kingdom. See Whately 1609:56

Considerations preliminary to the fixing the supplies. See Stair 1609:42

Considerations upon a proposal for lowering the interest 1608:21

Considerations upon a reduction of the land-tax. See Nugent 1608:47

Considerations upon the institution of marriage. See Warrington 181

Consolation of philosophy. See Boethius 148

Conspirators 1818:11

Constable, John:
Reflections upon style 682

Constant maid 1810:43

Constantia. See Poems 3222:9

Constantine I, Emperor of Rome. *See* Le Beau 1278

Constantine. See Francis 1818:13

Constantinople. *See* Banduri 3674; Craven 2168; *Letters* 1608:18

Constitution 1608:84

Constitution explain'd. See Tracts 400:9, 2475:6

Constitutional considerations on the power of Parliament 1609:56

Consultation on the subject of a standing army 1609:54

Contant d'Orville, André Guillaume:
Mariage du siècle 2669

Contemplatio. See Manchester 172

Contents of a folio history of the Moravians. See Wesley 1608:19

Contes à rire 1025

Contes de Guillaume Vadé. See Voltaire 2975

Contes françois 1783

Con-test. See Tracts 2968:8

Conti, Antonio, Abbé. *See* Montagu 1608:8

Conti, Armand de Bourbon, Prince de:
Works 2006, 2670

Conti, Louis François de Bourbon, Prince de:
Catalogue des tableaux. See Catalogues 3405:2

Conti, Louisa Margaret, Princess de. *See* Tracts 3054

Contile, Luca. *See* Raviglio 2937

Contini, Francesco:
Eleven plates of Hadrian's villa 3618

Contra Henricum Angliae Martinus Luther. See Henry VIII 84

Contract. See Francklin 1810:26

Controversy between Great Britain and her colonies reviewed. See Knox 1609:22

Convention Treaty. *See* Bath 1608:38; England 1608:23

Convict's address. See Johnson 1609:38

Conway, Lady Anne Seymour, Countess of Drogheda. *See* Drogheda

Conway, Anne Seymour. *See* Damer

Conway, Francis Ingram Seymour, 2d Marquess of Hertford. *See* Hertford

Conway, Henry Seymour:
Elegy on the death of Miss Caroline Campbell 3222:22
False appearances 1810:47
Speech 1609:42
See Adair 1609:10; Fox 1609:42; Guthrie 1609:8; Thompson 3222:6

Conway, Sir John:
Poesie of floured prayers 2361

Conybeare, John Bishop:
True patriotism 1608:6

Cook, James:
Death of Captain Cook 1810:47
Voyage towards the South Pole 3183
See Gianetti 4006; Hawkesworth 2869; Seward 3207

Cook, Robert. *See* Norfolk 2583

Cook, William, dramatist:
Capricious lady 1810:35
See Burke, William 1609:38

Cookbook. *See* Cookery

Cooke, Edward:
History of the successions of the kings of England. See Tracts 2146:4
Short historical account of the kings of England. See Tracts 2146:4

Cooke, George. *See* Middlesex 1608:69

Cooke, Thomas:
  Hymn to liberty. See Poems 280:17
  Letters of Atticus 1608:24
  See Marvell 1967; Plautus 1976
Cooke, William:
  Civil liberty 3410
  Sense of St. Peter considered 1379:10
Cooke, William, dramatist. *See* Cook
Cookery:
  Receipts in cookery 3165
Cooksey, Richard:
  Essay on John Lord Somers 3231
Cooper, Anthony Ashley, Earl of Shaftesbury. *See* Shaftesbury
Cooper, Elizabeth:
  Rival widows 1818:6
  See Muses Library 90
Cooper, John Gilbert:
  Letters concerning taste 1608:79
  Life of Socrates 1675
Cooper, Samuel. *See* Drawings 3567
Cooper, Thomas, Bishop:
  Chronicle. See Lanquet 1617
Cooper, William, bookseller:
  Catalogue of chymicall books 723
  Cooper 1810:18
Coote, Charles, Earl of Bellomont. *See* Bellomont
Coote, Sir Eyre:
  Letter from certain gentlemen 1609:55
Cope, Sir Anthony:
  Godly meditacion 834
Cope, Sir John:
  Report . . . of the Board of General Officers 1316
Copie. See Copy
Copies of various pedigrees. See Heraldry 2557
Copies taken from the records of the Court of King's Bench. See England 1609:55
Copley, John Singleton. *See* Pitt 3456
Copper Plate Magazine. See Antiquities 3485:4
Copper Plate Magazine, or monthly cabinet 3838
Copper Plate Magazine; or monthly treasure 3839
Copy of a letter from Lord Lovat 1608:54
Copy of a letter . . . from Master S. C. See Plays 1082:4

Copy of a letter to Sir Rowland G——n 1608: 94
Copy of the poll. See Westminster election
Corbet, Richard:
  Poëtica stromata 2671
Corbett, Thomas:
  Account of the expedition 1608:32
Corbinelli, Jean:
  Histoire généalogique de la Maison de Gondi 1139
Cordiner, Charles:
  Antiquities . . . of the North of Scotland 540
  Remarkable ruins 3840
Cori, Angelo Maria:
  New method for the Italian tongue 2099
Coriat, Junior. *See* Paterson 1234
Cork and Orrery, Ann (Courtenay) Boyle, Countess of:
  Trial 1609:42
Cork and Orrery, John Boyle, 5th Earl of:
  Letters from Italy 42
  One or more letters. *See* Letters 2576
  Remarks on Swift 43
  See Plinius 54
Corke, John Boyle, Earl of. *See* Cork and Orrery
Cornaro, Luigi:
  Sure . . . methods of attaining a long . . . life 1510
Cornazano, Antonio. *See* Cresswell 3778
Cornbury, Henry Hyde, Viscount:
  Mistakes 2362
Corneille, Pierre:
  Chef-d'oeuvres 1009
  Cid 1936
  Théâtre 937
  See Aspinwall 1810:7; Whitehead 1818:7
Corneille, Thomas:
  Théâtre 937
  See Young 1818:12
Cornélie. See Hénault
Cornish man. *See* Pitt 1608:32
Cornwall. *See* Borlase 559; Carew 651; Doddridge 1062; Heath 690; Norden 635; *Rural elegance* 2750
Cornwallis, Charles, 1st Marquess Cornwallis:
  Answer to Sir Henry Clinton 1609:44
  See O'Bryen 1609:43; Tracts 2968:4

Cornwallis, Sir William:
Essayes 2672
Coromandel. See Orme 3174
Corona Minervae. See Kynaston 2405
Corporation Act. See England 1609:53; Martin 1609:53
Corpus Christi College, Cambridge. See Cambridge University
Corpus Christi plays. See York 2628
Corpus juris civilis. See Classics 2207:18
Corpus Poetarum latinorum. See Maittaire 2159
Correspondance interceptée. See Dutens 2306
Correspondents. See Lyttelton 2899
Corsica. See Conquest of Corsica 1810:18; Fate of Corsica 1818:20
Cortese, Giacomo. See Drawings 3568
Cortona, Pietro da. See Drawings 3569
Cortona. Accademia Etrusca:
Saggi di dissertazioni accademiche 2076
Coryate, George:
Descriptio Angliae et descriptio Londini 3222:5
Coryate, Thomas:
Coryats crudities 1317
Corymbaeus, pseud. See Brathwait 2235
Cosens, John. See Tears 3222:7; Windsor 3222:16
Cosins, John. See Cosens
Cosmo I (Medici). See Baldini 2068
Cosmo II (Medici):
Descrizione delle feste fatte nelle nozze de Principi di Toscana D. Cosimo de' Medici, e Maria Maddalena 2304
Cosmo III (Medici):
Views. See Richard 3043
Costa, Giovanni. See Pope 3222:14
Coste, Doctor:
Traité. See Paulmier 3133
Coste, Gautier de, Sieur de La Calprenède. See Cassandra 367
Costumes et annales des grands théâtres de Paris. See Le Vacher 3119
Cosway, Maria. See Drawings 3678
Cosway, Richard:
Catalogue of paintings. See Tracts 3833:2
Cotes, Humphrey. See Enquiry 1609:15
Cotgrave, Randle:
Dictionarie of the French and English tongues 501

Cotolendi, Carlo. See Arlequiniana 1019
Cottagers. See Brunton 1810:45
Cotterell, Sir Charles. See Cassandra 367
Cottington, Robert. See Sherley 3828
Cotton, Charles. See Montluc 903
Cotton, John:
Covenant of God's free grace. See Sermons 2757:1
Cotton, Sir Robert Bruce:
Cottoni posthuma 1511
Exact abridgement 2167
Cotton family. See Mawson 2579
Council of Trent. See Le Vassor 3337
Count de Villeroi 1810:55
Counter-address to the public. See Walpole 1609:8
Counter-appeal to the public 1609:22
Counter-rat. See Tracts 3796:1
Counter-scuffle. See Tracts 3796:1
Countess of Pembrokes Yvychurch. See Fraunce 122
Country election. See Trusler 1810:12
Country girl. See Garrick 1810:9
Country Journal; or, the Craftsman. See Craftsman 2140
Country 'squire. See Gwinnett 1818:5
Country wife. See Lee 1810:7, 39
Coup de grace. See Henley 1608:31
Courcy, Gerald de, Lord Kinsale. See Kinsale
Courcy, John de. See Kinsale 2569
Court and character of King James. See Sanderson 1585, 1800; Weldon 1767
Court and city register 369
Court and country. See Masquerader 2416
Court convert. See Waring 1990
Court miscellany. See Miscellaneous tracts 89:1; Tracts 98:2
Court of adultery 3222:16
Court of Alexander. See Stevens 1810:15
Court of James I. See James I 850
Court register and statesman's remembrancer 1434
Court secret 1608:91
See Second Court Secret 1608:31
Court secrets. See Curll 1512
Court tales. See Oldmixon 1757
Courten, Lady Katharine. See Collinges 1782
Courtenay, Ann, Countess of Cork and Orrery. See Cork and Orrery

Courtenay, John:
  Philosophical reflections 1609:53
Courtenay family. *See* Cleaveland 589
Courtenay, Histoire de. See Du Bouchet
  895
Courteney, John:
  Rape of Pomona 3222:13
Courtilz, Gatien Sandras de. *See* Sandras de
  Courtilz
Covent Garden drolery. See Brome 1929
Covent Garden theatre. *See* Colman 1609:56;
  Drury Lane 1810:4; Harris 1609:56, 57;
  Managers 1609:56
Coventry, Francis:
  History of Pompey the Little 1556
  See Hill 1608:29
Coventry, George William, Earl of Coventry.
  See Thicknesse 1609:45, 46
Coventry, Henry:
  Philemon to Hydaspes 1608:33
  See Stebbing 1608:70
Coventry, William. *See* Halifax 83
Coverdale, Miles. *See* Werdmueller 212
Covolo, Giambattista dal, Conte:
  *Discourse concerning the irritability of
  some flowers* 1609:18
Cowdry, Richard. *See* Guides 2387
Cowley, Abraham:
  Select works 3917, 4001
  Works 1823
  See Oxford 2061
Cowley, Hannah:
  Albina 1810:30
  Belle's stratagem 1810:34
  Day in Turkey 1810:51
  Fate of Sparta 1810:44
  More ways than one 1810:36
  Runaway 1810:25
  School for Greybeards 1810:40
  Which is the man? 1810:35
  Who's the dupe 1810:30
Cowper, Judith. *See* Pope 1609:22
Cowper, William:
  Poems 2827
  Translation of Homer 2827
Cowper, Dr. William, of Chester:
  Il penseroso, 3222:8
Cox, James:
  Descriptive inventory 264
Cox, Sir Richard. *See* Munster 1608:61

Cox, Thomas:
  Magna Britannia 621
Coxe, William:
  Memoirs of Horatio Lord Walpole. See
  Geography 3423
  Memoirs of Sir Robert Walpole 3304
  Travels in Poland 31
Coyer, Gabriel François:
  De la prédication 3085
Coypel, Charles Antoine. *See* Cervantes 3081,
  3999
Cozens, Zechariah:
  Tour through the Isle of Thanet 3184
Crabbe, George:
  Library 3222:17
  News-paper 3222:19
  Village 3222:19
Cradock, Joseph:
  Zobeide 1810:18
Craftsman 1471, 2140
  See Bolingbroke 1608:13; *Observations*
  1608:24; Political tracts 94
Craftsman's doctrine. See Political tracts 94:9
Craftsmen: a sermon. See Miscellaneous
  tracts 89
Cranach, Lucas, the younger. *See* Saxony
  2468
Cranmer, Thomas, Archibishop of Canter-
  bury. *See* Gilpin 2855
Craven, Elizabeth (Berkeley), Baroness
  Craven, later Margravine of Anspach:
  Journey through the Crimea 2168
  Miniature picture 1810:33, 2363
  Modern anecdote 2364
  Philosophe moderne 2365
  Sleep-walker 1810:29. *See* Collection 2507:1
  See Muses 3222:13
Crawford, Mrs. Ann. *See* Barry
Crawford, Charles:
  Richmond Hill 3222:15
Crawford, David:
  Courtship à la mode 835
  Love at first sight 835
Crazy tales. See Stevenson 3222:2
*Créations des chevaliers de l'Ordre du St.
  Esprit. See* La Pointe 545
Crébillon, Claude Prosper Jolyot de:
  Ah! quel conte 977
  Catalina. See Almanach 1174
  Égaremens du coeur et de l'esprit 1026

Crébillon, Claude Prosper Jolyot de (*cont.*)
Le hazard du coin du feu 724
Lettres 978
Oeuvres 958, 3086
Le sopha. See Miscellaneous volumes 943:2
Tanzai et Néadarné 979
See Damours 1185
Creech, Thomas. See Lucretius 1831
Cresswell, Joseph:
Histoire de la vie du Père Henri Valpole 3778
See Philopatris 2590
Cresswell, Thomas Estcourt:
Three letters 1608:65
See Lee 1608:73
Creusa, Queen of Athens. See Whitehead 1818:13
Crévier, Jean Baptiste Louis:
Histoire des empereurs Romains 1184
Crewe, Emma, later Mrs. Offley. See Etchings 3588
Crewe, Mrs. Frances Anne. See Collection 2508; Muses 3222:13
Cries of London. See London
Crillon, Louis Balbe Berton de. See Lussan 1254
Crimea. See Craven 2168
Crisis 1608:82
Crisis, an ode 3222:5
Crisp, Henry, attributed author. See Crisp 1818:13
Crisp, Samuel:
Virginia 1818:13
Critical and historical account of libraries. See Libraries 2018
Critical and philosophical enquiry. See Warburton 211
Critical dissertation 1379:9
Critical examination of the pictures. See Royal Academy 3885:9
Critical, expatiatory, and interesting address 1608:38
Critical history of pamphlets. See Davies 370
Critical history of the administration of Sir Robert Walpole. See Ralph 2458
Critical observations on the buildings and improvements of London. See Stuart 1609:57
Critical observations on the pictures. See Royal Academy 3885:11

Critical review of the pictures. See Royal Academy 3885:7
Critical review of the pictures. By I. N. See Royal Academy 3885:6
Critical strictures on the new tragedy of Elvira. See Boswell 1810:4
Criticism on the Elegy. See Young 1609:45
Criticism on the Foundling 1818:9
Criticisms on the Rolliad. See Rolliad 2318; Tracts 2050
Crito. See Spence 1608:67
Crockat, Gilbert:
Scotch Presbyterian eloquence 1608:24
Croft, Sir Herbert:
Love and madness 2366
Crofts, Thomas:
Bibliotheca Croftsiana 2673
Crokatt, Gilbert. See Crockat
Croke, Sir George:
Arguments. See Tracts 3797
Cromarty, George Mackenzie, Viscount Tarbat, afterwards 1st Earl of:
Historical account of the conspiracies by the Earls of Gowry 116
Synopsis apocalyptica 77
Vindication of Robert III, King of Scotland 76
See Kilmarnock 2717
Crompton, Hugh:
Pierides, or the muses mount 1937
Crompton, Richard:
Star-Chamber cases. See Tracts 3797
Cromwell, Oliver:
One letter. See Letters 2576
Speech 1608:30
See Burrow 1609:6; England 1608:1; Harris 1645; Kimber 1648; Mathew 1336; Nickolls 1097; Peck 467
Cromwell, Richard:
Speech. See Tracts 2769:4
Cromwell, Thomas, Earl of Essex. See Essex
Cromwell family. See Noble 2913
Cronica Veneta. See Pacifico 2109
Crooke, Sir George. See Croke
Crooked six-pence. See Poems 3363
Crosfield, Miss A.:
History of North Allerton 2828
Cross, John C.:
Apparition 1810:56
Purse 1810:55

Cross partners 1810:51

Cross purposes. See O'Brien 1810:19

Crowe, Sir Sackville:
  Book of accompts 2544

Crowe, William:
  Lewesden Hill 3222:22

Crown law. *See* Foster 2851

Crowne, William:
  True relation 1061

Crozat, Joseph Antoine:
  Recueil d'estampes 3550
  See Mariette 303

Crozat, Pierre. *See* Crozat, Joseph Antoine

Crozat du Châtel, Louise Honorine, Duchesse
  de. *See* Choiseul

Crudeli, Tommaso:
  Raccolta di poesie 2077

Cruikshank, Isaac. *See* Bunbury 3563:2

Crussol de Florensac, Anne Charlotte de,
  Duchesse d'Aiguillon. *See* Aiguillon

Cruttenden, Robert:
  Principles and preaching of the Methodists
  1608:74

Cry aloud and spare not 1608:56

Cryptomenyses patefacta. See Falconer 734

Culloden:
  Particular account of the battle 1608:32

Cullum, Mrs.:
  Charlotte 1810:24

Cullum, Sir John:
  One letter. *See* Letters 2576

Culpeper, Sir Thomas:
  Humble proposal 2674

Cumberland, George:
  Attempt to describe Hafod 2829
  *Some anecdotes of the life of Julio Bona-
  soni* 2367

Cumberland, Henry Frederick, Duke of. *See*
  Henry Frederick

Cumberland, Richard, Bishop:
  Origines gentium antiquissimae 1640
  Reverend brethren 1608:8
  *To the Reverend the clergy of Peterbor-
  ough* 1608:8
  See Sanchoniathon 1653

Cumberland, Richard, dramatist:
  Amelia 1810:12
  Anecdotes of eminent painters in Spain
  3411
  Banishment of Cicero 3222:1

Cumberland, Richard (*cont.*)
  Battle of Hastings 1810:27
  Box-Lobby challenge 1810:55
  Brothers 1810:15
  Calypso 1810:30
  Carmelite 1810:37
  Catalogue of paintings at Madrid 2830
  Choleric man 1810:23
  Fashionable lover 1810:18
  Impostors 1810:46
  The Jew 1810:54
  Letter to R----- B----- Esq. 1810:2
  Letter to Richard Lord Bishop of Landaff
  1609:45
  Letter to the Bishop of O—d 1609:18
  Note of hand 1810:22
  Odes 3222:14
  Songs in the Widow of Delphi 1810:31
  Summer's tale 1810:8
  Timon of Athens 1810:18
  West Indian 1810:17
  Wheel of fortune 1810:56
  See Observer 3249, 3357

Cumberland, William Augustus, Duke of. *See*
  William Augustus

Cumberland. *See* Antiquities 3485:1; Burn
  3162; Hutchinson 2879, 3193; Robinson
  704

Cuningham, Josias. *See* Cunningham

Cunning man. See Burney 1810:9

Cunningham, Josias:
  Royal shepherds 1810:8

Cunningham, Timothy. *See* Owen 3359

Cunobelin. *See* Pegge 1609:56

Cunynghame, Mary Udney, Lady. *See* Etchings 3588

Cupid's revenge. See Gentleman 1810:18

Curate, Jacob, pseud. *See* Crockat

Cure of deism. See Smith 1383

Curio. See Akenside 3363:11

Curio, Joannes. *See* Salerno 2289

Curiosités historiques 3006

Curll, Edmund:
  Atterburyana 1512
  Miscellanea 1512
  See Rochester 176; *Whartoniana* 183

*Cursory animadversions upon a late contro-
  versy. See* Middleton 1337:6

Curtius Rufus, Quintus:
  Alexander Magnus. See Classics 2207:12

Curtius Rufus, Quintus (*cont.*)
De rebus gestis Alexandri Magni. See
Brindley 2120:3
Cuthbert, Saint. *See* Hegge 739
Cutts, John, Baron Cutts:
Poetical exercises 192
Cymon. See Garrick 1810:10
Cyphers. *See* Pigot 517; Sympson 312
Cyprus. *See* Loredano 1038
Cyrus. *See* Ramsay 1449

D***, Marquis. *See* Sandras 3144
D., M.:
Brief history of Mary Queen of Scots. See
Tracts 2146:4
D., T. *See* Dicey, Thomas
Dacier, André. *See* Plutarch 1718
Dacier, Anne Lefèvre. *See* Homer 1220
Dagenham Breach. *See* Duckett 683:5
Dagge, Henry:
Considerations on criminal law 2831, 3232
Daignan d'Orbessan, Anne Marie, Marquis.
See Orbessan
Daily advertiser. See London 2143
Daily observations or meditations, divine,
morall. See Capel 70, 109
Dale, Samuel:
History of Harwich and Dovercourt 654
Dallaway, James:
Inquiries into . . . the science of heraldry
3692
See Rundle 2947
Dalrymple, Sir David, Lord Hailes:
Account of the martyrs at Smyrna 2832
Annals of Scotland 3185
Catalogue of the Lords of Session 1609:56,
57
Discourse of the unnatural and vile con-
spiracie 1609:56
Examination of some of the arguments
1609:57
Historical memorials 1609:57
Memorials and letters 2368, 2675
Miscellaneous remarks 2676
One or more letters. *See* Letters 2576
Opinions of Sarah Duchess of Marlborough
2676
Remains of Christian antiquity 2832
Remarks on the history of Scotland 2833
Specimen of a glossary. See Tracts 2050:3

Dalrymple, Sir David (*cont.*)
See Atterbury 1609:57; Hales 2702; Lan-
guet 3333; Pinkerton 2925; Scotland 1609:
57
Dalrymple, Hugh:
Rodondo 1810:59
Dalrymple, James, Viscount Stair. *See* Stair
Dalrymple, John, 2d Earl of Stair. *See* Stair
Dalrymple, Sir John:
Memoirs of Great Britain 3186, 4002
Three letters 1609:39
See Observations 1609:58; Towers 1609:31
Dalrymple, William:
Travels through Spain and Portugal 3233
Dalton, James:
Life and actions 1818:3
Dalton, Richard:
Remarks on prints 1609:42
Damer, Mrs. Anne Seymour (Conway). *See*
Drawings 3641
Damiens, Robert François:
Pièces originales 781
Damours, Louis, *and* Crébillon, Claude Pros-
per Jolyot de:
Lettres de Ninon de Lenclos 1185
Danby, Thomas Osborne, Earl of; later Duke
of Leeds:
An account of the Earl of Danby's argu-
ments 15
Memoirs relating to the impeachment 117
Dance, James, afterwards James Love. *See*
Love, James
Dance of death. See Holbein 3715
Danchet, Antoine:
Sacre de Louis XV. See Mariette 3592
Dancing master:
Compleat country dancing master 1784
Dandini, Girolamo:
Voyage to Mount Libanus 1513
Dandré Bardon, Michel François:
Traité de peinture 329
Danger of the political balance of Europe.
See Mallet 2312
Dangerous situation of England or an address
to our landed, trading, and funded inter-
ests. See Rokeby 1609:50
Daniel, Gabriel:
Voyage du monde de Descartes 1214
Daniel, Samuel:
Poetical works 1891

Dante Alighieri:
    Inferno 3222:18
D'Anvers, Caleb, pseud. *See* Bath 1608:28;
    Craftsman 1471
Daphne and Amintor. See Bickerstaffe 1810:8
Daphnis and Chloe. See Longus 2411
D'Arblay, Frances Burney, later Mme. *See*
    Burney
Darby, Samuel:
    Letter to the Rev. Mr. T. Warton 1609:47
Darell, William:
    History of Dover Castle 551
Daret, Pierre. *See* Prints 3655
Dart, John:
    History and antiquities of the Cathedral
    Church of Canterbury 428
    Westmonasterium 566
Darwin, Erasmus:
    Botanic garden 3809
Dashwood, Helen Mary (Graham), Lady. *See*
    Tomkins 3471
D'Assigny, F.:
    Ladies miscellany 1818:3
Dati, Carlo Roberto:
    Vite de' pittore antichi 478
D'Auberval, Monsieur:
    Le cocq du village 1810:36
Daulby, Daniel:
    Descriptive catalogue of the works of
    Rembrandt 237
Dauncey, John:
    History of . . . Princess Henrietta Maria de
    Bourbon, Queen of England 1557
Davenant, Sir William:
    Man's the master 1810:24
    Works 1108, 3273
Davies, John:
    Ancient rites and monuments 725
Davies, Myles:
    Icon libellorum 370
Davies, Sneyd. *See* Hornby 692:2
Davies, Thomas:
    Dramatic miscellanies 3918
    Genuine narrative 1810:27
    Memoirs of Garrick. See Garrick 2380
    See Downes 3919
Davies, William:
    Plays 1810:41
Davila, Enrico Caterino:
    Historia delle guerre civili di Francia 872

Davis, Henry Edwards:
    Examination. See Gibbon 3188
    Reply to Mr. Gibbon's vindication 1609:41
    See Gibbon 1609:39
Davis, James:
    Origines Divisianae. See Hornby 692:2
Davis, John. *See* Hornby 692:2
Davison, Francis:
    Poetical rapsody 1938
Davison, William. *See Profitable instructions*
    2935
Davy du Perron, Jacques, Cardinal:
    Perroniana et Thuana 1273
Dawes, Sir William, Archbishop of York:
    Sermons 2268
Dawkes, Thomas:
    Prodigium Willinghamense 1514
Dawkins, James. *See* Wood 3548
Day, Robert:
    Free thoughts. See North 384:1
Day, Thomas:
    Devoted legions 3222:14
    See Veal 1609:32
Dazès, Abbé:
    Esprit des magistrats philosophes 3007
De la prédication. See Coyer 3085
De la vérité. See Herbert 35
De l'esprit. See Helvétius 552
De l'origine des loix. See Goguet 3100
De religione gentilium. See Herbert 85
De Rep. Anglorum instauranda libri decem.
    See Chaloner 112
De veritate. See Herbert 167
Dean and the squire. See Mason 3222:18
Death of Bucephalus. See Schomberg
    1810:7
Death of Captain Cook. See Cook 1810:47
Debate . . . on the motion of Mr. Fox. See
    England 1609:53
Debates in the Asiatic assembly 1609:17
De Bure, Guillaume. *See* La Vallière 3336
Decision of the Court of Session. See Scotland
    1609:58
Declaration of the libertyes of the English
    nation. See Edward I 1608:8
Declaration of the sense of the archbishops.
    See Tenison 1608:8
De Coetlogon, Charles Edward. *See* Coetlo-
    gon
De Coetlogon, Dennis. *See* Coetlogon

Dee, John:
　　True and faithful relation of what passed for many years 1109
Deering, Charles:
　　Nottinghamia vetus et nova 2834, 3305
Defence of F. Giardini 1609:56
Defence of Mr. Rousseau 1609:16
Defence of Mr. Sulivan's propositions 1609:17
Defence of Mr. Vansittart's conduct 1609:55
Defence of the administration 1609:20
Defence of the Bishop of London's connection. See Middleton 1379:4
Defence of the Crisis 1608:93
Defence of the Letter to Dr. Waterland. See Middleton 1379:1
Defence of the Letter to the Reverend Mr. John Jackson. See Middleton 1379:8
Defence of the majority in the House of Commons. See Lloyd 1609:8, 9
Defence of the minority in the House of Commons. See Townshend 1609:8
Defence of the New-England charters. See Dummer 1609:12
Defence of the people. See Egmont 119:1
Defence of the Right Honourable the Earl of Shelburne. See O'Bryen 1609:43
Defensative against the poyson of supposed prophecies. See Northampton 93
Defense de Milord Bollingbroke. See Voltaire 1608:76
Definitive treaty of peace. See England 1609:54
Defoe, Daniel:
　　And what if the Pretender should come 1608:9
　　Answer to a question 1608:9
　　Enquiry into the danger of a war with the Dutch 1608:9
　　Essay on the history of parties 1608:9
　　History of the union between England and Scotland 3306
　　Life and adventures of Robinson Crusoe 408
　　Memoirs of a cavalier 1704
　　Memoirs of D. of Shrewsbury 1608:14
　　Narrative of the proceedings in France 1608:29
　　Secret history of the October Club 1608:9
　　Shortest way with the dissenters. See Blackbird 2646:9

Defoe, Daniel (*cont.*)
　　Tour. See Beauties 716
　　Trade with France. See Detection 2677:10
　　See Carleton 1352; Detection 2677; Dictionary 1472
Deguisemens des auteurs. See Baillet 714
De Hooghe, Romeyn. *See* Hooghe
Deist doctor detected. See Middleton 1379:4
Dekker, Thomas. *See* Marlowe 1964
Delamayne, Thomas Hallie:
　　Patricians 3222:12
　　Senators 3222:12
Delamere, Henry Booth, 2d Baron, and 1st Earl of Warrington. *See* Warrington 182
Delany, Mary:
　　Catalogue of plants 1609:47, 2639
Delap, John:
　　Captives 1810:39
　　Hecuba 1810:2
　　Royal suppliants 1810:32
De Laune, Thomas:
　　Present state of London 726
De Leeuw, Thomas. *See* Prints 3626
Delfino family 3381
Delille, Jacques. *See* Lille
Delineatio pompae triumphalis. See Leicester 509
Della Bella, Stephano. *See* Sgrilli 3760
Della Crusca, pseud. *See* Merry, Robert
De Longueville, Henry Yelverton, Viscount. *See* Sussex 2600
Del Rio. *See* Rio 857
Demosthenes:
　　Demosthenis et Aeschinis opera 2153
　　Orations 463
　　Philippiques 1186
　　See Mounteney 1608:66
Dempster, George. *See* Boswell 1810:4
Denham, Sir John:
　　On Mr. Abraham Cowley his death. See Oxford 2061:4
Denina, Carlo Giovanni Maria:
　　Tableau des révolutions de la littérature 3008
Denis, Charles:
　　Siege of Calais 1810:7
Denisot, Nicolas. *See* Marguerite 2415
Denmark. *See* Caroline Mathilde 1609:29; Hofman 270; Mallet 3028

Denne, Samuel:
Historical particulars of Lambeth Parish and Lambeth Palace 3234
Dennis, John:
Appius and Virginia. See Plays 1623:2
See Concanen 1608:31
Dent, John:
Candidate 1810:34
Receipt tax 1810:35
Too civil by half 1810:35
Denton, Henry. *See* Georgirenes 1408
Deplorable life and death of Edward the Second. See Hubert 1953
Derby, Charles Stanley, Earl of:
Protestant religion 78, 79
Derby, Edward Smith-Stanley, Earl of. *See Fête* 3222:13
Derby, James Stanley, Earl of. *See* Winstanley 3668
Derby. *See* Hutton 2883
Derby Gallery. *See* Winstanley 3668
Derby House. *See Westminster* 1608:1
Derbyshire. *See Account* 1810:30; Bray 2345, 3400; Leigh 602; Pilkington 2922
Derham, William:
Astro-theology 1371
Physico and astro-theology 2835
See Ray 1689
Derniers sentiments des plus illustres personnages condamnés à mort. See Sabatier 2288
Desaguliers, John Theophilus. *See* Gravesande 1409
Desainliens, Claude:
Pretie and wittie historie of Arnalt and Lucenda 4003
Des Barres, Comtesse. *See* Choisy 1292
Descamps, Jean Baptiste:
Vie des peintres 295
Voyage pittoresque 295
Descartes, René. *See* Daniel 1214
Deschamps, Jean Baptiste. *See* Descamps
Descriptio Angliae et descriptio Londini. See Coryate 3222:5
Description de Nismes. See Arts 288:2
Description des tableaux du Palais Royal. See Du Bois 330
Description of a certain lady. See Particular description

Description of a new instrument. See Hadley 1608:37
Description of Holland. See Holland 1412
Description of Millennium Hall. See Scott 2469
Description sommaire . . . du cabinet de feu M. Crozat. See Mariette 303
Deseine, François Jacques:
Description de la ville de Rome 1027
Desert island. See Murphy 1818:18
Deserted daughter. See Holcroft 1810:56
Deserter. See Jerningham 3222:10
Desfontaines, Pierre François Guyot:
Dictionnaire néologique 3087
See Southwell 796; Swift 1456
Desgodetz, Antoine Babuty:
Les édifices antiques de Rome 3677
Deshoulières, Antoinette du Ligier de la Garde, Madame:
Poësies 1187
Deslandes, André François Boureau:
Poetae rusticantis literatum otium. See Arlequiniana 1019
Deslauriers, N. *See* Bruscambille 803
Des Maizeaux, Pierre:
Historical and critical account of John Hales 1608:14
Vie de M. Bayle 959
See Bayle 957; Saint-Evremonde 948; Whiston 1727:1
Des Marais, Paul Godet. *See* Maintenon 1280
Desmarest, Nicholas. *See* Dufour 1248
Des Noulis, N. Petrineau:
Histoire des rois de Sicile 918
Desormeaux, Joseph Louis Ripault:
Histoire de la maison de Bourbon 3088
Histoire de la maison de Montmorenci 794
Des Periers, Bonaventure:
Contes. See Contes 1025
Nouvelles récréations 1614
See Strawberry Hill 3469:6
Des Salles, Dom:
Mémoires . . . de France et de Bourgogne 919
Destouches, Philippe Néricault. *See* Holcroft 1810:50; O'Beirne 1810:34
Destrées, Jacques. *See* Estrées
Detached pieces printed at SH. *See* Collection 2506, 2508

Detection of the considerations 1608:27

Detection of . . . the Secret History of the White Staff 2677

Detector detected 1608:44

Dethick, Sir Gilbert. *See* Garter 2551

Dettingen, Battle of. *See Impartial review* 1608:46; *Operations* 1608:26

Deuce is in him. See Colman 1810:5

Deuchar, David. *See* Holbein 3715

De Vadis, Giles. *See* Duwes 118

Deveil, Sir Thomas. *See* Poems 3363:10

Devereux, Robert, Earl of Essex. *See* Essex

Devienne, Charles Jean Baptiste d'Agneaux, called Dom:
  Histoire d'Artois 3308
  Histoire de la ville de Bordeaux 3089

Devil upon crutches in England 1608:80

Deviliad. See Poems 3363:10

Devil's almanac 1608:4

Devizes. *See* Hornby 692:2

Devonshire, Dukes of. *See* Grove 1521

Devonshire, Charles Blount, Earl of. *See* Ford 1321

Devonshire, Christiana Cavendish, Countess of. *See* Pomfret 3900

Devonshire, Georgiana Cavendish, Duchess of. *See* Chatsworth 3222:21

Devonshire, William Cavendish, 1st Duke of. *See* Kennet 1750

Devonshire, William Cavendish, 4th Duke of. *See* Collection 2507:4; *London* 697

Devonshire:
  Description of Devon. See Risdon 703
  Worthies of Devon. See Prince 580
  See Heath 1609:54; Polwhele 2929, 3364; Pole 3205

De Vos, Marten:
  Portfolio of 641 engravings 3600
  See Prints 3605

Devoted legions. See Day 3222:14

Dewes, Giles. *See* Duwes 118

Dezallier d'Argenville, Antoine Joseph:
  Abrégé de la vie des peintres 265
  Théorie . . . du jardinage 920
  See Burgess 1608:78; De Piles 308

Diabo-lady. See Combe 3222:15

Diaboliad. See Combe 3222:15

Dialogue between a lieutenant and a captain 1608:27

Dialogue between Jack High and Will Low. See Black-bird 2646:12

Dialogue between Marcellus and Julia. See Marcellus 1609:51

Dialogue . . . between Puddle and Pepper. See Black-bird 2646:8

Dialogue between Thomas Jones and John Smith 1608:59

Dialogue between two great ladies. See Walpole 2050:21

Dialogue or rather a parley. See Black-bird 2646:8

Dialogues of the dead. See Lyttelton 131

Dialogues on the uses of foreign travel. See Hurd 1609:7

Diamond cut diamond. See Wallace 1810:42

Diamonds, Catalogue of. *See* Catalogues 2303:2

Diano, Carlo Calà, Duca di. *See* Calà 2072

Diatribe du docteur Akakia. See Voltaire 1608:76

Dibdin, Charles:
  Chelsea pensioner 1810:30
  Cobler 1810:23, 43
  Damon and Phillida 1810:13, 43
  Deserter 1810:10, 43
  Harvest home 1810:43
  Mirror 1810:31
  Poor Vulcan 1810:27
  Rose and Colin 1810:29
  Shepherdess of the Alps 1810:31
  Shepherd's artifice 1810:7, 43
  Songs, duets, and trios 1810:27
  Songs in Liberty-Hall 1810:37
  Songs in the Wedding Ring 1810:19
  Waterman 1810:22
  Wedding Ring 1810:19
  See Songs 1810:31

Dicey, Thomas:
  Case 1608:7
  Historical account of Guernsey 727
  See Loyalty 1608:60

Dickinson, John:
  Letters from a farmer in Pennsylvania 1609:22
  New essay 1609:32
  See Late occurrences 1609:12; *Regulations* 1609:11

Dictionarium polygraphicum. See Barrow 289

Dictionarium rusticum 1353

Dictionary:
Dictionarium sacrum 1472
Historical, genealogical, and classical dictionary 1551
Historical, genealogical, and poetical dictionary 1558
New and general biographical dictionary 1772
See Bailey 1463
Dictionary of husbandry. See Dictionarium 1353
Dictionnaire bibliographique. See Catalogues 2819
Dictionnaire d'anecdotes. See Lacombe de Prezel 3023
Dictionnaire des portraits historiques. See Lacombe 3023
Dictionnaire des théâtres. See Abguerbe 775
Dictionnaire néologique. See Desfontaines 3087
Diderot, Denis:
Dorval 1810:11
See Voltaire 3058
Dido 1810:11
Difficulties and discouragements which attend the study of the Scriptures. See Hare 1608:32
Digby, George, 2d Earl of Bristol. *See* Bristol
Digby, Lord George. *See* Digby, Sir Kenelm 159
Digby, John, 1st Earl of Bristol. *See* Bristol
Digby, Sir Kenelm:
Letters 159
See Browne 1732; Walpole 3730
Digges, Sir Dudley:
Compleat ambassador 1110
Dighton, Robert. *See* Bunbury 3563:2
Dilherr, Johann Michael:
Contemplations . . . of a Christian 2678
Dillingham, William. *See* Vere 492
Dillon, Sir John Talbot:
Travels through Spain 2836
Dimsdale, Thomas:
Present method of inoculating for the small-pox 1609:19
Diocletian, Emperor of Rome. *See* Adam 3531
Diodorus Siculus:
Bibliothecae historicae libri XV 2154

Dionysius Cassius Longinus. *See* Longinus 2089
Dionysius, of Halicarnassus:
Opera 2155
Dionysius Periegetes:
Orbis descriptio 2086
Discord. See Poems 280:13
Discourse concerning generosity. See Tracts 210
Discourse concerning the irritability of some flowers. See Covolo 1609:18
Discourse of infallibility. See Falkland 82, 120
Discourse of natural and moral impotency. See Truman 1804
Discourse of the general notions of money. See Clement 1608:8
Discourse of the unnatural and vile conspiracie. See Dalrymple 1609:56
Discourse on . . . Christian religion. See Collins 1402
Discourse on Providence 1608:29
Discourse, opening the nature of that episcopacie which is exercised in England. See Brooke 68
Discoverie of the treasons practised by Francis Throckmorton. See Cecil 111:2
The discovery. See Sheridan 1810:4
Disney, William:
Transcript of government 728
Dispute between the King and Senate. See Sweden 1608:83
Disquisitions on several subjects. See Jenyns 2892
Dissenters. *See* Protestant dissenters
Dissertation . . . de l'imprimerie primitive. See Fournier 3012:5
Dissertation sur . . . l'art de graver en bois. See Fournier 3012:4
Dissertation sur l'incertitude des cinq premiers siècles de l'histoire romaine. See Beaufort 1022
Dissertation upon Oriuna. See Stukeley 668:5
Dissertation upon 2 Peter i.19. See Middleton 1379:9
Distressed family 1810:42
Ditchley. See Guides 2387:2
Diversity. See Merry 3222:22
The Divorce. See Jackman 1810:33
Dixi, pseud. *See College exercise* 1609:23

Dobbs, Francis:
  Patriot king 1810:23
Dobneck, Johannes, Cochlaeus. *See* Cochlaeus
Docteur Pansophe. See Hume 1680:2
Doctor and the apothecary. See Cobb 1810:46
Doctor Last in his chariot. See Bickerstaffe 1810:14
Dr. Mead's Short Discourse explain'd. See Miscellaneous tracts 89
Dr. Mead's Short Discourse . . . exploded. See Miscellaneous tracts 89
Dodd, James Solas:
  Satyrical lecture on hearts 1609:17
Dodd, William:
  Sermon 2050:4
  See Johnson 1609:38; Villette 1609:38
Doddridge, Sir John:
  History of . . . Wales 1062
Doddridge, Philip:
  Some remarkable passages in the life of Colonel James Gardiner 1676
Dodington, George Bubb:
  Diary 429, 2837
  Epistle from John More. See Poems 881:13
  Examination of a letter 1608:87
  Honest grief of a Tory 1608:87
  Poetical epistle from the late Lord Melcombe 3222:15
Dodsley, Robert:
  Cave of Pope. See Poems 3363:4
  Cleone 1818:17
  Collection of poems 2370
  Fugitive pieces 1559
  King and the miller of Mansfield 1818:6
  Select collection of old English plays 1868
  Trifles in prose and verse 1824
  Triumph of peace 1818:10
  See Aesop 2208; Letters 1900; *London and its environs* 697; *London Chronicle* 538; Magazines 3338; *Museum* 2431; Pearch 3453; Roads 2287; *Theatrical* 3929
Dodwell, Henry, the elder:
  Dissertationes Cyprianicae 2087
Dodwell, Henry, the younger:
  Christianity not founded on argument 1608:25
Dodwell, William:
  Free answer. See Middleton 1379:8

Dodwell, William (*cont.*)
  Full and final reply 1372
  See Toll 1379:5
Dolben, John. *See Black-bird* 2646:11
Domenichi, Lodovico:
  Facecies et motz subtilz 3309
  Facetie, motti, et burle 2100
Domenichino. *See* Zampieri
Dominique de Colonia:
  Antiquités de la ville de Lyon 1246
Donaldson, Alexander. *See* Scotland 1609:58
Doncaster. *See* Paine 576
Donne, John:
  Biathanatos 1473
  Poems 1892
Donne, John, the younger. *See* Matthew 1441
Don Quixote. See Piguenit 1810:26
Don Saverio. See Arne 1623:1
Donzé de Verteuil, Joseph. *See* Sabatier 2288
Door, churches of. *See* Gibson 622
Doort, Abraham Van Der. *See* Van Der Dort
Dorando. See Boswell 1609:19
Dorchester, Dudley Carleton, Viscount:
  Letters 3310
  Letters during his embassy in Holland 3166
Dorothea Sophia (Neuburg), consort of Edward Farnese, Prince of Parma. *See* Cosmo II 2304:3
Dorrington, Theophilus:
  Excellent woman 2679
Dorset, Charles Sackville, Earl of. *See* Sprat 2760
Dorset, Charles Sackville, 2d Duke of:
  Treatise concerning the militia 1608:27, 48
Dorset, John Frederick Sackville, 3d Duke of. *See* Willis 2990
Dorset, Lionel Cranfield Sackville, 1st Duke of. *See* Letter 2146:3
Dorsetshire. *See* Coker 620; Hutchins 4
Dort, Abraham Van Der. *See* Van Der Dort
Dossie, Robert:
  Statesman foil'd 1810:13
Double déguisement. See Mélange 1045
Double disguise. See Hook 1810:36
Double mistake. See Griffith 1810:8
Douglas, Anne, Countess of Argyle. *See* Argyle 2329
Douglas, Archibald James Edward, Baron Douglas. *See* Douglas 1609:19

Douglas, Gawin. *See* Virgilius 101

Douglas, George, 4th Baron Mordington. *See* Mordington 134

Douglas, James, 4th Duke of Hamilton. *See* Hamilton

Douglas, Lady Jane:
Letters of the Right Honourable Lady Jane Douglas 1609:19

Douglas, John, Bishop:
Seasonable hints from an honest man 1609:2
Serious defence 1608:81
See Clarendon 1060

Douglas, house of. *See* Hume 2712

Douglas. See Home 1818:15

Douglas Cause:
Considerations on the Douglas Cause 1609:19
See Stuart 2471

Douglass, William:
Present state of the British settlements 1403
See Letter to Dr. Thomson 1608:89

Douxménil. *See* La Fayette 988:2

Dover Castle. *See* Darell 551

Dovercourt. *See* Dale 654

Dow, Alexander:
History of Hindostan 2838
Sethona 1810:22
Zingis 1810:13

Dowdeswell, William. *See* Sentiments 1609:57

Dowman, G.:
Answer 1608:89

Down, County. *See* Smith 396

Downe-fall of Dagon, or the taking downe of Cheap-side Cross. See Downfall of Dagon

Downes, John:
Roscius Anglicanus 3919

Downfal of the Association. See Downfall

Downfall of Dagon. See Tracts 2050

Downfall of Sejanus. See Masquerader 2416

Downfall of the Association 1810:17

Downing, George:
Parthian exile 1810:22
Volunteers 1810:31

Downman, Hugh:
Editha 1810:36
Lucius Junius Brutus 1810:30
See Pilon 3222:13

Downright, Sir Daniel, pseud. *See Bastard child* 1810:13

Doyle, John. *See* Tooke 1609:25

Drake, Francis:
Eboracum 567

Drake, James. *See* Miscellaneous tracts 89:2

Drakenborch, Arnold. *See* Silius Italicus 2198

Drama: a poem. See Pilon 3222:13

Dramatic execution of Agis 1818:16

Draper, Sir William:
Colonel Draper's answer 1609:9

Drapier, M. B., pseud. *See Letter* 1608:61

Drawings:
Drawings from coins, medals, bronzes, &c. 2371
Eight sketches in oil 3412
Portfolio of drawings by Dutch masters 3587
Portfolios of drawings 3567–9, 3641, 3678
See Vertue 2610

Drayton, Michael:
Historie of Lord Cromwell 3955
Works 1848

Dream and elegy on King Charles the First. See Quarles 2026

Dreamer. See King 1483

Dreux du Radier, Jean François:
Récréations historiques 3090
Tablettes anecdotes 3090
See Mémoires 1303

Drevet, Pierre. *See* Prints 3626

Drinkwater, John:
History of the late siege of Gibraltar 3311

Drogheda, Anne Seymour Conway, Countess of. *See* Etchings 3588

Droit le roy. See Brecknock 1609:7

Druids. *See* Airs 1810:22

Drumgold, John:
Avis aux vivants 3920
Charles et Vilcourt 3920
La gaieté 3920

Drummond, Alexander:
Travels 873

Drummond, John, 1st Earl of Melfort. *See* Melfort

Drummond, William, of Hawthornden:
Most elegant . . . poems 1893, 2839
Works 1111

Drunken Barnaby's four journeys. *See* Brathwait 2235, 2808

Drunken news-writer 1810:17

Drury Lane Theatre:
Historical . . . account of the late riots 1810:4
Three original letters 1810:4
See Mr. Garrick's conduct 1818:9

Dryden, John:
Alexander's feast. See Prior 2146:5
Astraea redux 238
Conquest of Granada. See Plays 1908:3
Don Sebastian, King of Portugal 1939
Dramatic works 1869
Fables 1849
Miscellaneous works 1812
Miscellany poems 1825
See Du Fresnoy 296; Garrick 1810:16; Hawkesworth 1818:15; Juvenalis 1874; Milbourne 1533; Ovidius 1904; Plutarch 1718; Poems 3363; Virgilius 1880; *Whittington's feast* 1810:26

Dryden, John (1668–1701):
Voyage to Sicily 1609:37

D—st D—ct—r detected. See Middleton 1379:4

Du Barry, Marie Jeanne, Comtesse. *See* Mairobert 3125

Du Bellay, Guillaume. *See Collection* 3084

Du Bellay, Martin:
Mémoires 894
See Collection 3084

Dublin. *See* Harris 689; Pool 3255; Wales 2976

Dublin. Theatres. *See* Victor 2973

Dublin. Trinity College:
Gratulationes juventutis academiae Dubliniensis 313

Du Bois de Saint-Gelais, Louis François:
Description des tableaux du Palais Royal 330

Dubos, Jean Baptiste:
Histoire de la ligue faite à Cambray 805
Réflexions critiques 1215

Du Bouchet, Jean:
Histoire généalogique de la Maison Royale de Courtenay 895

Du Buat-Nançay, Gabriel Louis:
Histoire ancienne des peuples de l'Europe 3009

Dubuy, Pierre Ancher Tobiésen:
Recueil général 3693
Traité des monnoies 3694

Ducarel, Andrew Coltee:
Anglo-Gallic coins 266. *See* Perry 248
Anglo-Norman antiquities 3274
One letter. *See* Letters 2576
Tour through Normandy. See Stukeley 668:6
See Bourget 2806

Ducatiana. See Le Duchat 1299

Du Cerceau, Jacques Androuet. *See* Androuet

Du Cerceau, Jean Antoine:
Conjuration de Nicolas Gabrini, dit de Rienzi 1293

Du Châtel, Louise Honorine Crozat, Duchesse de Choiseul. *See* Choiseul

Du Chesne, André:
Antiquitez et recherches 1247
Histoire généalogiques de la maison de Montmorency 896

Duchess of Devonshire's cow. See Combe 3222:15

Duck, Arthur:
Life of Henry Chichele 1705, 2680

Duck, Stephen:
Ode on the Battle of Dettingen. See Poems 881:9
Poems 1608:17
The Vision. See Poems 280:3

Duckett, George:
Summary of all the religious houses in England and Wales 683

Du Clercq, Jacques. *See Collection* 3084

Duclos, Abbé. *See* Catalogues 2819

Duclos, Charles Pineau:
Acajou et Zirphile 3091
Histoire de Louis XI 960
Mémoirs pour servir de suite aux Considerations 3092

Du Cros, Simon:
Histoire de la vie de Henry dernier Duc de Mont-Morency 921

Du Deffand, Marie de Vichy, Madame:
Collection of letters 2545
Journal 2545
Recueil de divers ouvrages ['Portraits'] 2545

Dudin, ——:
L'Art du relieur doreur de livres 3413

Dudley, Sir Henry Bate. *See* Bate, Henry

Dudley, Lady Jane. *See* Grey, Lady Jane

Dudley, John, Duke of Northumberland. *See* Northumberland 174

Dudley, Joshua:
Memoirs 1609:29

Dudley, Robert, Earl of Leicester. *See* Leicester 509

Duel. See O'Brien 1810:19

Duenna. See Pottinger 1810:26; Sheridan 1810:25

Duerer, Albrecht. *See* Dürer

Du Faur, Gui, Seigneur de Pibrac
Les quatrains 806

Dufour de Longuerue, Louis:
Longueruana ou recueil des pièces 1248

Du Fresnoy, Charles Alphonse:
Art of painting 296, 3890

Du Fresnoy, Nicolas Lenglet. *See* Lenglet du Fresnoy

Dugdale, Sir William:
Ancient usage . . . of . . . arms 729
Antiquities of Warwickshire 568
Baronage of England 590
History of St. Paul's Cathedral 591
Origines juridiciales 729
See Heraldry 2558; Hornby 692; Norfolk 2581

Du Guesclin, Bertrand, Comte de Longueville. *See* Collection 3084; Ménard 1076

Du Halde, Jean Baptiste:
Description . . . de la Chine 874

Du Jon, François. *See* Junius 221

Dukerus, Carolus Andreas. *See* Thucydides 535

Dulany, Daniel:
Considerations on the propriety of imposing taxes 1609:13

Du Laurens, Henri Joseph:
Balai 807

Du Maine, Sieur de la Croix. *See* La Croix 902

Dumaniant, A. J. *See* Wallace 1810:42

Dummer, Jeremiah:
Defence of the New-England charters 1609: 12

Du Molinet, Claude:
Cabinet de la Bibliothèque de Sainte-Geneviève 3679

Du Moulin. *See* Noailles 815

Du Moulin, Gabriel:
Conquestes . . . des Norman-François 897

Dumouriez, Antoine François Duperrier. *See* Ricciardetto 3041

Dumouriez, Charles François:
Coup d'oeil politique 2305

Dunch, Mrs. Elizabeth:
Catalogue of pictures. See Catalogues 3404

Duncombe, Giles:
Tryals per pais 2681

Duncombe, John:
Historical description of the Cathedral . . . [of] *Canterbury* 2840
Parody on Gray's Elegy 3222:14
See Cork 42; Herring 2872; Hughes 2876

Duncombe, William:
Junius Brutus 1818:6
See Herring 2872

Duncon, John:
Life . . . of . . . Lady Letice, Vi-Countess Falkland 1739

Dundas, Sir Lawrence:
Catalogue of paintings. See Tracts 3833:3

Dundee, John Graham, Viscount. *See* Graham 1565

Dunk, George Montagu, 2d Earl of Halifax. *See* Halifax

Dunkirk. *See* Detection 2677:8; Steele 1608:16

Dunning, John, 1st Baron Ashburton. *See* Ashburton

Du Noyer, Anne Marguerite Petit:
Letters from a lady at Paris. See Aulnoy 1462

Dunsford, Martin:
Historical memoirs of the town and parish of Tiverton 3187

Dunstaple. *See* Hearne 656

Dunster, Charles. *See* Aristophanes 3222:21

Dunster, Samuel. *See* Horatius 1854

Dunton, John:
Ox —— and Bull ——. See Black-bird 2646: 15

Dunwich. *See* Gardner 504

The dupe. See Sheridan 1810:5

Duperrier Dumouriez, Antoine François. *See* Ricciardetto 3041

Du Perron, Abraham Hyacinthe Anquetil. *See* Zand-Avastá 3155

Du Perron, Jacques Davy, Cardinal. *See* Davy 1273

Du Plessis, Armand Jean, Duc de Richelieu. *See* Richelieu

Du Plessis, Louis François Armand. *See* Richelieu 3368

Duplicity. See Holcroft 1853

Du Pont, Pierre:
Verification of an inventory 2546

Dupuy, Pierre:
Histoire de la condamnation des Templiers 1028

Dupuy-Demportes, Jean Baptiste:
Histoire du ministère du chevalier Robert Walpool 2269
See Walpole 2323

Dupuy la Chapelle, N.:
Caractères 1188

Durand, David. *See* Macé 1279

Durant, John:
Comfort & counsell for dejected soules 2682

Durell, David. *See* Whitefield 1609:20

Dürer, Albrecht:
Albert Durer revived 502
Portfolio of 296 engravings 3601
See Drawings 3567

Du Revest, Abbé. *See* La Monnoye 990

D'Urfey, Thomas:
Comical history of Don Quixote 2270
New collection of poems and songs 1940
See Pill 2446; Poems 3363

Durham. *See* Hutchinson 3330; Spearman 639

Durham Cathedral. *See* Davies 725; Hegge 739; Hunter 742

Durham. Coins. *See* Noble 243

Durham. St. Cuthbert's. *See* Hegge 739

Durham Cathedral as it was before the dissolution of the monastery. See Hunter 375, 742

Du Rondel, Jacques:
De vita et moribus Epicuri 2271

Durosoi, Barnabé Farmain. *See* Farmain 2689

Dury, John:
Reformed-School 193
See Hartlib 2390

Du Ryer, Sieur. *See* Koran 1484

Dusseldorf Gallery. *See* Pigage 3513

Dutch faith 1608:26

Dutch method of extinguishing accidental fires. See Heiden 529

Dutens, Louis:
L'Ami des étrangers 3414
Correspondance interceptée 2306
Histoire d'une regence 3093
History of the late important period 2841
Des pierres précieuses 3312
Recherches 2842

Du Terrail, Pierre, Seigneur de Bayard. *See* Bayard

Du Tillet, Evrard Titon. *See* Titon

Du Tillet, Jean:
Mémoires 898
Recueil des Roys de France 899

Du Tilliot. *See* Lucotte du Tilliot

Du Val, Michael:
Rosa Hispani-Anglica 1615

Du Verdier, Antoine:
Prosopographie 1063
See Bibliothèques 3068

Du Verdier, Gilbert Saulnier:
Love and armes of the Greeke princes 452, 2683

Du Villars, François de Boivin, Baron. *See* Collection 3084

Duwes, Giles:
Introductorie for to learne to rede 118

Dyde, William:
History and antiquities of Tewkesbury 3415

Dyer, John. *See* Poems 3363

Dymock, Thomas W.:
England's dust 1064

Dyson, Jeremiah:
Case of the late election for the County of Middlesex 1609:57

Dyson, Richard Randall:
History ... of Tottenham High Cross 2843

E., A. *See* Grey 1608:55

E., S. *See* Duncombe 2681

E., S. F., Mrs. *See* Egerton 1894

E., W. *See* Letters 1609:48

Eachard, John:
Mr. Hobb's State of Nature considered 1516
Works 1595

Eachard, Laurence. *See* Echard

Eagle found at Rome, engravings. *See* Antiquities 3485:9

Earbery, Matthias:
  Occasional historian 80
  Vindication of the history of clemency 2684

Earl of Essex. *See* Brooke 1810:1

Earl of Warwick. *See* Francklin 1810:9; Hiffernan 1810:9

Earlom, Richard. *See* Lorrain 3669

East India Bill. *See* Bunbury 3563:1; Burke 1609:46; Stuart 1609:46

East India Company:
  Address to the public 1609:18
  History of the administration 1609:55
  See Address 1609:55; Bengal 1609:7; Clive 1609:7, 58; Coote 1609:55; *Debates* 1609: 17; *East India Examiner* 1609:16; England 1609:30; Fox 1609:45; *Great Britain's poverty* 1608:64; Hastings 1609:49; Holwell 1609:55; *Letter* 1609:22; *Original papers* 1609:47A; Pownall 1609:31; Stuart 1609:46; Vansittart 1609:17

East India examiner 1609:16

East Indies. *See* Valle 2181

Easton, James. *See* Salisbury 2752

Easton Neston. *See* Nixon 485

Eastward Hoe. See Lennox 1810:25

Eboracensis. *See Letter* 1609:5

Eccardt, John Giles. *See* Drawings 3587

Echard, Laurence:
  Roman history 1641

Eckhel, Joseph Hilarius von:
  Choix des pierres gravées 3695

Éclaircissemens sur la vie de Jean d'Aranthon. See Le Masson 1252

Éclaircissement sur les moeurs. See Toussaint 2050:23

École de la volupté. See Almanach 1174

Economy. *See* Oeconomy

Eden, William, Baron Auckland. *See* Auckland

Edgar and Emmeline. See Hawkesworth 1810:1

Edgar, William:
  Vectigalium systema 1474

Edgcumbe, Richard:
  Epistle 881:33

Edict of the Grand Duke of Tuscany. See Tuscany 1609:52

Edinburgh. *See* Maitland 604

Edinburgh. Theatre Royal. *See* Fennell 1810: 46

Edmondson, Joseph:
  Baronagium genealogicum 527
  Complete body of heraldry 528
  Historical and genealogical account 2372
  One letter. *See* Letters 2576
  Precedency of princes 2373

Edmund, King of England. *See* Lydgate 3505

Éducation des femmes, Traité de l'. See Miremont 2284

Edward, the Confessor, King of England. *See* Keepe 377; Porter 391

Edward I, King of England:
  Charta de Foresta 2547
  Declaration of the libertyes of the English nation 1608:8
  See Topham 3382

Edward II, King of England:
  Anecdotes de la cour et du règne d'Edouard II 3010
  See Caesar 2815; Falkland 16; Hubert 1953; *Majesty misled* 1810:16

Edward III, King of England. *See* May 1969

Edward IV, King of England. *See* Habington 18; W., T. 1989

Edward V, King of England. *See Annalium* 3286; More 2247

Edward VI, King of England:
  Arguments against the Pope's supremacy 160
  Copies of letters 2509. *See* Collection 2508; Strawberry Hill 3469:1; Walpole 3476
  See Haynes 441

Edward, Prince of Wales (called the Black Prince). *See* Collins 1674; Shirley 1818:8

Edward [Farnese], Prince of Parma:
  L'Eta dell ora, balletto. See Cosmo II 2304: 3

Edwards, Edward. *See* Müntz 3575; Walpole 3582

Edwards, George:
  Gleanings of natural history 3872
  Natural history of uncommon birds 3873
  Some memoirs of ... George Edwards 3874

Edwards, John:
  British herbal 3492

Edwards, Thomas:
  Account of the trial 1608:79
  Canons of criticism 1608:66

Effingham, Thomas Howard, 3d Earl of:
Essay on the nature of a loan 1609:42
Égaremens du coeur. See Crébillon 1026
Egerton, John:
Theatrical remembrancer 3921
Egerton, Mrs. Sarah Fyge:
Collection of poems 1894
Egerton, Thomas, Baron Ellesmere. *See* Ellesmere
Egerton, William:
Memoirs of . . . Mrs. Anne Oldfield 1677
Eginhardus, Abbot of Seligenstadt:
De vita et gestis Caroli Magni 836
Eglinton, Alexander Montgomerie, 10th Earl of. *See* Campbell 1609:26
Eglisham, George:
Two petitions. See Letters 2576
Egmont, John Perceval, 1st Earl of. *See* Martyn 1608:40
Egmont, John Perceval, 2d Earl of:
Collection of tracts 119
Faction detected 2844
Memorial to the King. See Tracts 99:2
Question of the precedency of peers 44
See Anderson 2328; *Detector* 1608:44; Ruffhead 1609:6
Egotist: or, Colley upon Cibber 1608:90
Egremont, Charles Wyndham, 2d Earl of. *See* Bromfield 2534; *Letter* 1609:6
Egypt. *See* Dalton 1609:42; Pauw 3134; Rollin 1205
Ehret, Georg Dionysius. *See* Drawings 3587
Eidous, Marc Antoine. *See* Walpole 3908
Eight speeches. See Tracts 2769:13
Eijden, Jan van der. *See* Heiden
Eikon basilike. See Charles I 1507
Eisenberg, Baron d':
Description du manège moderne 3493
Eisenmenger, Johann Andreas. *See* Stehelin 1384
E—L of CH—M's apology. See Pitt 3222:7
Election. See Andrews 1810:22, 32
Election ball. See Anstey 3222:15
Election of 1784. *See* Westminster 557
Electrical eel. See Strong 3222:15
Elegiac monody. See Vyner 3834
Elegidia et poematia epidictica 331
Elegies and sonnets. See Knight 3222:20
Elegy on the death of Miss Caroline Campbell. See Conway 3222:22

Elegy on the death of Samuel Foote, Esq. See Foote 3222:16
Elegy on the late Right Honourable W . . . P . . . Esq. See Pitt 3222:7
Elegy to the memory of the Right Honourable William [Pulteney], *late Earl of Bath. See* Kelly 3222:6
Elegy upon the Earl of Granville. See Walpole 2489:4
Elegy written among the ruins of an abbey. See Jerningham 3222:6
Elegy written in Covent Garden 3222:11
Elements of architecture. See Wotton 103
Elements of modern gardening. See Gardening 3891:1
Elgin, Charles Bruce, Earl of. *See* Bruce
Élie de Beaumont, Anne Louise:
Lettres du Marquis de Roselle 938
See Edward II 3010
Eliot, Andrew:
Sermon preached 1609:11
Elizabeth, Princess of England and Landgravine of Hesse-Homburg. *See* Tomkins 3471
Elizabeth, Queen of England:
Passage to Westminster 1318
See Birch 1613; Camden 2166; Chettle 1315; Haynes 441; Marguerite 204; Nichols 3353; Sawyer 1100; Tower of London 2605; Townshend 1134
Ellesmere, Sir Thomas Egerton, Baron:
Certaine observations 161
Lord Chancellor Egerton's Observations 503
Speech. See Tracts 3797
Ellis, George:
Bath 3222:15
Specimens of the early English poets 2845
Ellison, —. *See Poems* 3222:17
Elmsley, Peter. *See* Wood 37
Éloge de l'yvresse. See Sallengre 763
Elogium heroinum. See Gerbier 2853
Elopement 1810:11
Elphinston, James. *See* Martialis 3341
Elphinstone, Arthur, Baron Balmerino. *See* Balmerino
Elsum, John:
Art of painting 332
Epigrams 333
Elvira. See Mallet 1810:4

Elwall, Edward:
  Supernatural incarnation 1608:60
Ely. *See* Bentham 11
Elyot, Sir Thomas:
  Bankette of sapience 782
  Boke named the governour 783
  Castell of helth 784, 2846
  Image of governance 785, 1319
  Knowledge whiche maketh a wise man 194, 2685
  See Bale 888
Emigrant in London 1810:57
Émile. See Rousseau 818
Emmanuel, King of Portugal. *See* Osorio 1419
Enchanted castle. See Andrews 1810:40
The enchanter. See Garrick 1810:1
'Endeavour,' ship. *See* Hawkesworth 2869
Enemy to all oppression. See Free apology 1608:31
Enfield Chace. *See* Stamford 521
Engeland beroerd. See James II 1331
England, George:
  Enquiry into the morals of the ancients 1320
England:
  Under this heading the entries have been grouped by alphabetized sub-headings.
  Administration of justice. *See Short view* 1608:6
  Army: *Regulations* 3416; *Rules* 2146:6. *See Ancient and present state* 1608:27; *Consultation* 1609:54; *Dorset* 1608:27; *England* 2146:3; *Morris* 1608:41; *Savile* 1609:54
  Assiento treaty 1608:94
  Assizes 1608:2
  Authors. *See* Marshall 3819
  Barrier treaty. *See* Swift 1608:13
  Board of Trade and Plantations. *See* Tracts 2050:14; Tracts 2146:6; *Two reports* 1609:58
  Chronicles. *See* Carion; Fabyan; Hardyng; Holinshed; Stow; Strutt
  Church of England. *See* Burnet 1105; Nelson 1445
  Civil War. *See* Heath 1118
  Committee of Safety. *See Westminster* 1608:1
  Constitution. *See* Harbin 1116
  Consulate. *See Memorials* 1609:15
  Convention Treaty with Spain. *See* Con-

England (*cont.*)
  vention Treaty
  Court of Chancery: *Select cases* 3313
  Court of King's Bench. *See Almon* 1609:28; *Circumstantial* 1609:26; *Considerations* 1609:21; England 1609:55; *Onslow* 1609:26; *Owen* 3359; *Raymond* 1128
  Court of Star Chamber. *See* Tracts 3797:4, 5
  Description. *See Beauties* 716; *Blome* 3271; Camden 563; Chamberlayne 1369; *Geography* 3423; Lambard 629; *Patching* 1608:83; Speed 534; Spelman 862; Sulivan 3829
  Fisheries. *See Letter* 1608:59
  Foreign Office 1609:57
  Forest Charter. *See* Edward I 2547
  History 1608:72. *See* Bath 1608:38; Dalrymple 3186; Defoe 3306; Dickinson 1609:32; England 1642; *Free conference* 3956; Fuller 1095; Gaillard 3013; Henry 543; Hume 3329; James II 1331; Knox 1609:21; Lee 1609:33; Macaulay 3197; Macpherson 3198–9; Martinelli 1161; *Measures* 1608:49; *Memoirs* 752; Milton 1338; *Observations* 1608:26; Rapin-Thoyras 1144; Raviglio 2937; *Revolution* 2593; Welwood 1768
  Kings 1608:66. *See* Baker 887; *Royal compendium* 762; Sandford 581; Tymme 1606
  Marriage Act. *See Letter* 1608:64
  Mutiny Bill. *See Seasonable* 1608:27
  Navy. *See* Bristol 1608:27
  Office of the Earl Marshal. *See* George III 3424
  Parliament: *Act* 2241; *Full report* 1609:43; *Journal* 2548; *List* 1608:23; *Most important transactions* 2146:1; *Motion* 2769:2; *Ordinance* 2686; *Parliamentary history* 1596; *View* 2146:1. *See Caveat* 1608:38; *Characters* 1609:37; *Collection* 1890; Cotton 2167; Dutens 2841; Hakewill 1608:2; *Important considerations* 1609:20; *Key* 1609:47; *Letter* 1608:56; *Letter* 1608:59; *Observations* 1608:50, 59; *Several proceedings* 2758; Townshend 1134; Tracts 2967
  Parliament. House of Commons: Debates 1354–5, 1609:53; *Genuine report* 1609:30; *Journals* 3275; Lists 1608:1, 23; *Minutes* 1608:39; *Observations* 1608:2; *Orders* 1608:2; *Rapport du Committé secret* 1249; *Report* 1609:51; *Substance of the speeches*

England (*cont.*)

1609:40. *See* Acherley 1698; Burke 1609: 40; *Coats of arms* 679; *Essay* 1609:25; Fox 1609:46; Jenyns 1609:46; Petyt 1716; Philips 1540; Ralph 1721

Parliament. House of Lords: *Compleat collection* 1608:2; *Perfect catalogue* 1608:1; *Protest* 2677:4; *Protests* 1740. *See* Byng 2146:3; Mauduit 1609:29; Pine 3552; *Sale* 3976

Peerage. *See* Brooke 2346; Collins 652–3; *England's glory* 2687

Privy Council. *See* Charles I 3797:6; Mauduit 1609:31; Swift 3984

Regency. *See* Regency

Registers. *See* True state 1608:72

Seven Years' War. *See* Case 1608:87

Sinking Funds. *See* Essay 1608:21

Treasury. *See* Kirke 2572

Treaties: *Definitive treaty* 1609:54; *Papers* 1609:54, 57; *Preliminary articles* 1609:54. *See* Anatomy 1609:54

Treaty of Aix-la-Chapelle. *See* Aix-la-Chapelle

Treaty of Paris. *See* Paris, Treaty of

Treaty of Seville. *See* Seville

Treaty of Utrecht. *See* Utrecht

Views. *See* Antiquities 3485; Birch 3837; Clarke 3852; Gilpin 3854; Hearne 3429; Kip 3573; Moore 3843; Strutt 3846; Watts 3849; *Topographer* 3831

Woollen manufacturers. *See* Tracts 2049:4

Year-books. *See* Annalium 3286

England's forewarning. *See* Cary 2536

England's genius 1608:17

England's glory 2687

England's Parnassus. *See* Allott 2326

England's remembrancer. *See* Political and satyrical history.

England's triumph. *See* Charles II 2004

England's worthies. *See* Lloyd 1752; Sandys 1763; Windover 2627; Winstanley 1769

English artists. *See* Vertue 3664

English baronage from William I to James I. *See* Heraldry 3499

English baronetage 655

English connoisseur. *See* Guides 2387:2

English garden: a poem, in four books. *See* Mason 3222:18

English globe. *See* Castlemaine 74

English green box 1609:40

English historical library. *See* Nicolson 1650

English loyalty 1608:46

English merchant. *See* Colman 1810:10

English officer. *See* Jardine 2891

English portraits. *See* Prints 3636

English protestant schools in Ireland. *See* Sermons 1346:10

English register. *See* Tracts 98:1

English topographer. *See* Rawlinson 664

Englishman. *See* Letter 1608:70, 1609:5; Sprat 2760

Englishman's complete guide to a parliamentary reform. *See* Every man 1609:47A

Engravings 3417. *See* Prints

Enquiry (*See also* Inquiry):

Short enquiry concerning the hermetick art 1517

Enquiry after happiness 1608:18

Enquiry into the conduct of a late Right Honourable Commoner 1609:15

Enquiry into the constitution . . . of the primitive church. *See* King 129

Enquiry into the customary-estates. *See* Burroughs 1608:21

Enquiry into the danger of a war with the Dutch. *See* Defoe 1608:9

Enquiry into the doctrine, lately propagated, concerning libels 1609:9

Enquiry into the life and writings of Homer. *See* Blackwell 1393

Enquiry into the present state of polite learning in Europe. *See* Goldsmith 1787

Enquiry into the present system 1608:82

Enquiry into the state of affairs 1608:56

Enquiry, or a discourse 1608:94

Enthusiasm. *See* Jerningham 3222:22

Entretiens sur l'état de la musique grecque. *See* Barthélemy 2999

Éon de Beaumont, Charles Geneviève Louis Anguste André Timothée, Chevalier d': *Lettres, mémoires et négotiations* 2374, 4004 *Note remise a son excellence Claude, Louis, Francois, Regnier comte de Guerchy* 1609: 54 *See* Catalogues 2819; Tracts 2966:4

Épernon, Bernard de Foix de la Vallette, Duc d'. *See* Girard 1010; Grignette 3745

Ephesian matron. *See* Bickerstaffe 1810:14

Epictetus:
    Enchiridion. See Classics 2207:13
Epicurus. *See* Du Rondel 2271; Gassendi 839
Epigrams. *See* Bruzen 1290
Epilogues. *See* Prologues
Epistle from a physician at Bath 1608:51
Epistle from Dick Poney 1608:92
Epistle from Mrs. B[ail]y 3222:12
Epistle from N---y P-----s 3222:9
Epistle from Schah Hussein to Nazro'din. See Tracts 2146:3
Epistle from the Honourable Charles Fox. See Tickell 3222:16
Epistle to Curio. See Poems 3363:11
Epistle to Dr. Shebbeare. See Mason 3222:16
Epistle to John Ranby 1608:51. *See* Walpole 2493:2
Epistle to Junius Silanus from Cornelius Scipio 1609:22
Epistle to Lord Holland 3222:10
Epistle to the dictator 1609:54
Epistle to the Reverend Mr. Brooke. See Middleton 1379:7
Epistle to the Right Honourable Lord G----- G----. See Germain 3222:16
Epitaphium Reginae Carolinae. See Tracts 2146:3
Épîtres diverses. See Baar 802
Erasmus, Desiderius:
    Colloquia 2243. *See* Classics 2207:14
    De conscribendis epistolis 2242
    De matrimonio Christiano 2242
    Epistolae 2169
    Moriae encomium 334, 2242
    Praise of folly 195, 334, 2688
    Proverbs. See Elyot 2685
    See Joly 1222; Jortin 554; Tracts 3986
Erreurs instructives. See Contes François 1783:1
Erskine, Andrew. *See* Boswell 1810:4
Erskine, David Stewart, Earl of Buchan. *See* Buchan
Erskine, Sir Henry:
    Story of Agis 1818:16
    See Thicknesse 1609:14
Erskine, John, Earl of Mar. *See* Mar
Escurial. *See* Santos 3759
Espion anglois. See Mairobert 3126
Esprit, Jacques:
    La fausseté des vertus humaines 730

Esprit de la Fronde. See Mailly 3124
Esprit des journaux 3011, 3314
Esprit des magistrats philosophes. See Dazès 3007
Essai historique sur la bibliothèque du Roi. See Le Prince 2217
Essai sur la peinture en mosaique. See Le Vieil 379
Essai sur l'étude de la littérature. See Gibbon 3015
Essay on acting. See Garrick 1818:19
Essay on design in gardening. See Mason 2903
Essay on faction. See Poems 280:1
Essay on medals. See Pinkerton 278–9
Essay on political lying 1608:86
Essay on the Constitution of England. See Ramsay 1609:9, 14
Essay on the Dunciad 1608:30
Essay on the history of parties. See Defoe 1608:9
Essay on the liberty of the press. See Hayter 1608:50
Essay on the life . . . of Dr. Samuel Johnson. See Towers 1609:50
Essay on the Middlesex election 1609:25
Essay on the publick debts. See Gould 1608:21
Essay on the several dispensations. See Barrington 106, 1608:19
Essay on the Sinking Fund 1608:21
Essay on the slave trade. See Thorkelin 1609:51
Essay on the writings and genius of Shakespear. See Montagu 1609:23
Essay on the writings of Pope. See Warton 2033, 3267
Essay on . . . tormenting. See Collier 2190
Essay on ways and means. See Fauquier 1608:82
Essay towards a new history of the Gunpowder Treason. See Taaffe 2763:3
Essay towards ascertaining the sense. See Middleton 1379:10
Essay towards fixing the true standards of wit. See Morris 1608:41
Essay towards illustrating the ancient history of the Britannic Isles. See Vallancey 1609:48

Essay towards illustrating the science of insurance. See Morris 1608:41

Essay towards the character of Her Late Majesty Caroline. See Clarke 1608:67

Essay upon prints. See Gilpin 338

Essays, moral and philosophical. See Pitsligo 139, 2745

Essays on gardening. See Gardening 2307

Essays on song-writing. See Aikin 2786

Essays on various subjects. See More 346

Essays upon pastoral ideas. See Suffolk 209

Essence of the Douglas Cause. See Boswell 1609:19

Essex, Arthur Capel, Earl of. *See* Somers 179

Essex, James. *See* Antiquities 3485:5; Letters 2576

Essex, Robert Devereux, 2d Earl of:
    Apology of the Earl of Essex to Mr. Anthony Bacon 81
    See Jones 1818:12; Letters 2576; *Profitable instructions* 2935

Essex, Thomas Cromwell, Earl of. *See* Collins 2543; Drayton 3955

Essex:
    Antiquities in Essex 3418
    See Salmon 7; Morant 22, 606

Este, Charles:
    Journey in the year 1793 409

Este, House of. *See* Berni 2069, 2186

Estienne, Charles:
    Agriculture 837

Estienne, Henri:
    Apologie pour Hérodote 1189

Estienne, Henri, Sieur des Fossés:
    Art of making devises 1065

Estimate of the times. See Another estimate 1609:23

Estoile, Pierre de l'. *See* Henry III 844

Estrades, Godefroy, Comte d':
    Ambassades en Italie, en Angleterre, et en Holland 1029
    Lettres et négociations 1216

Estrées, Abbé Jacques d':
    L'Europe vivant et mourant 2375

Estwick, Samuel:
    Letter to the Reverend Josiah Tucker 1609:37

Etchings by amateurs:
    Collection of prints 3588

Etherege, Sir George:
    Man of mode. See Plays 1910:3
    Works 1826

Etoffe, Henry. *See* Etough

Eton college:
    Musae Etonenses 2191, 2847
    See School books 3175; Walpole 2621

Etough, Henry:
    Reflections on Frederick, Prince of Wales 2549

Etruria pittrice. See Lastri 3540

Etruscan Academy. *See* Cortona 2076

Etymologist 1810:38

Euclid:
    Elementorum libri priores sex 2211

Euer, Sampson. *See* Duncombe 2681

Eugenia. See Francis 1818:7

Euphorbus. See Scotch 3222:16

Euphues, the anatomy of wit. See Lyly 2724

Euripides:
    Medea 838
    [*Opera*] 2170
    See Whitehead 1818:13

Europe:
    Compleat history 3419
    Green's map of Europe 3642
    See Broglie 3072; Campbell 1397; Du Buat 3009; Horsley 1329; Meyssens 3649; Perelle 3604; Pownall 1609:41; Thunberg 3262

L'Europe françoise. See Caraccioli 3077

L'Europe vivant et mourant. See Estrées 2375

European magazine. See Magazines 3338:3

Eurydice. See Mallet 1818:4

Eusden, Laurence. *See* Tracts 359:4

Evans, Caleb:
    Letter to the Rev. Mr. John Wesley 1609:35

Evans, Thomas. *See* Southerne 1917

Evelyn, Charles:
    Lady's recreation 731

Evelyn, John:
    Kalendarium hortense 1518
    Navigation and commerce 732
    Numismata 239
    Publick employment 733
    Sculptura 335
    Silva 3957
    See England 3956; Norfolk 486; Tracts 359:1

Ever, Sampson. *See* Duncombe 2681

Every man his own law-maker 1609:47A

Evesham. *See* Tindal 3210

Evidence of the common and statute laws 1609:35

Examen miscellaneum 1404

Examen of Mr. Sheridan's plan 1609:46

Examen of the new comedy, call'd the Suspicious husband 1818:19

Examen poeticum. See Dryden 1825

Examination and refutation of a late pamphlet 1608:27

Examination of a letter. See Dodington 1608:87

Examination of the commercial principles 1609:5

Examination of the consequences of Dr. Middleton's Free enquiry. See Middleton 1379:11

Examination of the principles . . . of a late Right Honourable Gentleman. See Lloyd 1609:15

Examination of the principles . . . of the two B*****RS. See Egmont 119:2

Examination of the rights of the colonies 1609:13

Examiner 1560

Excellencie of a free state. See Nedham 2730

Excellent contemplations. See Capel 151

Excellent woman. See Collings 1782

Excellent woman described. See Dorrington 2679

Excise Bill. *See Appeal* 1608:26, 32; England 1608:23; Tracts 2146:1; Vyner 3834; Walpole 1608:30

Excise scheme. *See Coats of arms* 679

Excise tax. *See* Heath 1609:54

Execution of justice in England. See Cecil 75, 111

Execution of Sir Charles Bawdin. See Chatterton 3222:12

Exhibition. *See* Royal Academy 3885:8

Exhibition in Hell 3222:11

Expeditio in Ream insulam. See Herbert 168, 202

Explication de divers monumens singuliers. See Martin 927

Explication des peintures. See Arts 288:2

Exposé succinct. See Hume 1680:1

Expostulatory address to John Ranby. 1608:51. *See* Walpole 2493:4

Expostulatory letter 1608:49

Expostulatory odes to a great duke. See Wolcot 3222:22

Extracts from various books. *See Reports* 2592

Extremities urging Sir Francis Vere 1608:1

Eyre, Edmund John:
    Maid of Normandy 1810:55

Eyre, Henry:
    Account of the mineral waters of Spa 1608:4

Ezzelino III. *See* Gherardo 3316

F., F. *See* Fauquier

F., S., Mrs. *See* Egerton 1894

Faber, Joannes, editor. *See* Schoppe 2293

Faber, John, Junior. *See* Kit-Cat Club 3501

Fabert, N. de, pseud. *See* Bruslé 1212

Fabius Pictor, Quintus, *See Some account* 1608:70

Fables for grown gentlemen. See Stevenson 3222:10

Fabricius, Nicolas Claude. *See* Gassendi 1743

Fabyan, Robert:
    Chronicle 240, 2171

Facecies et motz subtilz. See Domenichi 3309

Faction detected. See Egmont 119:1, 2844

Facts relating to the treaty of commerce 1609:55

Faerno, Gabriello. *See* Terentius 2226

Fair Circassian. See Pratt 1810:34

Fair orphan 1810:17

Fair Quaker. See Thompson 1810:20

Fair trial 1609:24

Fairfax, Thomas, 3d Baron Fairfax:
    Short memorials 162
    See Lenton 2575

Fairy favour. See Hull 1810:10

Fairy prince. See Colman 1810:18

Faith. See Nugent 3222:13

Faithful account of Mr. Bower's motives. See Baron 1608:31

Faithful account of the whole of the transactions 1609:31

Faithorne, William:
    Art of graveing and etching 336
    Portfolio of 280 engravings 3643

Falconer, John:
    Cryptomenyses patefacta 734

Falconer, William, M. D.:
    Historical view of the taste for gardening.
    See Gardening 3891:2
Falda, Giovanni Battista. *See* Rossi 3464–5,
    3515
Falkland, Henry Cary, 1st Viscount:
    History of Edward II 16
Falkland, Lady Letice Cary, Viscountess. *See*
    Duncon 1739
Falkland, Lucius Cary, Viscount:
    Discourse of infallibility 82, 120
Falkland Islands. *See* England 1609:57; John-
    son 1609:28; Penrose 1609:33
Fall of Mortimer. See Hatchett 1810:4
Falle, Philip:
    Account of the Isle of Jersey 735
False accusers 1608:74
False alarm. See Johnson 1609:25
Familiar epistle. See Bolingbroke 1608:13
Family party 1810:47
Fanshaw, Sir Richard. *See* Camoens 1809
Farington, Joseph. *See* Combe 3566
Farley, Robert:
    Lychnocausia. See King 1955
Farmain de Rosoi, Barnabé:
    Les sens 2689
Farmer, John:
    History of . . . Waltham 684
Farmer, Richard:
    Essay on the learning of Shakespeare
    1609:17
Farmer, Thomas:
    Plain truth 1609:54
Farmer in Pennsylvania. *See* Dickinson
    1609:22
Farmer's journey to London 1810:14
Farmer's return from London. See Garrick
    3222:2
Farnese, Edward, Prince of Parma. *See* Ed-
    ward, Prince of Parma
Farnese family. *See* Zuccaro 3560
Farnese Gallery:
    Portfolio of engravings 3619
Farnese Museum. *See* Pedrusi 457
Farquhar, George:
    Works 1870
Farther considerations upon a reduction. See
    Nugent 1608:47
*Farther illustration of the Analysis of my-
    thology. See* Bryant 1609:39

Fashionable lover. See Cumberland 1810:18
Fatal consequences of domestick divisions
    1608:24
Fatal discovery. See Home 1810:14
Fate of Corsica 1818:20
Father of Candor, pseud. *See Enquiry* 1609:9;
    Letter 1609:10
The fathers. See Fielding 1810:29
Faults on both sides. See Miscellaneous tracts
    89:2
Fauquier, Francis:
    Essay on ways and means 1608:82
Favart, Charles Simon. *See* D'Auberval
    1810:36; Plays 3972; *Reapers* 1810:16
Faversham. See Jacob 2888
Faversham Abbey. See Lewis 631; Southouse
    765
Favine, André. *See* Favyn
Favourite. See Scott 1810:15
Favyn, André:
    Theater of honour 592
F——d, Miss, i.e. Ann Ford. *See* Thicknesse
Feilding, Charles John:
    Brothers 3222:17
Félibien, André:
    Entretiens sur les vies et sur les ouvrages
    des . . . peintres 1294
    Tent of Darius explain'd 241
Félibien, Michel:
    Histoire de l'abbaye royale 875
Fell, John, Bishop:
    Privileges of the University of Oxford
    1608:8
    See Allestree 867
Fell, John (1735–1797). *See* Chatterton
    3690:11
Felle, Guillaume. *See Sage folie* 1306
Fellow commoner of St. John's College. *See*
    Essay 1379:10
Fellow of King's College, Cambridge. *See*
    Ashton, Thomas
Felton, Samuel:
    Imperfect hints 3922
    Miscellanies. See Gardening 3891:3
Female artifice 3222:13
Female deserters. See Plays 1909:3
Female duellist 1810:53
Female forgery 1609:35
*Female Quixote, or, the adventures of Ara-
    bella. See* Lennox 378

Female refugee. *See Carthusian friar* 1810:52

Fencing. *See* Alfieri 422

Fénelon, François de Salignac de la Mothe:
Abrégé des vies des anciens philosophes 961
Adventures of Telemachus. See Poems 3363:6
Avantures de Télémaque 3958
Dialogues sur l'éloquence 1193
Explication des maximes des saints 1217
Fables and dialogues of the dead 1741
Lettres sur divers sujets 1192
Oeuvres philosophiques 1190
Recueil des mandements 1191
Réfutation des erreurs de Benoît de Spinosa 1218
See Merry 1810:57

Fenin, Pierre de. *See* Collection 3084

Fenn, Eleanor (Frere), Lady:
Female guardian. See Manual 2414
School dialogues. See Manual 2414

Fenn, Sir John. *See* Paston 3251

Fennell, James:
Lindor and Clara 1810:50
Statement of facts 1810:46

Fenton, Elijah:
Mariamne 1895. *See History* 1608:17
Odyssey. See Homer 63
Plays 1895
See Milton 1833; Waller 472

Fer, Nicolas de:
Short . . . method to understand geography 1405

Ferdinand, Duke of Brunswick-Luneburg:
Operations of the allied army 3167

Ferdinand II, Grand Duke of Tuscany. *See* Zouch 3993

Ferdinand, Infanta of Spain, and Cardinal Archbishop of Toledo. *See* Gevartius 3620

Ferdinand V, King of Spain. *See* Godefroy 1066; Mignot 3032

Ferdinand IV, King of the Two Sicilies:
Interprétation des peintures 3709

Ferguson, Adam:
Essay on the history of civil society 2050:16

Ferishtah, Mohammed Kasim. *See* Dow 2838

Fermor, Henrietta Louisa, Countess of Pomfret. *See* Pomfret

Fermor, Lady Sophia. *See* Rigacci 2112

Ferrar, Nicholas. *See* Peckard 2917

Ferrari, Giovanni Battista:
Hesperides 900

Ferrerio, Pietro:
Palazzi di Roma. See Rossi 3465

Ferrero di Lavriano, Francesco Maria:
Augustae regiaeque Sabaudiae domus arbor gentilitia 3710

Ferrers, Laurence Shirley, Earl:
Trial of Laurence Earl Ferrers 1112

Ferriar, John:
Prince of Angola 1810:45

Ferrière, Claude Joseph de:
History of the Roman or civil law 1519

Ferriol, Antoine de. *See* Tencin 2295

Festeau, Paul. *See* Mauger 1229

Fête champêtre 3222:13

Feuquières, Antoine de Pas, Marquis de:
Mémoires 922

Few anecdotes and observations relating to Oliver Cromwell. See Burrow 1609:6

Ficoroni, Francesco de':
Bollo d'oro 479
Maschere sceniche 480

Fidanza, Paolo. *See* Raphael 3609

Field, Mrs. Sarah. *See* Egerton 1894

Fielding, —:
Asylum 3222:13

Fielding, Charles John. *See* Feilding, C. J.

Fielding, Henry:
Apology for the life of Mrs. Shamela Andrews 2474:6
Author's farce 1818:2
Charge to the jury 1608:51
Clear state of the case 1608:77
Dramatic works 1813
Enquiry into the causes of . . . robbers 1608:62
Examples of the interposition of Providence 1561
The Fathers 1810:29
Golden rump. See Cibber 450
History of Joseph Andrews 1562
History of Tom Jones 1785
Journal of a voyage to Lisbon 1742
Miscellanies 1814
Miss Lucy in town 1818:20
Proposal for . . . the poor 1608:72
Some papers 1608:45
Tom Thumb 1818:3
Tragedy of tragedies 1818:5

Fielding, Henry (*cont.*)
Works 2848
See *Champion* 1506; Fielding, Sir John 1608:88; *Jacobite's journal* 2142; Kenrick 1810:10; Poems 1835:1; Reed 1810:14
Fielding, Sir John:
Account of the origin 1608:88
Fielding, Sarah:
Adventures of David Simple 1563
See Collier 2190
Fiennes, Nathaniel:
Speech. See Tracts 2769:4
Fieschi, Giovanni Luigi, Conte de':
Conjuration 1030
Fifty queries concerning the present Oxfordshire contest 1608:61
Figaro. *See* Holcroft 1810:37
Filmer, Sir Robert:
Patriarcha. See Tyrrell 2770
Filosi, Giuseppe. *See* Venice 3662
Filtz-Moritz, Monsieur:
Lettres 1031
Finch, Anne, Countess of Winchilsea. *See* Winchilsea
Finch, Daniel, Earl of Nottingham. *See* Nottingham
Finch, Edward:
Petition and articles 1608:1
Finch, Heneage, Earl of Nottingham. *See* Nottingham
Finch, Heneage, 2d Earl of Winchilsea. *See* Winchilsea
Finesse of rantum-scantum 1608:61
Finett, Sir John:
Finetti Philoxenis 736, 2690
Fioravante, Benedetto:
Antiqui . . . denarii 481
See Vignolius 493
Firishtah, Mohammed Kasim. *See* Dow 2838
Firmanus, Hannibal Adamus:
Seminarii Romani Pallas purpurata 3740
First book of Fontenoy. See Stratford 3222:18
First chapter of Tear 'em 1608:69
First letter to the Duke of Grafton 1609:25
First of April. See Combe 3222:15
Fisher, John, Cardinal:
Funeral sermon of Margaret Countess of Richmond and Derby 685
Treatyse 121

Fitz-Adam, Adam, pseud. *See World* 911, 2501-2
Fitzgerald, George Robert:
Appeal to the Jockey Club 1609:33
Reply to Thomas Walker 1609:35
The riddle 3222:21
Fitzgibbon, John, Earl of Clare. *See* Clare
Fitzherbert, Maria Anne (Smythe). *See Marcellus* 1609:51
Fitz-Osborne, Sir Thomas, pseud. *See* Melmoth 1442
Fitzpatrick, Barnaby. *See* Edward VI, *Copies of letters*
Fitzpatrick, Richard:
Dorinda 2510
See Collection 2508
Fitzroy, Augustus Henry, 3d Duke of Grafton. *See* Grafton
Fitz-Thomas, Mr., supposed author. *See* Tindal 1609:42
Flagellum Dei 1608:8
Flamel, Nicolas:
Exposition of the hieroglyphicall figures 737
Flaminius, Marcus. *See* Knight 3331
Flamsteed, John. *See Black-bird* 2646:13
Flanders. *See* Bentivoglio 2644, 3290; Descamps 3307; Sandras 3144
Flatman, Thomas:
On the death of . . . George, Duke of Albemarle. See Oxford 2061:1
Poems and songs 1941
Flavell, John:
Token for mourners 2376
Fléchier, Valentin Esprit:
Histoire de Théodose le Grand 786
Lettres 1194
Mandemens et lettres pastorales 1195
Oraison funèbre de Henry Vicomte de Turenne. See Rémonstrance 1085
Vie du Cardinal Jean François Commendon 1156
See Graziani 3102
Flecknoe, Richard:
Erminia 1942
Fleetwood, Charles. *See* Tracts 2769:10
Fleetwood, Everard, pseud. *See* Burroughs 1608:21
Fleetwood, Martha. *See* Monk, Martha

Fleetwood, William, Bishop:
   Complete collection of the sermons 1094
   Life of St. Wenefred. See Whiston 1727:2
Fleetwood, William, Recorder of London:
   Annalium Edwardi V elenchus. See Annalium 3286
   How the Dukedom of Lancaster had commencement 2550
Fleming, Richard. *See* Stukeley 255
Fletcher, Andrew:
   Discourse of government 1608:80
Fletcher, Henry. *See* Casteels 3565
Fletcher, John:
   Beggar's bush. See Hull 1810:11; Plays 1623:2
   Island princess 1818:21
   Pilgrim 1818:21
   See Beaumont 1818:21, 2040; Colman 1810:5, 29; Cook 1810:35; *Female duellist* 1810:53; Garrick 1810:20; Kemble 1810:43
Fleury, André Hercule de, Cardinal. *See Ombre* 1608:53
Flight from Lapland. See O'Keeffe 1810:35
Flitner, John. *See* Murner 754
Flloyd, Thomas:
   Bibliotheca biographia 1678
Floravante. *See* Fioravante
Florence. *See* Gori 431; Malespini 2081, 3340; Zocchi 3530, 3583
Florence. Duomo. *See* Sgrilli 3520
Florence. Uffizi Gallery:
   Disegni originali 3570
   Galleria Imperiale e Reale 3570
   Portfolio of original drawings 3570
Florence Miscellany 3810
Florent d'Illiers. *See Collection* 3084
Florez, Henrique:
   Memorias de las Reynas Catholicas 3315
Florian, Jean Pierre Claris de. *See* Claris de Florian
Florio, Michel Angelo:
   Historia de la vita de Giovanna Graia 2101
Florio. See More 3222:20
Florizel. See Poetical epistle 3222:17
Florus, Lucius Annaeus:
   Epitome rerum Romanorum. See Classics 2207:15
   Opera 3959

Floyd, Philip:
   Prosperity to Houghton. See Strawberry Hill 3469:2
Floyer, Sir John:
   History of hot and cold bathing 1475
Fludyer, Sir Samuel. *See True Briton* 1609:5
Foeneste, Baron de. *See* Aubigné 776
Fog's Weekly Journal 2141
   Select letters from 1476
Foire. *See Théâtre* 1171
Foix de la Vallette, Bernard de, Duc d'Épernon. *See* Épernon
Folard, Jean Charles de. *See Almanach* 1174; Polybius 931
Folengo, Teofilo:
   Merlini Coccaii opus macaronicorum 2272
Folkes, Martin:
   Table of English silver coins 267
Follies of the day. See Holcroft 1853
Folly in print. See Raymund 1978
Folly of marrying widows. See Tracts 98:1
Fontanini, Giusto. *See* Stukeley 640:1
Fontenai, Claude de Nonney de:
   Lettres sur l'éducation des princes 980
Fontenelle, Bernard Le Bovier de:
   Oeuvres 808
   See Trablet 822
Fontenoy, a ballad. See Poems 881:11
Fontenoy, a poem. See Stratford 3222:18
Foord, William. *See* Forde, William
Foot, Ferdinando, pseud. *See* Pope 1912:4
Foot, Jesse:
   Life of John Hunter 2849
Foot, John, surgeon:
   Appeal to the public 1609:22
Foote, Catherine, Lady Herries. *See* Herries
Foote, Samuel:
   Author 1818:15
   Bankrupt 1810:26
   Capuchin 1810:28
   Commissary 1810:7
   Cozeners 1810:28
   Devil upon two sticks 1810:28
   Dramatic works 3420
   Englishman in Paris 1818:11
   Englishman return'd from Paris 1818:14
   Knights 1818:11
   Lame lover 1810:16
   Letter to the Reverend Author 1810:1

Foote, Samuel (*cont.*)
  The lyar 1810:6
  Maid of Bath 1810:28
  Mayor of Garret 1810:5
  Minor 1810:1
  Nabob 1810:28
  One letter. *See* Letters 2576
  The orators 1810:3
  The patron 1810:6
  Roman and English comedy . . . consider'd 1818:19
  Taste 1818:9
  Trip to Calais 1810:28
  Wilkes, an oratorio 1810:15
  See Bickerstaffe 1810:14; *Catalogue* 1818:9; Foote 3222:16; *Letter* 1818:19; *Tailors* 1810:28
Forbes, Alexander, Baron Pitsligo. *See* Pitsligo
Forbes, Duncan:
  Treatise 1608:93
  See Copy 1608:54
Forbin, Claude de, Comte:
  Mémoires 1157
Ford, Ann. *See* Thicknesse
Ford, John:
  Fames memoriall 1321
Forde, William:
  Sermon preached . . . at the funerall of Lady Anne Glover. See Sermons 2757:2
Forest, Ebenezer. *See* Forrest
Forest Charter. *See* Edward I 2547
Forest of varieties. See North 2734
Form of prayer used by his late Majesty King William III. See Tillotson 1546
Form of the proceeding to the Royal Coronation. See George III 3424
Forma, Giacomo Franco. *See* Franco
Forme of cury. See Pegge 1609:41
Formey, Jean Henri Samuel:
  France littéraire 1196
Forrest, Ebenezer. *See* Fuzelier 1818:3; Gostling 2385
Forrest, Thomas:
  Weathercock 1810:24
Forteguerri, Niccolò. *See* Ricciardetto 3041
Fortescue, Sir John. *See* Waterhouse 257
Fortune's tricks in forty-six 1818:19

Foster, James:
  Account 1608:54
Foster, John:
  Essay on accent and quantity 2850
Foster, Sir Michael:
  Report . . . on the Commission for the trial of the rebels in 1746 2851
Fothergill, John. *See* Lettsom 413; *Reflexions* 1609:13
Fougasses, Thomas de:
  General historie of Venice 3276
The Foundling. See Criticism 1818:9
Foundling Hospital:
  Account of the hospital. See Tracts 2049:1
Foundling Hospital for wit 2377
Fouquet, Charles Louis Auguste de, Duc de Belleisle. *See* Belleisle
Four letters in Old England. See Tracts 2050:8
Four original letters. See Cibber 1608:57
Four queries concerning miracles. See Middleton 1379:5
Four topographical letters. See Patching 1608:83
Fourdrinier, Pierre. *See* Ware 536
Fournier, Bernard. *See* Hoadly 1608:85
Fournier, Pierre Simon:
  Five tracts on printing 3012
Fourth letter to the people of England 1608:82
  See Shebbeare 3978
Fowler, William:
  Engravings of mosaic pavements 3421
Fox, Charles James:
  Beauties of Fox, North, and Burke 1609:46
  Speech in defence of his resignation 1609:42
  Speech on the Irish resolutions 1609:47
  State of the facts 1609:45
  Verses to Mrs. Crewe. See Collection 2508
  Warning voice 1609:45
  See Bunbury 3563:1; England 1609:53; *Female* 3222:13; Moir 3131; Tickell 3222:16; Tracts 2966:3
Fox, Edward:
  True dyfferēs 163
Fox, George:
  Journal 1113
Fox, Henry, Baron Holland. *See* Holland

Fox, John. *See Fox's martyrs* 1609:46
Fox, Luke:
    North-west Fox. See Crowne 1061
Fox's martyrs 1609:46
Foy, Louis Étienne de:
    Notices des diplômes 3094
Fragmens de lettres originales. See Charlotte 3298
Fragment 1609:57. *See* Stebbing 1608:70
Fragosa, King of Aragon. *See* Lyly 2724
France:
    Bibliothèque National: *Accounts and extracts of the manuscripts* 410
    History. *See* Chalons 975; Choiseul-Stanville 1609:54; *Collection* 3084; *Curiosités* 3006; Des Salles 919; Foy 3094; Gaillard 3013; Hénault 964; Hoey 1608:71; La Fayette 988; Le Feron 546; Millin 3721; Montfaucon 3683; Pasquier 907; *Tablettes* 3148
    Kings. *See* Bie 3735; Du Tillet 898; Sainte-Marthe 909; Vanel 954
    Theaters. *See* Beauchamps 1138
    Treaties. *See* England 1609:54
    Treaty of Seville. *See* Seville
    Treaty of Utrecht. *See* Utrecht
    See Bromley 291; Clavière 3230; Crozat 3550; Ireland 3857:2; Lavallée 3334; Necker 3035; Piganiol 1258
Francesco, called Il Guercino. *See* Bartolozzi 3398
Francini, Alexandre:
    New book of architecture 219
Francis, Duke of Anjou, and of Alençon:
    Joyeuse entrée de Monseigneur Françoys fils de France 3680, 3741
Francis I, King of France. *See* Clouet 2357; Lussan 811; Varillas 971
Francis II, King of France. *See* Hénault 2394
Francis de Sales, Saint. *See* Tauler 1589
Francis, Philip:
    Constantine 1818:13
    Eugenia 1818:7
    Letter from the anonymous author 1609:54
    Letter from the Cocoa-Tree 1609:54
    Letter to a Right Honourable person 1609:54
    See Constitution 1608:84; Demosthenes 463
Francis, Sir Philip. *See Letter* 1609:8
Franciscans, English. *See* Parkinson 636
Francisco de los Santos. *See* Santos 3759

Francklin, Richard:
    Act before the first act of Elvira. See Mallet 1810:4
    See Craftsman 2140; *New Year* 1608:73
Francklin, Thomas:
    Authentic narrative 1608:70
    Contract 1810:26
    Earl of Warwick 1810:9
    Matilda 1810:23
    See Kelly 1810:17; Lucian 3242; *Muses* 3222:13; Poems 3363; Sermons 1345; Sophocles 322; Stebbing 1608:70
Franco, Giacomo. *See* Venice 3987
Franco, Giovanni Battista. *See* Drawings 3569
Franco-Gallia. See Hotman 127
Franklin, Andrew:
    Mermaid 1810:51
Franklin, Benjamin:
    Interest of Great Britain considered. See Examination 1609:5
    Works 3235
    See Cicero 407; Dickinson 1609:22; *Faithful account* 1609:31; Tickell 1609:40
Franzini, Girolamo:
    Merveilles de la ville de Rome. See Arts 288:1
Fraser, Alexander, Baron Saltoun. *See* Saltoun
Fraser, James, of Inverness:
    Genuine narrative 1608:54
Fraser, S. *See* Duckett 683:2
Fraser, Simon, Baron Lovat. *See* Lovat
Fraunce, Abraham:
    Countess of Pembrokes Yvychurch 122
Fréart, Roland, Sieur de Chambray. *See* Chambray
Frédégonde et Brunéhaut. See Boutet 3295
Frederick I, King of Bohemia. *See* Caus 3777
Frederick II, the Great, King of Prussia:
    Antiquités . . . à Sans Souci 3422
    Correspondance avec Ulrich de Suhm 3095
    Letters on patriotism 2691
    Letters to the public 1608:76
    Matinées royales 3960
    Mémoires de la maison de Brandebourg 1140
    Memoirs of Brandenberg 1608:39
    Oeuvres du philosophe de Sans-Souci 1295
    Plan for reforming the administration of justice 1608:2

Frederick II (*cont.*)
  Rescript 1608:39
  Sylla. See Almanach 1174
Frederick, Prince of Wales. *See* Cambridge University 12, 498; Etough 2549; Oxford University 514
Frederick Henry, Prince of Orange:
  Mémoires 923
  See Post 3553
Frederick Louis, Prince of Wales. *See Letters* 1608:5
Frederick, Charles. *See* Lethieullier 3503
Free and impartial inquiry 1608:47
Free and Independent Artists of Great Britain. *See* Royal Academy 3885:14
Free apology 1608:31
Free conference touching the present state of England. See England 3956
Free enquiry into the nature and origin of evil. See Jenyns 1527
Free examination of the common methods. See Taaffe 2763:2
Free holder. *See* Freeholder
Free-holder. See Freeholder
Free Masons. *See* Anderson 2631
Free Society of Artists. *See* Royal Academy 3885:3
Free thoughts, and bold truths 1608:80
Free thoughts on the late treaty. See Worms 1608:44
Freedom of King's Lynn. *See* King's Lynn 2567
Freeholder, pseud. *See* Carlyle, Alexander
Freeholder. *See* Addison 1843; *Address* 1608:30; *Source* 1609:46; *Spectator* 1860
Freeman, W., pseud.:
  Comparison between Horace and the Roman father 1818:7
Freeman, Sir William, pseud.:
  Letters on several occasions 2007
Freind, Sir John, d. 1696. *See* Friend
Freind, John (1675–1728):
  Account of the Earl of Peterborow's conduct 123
  Epistle to Dr. Mead 1608:50
  History of physick 1406
  Opera omnia medica 2053
Freire de Andrade, Jacinto:
  Life of Dom John de Castro 2172
French catalogue. *See* Catalogues 2303

French comedians. *See Impartial* 1608:69
French King's dream. See Louis XIV 1608:23
French memorial. *See Reasons* 1608:81
French Revolution. *See* Wollstonecraft 3177
French theatre. *See Nouveau Théâtre François* 1232
Frere, Eleanor, Lady Fenn. *See* Fenn
Fresnoy, Nicolas Lenglet du. *See* Lenglet du Fresnoy
Fresny, Charles Rivière du. *See* Rivière du Fresny
Frey, Andreas:
  True account 1608:75
Frey, Johann Jacob:
  Portfolio of engravings 3602
  See Sacchi 3629
Frezza, Giovanni Girolamo. *See* Farnese 3619
Fribble, Timothy, pseud.:
  Tittle-tattle 1818:10
Fribbleriad. See Garrick 3222:1
Friend, Sir John. *See* Tenison 1608:8
Friend. *See* Grey 1608:55
Friend to the Army and the Constitution. *See Question* 1609:8
Friend to truth. *See Full and candid answer* 1609:54; *Plain answer* 1379:3
Friendly and honest advice 1608:70
Friendly call. See Brett 1367:6
Friendship 3222:9
Froissart, Jean:
  Chronicle 438, 2043
  See Lydgate 3505
Frontinus, Sextus Julius:
  Stratagemi militari. See Cosmo II 2304:4
Frosne, Jean. *See* Prints 3655
Frowde, Philip:
  Philotas 1818:4
Fry, Joseph:
  Specimen. See Jones 3784:2
Fryer, John:
  New account of East India and Persia 3277
Fugitive pieces (1785). *See* Headley 1609:47
Fugitive pieces, on various subjects. See Dodsley 1559
Fulham Church. *See* Antiquities 3485:7
Full account of the proceedings. See Steele 1608:16
Full and candid answer [to Kidgell] 1609:54
Full and candid answer to a pamphlet 1609:1

Full and clear answer to a book written by William Petyt. See Brady 2652

Full and impartial account of witchcraft. See Political tracts 94:13

Full clear . . . account of the late conspiracy. See Portugal 1343:3

Fuller, Francis:
Medicina gymnastica 1477

Fuller, Thomas:
Abel redevivus 2692
Church-history of Britain 1095
Fast sermon. See Sermons 2757:3
History of the worthies of England 1114
Holy state 2173
Sermon of reformation. See Sermons 2757:4
Sermon preached on the 27. of March. See Sermons 2757:5
See Sandys 1763

Fuller, William:
Original letters of the late King's 1608:10
Whole life of Mr. William Fuller 2693

Fulman, William:
Notitia Oxoniensis academiae 1608:3
See Charles I 13

Fun: a parodi-tragi-comical satire. See Kenrick 1818:10

Funebria Henrici Untoni 196

Funeral oration for Louis XVI. See Vyner 3834

Furber, Robert. *See* Casteels 3565

Furness Abbey. *See* West 258

Fuseli, Henry. *See* Winckelmann 421

Fuzelier, Louis:
Momus turn'd fabulist 1818:3

G., H. *See* John III 2715

G., Louis de, Capitaine, pseud. *See* Bruslé 1212

G., T. *See Letter* 1609:28

Gabalis, Count of. *See* Montfaucon 1756

Gabrini, Nicolas. *See* Du Cerceau 1293

Gaffarel, Jacques:
Curiositez inouyes 1219

Gage, Thomas, 1st Viscount Gage:
Speech 1608:93

Gage, Thomas. *See* Bernard 1609:25; Massachusetts 1609:23

Gahagan, Usher. *See* Brindley 2120

La Gaieté. See Drumgold 3920

Gaillard, Gabriel Henri:
Histoire de la rivalité 3013, 3096

Gainsford, Thomas:
History of Perkin Warbeck 1322

Galanteries des Rois de France. See Vanel 954

Gale, Roger:
Registrum . . . de Richmond 569

Gale, Samuel:
History . . . of the Cathedral Church of Winchester 686

Galerie de l'ancienne cour. See Louis XIV 3337

Gallaeus, Philippus. *See* Galle

Gallant Moriscoes 1810:57

Galle, Jan. *See* De Vos 3600; Prints 3461

Galle, Philipp. *See* Prints 3654; Stradanus 3659; Vries 3474

Galle, Theodor. *See* Meyssens 3649

Gallia orientalis. See Colomiès 833

Galliard, John Ernest. *See* Plays 1623:1

Galloway, Joseph:
Letter to Cicero. See Tracts 2966:3

Gallus, Cornelius. *See* Catullus 2267

Galluzzi, Jacopo Riguccio:
Istoria del Granducato di Toscana 32, 3097

Gambado, Geoffrey, pseud. *See* Bunbury 3913–4

Gambarini, Carlo, of Lucca:
Description of the Earl of Pembroke's pictures 297, 2378

Gambier, James:
Proceedings on the trial 1608:88

Gambold, John:
Works 2852

Games most in use in England 1564

The gamester. See Moore 1818:12

Gamon, Achille. *See* Collection 3084

Gandini, Ludovico. *See* Cresswell 3778

Gandini, Marco Antonio. *See* Cosmo II 2304:4

Ganganelli. *See* Clement XIV, Pope

Garampi, Giuseppe:
De nummo argenteo Benedicti III dissertatio 430

Garasse, François:
Doctrine curieuse 924

Garden of eloquence. See Peacham 136

Garden of the muses. See Bodenham 1997

Gardener, John. *See* Gardnor

Gardener's dictionary. See Dictionarium 1353

Gardener's labyrinth. See Hill 374, 2707

Gardening 1609:45, 2307, 3891. *See* Le Rouge 3433

Gardiner, Colonel James. *See* Doddridge 1676

Gardiner, William Nelson:
    Portraits of Royal and Noble authors 2379

Gardner, Thomas:
    Historical account of Dunwich 504

Gardnor, John. *See* Williams 3218

Garencières, Theophilus de. *See* Nostradamus 2177

Garland of pious and godly songs. See Hall 2011:3

Garnett, John, Bishop:
    One letter. *See* Letters 2576

Garrard, Marc. *See* Gheeraerts

Garrick, David:
    Albumazar 1810:20
    Bon ton 1810:25
    Catharine and Petruchio 1818:14
    Chances 1810:20
    Country girl 1810:9
    Cymon 1810:10
    Enchanter 1810:1
    Essay on acting 1818:19
    Farmer's return from London 3222:2
    Florizel and Perdita 1810:3
    Fribbleriad 3222:1
    Guardian 1818:17
    Irish widow 1810:18
    Isabella 1818:16
    King Arthur 1810:16
    Lethe 1818:9, 15
    Lilliput 1818:15
    Lying valet 1818:9
    Male-coquette 1818:16
    May-Day 1810:25
    Memoirs of the life of Garrick 2380
    Midsummer night's dream 1810:5
    Miss in her teens 1818:19
    Neck or nothing 1810:9
    New dramatic entertainment 1810:21
    Ode upon dedicating a building 3222:10
    One letter. *See* Letters 2576
    Peep behind the curtain 1810:11
    Shakespeare's garland 1810:15
    Songs and recitative of Orpheus 1810:11
    Songs in May-Day 1810:24
    Songs of the Institution of the Garter 1810:18
    Verses to Mr. Gray. See Collection 2508
    See Colman 1810:8; Fielding 1818:20; Griffith 1810:14; *Letter* 1810:18; *Letter* 1818:9;

Garrick, David (*cont.*)
    Mr. Garrick's conduct 1818:9; Poems 1835:5; *Politician* 1810:21; Sheridan 3222:16; Townley 1818:18

Garter, Order of the
    Arms of the Knights of the Garter 2551
    Procession 3551
    See Anstis 434; Ashmole 586; Garrick 1810:18; Heylyn 846; Windsor 2387:6

Garth, Sir Samuel:
    Dispensary 4005
    Works 371
    See Ovidius 1905

Gascoyne, Sir Crisp. *See* Liveryman 1608:77

Gassendi, Pierre:
    De vita et moribus Epicuri 839
    Mirrour of true nobility 1743

Gassion, Mareschal de. *See* Pure 2024

Gassmann, Florian Leopold:
    Gli Uccellatori. See Music 3448

Gastaldi, Giambattista. *See* Case 1608:44

Gastrell, Francis:
    Certainty of the Christian Revelation 1407

Gaultier, Leonard. *See* Prints 3626

Gautier, Solomon:
    Collection des vues 3779

Gay, John:
    Achilles 1818:5
    Fables 1827
    Poems on several occasions 1850
    Shepherd's week. See Tracts 2049:2
    Three hours after marriage. See Tracts 2474:2
    See Colman 1810:21

Gay, Joseph, pseud. *See* Breval

Gayot de Pitaval, François. *See* Pitaval

Gazetier cuirassé. See Morande 3033

Gazette littéraire de l'Europe 3014, 3098

Gazetteer and London Daily Advertiser. See London 2143

Gedde, Walter:
    Book of sundry draughtes. See Tracts 3797:3

Geddes, Michael:
    Miscellaneous tracts 1435

Gelée, Claude, called Le Lorrain. *See* Lorrain

Gellius, Aulus. *See* Beloe 3706

Genealogical table of the Kings and Princes of Wales. See Wales 2612

General. A poem. See Gentleman 3222:6

General Advertiser. See London 2143
General Evening Post. See Cresswell 1608:65
General instructions for preachers. See Reports 2592
General list of the officers. See Tracts 2146:6
General lover. See Marriott 1818:10
General Officer. *See* Cavan 3180
General opposition of the colonies 1609:56
General view of the present politics 1608:49
Generous impostor. See O'Beirne 1810:34
Geneva. *See* Keate 788; Senebier 3372
Genius of Britain 3222:13
Genoa. *See* Bréquigny 1181; *Case* 1608:44; Rubens 3466
Genoels, Abraham. *See* Drawings 3587
Gent, Thomas:
    History of the loyal town of Rippon 687, 2694
Gentleman, Francis:
    Cupid's revenge 1810:18
    The general 3222:6
    Modish wife 1810:27
    Pantheonites 1810:20
    Stratford Jubilee 1810:15
    Sultan 1810:15
Gentleman. *See* Harbin 1116
Gentleman at the Bar. *See Examination* 1609: 13
Gentleman long resident in India. *See Reflections* 1609:7
Gentleman of Cambridge. *See* Morris 1608:41; *Spirit* 1818:18
Gentleman of Oxford. *See Devil* 1608:80; *Germanicus* 1810:25
Gentleman of Wadham College. *See* Miller 1818:2
Gentleman's calling. See Allestree 3938
Gentleman's Magazine. See Magazines 3338:4
Gentleman's tour through Monmouthshire and Wales. See Wyndham 3481
Genuine account of the late secret expedition. See Guadaloupe 1608:87
Genuine and authentic account of the proceedings. See Westminster 1608:69
Genuine copies of all the letters. See Tooke 1609:25
Genuine copy of a letter. See Chatterton 3690: 13
Genuine copy of a letter written from Constantinople. See Montagu 1608:8

Genuine copy of the tryal of J‑‑‑‑ P‑‑‑‑‑l. See Egmont 119:2
Genuine legal sentence pronounced . . . upon the conspirators. See Portugal 1343:1
Genuine life of William Hawke 1609:32
Genuine narrative of the life of Mr. John Henderson. See Davies 1810:27
Genuine review of the political state of an unhappy country 1609:50
Genuine speech of an eminent Dutch patriot 1608:58
Genuine tryal of Dr. Nosmoth 1608:89
Geoffrey, of Monmouth:
    British history 1706
Geoffrin, Marie Thérèse (Rodet). *See* Tracts 2050:6
Geographical history of Nova Scotia. See Nova Scotia
Geography 2174, 3423
George I, King of England:
    Mémoires du règne de George I 1296
George II, King of England. *See* Almon 1609: 4; Casley 476; Harvard University 1325; *Letters* 1608:5; *Poems* 280:9; *Serious . . . considerations* 1608:59; Tracts 2146:1, 3
George III, King of England:
    Account of the ceremonies 3424
    Chronicle of George the 3d. See London Chronicle 538
    Form of the proceeding to the Royal Coronation 3424
    Poems published in the reign of George the 3d 3222
    Portraits in the reign of George the 3d 3636
    Print of the procession to St. Paul's 3424
    Theatre of George the 3d 1810
    Tracts published in the reign of George the 3d 1609
    See Dublin 313; Dutens 2841, 3093; England 1609:51; Harvard University 1325; *Heroic* 3222:16; MacFarlane 1609:27; *Royal* 3222:16; Williams 1609:51
George IV, King of England:
    One letter. *See Letters* 2576
    See Marcellus 1609:51; *Poetical epistle* 3222:17; Tooke 1609:51
George of Cappadocia, Saint. *See* Heylyn 846
Georgia. *See* Tracts 1608:40; Tracts 2146:6; Whitefield 1609:21

Georgirenes, Joseph:
  Description of ... Samos 1408
Gerardo, Pietro. *See* Gherardo
Gerbelius, Nicolaus:
  Icones imperatorum et breves vitae Ausonio, Jacobo Micyllo, Ursino Velio authoribus 337
Gerbier, Sir Balthazar:
  Counsel and advise 197
  Effets pernicieux 2383
  First lecture of geographie 2381
  Genealogie de Messire Balthazar Gerbier 3494
  Interpreter of the academie 124, 2381
  Lectures on fortification 2382, 3811
  None-such Charles his character 2383
  Sommary description off America. See Tracts 3797:2
  Subsidium peregrinantibus 198
  See Vade Mecum 2771
Gerbier, Charles:
  Elogium heroinum 2853
Gerbier d'Ouvilly, George:
  False favourite. See Plays 2451
Gerini, Andrea, Marchesa. *See* Zocchi 3583
Germain, Lady Elizabeth:
  Catalogue. See Tracts 2050
Germain, George Sackville, 1st Viscount Sackville:
  Epistle 3222:16
  Trial. See Ferrers 1112
  See Matrimonial 3222:16
German Empire. *See* Bancks 2637; Palazzi 3684
German hotel. See Holcroft 1810:49
German lessons 3425
German nobleman. *See Compleat view* 1608:44
Germanicus, Caesar. *See* Beaufort 1267
Germanicus 1810:25
Germany. *See* Pfeffel 1281; *Present* 1608:44
Germondo. See Plays 3972
Gersaint, Edme François:
  Catalogue raisonné 298
Gerund de Campazas, Friar. *See* Isla 2885
Gesner, Conrad:
  Bibliotheca 2157
  Pandectarum libri XXI 2156
Gesta Grayorum. See Canning 108

Gesta Romanorum:
  Hystorye of Gesta Romanorum 1597
Geta Britannicus. See Musgrave 2729
Gevartius, Joannes Casparus:
  Pompa ... honore ... Ferdinandi Austriaci 3620
Gheeraerts, Marcus. *See* Garter 3551
Gherardi, Evaristo:
  Théâtre italien 1250
Gherardo, Pietro, pseud.:
  Histoire d'Ezzelin III 3316
Ghiberti, Lorenzo. *See* Patch 3594
The Ghost 1810:11
Giaccone, Alfonso:
  Istoria ... dell' anima di Trajano 3426
Gianetti, Michel Angelo:
  Elogio del Capitano Cook 4006
  See Seward 3207
Giannini, J. *See* Gray 3893
Giannone, Pietro:
  Istoria civile del regno di Napoli 2078
Giardini, Felice. *See Defence* 1609:56
Giardini, Joannes:
  Promptuarium artis argentariae 220
Gibbon, Edward:
  Essai sur l'étude de la littérature 1786, 3015
  History of the decline and fall of the Roman Empire 3188
  Miscellaneous works 3189
  Vindication 1609:39
  See Davis 1609:41
Gibbon, John:
  Introductio ad Latinam blasoniam 738
Gibbs, James:
  Book of architecture 3535
  See Osorio 1419
Giblet, Henri. *See* Loredano 1038
Gibraltar. *See* Carter 2818; Drinkwater 3311; Tracts 2049:11
Gibson, Edmund, Bishop:
  Pastoral letter 1608:15
  See Camden 563
Gibson, Joseph:
  History of Glasgow 2854
Gibson, Matthew:
  View of ... churches of Door, Home-Lacy, and Hempsted 622
Gifford, William:
  Baviad. See Tracts 2050
  See Wright 3222:21

Gilbert, Sir Geoffrey:
Law of evidence 2695
Gilbert, John:
Sermon. See Sermons 1346:3
Gilbert, Thomas:
First satire of the second book of Horace.
See Poems 280:15
Poems 1828
Gildon, Charles. *See* Examen 1404; Langbaine 1899
Gillies, John:
History of ancient Greece 3191
Orations of Lysias and Isocrates 3190
Gillingwater, Edmund:
Historical account of the town of Lowestoft 3192
Gillot, Claude. *See* Aesop 2325; Drawings 3567, 3678
Gillray, James. *See* Bunbury 3563:2
Gilpin, Bernard. *See* Gilpin, William 1707
Gilpin, William:
Collection of works 3854
Essay on prints 2384
Essay upon prints 338
Life of Bernard Gilpin 1707
Life of Latimer 1608:78
Life of Thomas Cranmer 2855
Ginglecutt, John, pseud.:
Brief account of a treatise concerning . . .
scolding. See Political tracts 94:10
Giotto di Bondone. *See* Patch 3451
Giovannini, Giacopo. *See* Malvasia 3624
Giovannoli, Alo:
Roma antica 3495
Giovio, Paolo, Bishop of Nocera:
Elogia doctorum virorum 2273
Giraldi Cintio, Giovanni Battista:
Hecatommithi 3317
Girard, Gabriel:
Synonymes françois 3099
Girard, Guillaume:
Histoire de la vie du Duc d'Espernon 1010
Girard, Jean Baptiste. *See* Cadière 1023
Girardin, René Louis de:
De la composition des paysages. See Dezallier 920
Girardon, François:
Cabinet 3589
Gislenius, Augerius, Sieur de Busbecq:
Epistolae 2122

Giulianelli, Andrea Pietro:
Memorie degli intagliatori moderni 268, 505
Giulio, de Milano:
Sermon. See Tracts 210
G———k, Mr. *See* Letter 1818:9
Glamorgan, Edward Somerset, Earl of, later Marquess of Worcester. *See* Worcester
Glanvill, Joseph
Blow at modern Sadducism. See Tracts 2050:17
Glasgow. *See* Gibson 2854; MacUre 2725
Glasgow, University of. *See* Moor 1797
Glass Excise Act 1608:6
Glasse, George Henry. *See* Mason, William 2904
Glastonbury, History of. *See* Hearne 658
Glauber, Johannes, called Polydor. *See* Drawings 3587
Gleam of comfort. See O'Beirne 1609:47A
Glencoe. *See* Ridpath 1609:38
Glenie, James:
Reply to the Answer 1609:47A
Short essay on the modes of defence 1609: 47A
Gloucester, Henry, Duke of. *See* Henry
Gloucester, Humphrey, Duke of:
Complaynte made to Kynge Henry the VI 2552
Gloucestershire. *See* Atkyns 423; Bigland 526; Heraldry 3879; Lysons 3434–5; Rudder 530
Glover, Lady Anne. *See* Sermons 2757:2
Glover, Richard:
Athenaid 2856
Boadicia 1818:13
Leonidas, a poem 1616
Medea 3222:1
Glover, Robert. *See* Milles 605
Gnome. See Wewitzer 1810:46
Goat's beard. See Whitehead 3222:15
Godart de Beauchamps. *See* Beauchamps 1553
Godefroy, Denys:
Histoire des Connestables 876
Godefroy, François:
Recueil d'estampes 3742
Godefroy, Jean. *See* Louis XII 1227
Godefroy, Théodore:
Entreveues de Charles IV . . . et de Charles V 1066
See Seyssell 1088

Godet des Marais, Paul. *See* Maintenon 1280
Godfridus. *Knowledge of things unknowne.*
  See Hill 787
Godin d'Abguerbe. *See* Abguerbe
Godly medytacyon. See Marguerite 204
Godwin, Francis, Bishop:
  Annales of England 17
Godwin, Thomas:
  Moses and Aaron 1067
Goeree, Willem:
  *Inleydingh tot de practijck der algemeene
  schilder-konst* 3780
Goetze, Gottfried Christian:
  De bibliotheca senatus Lipsiensis 840
Goguet, Antoine Yves:
  De l'origine des loix 3100
Gold Coast. *See* Guinea
Golden Boke of Marcus Aurelius. *See* Gue-
  vara 199
Golden pippin. See O'Hara 1810:22
Golden Rump. See Cibber 450
Golding, Mrs. Mary. *See Authentic . . . narra-
  tive* 1609:29
Goldoni, Carlo:
  Germondo. See Plays 3972
  Gli Uccellatori. See Music 3448
  See Dibdin 1810:19; Toms 1810:9
Goldsmith, Oliver:
  Deserted village 3222:10
  *Enquiry into the present state of polite
  learning* 1787
  Essays. See Tracts 2768
  Good natur'd man 1810:12
  Haunch of venison 3222:14
  Impartial character 3222:13
  Poems 3711
  Retaliation 3222:13
  She stoops to conquer 1810:19
  Threnodia Augustalis 1810:18
  Traveller 3222:6
  See Parnell 3132; Scott 2469
Goldwin, William:
  Discourse against Popery 1608:60
  Scotch adventure. See Poems 3363
Goltzius, Hendrik. *See* Prints 3461, 3606
Gomersall, Robert:
  Poems 1943
Gondi, Jean François Paul de, Cardinal de
  Retz:
  Mémoires 962

Gondi, House of. *See* Corbinelli
  1139
Gontaut, Charles de. *See* Biron
Gonzaga, Aloysius. *See* Cepari 368
Gonzaga, Francesco, Archbishop:
  Lettere a prencipi 3318
Gooch, John. *See* Drawings 3641
Good humour 1609:13
Goodenough, Richard Josceline:
  Songs in William and Nanny 1810:35
  William and Nanny 1810:31
Goodridge, John:
  Phoenix 2857
Goodwin, John:
  Theomachia. See Sermons 2757
Gordon, Alexander:
  Itinerarium septentrionale 593
Gordon, Lord George:
  Trial of Lord George Gordon 439
  See Cassandra 1609:50; *Sketch* 1609:42
Gordon, Thomas:
  Cordial for low spirits 1744
  The craftsmen. See Miscellaneous tracts
  89:1
  Modest apology for Parson Alberoni. See
  Tracts 2050:5
  See Hervey 1608:11; *Independent Whig*
  1526; Sallustius 470; Tacitus 1103
Gordon, William:
  History of the . . . family of Gordon
  2696
Gordon, family of. *See* Gordon 2696
Gore, Thomas:
  *Catalogus . . . authorum qui de Heraldica
  . . . scripserunt* 1068
Gorges, Ferdinando:
  America painted to the life 3427
Gori, Antonio Francesco:
  Dactyliotheca Smithiana 3696
  Monumentum 3743
  Museum Florentinum 431
Goring, Henry. *See* Charles Edward Stuart
  1608:39
Gosling, William. *See* Gostling, William
Gospel-Shop. See Hill 1810:28
Gosson, Stephen:
  Schoole of abuse 1788
Gostling, George:
  *Extracts from the treaties between Great
  Britain and other kingdoms* 3697

Gostling, William:
Account of Hogarth's tour 2385
Walk in and about the City of Canterbury 2858
Gothic oration. See Coetlogon 1608:51
Goths. *See* Jornandes 1032; Pinkerton 2447
Goudar, Ange:
Histoires des grecs 3101
Gough, Richard:
Account of a rich illuminated Missal 3812
Anecdotes of British topography 3319
British topography 33
Catalogue of the coins of Canute. See Mead 3785
One or more letters. *See* Letters 2576
Sepulchral monuments 3644
See Camden 424; Hutchins 4; Martin 2902, 3200; Nash 6; Vertue 2479
Goujet, C. P. *See* Marolles 791
Gould, Sir Nathaniel:
Essay on the publick debts 1608:21
Goupy, Joseph:
Catalogue of pictures. See Catalogues 3404
Gourville, Jean Hérault:
Mémoires 939
Gout. *See* Paulmier 3133
Government of the tongue 3939
Gower, Granville, Viscount Trentham. *See* Trentham
Gower, Nathaniel:
Sermon. See Derby 79:3
Gower, Richard. *See* Le Boe 2279
Gowrie, John Ruthven, Earl of. *See* Cromarty 116; Dalrymple 1609:56
Graces 3222:13
Gracian, Baltasar:
Homme de cour 1197
Graevius, Johannes Georgius. *See* Classics 2207:9, 10, 11, 23
Grafton, Augustus Henry Fitzroy, 3d Duke of:
Hints, &c. 1609:52
See Epistle 3222:9; *First letter* 1609:25; Gray 3222:9
Grafton, Richard. *See* Mary, Queen of Scots 205
Graglia, Giuspanio. *See* Martialis 2107
Graham, Mrs. Catharine Macaulay, later Mrs. *See* Macaulay
Graham, George:
Telemachus, a mask 3222:4

Graham, Helen Mary, Lady Dashwood. *See* Dashwood
Graham, James:
Six odes presented to . . . Mrs. Catharine Macaulay 3222:15
Graham, James, Duke of Montrose. *See* Montrose
Graham, John, Viscount Dundee:
Memoirs 1565
Graham, Richard, Viscount Preston. *See* Boethius 148
Graham, Richard (*fl.* 1680–1720). *See* Piles 308
Grammaire . . . françoise. See Mauger 1229
Grammar of the English tongue. See Brightland 2000
Grammars. *See* School books 3175
Grammont, Philibert, Comte de. *See* Hamilton, Antoine, Count
Granby, Charles Manners, Marquess of. *See* Charity 3222:13; Rutland 1609:31
Grand Jury. *See* Hawkins 1609:25
Grand question stated. See Stillingfleet 56
Grand secret of precipitating the preliminaries 1608:56
Granger, James:
Apology 1609:36
Biographical history of England 541, 3813
One or more letters. *See* Letters 2576
Grantham, Thomas:
Hear the Church. See Tracts 2968:10
Grantham, Thomas Robinson, 2d Baron. *See* Etchings 3588
Granvelle, Antoine Perrenot de, Cardinal. *See* Lévêque 995
Granville, George, Baron Lansdowne. *See* Lansdowne
Granville, John Carteret, Earl. *See* Poems 3363:16; Walpole 2489:4
Granville, Mary, later Mrs. Delany. *See* Delany
Granville, Sir Richard. *See* Grenville
Granville, Lady Sophia Fermor, Countess. *See* Rigacci 2112
Gratius, Faliscus:
Cynegeticon 2008
Gratulatio Academiae. See Cambridge 498; Oxford 514
Graunt, John:
Observations . . . upon the bills of mortality

Graunt, John (*cont.*)
1069, 1520
See Hervey 1608:8; *Reflections* 1608:1
Gravelot, Henry. *See* Vertue 3663; Pine 3552
Graves, Richard:
Coalition 1810:54
Gravesande, Willem Jakob Storm van's:
Mathematical elements of natural philoso-
phy 1409
Gray, Charles:
Considerations on several proposals 1608:
48. *See* Tracts 2049:8
Gray, Lady Jane. *See* Grey
Gray, Thomas, Baron Gray. *See* Grey.
Gray, Thomas:
The Bard 3222:14
Catalogue of the antiquities 3892
Designs by Mr. R. Bentley for six poems
2044, 3698
Elegia Inglese 3699
Elegia scripta 3222:2
Elegy 3893
Eton, an ode. See Poems 881:12
Latin odes 3222:14
Ode on the death of Mr. Gray 3894
Ode performed at Cambridge 3222:9
Odes. See Collection 2506, 2508; Temple
2517
Poems 2859, 3700, 3841, 3895
See Duncombe 3222:14; *Irregular ode* 3222:
12; Poems 3363; Pope 3222:14; *Ruin* 3222:
16; Wright 3222:21; Young 1609:45
Gray Friars. *See* Grey Friars
Gray's Inn. *See* Canning 108
Graziani, Antonio Maria:
Vie du Cardinal Jean François Commen-
don 3102
See Fléchier 1156
Grazioli, Pietro:
De praeclaris Mediolani aedificiio . . . dis-
sertatio 3744
Grazzini, Antonio Francesco:
Tutti i trionfi, carri, mascherate 3320
Great blessing of a monarchical government.
See Mordington 134
Great Britain. *See* England
Great Britain's poverty and distress 1608:64
Great charter. See Blackstone 232
Great man's speech in Downing Street. See
Poems 280:12

Great Yarmouth. *See* Swinden 3208
Greatheed, Bertie:
Regent 1810:45
See Arno miscellany 3803; *Florence miscel-*
lany 3810; Walpole 3729
Greatrakes, William. *See Application* 1609:
13
Greaves, John:
Miscellaneous works 1436
Grecian daughter. See Murphy 1810:18
Greece:
See Chandler 2822; Choiseul-Gouffier 3586;
Gillies 3191; Pausanias 388; Pauw 3135;
Potter 1652; Wheeler 2497
Greece. Antiquities. *See* Le Roy 3541
Greek and Roman history illustrated by coins
and medals. See Walker 2774
Greek coinage. *See* Wren 2503
Greek poetesses. *See* Ursinus 2609
Green:
Map of Europe. *See* Europe 3642
Green, George Smith:
Nice lady 1810:3
Green, John:
New general collection of voyages and
travels 542
Green, John, engraver. *See* Engravings 3417
Green, Matthew:
Spleen 1608:35
Green, Thomas. *See* Greene
Green, Valentine:
History . . . of Worcester 3855
Survey of the city of Worcester 2697
Views in London. *See* Antiquities 3485:13
Green Box. See English green box 1609:40
Green Room scene. See Philoctetes 1810:57
Greene, Edward Burnaby. *See* Chatterton
3690:17; *Defence* 1609:16; Gray 3222:14,
3892
Greene, Robert:
Philomela 2386
Greene, Thomas (1658–1738), Bishop:
Poems 2553
Greenhill, Thomas:
Art of embalming 506
Green's Map of Europe. See Europe 3642
Greenwood, Jonathan. *See* Gulston 3876
Gregory, of Nazianzus, Saint:
Opera 2158
Gregory, George. *See* Chatterton 3690:8

Gregory, John. *See* MacGregory 698

Grenville, Anne, Countess Temple. *See* Temple

Grenville, George:
Speech of a Right Honourable gentleman 1609:24
See Almon 1609:54; Guthrie 1609:8; Hartley 1609:55; Knox 1609:21, 22; *Letter* 1609: 8, 54; Lloyd 1609:16; *Ode* 3222:9; *Regulations* 1609:11; *Reply* 1609:54; *Tears* 3222: 7; Whately 1609:56; Wilkes 1609:24

Grenville, Sir Richard:
Two original journals 45

Grenville, Richard Temple, Earl Temple. *See* Temple

Grenville, William Henry, Earl of Bath. *See* Bath

Grenville, William Wyndham, Baron Grenville:
Considerations on the establishment of a regency 1609:50

Grenville-Temple, Richard, Earl Temple. *See* Temple

Gresham College. *See* Ward 8

Gresset, Jean Baptiste Louis:
Oeuvres 963

Greville, Mrs. Frances. *See* Greville 2009

Greville, Francis, Earl of Warwick. *See* Warwick

Greville, Fulke, Baron Brooke. *See* Brooke

Greville, Fulke, of Wilberry:
Maxims 2009

Greville, Lady Louisa Augusta, later married to William Churchill. *See* Etchings 3588

Greville, Robert, Baron Brooke. *See* Brooke

Greville family. *See* Edmondson 2372

Grew, Nehemiah:
Musaeum Regalis Societatis 1115

Grey, Anchitell. *See* England 1354

Grey, Ford, Earl of Tankerville. *See* Tankerville

Grey, Lady Jane. *See* Florio 2101; Keate 3222:1; Plays 1623:2; Werdmueller 212

Grey, Richard:
Memoria technica 1789

Grey, Thomas, Baron Grey. *See* Plays 1082:4

Grey, Thomas, 2d Earl of Stamford. *See* Stamford

Grey, Zachary:
Critical . . . notes on Shakespeare 1829

Grey, Zachary (*cont.*)
Word or two of advice 1608:55
See Butler 1822; Masters 3820

Grey Friars. *See* Parkinson 636

Gribelin, Simon:
Judgment of Hercules. *See* Shaftesbury 1496
Livre de petite estampes 3875
See Zanetti 3801

Grievances of the American colonies. *See* Hopkins 1609:12

Griffet, Henri:
Recueil de lettres . . . du règne de Louis XIV 1297

Griffin, Benjamin:
Whig and Tory. *See* Plays 1909:2

Griffith, Mrs. Elizabeth:
Barber of Seville 1810:26
Double mistake 1810:8
Platonic wife 1810:6
School for rakes 1810:14
The times 1810:31
Wife in the right 1810:18

Griffith, Richard:
One letter. *See* Letters 2576
Variety 1810:34
See Masquerade 3222:9

Griffith, Richard, Jr.:
Thoughts on protecting duties 1609:46

Griffiths. *See also* Griffith

Griffiths, Ralph. *See* Ascanius 1500

Grignan, Comtesse de. *See* Sévigné 949

Grignan, Jacques Adhémar Monteil de. *See* Rémonstrance 1085

Grignette, Benigne:
Les armes triomphantes 3745

Grimaldi, Giovanni Francesco. *See* Drawings 3569

Grimston, Sir Harbottle:
Speech. *See* Tracts 2769:1

Grimston, James, Viscount Grimston:
One letter. *See* Letters 2576

Grimston, William Luckyn, 1st Viscount:
Lawyer's fortune 1896, 2861

Grimstone, Edward:
Generall historie of the Netherlands 2054

Groans of Britain 1608:56

Gronovius, Jacobus. *See* Classics 2207:22; Herodotus 3815

Gronovius, Joannes Fridericus. *See* Classics 2207:34

Groot, Hugo de. *See* Grotius

Grose, Francis:
Advice to the officers 2862
Antiquities of Ireland 3496
Classical dictionary of the vulgar tongue 2863
Collection of his works 3842
Guide to health 1609:47
The Olio 3923
See Antiquarian 3850; Bunbury 3913; Ledwich 3195

Grosley, Pierre Jean:
Londres 2274
Nouveaux mémoires sur l'Italie 3103

Grosseteste, Robert, Bishop. *See* Pegge 3252

Grosvenor, Richard, 1st Earl Grosvenor:
Copies of the depositions of the witnesses 1609:29
See Circumstantial 1609:26

Grotius, Hugo:
De jure belli ac pacis libri tres. See Classics 2207:16
See Burigny 1182

Grove, Henry:
Wisdom the first spring of action 1410

Grove, Joseph:
Lives of all the Earls and Dukes of Devonshire 1521

Grudé de la Croix du Maine, François. *See* La Croix

Gruel, Guillaume. *See Collection* 3084

Grunston, Lord. *See* Grimston

Grymston, Sir Harbottle. *See* Grimston

Gryphius, Christian. *See Vitae* 2137

Guadaloupe:
Genuine account 1608:87

Gualdi, Abbate, pseud. *See* Leti, Gregorio

Gualdo Priorato, Galeazzo, Conte:
Scena d'huomini illustri d'Italia 2079

Gualterotti, Raffaello:
Feste nelle nozze 3781

Gualterus, Petrus, pseud. *See* Fielding 1608:45

Gualtieri, Niccolò
Index 3621

Guardaloupe. *See* Guadaloupe

Guardian 1851, 1860

Guardian (1759). *See* Garrick 1818:17

Guarini, Giovanni Batista:
Il pastor fido 2123

Guasco, Octavien de, Comte de Clavières. *See* Montesquieu 2285

Guastaldi, Giambattista. *See* Gastaldi

Guay, Jacques. *See* Pompadour 3750

Guelard, J. B. *See* Huet 3647

Guerchy, Claude Louis François Regnier, Comte de. *See* Éon de Beaumont 1609:54

Guercino. *See* Bartolozzi 3398; Drawings 3569

Guérin de Tencin, Claudine Alexandrine. *See* Tencin

Guernsey, account of. *See* Dicey 727

Guerre d'Espagne, de Bavière, et de Flandres. See Sandras 3144

Gueudeville, Nicolas. *See* Chatelain 425

Guevara, Antonio de:
Diall of princes 2699
Golden boke 199, 1323
Spanish letters 1478

Guicciardini, Francesco:
Della istoria d'Italia 877

Guichard, Claude:
Funérailles . . . des Romains 841

Guide ou nouvelle description d'Amsterdam. See Amsterdam 3395

Guide to English juries 164

Guide to health. See Grose 1609:47

Guides 2387

Guidi, Tommaso, known as Masaccio. *See* Masaccio

Guienne, Ducs de. *See* Besly 889

Guilford, Francis North, 1st Baron:
Argument in the case 3321
See North 3355

Guilford, Francis North, 4th Earl of:
Kentish Barons 1810:47

Guilford, Frederick North, Lord North, later Earl of. *See* North

Guillim, John:
Display of heraldry 570

Guinea. *See* Thompson 1609:51

Guinement de Kéralio, Louise Félicité. *See* Kéralio

Guirlande de Julie. See Montausier

Guise, John. *See* Hervart 1608:7

Gulston, Eliza. *See* Etchings 3588

Gulston, Joseph:
Catalogue of [his] *collection of prints* 3876

Gunning, Elizabeth, Duchess of Argyle. *See* Argyle

Gunpowder Plot:
  Gunpowder-treason 2700
  See Taaffe 2763:3

Gunton, Simon:
  History of the Church of Peterburgh 594

Gurdon, Brampton:
  Christian religion supported 1608:22

Gurney, Joseph. *See* Onslow 1609:26

Gustavus III, King of Sweden. *See* Mallet 2312

Gustavus Adolphus, King of Sweden. *See* Harte 464

Gustavus Ericson, King of Sweden. *See* Scott 1654

Gutberleth, Tobias:
  Opuscula 2275

Gutch, John. *See* Wood 3219

Guthrie, William:
  Address to the public 1609:8
  Complete history of the English peerage. *See* Tracts 2968:1
  Reply to the Counter-Address 1609:8
  See Full and candid answer 1609:1

Guyot Desfontaines, Pierre François. *See* Desfontaines

Guzman, Gaspar de, Conde de Olivares. *See* Olivares 2586

Gwedir family, history of. *See* Wynn 2785

Gwinne, Matthew:
  Nero. See Plays 2131

Gwinnett, Richard:
  Country 'squire 1810:5

Gwynn, John:
  London and Westminster improved 3877
  See Tracts 2146:1

Gwynne, Matthew. *See* Gwinne

Gwynne, Sir Rowland. *See Copy of a letter* 1608:94

Gyllenborg, Carl, Count:
  Letters relating to the rebellion. See Tracts 2769:12

H., J. *See Private character* 1608:18
H., J., M. D. *See* Harvey, James
Habington, William:
  Castara 2388
  History of Edward IV 18
Habiti d'huomeni. See Venice 3987

Hackett, John:
  Collection of . . . epigrams 1944
  Select epitaphs 981

Hackman, James:
  Case and memoirs 1609:40

Haddington, Thomas Hamilton, 6th Earl of:
  Tales in verse 165
  Treatise on forest trees 2864

Hadley, George (1685–1768):
  Description of a new instrument 1608:37

Hadley, George (d. 1798):
  New and complete history of Kingston on Hull. See Cozens 3184

Hadrian, Emperor of Rome. *See* Contini 3618

Haendel, Georg Friedrich. *See* Händel

Hafod. *See* Cumberland 2829

Haggitt, John. *See Count de Villeroi* 1810:55

Hagley. See Maurice 3222:14

Hailes, David Dalrymple, Lord. *See* Dalrymple

Haistwell, E. *See Etchings* 3588

Hakewill, George:
  Comparison 3961

Hakewill, William:
  Order and course of passing bills 1608:2

Hale, John:
  Letter to the people of England 1609:42

Hale, Sir Mathew. *See* Burnet 1702

Hale, Thomas:
  Account of several new inventions 2701

Hales, John:
  Works 2702
  See Des Maizeaux 1608:14; Whiston 1727:1
  Half an hour after supper 1810:48

Halfpenny, Joseph:
  Gothic ornaments 3497

Halifax, Charles Montagu, 1st Earl of:
  Works 46

Halifax, George Montagu Dunk, 2d Earl of:
  Catalogue 3833:12
  See Letter 1609:6

Halifax, George Savile, 1st Marquess of:
  Character of a trimmer 83
  Character of Charles the Second 1608:67
  Miscellanies 47
  Miscellanies historical and philosophical 2010
  Some cautions 83

Halifax, William:
  Relation of the voyage to Tadmor 2554

Halifax, parish of. *See* Watson 3215
Hall, Anthony. *See* Cox 621; Leland 694;
Trivet 710
Hall, Antony. *See* Stevenson, John Hall
Hall, Francis. *See* Line, Francis
Hall, John:
Poems 2011
Hall, Joseph, Bishop:
Virgidemiarum 1945
Hall, Robert, pseud. *See* Heylyn 741
Hall-Stevenson, John. *See* Stevenson, John
Hall
Halle, Edward:
*Union of . . . families of York and Lan-
caster* 623
Hallifax, Samuel, Bishop. *See* Butler 1609:49
Ham, John. *See* Arbuthnot 1608:37
Hamet, Muley. *See* Sherley 3828
Hamilton, Antoine, Count:
Mémoires du comte de Grammont 2389,
2511
Memoirs 1479
Oeuvres meslées 982
Hamilton, Charles:
Patriot 1810:37
Hamilton, Gavin, artist:
Schola Italica picturae 3571
Hamilton, Gavin, Esq., of Killelagh. *See*
Tracts 2050:24
Hamilton, James, Viscount Paisley, later Earl
of Abercorn. *See* Abercorn
Hamilton, James Douglas, 4th Duke of. *See*
MacCartney 1608:5
Hamilton, John, 2d Baron Belhaven. *See*
Belhaven
Hamilton, John:
Case against Joseph Hickey 1608:28
Hamilton, Thomas, Earl of Haddington. *See*
Haddington
Hamilton, Sir William:
Campi Phlegraei 2865
Catalogue of Pictures. See Catalogues 3404
Collection of . . . antiquities 3536
Collection of engravings 3498
Observations on Mount Vesuvius 2865
See Etchings 3588
Hamilton, William, of Bangour:
Poems on several occasions 1946
Hamilton, William Gerard. *See* Opposition
1608:80, 81

Hammond, George. *See* Hamond
Hammond, Robert:
Letters . . . relating to King Charles I
1609:9
Hammond, William. *See* Hamond
Hamond, George:
Good minister of Jesus Christ. See Sermons
2756:1
Hamond, William:
Advice to a son 2555
Maxims, moral and political 2556
Hampden, John. *See* Tracts 3797:9
Hampden, Robert Trevor, 1st Viscount:
Britannia 3537
Hampshire. *See* Warner 2980
Hampton, James. *See* Polybius 319
Hancarville. *See* Hugues d'Hancarville
Händel, Georg Friedrich. *See* Burney 461;
Mainwaring 1608:36; Poems 3363:12
Hanmer, Meredith. *See* Ware 2182
Hanmer, Sir Thomas. *See* Hervey 1608:90;
Shakespeare 64
Hanover, Sophia Dorothea, called Duchess of.
See Pöllnitz 1282
Hanover. *See* English 1608:46; *Important*
1608:38; *Interest* 1608:43
Hanover, House of:
Memoirs 1608:9
See Second 1608:24
Hanover troops. *See* Free 1608:47; Waller
1608:43, 46
Hanway, Jonas:
Account of British trade 1324
*Account of the Society for the encourage-
ment of the British troops* 1790
Defects of police 3322
Proposals for county naval free-schools 440
Reflections on life and religion 2866
Happy bride. See Bramston 1886:1
Harbin, George:
Hereditary right of the Crown of England
1116
Harcouet de Longeville. *See* Longeville 380
Harcourt, George Simon, Earl Harcourt:
One or more letters. See Letters 2576
See Etchings 3588; Guides 2387:1
Harcourt, Simon, 1st Viscount Harcourt 1608:
94
Harding, Edward. *See* Shakespeare 3905
Harding, Samuel. *See* Persepolis 3756

Harding, Silvester. *See* Shakespeare 3905
Hardinge, Nicholas:
  Latin verses 3323
Hardouin, Jean:
  Mémoires d'Artois. See Tracts 2050:18
Hardwicke, Philip Yorke, 1st Earl of:
  Speech. See Tracts 2146:3
Hardwicke, Philip Yorke, 2d Earl of:
  Letters. See Letters 2576
  Miscellaneous state papers 3236
  Walpoliana 3924
  See Dorchester 3166, 3310
Hardyng, John:
  Chronicle 688
Hare, Francis, Bishop:
  Difficulties and discouragements 1608:32
  Sermon. See Derby 79:6
Hare, Henry, 3d Baron Coleraine. *See* Coleraine
Haren, Willem van:
  Leonidas. See Tracts 2146:5
Harenius, W. *See* Haren, Willem van
Hargrove, Ely:
  History of . . . Knaresborough 2867
Harington, Henry:
  Nugae antiquae 411, 3814
Harington, Sir John:
  History of Polindor and Flostella 1947
Harleian catalogue. *See* Oxford 318
Harleian Collection of manuscripts. *See* British Museum 218
Harlequin incendiary 1818:20
Harlequin premier 1810:14
Harlequin sorcerer. See Theobald 1818:17
Harlequin's gambols. See Airs 1810:21
Harlequin's jubilee. See Woodward 1810:15
Harley, Edward, Earl of Oxford. *See* Oxford
Harley, Margaret Cavendish, Duchess of Portland. *See* Portland
Harley, Richard. *See* Miscellaneous tracts 89:2
Harley, Robert, Earl of Oxford. *See* Oxford
Harley family. *See* Collins 565
Harrington, Barnaby. *See* Brathwait 2235
Harrington, Henry. *See* Harington.
Harrington, James (1611–1677):
  Oceana 1117
Harrington, James (1664–1693). *See* Oxford University 1608:3
Harrington, Sir John. *See* Harington

Harrington, William Stanhope, 1st Earl of. *See* Rival wives 2463; Tracts 2146:3
Harrington, William Stanhope, 2d Earl of. *See* Bevell 1609:56
Harris, James:
  Philological inquiries 3237
  The spring 1810:3
Harris, John:
  Collection of voyages and travels 432
  History of Kent 571
  See Pardies 1758
Harris, Thomas:
  Letter from T. Harris 1609:57
  Narrative of the disputes 1609:56
  See Linley 1810:43
Harris, Walter:
  Hibernica 595
  History and antiquities of Dublin 689
  See Smith 396; Ware 614
Harris, William:
  Historical and critical account of Hugh Peters 1608:20
  Life and writings of Charles I 1643
  Life and writings of James I 1644
  Life of Charles the Second 1356
  Life of Oliver Cromwell 1645
Harrison, Stephen:
  Arches of triumph 3428
Harrison, Susannah:
  Songs in the night. See Pye 2457
Harrison & Co. *See* Watts 3849
Harry, George Owen:
  Genealogy of . . . James, King of Great Brittayne 842
  See Clarke 1593
Harry the Ninth, pseud. *See* Tracts 2146:3
Hart, Mrs. Christian:
  Letter to Mrs. Rudd 1609:37
Harte, Walter:
  History . . . of Gustavus Adolphus, King of Sweden 464
Hartgyll, George:
  Astronomicall tables 2703
Hartley, David:
  Address to the Committee 1609:42
  The Budget 1609:55
  Right of appeal to juries 1609:8
  State of the nation 1609:56
  Two letters 1609:41
  See Whately 1609:9

Hartley, Elizabeth (White). *See* Vauxhall 1609:31

Hartley, Mary. *See* Etchings 3588

Hartlib, Samuel:
Chymical, medicinal, and chyrurgical addresses 372
Clavis apocalyptica 2390
Discours of husbandrie 125, 200
Discoverie for division of land 2391-2
Legacie 125, 1070
Reformed common-wealth of bees 125, 1071
See Beale 2333; Boate 147, 188, 1152, 2341; Dury 193

Hartly House, Calcutta 373

Hartson, Hall:
Countess of Salisbury 1810:11

Harvard University:
Pietas et gratulatio 1325

Harvest, George:
Collection of sermons 1598
Grounds and reasons. See Sermons 1346:4

Harvest is at hand. See Champneys 189

Harvey, Gideon:
Art of curing diseases by expectation 2012

Harvey, James:
Scelera aquarum 1608:8

Harvey, Thomas. *See* Owen 2022

Harwich, History of. *See* Dale 654

Harwood, Edward:
View of the Greek and Roman classics 2212

Harwood, Thomas:
Death of Dion 1810:42

Hassan, Abul, Persian ambassador:
One letter. *See* Letters 2576

Hassell, John:
Tour of the Isle of Wight 3856
See Antiquities 3485:1

Hasted, Edward:
History of Kent 3

Hastings, Francis, Earl of Huntington. *See* Huntington

Hastings, Warren:
Articles of charge 1609:49
Minutes of what was offered 1609:49

Hastings, Lady Winifred. *See* Letters 2576 (Pole)

Hastings:
Hastings guide 2868

Hastings, Battle of. *See* Cumberland 1810:27

Hastings guide. See Hastings 2868

Hatchett, William:
Fall of Mortimer 1810:4
See Bignon 2339

Hatsell, Henry. *See* Howard 1330

Hatton, Sir Christopher:
Treatise concerning statutes 166

Haudicquer de Blancourt, François:
De l'art de verrerie 1274

Havard, William:
King Charles the First 1818:6

Haven of pleasure. See Winchester 2499

Haverkamp, Sigebertus. *See* Classics 2207:39; Morel 226

Haversham, John Thompson, 1st Baron:
Account of the late Scotch invasion 1608:94
Speech 1608:94

Hawke, William. *See* Genuine life 1609:32

Hawkesworth, John:
Account of the voyages . . . in the southern hemisphere 2869
Amphitryon 1818:15
Edgar and Emmeline 1810:1
See Adventurer 2148; Swift 3379

Hawkesworth, Walter. *See* Plays 2131:4

Hawkins, Sir John:
Charge to the Grand Jury 1609:25
History of music 34
Life of Samuel Johnson 412
Memoirs of Agostino Steffani. See Tracts 2968:2
Observations on the state of the highways 2393
See Walton 2494

Hawkins, John Sidney. *See* Ruggle 2946

Hawkins, Thomas:
Origin of the English drama 2870

Hawkins, Sir Thomas. *See* Botero 2804; Horatius 1951

Hawkins, William (d. 1637):
Apollo Shroving. See Plays 2451

Hawkins, William (1722–1801):
Henry and Rosamond 1818:8

Hawksmoor, Nicholas:
Account of London Bridge 624

Hawkstone. See Rodenhurst 2944

Hawling, Francis:
Miscellany of original poems 1852

Haworth, Samuel:
True method of curing consumptions 2704

Hawtrey, Charles:
Letter to Earl Stanhope 1609:52
Hay, William:
Deformity 1608:79
Remarks 1608:48, 2049:10
Haydock, Richard. See Hilliard 2560
Hayes, Charles. See Tracts 2146:1
Hayes, Richard:
Estimate of places for life 1480
Hayley, William:
Essay on epic poetry 3222:18
Essay on history 3222:17
Ode inscribed to John Howard 3222:17
Philosophical essay on old maids 3104
Plays 3324
Poetical epistle 3222:16
Triumphs of temper 3222:17
Haym, Niccolò Francesco:
Del Tesoro Britannico parte prima 269
Hayman, Francis. See Tracts 2146:1
Haymarket. King's Theatre. See King's
Theatre, Haymarket
Haymarket Theatre. See Impartial 1608:69;
Letter 1608:63
Haynes, Samuel:
Collection of state papers 441
Hayter, Thomas, Bishop:
Essay 1608:50
See Catalogues 3404
Haython, Prince of Gorigos. See Hetoum
Haywood, Eliza:
Secret history of the . . . Court of Cara-
mania 1481
Head-dresses. See Lens 2574
Headley, Henry:
Fugitive pieces 1609:47
Select beauties of ancient English poetry
2871
Heads, Etchings of. See Zanetti 3801
Heard, Sir Isaac. See Collins 3888
Heard, William:
Sentimental journey to Bath, Bristol . . .
3222:16
Valentine's Day 1810:25
Hearne, Mary:
Female deserters. See Plays 1909:3
Hearne, Thomas:
Antiquities between Windsor and Oxford.
See Hornby 692:1
Antiquities of Great Britain 3429, 3645

Hearne, Thomas (cont.)
Chronicon de Dunstaple 656
Discourses by eminent antiquaries 657
Ectypa varia 596
History of Glastonbury 658
See Huddesford 2875; Rous 666; Spelman
1691; Sprott 2320; William of Newburgh
711
Heath, Benjamin:
Case of the County of Devon 1609:54
Heath, George. See Bristol 2809
Heath, James, engraver. See Bunbury 3563:2;
Goodridge 2857
Heath, James, historian:
Chronicle of the late intestine war 1118
Heath, Robert:
Account of the islands of Scilly and . . . of
Cornwall 690
Heathcote, Ralph:
Cursory animadversions. See Middleton
1337
Letter to the Honorable Mr. Horace Wal-
pole 1609:16
Some remarks on a book 1379:3
Sylva 1609:16
Hebrides. See Boswell 3069; Johnson 3108;
Pennant 547
Heckel, Augustin. See Drawings 3678
Hector. See Shepherd 3222:10
Hecquet, Robert:
Catalogue des estampes 3016
Hecuba. See Delap 1810:2
Hederich, Benjamin:
Lexicon manuale Graecum 843
Hedlinger, Johann Carl:
Oeuvre, ou recueil des medailles 453
Hegge, Robert:
Legend of St. Cuthbert 739
Heide, Jan van der. See Heiden
Heiden, Jan van der:
Beschryving der slangbrandspuiten 529
Heighington, Musgrave:
Six select odes 3878
Heince, Zacharie. See Vulson 3557
Heineken, Carl Heinrich von:
Idée générale d'une collection . . .
d'estampes 299, 3105, 3712
Heinsius, Daniel:
Laus asini 2244
See Horatius 2276

Heliopolis. *See* Wood 3547
Helman, Isidore Stanislaus:
 Abrégé historique des principaux traits de la vie de Confucius 3746
 Faits mémorables des Empereurs de la Chine 3747
Helmes, Henry. *See* Canning 108
Helmont, Jan Baptista van:
 Oriatrike 3325
Helvétius, Claude Adrien:
 De l'esprit 552
Helvicus, Christophorus:
 Historical and chronological theatre 1119
Helwich, Christopher. *See* Helvicus
Helyot, Pierre *and* Bullot, Maximilien:
 Histoire des ordres monastiques 1141
Hempstead. *See* Gibson 622
Hénault, Charles Jean François:
 Cornélie 2512
 François II 2394
 Nouvel abrégé chronologique de l'histoire de France 964
 Pièces du théâtre 3017
 See Cochin 3808
Henderson, Andrew:
 Arsinoe 1818:8
 Life of Earl of Stair 1608:20
Henderson, John. *See* Davies 1810:27
Henley, John:
 Coup de grace 1608:31
 Law and arguments 1608:70
Henniker, John Henniker Major, 2d Baron:
 Two letters on . . . Norman tiles 3106
Hennin, Heinrich Christian von. *See* Juvenalis 2195
Henrietta Maria de Bourbon, Queen of England. *See* Dauncey 1557
Henriques, Jacob. *See* Epistle 1609:54
Henry II, King of England. *See* Caesar 2815; Lyttelton 3173
Henry III, King of England:
 Charta de foresta. See Edward I 1608:8, 2547
Henry VII, King of England:
 Description of the coronation 3713
 Instructions given . . . to his embassadors 1609:54
 Will 1609:58
 See A. B. C. 141; Bacon 886; Macklin 1818: 20

Henry VIII, King of England:
 Assertio . . . adversus Martin Luther 84, 1608:6
 Necessary doctrine 201
 See Haynes 441; Herbert 19; Lewis 1794; Letters 1900; Paul III 1608:95; Tracts 2146:6
Henry II, King of France. *See* Lussan 812
Henry III, King of France:
 Recueil de diverses pièces 844
 See L'Estoile 1301
Henry IV, King of France:
 Amours. See Tracts 3054
 See Bury 3002; Du Pont 2546; La Boderie 3022; L'Estoile 1302; Péréfixe 930
Henry, Duke of Gloucester. *See* Manley 1573
Henry, Prince of Wales:
 True accompt 3962
 True report. See Harry 842
 See Birch 1666; Tracts 3797:1
Henry Frederick, Duke of Cumberland. *See* Circumstantial 1609:26; Epistle 3222:12
Henry, Robert:
 Five letters. See Letters 2576
 History of Great Britain 543
Hensbergh, Vincent 3963
Hentzner, Paul:
 Journey into England 2395, 2513
Heraclea. *See* Tracts 1348:11
Heraldry:
 Arms of the nobility 3782
 Collection of the coats of arms 3879
 Copies of various pedigrees 2557
 English baronage 3499
 Historical and heraldic documents 2558
 'Manuscript volume on heraldry' 2559
 Visitation of Norfolk. See Heraldry 3879
 See Cecil 2538; Peerage 2442; Seller 2754; Tilston 2604
Herbert, Edward, Baron Herbert of Cherbury:
 De la verité 35
 De religione gentilium 85
 De veritate 167
 Dialogue between a tutor and his pupil 3238
 Expeditio in Ream insulam 168, 202
 Letters. See Letters 2576
 Life 2514. See Strawberry Hill 3469:3
 Life of Henry VIII 19

Herbert, Edward (*cont.*)
Occasional verses 169
Religion of the Gentiles 48
Herbert, George:
Temple 2013
See Wit's recreations 2037
Herbert, Henry. Earl of Pembroke. *See* Pembroke
Herbert, Isaac. *See* Paine 3512
Herbert, Lady Lucy:
Several excellent methods of hearing mass 2396
Herbert, Mary, Countess of Pembroke. *See* Pembroke
Herbert, Philip, Earl of Pembroke. *See* Pembroke
Herbert, Thomas, Earl of Pembroke. *See* Pembroke
Herbert, Thomas (1597–1642):
Vox secunda populi 1326
Herbert, Sir Thomas (1606–1682):
Memoirs of the two last years of the reign of . . . King Charles I 1708
Herbert, William, bibliographer. *See* Ames 29
Herbert, William, Dean of Manchester. *See* Eton College 2847
Herbert, William, Earl of Pembroke. *See* Pembroke
Herbinius, Joannes:
Dissertationes 845
Herculaneum:
Catalogo degli antichi monumenti 3590
Four prints 3430
See Cochin 1433
Hercules, Judgment of. *See* Shaftesbury 1496
Hereditary right of the Crown of England. *See* Harbin 1116
Hereford. *See* Rawlinson 702
Herefordshire. *See* Antiquities 3485:2
Herefordshire orchards. See Beale 2333
Hermant, Godefroy:
Vie de Saint Athanase 1275
Vie de Saint Jean Chrysostome 1276
Hermeticall banquet 1745
Hermit of Warkworth. See Percy 3222:11
Herne, Samuel:
Domus Carthusiana 691
Hero and Leander. See Loves of Hero and Leander

Herodotus:
Historiarum libri IX 3815
History 1411
See Estienne 1189
Heroic answer from Richard Twiss. See Preston 3222:15
Heroic epistle from Donna Teresa Pinna y Ruiz. See Preston 3222:15
Heroic epistle to an unfortunate monarch 3222:16
Heroic epistle to Sir William Chambers. See Mason 3222:12
Heroic epistle to the noble author. See Combe 3222:15
Heroic epistle to the Rev. Martin M-d-n. See Madan 3222:17
Heroic postscript to the public. See Mason 3222:13
Heroine of the cave. See Hiffernan 1810:24
Heron, Robert, pseud. *See* Pinkerton 3825
Herrick, Robert:
Hesperides 1948
Herries, Catherine Foote, Lady:
One letter. *See* Letters 2576
Herring, Thomas, Archbishop:
Letters . . . to William Duncombe 2872
Sermon 1608:55
Herrnhuters. *See* United Brethren
Hertford, Francis Ingram Seymour-Conway, 2d Marquess of:
Letter 1609:45
Hertfordshire. *See* Chauncy 564; Norden 663
Hervart, Max:
Plain narrative 1608:7
Hervey, Augustus John, Earl of Bristol. *See* Bristol
Hervey, Carr, Lord Hervey. *See* Tracts 2050:5
Hervey, Elizabeth (Chudleigh), Duchess of Kingston. *See* Kingston
Hervey, Mrs. Elizabeth (March). *See Louisa* 2311; *Melissa and Marcia* 2314
Hervey, Frederick Augustus, Earl of Bristol. *See* Bristol
Hervey, George William, Earl of Bristol. *See* Bristol
Hervey, James:
Remarks 1608:34
Hervey, John, Baron Hervey:
Ancient and modern liberty 1608:28

Hervey, John (*cont.*)
Answer to the Country parson's plea 1608: 11
Answer to the Occasional writer. See Bolingbroke 1608:13
Letter to Mr. C--b--r 1608:90
Letters between Lord Hervey and Dr. Middleton 3168
Miscellaneous thoughts 1608:90
Quaker's reply 1608:35
Question stated 1608:28
Some remarks on the Minute philosopher 1608:90
To the occasional writer. See Bolingbroke 1608:13
See Political tracts 94:1; Tracts 2050:5; Tracts 2146:3; Yonge 1608:28
Hervey, Thomas:
Complaint 1609:14, 18
Letter from a patriot 1609:3
Letter from the Hon. Thomas Hervey 1609:6
Letter to a gentleman 1608:28
Letter to Sir Thomas Hanmer 1608:90
Letter to Sir William Bunbury 4007
Letter to William Pitt 1608:90
Mr. Hervey's answer 1609:9
See Hamilton 1608:28; Hickey 1608:28
Hervey, Mrs. William Thomas. *See* Hervey, Mrs. Elizabeth (March)
Hesiod:
Opera. See Classics 2207:17
Heskyns, Thomas:
Parliament of Chryste 2705
Hethum, Prince of Korghos. *See* Hetoum
Hetoum, Prince of Gorigos:
Chronicle 2397
Heuterus, Pontus:
Rerum Burgundicarum libri sex 2124
Hey, Richard:
Captive monarch 1810:54
Heyde, Jan van der. *See* Heiden
Heylyn, Peter:
Cosmographie 2055
Help to English history 740
Ἡρωολογια *Anglorum* 741
History of St. George of Cappadocia 846
See Sanderson 1585
Heyme, Francis. *See* Thynne 3726
Heynes, Samuel. *See* Haynes

Heywood, Thomas:
Life of Merlin 1599
Pleasant dialogues 1949
Hezekiah, Vision of. *See Black-bird* 2646:20
Hickey, Joseph. *See* Hervey 1608:28
Hickey against Hamilton and Hervey 1608: 28
Hickford, Rayner. *See* Chatterton 3690:11
Hiffernan, Paul:
Earl of Warwick 1810:9
Heroine of the Cave 1810:24
Lady's choice 1818:17
Wishes of a free people 1810:2
Higden, William:
Case of the admission of dissenters. See Derby 79:8
Higgons, Bevill:
Short view of English history 1679
Higgons, Thomas:
Ode upon the death of Mr. Cowley. See Oxford 2061:3
Higgs, William. *See Two letters* 1608:11, 15
High, Jack, pseud. See Black-bird 2646:12
High life below stairs. See Townley 1818:18
Highmore, Anthony:
One or more letters. *See* Letters 2576
Highmore, Joseph:
Critical examination. See Tracts 1348:2
Hilder, Thomas:
Conjugall counsell 2873
Hildesley, Mark:
Religio jurisprudentis 2706
Hildyard, Christopher. *See* Torr 669
Hill, Aaron:
Athelwold 1818:4
Merope 1818:7
Roman revenge 1818:12
Works 1815
Hill, Abraham:
Familiar letters 1609:18
Hill, John:
Account of a stone 1608:88
The actor 1522
Lucina sine concubitu 1608:29
The rout 1818:17
Story of Elizabeth Canning 1608:77
Thoughts concerning God and nature 465
See Tracts 2050:13; Woodward 1608:61
Hill, R., pseud.:
Gospel-Shop 1810:28

Hill, Sir Richard:
  Pietas Oxoniensis 1609:21
  See Rodenhurst 2944
Hill, Robert. *See* Spence 1608:79
Hill, Thomas:
  Briefe and pleasaunt treatise 787
  Gardener's labyrinth 374, 2707
  Profitable arte of gardeninge 2014
Hill, Dr. Thomas. *See* Sermons 2756:3
Hill, William, D. D. *See* Dionysius 2086
Hilliard, Nicholas:
  Treatise on the art of limning 2560
Hilliard d'Auberteuil, Michel René. *See* Le
  Vacher 3119
Hillier, Nathaniel:
  One letter. *See* Letters 2576
Hinchliffe, John, Bishop. *See* Platon 1609:57;
  Poems 3222:17
Hindustan. *See* Dow 2838; Orme 3174
Hingston, Mrs. Mary Shephard. *See* Baldwin
  1608:31
Hinton, John. *See* Scotland 1609:58
Hints, &c, submitted to the clergy. See Graf-
  ton 1609:52
Hippisley, John. *See* Connaught 1810:10
Hippolyto and Amynta. See Quintana 1582
Histoire ancienne des peuples de l'Europe.
  See Du Buat 3009
Histoire critique de la philosophie. See
  Boureau 974
Histoire de ce qui s'est passé. See Dutens
  3093
Histoire de César Germanicus. See Beaufort
  1267
Histoire de Jeanne première, Reine de
  Naples. See Mignot 3129
Histoire de la dernière guerre de Bohême.
  See Mauvillon 1162
Histoire de la ligue faite à Cambray. See
  Dubos 805
Histoire de la philosophie hermétique. See
  Lenglet 1199
Histoire de Madame la Comtesse des Barres.
  See Choisy 1292
Histoire des Camisards. See Camisards 1291
Histoire des comtes de Champagne et de Brie.
  See Le Pelletier 3117
Histoire des ducs de Bourgogne. See Bruslé
  1212
Histoire des grecs. See Goudar 3101

Histoire des modes françaises. See Molé 3344
Histoire des ordres monastiques. See Helyot
  1141
Histoire des personnes. See Longeville 380
Histoire des philosophes modernes. See Sa-
  vérien 3145
Histoire des quatres Cicérons. See Macé
  1279
Histoire des révolutions des Gênes. See
  Bréquigny 1181
Histoire des Rois Catholiques. See Mignot
  3032
Histoire des singes. See Alletz 3285
Histoire du docteur Akakia. See Voltaire
  1608:76
Histoire du ministère du chevalier Robert
  Walpool. See Dupuy-Demportes 2269
Histoire du Prince Apprius. See Beauchamps
  1553
Histoire du théâtre de l'Opéra-Comique. See
  Jullien 3110
Histoire et plaisante cronicque. See La Sale
  1277
Histoire secrète de la cour de Berlin. See
  Mirabeau 3343
Histoire secrette de la Duchesse d'Hanover.
  See Pöllnitz 1282
Histoires galantes de la Cour de Vienne. See
  Bougeant 1178:2
Historia Augustae scriptores sex. See Augus-
  tan 2084
*Historia delle cose occorse nel regno d'Inghil-
  terra. See* Raviglio 2460, 2937
Historia flagellantium. See Boileau 2209
Historical account of Mr. Rogers's three years
  travels. See Brome 717
Historical account of the conspiracies by the
  Earls of Gowry. See Cromarty 116
Historical account of the expedition against
  the Ohio Indians. See Smith 1609:56
Historical and critical account of Hugh
  Peters. See Harris 1608:20
Historical and critical account of John Hales.
  See Des Maizeaux 1608:14; Whiston 1727
Historical and critical account of the living
  authors of Great Britain. See Rider 1609:5
Historical and critical review of the paintings.
  See Royal Academy 3885:13
Historical and heraldic documents. See
  Heraldry 2558

Historical and poetical medley: or Muses library. See Muses 90

Historical and succinct account of the late riots. See Drury Lane 1810:4

Historical anecdotes of some of the Howard family. See Howard 128

Historical applications. See Berkeley 187, 2338

Historical compendium to 1726. See Compendium 1555

Historical description of Canterbury. See Duncombe 2840

Historical essay upon the ballance of civil power. See Squire 1608:59

Historical, genealogical, and classical dictionary. See Dictionary 1515

Historical, genealogical, and poetical dictionary. See Dictionary 1558

Historical register 1773

Historical view of the taste for gardening. See Gardening 1609:45; 3891:2

History and antiquities of Northampton. See Bridges 561

History and antiquities of Salisbury. See Rawlinson 665

History and antiquities of Tewkesbury. See Dyde 3415

History and antiquities of Winchester. See Winchester 2991

History and art of engraving. See Arts 288:2

History and description of the Isle of Man. See Waldron 139

History and progress of the four Indian Kings. See Black-bird 2646:23

History of an old lady. See Whitehead 1608: 74

History of England. See England 1642

History of Gustavus Ericson. See Scott 1654

History of Herod and Mariamne 1608:17

History of Jack Connor. See Chaigneau 1554

History of jewels. See Chappuzeau 779

History of King Lear. See Colman 1810:12

History of Nourjahad. See Sheridan 1586

History of the administration of the leader in the India direction. See East India 1609: 55

History of the Apostles' Creed. See King 129

History of the art of engraving in mezzotinto. See Arts 288:5

History of the castle of Knaresborough. See Hargrove 2867

History of the Cathedral Church at Chester. See Chester 2823

History of the Island of Anglesey. See Owen 513

History of the late important period. See Dutens 2841

History of the late minority. See Almon 363, 1609:14

History of the military transactions. See Orme 3174

History of the political life of Charles James Fox. See Moir 3131

History of the reign of George the Third. See MacFarlane 1609:27

History of the River Thames. See Combe 3566

History of the Westminster election. See Westminster 557

History of the world 2561

Hoadly, Benjamin, Bishop:
Answer 1608:25
Humble reply 1608:19
Letter to Clement Chevallier 1608:85
Measures of submission 1373
Nature and end of the Sacrament of the Lord's Supper 1374. *See* Warren 1387
Preservative 1608:15
See Black-bird 2646:10; Miscellaneous Tracts 89:2; Place 1608:35; Snape 1608:15

Hoadly, Benjamin (1706–1757):
Suspicious husband 1810:18

Hoadly, John, Archbishop. *See* Whitby 1608: 12

Hoamchi-van, pseud. *See Bonze*

Hobart, Lady Frances. *See* Collinges 1782

Hobart, John, 2d Earl of Buckinghamshire. *See* Buckinghamshire

Hobbes, Thomas:
Humane nature 1566
Leviathan 847, 2175, 2708
Tripos 1482
See Eachard 1516; Macaulay 1609:17; Thucydides 3470

Hobby horses 3222:17

Hobhouse, Thomas:
Kingsweston Hill 3222:19

Hoblyn, Robert:
Bibliotheca Hoblyniana 3326

Hoccleve, Thomas:
    Poems 1327
Hodges, William, lawyer:
    Historical account of Ludlow Castle 2874
Hodges, William, painter:
    Travels in India 3714
Hodgetts, John. *See* Luxborough 3896
Hodson, William:
    Adventures of a night 1810:35
    Arsaces 1810:24
    Zoraida 1810:31
Hoey, Abraham Van:
    Letters 1608:71
    Lettres. See Almanach 1174
Hofman, Tycho de:
    Portraits historiques 270
Hogarth, Mrs. Jane:
    Catalogue. See Tracts 2050
Hogarth, William:
    Analysis of beauty 3880
    Engravings of Lord Lovat's trial. See Tracts 2968:3
    Portfolio containing 365 original drawings or prints 3646
    Tour. See Gostling 2385
    See Butler 1822, 1865; Churchill *Epistle* 3222:5; Gostling 2385; Ireland 3857:1; Nichols 2435, 3860; Trusler 1810:11
Hogenberg, Franz. *See* Braun 3675
Hohenberg, Franz. *See* Hogenberg
Holbach, Paul Henri Thiry, Baron d':
    Christianisme dévoilé 3018
    See Akenside 2266
Holbein, Hans:
    Dances of death 3715
    Icones historiarum Veteris Testamenti 2398
    Imitations of original drawings 3500
    Oeuvre de Jean Holbein 3716
    Todten-Tanz 3717
    See Erasmus 334; Vertue 2772, 3581
Holbein, Jean. *See* Holbein, Hans 3716
Holbein Chamber. *See* Walpole 2619:4
Holcroft, Thomas:
    Choleric fathers 1810:38
    Deserted daughter 1810:56
    Duplicity 1810:33
    Follies of a day 1810:37
    German hotel 1810:49
    Love's frailties 1810:55

Holcroft, Thomas (*cont.*)
    Noble peasant 1810:36
    Plays 1853
    Road to ruin 1810:51
    School for arrogance 1810:50
    Seduction 1810:42
Holdsworth, Edward:
    Pharsalia and Philippi. See Tracts 2046:5
    Remarks on Virgil 3169
Holinshed, Raphael:
    Chronicles 597
Holkham Hall. *See* Brettingham 3401
Holland, Henry:
    Herwologia Anglica 3783
Holland, Henry Fox, Baron:
    One letter. *See* Letters 2576
    See Epistle 3222:10; *Letter* 1608:86; Tracts 2968:8
Holland. *See* Netherlands
Hollandus, Joannes Isaacus, called. *See* Weidenfeld 866
Hollar, Wenceslaus:
    Portfolio of 934 engravings 3622
    See Aesop 3670; Barlow 3771; Collins 2359:4; Drawings 3567; Garter 3551; Prints 3636; Vertue 2479:4
Holles, Denzil, Baron Holles:
    Letter of a gentleman 49
    Lord Hollis his remains 170
    Memoirs 50
    Speech in Parliament. See Tracts 2769:3
    True relation. See Tracts 100:2
Holles, Thomas Pelham, Duke of Newcastle. *See* Newcastle
Holles family. *See* Collins 565
Holliday, Barten. *See* Holyday
Hollins, Miss. *See* Poems 280
Hollis, Thomas:
    True sentiments of America 1609:21
    See Blackburne 3688; Locke 3172; Nedham 2730; Sidney 3176; Toland 1694; Wallis 2775
Holloway, John:
    Letter to the Rev. Dr. Price 1609:51
Holme, Randle:
    Academy of armory 598
Holroyd, John Baker, Earl of Sheffield. *See* Sheffield

Holt, Sir John:
  Arguments. See Stamford 521
Holt, Richard:
  Short treatise of artificial stone 1608:17
Holwell, John Zephaniah:
  Address to Luke Scrafton, Esq. 1609:17
  Address to the proprietors of East India stock 1609:55
  Important facts regarding the East-India Company's affairs 1609:55
  Interesting historical events 1609:12, 15
  Mr. Holwell's Refutation of a letter 1609: 55
  New experiment for the prevention of crimes 1609:50
  Vindication of Mr. Holwell's character 1609:55
Holy Ghost, Chapel of the, near Basingstoke. See Loggon 696
Holy Ghost, Order of the. See La Pointe 545; Saint-Foix 3143
Holy history. See Talon 97
Holy life and death of Lady Letice, Viscountess Falkland. See Duncon 1739
Holyday, Barten:
  Survey of the world 1950
Home, Henry, Lord Kames. See Kames
Home, John:
  Agis 1818:16
  Alfred 1810:27
  Alonzo 1810:19
  Douglas 1818:15
  Dramatic works 1871
  Fatal discovery 1810:14
  Siege of Aquileia 1810:14
  See Epistle 1609:22
Home-Lacy, churches of. See Gibson 622
Homer:
  Iliad, tr. by Pope 62
  Iliad and Odyssey 3964
  Iliad and Odyssey, tr. by Cowper. See Cowper 2827
  L'Iliade 1220
  Odyssey 2192
  Odyssey, tr. by Pope, Broome, and Fenton 63
  Opera 2399
  See Blackwell 1393; Wood 37
Homme dangereux. See Montenoy 3447
Hondius, Hendrik. See Verheiden 3727

Honest grief of a Tory. See Dodington 1608: 87
Honest man's reasons. See Lloyd 1609:11
Honeycomb, William, pseud.:
  History of Pudica. See Tracts 2049:7
Honeycombe, Polly. See Colman 1810:1
Honnêtetés littéraires. See Voltaire 3056
Honoria. See Jerningham 3222:18
Honour. See Poems 3363:8
Hood, Samuel, 1st Viscount Hood. See Bernard 1609:25
Hooghe, Romeyn de. See Miscellaneous volumes 943:3; William III 3800, 3529
Hook, Mrs. James:
  Double disguise 1810:36
Hooke, Andrew:
  Essay 1608:47
Hooke, Nathaniel:
  Account of the conduct of the Dowager Duchess of Marlborough 126
  Roman history 1328
Hooker, Richard:
  Of the lawes of ecclesiastical politie 2056
Hookes, Nathaniel:
  Amanda 1437
Hoole, John:
  Cleonice 1810:24
  Cyrus 1810:13
  Timanthes 1810:16
  See Tasso 1604
Hoole, Samuel:
  Poems 2709
Hooper, George, Bishop:
  Inquiry into the state of the ancient measures 2015
Hopkins, Stephen:
  Grievances of the American colonies 1609: 12
Horae. See Missal
Horae subsecivae. See Chandos 190
Horam, son of Asmar. See Ridley 392
Horatius Flaccus, Quintus:
  Art of poetry 3222:19. See Bramston 1886
  Comment on an ode of Horace. See Stukeley 640
  Emblemata Horatiana 2214
  Epistolae ad Pisones et Augustum 1791
  Odes and epodes 1951
  Opera 2088, 2193–4, 2213, 2276. See Brindley 2120:4

Horatius Flaccus, Quintus (*cont.*)
Opera omnia 2400
Satires and epistles 1854
See Baretti 1609:39; Heighington 3878;
Poems 280:45, 3363:7
Horn, George. *See* Classics 2207:38
Hornby, Charles:
Small specimen of the many mistakes 692
Horreus, Petrus. *See* Classics 2207:2
Horseman, Nicholas. *See* Whear 3478
Horsley, Samuel, Bishop:
*Review of the case of the Protestant dis-
senters* 1609:53. *See* Petre 1609:53
Horsley, William:
Political history of Europe 1329
Hortus Pembrochianus. See Wilton 3667
Hospital for the maintenance and education
of exposed and deserted young children.
See Foundling Hospital
Hoste, Paul. *See* Webster 1807
Hotman, François:
Franco-Gallia 127
Houbraken, Jacob. *See* Birch 3637; *Copper
Plate Magazine* 3839; Prints 3626; Weyer-
man 3766
Houdart de la Motte, Antoine. *See* La Motte
Houghton Gallery:
Set of prints 3572
Houghton Hall. *See* Strawberry Hill 3469:2;
Walpole 3546, 3931:2; Ware 536
Houghton hare-hunting. See Strawberry Hill
3469:2
Hour before marriage 1810:18
House, Samuel:
Letter to the electors 1609:46
House of Peeresses 3965
House of Peers. *See* Peers
Houston, Richard. *See* Walpole 3546
Howard, Charles, Earl of Carlisle. *See* Carlisle
Howard, Charles, Earl of Nottingham. *See*
Nottingham
Howard, Charles, later 10th Duke of Norfolk:
Historical anecdotes 128
Thoughts, essays and maxims 2308
Howard, Edward, 8th Earl of Suffolk. *See*
Suffolk
Howard, Edward:
Brittish Princes 1952
Howard, Frederick, Earl of Carlisle. *See*
Carlisle

Howard, Gorges Edmond:
Almeyda 1810:14
Siege of Tamor 1810:20
Howard, Henry, 6th Duke of Norfolk. *See*
Norfolk
Howard, Henry, 7th Duke of Norfolk. *See*
Norfolk
Howard, Henry, Earl of Northampton. *See*
Northampton
Howard, Henry, Earl of Surrey. *See* Surrey
Howard, Isabella (Byron), Countess of Car-
lisle. *See* Carlisle
Howard, John:
*Account of the principal lazarettos in Eu-
rope* 553
See Tuscany 1609:52
Howard, Leonard:
Collection of letters 86
Miscellaneous pieces 1330
Howard, Sir Robert:
Indian Queen. See Plays 1908:4
Life of King Richard the Second 2710
Poems 1872
Howard, Thomas, 4th Duke of Norfolk. *See*
Norfolk
Howard, Thomas, Earl of Arundel. *See*
Arundel
Howard, Thomas, 3d Earl of Effingham. *See*
Effingham
Howard, William, Viscount Stafford. *See*
Stafford
Howell, James:
Dodona's grove 2016
Epistolae Ho-Elianae 1438
Londinopolis 626
Precedency of kings 625
See Finett 736, 2690
Howell, Laurence:
History of the Holy Bible 1375
Howes, Edmond. *See* Stow 610
Hoyland, Francis:
Odes 3222:20
Poems. See Collection 2507:2
Hoyle, Edmond:
Games 1792
Short treatise of brag 1608:68
Hubert, Sir Francis:
*Deplorable life and death of Edward the
Second* 1953
Hübner, Johann. *See* Anderson 558, 615

Huddesford, George:
Salmagundi 3327
Huddesford, William:
Lives of antiquaries 2875
Hudson, Jeffrey. *See Microphilus* 2418
Hudson, John. *See* Dionysius 2155
Hudson, Michael:
Divine right of government 2711
Hue and cry after part of a pack of hounds
1608.24
Huebner, Johann. *See* Hübner
Huet, Christophe:
Singeries 3647
Huet, Pierre Daniel:
Histoire du commerce 983
Hughes, John:
*Letters by several eminent persons de-
ceased* 2876
Siege of Damascus. See Fenton 1895
See Spenser 1878
Hughes, Joseph:
Authentick letter. See Portugal 1343:4
Hugues, Pierre François, called D'Hancar-
ville. *See* Hamilton 3536
Hull, Thomas:
Edward and Eleonora 1810:24
Fairy favour 1810:10
Henry the Second 1810:21
The perplexities 1810:7
Pharnaces 1810:7
Richard Plantagenet 3222:13
Royal merchant 1810:11
Spanish lady 1810:7
See Luxborough 3896
Hull. *See* Cozens 3184
Hulle, Anselm van. *See* Van Hulle
Hulme Abbey. *See* Hulne Abbey
Hulne Abbey. *See* Percy 1609:19
Hulsius, Friedrich. *See* Carleton 3776
Humble address to the knights. See Bath
1608:26
Humble remonstrance to His Maiesty. See
Prynne 3797:8
Hume, David:
Concise and genuine account of the dispute
1609:16
Essays 1523
Four dissertations 1524
History of England 3328
Supplement to the life of 4008

Hume, David (*cont.*)
Tracts on his quarrel with Rousseau
1680
See Campbell 2659
Hume, David, of Godscroft:
*History of the Houses of Douglas and An-
gus* 2712
Hume, Hugh, Earl of Marchmont. *See* March-
mont
Hume, John:
Sermon. See Sermons 1346:5
Hume-Campbell, Hugh, Earl of Marchmont.
See Marchmont
Humorous lovers. See Newcastle 92
Humorous quarrel. See Pottinger 1810:1
Humours of Oxford. *See* Miller 1818:2
Humphrey, Duke. *See* Walpole *Letter from
Xo Ho* 2489:2
Hungary. *See* Nadanyi 2128
Hunter, Mrs. Anne:
One letter. *See* Letters 2576
Hunter, Christopher:
Durham Cathedral 375, 742
Hunter, Dr. John. *See* Catalogues 2819; Foot
2849
Hunter, William:
One or more letters. *See* Letters 2576
See Combe 3691
Hunting, hawking, and fishing. See Barlow
3771
Huntingdon, Catherine Pole, Countess of.
See Letters 2576 (Pole)
Huntingdon, Francis Hastings, Earl of:
One or more letters. *See* Letters 2576
Huntingford, George Isaac, Bishop:
Letter the first 1609:52
Second letter 1609:52
Huquier, Gabriel:
Catalogue de dessins 339
Hurault, Philippe. *See* Collection 3084
Hurd, Richard, Bishop:
Dialogues on the uses of foreign travel
1609:7
Letters on chivalry and romance 1609:6
Moral and political dialogues 1439
See Cowley 3917, 4001; Horatius 1791;
Warburton 3266, 3476
Hurdis, James:
Sir Thomas More 1810:51
Village curate 2877

Hurlstone, Thomas:
 Crotchet Lodge 1810:56
 Just in time 1810:50
 To arms 1810:52
Hurtley, Thomas:
 Concise account 2878
Husain, Shah of Persia. *See* Tracts 2146:3
Hutcheson, Francis:
 Essay 1525
Hutchett, William. *See* Hatchett, William
Hutchins, John:
 History of Dorset 4
Hutchins, Thomas. *See* Smith 1609:56
Hutchinson, Mrs. J. *See* *Private character* 1608:18
Hutchinson, Thomas (1698–1769). *See* Xenophon 2184
Hutchinson, Thomas (1711–1780). *See* Mauduit 1609:31, 34
Hutchinson, William:
 Excursion to the lakes 2879
 History of Cumberland 3193
 History . . . of . . . Durham 3329
 View of Northumberland 2880, 3170
Hutchinsonian. *See* *Letter* 1608:29
Huttichius, Joannes:
 Imperatorum Romanorum Libellus 340
Hutton, Matthew:
 Sermon. See Sermons 1346:6
Hutton, Sir Richard:
 Arguments. See Tracts 3797:9
Hutton, William:
 Battle of Bosworth Field 2881
 History of Birmingham 2882
 History of Derby 2883
Huybert, Pieter Antoni de:
 Parallel. See Tracts 2146:1
Huysum, Jan van. *See* Drawings 3587
Hyde, Edward, Earl of Clarendon. *See* Clarendon
Hyde, Henry, Viscount Cornbury. *See* Cornbury
Hymn to liberty. See Poems 280:17
The hypocrite. See Bickerstaffe 1810:13

Iamblichus of Chalcis:
 De vita Pythagorica liber 848
Iceland. *See* Troil 2969
Ickorngill, William, of Haworth:
 Address and remonstrance 2562

Icon libellorum. See Davies 370
Iconoclasts. *See* Manning 3439
Idea of arithmetic. See Beale 2333:1
Idée générale d'une collection complette d'estampes. See Heineken 299, 3105, 3712
Ignoramus. See Ruggle 3370
Ignotus, pseud. *See* Letters 2576 (Unidentified)
Iliad. See Homer
Illiers, Florent d'. *See* Collection 3084
Illustrium virorum elogia sepulchralia. See Popham 3365
Impartial character of the late Doctor Goldsmith. See Goldsmith 3222:13
Impartial enquiry, what is the test. See Middleton 1379:6
Impartial examination of a pamphlet 1608: 48, 2049:1
Impartial examination of the Bishop of London's late Appendix. See Middleton 1379: 11
Impartial hand. *See Argument of the Divine Legation; Attempt to prove a priori;* Towne, John
Impartial history of Michael Servetus. See Servetus 1655
Impartial inquiry. See Martyn 1608:40
Impartial review of the present troubles 1608:46
Impartial review of two pamphlets. See Chesterfield 1673:2
Impartial state of the case of the French comedians 1608:69
Impenetrable Secret 2401
Imperfect hints. See Felton 3922
Importance of . . . supporting the Royal African Company. See Tracts 2146:1
Importance of the colonies. See Ray 1609:56
Important considerations upon the act 1609: 20
Important facts regarding the East-India Company's affairs. See Holwell 1609:55
Important secret come to light 1608:38
Imposter detected 1608:13
Improved edition of the songs in Midas. See O'Hara 1810:47
Improvement of the mind. See Watts 420
Inchbald, Elizabeth:
 Appearance is against them 1810:38
 Child of nature 1810:45

Inchbald, Elizabeth (*cont.*)
  Every one has his fault 1810:52
  I'll tell you what 1810:37
  Midnight hour 1810:42
  Next door neighbours 1810:50
  Wedding day 1810:56
  Widow's vow 1810:39
  See Cross partners 1810:51
Inchofer, Melchior:
  Monarchie des solipses 1221
Incorporated Society of Artists. *See* Royal
  Academy 3885:1
Indagine, Joannes Ab:
  Book of palmestry 2017
Independent elector. *See Address* 1608:56
Independent free agent. *See Cry* 1608:56
Independent Whig, pseud. *See* Almon 1609:
  54; Tracts 2146:3
Independent Whig 1526
Index to the Records. See Strachey 767
India:
  See Bolts 2803; Cambridge 449; Fryer 3277;
  Hodges 3714; Orme 3174; Robertson 2941;
  Voltaire 3388
Indian Kings. *See Black-bird* 2646:23
Indignant liveryman. *See Letter* 1609:11
Indiscreet lover. See Portal 1810:13
*Information of a certain discourse. See De-
  tection* 2677:11
Ingenious and diverting letters. See Aulnoy
  364, 1461
Inglis, Alexander. *See* Bentivoglio 2096
Ingram, Charles, Viscount Irwin. *See* Irwin
Ingram, Dale:
  The blow 1609:22
Ingratitude 3222:5
Injur'd innocence. See Bellers 1818:4
Injured islanders 3222:16
Innocency of error. See Sykes 1608:12
Innocent XI, Pope:
  Decrees 1608:4
Innocent XII, Pope:
  Jubilé de l'an 1700 849
Ino et Themiste 2309
Inquiry. *See also* Enquiry
*Inquiry into the manner of creating peers.
  See* Tracts 2475:1, Tracts on Peerage Bill
  400:1
*Inquiry into the nature and effect of Habeas
  Corpus. See* Camden 1608:87

Inquiry into the origin and consequences
  1609:41
Inquiry into the share. See Birch 1665
Inscriptions on the monuments. See Le Neve
  695
Instructions for preachers. See Reports 2592
Instructions given . . . to his embassadors. See
  Henry VII 1609:54
Instructions to a celebrated laureat. See Wol-
  cot 3222:21
Instructions to a son. See Argyle 185
Interest book. See Castaing 1155
Interest of Great Britain. See Walpole 1608:
  43
Interest of Hanover 1608:43
Interprétation des peintures. See Ferdinand
  IV 3709
*Interpreter of the Academie for forrain lan-
  guages. See* Gerbier 124
Introduction to astronomy. See Astronomy
  1608:7
Introduction to the Carmen Seculare. See
  Baretti 1609:39
Introductorie for to learne to rede. See
  Duwes 118
Iphigenia. *See* Bunbury 3563:4
Irailh, Augustin Simon:
  Querelles 3019
Ireland, Samuel:
  Collection of works 3857
  Vindication. See Malone 1358
Ireland:
  Coins. *See* Stukeley 640:2
  History. *See Letter* 1608:86; Lucas 1609:20;
  Mountmorris 2909; Stevens 707; Vallancey
  1609:48
  Peerage. *See* Egmont 44; Lodge 660
  Protestant schools. *See Sermons* 1346:10
  See Boate 147, 188, 1152, 2341; Camden
  563; Cox 621; Dalrymple 3186; *College
  exercise* 1609:23; Fox 1609:47; Grose 3496;
  Harris 595; Ledwich 3195; *Letter* 1608:61;
  Milton 3508; Mountmorris 1609:47A;
  Smith 396; Stafford 3375; Taaffe 2763;
  Thoughts 1609:28; Twiss 2971; Walker
  3390; Ware 614, 2182; Wright 647; Young
  1364
Irelands naturall history. See Boate 147
Irish historical library. See Nicolson 1650
Irish register. See Tracts 98:1

Irish widow. See Garrick 1810:18

Irishman in London 1810:52

Irregular ode occasioned by the death of Mr. Gray 3222:12

Irwin, Charles Ingram, Viscount. *See Rise* 3222:8

Irwin, Eyles:
Occasional epistles 3222:19
Series of adventures 2884

Isaacus, Joannes. *See* Weidenfeld 866

Isabella. See Garrick 1818:16

Isabella Clara Eugenia, Infanta of Spain. *See* Hartlib 125:3

Isla, José Francisco de:
History of . . . Friar Gerund de Campazas 2885

Island of St. Marguerite. See St. John 1810:48

Isle of Pines. See Neville 1608:37

Isocrates. *See* Gillies 3190

Italy:
Theater. *See* Gherardi 1250; Riccoboni 1167
See Bromley 291; Capriata 3297; Grosley 3103; Gualdo Priorato 2079; Guicciardini 877; Marlow 3441; Misson 1230; Moore 2906; Northall 386; Richard 3043; Thomas 1090, 2472, 2765, 4016

Itinerarium. See Brathwait 2235

Ivan Czarowitz. See Catharine II 550

Ivar 1810:38

Ives, John:
Remarks upon the Garianonum of the Romans 2886
See Walpole 3476:2

J., E. *See* Johnson, Edward

J., R.:
Letter of advice. See Tracts 100:1

Jackman, Isaac:
All the world's a stage 1810:27
The divorce 1810:33

Jackson, John, controversialist:
Address to Deists 1608:55
Remarks on Dr. Middleton's Free inquiry. See Middleton 1379:8
Some reflections 1608:33

Jackson, John, printer:
History of . . . Lichfield 2887

Jackson, John Baptist:
Essay. See Tracts 1348:10

Jacob, Edward:
History of . . . Faversham 2888

Jacob, Giles:
Court beauties 1897
Memoirs of Addison 1608:5

Jacob, Hildebrand:
Fatal constancy 1818:2

Jacob, Louis:
Traicté des plus belles bibliothèques 3107

Jacobite's Journal 2142

Jacobitism. *See Letter from S—shire* 1608:70; *Some account* 1608:70

Jacobsz, Lucas, called Lucas van Leyden. *See* Prints 3608

Jago, Richard:
Edge-Hill 3222:8
Labour and genius 3222:9

James I, King of England:
Charges for work done in the palaces. *See* Caesar 2535:8
Connexion 1746
Copy of commission to the Earl of Worcester 2563
Court of the most illustrious James the First 850
Essayes of a prentise 376
Five years of the reign 87
Secret history 2889
Speech in the Starre-Chamber. See Tracts 3797:4
Workes 20
See Dalrymple 2368, 2675; Harris 1644; Harrison 3428; Harry 842; Plays 1082:2; *Reports* 2591; Robertson 321; Sawyer 1100; Tower of London 2605; Tracts 2050 (*Strange apparitions*); Weldon 1767; Wishart 1770; Wilson 910

James II, King of England:
Engeland beroerd 1331
Memoires of . . . his Royal Highness James, Duke of York and Albany 2713
Memoirs 51
Royal tracts 203
See Aquino 494, 3270; Bromley 3227; Caesar 2815; Fuller 1608:10; Keepe 377; Letters 2576 (Albemarle); Sandford 3517; Vertue 2479:2

James VI, King of Scotland. *See* James I, King of England

James Francis Edward Stuart, Prince of Wales, called the Pretender. *See Aeneas* 1608:91; *Black-bird* 2646:6; Burnet 1608:9; Defoe 1608:9; *Detection* 2677:1; Louis XIV 1608:9; *Miscellaneous tracts* 89:2; Shaftoe 1608:10

James, John. *See* Le Blond 1333

James, Robert:
Dissertation on fevers 2890

Jane I, Queen of Naples. *See* Mignot 3129

Janet, François Clouet, called. *See* Clouet

Janson van Almeloveen, Theodoor. *See* Almeloveen

Japan. *See* Kaempfer 1121

Jardine, Alexander:
Letters from Barbary 2891

Jealous wife. See Colman 1810:2

Jean de Troyes. *See Collection* 3084

Jeanne d'Arc. *See Collection* 3084

Jebb, Samuel:
Life of Robert Earl of Leicester 1709
See Bibliotheca 824, 2645; Bridges 561

Jefferson, Thomas:
Summary view 1609:32

Jeffreys, George, Baron Jeffreys. *See Life* 1609:8

Jekyll. See Townshend 3222:22

Jemmat, Catherine:
Miscellanies in prose and verse 3330

Jenkin, Thomas:
Impartial examination. See Middleton 1379:7

Jenkins, John. *See* Benlowes 2643

Jenkins, Sir Leoline. *See* Kirke 2572

Jenkins, Richard. *See* Chatterton 3690:15

Jenner, Charles:
Man of family 1810:17

Jennings, David:
Introduction to the knowledge of medals 300

Jennings, Henry Constantine. *See* Tracts 3833:8

Jenyns, Soame:
Disquisitions on several subjects 2892
Free enquiry 1527
Miscellaneous pieces 1793
Modern fine gentleman. See Poems 881:15

Jenyns, Soame *(cont.)*
Objections to the taxation of our American colonies 1609:11, 56. *See Reflexions* 1609:13
Ode 3222:17
Poems 1873
Scheme for the coalition of parties 1609:29
Short but serious reasons for a national militia. See Tracts 2146:3
Thoughts on a parliamentary reform 1609:46. *See* Tracts 2967:1
Thoughts on the causes of the present high price 1609:19
View of the Christian religion 2893
Works 2714
See Every man 1609:47A; Veal 1609:32

Jephson, Robert:
Braganza 1810:23, 4009
Count of Narbonne 2402, 1810:33
Julia 1810:43
Law of Lombardy 1810:30
Plays 1810:30
Roman portraits 466
Two strings to your bow 1810:50
See Walpole 3730

Jeremiah:
Lectiones 2564

Jernegan. *See* Jerningham, Edward

Jerningham, Edward:
Amabella 3222:9
Ancient English wake 3222:16
Deserter 3222:10
Elegy written among the ruins 3222:6
Enthusiasm 3222:22
Faldoni and Teresa 3222:12
Fall of Mexico 3222:14
Fugitive poetical pieces 1810:54
Funeral of Arabert 3222:11
Honoria 3222:18
Il Latte 3222:8
Lines on a late resignation 3222:22
Lines written in the album 3222:20, 22
Magdalens 3222:4
Margaret of Anjou 1810:54
The Nun, an elegy 3222:5
Nunnery 3222:2
Poems 2894
Rise and progress of the Scandinavian poetry 3222:19

Jerningham, Edward (*cont.*)
  Siege of Berwick 1810:56
  Swedish curate 3222:13
  Welch heiress 1810:57
  Yarico to Inkle 3222:7
  See Moore 2907
Jersey, William Villiers, Earl of. *See* Thicknesse 1609:2
Jersey, Isle of. *See* Falle 735
Jerusalem delivered. See Tasso 2066
Jessey, Henry. *See* Sermons 2756:4
Jesuit-Cabal farther opened. See Middleton 1337
Jesuits:
  Theses propounded at the Jesuits' College 2565
  See Cabinet 1269; *Love* 1608:31
Jesup, Edward:
  Lives of Picus and Pascal 1646
Jevon, Thomas. *See* Coffey 1818:5
Jewel, John, Bishop. *See* Heskyns 2705
Jobert, Louis:
  La science des médailles antiques et modernes 341
Jockey Club. *See* Fitzgerald 1609:33
Jodrell, Richard Paul:
  Knight and friars 3222:19
  Persian heroine 3222:20
  Seeing is believing 1810:39
  Widow and no widow 1810:31
John, Saint, of Jerusalem. *See* Bosio 435
John, Don, of Austria:
  Transactions of the Court of Spain 1710
John, King of England. *See* Cibber 1818:20
John, King of France. *See* Choisy 917
John III, King of Poland:
  Scanderbeg redivivus 2715
John Chrysostom, Saint. *See* Hermant 1276
John de Brienne, King of Jerusalem. *See* Lafitau 3114
John de Saintré. *See* La Sale 1277
John of Gaunt, Duke of Lancaster. *See* Collins 1674
John of Lancaster, Duke of Bedford. *See* Gough 3812
John Physiophilus's specimen. See Born 1609:45
Johnson, Abraham, pseud. *See* Hill 1608:29
Johnson, Ben, Jr., pseud. *See* S., W. 1980

Johnson, Charles:
  Sultaness. See Plays 1909:4
  Tragedy of Medaea 1818:4
  Village opera. See Bramston 1886:2
  See Kemble 1810:47
Johnson, Edward:
  Plain account of the Trinity 1608:33
Johnson, Captain Edward:
  Wonder working Providence. See Gorges 3427
Johnson, Henry:
  Introduction to logography 3431
Johnson, John. *See* Ferrers 1112
Johnson, Richard:
  Crown garland of golden roses. See Hall 2011:2
Johnson, Samuel (1691–1773):
  Hurlothrumbo 2403
Johnson, Samuel:
  Account of Richard Savage 1608:20
  Convict's address 1609:38
  Dictionary 5
  False alarm 1609:25
  Irene 1818:8
  Journey to the Western Islands of Scotland 3108
  Letters 3239
  Life of Roger Ascham. See Ascham 3157
  London. See Poems 280:6
  New prologue. See Poems 881:28
  The Patriot 1609:32
  Plan of a dictionary. See Tracts 2049:3
  Prayers and meditations 1609:48
  Prince of Abyssinia 1747
  Rambler 1748
  Rasselas 1747
  Taxation no tyranny 1609:33
  Thoughts on the late transactions 1609:28
  See Boswell 3069, 3294; Browne 2001; Hawkins 412; Hervey 1609:9; Oxford 318; Piozzi 3826; Poems 3363; Ritson 2939; Shakespeare 1360; Tindal 1609:42; Towers 1609:50; Wilkes 1609:25; Young 1609:45
Johnson, Thomas. *See* Sophocles 2224
Johnston, Andrew:
  Notitia Anglicana 659
Johnstone, Charles:
  Chrysal 984
  See Buthred 1810:29

Johnstone, James:
  Disbanded officer 1810:40
Johnstone, William, later William Pulteney.
  See Pulteney
Joinville, Jean, Sire de. *See Collection* 3084
Joly, Claude:
  Codicille d'or 1222
Joly, Guy:
  Mémoires 985
Jones, David:
  Secret history of Whitehall 1647, 1749,
  2566
  See Europe 3419
Jones, Edward:
  Musical and poetical relicks 3881
Jones, Henry:
  Earl of Essex 1818:12
  See Hiffernan 1818:24
Jones, Inigo:
  Designs 507, 3538
  Some designs 3784
  Stone-Henge, on Salisbury Plain 599
  See Palladio 3593
Jones, James:
  Sepulchrorum inscriptiones 1830
Jones, Mary:
  Miscellanies 1855
Jones, Robert, Lieutenant of artillery:
  Treatise on skating 1609:36
Jones, Thomas, pseud. *See Dialogue* 1608:59
Jones, Sir William:
  Muse recalled 3222:18. *See Collection* 2508;
  Strawberry Hill 3469:4
  Sacontalá 3194
Jonson, Ben:
  Three celebrated plays 1898
  Workes 1120
  See Acis 1810:22; Scott 1810:15; Sidney
  2956
Jonval. *See Contes François* 1783:1
Jordanes. *See* Jornandes
Jornandes:
  Histoire générale des Goths 1032
Jortin, John:
  Life of Erasmus 554
  Miscellaneous observations upon authors
  693
  Remarks on ecclesiastical history 3240
Joseph I, King of Portugal. *See Portugal* 1343

Joseph II, Emperor of Germany. *See* Catalogues 2303; Eckhel 3695
Josephus, Flavius:
  Works 2057
Journal étranger. See Magazines 3338:5
Journal historique de la révolution 3109
*Journal historique . . . du règne de Louis
  XV. See* Lévy 3121
Journal of a voyage for making discoveries
  1609:31
Journal of a voyage in the Endeavour. See
  Hawkesworth 2869
Journal of the Printing Office. See Collection
  2506
Journal of the Sessions in 1628. See England
  2548
Journal of the Virtuosi. See St. Luke's Club
  2595
*Journals of the House of Commons, 1558–
  1729. See* England 3275
Journeaulx, Philippe:
  Proceedings 1413
Journey through the head of a modern poet
  1608:31
Journey to the Western Islands. See Johnson
  3108
Jovi Eleutherio. See Poems 3363:14
Jovial poems. See Wit and drollery 1994
Jovien, Histoire de. See La Bléterie 965
Jovius, Paulus. *See* Giovio
Joyeuse, Anne de, Duc de Joyeuse. *See* Beaujoyeulx 2334, 3399
Jubilade. See Poems 3363:7
Jubilé de l'an 1700. See Innocent 849
Judgment of Hercules. See Shaftesbury 1496
Judgment of Paris. See Schomberg 1810:13
Judgment of the muse. See Poems 280:10
Jukes, Francis. *See* Antiquities 3485:13
Julian. See Warburton 1426
Julianus, Flavius Claudius, Emperor of
  Rome:
  Les Césars 925
Julie. See Rousseau 819
Julien, Vie de l'empereur. See La Bléterie
  986
Julienne, Jean de, Chevalier:
  Catalogue 3020
  See Watteau 3635
Julius II, Pope. *See* Dubos 805

Jullien des Boulmiers, Jean Auguste:
   Histoire du théâtre de l'Opéra-Comique
   3110
Jullienne. *See* Julienne
Junior's precedence 1608:2
Junius, Francis:
   De pictura veterum libri tres 221
   Painting of the ancients 482
Junius, pseud. (Author of the Letters):
   Letters 2215
   See Address 1609:24; Almon 1609:28;
   Letters 1609:24
Junius, pseud.:
   Serious letter to the public 1609:39
Junius Brutus. See Duncombe 1818:6
Junto 1810:29
Jurin, James:
   Account of the effects of soap-lye 1608:51.
   See Walpole 2493:8
*Justice and necessity of taxing the American
   colonies* 1609:13
Justification. See Combe 3222:15
Justification de Jean-Jacques Rousseau. See
   Hume 1680:3
Justinian I, Emperor:
   Corpus juris civilis. See Classics 2207:18
   Institutiones 2245
   See Procopius 759
Justinus:
   Justini historiae Philippicae. See Classics
   2207:19
Juvenal des Ursins, Jean:
   Histoire de Charles VI, Roy de France 901
Juvenalis, Decimus Junius:
   Opera 2277
   Satires 1874
   Satyrae 851, 2125, 2195–6, 2216. *See* Brind-
   ley 2120:5
   Sixteen satyrs 1954
Juvigny, Jean Antoine Rigoley de. *See* Rigo-
   ley

K., P. *See Nomenclatura* 1537
Kaempfer, Engelbert:
   History of Japan 1121
Kālidāsa. *See* Jones 3194
Kames, Henry Home, Lord:
   Elements of criticism 2895
Kane, Richard:
   Campaigns of King William 1608:50

Kate, Lambert ten:
   Beau ideal 3882
Kauffman, Angelica. *See* Keate 3222:17
Kearsly, George:
   Case of George Kearsly 1609:56
   See Copper Plate Magazine 3839; Sandby
   3844
Keate, George:
   Account of the Pelew Islands 271
   The Alps, a poem 3222:4
   Epistle from Lady Jane Grey 3222:1
   Epistle to Angelica Kauffman 3222:17
   Ferney 3222:9
   Monument in Arcadia 3222:13
   Netley Abbey 3222:9
   One or more letters. See Letters 2576
   [Poems] 3222:21
   Poetical works 1567
   Ruins of Netley Abbey 3222:6
   Short account of ... Geneva 788
   Sketches from nature 1568
   Temple-student 3222:6
Keate, Georgiana. *See* Etchings 3588
Keeffe, John. *See* O'Keeffe
Këen Lung, Emperor of China. *See* Kien
   Long 3222:13
Keepe, Henry:
   True and perfect narrative 377
Keill, John. *See* Euclid 2211
Kelly, D.:
   Molly White 3222:8
Kelly, Hugh:
   Amour a-la-mode 1810:11
   Clementina 1810:17
   Elegy 3222:6
   False delicacy 1810:12
   Romance of an hour 1810:23
   School for wives 1810:21
   Thespis 3222:7
   Thespis Book II 3222:8
   Word to the wise 1810:16
Kemble, John Philip:
   Coriolanus 1810:47
   Fugitive pieces 3966
   Lodoiska 1810:54
   Pannel 1810:46, 47
   Pilgrim 1810:43
   Short criticism on Hamlet 1810:48
Kempfer, Engelbert. *See* Kaempfer 1121

Ken, Thomas, Bishop:
Manual of prayers 1528
Kennedy, Archibald:
Serious considerations 1608:48
Kennedy, James:
Description of . . . Wilton-House 1072
Kennedy, John:
Dissertation upon Oriuna. See Stukeley 668:5
Kennet, Basil:
Romae antiquae notitia 2716
Kennet, White, Bishop:
History of the counties of Oxford and Bucks 627
Sermon 1750
See North 3354; Sermons 1451
Kennicott, Benjamin:
Letter to Dr. King 1608:77
Kennion, Edward. *See* Antiquities 3485:2
Kenrick, William:
Duellist 1810:21
Epistle to G. Colman 3222:9
Falstaff's wedding 1810:8
Fun 1818:10
Lady of the manor 1810:29
Widow'd wife 1810:1
Kent, Samuel:
Dictionary of arms 508
Grammar of heraldry 743
Kent, William. *See* Drawings 3567; Jones 3538, 3784; Spenser 323; Ware 536
Kent. *See* Harris 571; Hasted 3; Parsons 3203
Kentish Barons. See Guilford 1810:49
Kenwood. See Caen Wood
Kéralio, Louise Félicité Guinement de:
Collection des meilleurs ouvrages 3021
Kerdeston, Sir Thomas. *See* Heraldry 2559
Kew. See Chambers 3532
Key to the Lock 1810:46
Key to the Parliamentary debates 1609:47
Kidgell, John:
Genuine and succinct narrative 1609:54
Kien Long 3222:13
Killegrew, Thomas. *See* Killigrew
Killigrew, Mrs. Anne. *See* Poems 3363
Killigrew, Thomas:
Comedies and tragedies 1122
Killing noe murder. See Sexby 1608:8

Kilmarnock, William Boyd, Earl of:
Memoirs 2717
See Foster 1608:54
Kimber, Isaac:
Life of Oliver Cromwell 1648
Kinderley, Nathaniel. *See* Cole 1594
King, Daniel:
Churches of England and Wales 600
Vale-Royall of England 628
King, Edward:
Morsels of criticism 3241
Observations on ancient castles 544
One letter. *See* Letters 2576
Proposals for a marine school 1609:48
Remarks concerning stones 3816
Vestiges of Oxford Castle 222
King, Henry, Bishop:
Poems 1955
King, John Glen:
[Nummi familiarum et imperatorum Romanorum] 242
King, Peter, 1st Baron King:
Enquiry 129
History of the Apostles Creed 130
See Whatley 2496:4
King, Thomas:
Love at first sight 1810:5
Wit's last stake 1810:14
King, William (1663–1712):
Miscellanies, in prose and verse 1711
Original works 2896
See Examiner 1560
King, William (1685–1763):
Apology. *See* Tracts 2146:5
Dreamer 1483
Oratio in Theatro Sheldoniano. See Tracts 1348:4, 2146:5
Proposal for publishing 1608:61
Translation 1608:70
See Kennicott 1608:77
King Arthur. See Garrick 1810:16
King Charles the First. See Havard 1818:6
King Harry the Ninth's Speech to both Houses of P[arliamen]t. See Tracts 2146:3
King Henry the VII. See Macklin 1818:20
King of France's declaration of war. See Louis XV 1608:23
King Pepin's campaign. See Shirley 1818:14
King William and Queen Mary conquerors. See Blount 1608:1

King's Bench sermon 1609:28
King's Evil. See Duckett 683:1
King's library. See Casley 476
King's Lynn:
  Warrant constituting Walpole free of the Borough 2567
  See Cole 1594; Mackerell 699; Parkin 445
King's most gracious speech. See Tracts 2146:1
King's Theatre, Haymarket. See Taylor 1810:50
Kingsale, Gerald de Courcy, Lord. See Kinsale
Kingston, Elizabeth Chudleigh, Countess of Bristol, calling herself Duchess of:
  Brief for Her Grace the Duchess of Kingston 1609:58
  Kingston cause 1609:37
  See Bunbury 3563:4
Kingston, Evelyn Pierrepont, 1st Duke of:
  Catalogus 3278
Kingston on Hull. See Cozens 3184
Kingston cause. See Kingston, Duchess of
Kingsweston Hill. See Hobhouse 3222:19
Kinsale, Gerald de Courcy, Lord:
  Common-place books 2568
  Exercises in geometry 2569
  Introduction to algebra 2570
  Poems and songs 2571
Kip, John:
  Britannia illustrata 3573
  See London 3623, 3818
Kip, William. See Harrison 3428
Kippis, Andrew. See Biographia Britannica 217
Kirby, John:
  Suffolk traveller 744
Kirby, John Joshua:
  Dr. Brook Taylor's Method of perspective made easy 272
  Historical account of ... Suffolk 3858
  Perspective of architecture 3539
Kirke, Colonel Percy:
  Letter book 2572
Kirkley, Ralph. See Tracts 3833:6
Kirkman, Francis. See Marlowe 1964
Kit-Cat Club 3501
Klotz, Christian Adolphe:
  Historia numorum 1033
Knaresborough. See Hargrove 2867

Kneller, Sir Godfrey. See Kit-Cat Club 3501
Knight, Ellis Cornelia:
  Lettere di Marco Flaminio 3331
  Lines addressed to Victory. See Tracts 2968:4
  Marcus Flaminius 3718
  See Drawings 3641; Etchings 3588
Knight, Henrietta, Lady Luxborough. See Luxborough
Knight, Richard Payne:
  Account of the remains of the worship of Priapus 2404
  Progress of civil society 3432
  See Marshall 3245
Knight, Samuel (1675–1746):
  Life of Dr. John Colet 1681
Knight, Samuel (1755–1829):
  Elegies and sonnets 3222:20
Knole. See Willis 2990
Knollys, Sir Charles. See Knowles
Knollys, Hanserd:
  Life and death of Hanserd Knollys. See Sermons 2756:2
Know your own mind. See Murphy 1810:28
Knowledge of things unknowne. See Hill 787
Knowler, William. See Strafford 446
Knowles, Charles (1662–1740), called Earl of Banbury. See Stamford 521
Knowles, Sir Charles (d. 1777). See Authentick papers 1608:53; Gambier 1608:88
Knowles, Thomas. See Hervey 3168
Knowsley Hall. See Winstanley 3668
Knox, John. See Northampton 2584
Knox, Robert:
  Historical relation of the island of Ceylon 2718
Knox, William:
  Appendix to the Present state of the nation 1609:22
  Claim of the colonies 1609:12
  Controversy review'd 1609:22
  Letter to a Member of Parliament 1609:12
  Present state of the nation 1609:21
Knyff, Leonard. See Kip 3573
Knyvet, Katharine:
  Descent 2573
Koran:
  Alcoran of Mahomet 1484
Kuster, Ludolph. See Aristophanes 2151

Kynaston, Sir Francis:
  Constitutions of the Musaeum Minervae
  3817
  Corona Minervae 2405

La Barre de Beaumarchais, Antoine de. *See Temple* 3985
La Beaume le Blanc, Louis César de. *See* La Vallière
La Beaumelle, Laurent Angliviel de:
  Mes pensées 1223
  Vie de Mme. de Maintenon. See La Fayette 988:1
  See Maintenon 1255, 1280
La Blancherie, Flammès Claude Catherine Pahin-Champlain de:
  Extrait du journal de mes voyages 3111
La Blêterie, Jean Philippe René de:
  Histoire de l'empereur Jovien 965
  Vie de l'empereur Julien 986
La Boderie, Antoine le Fèvre de:
  Ambassade en Angleterre 3022
La Brune, Jean de:
  Mélanges historiques 1198
  Vie de Charles V, Duc de Lorraine 1298
Labyrinte de Versailles 301
Labyrinthus. See Plays 2131
La Calprenède, Gautier de Coste de:
  Cléopatre 1224
  See Cassandra 367
La Chaise, François d'Aix de. *See* Le Noble 1200
La Châtre, Claude de. *See* Collection 3084
La Chausse, Michel Ange de:
  Gemme antiche 3748
  Romanum Museum 3749
Lackington, James:
  Memoirs 2897
La Clos, Pierre Ambroise François Choderlos de. *See* Choderlos de Laclos
La Colombière, Marc Vulson de. *See* Vulson
Lacombe, François:
  Observations sur Londres 3112
Lacombe, Jaques:
  Abrégé chronologique de l'histoire du Nord 1034
  See Christina 804
Lacombe de Prezel, Honoré:
  Dictionnaire d'anecdotes 3023
  Dictionnaire des portraits historiques 3023

La Croix du Maine, François Grudé de:
  Bibliothèque du Sieur de la Croix 902
  See Bibliothèques 3068
Lactantius, Lucius Caecilius Firmianus:
  De mortibus persecutorum. See Classics 2207:21
  Opera. See Classics 2207:20
  Traité de la mort des persecuteurs 3967
La Curne de Sainte-Palaye, Jean Baptiste de:
  Histoire littéraire des troubadours 3113
  Mémoires sur l'ancienne chevalerie 809
Ladies cabinet. See Ruthven 177
Ladies miscellany. See D'Assigny 1818:3
Lady. See Celesia 1810:17; *Conquest of Corsica* 1810:18; *Cross partners* 1810:51; *Griffith* 1810:6; *Peruvian* 1810:39; *South Briton* 1810:22
Lady of quality. See Fate of Corsica 1818:20
Lady's head dresser. See Ritchie 1609:29
Lafargue, Étienne de:
  Oeuvres mêlées de littérature 3024
La Fayette, Marie Madeleine Motier, Comtesse de:
  Histoire de Mme. Henriette d'Angleterre 987
  Mémoires 988
  Oeuvres 2310
  Princesse de Clèves 2310
  Princesse de Montpensier 989
  Zayde. See Segrais 1005
  See Segrais 1005
Lafitau, Joseph François:
  Histoire de Jean de Brienne, Roi de Jérusalem 3114
Lafont, Joseph de. *See* O'Brien 1810:19
La Fontaine, Jean de:
  Contes 940, 2406
  Fables choisies 941
  Oeuvres 966
  See Apuleius 1151; Tracts 2050:25
La Force, Jean Aimar Piganiol de. *See* Piganiol 1258
La Fosse, Charles de. *See* Drawings 3567
La Guerre, Louis. *See* Drawings 3567
La Harpe, Jean François de:
  Eloge de la Fontaine 2050:25
  See Francklin 1810:9; Hiffernan 1810:9; Suetonius 3378

La Haye, Sieur de:
Policy and government of the Venetians 1751
Laird and farmer 2719
Lakes, English. *See* Gilpin 3854:2
La Live de Jully, Ange Laurent de:
Catalogue historique . . . de peinture et sculpture 3332
Lally, Thomas Arthur. *See* Voltaire 3388
La Marche, Olivier de. *See* Collection 3084
La Maria. *See* Malespini 3340
La Martelière, P. A. Pinel de. *See* Santeul 820
La Martinière, Antoine Augustin Bruzen de. *See* Bruzen 1290
Lambard, William:
Dictionarium Angliae topographicum 629
Lambart, Richard, Earl of Cavan. *See* Cavan 3180
Lambert, Anne Thérèse de. *See* Choisy 1292
Lambert, Claude François:
Recueil d'observations 3025
Lambert, Nicolas. *See* Le Brun 3648
Lambert, Hôtel de. *See* Le Brun 3648
Lambertini, Prospero. *See* Benedict XIV
Lambeth Palace. *See* Denne 3234
La Mettrie, Julien Offray de:
L'École de la Volupté. See Almanach 1174
La Monnoye, Bernard de:
Histoire de Mr. Bayle 990
La Mothe, Marie Catherine, Comtesse d'Aulnoy. *See* Aulnoy
La Mothe le Vayer, François de. *See* Lettres 1074
La Motte, Antoine Houdart de:
Fables nouvelles 926
Oeuvres 789
See Aesop 2325; Mallet 1810:4
La Motte, Marie Catherine de, Comtesse d'Aulnoy. *See* Aulnoy
La Mottraye, Aubry de:
Travels through Europe, Asia, and into part of Africa 442
Lancashire. *See* Leigh 602
Lancaster, John of Gaunt, Duke of. *See* Collins 1674
Lancaster, Nathaniel:
Public virtue. See Sermons 1346:7
Lancaster, House of. *See* Halle 623
Lancaster, Duchy of. *See* Fleetwood 2550

Lancelot, Antoine:
Naudaeana et Patiniana 745
Lancer, Edward:
Some particular remarks 1608:86
Landaff. *See* Llandaff
Landi, Ortensio. *See* Pazzia 2439
Lang, Joseph. *See* Juvenalis 851
Langage des bestes. See Bougeant 1178
Langbaine, Gerard (1609–1658), the elder. *See* Cheke 1608:1; Oxford University 1608:3
Langbaine, Gerard (1656–1692):
Lives . . . of the English dramatick poets 1899
Momus triumphans 1608:8
Langeais, —— de:
Réflexions sur Polibe. See Almanach 1174
Langford, Abraham, auctioneer. *See* Mead 3785; Royal Academy 3885:5; Tracts 2050
Langhorne, John:
Fables of Flora 3222:11
See Collins 3954
Langius, Josephus. *See* Martialis 2176
Langley, Batty and Thomas:
Ancient architecture, restored 630
Builder's bench-mate 342
Langley's Exactions detected. See Egmont 2844
Langton, Lewis:
Bellus homo. See Poems 881:3
Languet, Hubert:
Epistolae 3333
La Noue, François de:
Politicke and militarie discourses 2720
See Collection 3084
Lanquet, Thomas:
Cooper's Chronicle 1617
Lansdowne, George Granville, 1st Baron:
Genuine works in verse and prose 3171
See Ode 3222:19
Lansdowne, William Petty, Marquess of. *See* Address 1609:45; Bellomont 1609:43; Letter 1609:42, 43; Monitory hints 1609:44; O'Bryen 1609:43; Sketch 1609:42
Lanzi, Luigi Antonio:
La reale galleria di Firenze. See Florence 3570
La Place, Pierre Antoine de:
Pièces intéressantes 3115

Lapland. *See* Scheffer 1608:71

La Pointe, François de:
Créations des chevaliers de l'Ordre du St. Esprit 545

La Porte, Joseph de. *See Anecdotes* 3064

La Porte, Pierre de:
Mémoires 1225

Laquei ridiculosi. See Parrot 1906

L'Armessin, Nicolas de. *See* Prints 3655

La Roberdière, A. F.:
Voyage de l'amour en Angleterre 1251

La Rochefoucauld, François de:
Mémoires de la minorité de Louis XIV 991
Réflexions 992

Laroon, Marcellus. *See* Drawings 3678

La Roque, Jean de:
Voyage to Arabia 1569

La Sale, Antoine de:
L'histoire et plaisante cronicque 1277

Lascivious queen. See Marlowe 1964

La Serre, Jean Puget de. *See* Puget 608

Lassay, Armand de Madaillan de Lesparre, Marquis de:
Recueil de différentes choses 790

Lasso de la Vega, Garcia:
Royal commentaries of Peru 443

Last will and testament of Dr. Swift. See Tracts 98:1

Lastri, Marco:
L'Etruria pittrice 3540

La Suze, Henrietta de, Comtesse:
Recueil de pièces galantes 993

Late newes out of Barbary. See Barbary 3804

Late occurrences in North America 1609:12

Latimer, Hugh, Bishop:
Fruitfull sermons 1332
See Gilpin 1608:78

Latin classics. *See* Brindley 2120

Latouche, James Digges:
Address 1608:29

La Tour d'Auvergne, Henri de, Duc de Bouillon. *See* Bouillon

La Tour d'Auvergne, Henri de, Vicomte de Turenne. *See* Turenne

La Trémoille, Henri Charles de, Prince de Tarente:
Mémoires 2278
See Angola 1288

La Trémoille, Louis de. *See Collection* 3084

Il Latte. See Jerningham 3222:8

Lattré, Jean. *See* Atlas 447

Laud, William, Archbishop:
History of the troubles . . . of . . . William Laud 1123
See Tracts 2769:1

Lauderdale, Richard Maitland, 4th Earl of. *See* Virgilius 180, 1988

Laughton, Henry. *See* Virgilius 2204

Laurel 1816

Laurence, French. *See* Moir 3131

Laus asini. See Heinsius 2244

Laval, House of. *See* Du Chesne 896

Lavallée, Joseph:
Voyage dans les départemens de la France 3334

La Vallette, Bernard de Foix de, Duc d'Épernon. *See* Girard 1010; Grignette 3745

La Vallière, Louis César, Duc de:
Catalogues des livres 3335
See Bibliothèque 3001

Lavater, Johann Caspar:
Essais sur la physiognomonie 3701

Lavender, Theophilus. *See* Biddulph 3805

Lavenham Church:
Specimens of Gothic ornaments 3719

La Vergne, Louis Elisabeth de, Comte de Tressan. *See* Tressan

Lavinius, Lucius. *See* Du Val 1615

Law and arguments in vindication of the University of Oxford. See Henley 1608:70

Law MS. *See* Mawson 2579

Law of evidence. See Gilbert 2695

Law reports. *See Reports* 2591

Lawrence, Anthony:
Nurseries, orchards, profitable gardens. See Hartlib 125:6

Lawyer's fortune. See Grimston 1896, 2861

Layman. *See* Grafton 1609:52; Saunders 1608:12

Leaf, Jeremy:
Worldly compliances 1608:7

Leake, Stephen Martin:
Historical account of English money 302

Leapor, Mary:
Poems. See Poems 1835

Leave, R. *See* Müntz 3575

Le Bas, Jacques Philippe. *See* Teniers 3612; Wouwerman 3992

Le Beau, Charles:
  Histoire du Bas-Empire en commençant à Constantine-le-Grand 1278
  See Thou 3152
Le Blanc, François:
  Traité historique des monnoyes de France 1142
Le Blanc, Jean Bernard:
  Lettres d'un françois 1158
Le Blon, Jacques Christophe:
  Coloritto 2407, 3883
  See Kate 3882
Le Blond, Alexandre Jean Baptiste:
  Theory . . . of gardening 1333
Le Boe, Franciscus de, called Sylvius:
  New idea for the practice of physic 2279
Le Bossu, René:
  Traité du poème épique 1035
Le Bovier de Fontenelle, Bernard. *See* Fontenelle
Le Brun, Charles:
  Conference on expression. See Tracts 361:1
  La galerie de Monsr. le président Lambert 3648
  See Louis XIV 3574, 3591
Le Clerc, Jean:
  Parrhasiana 746
  See Classics 2207:3, 17
Le Clerc, Sébastien:
  Divers desseins de figures 2408
  See Labyrinte 301; Louis XIV 3591
Le Conte de Bièvre, Jean Joseph François:
  Histoires des deux Aspasies 994
Le Courayer, Pierre François. *See* Sarpi 933
Lectiones Jeremiae. See Jeremiah 2564
Lediard, Thomas:
  Life of John, Duke of Marlborough 1682
  See Mascou 1334
Le Duchat, Jacob:
  Ducatiana 1299
Ledwich, Edward:
  Antiquities of Ireland 3195
  See Grose 3496; Salisbury 2949
Lee, Arthur:
  Appeal to the justice and interests 1609:33
Lee, Elizabeth (Scrope):
  Answer to Mr. Cresswell's narrative 1608:73
Lee, Harriet:
  New peerage 1810:43

Lee, John:
  Country wife 1810:7, 39
  Letter to Mr. Sheridan. See Poems 1835:4
  Man of quality 1810:26
  See Squabble 1608:31
Lee, Nathaniel:
  Theodosius. See Plays 1623:2
Lee, Samuel. *See* Chelsea 1608:77
Lee, Sophia:
  Chapter of accidents 1810:32
Leeds, Francis Godolphin Osborne, 5th Duke of:
  Letter 1609:40
Leeds, Thomas Osborne, Earl of Danby; later Duke of. *See* Danby 15
Leeds. *See* Thoresby 612, 709
Leeke, Robert:
  Necessity of Christ's satisfaction 1608:35
Le Feron, Jean:
  Armoirs des connestables . . . de France 546
  See Godefroy 876
Le Fevre, Mlle. *See* Plautus 1013
Le Fèvre de la Boderie, Antoine. *See* La Boderie
Legend of Captaine Jones. See Lloyd 1957
Legend of St. Cuthbert. See Hegge 739
Legge, Henry Bilson. *See* Butler 1609:56;
  Observations 1609:56
Legh, Gerard:
  Accedence of armorie 1073
Legislative authority of the British Parliament. See Mauduit 1609:13
Legrand, Marc Antoine. *See* Fuzelier 1818:3
Legrand d'Aussy, Pierre Jean Baptiste:
  Fabliaux 3026
  Histoire de la vie privée des françois 3026
Leibnitz, Gottfried Wilhelm von, Baron:
  Collection of papers 1414
Leicester, John Sidney, 6th Earl of:
  Inventory of the pictures. See Walpole 2619:1
Leicester, Sir Peter:
  Historical antiquities 601
  Reply to Sir Thomas Mainwaring. See Mainwaring 751
Leicester, Robert Dudley, Earl of:
  Delineatio pompae triumphalis 509
  See Jebb 1709

Leicestershire. *See* Burton 618; Throsby 358, 3209

Leigh, Charles:
History of Lancashire, Cheshire, and the Peak in Derbyshire 602

Leigh, Gerard. *See* Legh 1073

Leigh, Peter. *See* Westminster election 1726

Leland, John:
Commentarii de scriptoribus Britannicis 694
Itinerary 3968
View of the principal Deistical writers 1376
See Huddesford 2875; Tracts 2049:5

Leland, Thomas:
History of Philip, King of Macedon 314

Le Long, Jacques:
Bibliothèque historique de la France 878

Leman, James. *See* Catalogues 3404

Le Masson, Innocent:
Éclaircissemens sur la vie de Jean d'Aranthon 1252

Lemery, Nicolas:
Modern curiosities 1529

Le Mierre, Antoine Marin. *See* Starke 1810: 50

Le Moine, Abraham:
Vindication of the literal account. See Middleton 1337

Le Moyne, Pierre:
Gallery of heroick women 3279

Lempereur, Magistrate. *See* Mariette 3592

Le Nain, Antoine. *See* Drawings 3567

Lenclos, Ninon de:
Lettres. See Damours 1185
Mémoires et lettres. See La Fayette 988:2

Le Neve, John:
Memoirs 748
Monumenta Anglicana 695

Leng, John, Bishop. *See* Terentius 2200

Lenglet du Fresnoy, Nicolas:
Histoire de la philosophie hermétique 1199
See Auvergne 801; Fénelon 1218; L'Estoile 1301

Lennard, Sampson. *See* Perrin 1079

Lennox, Charles, Duke of Richmond. *See* Richmond

Lennox, Charlotte:
Female Quixote, or, the adventures of Arabella 378
Old city manners 1810:25

Lennox, Charlotte (*cont.*)
Philander 1818:16
The sister 1810:14

Le Noble, Pierre:
Confession reciproque 1200

Le Noble de Tennelière, Eustache:
Contes 1036

Le Normand d'Etioles, Jeanne Antoinette, Marquise de Pompadour. *See* Pompadour

Lens, André:
Le costume 3116

Lens, Bernard:
Drawings of scenes in and near London 3502
New and compleat drawing book 510

Lens, Bernard, the younger:
Six views of ladies' head dresses 2574

Lenton, Francis:
Sacred history of Queen Esther 2575

Leo the Great, Pope. *See* Maimbourg 1039

Leominster. *See* Price 2934

Leonardo da Vinci. *See* Vinci

Leone, Gabriel. *See* Defence 1609:56

Leoni, Giacomo. *See* Palladio 3593

Leoni, Ottavio. *See* Lioni

Leopold William, Archduke of Austria. *See* Teniers 3633

Le Paon, Jean Baptiste. *See* Drawings 3567

Le Pautre, Jean:
Portfolio of architectural designs 3681
Portfolio of engravings 3603
See Louis XIV 3591:2

Le Pelletier, Robert Martin:
Histoires des comtes de Champagne et de Brie 3117

Le Petit, Nicolas:
La vie de monsieur le duc de Montausier 1226

Lépicié, François Bernard:
Catalogue . . . des tableaux du Roy 454
Vies des premiers peintres du Roi 343

Le Prince, Nicolas Thomas:
Essai historique 2217

Le Rouge, George Louis:
Détails des nouveaux jardins 3433

Le Roux, Philibert Joseph:
Dictionnaire comique 1159

Le Roy, David:
Les ruines . . . de la Grèce 3541

Le Sage, Alain René:
  Avantures de Monsieur Robert Chevalier 1300
  Devil upon two sticks 1570
  History of Gil Blas 1571
  Oeuvres choisies 3118
  See Devil 1608:80; Garrick 1810:9; Moore 1818:9; *Théâtre* 1171; Walpole 3730
Leslie, Charles. *See* Ridpath 1609:38
Lessing. *See* Raspe 1810:33
Lessons for the day. See Letter 1608:18; Walpole 2616
L'Estoile, Pierre de:
  Journal de Henri III, Roy de France 1301
  Journal du règne de Henri IV, Roi de France 1302
  See Henry III 844
L'Estrange, Sir Roger:
  Considerations 1608:1
  Observator 2058
  Word concerning libels 1608:8
  See Josephus 2057
Le Stue. *See Ode* 3222:10
Leszczynski. *See* Stanislaus 3053
Le Tessier, A. A. *See* Le Texier
Le Texier, A. A. *See Journal étranger* 3338:5
Lethieullier, Smart:
  Drawings of ancient buildings 3503
  See Catalogues 3404
Leti, Gregorio:
  Vita dell invittissimo imperadore Carlo V, Austriaco 2102
  Vita di Sisto V 2103
  See Northumberland 174
Le Tourneur, Pierre. *See* Shakespeare 3147
Letter balancing the causes. See Morris 1608:83
Letter concerning libels 1609:10
Letter, containing some reflections. See Burnet 1608:8
Letter describing the ride to Hulne Abbey. See Percy 1609:19
Letter from a by-stander. See Morris 1608:41
Letter from a friend in the country. See Bristol 1608:27
Letter from a gentleman at St. Germains. See Detection 2677:1
Letter from a gentleman in London 1608:58
Letter from a gentleman in town 1609:54

Letter from a Lady to her husband abroad. See Poems 280
Letter from a Member of Parliament 1608:80
Letter from a Member of Parliament, on the plate-tax 1608:82
Letter from a merchant in London to his nephew. See Tucker 1609:13
Letter from a patriot in retirement. See Hervey 1609:3
Letter from a person of distinction. See Egmont 119:2
Letter from a physician in town 1608:51, 2493:5
Letter from a Right Honourable person. See Francis 1609:54
Letter from Albemarle Street to the Cocoa-Tree 1609:55
Letter from an author. See Warburton 1608:18
Letter from an Hutchinsonian 1608:29
Letter from certain gentlemen of the Council. See Coote 1609:55
Letter from Dr. Rock 1608:51
Letter from Flanders 1608:26
Letter from Miss F——d. See Thicknesse 1609:2
Letter from Orford in the shades 1608:53
Letter from Rome. See Middleton 1574
Letter from S————shire 1608:70
Letter from the anonymous author of the letters versified. See Francis 1609:54
Letter from the Cocoa-Tree to the chiefs of the Opposition 1609:54
Letter from the Cocoa-Tree to the country-gentlemen. See Francis 1609:54
Letter from the late A** C**. See Middleton 1379:11
Letter from the late Earl of Harrington. See Tracts 2146:3
Letter from the rope-dancing monkey in the Hay-Market 1810:9
Letter from Xo Ho. See Walpole 2489
Letter in defence of Dr. Middleton. See Yate 1379:5
Letter of advice to a friend about clipt money. See Tracts 100:1
Letter of compliment 1818:19
Letter of consolation 1608:73
Letter the first addressed to the . . . Protestant Dissenters. See Huntingford 1609:52

Letter to ****** 1608:56

Letter to a certain distinguished patriot. See Walpole 1608:43

Letter to a certain eminent British sailor 1608:53

Letter to a clergyman 1608:6

Letter to a freeholder. See Political tracts 94:6

Letter to a friend in the country 1608:80

Letter to a gentleman in the country. See Hervey 1608:28

Letter to a gentleman occasioned by Dr. Middleton's Examination. See Middleton 1379:11

Letter to a late popular director 1609:22

Letter to a Member of Parliament [on Admiral Byng]. *See* Byng 3403

Letter to a Member of Parliament [on the colonies]. *See* Knox 1609:12

Letter to a Member of Parliament [on the fisheries] 1608:59

Letter to a Member of Parliament [on the Mutiny Bill] 1608:27

Letter to a member of the club, in Albemarle-Street 1609:55

Letter to a member of the late Parliament 1608:94

Letter to a noble lord 1608:59

Letter to a noble negotiator 1608:58

Letter to a Right Honourable person. See Francis 1609:54

Letter to Andrew Stone 1608:74

Letter to Cicero. See Tracts 2966:3

Letter to ——, *concerning the abuse of Scripture-terms* 1608:18

Letter to David Garrick 1810:18

Letter to Dr. Cadogan 1609:28

Letter to Dr. King. See Kennicott 1608:77

Letter to Dr. Sangrado 1608:89

Letter to Dr. Waterland. See Middleton 1379:1

Letter to Earl Stanhope. See Hawtrey 1609:52

Letter to Her R—l H—s the P—s D-w-g-r of W—— 1609:5

Letter to His G—e the D—e of B—d 1608:86

Letter to His Grace the D— of N—e. See Shebbeare 1608:86

Letter to His Grace the Duke of Grafton. See Wilkes 1609:18

Letter to Lord B—— 1609:20

Letter to Mr. C——b——r 1608:90

Letter to Mr. G————k 1818:9

Letter to Mr. Mason. See Poems 1835:6

Letter to Mr. Sheridan. See Poems 1835:4

Letter to R———— B———— Esq. See Cumberland 1810:2

Letter to Samuel Johnson, L.L.D. See Wilkes 1609:25

Letter to Sir John Phillips 1608:49

Letter to the author of a Letter 1609:54

Letter to the author of an Examination. See Egmont 119:2

Letter to the author of the Lucubrations 1609:42

Letter to the author of the Question stated. See Blackstone 1609:23

Letter to the Bishop of London. See Cassandra 1609:50

Letter to the Common-Council of London [1765] 1609:11

Letter to the Common Council of the City of London [1764] 1609:7

Letter to the Duke of Grafton. See First letter 1609:25

Letter to the Earl of B—— 1609:56

Letter to the Earl of Bute. See Almon 1609:28

Letter to the Earl of Chatham. See Meredith 1609:32

Letter to the Earl of O—d. See Tracts 400:10, 2475:12

Letter to the Earl of Shelburne 1609:43

Letter to the editor of . . . Chatterton. See Chatterton 3408, 3690:4; Strawberry Hill 3469:13; Walpole 1609:39

Letter to the editor of the Letters on the spirit of patriotism. See Warburton 1608:13

Letter to the First Belfast Company. See Hertford 1609:45

Letter to the gentlemen of the Committee of London Merchants 1609:13

Letter to the Hon. Author of the new farce 1818:17

Letter to the Honorable Mr. Horace Walpole. See Heathcote 1609:16

Letter to the Lord Viscount B———— ke. See Warburton 1608:13

Letter to the Members of the Society. See Royal Academy 3885:4

Letter to the Oxford Tories 1608:70

Letter to the people of England. See Shebbeare 1608:82

Letter to the proprietors of East-India stock. See Ashburton 1609:8

Letter to the proprietors of India stock 1609: 17

Letter to the public 1608:64

Letter to the Public Advertiser 1609:8

Letter to the Reverend Dr. Batteley. See Tenison 1608:8

Letter to the Reverend Dr. Conyers Middleton. See Wesley 1379:7

Letter to the Rev. Dr. Lowth. See Brown 1609:12

Letter to the Revd. Mr. G. R. See Spence 1608:79

Letter to the Reverend Mr. John Jackson. See Middleton 1379:8

Letter to the Rev. Mr. John Wesley. See Evans 1609:35

Letter to the Rev. Mr. T. Warton. See Darby 1609:47

Letter to the Rev. Mr. Thomas Carte. See Morris 1608:41

Letter to the Reverend Mr. Tong. See Saunders 1608:12

Letter to the Rev. Sir Thomas Broughton. See Tracts 2966:2

Letter to the Right Hon. Charles Townshend [1762] 1609:5

Letter to the Right Honourable Charles Townshend [1764] 1609:9

Letter to the Right Honourable Ch———s T———nd, Esq. 1609:6

Letter to the Right Honourable Earl Temple 1609:54

Letter to the Right Hon. George Grenville [1763]. *See* Almon 1609:54

Letter to the Right Honourable George Grenville [1764] 1609:8

Letter to the Right Honourable George Grenville [1769]. *See* Wilkes 1609:24

Letter to the Right Honorable H——y F——x 1608:86

Letter to the Right Honourable L—d Th—w. See Leeds 1609:40

Letter to the Right Honourable the Earl of B*** 1609:3

Letter to the Right Honourable the Earl of Shelburne 1609:42

Letter to the Right Honourable the Earls of Egremont and Halifax 1609:6

Letter to the Right Honourable the Lord ******** 1608:61

Letter to the Right Reverend Author. See Lowth 1609:12

Letter to the Right Reverend The Lord Bishop of O—d. See Cumberland 1609:18

Letter to the town 1608:63

Letter to the Whigs. See Walpole 3933

Letter to us 1609:38

Letter to Will Chat-em, Esq. 1609:15

Letter to William Pitt, Esq. See Hervey 1608: 90

Letter vindicating Queen Elizabeth. See Mary, Queen of Scots 205

Letter written to His Majesty's principal secretaries 1608:55

Lettera critica. See Cocchi 1608:52

Letters 2576

Letters:

    Collection of the letters of Atticus 1609:24

    Letters concerning the present state of England 3925

    Letters from a father 2409

    Miscellaneous unidentified letters. *See* Letters 2576 (*ad finem*)

    Original letters. See Vernon 1497

    Select collection of original letters . . . from the reign of Henry the Eighth 1900

    Useful and entertaining collection of letters 1440

Letters addressed to Sir Julius Caesar. *See* Caesar 2535:10, 11

Letters and poems upon political subjects. See Tracts 98:2

Letters between the Lord Chancellor and the sheriffs. See Tooke 1609:25

Letters by several eminent persons deceased. See Hughes 2876

Letters concerning mythology. See Blackwell 1394

Letters concerning poetical translations. See Benson 1845

Letters . . . concerning religion. See Digby 159

Letters concerning taste. See Cooper 1608:79

Letters concerning the present state of England. See Letters 3925

Letters concerning the present state of Poland. See Lind 1609:30

Letters describing the . . . English and French nations. See Muralt 1444

Letters from a farmer in Pennsylvania. See Dickinson 1609:22

Letters from a father to his daughter. See Letters 2409

Letters from a gentleman in the north of Scotland. See Burt 1430

Letters from a lady at Paris. See Aulnoy 1461

Letters from a Persian in England. See Lyttelton 3926–7

Letters from a young painter. See Russell 1540

Letters from Barbary. See Jardine 2891

Letters from Mons. La V——— 1609:6

Letters from the Right Honourable W— E— 1609:48

Letters historical and critical from Constantinople 1608:18

Letters, in the original, with translations 1608:5

Letters of Atticus. See Cooke 1608:24

Letters of Governor Hutchinson. See Mauduit 1609:31, 34

Letters of literature. See Pinkerton 3825

Letters of Valens. See Burke 1609:38

Letters on chivalry and romance. See Hurd 1609:6

Letters on patriotism. See Frederick II 2691

Letters on several occasions. See Freeman 2007

Letters on several subjects. See Melmoth 1442

Letters on the British Museum. See Thomson 2965

Letters, poems, and tales. See Tracts 98:2

Letters to a young nobleman. See Rivers 3257

Letters to His Grace the Lord Primate of All Ireland. See Brett 1367:3

Letters to Sir William Temple. See Arlington 104

Letters to the Right Honourable the Earl of Hillsborough. See Massachusetts 1609:23

Letters writ by a Turkish spy. See Turkish spy 1766

Lettice, James:
Letters on a tour through . . . Scotland 2898

Lettre de M. de Voltaire à M. Hume. See Hume 1680:4

Lettre sur l'origine de l'imprimerie. See Fournier 3012:3

Lettres d'amour d'une religieuse portugaise. See Alcoforado 1018

Lettres de cachet. See Mirabeau

Lettres de Monsieur de Montcalm. See Roubaud 1609:38

Lettres de Ninon de Lenclos au Marquis de Sévigné. See Damours 1185

Lettres diverses 1074

Lettres . . . du règne de Louis XIV. See Griffet 1297

Lettres d'un françois. See Le Blanc 1158

Lettres d'un inconnu. See Almanach 1174

Lettres historiques sur le Comtat Venaissin. See Moreau 3034

Lettres juives. See Argens 1007

Lettres sur la création de l'Arbre de Vie. See Mélange 1045

Lettres sur le caractère des Anglois. See Mélange 1045

Lettres sur l'éducation des princes. See Fontenai 980

Lettsom, John Coakley:
Memoirs of John Fothergill 413

Le Vacher de Charnois, Jean Charles:
Costumes et annales des grands théâtres 3119
Recherches sur . . . les théâtres 3120

Levant. *See* Perry 1098

Levant Company:
Letter books. See Caesar 2535:7
See Derby 79:2; *Some* 1608:50

Le Vassor, Michel:
Lettres . . . de François de Vargas 3336

Lévêque, Prosper:
Mémoires . . . du Cardinal de Granvelle 995

Lever, Thomas:
Three fruitfull sermons 749

Leveson-Gower, Granville, Viscount Trentham. *See* Trentham

Leveson-Gower, Margaret Caroline, Countess of Carlisle. *See* Carlisle

Lévesque de Burigny, Jean. *See* Burigny 1182

Lévesque de la Ravalière, Pierre Alexandre. *See* Theobald 798

Le Vieil, Pierre:
Essai sur la peinture en mosaique 379

Lévy, Jean Baptiste Michel de:
  Journal historique 3121
Lewesden Hill. See Crowe 3222:22
Lewis, Edward:
  Patriot king 1794
Lewis, George:
  Some general thoughts on government 1608:86
Lewis, Jenkin:
  Memoirs of Prince William Henry, Duke of Gloucester 1609:52
Lewis, John:
  History . . . of the Abbey of Favresham 631
  Life of . . . Caxton 273
  Life . . . of John Wicliffe 1683
  Life of Reginald Pecock 2721
  Translations of the Holy Bible into English 1415
Lewis, Matthew Gregory:
  The Monk. See Wollstonecraft 3177
Lewis, Paul. *See True . . . account* 1609:6
Lewis, Thomas:
  History of the Parthian Empire 1530
  Seasonable considerations on . . . burying in churches. See Duckett 683:3
Lewis, William. *See* Herbert 48
Lewis, Wilmarth S.:
  Collector's progress. See Theatre 1810
Lex Parliamentaria. See Petyt 1716
Lexiphanes. See Campbell 2658
Leyden, Lucas van. *See* Jacobsz, Lucas
Lhuyd, Edward:
  Archaeologia Britannica 21
Liaisons dangereuses. See Choderlos 3005
Libanus, Mount. *See* Dandini 1513
Liberty chastised. See Carey 1810:13
Liberty-Hall. See Dibdin 1810:37
Liberty invaded. See Baldwin 1608:31
Libraries:
  Critical and historical account 2018
Library. A poem. See Crabbe 3222:17
Lichfield. *See* Jackson 2887
Liebaut, Jean. *See* Estienne 837
Lien Chi. *See* Walpole 2489:1
Life, adventures, and amours, of Sir R— P— 1609:25
Life of Benjamin Hoadly. See Black-bird 2646:10
Life of Charles Price. See Price 1609:49

Life of Count Ulfeld of Denmark. See Rousseau 761
Life of Dr. George Abbot. See Oldys 417
Life of Edward Rainbow, late Lord Bishop of Carlisle. See Banks 2638
Life of Henry Jessey. See Sermons 2756:4
Life of John Buncle, Esq. See Amory 1636
Life of John Dolben. See Black-bird 2646:11
Life of Oliver Cromwell. See Kimber 1648
Life of Richard the Second [1681]. *See* Howard 2710
Life of Richard II [1713]. *See* Richard II 1608:9
Life of Robert Earl of Leicester. See Jebb 1709
Life of Sir Henry Vane. See Sikes 1089
Life of the late Lord Chancellor Jefferys 1609:8
Life of Théodore Agrippa d'Aubigné. See Scott 2953
Life of William Cavendish. See Newcastle 91
Lille, Jacques de:
  Les jardins. See Dezallier 920
Lilliput. See Garrick 1818:15
Lillo, George:
  Christian hero 1818:6
  Fatal curiosity 1810:36
  Silvia 1818:5
Lilly, William:
  True history of King James the first. See Tracts 360:2
  See Catastrophe 2352
Lima:
  True and particular relation of the earthquake 1485
Limborch, Philippus van:
  History of the Inquisition 1618
Limitation of the peerage. See Tracts 2475:10
Lincoln, Anna Maria Stanhope, Countess of, later Duchess of Newcastle. *See* Newcastle
Lincoln, Henry Fiennes Clinton, Earl of:
  One letter. See Letters 2576
Lincoln Cathedral. *See* Antiquities 3485:5
Lincolnshire. *See* Tilston 2048
Lind, John:
  Letters concerning Poland 1609:30
  Polish partition 1609:31
Lindor and Clara. See Fennell 1810:50

Lindsay, Colin. *See* Balcarras 105

Lindsey, Theophilus. *See* Lind 1609:31

Line, Francis, *alias* Hall:
Explication of the diall sett up in the King's garden at London 4010

Lines on a late resignation at the Royal Academy. See Jerningham 3222:22

Lines sent to Lady Miller's vase. See Bull 3222:18

Lines written at Twickenham. See O'Bryen 3222:22

Lines written in the Album, at Cossey-Hall. *See* Jerningham 3222:20, 22

Linguet, Simon Nicolas Henri:
Histoire du siècle d'Alexandre 810
See Théâtre 3150

Linley, Thomas:
Review 1810:43

Lionel and Clarissa. See Bickerstaffe 1810:12

Lioni, Ottavio:
Ritratti di alcuni celebri pittori del secolo XVII 274

Liques, David de. *See* Mornay 1078

Lisbon. *See* England 1609:15

L'Isle, Claude de:
Relation historique du Royaume de Siam 1037

List of officers kill'd . . . at Tournay. See Tracts 2146:6

List of ships taken. See Tracts 2146:3

List of the reduced officers. See Tracts 2146:6

Lists, army and navy. *See* Tracts 2146

Literary essays. See Moor 1797

Literary Museum. See Waldron 3389

Lithgow, William:
Travels 2722

Little John. *See* La Sale 1277

Littlebury, Isaac. *See* Herodotus 1411; Ludlow 1649

Littleton, Adam:
Linguae Latinae liber dictionarius 852

Littleton, Edward:
Sermons 1377

Littleton, G. *See* Discourse 1608:29

Liveryman's reply 1608:77

Lives and characters of illustrious persons. *See* Le Neve 748

Lives and characters of the Duchess of Marlborough's four daughters. See Black-bird 2646:24

Lives of . . . British, English, Scottish and Irish saints. See Challoner 619

Lives of John Leland, Thomas Hearne, and Anthony à Wood. See Huddesford 2875

Lives of the most eminent modern painters. *See* Burgess 1608:78

Livius, Peter. *See* England 1609:58

Livius, Titus:
Historiarum quod extat. See Classics 2207: 22

Livonia. *See* Blomberg 1467

Livoy, Timothée de. *See* Caimo 3075

Llandaff, Shute Barrington, Bishop of. *See* Barrington

Llandaff. Cathedral church. *See* Willis 2780

Llewellyn, Martin:
Men-miracles 1956

Lloyd, Charles:
Conduct of the late administration examined 1609:16
Defence of the majority 1609:8, 9
Examination of the principles 1609:15
Honest man's reasons 1609:11
See Letter 1609:8; Meredith 1609:9

Lloyd, David, biographer:
State worthies 1752

Lloyd, David, Dean of St. Asaph:
Legend of Captaine Jones 1957

Lloyd, Robert:
Arcadia 1810:2
Capricious lovers 1810:6
Epistle to Charles Churchill 3222:1
Tears and triumphs of Parnassus 1810:1
See Churchill 3222:1; *Phillis* 1810:10

Lloyd, T. A. *See* Bickerstaffe 1810:10, 38

Lloyd, William. *See* Castlemaine 110

Lobineau, Gui Alexis:
Histoire de Bretagne 879

Locke, John:
Abridgement of Mr. Locke's Essay 1753
Essay concerning human understanding 1124, 1486
Letters concerning toleration 3172
Some thoughts concerning education 1754

Lockhart, George:
Memoirs concerning the affairs of Scotland 1712

Lockman, John. *See* Apuleius 1151; Porée 1608:67; Swift 1456

Lodge, Edmund:
  Illustrations of British history, biography, and manners 455
  See Holbein 3500
Lodge, John:
  Peerage of Ireland 660
Lodge, Thomas:
  Rosalynd 2410
Lodge, W. *See* Barri 324
Logan, James. *See* Cicero 407
Logan, John:
  Runnamede 1810:35
Loggan, Samuel:
  History of the Brotherhood or Guild of the Holy Ghost 696
Logographic Press. *See* Defoe 408; Johnson 3431; Watts 420
Loménie de Brienne, Étienne Charles de:
  Oraison funèbre de Louis. See Tracts 2050: 19
London:
  Bills of mortality 1608:1
  Catch Club. *See* Catch Club
  Committee of London Merchants. *See* London Merchants
  Company of Parish Clerks. *See* Parish Clerks' Company
  Court of Common Council. *See* Letter 1609:7
  Cries of London. *See* Stradanus 3659
  Foundling Hospital. *See* Foundling Hospital
  Great Fire. *See* Duckett 683:4
  History. *See* De Laune 726; Maitland 573; Stow 611
  Opera House. *See* King's Theatre, Haymarket
  Portfolio of views 3623
  Prospects of the most remarkable places 3818
  Theatres. *See* Victor 2973–4
  Tower. *See* Tower of London
  Views. *See* Antiquities 3485:3, 13; Lens 3502; Smith 3521
  See Ambulator 2327; *Flagellum* 1608:8; Grosley 2274; Gwynn 3877; Lacombe 3112; Howell 626; Lysons 3859; Malton 3437; Parish Clerks 757; Pennant 3928; Stuart 1609:57; Tracts 2050; Warburton 2979
London Advertiser 2143

London and its environs described 697
London Belles. See Tracts 3832:2
London Bridge. *See* Hawksmoor 624
London Chronicle 538
London Daily Post and General Advertiser. See London Advertiser 2143
London Journal. See Collection 1608:24
London Magazine. See Magazines 3338:6
London Merchants, Committee of. *See* Letter 1609:13
Londres. See Grosley 2274
Long, Mrs. Anne. *See* Tracts 98:2
Long Parliament. *See* England 2686
Longeville, Harcouet de:
  Histoire des personnes 380
  See Samber 764
Longiano. *See* Gherardo 3316
Longinus, Caesar:
  Trinium magicum 2126
Longinus, Cassius, called Dionysius Cassius Longinus:
  De sublimitate 2089
Longmate, Barak:
  Supplement to the fifth edition of Collins's Peerage of England 414
Longueruana. See Dufour de Longuerue 1248
Longueville, Bertrand du Guesclin, Comte de. *See* Du Guesclin
Longueville, Henry Yelverton, Viscount de. *See* Sussex 2600
Longus:
  Amours pastorales de Daphnis et Chloe 2411
Lonsdale, Mark:
  Spanish rivals 1810:37
Loose remarks. See Macaulay 1609:17
Lord Mayor's Day. *See* O'Keeffe 1810:35
Lord of the manor. *See* Burgoyne 1810:32
Lord Stamford's charge. *See* Halifax 83
Lord's lamentation. See Poems 881:18
Lord's Supper:
  Week's preparation toward a proper receiving of the Lord's Supper 1531
Loredano, Giovanni Francesco:
  Histoire des rois de Chypre 1038
Lorrain, Claude:
  Liber veritatis 3669
  See Drawings 3569; Prints 3460
Lorraine, Duchy of. *See* Duckett 683:2

Lort, Michael:
  Forty letters. *See* Letters 2576
  Observations on celts 3504
  See Catalogues 2819
Lotteries. *See* Tracts 2146:6
Louis XI, King of France:
  Rozier des guerres 1253
  See Comines 1639; Duclos 960; Lussan 996
Louis XII, King of France:
  Lettres 1227
  See Godefroy 1066; Seyssel 1088
Louis XIII, King of France:
  Kings declarations 1608:1
  See Berton 1055; La Boderie 3022; Valdor 3525
Louis XIV, King of France:
  Cabinet du Roi 3591. *See* Labyrinte 301
  French King's dream 1608:23
  Galerie de l'ancienne cour 3337
  Lettres 967
  Promise to the Pretender 1608:9
  Two prints 3574
  See Amours 972; Caesar 497; Choisy 976; England 1608:94; Griffet 1297; La Pointe 545; La Rochefoucauld 991; Le Noble 1200; Lépicié 454; Voltaire 1149
Louis XV, King of France:
  Declaration of war 1608:23
  See Crozat 3550; Lévy 3121; Louis XIV 3337; Mariette 3592; Massillon 2313
Louis XVI, King of France. *See* France 410; Preston 1810:53; Vyner 3834
Louis, Dauphin of France, son of Louis XV. *See* Tracts 2050:19
Louisa 2311
Louisa Juliana, Consort of Frederick IV, Elector Palatine. *See* Spanheim 3467
Louisa Margaret, Princess de Conti. *See* Conti
Lousiad. See Wolcot 3222:20
Lousiad. Canto II. See Wolcot 3222:21
Louise de Savoie, Duchesse d'Angoulême. *See* Collection 3084
Louvre, Salon du. *See* Arts 288:3
Lovat, Simon Fraser, Baron:
  [Various tracts] 1608:54
  Whole proceedings in the House of Peers 1125
  See Kilmarnock 2717; Tracts 2146:3, 2968:3
Lovat's ghost 1608:54

Love, James:
  Cricket 3222:11
  Timon of Athens 1810:13
  Village wedding 1810:11
Love à la mode. See Kelly 1810:11
Love and folly. See Plays 1623:1
Love and innocence 1810:14
Love and madness. See Croft 2366
Love at first sight. See King 1810:5
Love in a village. See Bickerstaffe 1810:3
Love in all its shapes 1608:31
Love in its empire. See Chamberlen 1736
Love in the city. See Bickerstaffe 1810:10
Love in the East. See Cobb 1810:44
Love-letters. See Behn 1428
Love of fame. See Young 3934-5
Loveday, Robert:
  Letters 2723
Loveill, Mr. *See* Adventures 1551
Lovelace, Dudley Posthumus. *See* Lovelace, Richard 1959
Lovelace, Richard:
  Aramantha 1958
  Lucasta 1958-9
  Posthume poems 1959
Lover and reader. See Steele 1861
Lover of his country. See Bolingbroke 1608:13; Groans 1608:56; Plain matter 1608:38
Lover of Philalethes. See Enquiry 1517
Loves labyrinth. See Brathwait 1998
Loves of Cupid and Psyche. See Apuleius 1151
Loves of Hero and Leander 1960. *See* Ovidius 2021
Loves of Mirtil, son of Adonis 381
Low, Will, pseud. *See* Black-bird 2646:12
Low life above stairs 1810:11
Lower, Sir William:
  Amourous fantasme 1961
  Enchanted lovers 1962
  Noble ingratitude 1963
  Relation of the voiage 603
Lowestoft. *See* Gillingwater 3192
Lowhen, Baron von:
  Analysis of nobility 750
Lowth, Robert, Bishop:
  Letter to the Right Reverend Author 1609:12
  Life of William of Wykeham, Bishop of Winchester 1684

Lowth, Robert (*cont.*)
  Short introduction to English grammar 1795
  See Brown 1609:12; Cassandra 1609:50; Cumberland 1609:18
Lowther, Sir James. *See* Portland 1609:20
Loyal poems, collection of. See Collection of loyal poems 1935
Loyal songs. See Collection 1890
Loyalty to our king 1608:60
Loyd, Charles. *See* Lloyd, Charles
Lucan, Charles Bingham, Earl of:
  One or more letters. *See* Letters 2576
  See Muses 3222:13
Lucan, Margaret Bingham, Countess of:
  Verses on the present state of Ireland 3222:16
Lucanus, Marcus Annaeus:
  De Bello Civili 2218
  Pharsale 3027
  Pharsalia 1875, 1901, 2246. *See* Brindley 2120:6
  Pharsalia, printed at SH 2515. *See* Strawberry Hill 3469:5
Lucas, Charles:
  Address to the Lord Mayor of Dublin 1609:20
  See Swift 1693; Tracts 99:1
Lucas, Claude. *See* Paris 3578
Lucas, Henry:
  Earl of Somerset 3196
  Poems to Her Majesty 3196
Lucas, Theophilus:
  Memoirs of . . . gamesters and sharpers 1572
Lucian, of Samosata:
  Opera. See Classics 2207:23
  Works 3242
Lucina sine concubitu. See Hill 1608:29
Lucius, pseud. *See* Letters 1609:24
Luckyn, William, 1st Viscount Grimston. *See* Grimston
Lucotte du Tilliot, Jean Bénigne:
  Mémoires . . . de la Fête des Foux 1075
Lucretius Carus, Titus:
  De natura rerum. See Brindley 2120:7
  Della natura delle cose 2104
  Of the nature of things 1831

Ludlow, Edmund:
  Memoirs 1649
Ludlow Castle. *See* Hodges 2874
Lully's Spirit of wine. *See* Weidenfeld 866
Lulworth Castle. *See* Weymouth 2985
Lussan, Marguerite de:
  Anecdotes de la cour de François I 811
  Anecdotes de la cour de Philippe-Auguste 1011
  Annales galantes 812
  Histoire de la Révolution 813
  Histoire de Louis XI 996
  Vie de Louis Balbe Berton de Crillon 1254
  See Baudot 1241
Lust's dominion. See Marlowe 1964
Luther, Martin:
  Contra Henricum Angliae Martinus Luther. See Henry VIII 84
  See Henry VIII 1608:6; Perrin 1079; Woodhead 1635
Luti, Benedetto. *See* Drawings 3567
Luton House. *See* Adam 3597
Lutwidge, Skiffington. *See* Journal 1609:31
Luxborough, Henrietta Knight, Baroness:
  Letters . . . to William Shenstone, Esq. 3896
Luxembourg Gallery. *See* Rubens 3595
Luynes, Duc de. *See* Albert 713
Lydgate, John:
  Copies of limnings 3505
Lyly, John:
  Euphues 2724
  Euphues and his England 1160
Lynde, John. *See* Lind
Lynn, Co. Norfolk. *See* King's Lynn
Lynne, Walter. *See* Carion 831
Lyonnet, Pierre:
  Traité anatomique de la chenille 3750
Lyons. *See* Dominique 1246
Lysias. *See* Gillies 3190
Lysons, Daniel:
  Environs of London 3859
Lysons, Samuel:
  Account of the Roman antiquities 3434
  Views and antiquities 3435
  See Drawings 3641
Lyttelton, Charles, Bishop. *See* Letters 2576 (Foote); Prints 2454
Lyttelton, George, Baron Lyttelton:
  Court secret 1608:91

Lyttelton, George (*cont.*)
Dialogues of the dead 131
History of King Henry II 3173
Letters from a Persian 3926–7
Works 3173
See *Common Sense* 2360; *Ode* 3222:13;
Walpole 3933:2
Lyttelton, Thomas, Baron Lyttelton:
Letters 2899
Poems 3222:17
Speech of Lord Lyttelton 1609:58
See Meredith 1609:32

M. *See Address* 1609:40
M., A.:
Account of a dream at Harwich. See *Detection* 2677:2
M., B. L., Mr. See Bruzen 1290
M., E. See *Wit and drollery* 1994
M., J. See Blount 1608:1; *Guide* 164; Mauduit, Jasper 1609:13
M., M. L. C. See *Mélange* 1045
Mably, Gabriel Bonnot de:
De la manière d'écrire l'histoire 3122
Macartney, George. See MacCartney
Macaulay, Angus:
History of Claybrook 2900
Macaulay, Mrs. Catharine, later Mrs. Graham:
Address to the people 1609:33
History of England from the accession of James I 3197
Loose remarks 1609:17
Modest plea for the property of copy right 1609:58
Observations on a pamphlet 1609:26, 57
Treatise on the immutability of moral truth 3243
See Graham 3222:15
MacBean, William:
Constitution of Germany 1608:23
MacCartney, George:
Letter to a friend 1608:5
Macchiavelli, Niccolo:
Opere 2105
Macclesfield, George Parker, 2d Earl of. See Tracts 2769:14
McDonald, Andrew:
Vimonda 1810:46

Macdonald, Donald, pseud:
Three beautiful and important passages omitted 3222:2
Macé, François:
Histoire des quatres Cicérons 1279
Mace, Thomas:
Musick's monument 1126
MacFarlane, Robert:
History of the reign of George the Third 1609:27
MacGreggor, Malcolm, pseud. See Mason, William
MacGregory, John:
Account of the sepulchers of the antients 698
Mackenzie, George, Earl of Cromarty. See Cromarty
Mackenzie, George, M. D.:
Lives of writers of the Scots nation 444
Mackenzie, Henry:
Prince of Tunis 1810:20
See Lillo 1810:36
Mackerell, Benjamin:
History of King's Lynn 699
Monumental inscriptions 2577
Macklin, Charles:
King Henry the VII 1818:20
Man of the world 1810:53
See *Apology* 1810:21
Macky, John:
View of the Court of St. Germain 1608:10
Maclaine. See Maclean
Maclean, Archibald. See *True* 1608:65
Maclean, James. See Allen 1608:65; Tracts 2146:7; *True* 1608:65
MacNally, Leonard:
Fashionable levities 1810:37
Retaliation 1810:34
Robin Hood 1810:36
Tristram Shandy 1810:35
MacNeill, Hector:
Scotland's Skaith 1357
Macpherson, James:
Fingal 3222:2
Fragments of ancient poetry 3222:2
History of Great Britain 3198
Oithona 1810:12
Original papers 3199

Macpherson, James (*cont.*)
 Temora 3222:4
 See Shaw 1609:42
Macready, William:
 Irishman in London 1810:52
MacSwinny, Owen:
 Pyrrhus and Demetrius. See Plays 1623:1
MacUre, John, called Campbell:
 View of the city of Glasgow 2725
Madaillan de Lesparre, Marquis de Lassay.
 See Lassay 790
Madan, Martin:
 Heroic epistle 3222:17
 Thelyphthora 3244
 See Foote, *Letter* 1810:1
Madden, Samuel:
 Memoirs of the twentieth century 3123
Maddox, Isaac:
 Duty further considered. See Sermons 1346:
 9
 *Duty of encouraging public infirmaries.
 See* Sermons 1346:8
Madox, Thomas:
 Firma Burgi 572
Maetham, Jacobus. *See* Matham
Maffei, Francesco Scipione, Marchese:
 Verona illustrata 2080
Maffei, Paolo Alessandro. *See* Rossi 3628
Magazines 3338, 3436. *See* Miscellaneous
 3445; Tracts 2050
Magdalen College, Oxford. *See* Oxford University. Magdalen College
Magdalen Hospital. *See* England 2241
Magdalens. See Jerningham 3222:4
Maggots. See Wesley 1993
Magic cavern. See Wewitzer 1810:37
Magic girdle. See Carey 3222:10
Magna Britannia. See Cox 621
Magna Charta. *See* Blackstone 232
Magnet 3222:11
Magpie and her brood. See Collection 2508;
 Strawberry Hill 3469:6
Mahomet. *See* Mohammed
Mahon, Charles Stanhope, Viscount. *See*
 Stanhope, Charles, 3d Earl Stanhope
Maid of Kent. See Waldron 1810:28
Maid of the mill. See Bickerstaffe 1810:7
Maid of the oaks. See Burgoyne 1810:22
Maidstone. *See* Newton 634
Mailhol, Gabriel. *See* Contes François 1783:3

Mailly, Chevalier de. *See* Serendip 1237
Mailly, Jean Baptiste:
 Esprit de la Fronde 3124
Maimbourg, Louis:
 *Histoire du pontificat de Saint Leon-le-
 Grand* 1039
Maine, François Grudé de la Croix du. *See*
 La Croix du Maine
Maintenon, Françoise d'Aubigné, Marquise
 de:
 Lettres 942
 Lettres à diverses personnes 1280
 Mémoires 1255
 Two letters. *See* Letters 2576
 See Caraccioli 3077; La Fayette 988:1
Mainwaring, John:
 Memoirs of Handel 1608:36
Mainwaring, Sir Thomas:
 Defence of Amicia 751:1
 Legitimacy of Amicia 751
Mairobert, Mathieu François Pidansat de:
 Anecdotes sur M. la comtesse Du Barri
 3125
 Observateur anglois 3126
 See Journal 3109
Maisoncelle, — de. *See* Bougeant 1178:2
Maitland, Richard, 4th Earl of Lauderdale.
 See Lauderdale
Maitland, Sir Richard. *See* Pinkerton
 2925
Maitland, William:
 History of Edinburgh 604
 History of London 573
Maittaire, Michael:
 *Catalogue of the large and valuable library
 of Michael Mattaire* 344
 *Historia typographorum aliquot Parisien-
 sium* 275, 3339
 Opera et fragmenta 2159
 See Juvenalis 2277; Velleius 2261; Vir-
 gilius 2296
Majesty misled 1810:16
Major, John Henniker. *See* Henniker
Major, Thomas:
 Ruins of Paestum 3542
Makarony fables. See Stevenson 3222:9
Malaga. *See* Carter 2818
Malcolm. See Roberts 1810:35
Maldachini, Olimpia. *See* Northumberland
 174

Malespini, Ricordano:
  Historia antica dall'edificazione de Fio-
  renza 2081, 3340
Malham. *See* Hurtley 2878
Malheurs de l'amour. See Tencin 2295
Mallet, David:
  Elvira 1810:4
  Eurydice 1818:20
  Familiar epistle. See Bolingbroke 1608:13
  Life of Bacon 1713
  Mustapha 1818:20
  Poems 1378
  Two or more letters. *See* Letters 2576
  Works 1876
  See Bolingbroke 3159; *Laurel* 1816; Thom-
  son 1818:8; *Truth* 3222:1
Mallet, Dorothy. *See* Celesia, Dorothea
Mallet, Paul Henri:
  Histoire de Dannemarc 3028
Mallet du Pan, Jacques:
  Danger of the political balance of Europe
  2312
Malone, Edmond:
  Inquiry into Shakespeare 1358
  See Chatterton 3690:16; Shakespeare 1360
Malta. *See* Brydone 2810; Dryden 1609:37
Malta, Knights of. *See* Bosio 435; Vertot
  3055
Malton, Thomas:
  Picturesque tour 3437
  See Antiquities 3485:13
Malvasia, Carlo Cesare:
  Descrizione del Claustro di San Michele
  in Bosco 3624
Malvern. *See* Thomas 708
Malvern Hill. *See* Prospect 3222:15
Malvezzi, Virgilio:
  Romulus and Tarquin 171
Man, Henry:
  Cloacina 3222:14
Man, Isle of. *See* Robertson 3863; Waldron
  139
Man and wife. See Colman 1810:15
Man of family 1810:17
Man of Ross. *See* Tracts 2966:3
Man of taste. See Miller 1818:6
Man of the mill 1810:7
Managers: a comedy 1609:56
Manchester, George Montagu, 4th Duke of:
  Speech . . . against the bill 1609:58

Manchester, Henry Montagu, Earl of:
  Manchester al mondo 172
Manchester. *See* Whitaker 3217
Mandeville, Sir John:
  Voyages and travels 2412
Manfredi, Girolamo di:
  Liber de homine . . . de conservatione sani-
  tatis 2413, 3437
Manifesto. See Castlemaine 155
Manifesto of a certain power. See Tracts 98:1
Manifesto of the Cevennois. See Cevennes
  1608:93
Manley, Mrs. Mary de la Rivière. *See Con-*
  duct 1608:94; *Examiner* 1560; *Secret his-*
  tory 1608:91
Manley, Roger. *See* Turkish spy 1766
Manley, Thomas:
  Lives of Henry Duke of Gloucester and
  Mary Princess of Orange 1573
Mann, Sir Horace:
  Letters 2576
Manners, Charles, 4th Duke of Rutland. *See*
  Rutland
Manners, Charles, Marquess of Granby. *See*
  Granby
Manners, Robert. *See* Pignotti 2921
Manning, Robert:
  Rise and fall of the iconoclasts 3439
Manningham, Sir Richard. *See* Tracts 2146:1
Manpferdt, Jehan Paul Ernest Christian
  Lodovick. *See* Tracts 2050:2
Mansell, William:
  Fairy-Hill 1810:36
Mansfield, William Murray, 1st Earl of:
  The thistle 1608:49
  See King's Bench sermon 1609:28; *Missing*
  1609:28; *Stuart* 2471, 4015
Mantegna, Andrea. *See* Drawings 3568–9;
  Prints 3607; Sigismund 3632
Manual:
  Manuall of devotions 2414
Manuel, King of Portugal. *See* Osorio da
  Fonseca 1419
Map of Europe. *See* Europe 3642
Mar, John Erskine, Earl of:
  Letter 1608:10
Marana, Giovanni Paolo. *See* Turkish spy
  1766
Maratti, Carlo. *See* Drawings 3567–9; Sacchi
  3629

Marbodus, Bishop of Rennes:
  Dactyliotheca 2280
  De lapidibus pretiosis encheridion 2281
Marcellinus, Ammianus. *See* Ammianus
Marcellus and Julia 1609:51
March, Elizabeth. *See* Hervey, Mrs. Elizabeth (March)
Marchant, John:
  History of the present rebellion 3440
Marchetti, Alessandro. *See* Lucretius 2104
Marchetti, Marco. *See* Drawings 3567
Marchmont, Hugh Hume-Campbell, 3d Earl of:
  Present interest of the people 1608:38
  See Reflections 1608:80
Marcus Aurelius, Emperor. *See* Guevara 199, 1323
Margaret of Anjou, Queen of England. *See* Baudier 1608:36
Margat, Jean Baptiste:
  Histoire de Tamerlan 1040
Margery. See Carey 1818:20
Marguerite d'Angoulême [of Navarre]:
  Godly medytacyon of the Christen sowle 204
Marguerite de Valois, Queen of France:
  Mémoires 1041
  Tombeau de Marguerite de Valois 2415
  See Collection 3084
Maria. See Malespini 3340
Maria Maddalena, of Austria. *See* Cosmo 2304
Maria Theresa, Consort of Louis XIV. *See* Louis XIV 3574
Mariage du siècle. See Contant d'Orville 2669
Marian. See Brooke 1810:45
Marianne, Vie de. See Marivaux 997
Mariette, Pierre Jean:
  Description de la statue équestre 3592
  Description des desseins du cabinet de feu M. Crozat 303
  See Basan 3866; Boyer 3562; Vinci 3765
Marin, François Louis Claude:
  Histoire de Saladin 3029
  See Bibliothèque 3001; Richelieu 3044; Stanislaus 3053
Marinda. Poems and translations. See Monck 132
Marine Society, London. *See* King 1609:48

Marino, Giovanni Battista:
  L'Adone, poema 2106
Mariott. *See* Marriott
Marivaux, Pierre Carlet de Chamblain de:
  Paysan parvenu 1228, 1902
  Spectateur françois 1042
  Vie de Marianne 997
  See Colman 1810:44
Markham, Gervase. *See* Bernes 3772
Markham, Sir Griffin. *See* Plays 1082:4
Marlborough, Caroline (Russell) Spencer, Duchess of. *See* Brett 1367:7
Marlborough, George Spencer Churchill, 4th Duke of:
  Gemmarum antiquarum delectus 3625
  See Natter 276
Marlborough, Henrietta Churchill, Viscountess Rialton, Duchess of. *See Black-bird* 2646:24
Marlborough, John Churchill, 1st Duke of:
  Case 1608:9
  See Lediard 1682; *Reasons* 1608:94; Sandford 3282
Marlborough, Sarah Churchill, Duchess of. *See Black-bird* 2646:24; Dalrymple 2676; Hooke 126; *Secret history* 1608:91
Marlborough gems. *See* Marlborough 3625
Marliani, Giovanni Bartolommeo:
  Annales . . . Romanorum 2160
Marlow, William:
  Views in Italy 3441
  Views in London. *See* Antiquities 3485:13
Marlowe, Christopher:
  Lust's dominion 1964
Marmontel, Jean François:
  Les Incas 4011
  See Lucanus 3027
Marolles, Michel de:
  Mémoires 791
  See Temple des muses 3985
Marot, Clément. *See* Psalms 1283
Marot, Jean:
  Recueil des plans . . . des plusieurs palais . . . dans Paris 3751
Marriage of Figaro. See Holcroft 1810:37
Marriage of the Devil 1608:31
Marriot. *See* Marriott
Marriott, —:
  General lover 1818:10

Marriott, George:
Jesuit 3222:13
Marriott, Sir James:
Case of the Dutch ships 1608:87
Poems 1810:3, 1965
Political considerations 1609:5
Marsden, William:
History of Sumatra 2901
Marshall, —:
Catalogue of five hundred living authors 3819
See Holcroft 1810:49
Marshall, Jane:
Sir Harry Gaylove 1810:19
Marshall, William:
Review of the Landscape 3245
See Gardening 2307:2
Marsollier des Vivetières, Benoît Joseph. *See* Berkeley 1810:42
Marston, John:
Workes 1966
Marten, Henry:
Familiar epistles 1608:5
Martialis, Marcus Valerius:
Epigrammata 2219. *See* Classics 2207:24
Epigrammatum libri XV 2176
Epigrams 3341
Tutti gli epigrammi 2107
Martin, Elias:
Prints from his collection of drawings 3506
Martin, Jacques:
Explication de divers monumens 927
Martin, John:
Speech on the repeal of . . . the Test and Corporation Acts 1609:53
Martin, S. *See Letter* 1608:64
Martin, Thomas:
Drawings of antiquities 2578
History of the town of Thetford 2902, 3200
Martinelli, Vincenzio:
Istoria critica 1161
Istoria del governo d'Inghilterra 1161
Lettere familiari et critiche 2127
See Boccaccio 2070
Martini, Josephus:
Theatrum Basilicae Pisanae 3682
Martinique. *See* Guadaloupe
Martyn, Benjamin:
Account of . . . Georgia. See Account 2146:6
Impartial inquiry 1608:40

Martyn, Benjamin (*cont.*)
Timoleon 1817, 1818:2
See Laurel 1816
Martyn, Thomas:
English connoisseur. See Guides 2387:2
Marvell, Andrew:
Short historical essay 1608:93
Works 1967
Marville, pseud. *See* Argonne 1176
Mary, Princess of Orange. *See* Manley 1573
Mary I, Queen of England. *See* Duwes 118; Haynes 441
Mary II, Queen of England. *See* Burnet 1733
Mary, Queen of Scots:
Brief history of the life of Mary Queen of Scots. See Tracts 2146:4
[*Letter vindicating Queen Elizabeth*] 205
See Dalrymple 2676; James II 1331; Robertson 321; St. John 1810:47; Thoresby 2603
Mary de' Medici. *See* Baerle 587; Puget 608
Mary Magdalene, of Austria. *See* Cosmo 2304
Masaccio, Tommaso Guidi, known as. *See* Patch 3594
Masaniello:
Rebellion of Naples 2019
Mascherino, Ottavio. *See* Drawings 3568
Mascou, Johann Jacob:
History of the ancient Germans 1334
Masculus, Joannes Baptista:
Lyricorum sive odarum libri XV 2282
Mason, George:
Essay on design in gardening 2903
See Hoccleve 1327
Mason, William:
Caractacus 1810:26, 2904
Dean and the 'squire 3222:18
Elegies 3222:3
English garden 3222:12
English garden, Book II 3222:14
English garden, Book III 3222:16
English garden, in four books 3222:18, 3897
Epistle to Dr. Shebbeare 3222:16
Essays on English church music 3442
Heroic epistle to Sir William Chambers 3222:12
Heroic postcript to the public 3222:13
Jardin anglois 3127
Musaeus. See Poems 3363:3
Occasional discourse. See Collins 3888:1
Ode to Mr. Pinchbeck 3222:14

Mason, William (*cont.*)
   Ode to the Honourable William Pitt 3222:18
   Ode to the naval officers 3222:16
   One letter. *See* Letters 2576
   Poems 1619
   Pro-Pinchbeck's answer 3222:14
   Satirical poems 1619
   Secular ode. See Collins 3888:2
   See Du Fresnoy 3890; Gray 3841, 3892; *Kien Long* 3222:13; Poems 1835:6; Whitehead 2986
Masquerade 3222:9
Masquerader:
   C[ourt] and country 2416
Massachusetts:
   Letters to the Right Honourable the Earl of Hillsborough 1609:23
   See Bernard 1609:25; Boston 1609:26; Hollis 1609:21; Mauduit 1609:31; Tracts 2966
Massacre of Glencoe. *See* Ridpath 1609:38
Massenello. *See* Masaniello 2019
Massey, Edmund:
   Signs of the times. See Miscellaneous tracts 89:1
Massey, William:
   Origin and progress of letters 304
Massillon, Jean Baptiste:
   Mémoires de la minorité de Louis XV 2313
Massinello. *See* Masaniello 2019
Massingberd, Henry:
   Counsell 1335
Master of Arts. *See* Hill 1609:21
Master of Arts. *See* King 1608:61
Masters, Mary. *See Poems* 175
Masters, Robert:
   History of the College of Corpus Christi . . . in the University of Cambridge 632
   Memoirs . . . of Thomas Baker 3820
Match for a widow. See Atkinson 1810:44
Matham, Jacobus. *See* Prints 3606
Mathew, Francis:
   Passage between Lynn and Yarmouth 1336
Mathews, Thomas:
   Account of the action 1608:39
   Charge 1608:53
Mathews, Sir Tobie. *See* Matthew
Mathias, Thomas James. *See* Chatterton 3690:12

Matilda. *See* Francklin 1810:23
Matinées royales. See Frederick 3960
Matrimonial overtures 3222:16
Mattei, Domenico Barnaba:
   Memorie istoriche dell' antico Tuscolo oggi Frascati 483
Matteis, Paolo de. *See* Shaftesbury 1496
Matthew, Sir Tobie:
   Collection of letters 1441
Matthews, Thomas. *See* Mathews
Matthias, Emperor of Germany:
   Actus electionis 1043
Maty, Matthew:
   Authentic memoirs of R. Mead 1608:78
   One or more letters. *See* Letters 2576
   See Chesterfield 3915; Coyer 3085
Maubert de Gouvest, Jean Henri. *See* Walpole 2323
Mauclerc, John Henry:
   Power of imagination 1608:31
Mauclerc, Julian:
   New treatise of architecture 223
Maude, Thomas:
   Wensley-Dale 3222:12
Mauduit, Israel:
   Case of the Dissenting ministers 1609:29
   Considerations on the present German war 1609:1
   Letters of Governor Hutchinson 1609:31, 34
   Occasional thoughts 1609:1
Mauduit, Jasper:
   Legislative authority of the British Parliament 1609:13
Mauger, Claude:
   Grammaire angloise et françoise 1229
Maunsell, Andrew:
   Catalogue of English printed bookes 511
Maunsell, Dora. *See* Tenducci, Dora M.
Maupeou, René Nicolas Charles Augustin de. *See Journal* 3109
Maurice, Thomas:
   Hagley 3222:14
   Netherby 3222:14
Mauritius. *See* Saint-Pierre 3048
Mauvillon, Éléazar de:
   Histoire de la dernière guerre de Bohême 1162

GENERAL INDEX

Mavor, William Fordyce:
Blenheim 3222:21
Mawson, Richard:
Genealogy of the family of Cotton 2579
Maximilian I, Emperor of Germany. *See* Prints 3656
Maxims, characters and reflections. See Greville 2009
May, Thomas:
Tragedy of Cleopatra 1968
Tragedy of Julia Agrippina 1968
Victorious reigne of King Edward the Third 1969
See Lucanus 1901
May-Day. See Garrick 1810:24
Mayer, Charles Joseph. *See Cabinet* 3074
Maynard, Nancy Parsons, Viscountess. *See Epistle* 3222:9
Maynwaring, Arthur:
Life and posthumous works 1685
See Medleys 1487
Mazarin, Ortensia de la Porte, Duchesse de:
Mémoires 1044
Mazell, Peter. *See* Cordiner 3840
Mazière de Monville, Simon Philippe:
Vie de Pierre Mignard 998
Mazot, F. *See* Prints 3653
Mazzuoli, Francesco. *See* Drawings 3568
Mead, Richard:
Museum Meadianum 3785
See Freind 1406, 1608:50; Maty 1608:78; Miscellaneous tracts 89:1; Stukeley 668:2; Woodward 1608:48
Measures of the late administration 1608:49
Méchel, Chrétien de:
Catalogue des tableaux 2417
See Hedlinger 453; Holbein 3716; Pigage 3513
Mecheln, Israel van. *See* Prints 3607
Medallic history of England. See Pinkerton 3702
Medici, Alexander de'. *See* Ceccheregli 2121
Medici, Cosimo de'. *See* Cosmo 2304
Medici, Francesco de'. *See* Gualterotti 3781
Medici, Giovanni de'. *See* Mossi 2108
Medici, Lorenzo de':
Poesie 3821
See Grazzini 3320; Roscoe 3703
Medici, Marie de'. *See* Baerle 587; Puget 608

Medici family:
Secret history of the House of Medici 3720
See Allegrini 3584; Boissat 1244; Galluzzi 3097; Noble 416
Medland, Thomas. *See* Antiquities 3485:3
Medleys for the year 1711 1487
Medway, River. *See* Ireland 3857:3
Mehus, Laurentius. *See* Bruni 2071
Meilan, Mark Anthony:
Dramatic works 1810:17
Meilcour, — de. *See* Crébillon 1026
Meilhan, Gabriel Sénac de. *See* Sénac 3049
Mein, John. *See* Knox 1609:22
Mélange de pièces fugitives 1045
Mélanges d'histoire et de littérature. See Argonne 1176
Mélanges de littérature. See Alembert 799
Mélanges historiques. See Labrune 1198
Melcombe, George Bubb Dodington, Lord. *See* Dodington
Melcombe Regis. *See* Weymouth 2985
Melfort, John Drummond, 1st Earl of:
Some account 1609:10
Melinda. *See Adventures of Melinda*
Melissa and Marcia 2314
Melissus, Paulus:
Melissi Meletematum priorum libri VIII 2283
Melmoth, Courtney, pseud. *See* Pratt, Samuel Jackson
Melmoth, William:
Letters 1442
See Cicero 1399, 1432; Pliny 1446
Member of Parliament. *See* Conduct 1609:3; Hay 1608:48; *Letter* 1608:80, 82; Meredith 1609:23; *Reflections* 1608:80; Worms 1608:44
Member of the House of Commons. *See* Political tracts 94:2
Member of the Royal Society. *See* Burrow 1609:6
Member of the Society of Lincoln's Inn. *See* Brecknock 1609:7
Member of the University of Cambridge. *See* Cumberland 1609:18
Mémoire historique sur la negotiation. See Choiseul-Stanville 1609:54
Mémoires de la minorité de Louis XIV. See La Rochefoucauld 991

Mémoires de M. de ***. See Colbert 1272

Mémoires de Versorand. See Versorand 1208

Mémoires du règne de George I. See George I 1296

Mémoires historiques. See Collection 3084

Mémoires historiques, critiques, et anecdotes de France 1303

Mémoires politiques et militaires. See Millot 3130

Mémoires pour servir à l'histoire d'Espagne. See Bacallar 1266

Mémoires pour servir à l'histoire de la Maison de Brandebourg. See Frederick II 1140

Mémoires pour servir à l'histoire des révolutions. See Irailh 3019

Mémoires pour servir de suite aux 'Considerations.' See Duclos 3092

Mémoires secrets pour servir à l'histoire de la république des lettres 3030, 3128. *See* Memoirs 2315

Mémoires secrets tirés des archives. See Siri 3052

Mémoires sur la vie de Jean Racine. See Racine 969

Mémoires sur la vie de Loyse Juliane, Electrice Palatine. See Spanheim 3467

Memoirs 2315

Memoirs, British and foreign. See Le Neve 748

Memoirs concerning the affairs of Scotland. See Lockhart 1712

Memoirs for the curious. See Monthly Miscellany 853

Memoirs of a cavalier. See Defoe 1704

Memoirs of affairs of state. See Cole 869

Memoirs of an English missionary. See Thompson 1609:51

Memoirs of another unhappy old gentlewoman 1608:63

Memoirs of Father Richard Walpole. See Tracts 2050

Memoirs . . . of . . . persons who died in 1711. See Le Neve 748

Memoirs of publick transactions. See Defoe 1608:14

Memoirs of several ladies of Great Britain. See Amory 1054

Memoirs of the antiquities of Great Britain 752

Memoirs of the Court of Portugal 1609:18

Memoirs of the Dutch War. See Carleton 1352

Memoirs of the House of Hanover. See Hanover 1608:9

Memoirs of the life and ministerial conduct of Visc. Bolingbroke 52

Memoirs of the life and writings of Joseph Addison. See Jacob 1608:5

Memoirs of the life of Agostino Steffani. See Tracts 2968:2

Memoirs of the life of John Lord Somers. See Somers 1608:14

Memoirs of the life of Lord Lovat 1608:54

Memoirs of the life of the late George Frederic Handel. See Mainwaring 1608:36

Memoirs of the life of Thomas late Marquess of Wharton 1608:20

Memoirs of the revolution in Bengal. See Bengal 1609:2, 2642

Memoirs of the twentieth century. See Madden 3123

Memoirs of Thomas Hollis. See Blackburne 3688

Memoirs relating to the impeachment of Thomas Earl of Danby. See Danby 117

Memorial most humbly addressed to the sovereigns of Europe. See Pownall 1609:41

Memorial of the Chevalier de St. George. See James Edward Francis Stuart 1608:10

Memorial of the Church of England. See Miscellaneous tracts 89:2

Memorial sent from London to the Abbot Vertot. See Miscellaneous tracts 89:1

Memorial to the King. See Tracts 99:2

Memorials and characters. See Wilford 9

Memorials of the British consul and factory at Lisbon. See England 1609:15

Memorie degli intagliatori moderni. See Giulianelli 268

Memorie historiche dell' apparitione delle Croci prodigiose. See Calà 2072

Men-miracles. See Llewellyn 1956

Ménage, Gilles:
Ménagiana 999

Ménard, Claude:
Histoire de messire Bertrand du Guesclin 1076

Menart, pseud. *See* Hermant 1276

Mendes da Costa, Jacob:
Proceedings at large in the Arches Court 382

Mendez, Jael, later Mrs. Pye. *See* Pye

Mendez, Moses:
Robin Hood 1818:10

Menestrier, Claude François:
Traité des tournois 928, 1077
See Bartoli 3598

Mennes, Sir John:
Musarum deliciae 1970
See Wit 1994

Mensaërt, Guillaume Pierre:
Le peintre amateur et curieux 345, 3443

Mensonges imprimez. See Voltaire 1608:76

Mentet, Robert:
History of the troubles of Great Britain 1127

Merchant. *See* Clement 1608:8

Merchant in London. *See* Tucker 1609:13

Merchant of London. *See True interest* 1609: 13

Merchants. *See Protest* 1608:58

Merchants, Committee of London. *See* London Merchants

Mercier, Louis Sébastien:
Mon bonnet de nuit 3031
Tableau de Paris 3031
See Distressed family 1810:42; Inchbald 1810:50

Mercurius Politicus 2726

Mercurius Rusticus. See Ryves 1762

Meredith, Sir William:
Letter to the Earl of Chatham 1609:32
Question stated 1609:23
Reply to the Defence of the majority 1609: 9

Meres, Francis:
Palladis Tamia 1755

Meretriciad. See Thompson 3222:1

Mergey, Jean de. *See Collection* 3084

Merian, Matthew. *See* Holbein 3717

Merle, Mathieu. *See Collection* 3084

Merlin. *See Catastrophe* 2352; Heywood 1599; *Prophecy* 1609:5

Mermaid. See Franklin 1810:51

Merret, Christopher. *See Tracts* 361:2

Merrick, John:
Observationum medicinalium fasciculus 1609:55

Merry, Robert:
Diversity 3222:22
Fenelon 1810:57

Merry, Robert (*cont.*)
Lorenzo 1810:49
See Arno Miscellany 3803; *Florence Miscellany* 3810; Gianetti 4006; Pignotti 2921; Seward 3207

Merveilles de la ville de Rome. See Arts 288:1

Metamorphoses. See Ovidius

Metaphysics, treatise on. *See* Boehm

Metastasio, Pietro Antonio Domenico Bonaventura:
Opere 3342
Siroes. See Plays 1908:5
See Burney 2811; Murphy 1818:18; *Music* 3448

Methodism. *See* Hill 1609:21

A Methodist. *See* Wesley 1608:19

The Methodist. See Pottinger 1810:1

Methodist and mimick. See Adair 3222:7

Methodists. *See* Cruttenden 1608:74

Mexia, Pedro:
Treasurie of auncient and moderne times 2059. *See* Bristol 2533

Mexico. *See* Scawen 1810:47; Solis 3283

Mexio, Pedro. *See* Mexia

Meyssens, Joannes:
True effigies 3649

Michael Angelo. *See* Buonarroti

Mickle, William Julius:
Almada Hill 3222:18
Poems, and a tragedy 555
Pollio 3222:7

Microphilus:
New-yeeres gift 2418

Micyllus. *See* Mycillus

Midas. See O'Hara 1810:6, 47

Middiman, Samuel:
Select views in Great Britain 3507

Middle Temple, London:
Catalogus librorum bibliothecae 484

Middlesex, Charles Sackville, Earl of. *See* Dorset, Earl

Middlesex, Charles Sackville, Earl of, later 2d Duke of Dorset. *See* Dorset 1608:27, 48

Middlesex. *See* Bowack 560; Norden 663; Warburton 2979

Middlesex Election:
Collection of papers 1608:69
See Dyson 1609:57; *Essay* 1609:25

Middlesex. Grand Jury. *See* Grand Jury

Middleton, Conyers:
Defence of the letter to Dr. Waterland. See
Middleton 1379:1
History of the life of Cicero 315
Letter from Rome 1574
Letter to Dr. Waterland. See Middleton
1379:1
Miscellaneous works 316
On the origin of printing. See Printing
3459
Popery unmask'd 1574
Tracts and replies 1337
Tracts, with the answers 1379
See Church 1370; Cibber 451; Cicero 2666;
Dodwell 1372; Hervey 3168; *Military* 1608:
19; Sherlock 1422; Tunstall 1424
Middleton, Thomas:
Civitatis amor 1082:1
Tragi-coomodie called The Witch 2419
Midgley, Robert. *See* Turkish Spy 1766
Midnight hour. See Inchbald 1810:42
Midsummer night's dream. See Garrick 1810:
5
Miège, Guy:
Relation of three embassies 1532
Miel, Jan. *See* Castellamonte 3676
Mignard, Pierre, Vie de. See Mazière 998
Mignot, Vincent:
*Histoire de Jeanne première, Reine de
Naples* 3129
*Histoire des Rois Catholiques Ferdinand et
Isabelle* 3032
Mil sept cent quarante huit 1608:31
Milan. *See* Barbuo 3732; Grazioli 3744
Milbourne, Luke:
Notes on Dryden's Virgil 1533
Mildenhall, a poem. See Tracts 2968:6
Miles, William Augustus:
Artifice 1810:32
Military and other poems 1832
Military dictionary 1608:68
Military prophet's apology 1608:19
Millar, Andrew:
Question concerning literary property
1609:58
Millennium Hall. *See* Scott 2469
Miller, Anne, Lady:
Poetical amusements at a villa near Bath
415, 2420
See Bull 3222:18

Miller, Charles:
Verses to Lady Horatia Waldegrave. *See*
Collection 2508; Strawberry Hill 3469:7
Miller, James:
Humours of Oxford 1818:2
Man of taste 1818:6
Of politeness. See Rival wives 2463
Universal passion 1818:6
Miller, Philip:
Gardener's dictionary 1096
Gardener's kalendar 1488
Milles, Jeremiah. *See* Baynes 3222:18; Chatterton 3690:1
Milles, Thomas:
Catalogue of honor 605
See Mexia 2059
Millin, Aubin Louis:
Antiquités nationales 3721
Millot, Claude François Xavier:
Mémoires politiques et militaires 3130
See La Curne 3113
Milton, John:
Areopagitica. See Printing 3459
History of Britain 1338
Letters of state 1534
Paradise lost 224, 1833, 2421. *See* Richardson 1838
Paradise lost and Paradise regained
2197
Plates to *Paradise Lost. See* Antiquities
3485:15
Poems upon several occasions 2905
Poetical works 317, 1833
Tractate of Education 1833
See Blount 1608:1; Colman 1810:19; Nickolls 1097; Peck 467; Toland 1694
Milton, Thomas:
Collection of select views of Ireland 3508
Milward, Edward:
Trallianus reviviscens 3444
Miniature picture. See Craven 1810:33,
2363
Minister of state 3222:3
The minor. See Foote 1810:1
Minor poets. See Works of celebrated authors
1864; *Works of minor poets* 184
Minorca. *See* Armstrong 672; *Voice* 1608:81
The minstrel. See Beattie 3222:11
Minucius Felix, Marcus:
Octavius. See Classics 2207:25

Mirabeau, Honoré Gabriel Riquetti, Comte de:
  Ami des hommes 792
  Des lettres de cachet. See Mercier 3031
  Histoire secrète de la cour de Berlin 3343
Miracle plays. *See* York 2628
Miremont, Anne d'Aubourg de la Bove, Comtesse de:
  Traité de l'éducation des femmes 2284
The mirror. See Dibdin 1810:31
Mirror for magistrates 88
Mirtil. *See Loves of Mirtil* 381
Miscellanea sacra. See Barrington 107
Miscellaneous 3445–6
Miscellaneous:
  Letters, documents, and papers. See Letters 2576 (*ad finem*)
Miscellaneous letters. See Vernon 1497
Miscellaneous pieces. See Jenyns 1793
Miscellaneous poems. *See* Poems 280
Miscellaneous reflections upon the peace 1608:58
Miscellaneous thoughts on . . . foreign and domestic affairs. See Hervey 1608:90
Miscellaneous tracts 89
Miscellaneous views of the coins. See Snelling 243:2
Miscellaneous volumes 943
Miscellanies. *See* Miscellaneous tracts 89
Miscellanies historical and philological. See Halifax 2010
Miscellanies in prose and verse. See Whartoniana 183
Miscellanies in prose and verse by a person of quality. See Suffolk 57
Miscellanies on ancient and modern gardening. See Gardening 3891:3
Miscellany poems. See Dryden 1825; Winchilsea 61
Miss in her teens. See Garrick 1818:19
Miss Lucy in town. See Fielding 1818:20
Missal:
  Beatae Mariae Virginis officium 2422
  Book of hours 2423–6, 3786
  Psalter 2427, 3786:2
  See Gough 3812
Missing, John:
  Letter to the Right Honourable William Lord Mansfield 1609:28

Misson, François Maximilien:
  Memoirs 1416
  Nouveau voyage d'Italie 1230
The mistakes. See Cornbury 2362
Mr. Garrick's conduct considered 1818:9
Mr. Hobb's State of nature considered in a dialogue. See Eachard 1516
Mist's Weekly Journal 2144. *See Fog's* 2141
Mitchell, Joseph. *See* Waldron 1810:54
Mob in the pit 3222:13
Moderator. *See* Tracts 2475:14
Modern anecdote. See Craven 2364
Modern bill of fare for seven. See Tracts 2146:6
Modern quality. See Poems 280:11
Modern virtue. See Poems 3363:15
Modest and impartial reply. See Egmont 119:2
Modest apology for Parson Alberoni. See Tracts 2050:5
Modest apology for the prevailing practice of adultery. See Rutland 1609:31
Modest remarks upon the Bishop of London's letter 1608:19
Modish wife. See Gentleman 1810:27
Modius salium. See Pope 1912:3
Moetjens, Adriaan. *See* Estrades 1216
Moeurs. See Toussaint 2050:23
Mohammed. *See* Koran; Prideaux 1719
Mohun, Charles, Baron Mohun. *See* MacCartney 1608:5
Moir, John:
  History of Charles James Fox 3131
Moivre, Abraham de:
  Doctrine of chances 1620
Molé, Guillaume François Roger:
  Histoire des modes françaises 3344
Molesworth, Robert, 1st Viscount Molesworth. *See* Shaftesbury 1608:5
Molière, Jean Baptiste Poquelin de:
  Oeuvres 944
  [One volume unidentified] 3345
  Select comedies 1796
  See Bickerstaffe 1810:13, 14; *Hour* 1810:18; Miller 1818:6
Molinet, Claude du. *See* Du Molinet
  Geographia antiqua 2428
Molloy, Charles. *See Common sense* 2360
Moll, Herman:
Moltzer, Jacob. *See* Gerbelius 337

Momus, a poem 3222:8

Momus turn'd fabulist. See Fuzelier 1818:3

Monarchie des solipses. See Inchofer 1221

Monasteries, Pictures from suppressed. *See* Catalogues 2303:1

Monasticon Hibernicum, or, the monastical history of Ireland. See Stevens 707

Monck, George, Duke of Albemarle. *See* Albemarle

Monck, Hon. Mary:
   Marinda. Poems and translations 132

Moncornet, Balthazar. *See* Prints 3626, 3655

Moncreiff, John:
   Appius 1818:14

Moncrif, François Augustin Paradis de:
   Les chats 753

Le Monde. See World 2502

Monier, Pierre:
   History of painting, sculpture, architecture, graving. See Tracts 359:2

Monitor. See Tracts 2968:8

Monitory hints to the minister 1609:44

Monk, George, Duke of Albemarle. *See* Albemarle

Monk, Martha (Richardson) Fleetwood:
   Letter to the Rev. Mr. Madan 1609:19

The monk. See Wollstonecraft 3177

Monkeys 3884

Monkhouse, Thomas. *See* Clarendon 426

Monmouth, Henry Carey, Earl of. *See* Bentivoglio 2644, 3290; Biondi 3158; Boccalini 3293; Malvezzi 171; Paruta 3360; Senault 178

Monmouth, Robert Carey, Earl of:
   Memoirs 133

Monmouthshire. *See* Rogers 760; Williams 3218; Wyndham 3481

Monnoye, Bernard de la. *See* La Monnoye

Monod, Joel Gaspard. *See World* 2502

Monosyllable If. See Poems 881:21

Monro, Alexander:
   Observations on the structure and functions of the nervous system 225
   Works 3246

Monro, Thomas. *See* Alciphron 2996; *Philoctetes* 1810:57

Monroe, John. *See* Crockat

Monsey, Messenger:
   Sketch of the life . . . of the late Dr. Monsey 1609:53

Montagu, Lady Barbara. *See* Scott 2469

Montagu, Charles, Earl of Halifax. *See* Halifax

Montagu, Sir Charles:
   One or more letters. *See* Letters 2576

Montagu, Edward, 1st Earl of Sandwich. *See* Sandwich

Montagu, Edward Wortley:
   Observations upon a supposed antique bust at Turin 1609:56
   Reflections 2727
   See Payba 1608:65, 73

Montagu, Lady Elizabeth, later Duchess of Buccleugh. *See* Etchings 3588

Montagu, Elizabeth (Robinson):
   Essay on the writings and genius of Shakespear 1609:23
   See Pignotti 2921

Montagu, George, Duke of Manchester. *See* Manchester

Montagu, Henry, Earl of Manchester. *See* Manchester

Montagu, James, Bishop. *See* James I 20

Montagu, John, 4th Earl of Sandwich. *See* Sandwich

Montagu, Magdalena Browne, Viscountess. *See* Smith 2294

Montagu, Mary Churchill, Duchess of. *See Black-bird* 2646:24

Montagu, Lady Mary Wortley:
   Genuine copy of a letter 1608:8
   Letters 814
   Six town eclogues. See Poems 3363:2
   See Thicknesse 1609:14

Montagu, Walter:
   Shepheard's paradise. See Howard 1872

Montagu-Dunk, George, Earl of Halifax. *See* Halifax

Montaigne, Michel de:
   Essais 880
   Journal du voyage 880

Montalte, Louis de. *See* Pascal 1000

Montausier, Charles de Sainte-Maure, Duc de:
   Guirlande de Julie. See La Vallière 3336; *Le Petit* 1226

Montcalm, Louis Joseph de, Marquis de Saint-Véran. *See* Roubaud 1609:38

Monteage, Stephen:
   Debtor and creditor made easie 2720

Monteith, Robert. *See* Mentet 1127
Montelatici, Domenico:
  Villa Borghese 2316
Montenoy, Charles Palissot de:
  Homme dangereux 3447
  See Coyer 3085; Pope 3040
Montesquieu, Charles Louis de Secondat, Baron de:
  De l'esprit des loix 1163
  Lettres familières 2285
  Lettres persanes 1256
  Oeuvres 1621
  Persian letters 1443
  Reflections 1535
Montfaucon, Bernard de:
  Royal and ecclesiastical antiquities 3683
Montfaucon de Villars, Nicolas Pierre Henri:
  Count of Gabalis 1756
Montgomerie, Alexander, Earl of Eglinton. *See* Eglinton
Monthly Miscellany 853
Month's tour in North Wales. See Wales 2976
Montluc, Blaise de Lasseran Massencome, Seigneur de:
  Commentaries 903
  See Collection 3084
Montmaur, Pierre de. *See* Sallengre 2466
Montmorency, Henry, Duc de. *See* Du Cros 921
Montmorency, House of. *See* Du Chesne 896; Ripault 794
Montpensier, Anne Marie Louisa d'Orléans, Duchesse de:
  Divers portraits 4012
  Mémoires 1012
Montpleinchamp, Jean Chrysostome Bruslé de. *See* Bruslé 1212
Montrose, James Graham, 1st Marquess of. *See* Mentet 1127; Wishart 1770
Monument du costume. See Wouwerman 3992
Monvel, Jacques Marie Boutet de. *See* Boutet 3295
Monville, Simon Philippe Mazière de. *See* Mazière de Monville
Moor, James:
  Essays 1797
Moore, Edward:
  Fables for the female sex 1834

Moore, Edward (*cont.*)
  Foundling 1818:9
  Gamester 1818:12
  Gil Blas 1818:9
  Poems, fables, and plays 456
  See Gay 1827; *World* 911, 2501
Moore, James:
  Monastic remains 3843
Moore, John:
  View of society and manners in Italy 2906
Moore, Sir John Henry:
  Poetical trifles 2907
Moore, Sir Jonas:
  England's interest 1536
Moore, Joseph. *See* Ordinary 1609:56
Moore, Sir Thomas. *See* More
Moral and political dialogues. See Hurd 1439
Moralities: or, essays. See Spence 1608:79
Morande, Charles Théveneau de:
  Gazetier cuirassé 3033
  See Mairobert 3125
Morant, Philip:
  History ... of ... Colchester 606
  History of Essex 22
  See Biographia Britannica 2041; Essex 3418; Pine 3552 Mordaunt, Charles, 3d Earl of Peterborough. *See* Peterborough
Moravians. *See* United Brethren
Morbus Gallicus. See Hill 787
Mordington, George Douglas, 4th Baron:
  Great blessing of a monarchical government 134
More, Cresacre:
  Life and death of Sr. Thomas Moore 2429
More, Hannah:
  Bas bleu 3222:20, 3898
  Bishop Bonner's Ghost 2430. *See* Strawberry Hill 3469:8; Tracts 2968:7
  Essays on various subjects 346
  Florio 3222:20, 3898
  Inflexible captive 1810:22
  Ode to Dragon 3222:15
  Percy 1810:27
  Remarks 3969
  Sacred dramas 1856
  Search after happiness 1810:20
  Sensibility 1856
  Sir Eldred of the Bower 3222:14
  Slavery 3222:22

More, Sir Thomas, Saint:
  History of . . . Edward the Fifth 2247
  See More, Cresacre 2429; Tracts 3986
Moreau, Jacob Nicolas:
  Lettres historiques 3034
Moreau, Jean Michel:
  Monument du Costume. See Wouwerman 3992
Morel, André:
  Specimen universae rei nummariae antiquae 305
  Thesaurus Morellianus 226
Morel, Claude. *See* Le Feron 546
Morell, Sir Charles. *See* Ridley 392
Morellet, Abbé André:
  Portrait de Madame Geoffrin. See Tracts 2050:6
  See Beccaria 3066
Moréri, Louis. *See* Collier 3272
Mores, Edward Rowe:
  Dissertation upon English typographical founders 2908
Morgan, John:
  History of the . . . States of Barbary 1417
Morgan, Macnamara:
  Philoclea 1818:13
Morgan, Sylvanus:
  Armilogia 661
  Sphere of gentry 633
Morgan, Thomas:
  Various tracts 1608:12
Morgan, William. *See* Ogilby 1577
Morins, Richard de. *See* Hearne 656
Mornay, Philippe de:
  La vie 1078
Morocco, Kingdom of. *See* Torres 863
Morres, Hervey Redmond, Viscount Mountmorres. *See* Mountmorres
Morrice, John:
  Scriptural oration 2580
Morris, Corbyn:
  Letter balancing the causes 1608:83
  Various tracts 1608:41
Morris, Edward:
  Adventurers 1810:48
  False colours 1810:52
Morris, Matthew Robinson, Baron Rokeby. *See* Rokeby
Morris, Robert, of Twickenham:
  Rural architecture 3752

Morris, Robert (1744?–1793):
  Letter to Sir Richard Aston 1609:28
Morrison, Thomas. *See Pindarick ode* 3222:9
Mortimer, Thomas:
  Remarkable case of Thomas Mortimer 1609:26
Morton, Dr. *See College exercise* 1609:23
Morton, John:
  Natural history of Northamptonshire 574
Morton, Thomas:
  Columbus 1810:50
  Zorinski 1810:57
Moryson, Fynes:
  Itinerary 904
Mosaics. *See* Fowler 3421
Moseley, Richard. *See Impartial enquiry* 1379:6
Moses. *See* Warburton 1425
Moss, Theophilus, pseud. *See* Marriott 1818: 10
Mossi, Antonio:
  Compendio della vita del Sig. Giovanni de' Medici 2108
Mossom, Robert:
  King on his throne. See Sermons 2757:6
Most important transactions of the sixth session. See Tracts 2146:1
Most proper reply. See Sherwin 1608:30
Most wonderful wonder. See Tracts 3796:3
'The motion.' *See* Bunbury 3563:3
Motion . . . concerning the settlement of the Church. See England 2769:2
Motteux, Pierre Antoine:
  Temple of love. See Plays 1623:1
  Thamyris. See Plays 1623:1
Mottley, John:
  Antiochus. See Plays 1909:5
  See Coffey 1818:5
Mouffle d'Angerville. *See Journal* 3109
Mountain, D. *See* Hill 374
Mounteney, Richard:
  Dedication of . . . Demosthenes 1608:66
  Observations 1608:56
Mountfort, William. *See* Hatchett 1810:4
Mountmorres, Hervey Redmond Morres, 2d Viscount:
  Impartial reflections 1609:47A
  Letters of Themistocles 3822
  Principal transactions of the Irish Parliament from 1634 to 1666 2909

Mountmorres, Viscount (*cont.*)
 The prodigal. See Tracts 2050:7
 See Mallet 2312
Moxon, Joseph:
 Mechanick exercises 1339
Moyreau, Jean. *See* Wouwerman 3992
Moysie, David:
 Memoirs of the affairs of Scotland 1714
Mueller, Jan. *See* Müller
Muentz, John Henry. *See* Müntz
Muhammad. *See* Turkish spy 1766
Muhammad Ali Khan, Nabob of Arcot. *See*
 Original papers 1609:47A
Muley Hamet. *See* Sherley 3828
Mulgrave, Constantine John Phipps, 2d
 Baron. *See Journal* 1609:31
Mulgrave, John Sheffield, Earl of. *See* Buck-
 ingham, Duke of
Mulinari, Stefano. *See* Florence 3570
Müller, Jan. *See* Prints 3606
Mumford, Erasmus:
 Letter to the Club 1608:61
Mundy, Francis Noel Clarke:
 Needwood forest 3222:22
Munro, Alexander. *See* Monro, Alexander
Munro, John. *See* Monroe
Munster, Ireland:
 Address from the independent freeholders
 1608:61
Munster, Treaty of. *See* Prints 3656; Van
 Hulle 3580, 3661
Müntz, John Henry:
 Encaustic 347
 Portfolio of views 3575
 See Engravings 3417; Prints 3460; Walpole
 3582
Muralt, Béat Louis de:
 Letters 1444
Murdin, William. *See* Haynes 441
Murner, Thomas:
 Nebulo nebulonum 754
Murphy, Arthur:
 All in the wrong 1810:2
 Alzuma 1810:19
 Apprentice 1818:14
 Citizen 1810:4
 Desert island 1818:18
 Examiner 3222:1
 Grecian daughter 1810:18
 Know your own mind 1810:28

Murphy, Arthur (*cont.*)
 No one's enemy but his own 1810:5
 Ode to the Naiads of Fleet-Ditch 3222:1
 Old maid 1810:2
 Orphan of China 1818:17
 Rival sisters 1810:52
 School for guardians 1810:10
 Upholsterer 1818:16
 Way to keep him 1810:1, 1818:18
 What we must all come to 1810:5
 Zenobia 1810:12
 See Francis 1609:54; Tracts 2968:8
Murphy, James Cavanah:
 *Plans . . . of the Church of Batalha in
 Portugal* 3650
 Travels in Portugal 2910, 3247
Murray, Lord George. *See* Culloden 1608:32
Murray, Richard:
 Alethia 1575
Murray, William, 1st Earl of Mansfield. *See*
 Mansfield
Musae Etonenses. See Eton College 2191,
 2847
Musaeum hermeticum. See Lenglet du Fres-
 noy 1191
Musaeum Minervae. *See* Kynaston 3817
Musaeus. See Poems 3363:3
Musarum deliciae. See Mennes 1970
Musarum deliciae. See Suffolk 209
Museo Piccolomini. *See* Piccolomini 3757
*Muses and graces on a visit to Grosvenor
 Square* 3222:13
Muses en belle humeur 1201
Muses library 90
Muse's recreation. See Mennes 1970
Museum 2431
Museum Florentinum. See Gori 431
Musgrave, Samuel:
 Reply to a letter. See Tracts 2966:4
Musgrave, William (*d.* 1721), antiquary:
 Geta Britannicus 2729
Musgrave, William (*fl.* 1732):
 *Genuine memoirs of the life and character
 of Sir Robert Walpole* 2432
Music 3448
Musical lady. See Colman 1810:3
Musical travels through England. See Veal
 1609:32
Mustapha. See Mallet 1818:20
Mutiny Bill. *See* Seasonable 1608:27

Mutual deception. See Atkinson 1810:38

Mutual interest of Great Britain and the American colonies. See Bollan 1609:56

Mycillus. *See* Gerbelius 337

Myrrour for magistrates. See Mirror 88

Mysterious congress 1608:26, 44

Mysterious mother. See Lassay 790; Walpole 2490–1, 2528, 3469:15, 16

Mytens, Joannes. *See* Meyssens 3649

N., I. *See* Royal Academy 3885:6

N., N. *See* Cogan 722; Dickinson 1609:22

N., S. *See Plagiairiana* 3039; Shaftesbury 1764

Nabbes, Thomas:
  Playes 1600

Nadanyi, Joannes:
  Florus Hungaricus 2128

Nalson, John:
  Impartial collection of the great affairs of state 3346

Names of the knights. See England 1608:1

Names of the members of Parliament. See England 1608:1

Nandakumara, Maharaja. *See* Nundocomar

Nanni, Giovanni. *See* Drawings 3567

Napier, Archibald, 1st Baron Napier:
  Memoirs 3201

Naples:
  Reale Accademia della Scienze: *Istoria de' fenomeni* 3509
  Reale Accademia Ercolanese di Archeologia. *See* Herculaneum 3590
  See Bacco 3731; Des Noulis 918; Du Moulin 897; Giannone 2078; Hamilton 3498; Vergara 256

Nares, Robert. *See* Magazines 3338:2

Narrative in justification of injured innocence. See Tracts 2049:11

Narrative of facts. See Tracts 99:1

Narrative of some passages in the Long Parliament. See North 173

Narrative of some proceedings in . . . Chelsea Hospital. See Chelsea 1608:77

Narrative of the astonishing transactions. See Authentic . . . narrative 1609:29

Narrative of the proceedings in France. See Defoe 1608:29

Narrative of the rise and progress of the disputes. See Harris 1609:56

Narrative of what happened in Bengal. See Bengal 1609:7

Narrative of what passed between General Sir Harry Erskine and Philip Thicknesse. See Thicknesse 1609:14

Nash, Treadway Russell:
  Collections for the history of Worcestershire 6
  See Butler 3179

Nasmith, James:
  Catalogus 3347
  See Tractatus 3383

Naso Scarronnomimus, pseud. *See* Ovidius 1973

Nation, William:
  Dramatic pieces 1810:48

National prejudice, opposed to the national interest 1608:59

Natter, Lorenz:
  Catalogue des pierres gravées 276

Natural history of superstition. See Trenchard 1608:12

Natural probability of a lasting peace. See Political tracts 94:8

Naturalization Bill. See Tracts 2146:6

Nature displayed. See Pluche 1491

Naudaeana et Patiniana. See Lancelot 745

Naudé, Gabriel:
  Apologie 1231
  See Jacob 3107

Naunton, Sir Robert:
  Fragmenta regalia 1340

Navarre, Theobald IV, King of. *See* Theobald 798

Navy Bill. See Tracts 1608:27

Nayler, Sir George. *See* Heraldry 3879

Neagh, Lough. *See* Barton 1310

Neander, Joannes:
  Tabacologia 3970

Nebulo nebulonum. See Murner 754

Necessary doctrine and erudition for any Christen man. See Henry VIII 201

Necessity for lowering interest 1608:47

Necessity of repealing the American Stamp-Act 1609:12

Neck or nothing. See Garrick 1810:9

Necker, Jacques:
  De l'administration des finances 3035
  Sur la législation et le commerce des grains 3036

Nedham, Marchmont:
  Excellencie of a free state 2730
  See Mercurius 2726
Needham, Peter. *See* Classics 2207:40
Needwood forest. See Mundy 3222:22
Negro slave trade. See Tracts 2146:1
Nelson, James:
  Affectionate father 1810:40
Nelson, Robert:
  Companion for the festivals and fasts 1445
Nemours, Mary of Orleans, Duchess of. *See*
  Joly 985
Nepos, Cornelius:
  Excellentium imperatorum vitae. See
  Brindley 2120:8
  Vitae excellentium imperatorum 2248. *See*
  Classics 2207:26
Neri, Antonio:
  Art of glass. See Tracts 361:2
Néricault-Destouches, Philippe. *See* Des-
  touches
Nero, tragoedia. See Plays 2131:1
Ness, Loch. *See* Barton 1310
Netherlands:
  Description of Holland. See Holland 1412
  Theatre of the present war 1686
  History. *See* Bentivoglio 3290; *Case* 1608:
  87; Hoey 1608:71; *Important secret* 1608:
  38; Swift 1608:13
  See Aubery du Maurier 1008; Bowdler
  2807; Catalogues 2303:1; Gautier 3779;
  Gerbier 198; Grimstone 2054; Ireland 3857:
  2; Paterson 1234; Witt 1350
Netherlands. Southern Provinces:
  *True coppie of the transportation of the
  Lowe Countries* 125
  See Philip IV 488
Neufville, Nicolas de, Seigneur de Villeroi.
  See Collection 3084
Neuhoff, Theodore de, King of Corsica. *See*
  Theodore I
Neve, Richard:
  Art's improvement 1489
Nevile, Henry. *See* Neville
Nevill, Richard, Earl of Warwick. *See* War-
  wick
Neville, Arthur Jones. *See Letter* 1608:
  61
Neville, Edward:
  Plymouth in an uproar 1810:31

Neville, Henry:
  Isle of Pines 1608:37
  New and general biographical dictionary. See
  Dictionary 1772
  New and impartial collection. See Scott 1359
  New art of gardening. See Hill 2707
  New Bath guide. See Anstey 1810:59,
  3222:7
  *New collection of catches. See Whittington's
  feast* 1810:26
  New collection of poems 3971
  New Copper Plate Magazine. See Antiquities
  3485:4
  New essay on the constitutional power. See
  Dickinson 1609:32
New Forest:
  Two historical accounts 1608:66
  New Foundling Hospital for Wit 2317, 2433
  New general collection of voyages and travels.
  See Green 542
New Hampshire. *See* England 1609:58
  New martyrology. See Pitts 2746
  New musical interlude, called the Election.
  See Andrews 1810:32
  New postscript to Letter on libels. See Post-
  script 1609:10
  New remarks of London. See Parish 757
  New Spain. See Scawen 1810:49
  New system of military discipline. See Cavan
  3180
  New tale of a tub. See Pinkerton 2448
New Testament 945, 2249, 2434. *See Book of
  Common Prayer*, 1504, 1927; Burkitt 3870
  New Year's gift 1608:73
  New-Yeeres gift. See Microphilus 2418
Newbery, John. *See* Colman 1810:1
Newburgh, William of. *See* William of New-
  burgh 711
Newbury, John. *See* Newbery
Newcastle, Anna Maria Stanhope, Duchess of.
  See Etchings 3588
Newcastle, Margaret Cavendish, Duchess of:
  Letters 24
  Life of William Cavendish 91
  Plays 2060, 2731
  Poems and phancies 23
  World's olio 2732
  See Poems 175
Newcastle, Thomas Pelham-Holles, Duke of.
  See Coalition 1609:54; Fielding 1608:88;

Newcastle, Duke of (*cont.*)
   Finesse 1608:61; Marriott 1609:5; Shebbeare 1608:86
Newcastle, William Cavendish, Duke of:
   Humorous lovers 92
   Triumphant widow 92
Newcastle-upon-Tyne. *See* Brand 3160
Newcomb, Mrs., publisher. *See* Satires 2319
Newcome, Peter:
   History of the . . . Abbey of St. Alban 3202, 3248
Newgate Prison. *See* Ordinary 1608:24
Newnham, George Simon Harcourt, Viscount. *See* Harcourt
Newton, Hon. Catherine (Seymour):
   Trial 1609:43
Newton, Francis M. *See* Royal Academy 2146:1
Newton, Sir Isaac:
   Four letters to Dr. Bentley 1608:83
   Opticks 1418
Newton, Richard:
   Series of papers 1608:70
   Pluralities indefensible 1490
Newton, Thomas, Bishop:
   Works. See Milton 317
Newton, William, Vicar of Gillingham (*d.* 1744):
   History . . . of Maidstone 634
Newton, William (1735–1790). *See* Stuart 3544
Neyman, —, of Amsterdam. *See* Basan 3866
Nice. *See* Beaumont 2336
Nice lady. See Green 1810:3
Nicetas, the Physician:
   Graecorum chyrurgici libri 3449
Nicholas I, Pope. *See* Tracts 3986
Nicholas, John. *See* Rowland 1608:8
Nichols, Francis:
   British compendium 755
Nichols, John:
   Bibliotheca topographica Britannica 3348
   Biographical anecdotes of William Bowyer 3349
   Biographical anecdotes of William Hogarth 2435, 3860
   Collection of all the wills 3350
   Collection of ordinances 3351
   Liber quotidianus. See Topham 3382
   Miscellaneous tracts by William Bowyer

Nichols, John (*cont.*)
   3352
   One letter. See Letters 2576
   Progresses and processions of Queen Elizabeth 3353
   Select collection of poems 348
   Some account of the alien priories 2911
   See Atterbury 2791; Denne 3234; Gostling 2385; Hutchins 4; King 2896; *Tatler* 2963; Wolcot 3222:22
Nickolls, John (1710?–1745):
   Original letters . . . addressed to Oliver Cromwell 1097
Nickolls, Sir John. *See* Plumard 1761
Nicol, George. *See* Bosio 435
Nicolson, Joseph. *See* Burn 3162
Nicolson, William, Bishop:
   English historical library 1650
Nideck, A. van. *See* Van Nideck
Niebuhr, Carsten:
   Voyage en Arabie 2912
Night. See Churchill 3222:1
Nil dictum quod non dictum prius. See Disney 728
Nile River. *See* Bruce 4018
Nimeguen, Treaty of. *See* Estrades 1216
Nîmes. *See* Nismes
Nimmo, William:
   General history of Stirlingshire 1601
Nina. See Berkeley 1810:42
Nipclose, Sir Nicholas, pseud. *See* Theatres 3222:12
Nisbet, Alexander:
   Essay on the . . . use of armories 662
Nismes. *See* Arts 288:2
Nithard, Cardinal. *See* John 1710
Nivernois, Louis Jules Barbon Mancini-Mazarini, Duc de. *See* Walpole 2617
Nixon, Anthony:
   Oxfords triumph. See Plays 1082:2
Nixon, John:
   Marmor Estonianum 485
No abolition of slavery. See Boswell 3069
No one's enemy but his own. See Murphy 1810:5
No way more delightful 1608:74
Noailles, Adrien Maurice de, Duc de Noailles:
   Campagne . . . en Allemagne 815
   See Millot 3130

Noble, Mark:
  Memoirs of the illustrious House of Medici 416
  Memoirs of the protectorate-house of Cromwell 2913
  Two dissertations 243
Noble peasant. See Holcroft 1853
Noble pedlar. See Carey 3222:11
Nobleman. *See Mysterious* 1608:26, 44
Nolpe, Pieter. *See Post* 3553
Nomenclatura trilinguis 1537
None-such Charles his character. See Gerbier 2383
Norden, Frederick Lewis:
  Drawings of some ruins . . . at Thebes. See Tracts 1348:4
Norden, John:
  Description of Cornwall 635
  Description of Middlesex and Hartfordshire 663
  Surveyors dialogue 383, 2733
Norfolk, Charles Howard, 10th Duke of. *See* Howard 128
Norfolk, Henry Howard, 6th Duke of:
  Bibliotheca Norfolciana 486
  Case 512
Norfolk, Henry Howard, 7th Duke of:
  Charge 1608:5
Norfolk, Thomas Howard, 4th Duke of. *See* Mary, Queen of Scots 205
Norfolk:
  Visitations 2581–3
  See Blomefield 588; Heraldry 3879
Norfolk and Suffolk visitation. See Norfolk 2581
Norfolk tour. See Guides 2387:3
Norman tiles. *See* Henniker 3106
Normandy. *See* Stukeley 668:6
Norris, Charles:
  Dialogue 1608:12
  Reconciler 1608:12
Norris, Richard:
  Minutes 1608:39
North, Dudley, 3d Baron North:
  Forest of varieties 2734
North, Dudley, 4th Baron North:
  Light in the way of Paradise 384
  Narrative 173, 385
North, Sir Dudley. *See* North, Roger 3355

North, Francis, 1st Baron Guilford. *See* Guilford
North, Frederick, Lord North, later Earl of Guilford. *See* Bunbury 3563:1; Fox 1609:46
North, John. *See* North, Roger 3355
North, Roger:
  Examen 3354
  Life of the Right Honourable Francis North, Baron of Guilford 3355
North, Sir Thomas. *See* Guevara 2699
North Allerton. *See* Crosfield 2828
North Briton 1576
North Briton, an elegy. See Walpole 2489:3
North Wales. *See* Wales 2976
Northall, John:
  Travels through Italy 386
Northampton, Henry Howard, Earl of:
  Answere to the . . . invectyve 2584
  Defensative against the poyson of supposed prophecies 93, 3356
Northampton. *See* Bridges 1, 561; Morton 574
Northbrooke, John:
  Treatise against dicing 1341
Northumberland, Henry Algernon Percy, 5th Earl of:
  Regulations of the houshold 2436
Northumberland, John Dudley, Duke of:
  Saying 174
  See Raviglio 2460, 2937
Northumberland. *See* Hutchinson 2880, 3170; Wallis 3213
Norwich. *See* Browne 676; Mackerell 2577
Norwich Castle. *See* Wilkins 3836
Nosmoth, Dr., pseud. *See Genuine* 1608:89
Nostradamus, Michael:
  True prophecies 2177
Note of hand. See Cumberland 1810:22
Notes sur la lettre de M. de Voltaire. See Hume 1680:5
Notion of the judgment of Hercules. See Shaftesbury 1496
Notitia Oxoniensis academiae 1608:3
Notitia St. Johanniana 756
Notredame, Michel de. *See* Nostradamus 2177
Nottingham, Charles Howard, Earl of. *See* Treswell 2476
Nottingham, Daniel Finch, Earl of:
  Answer 1608:15

Nottingham, Heneage Finch, Earl of. *See*
England 3313; Norfolk 512
Nottingham. *See* Deering 2834, 3305
Nottinghamshire. *See* Thoroton 613, 3523
Noue, François de la. *See* La Noue
Nourjahad. *See* Sheridan 1586
*Nouveau recueil des épigrammatistes fran-
çois. See* Bruzen 1290
Nouveau théâtre françois 1232
Nouveau voyage de France. See Piganiol 1258
Nouveaux mémoires. See Grosley 3103
Nouvelle bigarure 1202
Nouvelle Héloise. See Rousseau 819
Nova Scotia:
Geographical history 1608:67
Nowell, Thomas:
Answer to a pamphlet 1609:21
Nugae antiquae. See Harington 411, 3814
Nugent, Nicholas:
Case of Nicholas Nugent 1609:36
Nugent, Robert:
Unnatural father 1608:78
Nugent, Robert, Viscount Clare and later
Earl Nugent. *See* Nugent, Robert Craggs
Nugent, Robert Craggs, Earl Nugent:
Considerations 1608:47
Faith 3222:13
Farther considerations 1608:47
Odes and epistles. See Tracts 2474:4
See Inquiry 1609:41; Poems 3363:8; *Rea-
sons* 1609:1
Nugent, Thomas. *See* Cellini 3181; Isla 2885
Numerus infaustus. See Caesar 2815
Numismatum antiquorum sylloge. See Wren
2503
The Nun, an elegy. See Jerningham 3222:5
Nundocomar Bahader:
Trial 3510
Nuneham, George Simon Harcourt, Viscount.
See Harcourt
Nuneham:
Account of Nuneham-Courtney. See Guides
2387:1
Nunnery. See Jerningham 3222:2
Nursery for gentry. See Brathwait 1999
Nut-cracker. See Pope 1912:4
Nuts cracked. See Tracts 98:1

O'Beirne, Thomas Lewis, Bishop:
Generous impostor 1810:34

O'Beirne, Thomas Lewis (*cont.*)
Gleam of comfort 1609:47A
Oberea, pseud.:
Epistle from Oberea 3222:13
*Objections to the taxation of our American
colonies. See* Jenyns 1609:11, 56
*Objections to the thirty-fourth article of the
Navy Bill* 1608:27
O'Brien, William:
Cross purposes 1810:19
Duel 1810:19
O'Bryen, Denis:
Defence of the Earl of Shelburne 1609:43
Lines written at Twickenham 3222:22
Obsequens, Julius:
De prodigiis. See Classics 2207:27
Observateur anglois. See Mairobert 3126
Observations and discourses. See Chandos
190
Observations made during a tour. See Sulivan
3829
*Observations on a book, intituled, an Intro-
ductory discourse. See* Stebbing 1379:3
Observations on a late publication 1609:58
Observations on a late state of the nation. See
Burke 1609:57
*Observations on a pamphlet, published by
Almon* 1609:56
Observations on modern gardening. See Gar-
dening 2307:1
Observations on the account given [of
R&NA]. *See* Tracts 2050:13
*Observations on the buyers . . . of stolen
goods* 1608:2
Observations on the conduct of Great-Britain
1608:26
Observations on the Craftsman. See Political
tracts 94:1
Observations on the last session of Parliament
1608:50, 59
*Observations on the Occasional Writer, the
Craftsman* 1608:24
*Observations on the papers relative to the
rupture with Spain. See* Wilkes 1609:5
*Observations on the probable issue of the
Congress. See* Mounteney 1608:56
Observations, rules, and orders 1608:2
Observations sur Londres. See Lacombe 3112
Observations sur un ouvrage. See Fournier
3012:2

Observations upon the state of the nation 1608:15

Observationum medicinalium fasciculus. See Merrick 1609:55

Observator. See L'Estrange 2058

Observer 3249, 3357

Occasional historian. See Earbery 80

Occasional letter from a gentleman in the country. See Egmont 119:2

Occasional patriot 1608:81

Occasional remarks 1608:6

Occasional thoughts on the present German war. See Mauduit 1609:1

Occasional verses. See Herbert 169

Occasional writer. See Bolingbroke 1608:13; *Observations* 1608:24

October Club. *See* Defoe 1608:9

Ode. See Jenyns 3222:17

Ode on the death of Mr. Gray. See Gray 3894

Ode performed in the Senate-house at Cambridge. See Gray 3222:9

Ode sacred to the memory of the late Right Honourable George Lord Lyttelton 3222: 13

Ode to Dragon. See More 3222:15

Ode to Duke Humphry. See Walpole 2489:2

Ode to Lansdown-Hill 3222:19

Ode . . . to Le Stue, cook to the Duke of Newcastle 3222:10

Ode to Mr. Handel. See Poems 3363:12

Ode to Mr. Pinchbeck. See Mason 3222:14

Ode to Palinurus 3222:10

Ode to the Legislator Elect of Russia. See Brown 3222:7

Ode upon dedicating a building. See Garrick 3222:10

Ode upon ode: or a peep at St. James's. See Wolcot 3222:21

Ode upon the present period of time 3222:9

Odes. See Poems 3363

Odes and epistles. See Tracts 2474:4

Odescalchi, Baldassar. *See* Knight 3332

The Odyssey. See Homer

Oeconomy of a winter's day 1608:63

Oeuvres du philosophe de Sans-Souci. See Frederick II 1295

Oeyras, Sebastião José de Carvalho e Mello, Conde d'. *See* Memoirs 1609:18

Of politeness. See Rival wives 2463

Of the laws of chance. See Arbuthnot 1608:37

Officer. *See* Ferdinand 3167; Glenie 1609: 47A; *Voyage* 1609:17

Officer at Hanover. *See Popular* 1608:43

Officium. *See* Missal

Offley, Mrs. Emma. *See* Crewe, Emma

Offray de la Mettrie, Julien. *See* La Mettrie

Ogborne, David:
Merry midnight mistake 1810:8

Ogden, Samuel. *See* Ashton 1379:10

Ogilby, John:
Britannia depicta 2437
Entertainment of Charles II 575, 3280
Pocket-book of the roads 1577. *See* Roads 2287
See Aesop 3670

Ogilvie, John:
Poems on several subjects 3222:3

Ogle family. *See* Collins 565

O'Hara, Kane:
April-Day 1810:27
Golden Pippin 1810:22
Midas 1810:6
Songs in Midas 1810:47
Two misers 1810:23

Ohio project. *See* Tracts 2050:14

Oiselius, Jacobus. *See* Wren 2503

Oithona. *See* Macpherson 1810:12

O'Keeffe, John:
Castle of Andalusia 1810:55
Irish mimic 1810:57
Life's vagaries 1810:56
London hermit 1810:53
Prisoner at large 1810:46
She-gallant 1810:10
Songs, duets, &c. in the Lord Mayor's Day 1810:35
Songs, duets . . . in the Siege of Curzola 1810:39
Sprigs of laurel 1810:53
Tony Lumpkin in town 1810:32
Wild oats 1810:55
World in a village 1810:53

Old Bailey. *See* Trials 1723

Old England. See Spectator 1860; Tracts 2050:8; Walpole 2616

Old lady and her niece 1608:63

Old maid. See Murphy 1810:2

Old Member of Parliament. *See* Lee, Arthur

Old Tory. *See Friendly* 1608:70

Old Whig. *See* Tracts 400:3, 2475:4

Old women weatherwise. See Carey 1810:16

Oldcastle, Sir John, Baron Cobham:
    Brefe chronycle 3450

Oldfield, Mrs. Anne. *See* Egerton 1677

Oldfield, Henry George. *See* Dyson 2843

Oldham, John:
    Works 1857

Oldisworth, Michael:
    Thanks-giving for Earl of Pembroke 1608:8

Oldisworth, William:
    State and miscellany poems 135
    State tracts 135
    See Examiner 1560

Oldmixon, Sir John:
    Apollo turn'd stroller 1810:43

Oldmixon, John:
    Clarendon and Whitlock compar'd 1651
    Court tales 1757
    See Maynwaring 1685

Oldys, William:
    British librarian 700, 2735
    Catalogue of his engraved portraits 2585
    Commonplace books 2585
    Life of Dr. George Abbot 417
    See Libraries 2018; Muses Library 90; Oxford 318

Olearius, Adam:
    Voyages 905

Olivares, Gaspar de Guzman, Duque de San Lucar and Conde de:
    Historia de la monarchia 2586

Oliver, Andrew. *See* Mauduit 1609:31

Oliver, Edward. *See* Rowland 1608:8

Oliver, Isaac. *See* Drawings 3567

Oliver, William. *See* Tracts 99:1

Ombre du feu cardinal 1608:53

On the abuse of unrestrained power. See Temple 1609:39

On the . . . death of the Marquis of Tavistock. See Anstey 3222:8

On the employment of time. See Bolton 1608: 62, 3949

One thousand seven hundred and fifty six. See Poems 1835:3

O'Neil, Elizabeth, pseud. *See* Tracts 2966:7

Onslow, Arthur:
    Speech 1608:93
    See Middleton 1574; Oldys 417

Onslow, George, 1st Earl of Onslow:
    Whole proceedings 1609:26

Opera House, London. *See* King's Theatre, Haymarket

Operations of the allied army. See Ferdinand 3167

Operations of the British 1608:26

Opposition 1608:80, 81

Opposition mornings. See Tracts 2966:7

Oraisons funèbres 929

Orandus, Eirenaeus. *See* Flamel 737

Orange, Louisa Juliana, Princess of. *See* Spanheim 3467

Orange, William, Prince of. *See* William IV

Orations spoke at Will's Coffee House. See Tracts 2146:3

Orbessan, Anne Marie Daignan d', Marquis:
    Mélanges historiques et critiques 3037

Orde-Powlett, Thomas, 1st Baron Bolton. *See* Bolton

Order and course of passing bills 1608:2

Order of the Garter. *See* Garter

Order of the Holy Ghost. *See* Holy Ghost

Orders, standing orders, and resolutions 1608: 2

Ordinary of Newgate's account 1608:24, 56

Ordo Baptismi Parvulorum. See Deseine 1027

Ordonnance de 1627. *See* Philip IV 488

Ordre du Saint Esprit. *See* La Pointe 545

Orford, George Walpole, 3d Earl of. *See* Houghton 3572

Orford, Horace Walpole, 4th Earl of. *See* Walpole

Orford, Margaret (Rolle) Walpole, Countess of. *See* Rigacci 2111

Orford, Robert Walpole, 1st Earl of. *See* Walpole

Orford, Robert Walpole, 2d Earl of. *See* Walpole

Original letters and papers of state. See Nickolls 1097

Original letters to an honest sailor. See Vernon 1497

Original papers relative to the Nabob of Arcot 1609:47A

Original Weekly Journal. See Applebee 2139

Origines Divisianae. See Hornby 692:2

Origins of moral virtue 1608:33

Oriuna, supposed wife of Carausius. *See* Stukeley 668:5

Orkney, isles of. *See* Wallace 770

Orlandi, Pellegrino Antonio:
  L'Abecedario pittorico 2082
  See Arts 288:2; *Repertorium* 354
Orléans, Anne Marie Louisa d', Duchesse de
  Montpensier. *See* Montpensier
Orléans, Charlotte Elizabeth, of Bavaria,
  Duchesse d'. *See* Charlotte 3298
Orléans, Louis, Duc d'. *See* Crozat 3550
Orléans, Louis Philippe Joseph, Duc d':
  Orleans Gallery. See Tracts 3833:4
Orléans, Pierre Joseph d':
  Histoire des révolutions d'Espagne 3358
Orleans Gallery. *See* Bonafons 3488
Orme, Robert:
  History of the military transactions in In-
  dostan 3174
Ormonde, James Butler, 1st Duke of. *See*
  Carte 1672
Ormonde, James Butler, 2d Duke of:
  Clamour of the Whigs. See Black-bird 2646:
  21
  See Conduct 1608:94
Orphan of China. See Murphy 1818:17
Orpheus. See Garrick 1810:11
Orpheus Caledonius 2045
Orpheus, priest of nature 3222:18
Orrery, Charles Boyle, 4th Earl of:
  Dr. Bentley's dissertations on the Epistles
  of Phalaris 1380
  See Budgell 1670
Orrery, John Boyle, Earl of Cork and. *See*
  Cork and Orrery
Orrery, Roger Boyle, 1st Earl of:
  Collection of state letters 25
  Dramatic works 53
  Several copies of verses on the death of
  Cowley. See Oxford University 2061:2
  Tragedy of Saul. See Trapp 1623:1
  Treatise of the art of war 26
Orsini Rosenberg, Justine, Countess:
  Alticchiero 3753
Orsino, Cesare:
  Epistole amorose 2129
Orsino, Fulvio. *See* Ursinus, Fulvius
Orville, André Guillaume Contant d'. *See*
  Contant d'Orville
Osborn, George:
  Remarks on Royal and noble authors. See
  Tracts 2050:13

Osborne, Francis:
  Works 1715
Osborne, Francis Godolphin, Duke of Leeds.
  See Leeds
Osborne, Thomas, Earl of Danby. *See* Danby
Osnaburg. *See* Munster, Treaty of
Osney Abbey. *See* Swaine 2761
Osorio da Fonseca, Jeronimo:
  History of the Portuguese 1419
Ossian. *See* Macpherson, James
Ostend, Siege of. *See* Vere 1608:1
Otis, James:
  Considerations on behalf of the colonists
  1609:11
  Rights of the British colonies 1609:13
Oudart Feudrix de Bréquigny, Louis George.
  See Bréquigny 1181
Oudendorp, Franciscus van. *See* Classics 2207:
  27
Oulton, Walley Chamberlaine:
  All in good humour 1810:51
  As it should be 1810:47
Overbeke, Bonaventura van:
  Degli avanzi dell' antica Roma 306
  Reliquiae antiquae urbis Romae 3576
  Stampe degli avanzi dell' antica Roma 3576
Overbury, Sir Thomas:
  Wife, with new elegies 2020
  See James I 87; Woodfall 1810:27
Overton, Benjamin:
  Good advice to the Whigs 1608:9
Overton, Henry. *See* London 3623, 3818
Ovid travestie. See Ovidius 1973
Ovidius Naso, Publius:
  Chaucer's ghoast 1971
  Opera 2286
  Opera omnia. See Classics 2207:28
  Opera quae extant. See Brindley 2120:9
  Ovid de arte amandi 2021
  Ovidius exulans 1973
  Ovid's Art of love paraphrased. See Poems
  1835:1
  Ovid's Epistles 1904
  Ovid's heroical epistles 1972
  Ovid's Metamorphoses 1905
  See Hall 2011:1; *Loves of Hero* 1960;
  Passe 3788
Ovington, John:
  Voyage to Suratt 1774

Owen, Charles:
Plain reasons. See Miscellaneous tracts 89:1
Owen, Henry:
Sixteen sermons 3250
Owen, John (1560?–1622):
Epigrammata 2250
Latine epigrams 2022
Owen, John, of the Middle Temple. *See*
Ogilby 2437
Owen, Nicholas:
Caernarvonshire 2914
History of the Island of Anglesey 513
Owen, Robert. *See* Owen 3359
Owen, Thomas, chaplain:
Sermon. See Derby 79:2
Owen, Thomas, judge:
Reports 3359
Owen, William. *See* Owen 3359; Zenger 1609:
10
Ox — and Bull —. See Dunton 2646:15
Oxford, Earls of. *See* Collins 565, 2359
Oxford, Edward Harley, 2d Earl of. *See* Collins 2359
Oxford, Henrietta Holles, Countess of. *See*
Collins 2359
Oxford, Robert Harley, Earl of:
Catalogus bibliothecae Harleianae 318
See Black-bird 2646:15; Burnet 1779; Collins 2359
Oxford:
New Oxford guide. See Guides 2387:2
Pocket companion for Oxford. See Tracts
100:3
Views. See London 3623
Oxford University:
Defence of the rights and privileges 1608:3
Epicedia Universitatis Oxoniensis 2061
Gratulatio Academiae Oxoniensis 514
*Pietas Academiae Oxoniensis in obitum
Reginae Carolinae* 2046
See Amhurst 1729; Ayliffe 674; Fell 1608:8;
Fulman 1608:3; Henley 1608:70; Miller
1818:2; Newton 1608:70; Wood 584, 3219
Oxford University:
Balliol College. *See* Savage 1608:3, 1629
Magdalen College. *See Conduct* 1609:26;
Swaine 2761
St. Edmund Hall. *See* Hill 1609:21
University College. *See* Smith 706
Oxford Almanack 3511

Oxford sausage: or, select poetical pieces 387
Oxfords triumph. See Plays 1082:2
Oxfordshire. *See Address* 1608:61; Hornby
692:1; Kennet 627
Oxfordshire election. *See Fifty queries* 1608:
61
Oxonian in town. See Garrick 1810:11
Oxoniensis. *See Philoctetes* 1810:57
Oxoniensis, pseud. *See* Randolph, Thomas
(1701–1783)
Ozell, John. *See* Brantôme 2653; Montesquieu 1443; Misson 1416; Tracts 2474:3;
Vertot 1662

P., Madame de. *See* Puisieux 1203
P., A. *See* Parkinson 636
P., H. *See* Parrot 1906
P., P. *See Political* 1608:86
P., R. *See Defence* 1609:56; Patching, Resta
P., Sir R. *See Life* 1609:25
P., W., Esq.:
Epistle from Schah Hussein. See Hussain
2146:3
Pacifico, Pietro Antonio:
Cronica Veneta 2109
The pad 1810:53
The padlock. See Bickerstaffe 1810:13
Paestum. *See* Major 3542
Page, Thomas:
Art of painting. See Tracts 361:4
Page, William, highwayman:
Genuine narrative. See Tracts 2049:6
Pagni, Niccolo. *See* Lastri 3540
Pagnino, Guglielmo. *See* Gonzaga 3318
Pahin-Champlain de la Blancherie, Flammès
Claude Catherine. *See* La Blancherie
Paine, James:
Plans, elevations, and sections 3512
*Plans . . . of the Mansion-House . . . of
Doncaster* 576
Paine, Thomas:
Common sense 1609:37
Painters. *See* Meyssens 3649
Painting illustrated. See Aglionby 474
Painting, Tracts on 359
Paintings. *See* Vertue 2772
Paisiello, Giovanni. *See* Music 3448
Paisley, James Hamilton, Viscount, later Earl
of Abercorn. *See* Abercorn
Pakington, Dorothy, Lady. *See* Allestree 3938

Palairet, John:
New royal French grammar 1233
Palais Royal. *See* Bonafons 3488; Du Bois 330
Palatius, Joannes. *See* Palazzi, Giovanni
Palazzi, Giovanni:
Fasti ducales 3754
Monarchia imperii occidentalis 3684
Palissot de Montenoy, Charles. *See* Montenoy
Palladio, Andrea:
Architecture 3593
Fabbriche antiche 3577
Palladis Tamia. See Meres 1755
Palladius and Irene 1810:21
Palma Cayet, Pierre Victor. *See* Cayet
Palmer, John. *See* Linley 1810:43
Palmer, Roger, Earl of Castlemaine. *See* Castlemaine
Palmer, Samuel:
General history of printing 515
Palmyra. *See* Halifax 2554; Seller 1603; Wood 3548
Palomino de Castro y Velasco, Aciscle Antonio:
Histoire abrégée des plus fameux peintres 349
Pamfili, Olimpia, Princess. *See* Maldachini
Pamphilia. *See Villa* 3527
Pamphlets. *See* Tracts
Pancirollus, Gulielmus:
History of many memorable things 1538
Pandora. See Songs 1810:31
Panedonius, Philogenes, pseud. *See* Brathwait 1592
The pannel. See Kemble 1810:46, 47
Pansmouzer, Gotlieb, pseud. *See* Lind, John 1609:31
Pantheon. *See* Burney 461
The Pantheon, a poem 3222:13
The Pantheonites. See Gentleman 1810:20
Pantin. See Poems 881:24
Paoli, Pasquale. *See Review* 1609:24
Papers laid before the House of Commons [on African trade.] *See* Tracts 2146:6
Papers, parliamentary. *See* Tracts 2050
Papers relating to state affairs. *See Choice collection* 114
Papers relative to the late negotiation with Spain. See England 1609:57
Papers relative to the rupture with Spain. See England 1609:54

Papillon, Jean Baptiste Michel:
Traité . . . de la gravure en bois 3722
Paradis, Marie Thérèse von. *See Account* 1609:47A
Paradis de Moncrif, François Augustin. *See* Moncrif 753
Paragraph, Peter, pseud. *See* Adair 3222:7
The parallel 1608:45
Parallel between the power of a King of England and that of a Statholder. See Tracts 2146:1
Pardies, Ignace Gaston:
Short . . . elements of geometry and . . . trigonometry 1758
Pardo, Filippo. *See* Bernardino 3067
Pardo, El, Treaty of. *See* Bath 1608:38
Parentalia Mariae Clementinae. See Clementina 3491
Parfaict, François. *See* Abguerbe 775
Paris, John:
True state of Trinity College 1608:11
Paris, Matthew:
Historia major 607
Paris, son of Priam. *See* Schomberg 1810:13
Paris:
Académie des inscriptions. *See* Académie des inscriptions
Louvre. *See* Arts 288:3
Plan de la Ville de Paris 3578
Theatres. *See* Abguerbe 775; Jullien 3110; Le Vacher 3119; Théâtre 1171
Treaty of Paris [1763]. *See Anatomy* 1609:54; England 1609:54 (two); *Letter* 1609:5
Treaty of Paris [1783]. *See* England 1609:43; *Letter* 1609:43
See Atlas 447; Brice 3071; Marot 3751; Mercier 3031; Saint-Foix 1261; Sandras de Courtilz 1236
Parish Clerks' Company:
New remarks of London 757
Parker, George, Earl of Macclesfield. *See* Macclesfield
Parker, George, almanac maker. *See World* 1608:1
Parker, Henry:
Case of ship mony. See Tracts 3797:7
Parker, J.:
History of eclipses. See Black-bird 2646:14
Parker, Matthew. *See* Nasmith 3347; Stanley 583

Parker, Richard. *See* Cambridge University 678

Parker, Samuel, Bishop:
History of his own time 1687
Letter to Mr. Mason. See Poems 1835:6

Parker, William:
Expediency of some divine interpositions. *See* Middleton 1379:8
See Sermons 1345

Parkes, Joseph. *See* Junius 1609:39

Parkin, Charles:
Account of the invasion under William Duke of Normandy. See Tracts 1348:5
Topography of Freebridge Hundred and Half, in Norfolk 445
See Blomefield 588

Parkins, Sir William. *See* Tenison 1608:8

Parkinson, Anthony:
Collectanea Anglo-Minoritica, or . . . the antiquities of the . . . Gray Friers 636

Parkinson, John:
Paradisi in sole 3723

Parkyns, George Isham. *See* Moore 3843

Parliament. *See* England. Parliament

Parliamentary history. See England 1596

Parliamentary papers. *See* Tracts 2050

Parnassus. *See* Titon 3153

Parnell, Thomas:
Poems on several occasions 3132
Posthumous works 1858
See Goldsmith 3711

Parnell, Thomas, i.e. Pownall. *See* Pownall 2931

Parodies du nouveau théâtre Italien 816

Parody on Gray's Elegy. See Duncombe 3222:14

Parr, Catherine, Consort of Henry VIII. *See* Catherine Parr

Parr, Richard:
Life of . . . James Usher 906

Parr, Samuel:
Praefationis ad tres libros De Statu 2915
See Bellendenus 405, 2797

Parrhasiana. See Le Clerc 746–7

Parrot, Henry:
Laquei ridiculosi 1906

Parrot, Sir James:
Speech. See Tracts 2769:2
The parrot and the owl 2438

Parry, Edward, Bishop:
David restored 2736

Parry, James:
True anti-Pamela 1759

Parry, William:
A true and plaine declaration. See Cecil 111:1

Pars, William. *See* Chandler 3534

Parsons, Nancy, later Viscountess Maynard. *See* Epistle 3222:9

Parsons, Philip:
Monuments and painted glass of . . . Kent 3203

Parsons, Robert. *See* Philopatris 2590

Parsons, Colonel William. *See* Félibien 241

Parsons, William, poet:
Poetical tour 2916
See Arno Miscellany 3803; Florence Miscellany 3810

Parthenia; or the lost shepherdess 1810:7

Parthia. *See* Lewis 1530

Particular account of the battle of Culloden. See Culloden 1608:32

Particular description of a certain lady 1608:63

Particulars composing the prizes in the Adelphi lottery 1609:58

Particulars of the charges. *See* Caesar 2535:6

Partridge, John. *See* World 1608:1

Partridge, Seth:
Rabdologia, or the art of numbering by rods. See Beale 2333:2

Paruta, Filippo:
La Sicilia 244

Paruta, Paolo:
History of Venice 3360
Politick discourses 3361

Pascal, Blaise:
Provinciales 1000
See Jesup 1646

Pasquier, Etienne:
Recherches de la France 907

Pasquin, Anthony, pseud. *See* Williams, John

Pasquin and Marforio on the peace 1608:58

Passe, Crispin de:
Della luce del dipingere 3787
Metamorphoseon Ovidiarum figurae 3788
Les vrais pourtraits 3789
See De Vos 3600; *Elegidia* 331; Holland

Passe, Crispin de (*cont.*)
3783; Pluvinel 3794; Prints 3605
Passe-temps agréable 1046
Passerano, Alberto Radicati, Conte di:
Recueil de pièces curieuses 1164
Passeri, Giovanni Battista:
Lucernae fictiles Musei Passerii 3755
Paston letters 3251
Pastoral cordial. See Stevenson 3222:4
Pastoral puke. See Stevenson 3222:6
Patagonians. *See* Pennant 2443; *Voyage* 1609:
17; Walpole 2614
Pataroli, Lorenzo:
Series Augustorum 307
Patch, Thomas:
Engravings after Masaccio 3594
Engravings from Fra Bartolommeo and
Giotto 3451
Series of 24 caricatures 3452
Patching, Resta:
Four topographical letters 1608:83
Paterson, Mr. *See* Tucker 1609:13
Paterson, Samuel:
Another traveller 1234
Patin, Charles:
Imperatorum Romanorum numismata 245
See Erasmus 334
Patin, Gui:
Nouvelles lettres 1257
Patin, Jacques. *See* Beaujoyeulx 3399
Patriarcha non monarcha. See Tyrrell 2770
The Patricians. See Delamayne 3222:12
Patrick, Samuel. *See* Hederich 843
Patrick, Simon, Bishop. *See* Gunton 594
The Patriot. See Anstey 3222:8
The Patriot. See Johnson 1609:32
The Patriot; or, The Irish packet open'd
1608:61
Patriot unmasked. See Trott 1609:3
Patriotism. See Bentley 1810:59, 3222:5
Patten, Robert:
History of the Rebellion 1608:10
Paul III, Pope:
Two bulls 1608:95
See Fioravante 481
Paul, George. *See* Ellesmere 503
Paul Sarpi, Father. *See* Sarpi 933
Paulden, Thomas:
Pontefract Castle 1608:1

Paulet, John, Marquess of Winchester. *See*
Winchester
Paulet, William, Marquess of Winchester. *See*
Winchester
Paulmier, François:
*Traité methodique et dogmatique de la
goutte* 3133
Paulmy, René Louis de Voyer de, Marquis
d'Argenson. *See* Argenson
Paul's Cross:
Account of St. Paul's Cross 2587
Pausanias:
Extract out of Pausanias 388
Pauw, Cornelius de:
*Recherches philosophiques sur les Egyp-
tiens et les Chinois* 3134
Recherches philosophiques sur les Grecs
3135
Pawn-Broker. See Apology 1608:53
Paxton, Nicholas. *See Epistle* 1608:92
Payba, Abraham, called James Roberts:
Memorial 1608:73
Sentence 1608:65
Payne, Sir Ralph. *See Loves of Mirtil* 381
Payne, William:
Texts examined 1608:1
Pazzi, Pietro Antonio. *See* Gualtieri 3621
La Pazzia 2439
Peace considered 1608:94
Peacham, Henry, the Elder:
Garden of eloquence 136
Peacham, Henry:
Compleat gentleman 487, 2440, 2737
Gentlemans exercise 487, 2738-9
Graphice 2738
Minerva Britanna 1342, 3790
Period of mourning. See Tracts 3797:1
Thestylis atrata. See Ford 1321
Truth of our times 2251, 3791
Valley of varietie 389, 2252, 2740
Worth of a peny 2441
Peacock, Reginald, Bishop. *See* Lewis 2721
Peak, The, in Derbyshire. *See* Leigh 602
Pearce, William:
Arrived at Portsmouth 1810:54
Hartford-Bridge 1810:52
Midnight wanderers 1810:53
Netley Abbey 1810:54
Windsor Castle 1810:56

Pearce, Zachary:
  Reply to the Defence 1379:1
  Reply to the Letter 1379:1
  See Classics 2207:11; Longinus 2089
Pearch, George:
  Collection of poems 3453
Pearson, Mr. and Mrs., of Highgate:
  Catalogue of Stained Glass. See Tracts 3833:5
Peck, Francis:
  Academia tertia Anglicana 577
  Desiderata curiosa 578
  Memoirs . . . of Oliver Cromwell 467
  New memoirs of . . . John Milton 467
Peckard, Peter:
  Memoirs of the life of Mr. Nicholas Ferrar 2917
Pecke, Samuel:
  Perfect Diurnal. See Perfect Diurnal 2741
Pecock, Reginald, Bishop. *See* Lewis 2721
Pedro II, King of Portugal. *See* Colbatch 680
Pedrussi, Paolo:
  I Cesari in oro raccolti nel Farnese Museo 457
A Peep behind the curtain. See Garrick 1810:11
Peerage:
  Coats of Arms of the King 2442
  See Heraldry 3782
Peerage Bill. *See* Steele 1608:16; Tracts 400, 2475
Peeresses. *See* House of Peeresses
Peers. *See Sale of the House of Peers* 3976
Pegge, Samuel:
  Assemblage of coins 246
  Essay on the coins of Cunobelin 1609:56
  The forme of cury 1609:41
  Life of Robert Grosseteste 3252
  Memoirs of Roger de Wesecham 516
Peintures de l'Académie. See Arts 288:2
Peirce, James:
  Essay 1608:22
Peiresk, Nicolas Claude Fabricius, Lord of. *See* Gassendi 1743
Pelew Islands. *See* Keate 271
Pelham, Henry. *See Finesse* 1608:61
Pelham-Holles, Thomas, Duke of Newcastle. *See* Newcastle
Pellerin, Joseph:
  Recueil de médailles 277

Pellisson-Fontanier, Paul:
  Lettres historiques 946
Pembroke, Henry Herbert, 10th Earl of:
  Method of breaking horses 206
Pembroke, Mary (Sidney) Herbert, Countess of. *See* Fraunce 122
Pembroke, Philip Herbert, 4th Earl of. *See* Du Verdier 2683; Herbert 1326; Oldisworth 1608:8; Wilton 3667
Pembroke, Thomas Herbert, 8th Earl of:
  Numismata antiqua 247
  See Gambarini 297; Guides 2387:6; Kennedy 1072
Pembroke, William Herbert, 3d Earl of:
  Poems 207
Penang. *See* Trapaud 1609:51
Pencz, Georg. *See* Prints 3608
Pendarves, Mary Granville. *See* Delany
Penitent Tory. *See Letter* 1609:54
Penmanship:
  Specimens of penmanship 3651
Penn, William. *See* Fox 1113
Pennant, Thomas:
  Miscellanies 3454
  Of London 3928
  Of the Patagonians 2443
  Tour in Scotland 2918
  [Works] 547
  See Cordiner 540
Pennicote, William. *See* Pennicott
Pennicott, William:
  One or more letters. See Letters 2576
Pennsylvania. *See* Dickinson 1609:32; Smith 1608:82
Pennsylvania farmer. *See* Dickinson, John
Penny, Anne Hughes (Christian):
  Poems. See Lucas 3196
Pennyman, Margaret:
  Miscellanies 1974
Penrose, Bernard:
  Account of the last expedition 1609:33
Pensées. See La Beaumelle 1223
Pensées ingénieuses. See Bouhours 1179
Il Penseroso. See Cowper 3222:8
Pentycross, Thomas:
  Wittenham-Hill 3222:14
Penz, Georg. *See* Pencz
People's answer to the court pamphlet 1609:50

Pepusch, Johann Christoph:
Short treatise on harmony 2444
Pepys, Samuel:
Memoirs 1760
See James II 51; Kirke 2572
Perceval, John, 2d Earl of Egmont. *See* Egmont
Perchè, Libro del. *See* Manfredi 2413, 3437
Percy, Henry Algernon, Earl of Northumberland. *See* Northumberland
Percy, Thomas, Bishop:
Essay on the origin of the English stage 2050:9
Hermit of Warkworth 3222:11
Letter describing the ride to Hulne Abbey 1609:19
Miscellaneous pieces relating to the Chinese 1578
Reliques of ancient English poetry 2919, 3455
See Northumberland 2436
Percy. See More 1810:27
Perdita. *See* Robinson, Mrs. Mary
Péréfixe, Hardouin de Beaumont de:
Histoire du Roy Henry le Grand 930
Peregrine, the elder, pseud. *See* Heroic 3222:16
Perelle, Gabriel:
Portfolio of 225 engravings 3604
Perez, Antonio:
Las obras y relaciones 2130
Perfect catalogue of the peeres 1608:1
Perfect Diurnal 2741
Pergolesi, Giovanni Battista:
Stabat Mater 2588
Periander. See Tracy 1818:4
Pericles. *See* Campbell 1608:53
Periers, Bonaventure des. *See* Des Periers
Perkin Warbeck, History of. *See* Gainsford 1322
Perkins, William:
Art of prophesying 2589
Perondinus, Petrus:
Magni Tamerlanis Scytharum imperatoris vita 2445
The perplexities. See Hull 1810:10
Perrault, Charles:
Les hommes illustres 3792
See Labyrinte 301

Perreau, Daniel:
Narrative 1609:35
See Female forgery 1609:35
Perreau, Robert. *See Female forgery* 1609:35
Perrin, Antoine. *See Collection* 3084
Perrin, Jean Paul:
Luthers fore-runners 1079
Perrinchief, R. *See* Charles I 13
Perroniana. See Davy 1273
Perrot, Sir Richard. *See Life* 1609:25
Perrott, Sir John:
History of Sir John Perrott 1688
Perry, Charles:
View of the Levant 1098
Perry, Francis:
Series of English medals 248
See Ducarel 266
Perry, James. *See* Strong 3222:15
Perry, John:
Account of the stopping of Daggenham Breach. See Duckett 683:5
Persepolis illustrata 3756
Persia. *See* Fryer 3277; Sherley 3827
Persian and Turkish tales. See Pétis de la Croix 2742
Persian letters. See Lyttelton 3926:7
Persian letters. See Montesquieu 1443
Persio, Ascanio. *See Pazzia* 2439
Persius. *See* Juvenalis
Person of Quality. *See* Camus 2816
Person of quality. *See Guide* 164
Peru. *See* Lasso de la Vega 443
Perugino. *See* Bartoli 3486
Peruvian 1810:39
Pervigilium Veneris. See Classics 2207:29
Peter I, the Great, Emperor of Russia. *See* Alexis 1608:20
Peter III, Emperor of Russia:
Original letter. *See* Letters 2576
Peter Leopold, Grand Duke of Tuscany. *See* Tuscany 1609:52
Peterborough, Charles Mordaunt, 3d Earl of:
Remarks on . . . the Thoughts of a Member of the lower House. See Tracts 400:5, 2475:9
See Freind 123
Peterburgh, Church of. *See* Gunton 594
Peters, Hugh. *See* Gerbier 2383; Harris 1608:20
Peter's pension. See Wolcot 3222:22

Peter's prophecy. See Wolcot 3222:22

Pétis de la Croix, François:
    Persian and Turkish tales 2742

Petit, Nicolas. *See* Le Petit 1226

Petit, William. *See* William of Newburgh 711

Petit de Bachaumont, Louis. *See* Bachaumont

Petit du Noyer, Anne Marguerite. *See* Du Noyer

Petit réservoir 1304

Petiver, James. *See Monthly miscellany* 853

Petrarch. *See* Cresswell 3778; Sade 932

Petre, Edward, Father Petre:
    One letter. *See* Letters 2576

Petre, Robert Edward, Baron Petre:
    Letter . . . to the Right Reverend Dr. Horsley 1609:53

Petrineau des Noulis. *See* Des Noulis 918

Petronius Arbiter, Titus:
    Satyrical works 1539
    Satyricon 2207:30, 2253

Pett, Sir Peter. *See* Anglesey 143

Pettingal, John:
    Dissertation on the equestrian figure. See Tracts 1348:6
    Dissertation upon the tascia 1609:54
    Latin inscription . . . near Heraclea. See Tracts 1348:11

Petty, William, Marquess of Lansdowne. *See* Lansdowne.

Petyt, George:
    Lex Parliamentaria 1716

Petyt, William:
    Ancient right of the Commons. See Brady 2652

Peyton, Thomas:
    Glass of time 2743

Pfeffel von Kriegelstein, Christian Friedrich:
    Abrégé chronologique de l'histoire 1281

Phaedrus:
    Fabulae. See Brindley 2120:10
    Fabularum Aesopicarum libri V. See Classics 2207:31

Phalaris, Letters of. *See* Orrery 1380

Pharmacopola. See Good humour 1609:13

Philalethes, pseud. *See* Enquiry 1517; *Profit* 1608:38; *Some reflexions* 1379:9; Stackhouse 1608:16; Tyrrell 2770

Philalethes, Eirenaeus, pseud. *See Tomb* 1547

Philalethes, Eugenius, pseud. *See* Rosicrucians 1542; Samber 764; Sykes 1608:12

Philaster. See Colman 1810:5

Philathes, pseud. *See Majesty misled* 1810:16

Phileleutherus Londinensis, pseud. *See* Burton 1608:70

Philemon to Hydaspes. See Coventry 1608:33

Philip, King of Macedon. *See* Leland 314

Philip II, King of Spain. *See* Hartlib 125:3; Watson 3216

Philip IV, King of Spain:
    Carte ou liste [of coins] 488
    See Louis XIV 3574

Philip V, King of Spain. *See* Bacallar 1266; England 1608:94

Philipot, John:
    Catalogue of the Chancellors of England 1080, 1608:1

Philipot, Thomas:
    Brief discourse of heraldry 758

Philippe-Auguste. *See* Lussan 1011

Philippi, Jean. *See Collection* 3084

Philipps, Henry:
    Grandeur of the law 793

Philipps, Jenkin:
    Rational grammar 1579

Philipps, Sir John. *See Letter* 1608:49; Walpole 2624

Philipps, Mary:
    One letter. *See* Letters 2576

Philips, Ambrose:
    Life of John Williams 1717
    Pastorals 1975
    See Boulter 2805

Philips, George:
    Lex parliamentaria 1540

Philips, John:
    Ode to St. John. See Shenstone 3979
    Whole works. See Shenstone 3979
    See Poems 3363:9

Philips, Mrs. Katharine:
    Poems 2178
    See Poems 3363:9

Philips, William:
    Belisarius 1818:16

Phillip, Arthur:
    Voyage to Botany Bay 2920

Phillipps, Sir Thomas. *See* Dorchester 3310

Phillips, Sir John. *See* Philipps

Phillips, Thomas:
    History of Shrewsbury 3204

Phillis at court 1810:10

Philo-Christus, pseud. *See Impartial enquiry* 1379:6

Philo-patriae. *See* Philopatriae

Philocronos. *See Memoirs* 1608:63

Philoctetes in Lemnos 1810:57

Philodamus. See Bentley 3222:8, 19

Philopatriae. *See Observations* 1608:2

Philopatris, John, pseud:
 Advertisement 2590

Philosophe moderne. See Craven 2365

Philosophical . . . essay on old maids. See Hayley 3104

Philosophical inquiry concerning human liberty. See Collins 1509

Philosophical transactions. See Royal Society 1628

Philostratus:
 Les Images 2161

Philostratus, Flavius:
 Two first books of Philostratus 249

Philotheos, pseud. *See Dissertations* 1379:9; D–st D-ct-r 1379:4

Philpot, John:
 Examinacion 1541

Phipps, Constantine John, Baron Mulgrave. *See* Mulgrave

Phoenix of these times. See Welby 2777

Physic in danger 1608:89

Physiognomy. See Clubbe 1609:55

Physiophilus, Joannes, pseud. *See* Born 1609: 45

Piazza, Girolamo Bartolomeo:
 Short and true account of the Inquisition 854

Picardy. *See* Verité 2050:20

Picart, Bernard:
 Cérémonies et coutumes religieuses 3685
 See Bartholomaeus 1021; Cervantes 3081; Le Brun 3648; Stosch 3762; *Temple des muses* 3985

Picart, Etienne. *See* Canini 3738; Cervantes 3081; Sacchi 3629

Piccolomini Museum:
 Engravings 3757

Pichler, Giovanni. *See* Rossi 2114

Pico della Mirandola, Giovanni Francesco. *See* Jesup 1646

Pictures, Catalogue of. *See* Catalogues 2303

Picturesque Views. See Watts 3849

Pidansat de Mairobert, Mathieu François. *See* Mairobert

Pièces de Théâtre. See Plays 3139

Pièces de théâtre en vers et en prose. See Hénault 3017

Pièces diverses françoises 817

Pièces françoises 3136. *See Muses* 1201; Puisieux 1203

Pièces intéressantes. See La Place 3115

Pielat, B.:
 Sécrétaire inconnu 1305

Pierre de Bernis, François Joachim. *See* Bernis

Pierrepont, Evelyn, 1st Duke of Kingston. *See* Kingston

Pierrepont, Lady Mary. *See* Montagu, Lady Mary Wortley

Piers, Sarah, Lady:
 George for Britain, a poem 390

Pietas Academiae Cantabrigiensis in funere . . . Wilhelminae Carolinae. See Cambridge University 2042

Pietas Academiae Oxoniensis in obitum Reginae Carolinae. See Oxford University 2046

Pietas Oxoniensis. See Hill 1609:21

Pigage, Nicolas de:
 Galerie Electorale de Dusseldorff 3513

Piganiol de la Force, Jean Aimar:
 Nouveau voyage de France 1258

Pignotti, Lorenzo:
 Robert Manners, a poem 2921
 Shakespear 2921

Pigot, James:
 Complete alphabet of cyphers 517

Piguenit, D. J.:
 Don Quixote 1810:26

Pikler, Giovanni. *See* Rossi 2114

Piles, Roger de:
 Abrégé de la vie des peintres 350
 Art of painting 308
 Cours de peintures par principes 351
 See Burgess 1608:78

Pilkington, James:
 View of the present state of Derbyshire 2922

Pilkington, Laetitia:
 Memoirs 1798

Pilkington, Matthew:
 Gentleman's dictionary of painters 3362

Pill to purge state-melancholy 2446

Pilon, Frederick:
    Aerostation 1810:36
    Barataria 1810:37
    Drama 3222:13
    Fair American 1810:37
    He would be a soldier 1810:39
    Humours of an election 1810:32
    Illumination 1810:30
    Invasion 1810:29
    Liverpool prize 1810:30

Pincot, Daniel:
    Essay on the origin . . . of artificial stone
    1609:26

Pindar:
    Odes 1622
    [One volume] 2923

Pindar, Peter, pseud. *See* Wolcot, John

Pindarick ode on painting 3222:9

Pine, George, pseud. *See* Neville, Henry

Pine, John, engraver:
    Procession and ceremonies 3652
    Tapestry hangings of the House of Lords
    3552
    See Horatius 2088

Pineau-Duclos, Charles. *See* Duclos 960

Pinel de la Martelière, P. A. *See* Santeul
820

Pinelli, Maffeo:
    Bibliotheca Pinelliana 2744, 2924

Pinkerton, John:
    Ancient Scotish poems 2925
    Dissertation 2447, 2926
    Essay on Medals 278–9, 3823
    Iconographia Scotica 3824
    Inquiry into the history of Scotland 3253
    Letters of literature 3825
    Medallic history of England 3702
    New tale of a tub 2448
    Rimes 2927
    Treasury of wit 2449
    Vitae antiquae sanctorum 2450
    See Paine 3512

Pinna y Ruiz, Donna Teresa. *See* Preston
3222:15

Pinson, Pierre:
    Vie et aventures 3137

Piobbici, Salustio. *See* Vecelli 2477

Piozzi, Hester Lynch (Thrale):
    Anecdotes 3826

Piozzi, Hester Lynch (*cont.*)
    British synonymy 3254
    Observations and reflections 3138
    See Arno Miscellany 3803; *Florence Miscel-
    lany* 3810; Johnson 3239

Pipe of tobacco. See Tracts 2474:7

Piranesi, Giovanni Battista:
    Le Antichità Romane 3543

Piron, Alexis:
    Gustave 1818:15

Pisa. *See* Martini 3682

Pisan, Christine de:
    Le Trésor 3899
    See Collection 3084

Pitaval, François Gayot de:
    Saillies d'esprit 3038

Pitiscus, Samuel, editor. *See* Classics 2207:6;
    Suetonius 2225

Pitsligo, Alexander Forbes, Baron:
    Essays 137, 2745

Pitt, Anne. *See Letter* 1609:15

Pitt, Christopher. *See* Virgilius 1921

Pitt, George, Baron Rivers. *See* Rivers

Pitt, Thomas (*d.* 1760):
    State of the proceedings 1608:32

Pitt, Thomas (1737–1793), 1st Baron Camelford. *See* Camelford

Pitt, William, Earl of Chatham:
    Death of Lord Chatham 3456
    E—l of Ch—m's apology 3222:7
    *Elegy on the late Right Honourable W . . .
    P . . .* 3222:7
    Plan offered by the Earl of Chatham 1609:
    58
    Political debates 1609:13
    Speech 1609:58
    See Almon 1609:5, 6; *Coalition* 1609:54;
    Constitution 1608:84; England 1609:54;
    Enquiry 1609:15; *Epistle* 1609:54; Francis
    1609:54; Hervey, Thomas 1608:90; Mere-
    dith 1609:32; *Political conduct* 1609:23;
    Trott 1609:3; *Verses* 3222:5

Pitt, William, the younger:
    Mr. Pitt's reply to Mr. Orde 1609:47A
    Speech 1609:43
    See House 1609:46; Mason 3222:18; Priest-
    ley 1609:50; Wolcot 3222:22

Pitts, Thomas:
    Western martyrology 2746

Pizzoli, Pietro Paolo. *See* Bologna 2532

Place, Conyers:
  Remarks on a treatise 1608:35
Plagiairiana 3039
Plain account of the Sacrament. See Hoadly 1374
Plain account of the Trinity. See Johnson 1608:33
Plain and seasonable address to the freeholders 1609:13
Plain answer to Dr. Middleton's Letter from Rome 1379:3
Plain dealer, pseud. *See Letter* 1609:56
Plain dealer. See Bickerstaffe 1810:8
Plain matter of fact [1742] 1608:38
Plain matter of fact [1748]. *See* Spence 1608:60
Plain narrative, or a true state of the case 1608:7
Plain reasons. See Miscellaneous tracts 89:1
Plain truth [1747]. *See* Poems 3363:16
Plain truth [1776]. *See* Paine 1609:37
Plan of a Supplement to Dr. Middleton's Free Enquiry 1379:7
Plan of an academy. See Tracts 2146:1
Plantagenet's tragicall story. See W., T. 1989
Plantavit de la Pause de Margon, Guillaume. *See* Filtz-Moritz 1031
Planting and ornamental gardening. See Gardening 2307:2
Plat, Sir Hugh. *See* Platt
Platina, Baptista Sacchi, de. *See* Sacchi, Bartholomaeus
Platon, Metropolitan of Moscow:
  Sermon 1609:57
Platonic wife. See Griffith 1810:6
Platt, Sir Hugh:
  Garden of Eden 2928, 3793
  Jewel house of art and nature 855
Plautus, Titus Maccius:
  Comédies 1013
  Comedies, tr. by Cooke 1976
  Comedies, tr. by Thornton 2023
  Comoediae. See Classics 2207:32
Playford, John:
  Brief introduction to the skill of musick 2747
Plays 856, 1081–3, 1623, 1810, 1818, 1907–10, 2451, 3139, 3457, 3972
Plays:
  French plays 1083, 1259

Plays (*cont.*)
  Latin plays 2131
  Theatre of the reign of George the 3d 1810
Pleasant comedie, called, Wily Beguilde. See Plays 2451:2
Plebeians. See Tracts 400:2, 2475:3
Plinius Caecilius Secundus, Caius:
  Epistolarum libri X 2220
  Letters 54, 1446
  Libri epistolarum novem 518
  Panegyricus. See Classics 2207:33
Plinius Secundus, Caius:
  Histoire naturelle de Pline 3140
  Naturalis historiae tomus primus. See Classics 2207:34
Plot, Robert:
  Natural history of Staffordshire 579
Pluche, Noël Antoine:
  Histoire du ciel 1001
  Spectacle de la nature 1491
Plumard de Dangeul:
  Remarks on . . . commerce 1761
Pluralities indefensible. See Newton 1490
Plutarch:
  Lives 1718
Pluvinel, Antoine de:
  Instruction du Roy 3794
Plymouth in an uproar 1810:31
Pocket Books. *See* Walpole 2622
Pocket Companion for Oxford. *See* Tracts 100:3
Pococke, Richard, Bishop:
  Description of the East 1099
Poellnitz, Baron von. *See* Pöllnitz
Poem on satire. See Walpole 3222:6
Poems and Phancies. See Newcastle 23
Poems. By a Lady. See Pye 2457
Poems by a young nobleman. See Lyttelton 3222:17
Poems by eminent ladies 175
Poems by J. C. See Cleveland 1933
Poems by several Gentlemen at Oxford. See Poems 1835:2
Poems, elegies, paradoxes, and sonets. See King 1955
Poems fit for a bishop 3222:17
Poems:
  Miscellaneous Poems 280, 881, 1624, 2748
Poems, Odes, and Tracts 3363

Poems of the reign of George the 3d 1810:59, 3222

Poems on affairs of state 1836. See New collection 3971

Poems on several occasions by Mrs. S. F. See Egerton 1894

Poems published in the Reign of King George the 3d. *See* Poems of the reign of George the 3d

Poems written . . . at . . . Cambridge. See Marriott 1810:59

Poëtica stromata. See Corbet 2671

Poetical amusements at a villa near Bath. See Miller 415, 2420

Poetical and congratulatory epistle to James Boswell. See Wolcot 3222:20

Poetical epistle from Florizel to Perdita 3222:17

Poetical epistle to a falling minister. See Wolcot 3222:22

Poetical epistle to an eminent painter. See Hayley 3222:16

Poetical epistle to His Excellency George Washington. See Wharton 3222:19

Poetical epistle to Sir Joshua Reynolds. See Combe 3222:15

Poetical excursions in the Isle of Wight 3222:15

Poetical miscellanies. See Dryden 1825

Poetical tour, in the years 1784–6. See Parsons 2916

Poetical tracts. *See* Tracts 98

Poets, Minor. *See Works of Minor Poets* 184; *Works of celebrated authors* 1864

Poinsinet, Antoine Alexandre Henri:
Tom Jones. See Reed 1810:14

Poinsinet de Sivry, Louis. *See* Sivry

Pointed arch. *See* Agincourt 3994

Poisson, Jeanne Antoinette, Marquise de Pompadour. *See* Pompadour

Poitou, Comtes de. *See* Besly 889

Poland. *See* Lind 1609:30, 31

Pole, Catherine, Countess of Huntingdon. *See* Huntingdon

Pole, Reginald, Cardinal:
Three letters. *See* Letters 2576

Pole, Sir William:
Collections toward a description of the County of Devon 3205

Policy of Popish Priests. See Champneys 189

Polignac, Melchior de, Cardinal:
Anti-Lucretius 2132

Poliphilus. *See* Colonna 2075

Polish partition. See Lind 1609:31

Political and satyrical history of the years 1756 and 1757. See Tracts 361:3

Political conduct of the Earl of Chatham 1609:23

Political considerations. See Marriott 1609:5

Political debates. See Pitt 1609:13

Political prints. *See* Bunbury 3563; Poems 3363

Political Tracts. *See* Tracts

Political truths humourously delineated 1608:86

Politician reformed 1810:21

Politicks on both sides. See Bath 1608:26

Politique de tous les cabinets de l'Europe. See Broglie 3072

Poll of Plympton. *See* Constant maid 1810:43

Pollard, Robert. *See* Defoe 408

Pollio. See Mickle 3222:7

Pöllnitz, Karl Ludwig, Baron von:
Histoire secrette de la Duchesse d'Hanover 1282

Polly Honeycombe. See Colman 1810:1

Polwarth, Amabel Yorke, Viscountess. *See* Etchings 3588

Polwhele, Richard:
Historical views of Devonshire 3364
History of Devonshire 2929

Polwhele, Sir William. *See* Pole, Sir William 3205

Polyaenus:
Stratagematum libri octo. See Classics 2207:35

Polybius:
General History 319
Histoire 931
See Almanach 1174

Polydor, Johannes Glauber, called. *See* Glauber

Pombal, Sebastião José de Carvalho e Mello, Conde d'Oeyras and Marques de. *See* Oeyras

Pomey, François Antoine:
Pantheum mythicum 2254
See Tooke 399

Pomfret, Henrietta Louisa Fermor, Countess of. *See* Nixon 485

Pomfret, John:
Poems 1911

Pomfret, Thomas:
Life of . . . Lady Christian late Countess Dowager of Devonshire 3900

Pompadour, Jeanne Antoinette Poisson Le Normand d'Etioles, Marquise de:
History of the Marchioness de Pompadour 1799
Mémoires . . . écrits par elle-même 3141
Suite d'estampes gravées 3758

Pompey, the Little. *See* Coventry 1556

Pomponne, Simon Arnauld, Marquis de. *See* Sévigné 2597

Ponce, Nicolas. *See* Godefroy 3742

Poney, Dick. *See* Epistle 1608:92

Ponsonby, William, 2d Earl of Bessborough. *See* Natter 276

Pont-de-Veyle, Antoine de Ferriol, Comte de. *See* Collection 2507:1; Craven 1810:29; Tencin 2295

Ponteach, or the savages of America. See Rogers 1810:8

Pontefract Castle 1608:1

Pontiac, Chief of the Ottawas. *See* Rogers 1810:8

Pool, Robert, *and* Cash, John:
Views of . . . public buildings . . . of Dublin 3255

Poole, Sir William. *See* Pole, Sir William

Poor Laws. *See* Tracts 2049:10–12; 3797:6

Poor Robin. See Black-bird 2646:4

Poor Vulcan. See Dibdin 1810:27

Pope, Alexander:
Additions to the works 2452, 3901
Dunciad. See Essay 1608:30
La Dunciade 3040
Essay on criticism 1912:1
Essay on man 1912
First epistle of Horace. See Poems 881:4
First epistle of the second book of Horace. See Poems 280:5
Letters to a lady 1609:22
Poema 3222:14
Il riccio rapito 2110
Sixth epistle of the first book of Horace. See Poems 280:4
Supplement to the works 1913

Pope, Alexander (*cont.*)
Universal prayer. See Poems 881:5
Verses on the grotto. See Poems 3363:4
Works 320, 1819, 2453
See Cibber 1608:90; Concanen 1608:31; Dryden 1825; Homer 62–3, 3964; Ovidius 1904; Ruffhead 2945; Shakespeare 65, 1915; Spence 1608:13; Swift 1862; Tracts 2474:2; Warburton 1608:13; Warton 2033, 3267; Young 1818:3

Pope, Sir Thomas. *See* Warton 2981–2

Popery. *See* Goldwin 1608:60; *Letter* 1608:55; *Serious* 1608:60; Trebeck 1608:60

Popery unmasked. See Middleton 1574

Popes. *See* Sacchi 1129

Popham, Edward:
Illustrium virorum elogia sepulchralia 3365

Popish Plot. *See* Collection 2358

Popular prejudice concerning partiality 1608:43, 46

Porée, Charles:
Oration 1608:67

Porrett, Robert:
Clarissa 1810:45

Porsenna's invasion 1818:8

Portal, Abraham:
Indiscreet lover 1810:13
Songs, duets, and finale 1810:27

Porter, Jerome:
Edwardus redivivus 391

Portfolio for prints and drawings 3458

Portfolio of original drawings by Dutch masters. *See* Drawings 3587

Portfolios of original drawings. *See* Drawings 3567–9

Portius, pseud. *See* Letter 1609:43

Portland, Margaret Cavendish (Harley) Bentinck, Duchess of:
Catalogue of the Portland Museum 3902
Two or more letters. *See* Letters 2576

Portland, William Henry Cavendish Bentinck, Duke of:
Case of His Grace the Duke of Portland 1609:20
See Defence 1609:20

Portlock, Nathaniel:
Voyage round the world 2930

Portocarrero, Luis Manuel, Cardinal:
History . . . of the famous Card. Portocarrero 1580

Portrait. See Colman 1810:16

Portraits historiques. See Hofman 270

Portraits in the reign of George the 3d 3636

Portugal:

Five tracts on the conspiracy against King Joseph I 1343

Kings. *See* Sainte-Marthe 250, 3281; Vasconcellos 3386

See Colbatch 680; Dalrymple 3233; *Memoirs* 1609:18; Murphy 2910, 3247; Orléans 3358; Osorio da Fonseca 1419; Rhys 1420; Twiss 2972; Vertot 1661

Post, Pieter:

Begraeffenisse 3553

De Sael van Orange 3142

Post-Chaise. *See Travels* 1608:74

Postlethwayt, Malachy:

African trade. See Tracts 2146:1

Great Britain's true system 1447

Postscript to the Letter, on libels 1609:10

Pote, Joseph:

History . . . of Windsor Castle 637

See School Books 3175

Pott, Joseph Holden:

Elegies, with Selmane 1810:34

Potter, John (1674?–1747), Archbishop:

Archaeologia Graeca 1652

Potter, John (*fl.* 1754–1804):

Choice of Apollo 3222:6

Potter, Robert. *See* Aeschylus 3156

Potter, William. *See* Hartlib 2391

Pottinger, Israel:

Duenna 1810:26

Humorous quarrel 1810:2

The Methodist 1810:1

Poulett, John, 2d Earl Poulett:

Sibylline leaves 1608:50

Poulett, Vere, 3d Earl Poulett. *See Letter* 1609:17

Poullain de Saint-Foix, Germain François. *See* Saint-Foix

Le Pour et le Contre. See Royal Academy 3885:10

Poussin, Nicolas. *See* Drawings 3567, 3569

Povey, Charles:

Visions of Sir Heister Ryley 95

Powel, Robert. *See* Burnet 1779

Powel, William. *See* Fleetwood 1094

Powell, James:

The Narcotic and Private theatricals 1810:52

Pownall, Thomas:

Administration of the colonies 1609:7, 11

Memorial 1609:41

Right of the state 1609:31

Topographical description of . . . North America. See Tracts 2968:5

Treatise on the study of antiquities 2931

Poynings, Henry. *See* Letters 2576 (Pole)

Practice of piety. See Manual 2414

Pratolino. *See* Sgrilli 3760

Pratt, Charles, 1st Earl of Camden. *See* Camden

Pratt, Robert. *See Another estimate* 1609:23

Pratt, Samuel Jackson:

Fair Circassian 1810:34

Tears of genius 3222:14, 3973

See Hume 4008

Prayer. *See* Topping 2473

Precedents of writs. See Reports 2591

Precepts. See Cecil 157, 2820

Preces, catechismus, et hymni. See St. Paul's School 2751

Précis pour Jean-Jacques Rousseau. See Hume 1680:6

Prédiction tirée d'un ancien manuscrit. See Borde 2050:15

Preliminaries productive of a premunire 1608:58

Preliminary articles of peace. See England 1609:54

Prenner, Giorgio Gasparo. *See* Zuccaro 3560

Presbyter of the Church of England. *See* Hare 1608:32; *Some reflexions* 1379:4

Prescot, Kenrick:

Letters concerning Homer 2932

Mildenhall. See Tracts 2968:6

St. Paul at Athens. See Manual 2414

Prescott, Isaac:

Trial 1609:48

Present conduct of the war 1608:44

Present for an apprentice. See Manual 2414

Present interest of the people of Great-Britain. See Marchmont 1608:38

Present measures proved 1608:44

Preston, Richard Graham, Viscount. *See* Boethius 148

Preston, William:
Democratic rage 1810:53
Heroic epistle from Donna Teresa Pinna y Ruiz 3222:15
Poems on several occasions 2933
Pretender, Old. See James Edward Francis Stuart
Pretender, Young. See Charles Edward Stuart
Pretie and wittie historie of Arnalt and Lucenda. See Desainliens 4003
Prévost d'Exiles, Antoine François:
Life of Mr. Cleveland 1581
Prezel, Honoré Lacombe de. See Lacombe de Prezel
Priapeia 2255
Price, Charles, forger:
Life 1609:49
Price, Francis:
Series of observations upon the Cathedral Church of Salisbury 519
Price, John, of Penzance:
One letter. See Letters 2576
Price, John (1773–1801):
Historical account of Leominster 2934
Price, Richard:
Additional observations 1609:37
Discourse on the love of our country 1609: 51
Observations 1609:34
Price, Uvedale. See Repton 2938
Pricke, Robert. See Francini 219; Mauclerc 223
Prideaux, Humphrey:
True nature of imposture 1719
Priest dissected. See Anstey 3222:13
Priestcraft in perfection. See Collins 1608:19
Priestley, Joseph:
Letter to the Right Honourable William Pitt 1609:50
See Bryant 1609:41; Courtenay 1609:53
Primaticcio, Francesco. See Thulden 3524
Prince, —. See Orme 3174
Prince, John:
The beauty of God's house. See Derby 79:7
Danmonii orientales illustres 580
Prince Arthur. See Blackmore 2052
Prince of Abyssinia. See Johnson 1747
Prince of Peace. See Cartwright 3222:16
Prince of Tunis. See Mackenzie 1810:20

Princesse de Montpensier. See La Fayette 989
Principles and preaching of the Methodists. See Cruttenden 1608:74
Principles of philosophy 1608:29
Principles of the late changes. See Temple 1609:11
Pringle, Sir John:
Observations on the diseases of the army 1492
Prinsep, J. See Eton College 2191
Printer's grammar. See Smith 311
Printing 3459. See Jones 3784:2; Palmer 515; Perkins 2589
Prints:
English portraits 3636
Engravings after Claude, Zoffany, Müntz, Wilson 3460
Engravings after Guercino. See Bartolozzi 3398
Miscellaneous prints 468, 2454, 3461, 3605–8, 3626, 3653–6. See Antiquities 3485; Poems 3363
Prior, Matthew:
Memorial against fortifying Dunkirk. See Detection 2677:8
Miscellaneous works 1837
Poems 1877, 2047
Solomon de mundi vanitate. See Tracts 2146:5
Priorato, Galeazzo Gualdo. See Gualdo Priorato
The prisoner. See Rose 1810:51
Private character of Admiral Anson 1608:18
Privileges of the House of Lords and Commons. See Anglesey 144
Privileges of the University of Oxford. See Fell 1608:8
Pro Bono Publico. See Epistle 1609:54
Pro-Pinchbeck's answer. See Mason 3222:14
Probationary ode for the laureatship. See Keate 3222:21
Probationary odes. See Rolliad 2318
Proceedings at the Court of Apollo. See Poems 881:32
Proceedings in a cause . . . of a ravishment of a ward. See Journeaulx 1413
Proceedings on the trials of the conspirators. See Portugal 1343:5
Proclamation. See Poems 881:27

Procopius, of Caesarea:
Secret history of the Court of the Emperor Justinian 759
Prodicus. *See* Shaftesbury 1496
Prodigal. See Waldron 1810:54
Profit and loss of Great-Britain 1608:38
Profitable instructions 2935
Project. See Tickell 3222:16
Prologues:
Collection of English prologues and epilogues 2936
Collection of prologues and epilogues 1810:58
Prologues and epilogues. See Poems 3363
Prolusions; or select pieces of antient poetry. See Capell 2003
Promenade de Versailles. See Bougeant 1178
Promptuaire des medailles. See Rouillé 490
Proofs on the enquiry into Homer's life. See Blackwell 1393
Propagation of the Gospel, Society for. *See* Sermons 1346:3
Proper reply 1608:73
Proper reply to a late scurrilous libel. See Bath 1608:28, 30
Propertius. *See* Catullus
Property re-asserted. See Brett 1367:2
Prophecies. *See* Catastrophe 2352
Prophecy of Merlin 1609:5
Proposal for publishing a poetical translation. See King 1608:61
Proposal to the ladies. See Astell 2633
Proposals for a tax upon liberty of conscience. See Black-bird 2646:19
Proposals for establishing at sea a marine school. See King 1609:48
Proposals for remedying the great charge and delay. See Political tracts 94:12
Proprietor. *See* Letter 1609:22
Prospect from Barrow Hill. See Astle 1609:39
Prospect from Malvern Hill 3222:15
Prospects of London. See London 3818
Protest 1608:84
Protest of the Lords. See Detection 2677:4
Protest of the Merchants 1608:58
Protestant Association, London. *See* Sketch 1609:42
Protestant dissenters. *See* Horsley 1609:53; Huntingford 1609:52; Withers 1609:53

Protestant Divine. *See Defence* 1379:4; *Remarks* 1379:4
Protestant of Eton. *See* Goldwin, William
Protestant Religion is a sure foundation. See Derby 79
Protestant Schools in Ireland. *See* Sermons 1346:10
Protestant volunteer. *See* Serious 1608:60
Pr-t-st. *See* Protest
Prunaeus, Jacobus Billius. *See* Gregory 2158
Prynne, William:
Humble remonstrance . . . against the tax of ship-money. See Tracts 3797:8
Mount-Orgueil 1625
Survay . . . of . . . Mr. Cozens's . . . devotions 1084
Unloveliness of love-lockes. See Tracts 2968:10
See Cotton 2167
Psalms 3974
Psalms:
Les Psaumes de David 1283
Psalter. *See* Missal 2427
Public Advertiser. See London 2143
Public Ledger. See Shebbeare 1609:32
Publick spirit of the Whigs. See Swift 1608:93–4
Puddle. *See Black-bird* 2646:8
Pudica. *See* Honeycomb, William, pseud.
Puffendorf, Samuel von, Baron:
Introduction to the history of . . . Europe 1720
Law of nature and nations 2062
Puget de la Serre, Jean:
L'entrée de la Reyne Mère 608
Puisieux, Madeleine de:
Caractères 1203
Puissance d'un Roi d'Angleterre mise en paralelle. See Tracts 2146:1
Pulteney, William, Earl of Bath. *See* Bath
Pulteney, William, Esquire:
Considerations on the present state of public affairs 1609:39
Thoughts on the present state of affairs 1609:38
Puppet-Shew. See Poems 881:23
Pure, Michel de:
Vie du Mareschal de Gassion 2024
Purpoole, Henry Helmes, Prince of. *See* Canning 108

Puttenham, George:
  Arte of English poesie 2455–6
The puzzle. *See* Tracts 98:1
Pybrac, Seigneur de. *See* Du Faur 806
Pye, Henry James:
  Siege of Meaux 1810:54
  See Rosciad 3222:1
Pye, Jael Henrietta (Mendez):
  Poems 2457
  Short account of Twickenham. See Guides 2387:3
  Short view of Twickenham 2457
Pyke, Joseph. *See* Morgan 1608:12
Pyle, Thomas:
  Paraphrase . . . on the Acts of the Apostles and . . . the Epistles 1381
Pym, John. *See* Tracts 2769:5
Pynson, Richard. *See* Hetoum 2397
Pyrrhus and Demetrius. See Plays 1623:1
Pythagoras. *See* Hill 787; Iamblichus 848

The Quaker. See Dibdin 1810:27
Quaker's reply to the Country Parson's plea.
  See Hervey 1608:35
Quane, Richard. *See* Journeaulx 1413
Quarles, Francis:
  Divine poems 2025
Quarles, John:
  Regale lectum miseriae 2026
Quarter of an hour before dinner. See Rose 1810:46
Quebec. *See* Roubaud 1609:38
Quebec Act. *See* Lyttelton 1609:58; Meredith 1609:32
Queensberry, Catherine Hyde, Duchess of. *See Venus* 3222:15
Quentin, M. *See* Gersaint 298
Querelles littéraires. See Irailh 3019
Quesnel, Pierre. *See Almanach* 1174
Question concerning literary property. See Millar 1609:58
Question of the independency of military officers 1609:8
Question of the precedency of peers. See Egmont 44
Question on some late dismissions truly stated 1609:8
Question relating to a Scots militia considered. See Carlyle 1609:5
Question stated. See Meredith 1609:23

Question stated with regard to our army. See Hervey 1608:28
Questions sur l'Encyclopaedie. See Voltaire 3058
Quinault, Philippe. *See* Lower 1963
Quintana, Francisco de:
  History of Hippolyto and Aminta 1582
Quintilianus, Marcus Fabius:
  Institutionum oratoriarum libri duodecim 2221
Quintus Curtius. *See* Curtius
La quinzaine angloise à Paris. See Rutledge 3046

R., B., Esquire. *See* Hegge 739
R., T. *See Politician* 1810:21
Rabelais, François:
  Works 1583
Rabutin, François de. *See* Collection 3084
Rabutin, Roger de, Comte de Bussy:
  Histoire amoureuse des Gaules 1235
  Mémoires 1002
  Nouvelles lettres 968
Rabutin-Chantal, Marie de, Marquise de Sévigné. *See* Sévigné
Raccolta di lettere. See Bottari 2342
Racine, Jean:
  Oeuvres 947
Racine, Louis:
  Mémoires sur la vie de Jean Racine 969
Radcliffe, Alexander. *See* Ovidius 1973
Radcliffe, Ann. *See* Boaden 1810:54
Radcliffe, Sir George. *See* Strafford 446
Radcliffe Library. *See* King 1608:70; Tracts 1348:3; Tracts 2146:5
Rademaker, Abraham. *See* Gautier 3779
Rademaker, Gerard. *See* Drawings 3587
Radicati, Alberto. *See* Passerano 1164
Radstock, William Waldegrave, Baron. *See* Waldegrave
Raffaello. *See* Raphael, of Urbino
Raftor, Catherine, later Mrs. Clive. *See* Clive
Ragionamenti 3366
Raimondi, Marc Antonio. *See* Dürer 3601
Rainbow, Edward, Bishop. *See* Banks 2638
Raleigh, Sir Walter:
  History of the world 2063
  Works 1448
Ralph, Dr., pseud. *See* Voltaire 1307

Ralph, servant to Reynolds. *See* Kirkley, Ralph

Ralph, James:
Case of our present theatrical disputes 1608:45
Court secret 1608:91
Critical history of the administration of Sir Robert Walpole 2458
Defence of the people. *See* Egmont 119:1
Miscellaneous poems 1914
Of the use and abuse of parliaments 1721
See Champion 1506; Remembrancer 2145

Rams all. See Poems 881:29

Ramsay, Allan (1686–1758):
Poems 1626

Ramsay, Allan, painter:
Essay on ridicule. *See* Tracts 2050:10
Essay on the Constitution 1609:9, 14
Investigator 352. *See* Tracts 2050:11
Thoughts on the origin and nature of government 1609:21
See Arno Miscellany 3803; Meredith 1609:32

Ramsay, Andrew Michael:
Histoire du Vicomte de Turenne 1003, 1143
Travels of Cyrus 1449

Ramsay, Charlotte, later Mrs. Lennox. *See* Lennox

Ramsgate Harbour 1608:7

Ranby, John:
Appendix to the narrative. *See* Tracts 2050:12: Walpole 2493:6
Narrative of the last illness of . . . the Earl of Orford. *See* Tracts 1608:51; Walpole 2492:3, 2493:1
Various tracts 1608:51

Rand, William. *See* Gassendi 1743

Randolph, Thomas (1605–1635):
Cornelianum dolium. *See* Plays 2131:3
Poems 1977

Randolph, Thomas (1701–1783). *See* Newton 1608:70

Ranzovius, Henricus:
Catalogus imperatorum 1584, 3367

Rape of Pomona. See Courteney 3222:13

Raphael, of Urbino:
Essays of character 3514
Portfolio of 460 engravings 3609
Teste scelte 3609
See Bartoli 3486; Farnese 3619

Rapin-Thoyras, Paul de:
Histoire d'Angleterre 1144
History of England . . . to . . . George II 433
See Vertue 3663

Rasbotham, Dorning:
Codrus 1810:22

Rashīd, Maulāy, Sultan of Morocco:
Life of Tafiletta . . . Emperor of Barbary 1344

Raspe, Rudolph Erich:
Critical essay on oil-painting 2459
Nathan the wise 1810:33

Raspono, Cesare:
De basilica et patriarchio Lateranensi 3462

Rasselas. See Johnson 1747

Rational Rosciad 3222:7

Ratts rhimed to death. See Collection 1890

The raven. See Black-bird 2646:5

Raviglio Rosso, Giulio:
Historia delle cose occorse nel regno d'Inghilterra 2460, 2937. *See* Martinelli 1161

Rawlinson, Richard:
English topographer 664
History . . . of the Cathedral Church of Salisbury 665
History . . . of the Cathedral Church of Rochester 701
History . . . of the City and Cathedral Church of Hereford 702
See Aubrey 648; Hornby 692; Perrott 1688

Ray, John:
Collection of English words not generally used 2027
Select remains 1689

Ray, Martha. *See* Hackman 1609:40

Ray, Nicholas:
Importance of the colonies 1609:56

Raymond, Henry Augustus, pseud. *See* Scott 1654

Raymond, Sir Thomas:
Reports of divers special cases 1128

Raymund, John:
Folly in print 1978

Raynal, Guillaume Thomas François:
Anecdotes historiques 1166
Anecdotes littéraires 1165
See Irailh 3019

Rayner, John:
History and antiquities. *See* Dugdale 729

GENERAL INDEX

Reading, William:
Catalogue of the Sion College Library 908
Real happiness of a people. See Wolff 1608:72
Reale Accademia delle Scienze. *See* Naples 3509
The reapers 1810:16
Reasonable animals 1810:31
Reasons humbly offered for the liberty of unlicens'd printing. See Blount 1608:1
Reasons humbly offered to prove 1608:81
Reasons humbly offer'd to the Parliament. See Charles VI 1608:26
Reasons in support of the war in Germany. 1609:1
Reasons why the Duke of Marlborough cannot lay down his commands 1608:94
Reay, Martha. *See* Ray
Rebellion of Naples. See Masaniello 2019
Receipt tax. See Dent 1810:35
Receipts in cookery. See Cookery 3165
Recherches philosophiques sur les Egyptiens. See Pauw 3134
Recherches sur les costumes et sur les théâtres de toutes les nations. See Le Vacher 3120
Récréations historiques. See Dreux du Radier 3090
Recreations of his age. See Thoresby 2603
Recruiting serjeant. See Bickerstaffe 1810:16
Recueil d'estampes. See Crozat 3550
Recueil d'observations . . . sur les moeurs . . . de differens peuples de l'Asie. See Lambert 3025
Recueil de diverses pièces. See Henry III 844
Recueil de lettres. See Griffet 1297
Recueil de médailles. See Pellerin 277
Recueil des lettres. See Racine 969
Recueil des pièces du Régiment de la Calotte. See Calotte 1270
Recueil des pièces les plus curieuses. See Albert 713
Recueil des plus beaux tableaux de France. See Crozat 3550
Recueil historique 1047
Recueil nécessaire. See Voltaire 3059
Red Sea. *See* Irwin 2884
Redmond, Jean de, Chevalier. *See* Walpole 2614
Reed, Isaac. *See* Baker 3912; Middleton 2419
Reed, Joseph:
Dido 1810:11

Reed, Joseph (*cont.*)
The register-office 1810:2
Tom Jones 1810:14
Reeve, Clara:
Old English Baron 2461
Reeve, Joseph:
Ugbrooke Park 3222:14
Reeve, Sir Thomas. *See* Etchings 3588
Reflections concerning innate moral principles. See Bolingbroke 1608:13
Reflections on the case of Mr. Wilkes 1609:20
Reflections on the Letter to Dr. Waterland 1379:1
Reflections on the present commotions in Bengal 1609:55
Reflections on the present state of our East India affairs 1609:7
Reflections on the weekly Bills of Mortality 1608:1
Reflections upon learning. See Baker 3887
Reflections upon the present state of affairs 1608:80
Reflexions on representation in Parliament 1609:13
Réflexions sur Polibe. See Almanach 1174
Regencies. *See* England 1608:66
Regency. *See* Dutens 2841
Regenfuss, Franz Michael:
Choix de coquillages 3554
Regimen sanitatis. *See* Salerno 2289
Register of reports. *See* Caesar 2535:4, 5
Register-office. See Reed 1810:2
Registrum brevium. *See* Reports 2591
Regnier, Claude Louis François, Comte de Guerchy. *See* Guerchy
Regnier, Mathurin:
Satyres 1204
Regulations lately made concerning the colonies 1609:11
Reid, Thomas:
Inquiry into the human mind 1602
Relandus, Petrus:
Fasti consulares ad illustrationem Codicis Justinianei ac Theodosiani. See Classics 2207:36
Relation of the earthquake. See Lima 1485
Relation of the voyage to Tadmor. See Halifax 2554
Relation of three embassies. See Miège 1532
Relief of debts. See Culpeper 2674

[491]

Religio jurisprudentis. See Hildesley 2706

Religion of nature delineated. See Wollaston 1363

Religion of the Gentiles. See Herbert 48

Religious tracts. *See* Grove 1410

Remains of Christian antiquity. See Dalrymple 2832

Remarkable satires. See Satires 2319

Remarks critical and illustrative on . . . Shakespeare. See Ritson 2939

Remarks in the grand tour of France and Italy. See Bromley 291

Remarks on a false, scandalous, and seditious libel, intituled, The conduct of the allies 1608:13

Remarks on a pamphlet, entitled, The Thoughts of a Member of the lower House. See Tracts 400:5, 2475:9

Remarks on a pamphlet intituled A Short view of a dispute 1608:6

Remarks on a scurrilous postscript 1379:3

Remarks on Dr. Johnson's Life of Gray. See Tindal 1609:42

Remarks on Dr. K——'s speech. See Burton 1608:70

Remarks on Dr. Middleton's Examination 1379:4

Remarks on Dr. Sherlock's first dissertation 1379:11

Remarks on Italy. See Spectator 1860

Remarks on . . . Royal and Noble Authors. See Tracts 2050:13

Remarks on the Budget. See Whately 1609:9

Remarks on the conduct of the B*** M*** 1608:59

Remarks on the controversial writings of Dr. Middleton 1379:9

Remarks on the Craftsman's vindication. See Political tracts 94:4

Remarks on the Journal of a Tour 1609:48

Remarks on the laws relating to the poor. See Hay 1608:48; Tracts 2049:10

Remarks on the preliminary articles 1608:58

Remarks on the writings . . . of J. J. Rousseau. See Hume 1680:7

Remarks upon Mr. Carte's specimen. See Squire 1608:61

Remarques sur un ouvrage. See Fournier 3012:1

Rembrandt van Rijn, Harmensz. *See* Daulby 237; Drawings 3587

Remembrancer 2145

Remicius. *See* Aesop 1728

Rémonstrance du clergé de France 1085

Remy, Pierre:
    Catalogue raisonné 353
    See Julienne 3020

Renan, Barthélémi. *See* Lastri 3540

Renard, Louis. *See* Geography 2174

Reni, Guido:
    Portfolio of 160 engravings 3610
    See Frey 3602

Renowned history of Fragosa. See Lyly 2724

Repertorium sculptile-typicum 354. *See* Arts 288:2; Orlandi 2082

Reply to a Letter addressed to the Right Hon. George Grenville 1609:54

Reply to Dr. Middleton's Examination 1379:4

Reply to the Answer to A short essay. See Glenie 1609:47A

Reply to the Counter-address. See Guthrie 1609:8

Reply to the Defence of the Letter. See Pearce 1379:1

Reply to the Defence of the majority. See Meredith 1609:9

Reply to the Letter to Dr. Waterland. See Pearce 1379:1

Réponse aux questions d'un Provincial. See Bayle 934

Report from the Committee appointed to examine the physicians. See England 1609:51

Report of the Committee on lotteries. See Tracts 2146:6

Reports and documents 2591

Reports and Letters 2592

Reports, letters, and documents, especially Scottish. *See* Caesar 2535:2

Reports, letters, and documents, of the time of King James I. *See* Caesar 2535:1

Representation of the Board of Trade relating to . . . America. See Tracts 2146:6

Reprisal. See Smollett 1818:15

Repton, Humphry:
    Letter to Uvedale Price, Esq. 2938
    Sketches and hints on landscape gardening 3861

Repton, Humphrey (*cont.*)
See Gillray 3563:2
Requier, Jean Baptiste. *See* Siri 3052
Reresby, Sir John:
Memoirs 469
Reresby, Tamworth:
Miscellany of ingenious thoughts 1627
Resignation discussed. See Chesterfield 1673:3
Resta, Sebastiano. *See* Meyssens 3649
Restout, Jean. *See* Drawings 3567
Retz, Jean François Paul de Gondi, Cardinal
de. *See* Gondi 962
Reveley, Willey. *See* Stuart 3544; Walpole
2486
Reverend Brethren. See Cumberland 1608:8
Revett, Nicholas. *See* Chandler 3534; Stuart
3544
Review of all that hath pass'd. See Bath 1608:
38
Review of Lord Bute's administration. See
Almon 1609:6
Review of Mr. Pitt's administration. See
Almon 1609:5
Review of Mrs. Crawford and Mrs. Siddons
1810:34
*Review of the Case of the Protestant Dis-
senters. See* Horsley 1609:53
Review of the conduct of Pascal Paoli 1609:
24
Review of the Landscape. See Marshall 3245
Review of the passage in Tully 1608:55
Review of the reign of George the Second.
See Almon 1609:4
Review of the whole political conduct 1608:
44
Review, or Memoirs. See Castlehaven 152
Reviews. *See* Tracts 2050
Revolution:
Some Account of the Revolution 2593
Revolution of Sweden. See Cockburn 1818:21
Revolution politicks 96
Revolutions in Spain. See Orléans 3358
Reynolds, Frederick:
Dramatist 1810:51
How to grow rich 1810:52
Notoriety 1810:52
Reynolds, Sir Joshua:
Catalogue of Ralph's exhibition. See Tracts
3833:6, 9

Reynolds, Sir Joshua (*cont.*)
Discourses. See Royal Academy 3885
Seven discourses 281
See Combe 3222:15; Du Fresnoy 3890;
Pindarick 3222:9; Warton 3222:18
Reynst, Gerard:
Variarum imaginum . . . caelaturae 3579
The rhapsody. See Pope 1912:2
Rhapsody of free thoughts 1608:63
The Rhine. See Cogan 3853
Rhodes. See Caoursin 3739
Rhodes, Knights of. *See* Vertot 3055
Rhodomannus, Laurentius. *See* Diodorus 2154
Rhys, Udal ap:
Account of . . . Spain and Portugal
1420
Rialton, Henrietta Churchill, Viscountess;
later Duchess of Marlborough. *See* Marl-
borough
Ricci, Marco. *See* Drawings 3567
Ricciardetto:
Richardet 3041
Riccoboni, Luigi:
Histoire du théâtre italien 1167
Riccoboni, Marie Jeanne:
Lettres de My-Lord Rivers 3042
See Marivaux 997
Rice, John. *See* True . . . account 1609:6
Rich, John:
One or more letters. *See* Letters 2576
See Spirit 1818:18
Rich, Mary, Countess of Warwick. *See* War-
wick
Rich, Sir Robert:
*Letter . . . to the Right Honourable Lord
Viscount Barrington* 1609:58
See Defence 1609:56
Richard II, King of England:
Life and reign 1608:9
See Caesar 2815; Howard 2710
Richard III, King of England:
Paradoxe in prayse of Richard III 2594
See Buck 475; More 2247; Walpole 2487
Richard, Jérôme:
Description . . . de l'Italie 3043
Richard of Cirencester. *See* Tracts 1348:8
Richard Coeur de Lion. See Burgoyne 1810:
39
Richardet. See Ricciardetto 3041

Richardson, Francis:
Appeal to the officers of the Guards 1609:
58
Richardson, Jonathan:
Account of some of the statues . . . in Italy
309
*Explanatory notes . . . on Milton's Paradise
Lost* 1838
Two discourses 310
See Drawings 3567
Richardson, Joseph:
Fugitive 1810:51
See Townshend 3222:22
Richardson, Martha. *See* Monk, Martha
(Richardson)
Richardson, Samuel. *See* Porrett 1810:45
Richelieu, Armand Jean du Plessis, Cardinal,
Duc de:
Maximes d'état 3044
Mémoires 3368
See Girardon 3589; Vulson 3557
Richmond, Charles Lennox, 3d Duke of:
Answer 1609:47A
Richmond, Margaret Beaufort, Countess of.
See Fisher 685
Richmond. *See* Gale 569
Richmond, a vision. See Poems 881:20
Richmond Park. *See* New Forest 1608:66
Rickard, Sir Andrew. *See* Caesar 2535:7
Ride and walk through Stourhead 3222:16
Rider, Cardanus. *See* Walpole 2622
Rider, William:
*Historical and critical account of . . . the
living authors of Great-Britain* 1609:5
The rider 1810:12
Ridley, Glocester:
Life of Dr. Nicholas Ridley 3256
See Poems 3363:14
Ridley, James:
Tales of the genii 392
Ridley, Nicholas, Bishop. *See* Ridley, Glocester 3256
Ridolfi, Carlo:
Maraviglie dell'arte 489
Ridpath, George:
Massacre of Glencoe 1609:38
See Rowland 1608:8
Rienzi. *See* Du Cerceau 1293
Rigacci, Giuseppe:
Raccolta di varie canzoni . . . A sue

Rigacci, Giuseppe *(cont.)*
Eccellenza Myledy Walpole [Margaret
Rolle] 2111, 2462, 3463
Raccolta . . . A Mylady Sofia Farmor 2112
Rigault, Nicholas. *See* Thou 3152
Rigby, Joseph:
Ingenious poem 1979
Rigby, Richard:
Authentic memoirs 3903
Right Honourable annuitant vindicated
1609:3
Right of appeal to juries. See Hartley
1609:8
Rightful monarchy. See Tracts 98:2
Rights of Britons. *See* Evidence 1609:35
Rights of Parliament vindicated 1609:13
Rights of the British colonies considered
1609:11
Rigoley de Juvigny, Jean Antoine. *See* Bibliothèques 3068
Riley, John. *See* Drawings 3567
Rimius, Heinrich:
Candid narrative 1608:75
Rinucius. *See* Remicius
Rio, Martinus Antonius Del:
Disquisitionum magicarum libri sex 857
Ripault-Desormeaux, Joseph Louis. *See*
Desormeaux
Ripley, James:
Select original letters 2749
Ripley, Thomas. *See* Walpole 3546; Ware 536
Ripon. *See* Gent 687, 2694
Riquetti, Honoré Gabriel, Comte de Mirabeau. *See* Mirabeau
Risdon, Tristram:
Chorographical description of Devon 703
*Rise and fall of the heresy of the iconoclasts.
See* Manning 3439
Rise and fall of the late projected excise. See
Walpole 1608:30
*Rise and progress of the present taste in
planting parks* 3222:8
Ritchie, David:
Lady's head dresser 1609:29
Ritson, Joseph:
*Remarks . . . on the text and notes of the
last edition of Shakespeare* 2939
See Robin Hood 1493
Rival wives 2463
The rivals. See Sheridan 1810:23

Rivers, George Pitt, Baron:
  Letters to a young nobleman 3257
Rivière du Fresny, Charles. *See Amusemens* 3940
Roach, Deodata and Elizabeth. *See* Journeaulx 1413
Roads:
  Book of English roads 2287
Robert III, King of Scotland. *See* Cromarty 76
Robert the Devil 3975
Roberts, James, dramatist:
  Rule Britannia 1810:54
Roberts, James, pseud. *See* Payba
Roberts, Miss R.:
  Malcolm 1810:35
Roberts, Samuel:
  Love to our country 1608:25
Roberts, William Hayward:
  Judah restored 2940
Robertson, Archibald:
  Topographical survey of the Great Road 3862
Robertson, David:
  Tour through the Isle of Man 3863
Robertson, William:
  Historical disquisition concerning India 2941
  History of America 2942
  History of Scotland 321
  History of the reign of the Emperor Charles V 2943
  One or more letters. *See* Letters 2576
Robin Hood. *See* Mendez 1818:10
Robin Hood: a collection of . . . poems 1493
Robin Hood Society:
  Genuine and authentick memoirs 1608:63
Robin-Red-Breast's answer. *See* Black-bird 2646:2
Robinson, Christopher:
  Considerations 1608:39
Robinson, Elizabeth. *See* Montagu, Elizabeth (Robinson)
Robinson, John:
  Account of Sueden 1421
Robinson, Mrs. Mary. *See* Poetical epistle 3222:17
Robinson, Matthew, Baron Rokeby. *See* Rokeby

Robinson, Pollingrove:
  Beauties of painting 3222:18
Robinson, Robert:
  Case of the Chief Justice of Gilbraltar. See Tracts 2049:11
Robinson, Thomas, 2d Baron Grantham. *See* Grantham
Robinson, Thomas:
  History of Westmorland and Cumberland 704
Robinson-Morris, Matthew, Baron Rokeby. *See* Rokeby
Robson, Horatio:
  Look before you leap 1810:46
Rocester, Staffordshire. *See* Astle 1609:39
Rochechouart, Guillaume de. *See Collection* 3084
Rochefort, Jean de. *See Passe-tems* 1046
Rochester, John Wilmot, Earl of:
  Works 176
  See Burnet 1703
Rochester Cathedral. *See* Rawlinson 701
Rochette de la Morlière, Jacques. *See Angola* 1288
Rochford, Lucy Young, Countess of:
  One or more letters. *See* Letters 2576
Rock, Richard, pseud. *See Epistle* 1608:51
Rodenhurst, T.:
  Description of Hawkstone 2944
Rodet, Marie Thérèse, Mme. Geoffrin. *See* Geoffrin
Rodogune: or, the rival brothers. *See* Aspinwall 1810:7
Rodondo. See Dalrymple 1810:59
Roe, Sir Thomas:
  Negotiations 882
  See Valle 2181
Rogers, Charles:
  Collection of prints 3627
  See Dante 3222:18
Rogers, Nathan:
  Memoirs of Monmouth-Shire 760
Rogers, Mr. R., pseud. *See* Brome 717
Rogers, Robert:
  Ponteach 1810:8
Rogers, Samuel:
  Ode to superstition. See Tracts 2968:7
  Pleasures of memory 2464. *See* Tracts 2968:7
Rogers, William. *See* Walpole 3582

Rogissard, Sieur de:
   New French grammar 1260
Rohan, Marie Eléanor de, Abbesse de
   Malnouë. *See Oraisons* 929
Rokeby, Matthew Robinson, Baron:
   Considerations 1609:32, 33
   Dangerous situation of England 1609:50
   Further examination 1609:34
   Peace the best policy 1609:38
Rolle, Margaret, Countess of Orford. *See*
   Orford
Rolli, Paolo Antonio:
   Di canzonette e di cantate libri due 2113
   See Overbeke 306; Plays 3972; Steele 2115
Rolliad:
   Criticisms on the Rolliad 2318
   See Tracts 2050
Rollin, Charles:
   De la manière d'enseigner et d'étudier les
   belles-lettres 1206
   Histoire ancienne des Egyptiens 1205
Rolt, Richard:
   Almena 1810:6
   The royal shepherd 1810:6
Roman de la rose. See Robert the Devil 3975
Roman eagle, engravings of. *See* Antiquities
   3485:9
Romano, Giulio. *See* Drawings 3567-8
Romans, Jacob. *See* Schenk 3657
Romans et contes 3045
Romant of romants. See Du Verdier 452, 2683
Romanus, Jacobus. *See* Romans, Jacob
Rome:
   Antiquities. *See* Bartoli 3598; Desgodetz
   3677; Giovannoli 3495; Kennet 2716; Over-
   beke 3576; Piranesi 3543; Rossi 3516;
   Schenk 3518; Van Nideck 3686; Venuti
   3545
   Church of Rome. *See* Cogan 722; Innocent
   XII 849
   Corpus Juris Civilis. See Classics 2207:18
   See Arts 288:1; Boissard 495; Deseine 1027;
   Echard 1641; Lucanus 1901; Rossi 3464-5,
   3515; Rubens 3466; Tracts 361:5; Venice
   3662; Vertot 1662
Romney, George. *See* Hayley 3222:16
The romp. See Bickerstaffe 1810:10, 38
Romulus and Tarquin. *See* Malvezzi 171
Rondellus, Jacobus. *See* Du Rondel

Rooke, John. *See* Arrian 3995; Egerton 1677
Rooker, Edward. *See* Antiquities 3485:15;
   Copper Plate Magazine 3839
Rooker, Michael Angelo. *See Copper Plate*
   Magazine 3839
Rosa, Salvatore. *See* Drawings 3569
Rosciad of C--v--nt—g--rd--n 3222:1
Roscius Anglicanus. See Downes 3919
Roscoe, William:
   Life of Lorenzo de' Medici 3703
   See Medici 3821
Rose, John:
   Prisoner 1810:51
   Quarter of an hour before dinner 1810:46
Rose, M. *See* Louis XIV 967
Rose and Crown Club. *See* St. Luke's Club
   2595
Roselle, Marquis de. *See* Elie de Beaumont
   938
Rosenberg, Justine Wynne, Countess Orsini.
   See Orsini 3753
Rosicrucians:
   Fame and confession of the Fraternity of
   . . . the Rosie Cross 1542
Rosina. See Brook 1810:35
Rosoi, Barnabé Farmain de. *See* Farmain
Ross, Anna, Mrs. Brunton. *See* Brunton
Rossi, Domenico de, engraver:
   Raccolta di statue antiche e moderne 3628
   Romanae magnitudinis monumenta. See
   Rubens 3466
Rossi, Giovanni Gherardo de:
   Vita del Cavaliere Giovanni Pikler, intag-
   liatore 2114
Rossi, Giovanni Giacomo de:
   Fontane di Roma 3464, 3515
   Nuovo teatro delle fabriche ed edificii 3465
Rossi, Lorenzo Filippo de:
   Raccolta di vasi diversi 3516
Rosso, Giulio Raviglio. *See* Raviglio Rosso
Rossus, John. *See* Rous
Roubaud, Pierre Joseph Antoine:
   Lettres de Monsieur de Montcalm 1609:38
Roucher, Jean Antoine. *See* Collection
   3084
Rouillé, Guillaume:
   Promptuaire des medailles 490
Rouquet, André:
   Present state of the arts in England 355

Rous, George, supposed author. *See Essay* 1609:25

Rous, John:
Historia regum Angliae 666

Rousseau, Jean Baptiste:
Oeuvres diverses 1145

Rousseau, Jean Jacques:
Emile 818
Lettres de deux amans 819
Pygmalion 3222:16
Rousseau juge de Jean Jacques 3369
See Burney 1810:9; Hume 1609:16, 1680; Wollstonecraft 3177

Rousseau de la Valette, Michel:
Life of Count Ulfeld of Denmark 761

Roussel, Pierre Joseph Alexis. *See* Broglie 3072

Rousset de Missy, Jean:
Intérêts présens des puissances de l'Europe 1014

The rout. See Hill 1818:17

Rouvroy, Louis de, Duc de Saint-Simon. *See* Saint-Simon

Rowe, Nicholas:
Ambitious step-mother 1818:21
Fair penitent 1818:21
Jane Shore. See Plays 1907:4
Royal convert. See Plays 1910:5
Tamerlane 1818:21
Tragedy of Lady Jane Grey. See Plays 1623:2
Ulysses 1818:21
See Lucanus 1875

A Rowland for an Oliver 1608:8

Rowlands, Henry:
Mona antiqua restaurata 3206
See Owen 513

Rowlands, Richard, alias Verstegan. *See* Verstegan, Richard

Rowlandson, Thomas. *See* Bunbury 3563:2; Grose 2862; Westminster 557

Rowley, Thomas, pseud. *See* Barrett 539; Chatterton 3690

Rows, John. *See* Rous

Royal Academy of Arts:
Collection of catalogues 3885
Plan of an academy. See Tracts 2146:1
See Reynolds 281; Strange 3468; Tracts 3833

Royal African Company. *See* Tracts 2146:1, 6

Royal compendium 762

The royal garland. See Bickerstaffe 1810:13

Royal Incorporated Society of Artists. *See* Royal Academy 3885:1

The royal merchant. See Hull 1810:11

Royal perseverance 3222:16

Royal recollections on a tour to Cheltenham. See Williams 1609:51

The royal shepherd. See Rolt 1810:6

Royal Society, London:
Diplomata 1608:50
Philosophical transactions 1608:7, 1628
See Birch 1056; Fielding 1608:45; Grew 1115; Norfolk 486; Sprat 1632

Royal Society of Arts. *See* Royal Academy 3885:3, 4; Society 2957

Royal suppliants. See Delap 1810:32

Royal tracts. See James II 203

Royalty Theatre. *See* Linley 1810:43

Royston, Philip Yorke, Viscount, 2d Earl of Hardwicke. *See* Hardwicke

Royston. *See* Stukeley 668

Rubeis, Bernardo Maria de:
De nummis. See Arts 288:4

Rubens, Peter Paul:
La gallerie du Palais du Luxembourg 3595
Palazzi di Genova 3466
See Drawings 3568–9; Gevartius 3620; Hecquet 3016

Rubeus, Joannes:
Bonifacius VIII 858

Rudd, Mrs. Margaret Caroline (Young):
Genuine letter 1609:34
See Female forgery 1609:35; Hart 1609:37

Rudd, Sayer:
Certain method to know the disease. See Tracts 2146:1

Rudder, Samuel:
New history of Gloucester 530

Ruddier, Benjamin. *See* Rudyerd

Ruddiman, Thomas. *See* Anderson 3549; Chalmers 2821

Rudyerd, Benjamin. *See* Pembroke 207

Ruffhead, Owen:
Considerations on the present dangerous crisis 1609:6
Life of Alexander Pope 2945
See Tracts 2968:8

Ruggieri, Ferdinando:
  Studio d'architettura civile 531
Ruggle, George:
  Ignoramus 2256, 2946, 3370. *See* Grimston
  1896:1
Ruin seize thee 3222:16
Rules and articles for . . . his Majesty's forces.
  See Tracts 2146:3
Rules for being a wit 1608:74
Rules for speaking 1608:29
The runaway. See Cowley 1810:25
Rundle, Thomas, Bishop:
  Letters to Mrs. Barbara Sandys 2947
Runnamede. See Logan 1810:35
Rupert to Maria. See Poems 881:19
Rural elegance display'd 2750
Ruscelli, Girolamo:
  Epistres des princes 1086
  See Alexis 2629
Russell, Alexander:
  Natural history of Aleppo 2948
Russell, Lady Caroline, later Duchess of Marl-
  borough. *See* Marlborough
Russell, Francis, Marquess of Tavistock. *See*
  Tavistock
Russell, James. *See* Russell, John
Russell, John:
  Letters 1450
Russell, Rachel, Baroness Russell:
  Letters 3258
Russell, William, Lord Russell. *See* Towers
  1609:31
Russia. *See* Hanway 1324; Schérer 3146;
  Whitworth 2324, 2530, 3469:17
Rutherford, John. *See* Harris 1609:56
Rutherforth, Thomas:
  Defence of the Lord Bishop of London's
  Discourses. See Middleton 1379:11
Ruthven, John, Earl of Gowrie. *See* Gowrie
Ruthven, Thomas, Baron Ruthven:
  Ladies cabinet 177
Rutland, Charles Manners, 4th Duke of:
  Modest apology 1609:31
Rutland, County of. *See* Wright 585
Rutledge, Jean Jacques:
  La quinzaine angloise à Paris 3046
Rutter, Joseph. *See* Corneille 1936
Ruyssen, Nicolas Joseph. *See* Raphael 3514
Ruyter, Michel de. *See* Brandt 891

Ryall, John. *See* Withy 259
Rycaut, Paul. *See* Lasso de la Vega 443;
  Sacchi 1129
Ryder, Thomas. *See* Connaught 1810:10
Rye House Plot. *See* Sprat 1132; Tankerville
  1608:71
Ryley, Sir Heister. *See* Povey 95
Rymer, Thomas. *See* Ralph 1721; *Whole*
  Prophecies 1608:45
Rymsdyk, Andreas van. *See* Rymsdyk, Jan van
Rymsdyk, Jan and Andreas van:
  Museum Britannicum 3555
Rysbrack, John Michael. *See* Müntz 3575
Ryves, Bruno:
  Mercurius rusticus 1762
Ryves, Elizabeth:
  Ode to the Rev. Mr. Mason 3222:17
  Poems 2465

S., C. *See* Dorset 1608:27; Plays 1082:4
S., G. *See* Broughton 718
S., H. *See Reasons* 1608:94
S., L. *See* Cooke 2146:4
S., P. *See Letter* 1818:17
S., R. *See* Speed, R.; Strange, Richard
S., R. *See* Barbary 3804
S., T. *See* Neve 1489
S., W.:
  Poems of Ben. Johnson, Junior 1980
Sabatier de Castres, Antoine:
  Derniers sentiments 2288
  Trois siècles de notre littérature 1168
Sablier, Charles:
  Variétés sérieuses et amusantes 3047
Sacchi, Andrea:
  Portfolio of 20 engravings 3629
  See Drawings 3569
Sacchi, Bartholomaeus:
  Lives of the Popes 1129
Sacheverell, Henry:
  Tryal of Dr. Henry Sacheverell 1130
  See Tracts 98:2; Tracts 3832:3
Sachs, Hans. *See* Amman 3769
Saci, Le Maistre de. *See* Bible 915
Sackville, Charles, Earl of Dorset. *See* Dorset
Sackville, Charles, 2d Duke of Dorset. *See*
  Dorset
Sackville, Lord George. *See* Germain, George
  Sackville, 1st Viscount Sackville

Sackville, George Germain, Viscount Sackville. *See* Germain, George Sackville, 1st Viscount Sackville

Sackville, John Frederick, 3d Duke of Dorset. *See* Dorset

Sackville, Lionel Cranfield, 1st Duke of Dorset. *See* Dorset

Sacre de Louis XV. See Mariette 3592

Sadducism. *See* Glanvill 2050:20

Sade, Jacques François Aldonçe de:
Mémoires pour la vie de François Pétrarque 932

Sadeler, Aegidius. *See* Prints 3606

Sadeler, Jan. *See* De Vos 3600; Prints 3605

Sadeler, Raphael. *See* Gislenius 2122

Sadoleto, Jacopo, Cardinal:
Epistola 859

Saenredam, Joannes. *See* Prints 3606

La sage folie 1306

Saggi di dissertazioni. See Cortona 2076

St. Albans, Francis Bacon, Viscount. *See* Bacon

St. Albans. *See* Newcome 3202, 3248

St. Asaph. *See* Willis 2780

St. Aubyn, Catherine. *See* Etchings 3588

St. Denys, Abbaye Royale. *See* Félibien 875

St. Edmund Hall. *See* Oxford University

St. Edmundsbury. *See* Battely 616

Saint-Evremond, Charles Marguetel de Saint-Denis, Seigneur de:
Oeuvres 948

Saint-Foix, Germain François Poullain de:
Essais 1261
Histoire de l'Ordre du Saint-Esprit 3143
See Cibber 1818:10

St. Germain, Abbaye Royale. *See* Bouillart 868

St. Innocent's Church, Paris. *See* Flamel 737

St. John, Henry, Viscount Bolingbroke. *See* Bolingbroke

St. John, Hon. John:
Island of St. Marguerite 1810:48
Mary, Queen of Scots 1810:47

St. John family. *See Notitia* 756

St. John of Jerusalem, Knights of. *See* Bosio 435; Vertot 3055

St. John the Baptist, Church of, in the Lateran. *See* Raspono 3462

St. Laurence, Monastery of. *See* Santos 3759

St. Luke's Club:
Journal of the Virtuosi 2595

St. Mark's, Venice. *See* Zanetti 3559

St. Paul's Cathedral, London. *See* Dugdale 591; George III, 3424

St. Paul's Cross. *See* Paul's Cross 2587

St. Paul's School, London:
Preces, catechismus, et hymni 2751
See Knight 1681

St. Peter's, Abbey church of, Westminster. *See* Dart 566

Saint-Philippe, Vincente Bacallar y Sanna, Marquis de. *See* Bacallar 1266

Saint-Pierre, Jacques Henri Bernardin de:
Voyage à l'Isle de France 3048

Saint Réal, César Vischard de:
Oeuvres 1004

Saint-Simon, Louis de Rouvroy, Duc de:
Mémoires 3259, 3371
Supplément 3371
See Louis XIV 3337

St. Stephen's Chapel, Westminster. *See* Topham 3472

Saint-Véran, Louis Joseph de, Marquis de Montcalm. *See* Montcalm

Sainte-Geneviève, Bibliothèque de. *See* Du Molinet 3679

Sainte-Marthe, Denis de:
Vie de Cassiodore 1207

Sainte-Marthe, Louis de. *See* Sainte-Marthe, Scévole de

Sainte-Marthe, Scécole de:
Genealogical history of the kings of Portugal 250, 3281
Histoire généalogique de la Maison de France 909
Oeuvres poetiques 1048

Sainte-Maure, Charles de, Duc de Montausier. *See* Montausier

Sainte-Palaye, Jean Baptiste de la Curne de. *See* La Curne 809

Saintré, John de. *See* La Sale 1277

Saints, Lives of. *See* Challoner 619

Saladin, Sultan of Egypt. *See* Marin 3029

Sale of authors, a dialogue. See Campbell 366, 2658

Sale of the House of Peers 3976

Salerno. Schola Salernitana 2289

Sales, Francis de, Saint. *See* Tauler 1589

Salignac, Bertrand de. *See Collection* 3084

Salisbury, Robert Cecil, Earl of:
Answere to certaine scandalous papers 1169

Salisbury:
Antiquitates Sarisburienses 2949
Salisbury guide 2752

Salisbury Cathedral:
Description of that admirable structure 556
See Price 519; Rawlinson 665

Salisbury guide. See Salisbury 2752

Sallengre, Albert Henri de:
Eloge de l'yvresse 763
Histoire de Pierre de Montmaur 2466

Sallustius Crispus, Caius:
Opera 2222, 2290
Works 470
See Brindley 2120:11

Salmagundi. See Huddesford 3327

Salmon, Nathaniel:
Antiquities of Surrey 705, 2753
History and antiquities of Essex 7
See Essex 3418

Salmon, Thomas, the elder:
Essay to the advancement of musick 393

Salmon, Thomas, the younger:
Chronological historian 1690
See Collection 870

Salmon, William:
Polygraphice 1494
Seplasium 1495

Saltern, George:
Of the ancient lawes of Great Britaine. *See*
Tracts 3797:1

Saltonstall, Wye. *See* Ovidius 1972

Saltoun, Alexander Fraser, 15th Baron:
Thoughts on the disqualification of the eldest sons of the peers of Scotland 2950

Salusbury, Thomas. *See* Ovidius 1904

Salzburg:
Account of the sufferings. *See* Villars 1550

Samber, Robert:
Long livers 764
Roma illustrata. *See* Tracts 361:5

Sambucus, Joannes:
Emblemata 2291

Samos. *See* Georgirenes 1408

Samuel Hartlib his Legacie. See Hartlib 125

San Lorenzo. *See* Santos 3759

San Lucar, Gaspar de Guzman, Conde de
Olivares and Duque de. *See* Olivares 2586

San Michele Cloister. *See* Malvasia 3624

San Pedro, Diego de:
Castell of love 208, 2467

San Severino, Giulio Roberto di:
Vies des hommes et des femmes illustres
d'Italie. *See* Tracts 359:5

Sanchez, Francisco:
Minerva 2257

Sanchoniathon:
Sanchoniatho's Phoenician history 1653

Sandby, Paul:
Virtuosi's Museum 3844
See Antiquities 3485:12; *Copper Plate
Magazine* 3839

Sandby, William. *See* Horatius 2194; Terentius 2202; Virgilius 2205

Sanderson, Robert (1587–1663), Bishop. *See*
Walton 1725

Sanderson, Robert (1660–1741). *See* William
III 2035, 2779

Sanderson, Sir William:
Aulicus coquinariae 1585, 1800
Compleat history of Charles I 1585
Graphice: the use of pen and pencil 251

Sanderus, Antonius:
Grand théâtre sacré du Duché de Brabant
532

Sandford, Francis:
Genealogical history of the kings of Eng-
land 581
History of the coronation of James II
3517
Order and ceremonies 3282
See Sainte-Marthe 250, 3281

Sandisson. *See* Bignon 2339

Sandrart, Joachim von:
Academia nobilissimae artis pictoriae 3630

Sandras de Courtilz, Gatien:
Annales de la Cour et de Paris 1236
Guerre d'Espagne 3144

Sandwich, Edward Montagu, 1st Earl of. *See*
Barba 145

Sandwich, John Montagu, 4th Earl of:
One letter. *See* Letters 2576
See Letter 1608:58

Sandwich. *See* Boys 234

Sandys, Mrs. Barbara. *See* Rundle 2947

Sandys, George (1578–1644):
Travels 2064
See Ovidius 1905

Sandys, George (*fl.* 1684):
Anglorum speculum 1763
Sandys, Sir Miles:
Prima pars parvi opusculi 394
Sandys, Samuel, Baron Sandys. *See* Poems 280:12
Saneredam, Joannes. *See* Saenredam
Sangrado, Dr., pseud. *See Letter* 1608:89; *Thomsonus* 1608:89
Sans Souci. *See* Frederick II 3422
Sanson, Guillaume and Nicolas:
Atlas nouveau 533
Sanson, Nicolas:
Table alphabétique 4013
Sansovino, Francesco. *See* Mexia 2059
Santeul, Jean de:
Oeuvres 1284
Vie et bon mots 820
Santi Bartoli, Pietro. *See* Bartoli
Santos, Francisco de los:
Descripcion breve del Monasterio de San Lorenzo del Escorial 3759
Sanzio, Raffaello. *See* Raphael
Sapientia Salomonis 2596
Sappho. *See* Anacreon 2232
Sarendip. *See* Serendip 1237
Sargent, John:
The mine 2951, 3222:19
Sarpi, Father Paolo:
Histoire du Concile de Trente 933
Sartine, Antoine Raymond Jean Gualbert Gabriel de, Comte d'Alby. *See* Tickell 1609:40
Sarto, Andrea del. *See* Drawings 3568
Sarum, Bishop of. *See* Burnet 830
Satires:
Remarkable satires 2319
See Collection 2358
Satires on several occasions. See Satires 2319
Satiric prints. See Bunbury 3563:1
Satyre Menippée de la vertu du Catholicon d'Espagne 1049
Satyrical lecture on hearts. See Dodd 1609:17
Satyrist. See Poems 280:2
Saul, King of Israel. *See* Trapp 1623:1
Saulnier du Verdier, Gilbert. *See* Du Verdier
Saulx, Gaspard de, Seigneur de Tavannes. *See* Tavannes
Saunders, Sir Edmund:
Summus Angliae seneschallus 1608:54

Saunders, John. *See* Tracts 359:4
Saunders, R.:
View of the soul 27
Saunders, Samuel:
Letter 1608:12
Saurin, Bernard Joseph:
Orpheline léguée. See Plays 1259
Savage, Henry:
Balliofergus 1608:3, 1629
Savage, John. *See* Guevara 1478
Savage, Richard. *See* Johnson 1608:20; Woodfall 1810:27
Savérien, Alexandre:
Histoire des philosophes modernes 3145
Savile, Dorothy, Countess of Burlington. *See* Burlington
Savile, George, Marquess of Halifax. *See* Halifax
Savile, Sir George:
Argument concerning the militia 1609:54
Savile, Henry. *See* Sidney 1452
Savoy, Louise de. *See* Louise de Savoie
Savoy. *See* Ferrero 3710
Sawyer, Edmund:
Memorials of affairs of state 1100
Saxe-Gotha, Augusta, Princess of. *See* Cambridge 498
Saxony, Dukes of:
Illustrissimorum ducum Saxoniae . . . effigies 2468
Sayer, James. *See* Bunbury 3563:2
Scacciati, Andrea. *See* Florence 3570
Scaliger, Joseph Justus:
Epistola. See Tracts 3986
Scaligerana, Thuana, Perroniana, Pithoeana, et Colomesiana 1262
Scaligeriana 1285, 2223
Scaliger, Julius Caesar:
De causis linguae Latinae 2258
Oratio pro Cicerone contra Erasmum 2292
See Tracts 3986
Scanderbeg, Prince of Epirus. *See* Lillo 1818:6
Scanderbeg. See Whincop 1842
Scanderbeg redivivus. See John III 2715
Scarlet gown: or the history of all the present cardinals of Rome. See Cogan 722
Scarron, Paul:
Virgile travesty 1087
Scarronnomimus, pseud. *See* Ovidius 1973

Scawen, John:
New Spain 1810:49
Scelera aquarum. See Harvey 1608:8
Scepeaux, François de, Sire de Vieilleville.
See Vieilleville
Schede, Paul. *See* Melissus 2283
Scheffer, Joannes:
History of Lapland 1608:71
Schellincks, William. *See* Drawings 3567
Scheme for the coalition of parties. See Jenyns
1609:29
Schenk, Peter:
Paradisus oculorum 3657
Roma aeterna 3518
Schenkius, Petrus. *See* Schenk
Schérer, Jean Benoît:
*Anecdotes et recueil de coutumes . . . de la
Russie* 3146
Schiller, Johann Christoph Friedrich von. *See
Cabal* 1810:57
Schmincke, Johann Hermann. *See* Eginhar-
dus 836
Schnebbelie, Jacob:
Antiquaries Museum 3519
Schoepflin, Johann Daniel:
Vindiciae typographicae. See Fournier
3012:2
Schola Salernitana. *See* Salerno
Schomberg, Raphael:
Death of Bucephalus 1810:7
Judgment of Paris 1810:13
See Advice 1608:51; Walpole 2493:3
Schongauer, Martin. *See* Prints 3607
School books 3175. *See* Manual 2414
School for guardians. See Murphy 1810:10
School for rakes. See Griffith 1810:14
School for scandal 1810:29
School for wives. See Kelly 1810:21
School of miniature 1608:91
Schoolmaster. See Twyne 1605
Schoppe, Caspar:
Comitis Clarae Vallae infamia Famiani
2293
*De paedia humanarum ac divinarum liter-
arum* 2259
See Priapeia 2255; Sanchez 2257
Schopperus, Hartmannus:
Speculum vitae aulicae 2260
Schottus, Andreas. *See* Demosthenes 2153

Schreber, Johann Christian Daniel von:
Die Säugthiere. See Monkeys 3884
Schrijver, Pieter:
Principes Hollandiae. See Prints 3656
Veteres de re militari scriptores. See Classics
2207:37
Schutz, Charles. *See Silver* 3222:13
Science des médailles. See Jobert 341
Scilly Islands. *See* Borlase 617; Heath 690
Scioppius, Gaspar. *See* Schoppe
Scipio, Cornelius, pseud. *See Epistle* 1609:22
Scobell, Henry. *See Several proceedings* 2758
Scot, Thomas:
Philomythie 1981
Scotch adventure. See Poems 3363:1
Scotch excise. See Blessings 1810:4
Scotch hut 3222:16
Scotch Presbyterian eloquence. See Crockat
1608:24
Scotland:
Church of Scotland 1609:57. *See* Crockat
1608:24
Court of Session 1609:58. *See* Dalrymple
1609:56
Heritable jurisdictions. *See Letter* 1608:59
High Court of Justiciary. *See* Campbell
1609:26
History. *See* Anderson 3549; Astle 3396;
Buchan 1609:42; Dalrymple 2833, 3185;
Lockhart 1712; Mentet 1127; Moysie 1714;
Pinkerton 2450, 3253; Robertson 321; Wal-
lace 3154
Union with England. *See* Belhaven 1608:9;
Black 1608:8; Defoe 3306
See Cordiner 540, 3840; Gilpin 3854:3;
Haversham 1608:94; Lettice 2898; Mans-
field 1608:49; Pennant 547, 2918; Pinkerton
3824; Slezer 582; Stair 3376; Sulivan 3829;
Ubaldini 523; Walker 3835; *Whole Proph-
ecies* 1608:45; Williams 1609:39
Scotland's skaith. See MacNeill 1357
Scott, ——, printer. *See* Charlotte 2356
Scott, George. *See* Ray 1689
Scott, James:
Every man the architect of his own fortune
3222:4
The favourite 1810:15
*How far a state of dependence . . . should
influence our conduct* 1609:55

Scott, James (*cont.*)
  Letters from the public papers 1359
  See Plain and seasonable address 1609:13
Scott, John:
  Foundation of Cambridge 4014
Scott, John, of Amwell:
  Amwell 3222:14
  Poetical works 2952
Scott, Samuel. *See* Müntz 3575
Scott, Mrs. Samuel. *See* Letters 2576 (Walpole, E.)
Scott, Mrs. Sarah:
  Description of Millennium Hall 2469
  History of Gustavus Ericson 1654
  Life of Théodore Agrippa d'Aubigné 2953
Scottish historical library. See Nicolson 1650
Scotus, Julius Clemens. *See* Inchofer 1221
The scourge 3222:7
The scourge of Venus. See Hall 2011
Scrafton, Luke:
  Observations on Mr. Vansittart's Narrative 1609:17
  See Bengal 1609:7
Scribbler. See Whittington's Feast 1810:26
Scriblerus Secundus, pseud. *See* Fielding 1818:2
Scrijver, Pieter. *See* Schrijver
Scriptores de re militari. See Classics 2207:37
Scriptores rei rustici 3977
Scripture vindicated. See Waterland 1607
Scrope, Eliza, later Mrs. Lee. *See* Lee, Elizabeth (Scrope)
Scrope, Richard. *See* Clarendon 3229
Scrubb, Timothy, pseud. *See* Robin Hood Society
Scudéry, George de:
  Alaric ou Rome vaincue 1050
Scudéry, Madeleine de. *See* Bougeant 1178
Sculptura historo-technica. See Arts 288:2
Scythians. *See* Pinkerton 2447
Sea Officer. *See Considerations* 1608:27; *Examination* 1608:27
Sea-sick ministrel. See Tresham 3211
Seacome, John:
  Memoirs of the House of Stanley 471
Seaman. *See Detection* 1608:27
Seasonable advice to the disinterested freeholders 1608:49
Seasonable and affecting observations 1608: 27, 48

Seasonable considerations on . . . burying in churches. See Duckett 683:3
Seasonable hints from an honest man. See Douglas 1609:2
Seasonable recapitulation 1608:64
Seasonable reflections on the present state of affairs 1609:15
Sebright, Henrietta. *See* Drawings 3641
Secker, Thomas, Archbishop:
  Letter to the Right Honourable Horatio Walpole 1609:22
Second advertisement. See Bedford 1608:64
Second and third letter to the Whigs. See Walpole 3933
Second answer. See Copy 1608:54
Second Court Secret 1608:31
Second epistle to the Reverend Mr. Brooke. See Middleton 1379:7
Second letter. See Egmont 119:2
Second letter addressed to the . . . Protestant Dissenters. See Huntingford 1609:52
Second letter from a physician. See Letter from a physician 1608:51; Walpole 2493:7
Second letter to the people of England. See Shebbeare 1608:82
Second letter to the Right Honourable the Earl of B*** 1609:3
Second part of the advantages [of the Hanover Succession] 1608:24
Second postscript to a late pamphlet 1609:28
Second series of facts and arguments. See Egmont 119:2
Secondat, Charles Louis de, Baron de Montesquieu. *See* Montesquieu
Secousse, Denis François:
  Mémoires 1146
Secret. See Important secret
Secret booke of Artephius. See Flamel 737
Secret history of King James I and King Charles I. See James I 2889
Secret history of Lewis XI. See Comines 1639
Secret history of Queen Zarah 1608:91
Secret history of the . . . Court of Caramania. See Haywood 1481
Secret history of the October Club. See Defoe 1608:9
Secret history of the White Staff. See Detection 2677
Security of Englishmen's lives. See Somers 179

Sedaine, Michel Jean:
   Philosophe sans le savoir. See Plays 1259
   See Burgoyne 1810:39; Dibdin 1810:20;
   Key 1810:46; O'Brien 1810:19
Sedition and defamation display'd. See Yonge
   1608:28
Sedley, Sir Charles:
   Miscellaneous works 1859
Seduction. See Holcroft 1853
Seeing is believing. See Jodrell 1810:39
Segar, Sir William:
   Honor, military and civil 638
   See Edmondson 527
Segrais, Jean Regnauld de:
   Zayde 1005
Seissel, Claude de. *See* Seyssel
Sejanus. See Masquerader 2416
Selborne. See White 3393
Selden, John:
   Duello 1608:67
   Table talk 1801
   Titles of honor 609
   Tracts 1131
   See Vincent 642
Seldom comes a better. See Black-bird 2646:
   18
Select collection of original letters. See Letters
   1900
Select letters. See Fog's Journal 1476
Select letters. See Luxborough 3896
Select trials. See Trials 1723
Seller, Abednego:
   Antiquities of Palmyra 1603
Seller, John:
   Heraldry epitomized 2754
Sellwood, Thomas. *See* Russell 3258
Semiramis. See Tomb of Semiramis 1547
Sénac de Meilhan, Gabriel:
   Mémoires d'Anne de Gonzagues 3049
The senators. See Delamayne 3222:12
Senault, Jean François:
   Use of the passions 178
Senebier, Jean:
   Catalogue des manuscrits 3372
Seneca, Lucius Annaeus:
   Opera quae exstant 2090
   Thyestes 2028
   Tragoediae 2091
Les sens, poëme. See Farmain 2689

Sentimental mother. See Baretti 1810:48
*Sentiments des . . . personnages condamnés à
   mort. See* Sabatier 2288
Sentiments of an English freeholder 1609:57
Septennial Act. See England 1608:23
Sequel to Arms and the man. See Poems 881:
   17
Serendip:
   Voyage . . . des trois Princes de Sarendip
   1237
Series of papers. See Newton 1608:70
*Serious advertisement concerning the . . .
   play-houses. See* Bedford 1608:64
Serious and impartial considerations 1608:59
Serious considerations on the measures. See
   Butler 1609:54
Serious defence of some late measures. See
   Douglas 1608:81
Serious letter to the public. See Junius 1609:
   39
Serious proposal to the ladies. See Astell 2633
Serious remonstrance. See Westminster 1608:
   69
Serious thoughts on . . . Popery 1608:60
*Serious thoughts on the trial of William
   Barnard. See* Barnard 1608:88
Serle, John:
   Plan of Mr. Pope's garden. See Poems
   3363:5
Sermon preach'd at the annual Visitation. See
   Brett 1367:1
Sermon preach'd on Easter Day. See Brett
   1367:4
Sermon preached to a large congregation. See
   Blackburne 1608:74
Sermons 1345–6, 1451, 2755–7
Sermons of Mr. Yorick. See Sterne 1803
Sermons of the time of Charles II 2757
Seroux d'Agincourt. *See* Agincourt
Serre, Puget de la. *See* Puget 608
Sersale, Antonio, Cardinal. *See* Benedict XIV
   3487
Sertor, Gaetano. *See* Music 3448
Servant of the Company. See Defence 1609:55
Servetus, Michael:
   Impartial history of Michael Servetus 1655
Sethona. See Dow 1810:22
Settala. See Terzago 284
Sevarambians. See Serendip 1237

Seventeen hundred forty-two 1608:43
Several assertions proved. See Tracts 100:1
Several copies of verses. See Oxford 2061:2
Several declarations. See Miscellaneous tracts 89:2
Several proceedings in Parliament 2758
Several years travels. See Bromley 1396
Severn River. *See* Congreve 681
Severus, Alexander. *See* Elyot 785
Severus, Sulpicius:
   Opera omnia. See Classics 2207:38
Sévigné, Marie de Rabutin-Chantal, Marquise de:
   Four letters. See Letters 2576
   Lettres à Monsieur de Pomponne 2597
   Lettres nouvelles 950
   Lettres nouvelles ou nouvellement recouvrés 952
   Portfolio of 144 portraits 3631
   Recueil de lettres choisies 951
   Recueil des lettres 949
   Sévigniana 1015
   See Curll 1512; Memoirs 2315
Sévigniana. See Memoirs 2315; Sévigné 1015
Sévigniana, or a collection of portraits. See Sévigné 3631
Seville, Treaty of. *See* England 1608:23
Seward, Anna:
   Elegy on Captain Cook 3207
   Poem to the memory of Lady Miller 3222:18
Seward, William:
   Anecdotes 821
Sexby, Edward:
   Killing noe murder 1608:8
Seymour, Lady Anne. *See* Marguerite 2415
Seymour, Hon. Catherine, later Mrs. Newton. *See* Newton
Seymour, Charles, Duke of Somerset. *See* Somerset
Seymour, Edward, Duke of Somerset. *See* Werdmueller 212
Seymour, Henry, d. 1805. *See* Ode 3222:9
Seymour, Thomas, Baron Seymour. *See* Letters 2576 (Catherine Parr)
Seymour-Conway, Francis Ingram, Marquess of Hertford. *See* Hertford
Seyssel, Claude de:
   Histoire de Louys XII 1088

Sgrilli, Bernardo Sansone:
   Descrizione della regia villa . . . di Pratolino 3760
   Descrizione e studi 3520
Shadwell, Charles. *See* Thompson 1810:20
Shadwell, Thomas:
   The libertine. See Plays 1623:2
Shaftesbury, Anthony Ashley Cooper, 1st Earl of:
   Delenda est Carthago 1608:5
   Letter to the Lord Fleetwood. See Tracts 2769:10
   Rawleigh redivivus 1764
Shaftesbury, Anthony Ashley Cooper, 3rd Earl of:
   Characteristicks 55
   Judgment of Hercules 1496
   Letters to Molesworth 1608:5
Shaftoe, Frances:
   Narrative 1608:10
Shakespeare, William:
   Collection of prints 3904
   Comedies, histories and tragedies [2d Folio] 2470
   Plays, ed. Johnson 1360
   Plays, ed. Malone 1360
   Romeo and Juliet. See Cibber 1608:57
   Series of Prints 3905
   Shakespeare traduit de l'anglois 3147
   Works, ed. Hanmer 64
   Works, ed. Pope 65, 1915
   Works (Bell's edition). *See* Ritson 2939
   See Carey 1810:15; Cibber 1818:20; Colman 1810:12; Cumberland 1810:18; Edwards 1608:66; Garrick 1810:3, 5; 1818:14; Grey 1829; Kemble 1810:47; Love 1810:13; Malone 1358; Montagu 1609:23; Victor 1810:4; Whiter 2987
Shakespeare's garland. See Garrick 1810:15
Shamela. See Tracts 2474:6
Shannon, Francis Boyle, Viscount:
   Discourses and essays 395, 2759
Sharp, John, Archbishop. *See* Sermons 1451
Sharpe, Gregory:
   Short dissertation 1608:26
Sharpe, William. *See* Drawings 3678
Shaw, Peter. *See* Boyle 1311
Shaw, Stebbing:
   Tour to the West of England 2954

Shaw, William:
  Enquiry into the authenticity [of Ossian] 1609:42
The She-gallant. See O'Keeffe 1810:10
Shebbeare, John:
  Answer to the queries 1609:32
  Candid inquiry 1609:31
  Fourth letter 3978
  Letter to His Grace [Newcastle] 1608:86
  Letters to the people of England 1608:82
  The Monitor. See Tracts 2968:8
  See Beard 1810:10
Sheffield, John, Duke of Buckingham. *See* Buckingham 448
Sheffield, John Baker Holroyd, Earl of. *See* Gibbon 3189
Shelburne, William Petty, Earl of, Marquess of Lansdowne. *See* Lansdowne
Shelton, Thomas (*fl.* 1610). *See* Cervantes 1735
Shelton, Thomas (1601–1650?):
  Short-writing. See Tracts 210
  Zeiglographia 795
Shenstone, William:
  Poems 3979
  Works 2029
  See Luxborough 3896; Poems 3363
Shepherd, Richard:
  Hector 3222:10
Shepherdess of the Alps. See Dibdin 1810:31
Sherburne, Sir Edward:
  Salmacis . . . with other poems 2030
Sheridan, Charles Francis:
  History of the late Revolution in Sweden 2955
Sheridan, Mrs. Frances:
  The discovery 1810:4
  The dupe 1810:5
  History of Nourjahad 1586
Sheridan, Richard Brinsley:
  The critic 1810:33
  The rivals 1810:23
  Songs, duets, trios in the Duenna 1810:25, 3222:14
  Verses to the memory of Garrick 3222:16
  See Poems 1835:4; Pottinger 1810:26
Sheridan, Thomas:
  British education 1382
  See Examen 1609:46

Sherley, Sir Anthony:
  Relation of his travels into Persia 3827
  True historical discourse 3828
Sherlock, Martin:
  Consiglio ad un giovane poeta 3373
  Letters on several subjects. See Tracts 361:6
  Lettres d'un voyageur Anglois 3050
  Nouvelles lettres 3051
Sherlock, Thomas, Bishop:
  Condition of our Blessed Saviour 1608:25
  Tryal of the witnesses 1608:25
  Use and intent of prophecy 1422
  See Norris 1608:12; Remarks 1379:11; Reply 1379:4; Rutherforth 1379:11; Tracts 1608:19
Sherwin, William:
  Reply to the nobleman's epistle 1608:30
  See South 1347
Shiels, Robert. *See* Cibber 2005
Shipley, Jonathan, Bishop:
  Speech. See Tracts 2966:5
  See Poems 3222:17
Shipton, William:
  Dia 1982
The shipwreck. See Lillo 1810:36
Shirley, Sir Anthony. *See* Sherley
Shirley, Laurence, Earl Ferrers. *See* Ferrers 1112
Shirley, William:
  Edward the Black Prince 1818:8
  Electra 3222:6
  King Pepin's campaign 1818:14
  Observations on . . . 'The genuine and legal sentence.' See Portugal 1343:2
Shore, Jane:
  Life 1802
Short and strange relation. See Rashīd 1344
Short and true account. See Castlemaine 156
Short answer to . . . Buckingham. See Buckingham 69:1
Short but serious reasons for a national militia. See Tracts 2146:3
Short character of the late M----s of W-------n. See Swift 1608:20
Short character of Thomas Earl of Wharton. See Swift 3983
Short considerations upon some late extraordinary grants 1609:15

Short criticism on the performance of Hamlet. See Kemble 1810:48

A Short discourse. See Buckingham 69

Short dissertation upon . . . oligarchy. See Sharpe 1608:26

Short enquiry concerning the hermetick art. See Enquiry 1517

Short essay on the modes of defence. See Glenie 1609:47A

Short historical account of the Kings of England. See Tracts 2146:4

Short history of standing armies. See Trenchard 1608:93

Short memorials. See Fairfax 162

Short narrative of the horrid massacre. See Boston 1609:26

Short review of the political state of Great Britain. See Genuine review 1609:50

Short state of the war. See Brodrick 1638

Short treatise on harmony. See Pepusch 2444

Short view of Dr. Beveridge's writings. See Whitby 1608:12

Short view of the dispute . . . concerning the regulation of the African trade. See Tracts 2146:1

Short view of the frauds 1608:6

Short view of the political life [of Pitt] 1609: 15

Short view of the trade and taxes of Scotland. See Black 1608:8

Short view of Twickenham. See Pye 2457

Shorter, Catherine, later Lady Walpole. *See* Walpole

Shorter, Sir John. *See* Tracts 3832:1

Shrewsbury, Charles Talbot, Duke of. *See* Defoe 1608:14

Shrewsbury. *See* Phillips 3204

Shute, John:
  First and chief grounds of architecture 520

Shute, W. *See* Fougasses 3276

Shuter, Edward:
  Shuter's jests 1608:88

Siam. *See* Kaempfer 1121; L'Isle 1037

Sibylline leaves. See Poulett 1608:50

Sicily. *See* Brydone 2810; Corbett 1608:32; Des Noulis 918; Dryden 1609:37; Du Moulin 897; Paruta 244; Swinburne 2961

Sick Laureat 3222:22

Sick monkey. See Stevenson 3222:6

Siddons, Henry:
  Sicilian romance 1810:54

Siddons, Sarah. *See Review* 1608:34

Siderston, Sir Thomas. *See* Heraldry 2559

Sidney, Algernon:
  Discourses concerning government 3176
  Letters to the Honourable H. Savile 1452
  Sidney redivivus 1608:8
  See Ralph 1721; Towers 1609:31

Sidney, Sir Henry. *See* Collins 871; White 214, 773

Sidney, Mary, later Countess of Pembroke. *See* Fraunce 122

Sidney, Sir Philip:
  Defence of poetry 2956
  Works 1839
  See Brooke 1931; *Funebria* 196; Hamond 2556; *Profitable instructions* 2935

Siège de Calais. See Tencin 3149

Siege of Aquileia. See Home 1818:18

Siege of Calais. See Denis 1810:7

Siege of the Castle of Aesculapius 1810: 12

Sigismund, Emperor of Germany:
  Profectio 3632

Signs of the times, a sermon. See Miscellaneous tracts 89:1

Sigrilli, Bernardo Sansone. *See* Sgrilli

Sikes, Arthur Ashley. *See* Sykes

Sikes, George:
  Life . . . of Sir Henry Vane 1089

Silius Italicus, Caius:
  Punicorum libri XVII 2198

Silver tail 3222:13

Silvester, Joshua. *See* Sylvester

Silvestre, Israel:
  Portfolio of 410 engravings 3611
  See Louis XIV 3591:2

Silvia. See Lillo 1818:5

Simco, John. *See* Antiquities 3485:7

Simeon, Simon. *See* Tractatus 3383

Simiane, Marquise de. *See* Sévigné 952

Simler, Josias. *See* Gesner 2157

Simon, James:
  Essay [on] *Irish coins* 252, 282. *See* Stukeley 640:2

Simon, Richard:
  Histoire critique du Vieux Testament 1147

Simon, Thomas. *See* Vertue 2480

Simple, Adventures of David. See Fielding, Sarah 1563

Simpson, Christopher:
    Compendium of practical musick 1543

Simpson, Samuel. *See* Sympson

Sinclair, Sir John. *See Letter* 1609:42

Singleton, John:
    Description of the West Indies 3222:15

Sion College. *See* Reading 908

Sion House. *See* Adam 3597

Sir Harry Gaylove. See Marshall 1810:19

Sir Joseph Banks and the Emperor of Morocco. See Wolcot 3222:22

Sir Thomas Overbury. See Woodfall 1810:27

The sirens. See Thompson 1810:25

Siri, Vittorio:
    Mémoires secrets 3052

Siriès, Louis:
    Catalogue des pierres gravées. See Tracts 3833:10

Sivrac, Jean. *See* Walpole 3728

Sivry, Louis Poinsinet de. *See* Plinius 3140

Six odes presented to . . . Mrs. Catharine Macaulay. See Graham 3222:15

Six questions, stated and answered. See Tracts 400:11, 2475:2

Six weeks tour. See Young 2995

Sixtus V, Pope. *See* Leti 2103

Skelton, John:
    Pithy . . . workes 1916

Skerrett, Maria. *See Rival Wives* 2463

Skerrett, Thomas:
    Poem on the much lamented death of Thomas Skerrett. See Walpole 2619:2

Sketch of a conference 1609:42

Sketch of a tour into Derbyshire. See Bray 2345, 3400

Sketch of the life . . . of the late Dr. Monsey. See Monsey 1609:53

Sketch of the times. See Walpole 3222:12

Sketches and characters of . . . persons now living. See Thicknesse 3906

Sketches: or essays. See Armstrong 1608:85

Skewball, Peter, pseud. *See Catalogue* 1818:9

Skinner, Thomas:
    Life of General Monk 1656

Slade, John:
    Love and duty 1818:15

Slater, ——. *See* Microphilus 2418

Slavery: a poem. See More 3222:22

The sleep-walker. See Craven 1810:29

Slezer, John:
    Theatrum Scotiae 582

Sliford, William. *See Court Register* 1434

Sloane, Sir Hans:
    Account 1608:48
    Authentic copies of the codicils 1608:50
    Will 1808:50

Small garland of pious and godly songs. See Hall 2011:3

Small specimen of . . . mistakes in Sir William Dugdale's Baronage. See Hornby 692

Smalridge, George, Bishop:
    Some remarks 1608:6
    See Atterbury 1608:16

Smart, Christopher:
    Occasional prologue. See Poems 881:30

Smellie, William:
    Account of the Society of the Antiquaries of Scotland. See Buchan 1609:42

Smelt, Leonard:
    Account of some particulars 1609:41
    See System 1609:40

Smith, Adam:
    Inquiry into the . . . wealth of nations 3260
    Theory of moral sentiments 1453

Smith, Charles:
    Ancient and present state of the County of Down 396

Smith, Charlotte:
    Elegiac sonnets. See Kemble 3966

Smith, Elisha:
    Cure of deism 1383

Smith, Francis, publisher. *See* Tracts 2146:2

Smith, George:
    Six pastorals 3222:11

Smith, James (1605–1667). *See Loves of Hero* 1960; Mennes 1970; *Wit* 1994

Smith, John (1652–1742), engraver. *See* Sacchi 3629

Smith, John (1655–1723), politician. *See* Tracts 400:4, 2475:8

Smith, John (*fl.* 1673–1680):
    Art of painting in oyl. See Tracts 359:3

Smith, John (*fl.* 1755):
    Printer's grammar 311

Smith, John, M. D.:
    Choir Gaur. See Tracts 1348:7

Smith, John Christopher. *See* Garrick 1810:1
Smith, John Thomas:
Antiquities of London 3521
Smith, Joseph, called Consul Smith. *See* Gori 3696
Smith, Richard, Bishop of Chalcedon:
Vitae Dominae Magdalenae Montis-Acuti 2294
Smith, Sir Thomas (1513–1557). *See* Strype 1692
Smith, Thomas (1638–1710):
Vitae quorundam . . . virorum 860
Smith, William (1651?–1735), antiquary:
Annals of University College [Oxford] 706
Smith, William (*d.* 1750):
Authentic account of the life 1608:65
Smith, William (*fl.* 1761):
Authentic journal of the expedition to Belleisle 1609:2
Smith, William (1727–1803):
Brief view 1608:82
Historical account of the expedition against the Ohio Indians 1609:56
Plain truth. See Paine 1609:37
Smith-Stanley, Edward, Earl of Derby. *See* Derby
Smollett, Tobias George:
The reprisal 1818:15
Smyrna. *See* Dalrymple 2832
Smythe, Maria Anne, later Mrs. Fitzherbert. *See* Fitzherbert
Snape, Andrew:
Letter 1608:15
Second letter 1608:15
Snelling, Thomas:
Collection of works on coins 253
See Pinkerton 3702
Snow, Thomas. *See* Neve 1489
Soames, Sir William. *See* Guilford 3321
Sobieski, Princess Clementina Maria. *See* Clementina
Sobieski, John, King of Poland. *See* John III 2715
Society for promoting English Protestant working-schools in Ireland. *See* Sermons 1346:10
Society for the encouragement of arts, manufactures, and commerce:
Transactions 2957
See Barry 325; Royal Academy 3885:3, 4

Society of Antiquaries:
Minutes 2598
Vetusta monumenta 3658
See Archaeologia 3223; Astle 3396; Gale 569; Topham 3472; Vertue 2772
Society of Antiquaries of Scotland. *See* Buchan 1609:42
Society of Artists of Great Britain. *See* Royal Academy 3885:1, 2
Society of Arts. *See* Society for the encouragement of arts
Society of Dilettanti, London. *See* Chandler 3534; Knight 2404
Society of Noblemen and Gentlemen. *See* Catch Club
Socrates. *See* Cooper 1675; Xenophon 1697, 2229
Socrates triumphant. See Military 1832
The sofa. See Sopha, conte moral
Soldier. A Poem, inscribed to the Hon. General Conway. See Thompson 3222:6
Solis y Ribadeneyra, Antonio de:
History of the conquest of Mexico 3283
Solomon, King of Israel. *See* Sapientia 2596
Some account of the alien priories. See Nichols 2911
Some account of the character of Henry Bilson Legge. See Butler 1609:56
Some account of the Revolution. See Revolution 2593
Some account of the Roman history of Fabius Pictor 1608:70
Some cautions offered. See Halifax 83:1
Some considerations concerning the publick funds. See Walpole 1608:21, 39
Some considerations humbly offer'd. See Tracts 400, 2475:13
Some considerations on the establishment of the French strolers 1608:69
Some considerations on the law. See Yorke 1608:62
Some enquiries concerning the first inhabitants. See Tracts 1348:9
Some general thoughts on government. See Lewis 1608:86
Some new proofs. See Burnet 1608:9
Some observations on a book intitled an Essay. See Ashton 1379:10
Some papers proper to be read. See Fielding 1608:45

Some proceedings in the last Parliament 1608:49

Some reflections on prescience. See Jackson 1608:33

Some reflections upon a pamphlet called the Old Whig. See Tracts on Peerage Bill 400:6, 2475:5

Some reflexions upon a late pamphlet 1379:4

Some reflexions upon the . . . second chapter of Genesis 1379:9

Some remarks on a book, entitled, A View of miraculous powers. See Heathcote 1379:3

Some remarks on a late pamphlet 1608:50

Some remarks on the Barrier Treaty. See Swift 1608:13

Some remarks on the Minute Philosopher 1608:90

Some remarks upon the temper of the late writers 1608:6

Some rules for speaking and action 1608:29

Some strictures on the late occurrences in North America 1609:13

Somers, John, Baron Somers:
  Argument 1630
  Collection of scarce and valuable tracts 1631
  Discourse concerning generosity. See Tracts 210
  Guide to the knowledge of the rights of Englishmen 397
  Memoirs 1608:14
  Security of Englishmen's Lives 179
  See Cooksey 3231

Somerset, Charles Seymour, Duke of. *See Detection* 2677:4

Somerset, Edward, 4th Earl of Worcester. *See* Worcester

Somerset, Edward, 2d Marquess of Worcester. *See* Worcester

Somerset, Edward Seymour, Duke of. *See* Marguerite 2415; Werdmueller 212

Somerset, Henry, Marquess of Worcester. *See* Worcester

Somersetshire. *See* Collinson 3164

Somerville, William:
  The chase, a poem 3724

Somner, William:
  Antiquities of Canterbury 667

Son of Candor. *See* Temple 1609:11

Songs and chorusses in May-Day. See Garrick 1810:24

Songs and poems of love and drollery. See Weaver 1992

Songs and recitative of Orpheus. See Garrick 1810:11

Songs, &c. in Pandora 1810:31

Songs, chorusses, &c. in Belphegor. See Andrews 1810:27

Songs, choruses . . . of the Institution of the Garter. See Garrick 1810:17

Songs, duets, and finale, in the Cady of Bagdad. See Portal 1810:27

Songs, duets, and trios, in the Quaker. See Dibdin 1810:27

Songs, duets, &c. in the new pantomime called Lord Mayor's Day. See O'Keeffe 1810:35

Songs, duets, trios, &c. in the Siege of Curzola. See O'Keeffe 1810:39

Songs, duets, trios in the Duenna. See Sheridan 1810:25

Songs in the night. See Pye 2457

Songs in the Widow of Delphi. See Cumberland 1810:31

Songs in William and Nanny. See Goodenough 1810:35

Sonnets, printed for the author 3222:14

Sopha, conte moral. See Miscellaneous volumes 943:2

Sophia Dorothea, Consort of George I. *See* Pöllnitz 1282

Sophocles:
  Tragedies of Sophocles from the Greek 322
  Tragoediae 2224

Soprani, Raffaello:
  Vite de' pittori 3374

Sorbière, Samuel de:
  Lettres et discours 861
  Relation d'un voyage en Angleterre 1052
  Sorberiana 1051
  Voyage to England 1454

The sorcerer. See Theobald 1818:17

Sorrowfull ditty. See Poems 881:22

Sorrows sacred to the memory of Penelope. See Boothby 3707

Soulavie, Jean Louis Giraud. *See* Richelieu 3368; Saint-Simon 3259

Source of the evil 1609:46

Sousa Coutinho, Manoel de. *See* Murphy 3650

South, Robert:
  Animadversions upon Dr. Sherlock's book
  1347
  Maxims 1608:19
  Sermons 1347
South Briton 1810:22
South Lambeth. *See* Tradescant 769
South Pole. *See* Cook 3183
South Sea Company. *See* Steele 1608:16
Southerne, Thomas:
  Plays 1917
  See Ferriar 1810:45; Garrick 1818:16
Southgate, Richard:
  Museum Southgatianum 3261
Southouse, Thomas:
  Monasticon Favershamiense 765
Southwell, Robert:
  Histoire du détrônement d'Alphonse VI
  796
Soyres, François de:
  Reponse critique 1609:52
Spa. *See* Eyre 1608:4
Spain:
  Painters. *See* Cumberland 3411
  Theatre. *See* Théâtre 3150
  Treaties. *See* England 1608:23, 94; 1609:
  54, 57
  See Aulnoy 364, 1461; Bacallar 1266; Bar-
  etti 2792; Caimo 3075; Clarke 3301; Dal-
  rymple 3233; Dillon 2836; Orléans 3358;
  Rhys 1420; Sandras 3144; Swinburne 2960;
  Twiss 2972; Wilkes 1609:5
Spalatro. Palace of Diocletian. *See* Adam 3531
Spanheim, Ezechiel. *See* Julianus 925; Morel
  305
Spanheim, Friedrich:
  Mémoires sur la vie . . . de . . . Loyse
  Juliane 3467
Spanish-English Rose. See Du Val 1615
Spanish history. See John 1710
Spanish lady. See Hull 1810:7
Spanish Succession, War of. *See* Brodrick
  1638; Kane 1608:50
Sparks. See Poems 881:31
Spearman, John:
  Enquiry into . . . the County Palatine of
  Durham 639
Specimen of a Glossary of the Scottish lan-
  guage. See Tracts 2050:3

Specimen of the natural history of monks.
  See Born 1609:45
Specimens of Gothic ornaments. See Laven-
  ham 3719
Specimens of penmanship. *See* Penmanship
  3651
Specimens of printing types. *See* Type Speci-
  mens
Spectacle de la nature. See Pluche 1491
Spectateur françois. See Marivaux 1042
The Spectator 1860
Speculation. See Anstey 3222:17
Speech at the General Quarter Sessions. See
  Halifax 83:2
Speech intended to have been spoken [by
  Bishop Shipley]. *See* Tracts 2966:5
Speech of a Right Honourable Gentleman.
  See Grenville 1609:24
Speed, John:
  Theatre of . . . Great Britain 534
Speed, R. *See* Tracts 3796
Speedy post 1608:5
Speer, Joseph Smith:
  West-India pilot 3284
Speke, Hugh:
  Some memoirs . . . of the Revolution 398
Spelman, Sir Henry:
  English works 2065
  Villare Anglicum 862
Spelman, Sir John:
  Life of Aelfred the Great 1691
Spence, Joseph:
  Apology for the late Mr. Pope 1608:13
  Crito 1608:67
  Letter to the Rev. Mr. G. R. 1608:79
  Moralities 1608:79
  Parallel 2516. *See* Strawberry Hill 3469:9
  Plain matter of fact 1608:60
  Polymetis 1101
  See Attiret 1608:71; Webb 362
Spencer, Mary Beauclerk, later Lady Charles.
  See Collection 2508; Temple 2517
Spencer, Lady Diana, later Beauclerk. *See*
  Beauclerk
Spencer, George. *See* Natter 276
Spencer, Lavinia Bingham, Countess. *See*
  Etchings 3588
Spencer, Oliph Leigh:
  Life of Henry Chichele 2958

Spencer, Robert, Earl of Sunderland. *See* Sunderland

Spencer, William Robert. *See* Bürger 2349

Spenser, Edmund:
Faerie Queene 323. *See* Warton 1840
Works 1878
See Ware 2182

Spiller, James:
Jests. See Plays 1907:5

Spilsbury, John:
Collection of fifty prints 3761

Spinoza, Benedictus de. *See* Fénelon 1218

Spintrian medals:
Collection of the Spintrian medals of Tiberius 2599

Spirit of contradiction 1818:18

Spon, Charles. *See* Patin 1257

Spon, Jacob. *See* Wheeler 2497

Sports of the muses 1918

Spranger, Bartholomaeus. *See* Prints 3606

Sprat, Thomas, Bishop:
History of the Royal Society 1632
[Letters] *to the Earl of Dorset* 2760
True account of the conspiracy 1132
See Sermons 1451; Sorbière 1454

Sprigge, Joshua:
Anglia rediviva 2179

The spring. See Harris 1810:3

Sprott, Thomas:
Chronica 2320

Spyers, James. *See* Hearne 3645

Squabble of the Richmond players 1608:31

Squallini, Seignior, pseud. *See* Man 1810:7

Squire, Jane:
Proposal for discovering our longitude 1455

Squire, Samuel, Bishop:
Historical essay 1608:59
Remarks upon Mr. Carte's specimen 1608:61
See Burton 1608:70

Staal, Marguerite Jeanne de, Baroness:
Mémoires de Madame de Staal 1286

Stackhouse, Thomas:
Memoirs of Atterbury 1608:16

Stadler, Joseph Constantine. *See* Combe 3566

Stafford, Edward, 3d Duke of Buckingham. *See* Buckingham

Stafford, Granville Leveson-Gower, Marquess of. *See* Trentham

Stafford, Henry, Baron Stafford. *See* Fox 163

Stafford, Humphrey:
Arraignement. See Plays 1082:5

Stafford, Thomas:
Pacata Hibernia 3375

Stafford, William Howard, Viscount:
Stafford's Memoirs 1765

Staffordshire. *See* Letter 1608:70; Plot 579

Stahl. *See* Staal 1286

Stair, James Dalrymple, later Viscount:
Institutions of the law of Scotland 3376

Stair, John Dalrymple, 2d Earl of. *See* Henderson 1608:20

Stair, John Dalrymple, 5th Earl of:
Address to the public 1609:46
Claims of the public 1609:47A
Considerations 1609:42
Facts and their consequences 1609:42
State of the public debts 1609:44

Stamford, Thomas Grey, 2d Earl of:
Case of the Earl of Stamford considered 521
Speech at the General Quarter Sessions. See Halifax 83:2

Stamford, Lincolnshire. *See* Butcher 650; Peck 577

Stamma, Louis:
Kellyad 3222:7

Stamma, Philip:
Essai 1608:68

Stamp Act. *See* Tracts 1609:12, 13, 56

Standish, Arthur:
The Commons Complaint. See Hartlib 125

Stanford, R. *See* Cepari 368

Stanford, Antiquarian annals of. See Peck 577

Stanhope, Anna Maria, Duchess of Newcastle. *See* Newcastle

Stanhope, Charles, 3d Earl Stanhope:
Considerations on the means of preventing fraudulent practices on the gold coin 1609:58
Letter 1609:53
See Hawtrey 1609:52

Stanhope, James Stanhope, 1st Earl:
Memorial sent . . . to the Abbot Vertot at Paris. See Miscellaneous tracts 89:1

Stanhope, Philip Dormer, 4th Earl of Chesterfield. *See* Chesterfield

Stanhope, William, 1st Earl of Harrington. *See* Harrington

Stanhope, William, 2d Earl of Harrington. *See* Harrington

Stanislaus I (Leszczynski), King of Poland: *Oeuvres* 3053

Stanislaus Augustus [Poniatowski], King of Poland: Two letters. *See* Letters 2576

Stanley, Charles, Earl of Derby. *See* Derby

Stanley, Hans: Two letters. *See* Letters 2576

Stanley, James, Earl of Derby. *See* Derby

Stanley, Thomas: *History of philosophy* 1102 *See* Aeschylus 2165

Stanley, William: *Catalogus librorum manuscriptorum* 583

Stanley, House of. *See* Seacome 471

Stanmer, ——: One or more letters. *See* Letters 2576

Stannaries. *See* Pitt 1608:32

Stapleton, Sir Robert. *See* Juvenalis 1954

Star Chamber. *See* England. Court of Star Chamber

Star-Chamber cases. See Tracts 3797

Starke, Mariana: *Sword of peace* 1810:48 *Widow of Malabar* 1810:50

State and Miscellany Poems. See Oldisworth 135

State necessity considered 1609:16

State of facts. See Fox 1609:45

State of the nation consider'd 1608:49

State of the nation, with a general ballance 1608:56

State of the nation, with a preliminary defence of the budget. See Hartley 1609:56

State of the proceedings of the convocation. See Pitt 1608:32

State of the province of Georgia. See Stephens 1608:40

State papers, A collection of. See Haynes 441

State papers relative to the late negotiations with Spain. See England 1609:57

State poems. See Poems on affairs of state 1836

State tracts 1170, 2180

State tracts. See Oldisworth 135

State trials. *See* Collection 870; Trials 1724

Statesman foil'd. See Dossie 1810:13

Statius, Publius Papinus: *Opera* 2092

Stearne, Docteur, pseud. *See* Rutledge 3046

Stebbing, Henry: *Fragment* 1608:70 *Observations on a book* 1379:3

Steel, Rev. Richard. *See* Sermons 2756:1

Steele, Joshua, supposed author: *Account of a late conference* 1609:13

Steele, Sir Richard: *Amanti interni* 2115 *Apology* 1608:6 *The crisis* 1608:93, 94 *The Englishman* 1608:6 *Full account of the proceedings against* 1608:16 *The funeral* 1910:5 *Importance of Dunkirk* 1608:16 *Letter to a Member of Parliament* 1608:6 *Letter to the Earl of O——d* 1608:16. *See* Tracts 400:10, 2475:12 *Lover and Reader* 1861. *See Spectator* 1860 *Nation a family* 1608:16 *Plebeians. See* Tracts 400:2, 2475:3 *Poetical miscellanies* 1919 *State of the case* 1608:16 *See* Brightland 2000; Jacob 1608:5; Mar 1608:10; Wharton 1608:20

Steevens, George: *Account of the Felton portrait of Shakespeare. See* Felton 3922 One letter. *See* Letters 2576 *See* Etymologist 1810:38; Nichols 2435; Ritson 2939

Steffani, Agostino. *See* Tracts 2968:2

Stehelin, John Peter: *Traditions of the Jews* 1384

Stell, I. *See* Hastings 2868

Stephen, James. *See King's Bench* 1609:28

Stephens, Thomas: *Brief account* 1608:40

Stephens, William: *State of the province of Georgia* 1608:40

Sterling, Earl of. *See* Stirling

Sterne, Laurence: *Life and opinions of Tristram Shandy* 356 *Sermons of Mr. Yorick* 1803

Sterne, Richard, Archbishop. *See* Allestree 3938–9

Stevens, George Alexander:
  Court of Alexander 1810:15
  Songs, &c. in the Cabinet of Fancy 1810:35
  Trip to Portsmouth 1810:20
Stevens, John:
  Monasticon Hibernicum 707
  See Quintana 1582
Stevenson, John Hall:
  Crazy tales 3222:2
  Fables 3222:10
  Makarony fables 3222:9
  Pastoral cordial 3222:4
  Pastoral puke 3222:6
  Sick monkey 3222:6
  Works 2959
Stevenson, Matthew:
  Wits 1983
Stewart. *See also* Stuart
Stewart, James, defendant:
  Trial of James Stewart 1722
Stewart, James, hairdresser:
  Plocacosmos 1361
Stillingfleet, Benjamin:
  Calendar of Flora 1609:4
  See Covolo 1609:18
Stillingfleet, Edward:
  The grand question stated 56
Stirling, William Alexander, Earl of:
  Recreations with the muses 3377
Stirlingshire. *See* Nimmo 1601
Stockdale, John:
  Whole proceedings . . . for a libel 418
Stockdale, Percival:
  Ximenes 1810:44
  See Waller 2977
Stockwell, Surrey. *See Authentic . . . narrative* 1609:29
Stone, Andrew. *See Letter* 1608:74
Stone, George, Archbishop. *See* Brett 1377:3
Stonehenge. *See* Jones 599; Tracts 1348:7
Story of the tragedy of Agis. See Erskine 1818:16
The story on which the Roman father is founded 1818:7
Stosch, Philipp von, Baron:
  Pierres antiques gravées 3762
  See Catalogues 3404; Winckelmann 3767
Stourhead. *See Ride* 3222:16
Stow, John:
  Annals . . . of England . . . continued . . .

Stow, John (*cont.*)
  by Edmond Howes 610
  Summarye of the Chronicles of England 766
  Survey of London 611
Stowe:
  Stowe: a description. See Guides 2387:5
  Views by Chatelain. See Antiquities 3485
Strachey, —:
  Index to the records 767
Strada, Famiano. *See* Schoppe 2293
Stradanus, Johannes:
  Portfolio of 62 engravings 3659
Strafford, Thomas Wentworth, Earl of:
  Letters 446
Strafford, William Wentworth, Earl of:
  One or more letters. See Letters 2576
Strahan, George. *See* Johnson 1609:48
Strahan, William:
  Toleration in Scotland 1608:94
Strange, Richard. *See* Cantelupe 1505
Strange, Sir Robert:
  Descriptive catalogue 283
  Inquiry into . . . the Royal Academy 3468
  See Drawings 3678
Strange apparitions. See Tracts 2050
Straparola, Giovanni Francesco 3980
Stratford, Agnes. *See* Stratford 3222:18
Stratford, Thomas:
  First book of Fontenoy 3222:18
Stratford. *See* Garrick 1810:15
Strauch, Aegidius 3981
Strawberry Hill:
  Catalogue. See Collection 2506
  Catalogue of pictures. See Walpole 2162
  Catalogue of the English portraits. See Walpole 2163
  Catalogue of the Library. See Walpole 2164
  Collection 2506–8
  Description. See Walpole, *Description of the villa*
  Detached pieces. See Collection 2506, 2508
  Drawings. See Drawings 3678
  Journal of the Printing Office. See Collection 2506
Strawberry Hill Press:
  Remainders 3469
Strong, Adam, pseud.:
  Electrical eel 3222:15

Strutt, Joseph:
  Biographical dictionary 254
  Chronicle of England 3845
  Complete view of the manners . . . of England 3846
  Regal and ecclesiastical antiquities 3847
  See Antiquities 3485:8
Strype, John:
  Ecclesiastical memorials 883
  Life of John Aylmer 1657
  Life of Sir John Cheke 1658
  Life of Sir Thomas Smith 1692
Stuart. See also Stewart
Stuart, Andrew:
  Considerations on the present state of East-India affairs 1609:46
  Letters to Lord Mansfield 2471, 4015
Stuart, Charles:
  Cobler of Castlebury 1810:30
  Distress'd baronet 1810:42
  Irishman in Spain 1810:47
  Stone eater 1810:45
Stuart, Charles Edward, the Young Pretender. See Charles Edward Stuart
Stuart, James:
  Antiquities of Athens 3544
  Critical observations 1609:57
Stuart, James Francis Edward, the Pretender. See James Francis Edward Stuart
Stuart, John, 3d Earl of Bute. See Bute
Stubbe, Edmund:
  Fraus honesta. See Plays 2131:2
Student of Gray's Inn. See Kingston 1609:58
Stukeley, William:
  Account of Richard of Cirencester. See Tracts 1348:8
  Medallic history of Carausius 522
  Palaeographia Britannica 668
  Palaeographia sacra 640
  Twenty-three plates of coins 255
Style, William. See Dilherr 2678
Suard, Jean Baptiste Antoine. See Du Buat 3009; Gazette 3014; Hume 1680:1
Suarès, Joseph Marie:
  Praenestes antiquae libri duo 3763
Subjects for painters. See Wolcot 3222:22
Substance of the speeches. See England 1609: 40
Succinct and impartial history of all the regencies. See England 1608:66

Sudbury, John Chapman, Archdeacon of. See Chapman
Sudeley Castle. See Willyams 3558
Suetonius Tranquillus, Caius:
  Les douze Césars 3378
  Opera 2225
Suffolk, Edward Howard, 8th Earl of:
  Miscellanies 57
  Musarum deliciae 209
Suffolk, Dukes of. See Wilson 402
Suffolk. See Kirby 744; Kirby 3858; Norfolk 2581
Suhm, Ulrich Friedrich von. See Frederick II 3095
Sulivan, Lawrence. See Sullivan, Lawrence
Sulivan, Richard J.:
  Observations made during a tour 3829
Sulla, Lucius Cornelius. See Sylla
Sullivan, Lawrence. See Defence 1609:17; East India 1609:55; Letter 1609:22
Sullivan, Richard J. See Sulivan
Sully, Maximilien de Bethune, Duc de:
  Mémoires 1016
Sumatra. See Marsden 2901
Summary of all the religious houses. See Duckett 683
Summary view of the rights of British America. See Jefferson 1609:32
Summer's tale. See Cumberland 1810:8
Summus Angliae seneschallus. See Saunders 1608:54
Sunder, Lucas, called Cranach. See Cranach
Sunderland, Anne Churchill, Countess of. See Black-bird 2646:24
Sunderland, Robert Spencer, 2d Earl of. See Etchings 3588
Supplement to the Narrative. See Bengal 1609:7
Supplement to the Papers. See Tracts 400, 2475:16
Supplement to the State of the nation 1608: 56
Sur la législation et le commerce des grains. See Necker 3036
Surrey, Henry Howard, Earl of:
  Poems 58
  Songes and sonettes 1920
Surrey. See Aubrey 648; Salmon 705, 2753

Sussex, George Augustus Yelverton, Earl of:
  *Catalogue of the Library at Easton Mau-
  duit* 2600
Sutherland, David:
  Tour up the Straits 1385
Sutton, Daniel. *See Tryal* 1609:19
Suyderhoef, Jonas. *See Prints* 3626
Swaine, John:
  Memoirs of Osney Abbey 2761
Swan marks 2601
Sweden:
  Dispute between the King and Senate 1608:
  83
  See Consett 3303; Harte 464; Robinson
  1421; Sheridan 2955; Vertot 1663
Swedish curate. See Jerningham 3222:13
Sweete savor for woman. See Walker
  2613
Swift, Deane:
  *Essay upon the life . . . of Dr. Jonathan
  Swift* 1659
  See Swift, J. 3379
Swift, Jonathan:
  Ars pun-ica. See Tracts 2474:5
  Conduct of the allies. See Remarks 1608:13
  Directions to servants 1608:45
  Gulliver's travels 1456
  History of . . . the Queen 1693
  Letter 3982
  Letters 3380
  Miscellanies 1862
  Publick spirit of the Whigs 1608:93, 94
  Short character of Wharton 1608:20, 3983
  Some observations upon a paper 3984
  Some remarks on the Barrier Treaty 1608:
  13
  Tale of a tub 1587
  Works 3379
  See Berkeley 2799; Cork 43; *Examiner* 1560;
  Fribble 1818:10; Swift 1659; Tracts 98:1;
  Tracts 3796:3
Swinburne, Henry:
  Travels in the two Sicilies 2961
  Travels through Spain 2960
Swinden, Henry:
  History . . . of Great Yarmouth 2962, 3208
Swinton, John:
  Metilia. See Stukeley 668:4
Switzerland. *See* Bate 1810:55
Sword of peace. See Starke 1810:48

Swordfeager, Martha Sophia:
  Case 3522
Sydney. *See* Sidney
Sykes, Arthur Ashley:
  Innocency of error 1608:12
  Two questions 1379:6
Sykes, George. *See* Sikes
Sylla, pièce dramatique. See Almanach 1174
Sylphs. See Airs 1810:21
Sylvae. See Dryden 1825
Sylvester, Joshua:
  Maiden's blush 1984
  Memorials of mortality 2762
  Parliament of vertues royal 1984
Sylvius, Franciscus de le Boe, called. *See* Le
  Boe
Symon Simeonis. *See Tractatus* 3383
Sympson, Christopher. *See* Simpson
Sympson, Samuel:
  New book of cyphers 312
Synopsis Apocalyptica. See Cromarty 77
The Syren 1588
The Syrens. See Sirens
Syria. *See* Vaillant 491
*System, occasioned by the speech of Leonard
  Smelt* 1609:40

T., Marquis de. *See* Trévié
T., I.:
  Haven of pleasure. See Winchester 2499
T., J. *See Letter* 1818:19
T., N. *See Collection* 1935
T., N., pharmacopola. *See Good humour*
  1609:13
T., S. *See Tracts* 2475:14; Walpole 1609:15
T., T. *See* Tymme, Thomas
Taaffe, Nicholas, Viscount Taaffe:
  Observations on affairs in Ireland 2763
Taaffe, Theobald. *See* Payba 1608:65, 73
Tabago. *See* Tobago
Tableau de famille. See Tracts 3054
Tableau de Paris. See Mercier 3031
Tableau des révolutions de la littérature. See
  Denina 3008
Tableau des riches inventions. See Colonna
  2075
Tableau historique du Roi. See Le Prince
  2217
Tablettes anecdotes et historiques. See Dreux
  du Radier 3090

Tablettes historiques et chronologiques 3148
Tacitus, Publius Cornelius:
   Opera 2093, 2133
   Works 1103
Tadmor. *See* Halifax 2554; Wood 3548
Tafiletta, Emperor of Barbary. *See* Rashīd 1344
The tailors 1810:28
Talbot, Charles, Duke of Shrewsbury. *See* Shrewsbury
Talbot, James. *See* Horatius 2193
Talbot, William:
   Narrative of . . . his proceedings 1609:29
Tale of a tub. See Swift 1587
Talemik et Zinéra. See Contes François 1783: 3
Tales in verse. See Haddington 165
Tales of genii. See Ridley 392
Tallents, Francis:
   View of universal history 227
Talman, John. *See* Drawings 3567
Talon, Nicholas:
   The holy history 97
Tamerlane, Emperor of the Monguls. *See* Margat 1040; Perondinus 2445
Tamor. *See* Howard 1810:20
Tandon, J. E.:
   New French grammar 1238
Tangier. *See* Kirke 2572
Tanjore, Tulaji, Rajah of. *See* Tulaji
Tankerville, Ford Grey, Earl of:
   Secret history 1608:71
   See Behn 1428
Tanner, Thomas:
   Bibliotheca Britannico-Hibernica 884
Tanzai et Néadarné. See Crébillon 979
Tapestries:
   Succinte description des tapisseries 3381
Tarbat, Viscount, 1st Earl of Cromarty. *See* Cromarty
Tarente, Henri Charles de La Trémoille, Prince de. *See* La Trémoille
Tasker, William:
   Annus mirabilis 3222:19
   See Pindar 2923
Tasnière, G. *See* Castellamonte 3676
Tasso, Torquato:
   Aminta 2134
   Gerusalemme liberata 2066
   Jerusalem delivered 1604

Tassoni, Alessandro:
   Secchia rapita. See Tracts 2474:3
Taswell, Mr.:
   Deviliad. See Poems 3363:10
Tatham, John:
   Fancies theater 1985
Tatler 1863, 2963. *See Spectator* 1860
Taubman, Matthew:
   London's triumph. See Tracts 3832:1
Tauler, Johann:
   History 1589
Taunton. *See* Toulmin 3263
Tavannes, Gaspard de Saulx, Seigneur de. *See Collection* 3084
Tavannes, Guillaume de Saulx, Seigneur de. *See Collection* 3084
Taverner, Richard:
   Confessyon of the fayth of the Germaynes 797
   Proverbs. See Elyot 2685
Tavistock, Francis Russell, Marquess of. *See* Anstey 3222:8; *Vanity* 3222:8
Taxation no tyranny. See Johnson 1609:33
Taylor, Brook:
   Contemplatio philosophica 3830
   See Kirby 272, 3539
Taylor, George Watson. *See* Watson
Taylor, Isaac. *See* Lavenham 3719
Taylor, Jeremy:
   Golden grove 1544
Taylor, John, mathematician:
   Thesaurarium mathematicae 2764
Taylor, John, the Water Poet (1508–1653):
   Verry merry wherry-ferry voyage 1986
   See Tracts 3796
Taylor, John (1704–1766). *See* Sermons 1345
Taylor, John (1757–1832):
   Verses on various occasions 2964
Taylor, Robert. *See* Millar 1609:58
Taylor, Silas. *See* Dale 654
Taylor, William:
   Concise statement of transactions 1810:50
Taylour, Charles. *See* Keepe 377
Tear 'em. See First chapter 1608:69
Tears and triumphs of Parnassus. See Lloyd 1810:1
Tears of genius. See Pratt 3222:14, 3973
Tears of Twickenham 3222:7
Teatro delle fabbriche . . . di Venezia. See Venice 3662

Tedmor. *See* Tadmor

Teinturier parfait 357

Teissier, Antoine:
    Catalogus auctorum 2199

Telemachus. *See* Fénelon 3958

Tell-truth, Paul, pseud. *See* Carey 1810:13

Tempesta, Antonio. *See* Drawings 3569; Zuccaro 3615

Temple, Anne Grenville, Countess:
    Poems 2517. *See* Collection 2508

Temple, Sir John. *See Faithful account* 1609: 31

Temple, Launcelot, pseud. *See* Armstrong

Temple, Richard Temple Grenville, Earl:
    Principles of the late changes 1609:11
    See Enquiry 1609:15; *Letter* 1609:54

Temple, Sir William:
    Works 1133
    See Arlington 104

Temple, William Johnson:
    On the abuse of unrestrained power 1609: 39

The temple. See Herbert 2013

Temple des muses 3985

Temple of corruption. See Churchill 3222:10

Temple-student. See Keate 3222:6

Tencin, Claudine Alexandrine Guérin, Marquise de:
    Malheurs de l'amour 2295
    Siège de Calais 3149
    See Edward II 3010

Tencin, Pierre Guérin de, Cardinal. *See Ombre* 1608:53

Tenducci, Dora Maunsell:
    True and genuine narrative 1609:20

Teniers, David:
    Portfolio of engravings 3612
    Theatrum pictorum 3633

Tenison, Thomas, Archbishop:
    Declaration of the sense of the archbishops 1608:8
    Letter to the Reverend Dr. Batteley 1608:8

Terentius Afer, Publius:
    Comoediae 2094, 2200–2, 2226
    See Brindley 2120:12

Teres, T.:
    Richard in Cyprus 1810:15

Terrae Filius. See Amhurst 1729

Terrick, Richard, Bishop. *See* Sermons 1345

Terry, Edward. *See* Valle 2181

Tertullianus, Quintus Septimus Florens:
    Apologeticus. See Classics 2207:39

Terzago, Paolo Maria:
    Museo . . . del Sig. . . . Manfredo Settala 284

The Test. See Protest 1608:84; Tracts 2968:8

Test Act. *See* England 1609:53; Martin 1609: 53; Tracts 2769:8

Testa, Pietro:
    Portfolio of 79 engravings 3613

Testament politique du Chevalier Walpoole. See Walpole 2323

Tetherington, —. *See* Fox 1609:45

Tetius, Hieronymus:
    Aedes Barberinae ad Quirinalem . . . descriptae 3725

Tewkesbury. *See* Dyde 3415

Thames River. *See* Combe 3566; Ireland 3857:4

Thamyris, Queen of Scythia. See Plays 1623:1

Thanet, Isle of. *See* Cozens 3184

Thauler, Johann. *See* Tauler

Théâtre de Brabant. See Sanderus 532

Théâtre de campagne. See Carmontelle 3004

Théâtre de la Foire 1171

Théâtre espagnol 3150

Théâtre françois. See Bibliothèque 3001; *Nouveau théâtre* 1232

Theatre of the reign of George the 3d 1810

The theatres 3222:12

Theatrical campaign 1810:10

Theatrical candidates. See Garrick 1810:25

Theatrical monopoly 1810:30

Theatrical prints. *See* Poems 3363

Theatrical records 3929

Theatrum Scotiae. See Slezer 582

Thebes. *See* Tracts 1348:4

Thelyphthora. See Madan 3244

Themistocles, pseud. *See* Mountmorres 3822

Theobald IV, King of Navarre:
    Poesies 798

Theobald, Lewis:
    Fatal secret 1987
    Harlequin sorcerer 1818:17

Theodore I, King of Corsica:
    History 1608:5
    See Music 3448

Theodosius, the Great. *See* Fléchier 786

Theodosius: or a solemn admonition to Protestant dissenters. See Withers 1609:53

Theodosius, or the force of love. See Plays 1623:2

Theophila. See Benlowes 2643

Théophile de Viau, Sieur:
Oeuvres 1053

Theophrastus:
Caractères 953
Characteres ethici. See Classics 2207:40

Théorie et la pratique du jardinage. See Dezallier 920

Theosebia 1608:63

Theses propounded at the Jesuits' College. See Jesuits 2565

Thespis. See Kelly 3222:7

Thespis. See Brownsmith 3222:8

Thetford. *See* Martin 2902, 3200

Théveneau de Morande, D. *See* Morande

Thicknesse, Ann (Ford):
Letter from Miss F - - d 1609:2

Thicknesse, Philip:
Letter to the Earl of Coventry 1609:46
Memoirs. See Tracts 3834:7
Narrative of what passed 1609:14
Pere Pascal vindicated 1609:45
Sketch of . . . Thomas Gainsborough. See Tracts 3834:7
Sketches and characters of . . . persons now living 3906

Thiers, Jean Baptiste:
Histoire des perruques 768

Third letter to the people of England. See Shebbeare 1608:82

Third letter to the Right Honourable the Earl of B*** 1609:5

Thirlby, Styan:
University of Cambridge vindicated 1608:11
See Walpole 3933:2

Thirty-nine articles. See Tracts 2967:2

Thirty-three plates of English medals by the late Mr. Thomas Snelling. See Snelling 253:4

Thiry, Paul Henri, Baron d'Holbach. *See* Holbach

The thistle. See Mansfield 1608:49

Thomas, Antoine Léonard:
Oeuvres 3151

Thomas, John, Bishop of Winchester:
Sermon 1346:10
See Conduct 1609:26; Swaine 2761

Thomas, Nathanael. *See* Ainsworth 3936

Thomas, William (*d.* 1554):
Historie of Italie 1090, 2472, 2765, 4016

Thomas, William (1670–1738):
Antiquitates prioratus majoris Malverne 708
Cathedral-church of Worcester 641
See Dugdale 568

Thomas and Sally. See Bickerstaffe 1810:1

Thompson, Mrs. *See* Baudier 1608:36

Thompson, Aaron. *See* Geoffrey of Monmouth 1706

Thompson, Charles:
Travels 1545

Thompson, Edward:
Airs in the Sirens 1810:25
Fair Quaker 1810:20
Meretriciad 3222:1
Soldier 3222:6
Syrens 1810:26
Trinculo's trip to the Jubilee 3222:10
See Whitehead 3269

Thompson, George:
Description of the Escurial. See Santos 3759

Thompson, John, 1st Baron Haversham. *See* Haversham

Thompson, Nathaniel. *See* Collection 158, 1935

Thompson, Dr. Thomas:
Case of Thomas Winnington 1608:89

Thompson, Thomas, missionary:
Memoirs of an English missionary 1609:51

Thompson, William. *See* Browne 2656; Hall 1945

Thomson, Alexander:
Letters on the British Museum 2965

Thomson, George:
Syllabus 1608:64

Thomson, James:
Alfred 1818:8
Coriolanus 1818:7
Lodi d'Isacco Neuton 1608:52
Seasons 66
Sophonisba 1818:2
See Hull 1810:24; Kemble 1810:47; Millar 1609:58; Pope 3222:14; Poems 3363

Thomson, Thomas. *See* Thompson

Thomson, William. *See* Orpheus Caledonius 2045

Thomsonus redivivus 1608:89
Thoresby, John. *See* Throsby
Thoresby, Ralph:
  Ducatus Leodiensis 612
  Miscellaneous volumes 2602
  Vicaria Leodiensis 709
  See Catalogues 3404
Thorkelin, Grimur Jónsson:
  Essay on the slave trade 1609:51
Thornton, Bonnell:
  Battle of the wigs 3222:9
  City Latin 1609:2
  Ode 3222:4
  See Plautus 2023; *Poems* 175
Thoroton, Robert:
  Antiquities of Nottinghamshire 613
  History of Nottinghamshire 3523
Thou, Jacques Auguste de:
  Histoire universelle 3152
  Historia sui temporis 3556
  See Collection 3084; Davy du Perron 1273
Thoughts, English and Irish 1609:28
Thoughts of a Member of the lower House.
  See Tracts 400:4; 2475:8
Thoughts on a parliamentary reform. See
  Tracts 2967:1
Thoughts on hunting. See Beckford 2796
Thoughts on parliamentary reform. See
  Jenyns 1609:46
Thoughts on the affairs of Ireland. See Letter
  1608:61
Thoughts on the cause of the present discon-
  tents. See Burke 1609:57
Thoughts on the causes and consequences of
  the present high price of provisions. See
  Jenyns 1609:19
Thoughts on the dismission of officers. See
  Adair 1609:10
Thoughts on the late transactions respecting
  Falkland's Islands. See Johnson 1609:28
Thoughts on the origin and nature of govern-
  ment. See Ramsay 1609:21
Thoughts on the present state of affairs. See
  Pulteney 1609:38
Thoughts upon the Bill for general natural-
  ization. See Tracts 2146:6
Thoyras, Paul de Rapin. *See* Rapin-Thoyras
Thrale, Mrs. Hester Lynch, later Mrs. Piozzi.
  See Piozzi

Three conjurors 3222:5
Three hours after marriage. See Tracts 2474:2
Three letters published in the General Eve-
  ning Post. See Cresswell 1608:65
Three original letters to a friend. See Drury
  Lane 1810:4
Threnodia Augustalis. See Goldsmith 1810:18
Throckmorton, Francis:
  Discoverie of the treasons. See Cecil 111:2
Throsby, John:
  Memoirs of the town and county of Leices-
  ter 358
  Select views in Leicestershire 3209
  See Thoroton 3523
Thuana. See Davy 1273
Thuanus, J. A. *See* Thou, Jacques Auguste
  de
Thubières. *See* Tubières
Thucydides:
  De bello Peloponnesiaco 535
  History of the Grecian war 3470
Thuillier, Dom Vincent. *See* Polybius 931
Thulden, Theodor van:
  Travaux d'Ulysse 3524
Thunberg, Carl Peter:
  Travels in Europe, Africa, and Asia 3262
Thurloe, John:
  Collection of the state papers of John
  Thurloe 1104
Thurlow, Edward, 1st Baron Thurlow. *See*
  Cassandra 1609:50; *English green box*
  1609:40; Leeds 1609:40
Th—w, L—d. *See* Leeds 1609:40
Thyer, Robert. *See* Butler 1821
Thyestes. See Seneca 2028
Thynne, Francis:
  Plea . . . concerning the Bathe and Bach-
  eler Knights 3726
  See Heraldry 2558
Thynne, Thomas, Marquess of Bath. *See*
  Bath
Thysius, Antonius. *See* Seneca 2091; Valerius
  2095
Tiberius, Emperor. *See* Spintrian 2599
Tibullus, Albius. *See* Catullus
Tickell, Richard:
  Anticipation 1609:39, 2966:6
  Casette verte 1609:40
  Epistle from Charles Fox 3222:16

Tickell, Richard (*cont.*)
  Opposition mornings 2966:7
  The project 3222:16
  Wreath of fashion 3222:16
  See English green box 1609:40
Tiepolo, Giovanni Battista. *See* Drawings 3568
Tillemans, Pieter. *See* Drawings 3567
Tilliot, Jean Bénigne Lucotte du. *See* Lucotte du Tilliot 1075
Tillotson, John, Archbishop:
  Form of prayer 1546
  Works 28
  See Birch 1667; Sermons 1451
Tilston, John:
  Booke of Petigrees 2604
  Pedigrees of the gentry of Lincolnshire and Warwickshire 2048
Timaeus, Johann Jacob Carl. *See* Cabal 1810:57
The Times, London. *See* Vyner 3834
Timme, Thomas. *See* Tymme
Timoleon. See Martyn 1817, 1818:2
Timon of Athens. See Love 1810:13
Tin mines. *See* Stannaries
Tindal, Matthew:
  Christianity as old as the Creation. See Waterland 1607
  See Tracts 400:9, 2049:5
Tindal, Nicholas. *See* Rapin-Thoyras 433
Tindal, William:
  History . . . of Evesham 3210
  Remarks on Dr. Johnson's Life 1609:42
Tippoo Sultan. *See* Tracts 2968:4
'Tis well it's no worse. See Bickerstaffe 1810:16
Tit for tat. See Colman 1810:43
Titian. *See* Vecelli, Tiziano
Titon du Tillet, Evrard:
  Description du Parnasse françois 3153
Tittle-tattle. See Fribble 1818:10
Titus, Silius. *See* Sexby 1608:8
Tiverton. *See* Dunsford 3187
To Lady Horatia Waldegrave. See Collection 2508; Strawberry Hill 3469:7
To the author of a libel. See Warburton 1608:13
To the Occasional Writer. See Bolingbroke 1608:13

To the Reverend the Clergy of the Diocese of Peterborough. See Cumberland 1608:8
Tobacco Bill. *See Appeal* 1608:32
Tobago:
  Tabago: or, a geographical description 1608:67
Tobiésen Dubuy, Pierre Ancher. *See* Dubuy
Tobin, J., engraver. *See* Etchings 3588
Token for mourners. See Flavell 2376
Toland, John:
  Art of governing by partys 2766
  Art of restoring. See Detection 2677:3
  Christianity not mysterious 1423
  Life of John Milton 1694
  Miscellaneous works 1660
Toll, Frederick:
  Defence of Dr. Middleton's Free Enquiry 1379:5
  Sermon 1379:5
  Some remarks upon Mr. Church's Vindication 1379:5
  See Dodwell 1372
Tollendal, Thomas Arthur Lally, Comte de. *See* Lally
Tom, Whipping. *See* Whipping Tom
Tom Thumb. See Fielding 1818:3
Tomb of Semiramis 1547
Tombeau de Marguerite de Valois. See Marguerite 2415
Tomkins, Charles:
  Tour to the Isle of Wight 3848
Tomkins, Peltro William:
  Birth and triumph of Cupid 3471
Tomkis, Thomas. *See* Garrick 1810:20; Plays 2451
Toms, Edward:
  Accomplished maid 1810:9
Tong, William. *See* Saunders 1608:12
Tonson, Jacob. *See Works of celebrated authors* 1864
Tooke, Andrew:
  Pantheon 399
Tooke, John Horne:
  Genuine copies of all the letters 1609:25
  Letter to a friend 1609:51
  Sermon 1609:57
  See Foot 1609:22; Onslow 1609:26; Ridpath 1609:38
Tooke, William. *See* France 410

Topham, Edward:
Fool 1810:39
Topham, John:
Liber quotidianus 3382
Some account of the Collegiate Chapel of Saint-Stephen 3472
The Topographer 3831
Topographical miscellanies. Ed. by Sir Samuel Egerton Brydges 3795
Topping, Henry:
Sermon 2473
Torcy, Jean Baptiste Colbert, Marquis de. *See* Colbert 1272
Torelli, Giuseppe. *See* Gray 3699
Torlonia Palace. *See* Verospi Palace
Torr, James:
Antiquities of York 669
Torres, Diego de:
Relation 863
Torrington, George Byng, 1st Viscount. *See* Corbett 1608:32
Tory pill to purge Whig melancholy. See Tracts 98:2
Toscanella, Orazio:
Dittionario volgare e Latino 2321
Tosi, Pier Francesco:
Observations on the florid song 2031
Tottel's *Miscellany. See* Surrey 58, 1920
Tottenham High Cross. *See* Butcher 650; Dyson 2843
Touchet, James, Earl of Castlehaven. *See* Castlehaven 152
Toulmin, Joshua:
History of the town of Taunton 3263
Tour through Normandy. See Stukeley 668:6
Tour through the Isle of Thanet. See Cozens 3184
Tour through the South of England. See Clarke 3852
Tournay. *See* Tracts 2146:6
Tourreil, Jacques de, editor. *See* Demosthenes 1186
Toussaint, François Vincent:
Eclaircissement sur les Moeurs 2050:23
Les Moeurs 2050:23
Tower of London:
Copies of State Papers 2605
See Caesar 2535:9; Cotton 2167

Towers, Joseph:
Essay on the life of Dr. Samuel Johnson 1609:50
Examination of the charges 1609:31
See Letter 1609:42
Towne, John:
Argument of the Divine Legation 1379:3
Townley, James:
High life below stairs 1818:18
Low life 1810:11
Townsend, Heywood. *See* Townshend
Townsend, Thomas. *See* Solis 3283
Townshend, Charles:
Defence of the minority 1609:8
See Letter 1609:5, 6, 9; Tracts 2968:8
Townshend, George, 1st Marquess Townshend:
Brief narrative 1608:32
See Essay 1608:86; Grose 2862; Tracts 361:3
Townshend, Heywood:
Historical collections 1134
Townshend, Lord John:
Jekyll 3222:22
See Tickell 3222:16
Trablet, Nicholas Charles Joseph:
Mémoires . . . de M. de Fontenelle 822
Tractatus:
Tractatus de metro 3383
Tracts 98–100, 210, 1348, 1608, 2049–50, 2146, 2474, 2767–9, 2966–8, 3054, 3796–7, 3832, 3986
See Detection 2677; Miscellaneous volumes 3445–6; Music 3448; Plays 1082; State tracts 1170, 2180, 2606; Walpole 2492–3
Tracts of the reign of George the 3d 1609
Tracts on the Arts 359–61, 3833
Tracts on the Peerage Bill 400, 2475
Tracts, Parliamentary 2967
Tracy, John:
Periander 1818:4
Trade with France . . . considered. See Detection 2677:10
Tradescant, John:
Museum Tradescantium 769
Tragedy of Chrononhotonthologos. See Carey 1818:5
Tragedy of King Saul. See Trapp 1623:1
Traité de l'éducation des femmes. See Miremont 2284

Traité des tournois. See Menestrier 928, 1077

Trajan, Emperor of Rome. *See* Giaccone 3426

Trallianus, Alexander. *See* Alexander

Transactions of the Society for the encouragement of arts. See Society 2957

Transcript of government. *See* Disney 728

Transcripts of historical letters 2607

Trapaud, Elisha:
Short account of the Prince of Wales's Island 1609:51

Trapp, Joseph:
Abra-mule 1818:21
Praelectiones poeticae 2135
Tragedy of King Saul. See Plays 1623:1
See Virgilius 1922

Travels into Spain. See Aulnoy 364, 1461

Travels of Mons. le Post-Chaise 1608:74

Travels through Flanders. See Tracts 360:3

Treasury of auncient and moderne times. See Bristol 2533; Mexia 2059

Treasury of wit. See Pinkerton 2449

Treatise concerning statutes. See Hatton 166

Treatise concerning the dignities and yearly revenues 1608:93

Treatise concerning the militia. See Dorset 1608:27, 48

Treatise on the prerogatives of a Queen Consort 1609:2

Treaty of navigation and commerce. See England 1608:94

Treaty of peace and friendship. See England 1608:94

Treatyse concernynge the fruytfull sayinges of Davyd. See Fisher 121

Trebeck, Andrew:
Preservative against Popery 1608:60
Sermon. *See* Sermons 1346:1

Trenchard, John:
Essays 1608:42
Natural history of superstition 1608:12
Short history of standing armies 1608:27, 93
See Independent Whig 1526; Tracts 400:11

Trenchard, Thomas:
Short history. See Trenchard, John 1608:27

Trent, Council of. *See* Baphius 3944; Le Vassor 3336; Sarpi 933

Trent River. *See* Congreve 681

Trentham, Granville Leveson-Gower, Viscount. *See* Westminster 1608:69, 1726, 2146:1

Tresham, Henry:
Sea-sick minstrel 3211

Tressan, Louis Elisabeth de la Vergne, Comte de. *See Bibliothèque* 2801

Treswell, Robert:
Relation of . . . the journey 2476

Trévié, Marquis de. *See* Political tracts 94:11

Trevisa, John. *See* Bartholomaeus 1612

Trevor, John. *See* Hampden 3537

Trevor, Robert, 1st Viscount Hampden. *See* Hampden 3537

Treyssac de Vergy, Pierre Henri:
Lettre à Monseigneur le duc de Choiseul 1609:56

Trial. *See also* Tryal

Trial for murder 3222:6

Trial of the important question. See Fair trial 1609:24

Trial of the witnesses. *See* Sherlock 1608:25

Trials:
Select trials . . . in the Old Bailey 1723
Tryals for high-treason 1724
See Collection 870

Tribunus, pseud. *See* Jefferson, Thomas

Trinculo's trip to the Jubilee. See Thompson 3222:10

Trinity College, Dublin. *See* Dublin 313

Trip to Portsmouth. See Stevens 1810:20

Trip to Scotland. See Whitehead 1810:15

Triumphant campaign 1608:46

Triumphant widow. See Newcastle 92

Triumphs of Bute 3222:11

Trivet, Nicholas:
Annales sex regum Angliae 710

Troil, Uno von:
Letters on Iceland 2969

Trois siècles de notre littérature. See Sabatier 1168

Tronchin du Breuil, Jean. *See* William III 3529

Trott, John, pseud.:
Patriot unmasked 1609:3

Trotter, Catharine, later Mrs. Cockburn. *See* Cockburn

Troyes, Jean de. *See* Collection 3084

True account and declaration of the . . . conspiracy against the late king. See Sprat 1132

True and exact copy of a genuine letter 1608: 65

True and exact relation of the late earthquake and eruption of Mount Aetna. See Winchilsea 102

True and exact relation of the strange finding out of Moses his tombe. See Tracts 210

True and genuine narrative of Mr. & Mrs. Tenducci. See Tenducci 1609:20

True and particular relation of the earthquake. See Lima 1485

True and perfect narrative. See Keepe 377

True and plaine declaration. See Cecil 111

True Briton 1609:5

True coppie of the transportation of the Lowe Countries. See Hartlib 125:3

True dyfferēs between the regall power and the ecclesiasticall power. See Fox 163

True Englishman. *See Letter* 1609:54

True, genuine, and authentic account . . . of John Rice 1609:6

True historical discourse of Muley Hamet. See Sherley 3828

True interest of Great Britain 1609:13

True interest . . . of Ireland. See Brett 1367: 5

True Protestant. *See* Owen, Charles

True relation of the unjust accusation. See Tracts 100:2

True sentiments of America. See Hollis 1609:21

True state of England. See England 1608:72

True state of facts relating to Ramsgate Harbour 1608:7

True state of the question 1609:46

True state of Trinity College. See Paris 1608: 11

Truman, Joseph:
  Discourse 1804

Trusler, John:
  Country election 1810:12
  See Gardening 3891:1

Truth in rhyme 3222:1

Truth triumphant. See Derby 79:1

Tryal. *See also* Trial

Tryal at Paris. See Journeaulx 1413

Tryal of Mr. Daniel Sutton 1609:19

Tryals for high-treason 1724

Tryals per pais. See Duncombe 2681

Tryon, Thomas:
  Memoirs 2970

T——t——m and V——d—t [i. e. Trentham and Vandeput]. *See* Tracts 2146:1

Tubières, Anne Claude Philippe de, Comte de Caylus. *See* Caylus

Tubières, Marthe Marguerite Hippolyte de, Marquise de Caylus. *See* Caylus

Tucker, Josiah:
  Cui bono 1609:42
  Four letters 1609:45
  Humble address 1609:35
  Letter from a merchant in London 1609:13
  Letter to Edmund Burke 1609:35
  Reflections 1608:64
  See Estwick 1609:37; *Some remarks* 1608: 50

Tuckney, Anthony:
  Death disarmed. See Sermons 2756:3

Tuke, Sir Samuel:
  Adventures of five hours 1818:21. *See* Hull 1810:10

Tuke, Thomas. *See* Perkins 2589

Tulaji, Rajah of Tanjore. *See Original papers* 1609:47A

Tunbridge walks. See Plays 1623:1

Tunbridge Wells. *See* Burr 677

Tunis. *See* Mackenzie 1810:20; Waldegrave 2611

Tunstall, James:
  Observations . . . between Cicero and M. Brutus 1424

Turenne, Henri de la Tour d'Auvergne, Vicomte de:
  Military memoires 1548
  See Ramsay 1003, 1143; *Rémonstrance* 1085

Turkey. *See* Castlemaine 2660; *see also* Levant Company

Turkish spy:
  Letters writ by a Turkish spy 1766

Turkish wives. See Songs 1810:31

Tuscany:
  Edict of the Grand Duke of Tuscany 1609: 52
  See Galluzzi 32, 3097

Tutti i trionfi, carri, mascherate. See Grazzini 3320

Tuvil, Daniel:
Vade Mecum, a manuall of essayes. See
Vade Mecum 2771
Twickenham. See Antiquities 3485:10; En-
gravings 3417; Guides 2387:3; Müntz 3575;
O'Bryen 3222:22; Pye 2457
Twiss, Richard:
Tour in Ireland 2971
Travels through Portugal and Spain 2972
See Preston 3222:15
Two bulls roaring out excommunications.
See Paul III 1608:95
Two candidates. See Tracts 2146:1
Two discourses. See Woodhead 1635
Two epistles to Mr. Pope. See Young 1818:3
Two gentlemen of Verona. See Victor 1810:4
Two historical accounts of the making New
Forest. See New Forest 1608:66
Two letters to the Reverend Dr. Bentley
1608:11, 15
Two misers. See O'Hara 1810:23
Two questions, previous to Dr. Middleton's
Free Enquiry. See Sykes 1379:6
Two reports on the matter of complaint of
Mr. Livius. See England 1609:58
Two Sicilies. See Naples
Twyne, Thomas:
Schoolmaster 1605
Tymme, Thomas:
Booke containing the true portraiture of
the ... Kings of England 1606
Type specimens. See Caslon 292; Jones 3784
Tyrrell, James:
Patriarcha non monarcha 2770
Tyrwhitt, Thomas. See Chatterton 3690;
Chaucer 1431
Tyson, Michael:
Account of an illuminated manuscript
1609:57
Tytler, William. See Dalrymple 2666

Ubaldini, Petruccio:
Descrittione del regno di Scotia 523, 3384
Vite delle donne illustri del regno d'Inghil-
terra 2322, 3385
Udney, Mary, later Lady Cunynghame. See
Cunynghame
Uffizi Gallery. See Florence 3570
Ugbrooke Park. See Reeve 3222:14

Ulfeld, Count, of Denmark. See Rousseau
761
Ulysses. See Thulden 3524
Umphreville, Edward:
Law collections 2608
See Mawson 2579
Unconnected Whig's address 1609:38
Undertakers, Company of. See Physic 1608:
89
Union; or, select Scots and English poems.
See Grimston 1896:2
United Brethren. See Frey 1608:75; Rimius
1608:75; Wesley 1608:19
United States. See Clavière 3230; Godefroy
3742
United States. Continental Congress:
Extracts from the votes 1609:32
Journal 1609:36
Universal history. See Tallents 227
Universal passion. See Miller 1818:6
University College, Oxford. See Oxford Uni-
versity. University College
University of Cambridge vindicated. See
Thirlby 1608:11
Unton, Henry. See Funebria 196
The upholsterer. See Murphy 1818:16
Urban VIII, Pope:
Poemata 1362
Urban, Sylvanus, pseud. for John Nichols.
See Wolcot 3222:22
Urquhart, Sir Thomas:
Discovery of a most exquisite jewel 3798
Ursinus, Fulvius:
Carmina novem poetriarum 2609
Use of passions. See Senault 178
Useful and entertaining collection. See Let-
ters 1440
Ussher, James, Archbishop of Armagh. See
Bernard 1699; Parr 906
Utrecht, Treaty of. See Brodrick 1638; Eng-
land 1249, 1608:94, 96
Uvedale, Thomas. See Comines 1639

V., C. See Vallancey
Vadé, Guillaume. See Voltaire 2975
Vade mecum 2771
Vaenius, Otho. See Veen
Vaillant, Jean Foi:
Numismata aerea imperatorum Augusta-
rum et Caesarum in coloniis 228

Vaillant, Jean Foi (*cont.*)
Numismata imperatorum Romanorum 285
Seleucidarum imperium 491
Vaillant, Paul. *See* Ferrers 1112
Vairasse, Denis:
Histoire des Sevarambes. See Serendip 1237
Valdor, Jean:
Triomphes de Louis XIII 3525
Valens, pseud. *See* Burke, William
Valentine's Day. See Heard 1810:25
Valerius Maximus:
Opera 2095
Valesius, Hadrianus. *See* Valois, Adrien de
Vallancey, Charles:
Essay towards illustrating the ancient history of the Britannic Isles 1609:48
Valle, Pietro della:
Travels 2181
Valline, John. *See* Tooke 1609:25
Valois, Adrien de:
Valesiana 1287
See Ammianus 2150
Valois, Charles de, Duc d'Angoulême. *See* Collection 3084; Torres 863
Valois, Marguerite de. *See* Marguerite
Valois, Philippe de. *See* Choisy 917
Valpole, Father Henry. *See* Walpole
Vanbrugh, Sir John:
Plays 1879
See Kemble 1810:43; Lee 1810:26
Vandeput, Sir George. *See* Tracts 2146:1; Westminster 1726
Van de Velde, Jan. *See* Prints 3461
Van Der Dort, Abraham:
Catalogue of paintings 3526
See Vertue 2478–9, 3704
Van der Heyden, Jan. *See* Heiden
Van der Meulen, Adam Frans. *See* Drawings 3567; Louis XIV 3591:3
Van der Straet, Jan. *See* Stradanus
Van Dyck, Sir Anthony:
Portfolio of 59 prints 3660
Portfolio of 150 engravings 3634
See Drawings 3569; St. Luke's Club 2595
Van Hoey, Abraham. *See* Hoey
Van Hulle, Anselm:
Portraicts 3580, 3661
Van Nartow, André. *See* Van Nideck 3686

Van Nideck, A.:
Antiquitates . . . Romanorum 3686
Van Schuppen, Pieter. *See* Prints 3626
Van Thulden, Theodor. *See* Gevartius 3620
Van Westerhout, Arnold. *See* Wright 3687
Vane, Sir Henry. *See* Sikes 1089
Vanel, —:
Galanteries des rois de France 954
Vanity of human life 3222:8
Vansittart, Henry:
Letter to the proprietors of East-India stock 1609:17
See Facts 1609:55; Defence 1609:55
Vanvitelli, Luigi:
Dichiarazione dei disegni 3596
Vardy, John. *See* Jones 3784
Vargas, François de. *See* Le Vassor 3336
Variétés historiques. See Boucher 1153
Variétés sérieuses et amusantes. See Sablier 3047
Variety. See Griffith 1810:34
Varillas, Antoine:
Histoire de Charles IX 970
Histoire de François I 971
Varotari, Alessandro. *See* Drawings 3567
Varsovie ridicule. See Mélange 1045
Vasari, Giorgio:
Ragionamenti. See Ragionamenti 3366
See Aglionby 474; Drawings 3568
Vasconcellos, Antonio de:
Anacephalaeoses 3386
Vatican. *See* Raphael 3609
Vatican Library. *See* Venuti 229
Vattel, Emerich de:
Pièces diverses 1006
Vaughan, Henry:
Olor Iscanus 2032
Vaughan, Samuel:
Appeal to the public 1609:25
Vaughan, Thomas (1622–1666). *See* Rosicrucians 1542
Vaughan, Thomas (*fl.* 1772–1820):
Hotel 1810:26
Vauxhall affray 1609:31
Vavasseur, François:
De epigrammate liber 2136
Veal, George:
Musical travels 1609:32
Vecelli, Cesare. *See* Vecelli, T. 2477

Vecelli, Tiziano:
  Habiti antichi 2477
  Portfolio of 165 engravings 3614
  See Drawings 3569
Veen, Otto van:
  Amorum emblemata 3799
  See Horatius Flaccus 2214
Vegetius, Flavius. *See* Classics 2207:37
Velleius Paterculus, Caius:
  Historia Romana 2261. *See* Classics 2207:41
Venaissin. *See* Moreau 3034
Veneroni, Giovanni:
  Dictionnaire Italien et François 2083
  Il maestro Italiano 2116
  Le maître Italien 2117
Venice:
  Arme overo insegne di tutti li nobili 2051
  Habiti d'huomeni 3987
  Teatro delle fabbriche 3662
  See Castlemaine 2660; Fougasses 3276; La Haye 1751; Pacifico 2109; Paruta 3360
Venice. St. Mark's. *See* St. Mark's, Venice
Venus attiring the Graces 3222:15
Venus, Vigil of. *See* Classics 2207:29
Venuti, Ridolfino:
  Antiqua numismata 229
  Collectanea antiquitatum Romanarum 3545
Verax, pseud. *See* Remarks 1609:48
Verdere, Mr. *See* Du Verdier
Verdier, Gilbert Saulnier du. *See* Du Verdier
Verdizotti, Giovanni Mario:
  Cento favole morali 3988
Vere, Sir Francis:
  Commentaries 492
  Extremities 1608:1
Vere family. *See* Collins 565
Vergara, Cesare Antonio:
  Monete del regno di Napoli 256
Vergetius, Angelus. *See* Ursinus 2609
Vergilius. *See* Virgilius
Verheiden, Jacobus:
  Praestantium aliquot theologorum . . . effigies 3727
  See Holland 3783
Verité, Louis Alexandre de:
  Essai sur l'histoire de Picardie. See Tracts 2050:20
Verney, Richard, Baron Willoughby de Broke. *See* Willoughby de Broke

Vernon, Edward, Admiral:
  Original letters 1497
  See Authentick papers 1608:53; *Letter* 1608:53
Verona. *See* Maffei 2080
Vérone, François de, pseud. *See* Boucher 2343
Verospi Palace. *See* Farnese 3619
Verres, Caius Cornelius. *See* Cicero 3300
Verrue, Jeanne Baptiste de. *See* Bougeant 1178:1
Versailles. *See* Labyrinte 301; Louis XIV 3591:2
Versailles, Promenade de. See Bougeant 1178:1
Verses addressed to no Minister 3222:5
Verses addressed to the — 3222:13
Verses on Sir Joshua Reynolds's painted window. See Warton 3222:18
Verses on the present state of Ireland. See Lucan 3222:16
Verses to Lady Charles Spencer. See Collection 2508
Verses to the memory of Garrick. See Sheridan 3222:16
Verses written on several occasions. See Burnet 3222:15
Versorand:
  Mémoires de Versorand 1208
Verstegan, Richard:
  Restitution of decayed intelligence 1549
  Theatre des cruautez 3989
Vertot, René Aubert de:
  Histoire des Chevaliers Hospitaliers 3055
  History of the revolutions in Portugal 1661
  History of the revolutions in Sweden 1663
  History of the revolutions . . . of the Roman republic 1662
  Miscellanies 3473
  See Miscellaneous tracts 89:1
Vertue, George:
  Abstracts of MSS. *See* Walpole 2488
  Anecdotes of painting. See Walpole, Horace. *Anecdotes.*
  Catalogue of engravers. See Walpole, Horace. *Anecdotes.*
  Catalogue of his works 3665
  Catalogue . . . of King Charles the First's capital collection 2478-9

Vertue, George (*cont.*)

Catalogue of . . . *pictures . . . belonging to King James the Second* 2479

Catalogue of the curious collection of pictures of George Villiers, Duke of Buckingham 2479

Collection of catalogues 2479

Collection of notebooks 3704

Description of the works of Wenceslaus Hollar 2479:4

Drawings 2610

Explanations of historic prints 2772

Heads of the Kings of England 3663

Index of engravers. See Walpole, Horace 2488

Letters to. *See* Collection of fees 2540

Medals, coins, great seals 2480. *See* Snelling 253

Portfolio of original drawings 3581

Portfolios of prints 3664–5

See Birch 3637; Collins 2359; Garter 3551; Society 3658

Vesuvius, Mount. *See* Hamilton 2865

Veteranus, pseud. *See* Tracts 3796:3

Veteres de re militari scriptores. See Classics 2207:37

Veterum medicorum chirurgica. See Nicetas 3449

Vetusta monumenta. See Society 3658

Vices of the town. See Poems 280:14

Vichy-Champrond, Marie de, later Mme. du Deffand. *See* Du Deffand

Victor Amadeus II, King of Sardinia. *See* Political tracts 94:11

Victor, Benjamin:

History of the theatres of London and Dublin 2973

History of the theatres of London from 1760 2974

Original letters 3930

Two gentlemen of Verona 1810:4

Widow of the wood 1805

Victoria, Consort of Ferdinand II, Grand Duke of Tuscany. *See* Zouch 3993

Vida, Marco Girolamo, Bishop of Alba:

Poemata 2262

Vie de Cassiodore. See Sainte-Marthe 1207

Vie de Charles V, Duc de Lorraine. See La Brune 1298

Vie de Louis Balbe Berton de Crillon. See Lussan 1254

Vie de Monsieur le duc de Montausier. See Le Petit 1226

Vie de Saint Jean Chrysostome. See Hermant 1276

Vie et aventures de Pierre Pinson, dit le Chevalier Bero. See Pinson 3137

Vieilleville, François de Scepeaux, Sire de. *See* Collection 3084

Vienna:

Court. *See* Bougeant 1178:2

Imperial Collection. *See* Eckhel 3695; Méchel 2417

Vientanus. *See* Giovannoli 3495

Vies de plusieurs saints illustrés. See Arnauld d'Andilly 1265

Vies des premiers peintres du Roi, depuis Lebrun jusqu'à présent. See Lépicié 343

View of Lord Bolingbroke's philosophy. See Warburton 1608:34

View of the City of Glasgow. See MacUre 2725

View of the controversy 1379:5

View of the Court of St. Germain. See Macky 1608:10

View of the internal evidence of the Christian religion. See Jenyns 2893

View of the origin, nature, and use of jettons. See Snelling 253:2

View of the several changes 1609:18

View of the silver coin and coinage of England. See Snelling 253:1

View of the silver coin and coinage of Scotland. See Snelling 253:3

View of the soul. See Saunders 27

View of the taste for gardening. See Gardening 1609:45

View of the taxes. See Tracts 2146:1

Views of English seats. *See* Antiquities 3485

Views of the lakes in Cumberland. *See* Antiquities 3485:1

Vigenère, Blaise de. *See* Philostratus 2161

Vigneul-Marville, pseud. *See* Argonne 1176

Vignier, Nicolas:

Rerum Burgundiorum chronicon 864

Vignola, Giacomo Barozzi da:

Regla de las cinco orderes de architectura 3764

Vignolius, Joannes:
Antiquiores 493
Villa Borghese. *See* Montelatici 2316
Villa Nova, Arnaldus de. *See* Salerno 2289
Villa Pamphilia 3527
Villa Real, Mrs. Catherine da Costa. *See* Mendes 382
Village curate. See Hurdis 2877
Village wedding. See Love 1810:11
Villars, Claude Louis Hector, Duc de:
Memoirs 1550
Vie du maréchal duc de Villars 3387
Villars, François, Baron du. *See* Du Villars
Villegagnon, Nicolas Durand de:
Caroli V expeditio 138
Villeneuve, Guillaume de. *See* Collection 3084
Villeroi. *See Count de Villeroi* 1810:55
Villeroi, Nicolas de Neufville, Seigneur de. *See* Neufville
Villette, John:
Genuine account 1609:38
Villiers, George, Duke of Buckingham. *See* Buckingham
Villiers, John Charles, Earl of Clarendon:
Chaubert 1810:49
Villiers, Thomas, Earl of Clarendon. *See* Clarendon
Villiers, William, Earl of Jersey. *See* Jersey
Vincent, Augustine:
. . . Errours in . . . the Catalogue of the nobility published by Raphe Brooke 642
Vincent, Nathaniel:
Conversion of the soul 2773
Vinci, Leonardo da:
Recueil de testes de caractère 3765
See Drawings 3567, 3569
Vinciolo, Federico di:
Excellentes eschantillons, patrons, et modeles 2481
Vindication in answer to . . . The Court and Character of King James. See Sanderson 1585
Vindication of a late pamphlet. See Waller 1608:43
Vindication of Lord Taaffe's civil principles. See Taaffe 2763:1
Vindication of Mr. Holwell's character. See Holwell 1609:55

Vindication of Robert III, King of Scotland. See Cromarty 76
Vindication of some passages. See Gibbon 1609:39
Vindication of the conduct of the present war 1609:1
Vindication of the rights of women. See Wollstonecraft 3177
Vinnius, Arnoldus:
Commentarius 2203
Virgilius Maro, Publius:
Aeneid 1921
Bucolica, Georgica, et Aeneis 2204–6, 2482
Georgics. See Tracts 2146:5
Opera 2263–4, 2296. *See* Brindley 2120:13; Classics 2207:42
The XIII Bukes of Eneados 101
Works 180, 1880, 1922, 1988
See Bartoli 3598; Holdsworth 3169; Scarron 1087
Virginia. *See* Beverly 1392; Crisp 1818:13; Jefferson 1609:32
Virtue. *See Modern virtue*
Virtuosi. *See* St. Luke's Club 2595
Virtuosi's Museum. See Sandby 3844
Virtuous woman found. See Walker 140
Virtu's Explication des peinteurs. *See* Vertue 2772
Vision of King Hezekiah. See Black-bird 2646: 20
Visions of Sir Heister Ryley. See Povey 95
Visions of Zabdeel 1608:91
Visitation of Norfolk. See Heraldry 3879; Norfolk 2581–3
Visscher, Cornelis. *See* Reynst 3579
Vitae selectae 2137
Vitruvius Pollio, Marcus:
Architecture. See Mauclerc 223
Voice of the people 1608:81
Voiture, Vincent de:
Oeuvres 955
Voix de la nature. See Mélange 1045
Voltaire, François Marie Arouet de:
Abrégé de l'histoire universelle 1173
Alzire. See Plays 1908:6
Amelie 1818:11
Candide 1172, 1307
Contes de Guillaume Vadé 2975
Defense de Milord Bollingbroke 1608:76
Diatribe du docteur Akakia 1608:76

Voltaire, François Marie Arouet de (*cont.*)
  Essai sur l'histoire générale 1172
  Fragments sur l'Inde 3388
  Henriade 1148
  Histoire de la guerre de 1741 1308
  Histoire du docteur Akakia 1608:76
  Honnêtetés littéraires 3056
  Lettres. *See* Du Deffand 2545
  Lois de Minos 4017
  Mémoires 3990
  Mensonges imprimez 1608:76
  Nanine 1818:10
  Oeuvres 1172, 3057
  One or more works 4017
  Orphan of China 1818:17
  Orphelin de la Chine 1263
  Porte-feuille trouvé 1239
  Pucelle d'Orléans 1263
  Questions sur l'Encyclopaedie 3058
  Recueil nécessaire 3059
  Siècle de Louis XIV 1149
  See Ayscough 1810:26; Borde 2050:15;
    Caylus 2353; Celesia 1810:17; Colman
    1810:10; Duncombe 1818:6; Hill 1818:7;
    Hume 1680; Keate 3222:9; *Romans* 3045;
    Songs 1810:31
  Voluntary exile 3222:19
  The volunteers. See Downing 1810:31
Vos, Marten de. *See* De Vos
Vossius, Isaac:
  De Sibyllinis . . . oraculis 2227
Voyage dans les départemens de la France.
  See Lavallée 3334
Voyage du jeune Anacharsis en Grèce. See
  Barthélemy 262
Voyage du monde de Descartes. See Daniel
  1214
Voyage et les aventures des trois Princes de
  Sarendip. See Serendip 1237
Voyage round the world 1609:17
Voyage to the North Pole. See Journal 1609:
  31
Voyages and travels. See Green 542
Voye de laict ou les chemins des héros. See
  Berton 1055
Voyer de Paulmy, René Louis de, Marquis
  d'Argenson. *See* Argenson
Vries, Jan Vredeman de:
  Hortorum viridariorumque elegantes . . .
  formae 3474

Vries, Jan Vredeman de (*cont.*)
  See Prints 3654
Vroom, Cornelis. *See* Drawings 3567
Vulcan's wedding. See Fuzelier 1818:3
Vulson, Marc de:
  Portraits des hommes illustres françois 3557
  Vray théâtre d'honneur 3557
Vyner, Robert, pseud.:
  Sermon (on Excise Bill) 3834

W., Lady. *See* Wallace 1810:42
W., A. *See* Walker 2613
W., E. *See* Plays 2451
W., F. *See Friendship* 3222:9
W., H. *See* Hartlib 125:3
W., J. *See* Sermons 2756:5
W., J., Esq. *See Military* 1608:68
W., J., Gent. *See Speedy post* 1608:5
W., O. *See* Walker 2774
W., T.:
  Plantagenets tragicall story 1989
Wake, William:
  Principles of the Christian religion ex-
  plained 1386
Wakefield, Gilbert. *See* Gray 3895
Waldegrave, George, 4th Earl Waldegrave:
  Portrait 3475
Waldegrave, Lady Horatia. *See* Collection
  2508; Strawberry Hill 3469:7
Waldegrave, James, 2d Earl Waldegrave:
  Catalogue of pictures. See Catalogues 3404
  Portrait 3475
Waldegrave, Admiral William, later Baron
  Radstock:
  Account of his embassy to Tunis 2611
Waldegrave family 3475
Waldegrave manuscripts. *See* Walpole 2616
Waldron, Francis Godolphin:
  Heighho for a husband 1810:54
  Literary museum 3389
  Maid of Kent 1810:28
  Prodigal 1810:54
  See Downes 3919
Waldron, George:
  History . . . of the Isle of Man 139
Wales, Frederick, Prince of. *See* Frederick,
  Prince of Wales
Wales:
  Genealogical table of the kings and princes
  2612

Wales (cont.)
  Month's tour in North Wales 2976
  See Antiquities 3485:11; Baker 3178; Dod-
  dridge 1062; Duckett 683; Gilpin 3854:4;
  Lambard 629; Moore 3843; Pennant 547;
  Sulivan 3829; Warrington 419; Wyndham
  3221, 3481
Walker, Anna:
  Sweete savor for woman 2613
Walker, Anthony:
  The virtuous woman found 140
Walker, Sir Edward:
  Historical discourses 1135
  See Heraldry 2558
Walker, George, painter:
  Select views of picturesque scenery 3835
Walker, Henry. See Several proceedings
  2758
Walker, John. See Antiquities 3485:4; Copper
  Plate Magazine 3838
Walker, Joseph Cooper:
  Historical essay on the dress of . . . the
  Irish 3390
  Historical memoirs of the Irish bards 3212
Walker, Obadiah:
  Greek and Roman history 2774
  See Woodhead 1635
Walker, Richard. See Conduct 1609:26;
  Swaine 2761
Walker, Thomas, Cornet:
  Answer to Mr. Fitzgerald's appeal 1609:33
Wallace, Eglantine, Lady Wallace:
  Diamond cut diamond 1810:42
  The ton 1810:45
  Whim 1810:57
Wallace, George:
  Nature and descent of ancient peerages
  3154
  Thoughts on the origin of feudal tenures
  3264
Wallace, James:
  Description of the isles of Orkney 770
Waller, Edmund:
  Case of the Hanover forces 1608:43, 46
  Of love. See Poems 3363:3
  Vindication 1810:43
  Works 472, 2977
  See Free 1810:47
Waller, Sir William:
  Vindication of . . . Sir William Waller 3907

The wallet 1609:55
Wallis, John, D. D. (1616–1703):
  Grammatica linguae Anglicanae 2775
  Sermons 3265
Wallis, John, A. M. (1714–1793):
  Natural history . . . of Northumberland
  3213
Wallis, Captain Samuel. See Injured 3222:16
Walpole, Catherine (Shorter), Lady. See Rival
  wives 2463
Walpole, Sir Edward:
  Letters. See Letters 2576
  Poem on satire 3222:6
  Sketch for A.D. 1769 3222:12
  Sketch of the times 3222:12
  See Drawings 3641; Jesuits 2565; Poems 280
Walpole, George, Earl of Orford. See Orford
Walpole, Father Henry. See Cresswell 3778
Walpole, Horace, 4th Earl of Orford:
  Abstracts of Vertue's notebooks 2488
  Account of the giants 1609:15; 2614. See
  Collection 2507:3
  Aedes Walpolianae 2483, 3546, 3931–2. See
  Houghton 3572
  Alphabetical catalogue of the pictures at
  SH 2162
  Anecdotes of painting 2484, 2518–20. See
  Bromfield 2534; Vertue 3664
  Book of visitors. See Walpole 2488, 2616
  'Books of materials' 2615
  Castello di Otranto 3728
  Castle of Otranto 2485–6; 3391
  Castle of Otranto, printed by Bodoni 3729
  Castle of Otranto, various editions 3730,
  3908
  Catalogue of engravers. See his Anecdotes
  of painting
  Catalogue of pictures and drawings in the
  Holbein Chamber 2619:4
  Catalogue of Sir Robert Walpole's pictures.
  See Walpole 3931
  Catalogue of the collections of the Duke
  of Devonshire. See Collection 2507:4
  Catalogue of the English portraits 2163
  Catalogue of the Library at SH 2164
  Catalogue of the pictures at SH 2162
  Catalogue of the royal and noble authors
  of England 2521, 2978. See Gardiner 2379
  Catalogue of the royal and noble authors:
  Observations on and Remarks on. See

Walpole, Horace (*cont.*)

Tracts 2050:13

Catalogues of the collections of Charles I, &c. *See* Vertue 2478–9

Château d'Otrante 3908

Commonplace books 2616. *See also* Bayle 2039

Counter-address to the public 1609:8

Description of the villa 2522–5, 3582, 3932. *See* Strawberry Hill 3469:10; Walpole 2162

Dialogue between two great ladies. See Tracts 2050:21

Epilogue to Tamerlane. See Tracts 2968:9

Essai sur l'art des jardins modernes 2617

Essay on modern gardening 2526. *See* Gardening 3891; Strawberry Hill 3469:11

Fragment of a play 2618

Fugitive pieces 1881, 2527. *See* Strawberry Hill 3469:12

Hieroglyphic tales 2507:5

Historic doubts 2487, 2620, 3909

Index of engravers 2488

Journal of the Printing Office 2506

Lessons for the day. See Letter 1608:18; Walpole 2616

Letter from Xo Ho 2489

Letter on Chatterton 1609:39. *See* Chatterton 3408, 3690:4; Strawberry Hill 3469:13

Letter to the Whigs 3933

Letters. *See* Bromfield 2534; Letters 2576; Walpole 2620

List of the principal pictures 2162

Manuscript catalogue 2164

Memoirs of Grammont 3991. *See* Hamilton 2511

Miscellaneous antiquities 2508–9, 3469:14, 3476

Mysterious mother 2490–1, 2528, 3469:15, 16

Narrative of the quarrel between Hume and Rousseau. See Walpole 2623

Notes to Mason's later poems. *See* Mason 1619

Notes to the portraits at Woburn Abbey 2619

Old England, contributions to. *See Old England*

Paris Journals. *See* Walpole 2616

Parody of Lord Chesterfield. See Walpole 2623

Walpole, Horace (*cont.*)

Pocket books 2622

Poems addressed to HW 2619:3

Postscript to Royal and noble authors 2521

Reminiscences. See Walpole 2623

Royal and noble authors. See Catalogue of *royal and noble authors*

School exercises 2621

Visitors, Lists of. *See* Walpole 2488, 2616

See Collection 2506; Hayter 1608:50; Heathcote 1609:16; King's Lynn 2567; Opposition 1608:80; Ranby 1608:51; *Vindication* 1609:1; Walpole 2622; *World* 911, 2501

Walpole, Horatio, 1st Baron Walpole:

Answer to Lord Bolingbroke's Letters 59

Considerations on the present state of affairs 1608:43

Interest of Great Britain 1608:43

Letter 1608:43

Rise and fall of the . . . excise 1608:30

See Impostor 1608:13; Secker 1609:22; Whytt 1608:42

Walpole, Margaret (Rolle), Lady. *See* Rigacci 2111, 2462, 3463

Walpole, Lady Maria, later Churchill. *See* Churchill, Lady Mary

Walpole, Richard, Jesuit:

Authentic memoirs of . . . Father Richard Walpole 3910

See Tracts 2050

Walpole, Robert (1650–1700):

Pocket account book 2622

Walpole, Sir Robert, 1st Earl of Orford:

Mr. Walpole's case. See Detection 2677:5

Some considerations 1608:21, 39

Some reflections upon a pamphlet called the Old Whig 400:6, 2475:5

Testament politique 2323

Thoughts of a Member of the lower House 400:4, 2475:8

Tracts 2492

Tracts on his last illness 2493. *See* 1608:51

See Authentick 1608:51; Bunbury 3563:3; Coxe 3304; Dupuy-Demportes 2269; England 1249; *Fragment* 1609:57; Hardwicke 3924; Masquerader 2416; Mounteney 1608: 66; Musgrave 2432; Ralph 2458; Ranby 1608:51; *Reflections* 1609:20; Vyner 3834; Ware 536; Whatley 2496

Walpole, Robert (1701–1751), 2d Earl of Orford:
Patent of appointment to Exchequer 2623
See Poems 3363:13
Walpole, Thomas:
Letter 2508, 2529
Report of the Lords Commissioners on the petition. See Tracts 2050:14
Walpole, Thomas, Jr. *See* Drawings 3641
Walpole family:
Pedigree 2624
See Collins 3888; Engravings 3417; Geography 3423
Walsingham, Sir Francis. *See* Tracts 2146:4
Walter, John. *See* Watts 420
Walter, Peter. *See* Gualterus, Petrus
Walter, Richard. *See* Anson 458
Waltham, town and Abbey of. *See* Farmer 684
Walton, Isaac:
Complete angler 2494
Life of Dr. Robert Sanderson 1725
Walton, Peter:
List of the pictures belonging to the Crown 3911
Walwyn, B.:
Chit-chat 1810:33
Wanley, Humfry. *See* British Museum 218; Henry VII 1609:58
Warbeck, Perkin. *See* Macklin 1818:20
Warburton, John:
London and Middlesex illustrated 2979
Warburton, William, Bishop:
Alliance between church and state 1608:34
Critical and philosophical enquiry 211
Divine legation of Moses 1425
Doctrine of grace 1806
Julian 1426
Letter from an author 1608:18
Letter to the editor of the Letters on the Spirit of Patriotism 1608:13
Letter to the Lord Viscount B------ke 1608:13
Supplemental volume of Bishop Warburton's Works 3266, 3477
View of Lord Bolingbroke's philosophy 1608:34
Vindication 1608:55
See Cibber 1608:90; Edwards 1608:66; Gray 1608:55; Lowth 1609:12; Pope 1819, 1912, 2452, 3901; *Review* 1608:55

Ward, Caesar:
One letter. *See* Letters 2576
Ward, Edward. *See* World bewitched 1608:1
Ward, John:
Four essays 1457
History of the Professors of Gresham College 8
Ward, Thomas:
Englands reformation 1633
Ward, Samuel. *See* Hopkins 1609:12
Warde, William. *See* Alexis 2629
Warder, Joseph:
True Amazons 1608:29
Ware, Isaac:
Plans . . . of Houghton in Norfolk 536
See Jones 507
Ware, Sir James:
Historie of Ireland 2182
Works concerning Ireland 614
Warhaffte Bildnis. See Venice 3662
Waring, Henry:
Court convert 1990
Warmstry, Thomas:
Baptized Turk 2776
Warnefridus, Paulus:
De gestis Langobardorum 2138
Warner, Ferdinando. *See* Isla 2885
Warner, John. *See* Isla 2885
Warner, Richard (1713?–1775). *See* Plautus 2023
Warner, Richard (1763–1857):
Topographical remarks 2980
Warning voice. See Fox 1609:45
Warrant constituting Walpole free of the Borough. See King's Lynn 2567
Warren, Richard:
Answer to a book intituled, a Plain Account 1387
Warrington, George Booth, 2d Earl of:
Considerations upon the Institution of Marriage 181
Warrington, Henry Booth, 2d Baron Delamere and 1st Earl of:
Works 182
Warrington, William:
History of Wales 419
Warton, Joseph:
Essay on the writings and genius of Pope, Vol. I 2033; Vol. II 3267
See Sidney 2956

Warton, Thomas:
  Companion to the Guide. See Guides 2387
  History of English poetry 3214
  Life . . . of Ralph Bathurst 1695
  Life of Sir Thomas Pope 2981–2
  Observations on the Fairy Queen of Spenser 1840
  Poems 2983
  Verses on Sir Joshua Reynolds's painted window 3222:18, 19
  See Chatterton 3690:10; Darby 1609:47; Grimston 1896:2; Milton 2905; *Oxford Sausage* 387; Winchester 2991; Wolcot 3222:22
Warville, Jean Pierre Brissot de. *See* Brissot
Warwick, Comte de. *See* Aulnoy 3065
Warwick, Earls of. *See* Edmondson 2372
Warwick, Frances Rich, Countess of. *See* Ford 1321
Warwick, Francis Greville, 1st Earl of:
  One letter. *See* Letters 2576
Warwick, Mary (Boyle) Rich, Countess of. *See* Walker 140
Warwick, Richard Nevill, Earl of. *See* Francklin 1810:9; Hiffernan 1810:9
Warwick, Thomas:
  Abelard to Eloisa 3222:20
Warwick Castle. *See* Antiquities 3485:12; Edmondson 2372
Warwickshire. *See* Dugdale 568; Tilston 2048
Wase, Christopher. *See* Gratius 2008
Washington, George. *See* Wharton 3222:19
Watelet, Claude Henri:
  Essai sur les jardins 3060
Waterhouse, Edward:
  Discourse and defence of arms and armory 771
  Fortescutus illustratus 257
Waterland, Daniel:
  Scripture vindicated 1607
  See Middleton 1379:1
The waterman. See Dibdin 1810:22
Watkins, John:
  Essay towards a history of Bideford 2984
Watkins, Rowland:
  Flamma sine fumo 1991
Wats, William. *See* Watts
Watson, George:
  England preserved 1810:56

Watson, James:
  History of the art of printing 772
Watson, John:
  Apology 1608:83
  History of the parish of Halifax 3215
Watson, Richard, Bishop. *See* Cumberland 1609:45
Watson, Robert:
  History of the reign of Philip the Second, King of Spain 3216
Watson, Thomas:
  Intimations and evidences of a future state 2495
Watson, Sir William:
  Experiments 1608:48
Watt, James. *See* Williams 1609:39
Watteau, Antoine:
  Collection of 595 engravings 3635
  Figures de différents caractères 3635
  Figures de modes 3666
  Oeuvre 3635
  See Drawings 3567, 3678
Watts, Isaac:
  Improvement of the mind 420
Watts, William, D. D. *See* Paris 607
Watts, William, engraver:
  Seats of the nobility 3849
  Views of Bath and Bristol 3528
  See Copper Plate Magazine 3839; Sandby 3844
Watts, William, of the East India Company. *See* Bengal 1609:2, 2642
Way to keep him. See Murphy 1810:1, 1818:18
Weakest goeth to the wall. See Plays 2451:1
Weathercock. See Forest 1810:24
Weaver, Thomas:
  Songs and poems 1992
  See W., T. 1989
Webb, Daniel:
  Inquiry into the beauties of painting 362
  Literary amusements 1609:50
Webb, John. *See* Jones 599
Webb, Philip Carteret. *See* Coalition 1609:54; England 1609:55
Webster, Thomas. *See* Henry VIII 1608:6
Webster, William:
  Compendious course of practical mathematics 1807

Webster, William, D. D.:
Casuistical essay 1608:60
See Skinner 1656
Wedding ring. See Dibdin 1810:19
Weekly Journal 2147. See Mist's Weekly Journal 2144
Weekly pacquet of advice from Rome 865
Week's preparation 1608:15. See Lord's Supper 1531
Weever, John:
Ancient funerall monuments 643
Weidenfeld, Johann Seger von:
Four books 866, 1634
Welby, Henry:
Phoenix of these times 2777
Welch, Joseph:
List of scholars of St. Peter's College, Westminster 286
Weldon, Sir Anthony:
Court and character of King James 1767
See Sanderson 1585
Well-wishers to the University of Oxford. See Newton 1608:70
Wells, Edward. See Xenophon 2228
Wells. See Bristol 2809
Welwood, James:
Memoirs 1768, 2625
Wenceslaus, Emperor. See Godefroy 1066
Wenham, Jane. See Political tracts 94:13
Wensley-Dale. See Maude 3222:12
Wentworth, Sir John. See England 1609:58
Wentworth, Thomas, Earl of Strafford. See Strafford
Wentworth, William, Earl of Strafford. See Strafford
Werdmueller, Otto:
How a Christen man ought to behave 212
Spiritual and most precious perle 212
Weseham, Roger de. See Pegge 516
Wesket, John. See Westcote
Wesley, John:
Calm address 1609:35
Contents of a folio history 1608:19
Journal 1608:42
Letter to Middleton 1379:7
Wesley, Samuel (1662–1735):
Life of our Blessed Lord and Saviour Jesus Christ 2778
Maggots 1993

Wesley, Samuel (1766–1837). See Withers 1609:53
West, Benjamin:
Discourses. See Royal Academy 3885
See Smith 1609:56
West, Gilbert. See Garrick 1810:18; Pindar 1622
West, James:
Catalogues. See Tracts 2050
West, Richard (d. 1726):
Inquiry into the manner of creating peers. See Tracts 400:1, 2475:1
West, Richard (1716–1742). See Poems 3363
West, Temple. See Examination 1608:27
West, Thomas:
Antiquities of Furness 258
West-India pilot. See Speer 3284
West Indian. See Cumberland 1810:17
West Indies. See Singleton 3222:15
Westall, Richard. See Antiquities 3485:15
Westcote, John:
Account of John Westcote 1609:9
See Bevell 1609:56; Ordinary 1609:56
Westerhout, Arnold van. See Van Westerhout
Western counties. See Rural elegance 2750
Western martyrology. See Pitts 2746
Westley, Samuel. See Wesley
Westminster. See Malton 3437
Westminster Abbey. See Burney 461; Dart 566
Westminster Election:
Copy of the poll for a citizen for the city and liberty of Westminster 1608:69, 1726
Genuine account 1608:69
Serious remonstrance 1608:69
T--t--m and V--d-t. See Tracts 2146:1
Two candidates. See Tracts 2146:1
See Cry 1608:56; First chapter 1608:69
Westminster Election of 1784:
History of the Westminster Election 557
See Bunbury 3563:1
Westminster projects 1608:1
Westminster School:
Latin grammar 2265
See Welch 286
Westmorland. See Burn 3162; Hutchinson 2879; Robinson 704
Weston, Sir Richard. See Hartlib 200

Weston, Stephen:
  Letters from Paris 3268
Wetenhall, Edward:
  Of gifts and offices in the publick worship of God 213
Wewitzer, Ralph:
  Songs in the Gnome 1810:46
  Songs in the Magic Cavern 1810:37
Weyerman, Jacob Campo:
  De levens-beschryvingen der Nederlandsche konst-schilders 3766
Weymouth, Thomas Thynne, Viscount, later Marquess of Bath. *See* Rudd 1609:34
Weymouth:
  Weymouth guide 2985
Whaley, John:
  Collection of original poems 1841
  Collection of poems 1820
Whalley, Peter. *See* Bridges 1
Whalley, Stephen. *See* Journeaulx 1413
Wharton, Anne:
  Love's martyr 2626
Wharton, Charles Henry:
  Poetical epistle 3222:19
Wharton, Henry. *See* Laud 1123
Wharton, Philip, Duke of Wharton:
  His Grace the Duke of Wharton's speech. *See* Tracts 2146:4
  Life and writings 60
  See Whartoniana 183
Wharton, Thomas, Marquess of Wharton:
  Memoirs 1608:20
  See Swift 3983
Whartoniana: or, Miscellanies in prose and verse 183
What we must all come to. See Murphy 1810:5
Whately, Thomas:
  Considerations on the trade and finances of the kingdom 1609:56
  Observations on modern gardening. See Gardening 2307:1
  Remarks on Shakespeare. See Gardening 2307:1
  Remarks on the Budget 1609:9
  See Knox 1609:21, 22
Whately, William. *See Faithful account* 1609: 31

Whatley, Robert:
  Collection of tracts against Sir Robert Walpole 2496
Whear, Diggory:
  Method and order of reading histories 1664, 3478
Wheeler (Wheler), Sir George:
  Journey into Greece 2497
Whichcot, Thomas. *See* W., T. 1989
Whig. *See* Butler 1609:54; *Unconnected Whig's address* 1609:38
Whig Examiners. See Medleys 1487
Whiggism. *See Plain matter* 1608:38
Whincop, Thomas:
  Scanderbeg 1842
Whipping Tom 1608:63
Whiston, Edward:
  Life and death of Mr. Henry Jessey. See Sermons 2756:4
Whiston, William:
  Account of the exact time when miraculous gifts ceas'd. See Middleton 1379:8
  Calculation 1608:37
  Historical memoirs of the life of Dr. Samuel Clarke 1727
  Memoirs 2498, 3392
  See Nottingham 1608:15
Whiston, William, Clerk of the Records. *See* Anderson 2328
Whitaker, John, historian:
  History of Manchester 3217
Whitaker, John, M. A.:
  Survey of the doctrine 1379:9
Whitby, Ann. *See* Victor 1805
Whitby, Daniel:
  Short view 1608:12
Whitby. *See* Charlton 3182
Whitchcot, Thomas. *See* Whichcot
White, Elizabeth, later Mrs. Hartley. *See* Hartley
White, George:
  Theological remarks. See Middleton 1337
White, Gilbert:
  Natural history . . . of Selborne 3393
White, James (d. 1799):
  Conway Castle 3222:22
  See Cicero 3300
White, Samuel. *See* Paris 1608:11
White, Thomas:
  Godlie sermon 214, 773

GENERAL INDEX

White Horse. *See* Stukeley 668:2
White Staff. See Detection 2677
Whitefield, George:
    Continuation of the Journal 1608:55
    Expostulatory letter 1608:74
    Further account 1608:55
    Letter to His Excellency Governor Wright
    1609:21
    Letter to the Reverend Dr. Durell 1609:20
    Sermons 1427
Whitehall. *See* Jones 1647, 1749, 2566; Tracts
    1348:2
Whitehead, Paul:
    History of an old lady 1608:74
    Poems and miscellaneous compositions 3269
Whitehead, William:
    Charge to the poets 3222:1
    Creusa 1818:13
    Dissertation. See Animadversiones 2185
    Goat's beard 3222:15
    Poems 1882, 2986
    Roman father 1818:7
    School for lovers 1810:3
    Trip to Scotland 1810:15
    Variety 3222:14
    See Poems 3363
Whitelocke, Bulstrode:
    Essays ecclesiastical and civil 2034
    See Oldmixon 1651
Whiter, William:
    Specimen of a commentary on Shake-
    speare 2987
White's Club, London. *See* Mumford 1608:
    61; Tracts 2146:6
Whittington, Richard. *See Whittington's*
    feast 1810:26
Whittington, Robert:
    Grammatice Whitintoniane liber secundus
    1349
    See Cicero 780
Whittington's feast 1810:26
Whitworth, Charles, Baron Whitworth:
    Account of Russia 2324, 2530, 3469:17
Whitworth, Sir Charles:
    List of ... nobility. See Tracts 2768:2
Whole body of arts regularly digested. See
    Barrow 289
Whole duty of man. See Allestree 867, 1389
Whole prophecies of Scotland 1608:45
Wholesworth, Edward. *See* Holdsworth 3169

Whytt, Robert:
    Essay on the virtues of lime-water 401,
    1608:42
Wiclif, John. *See* Wycliffe
Wicquefort, Abraham de. *See* Olearius 905
Widow of Delphi. See Cumberland 1810:31
Widow of the wood. See Victor 1805
Widow of Wallingford 1810:24
Widow's vow. See Inchbald 1810:39
Wierix, Antony. *See* De Vos 3600
Wierix, Hieronymus. *See* Dürer 3601; De Vos
    3600
Wierix, Jan. *See* De Vos 3600
Wight, Isle of. *See* Hassell 3856; *Poetical*
    3222:15; Tomkins 3848; Worsley 3220;
    Wyndham 2994
Wigmore, Michael:
    Holy citie 1608:8
Wildman, Thomas:
    Treatise on the management of bees 3394
Wilford, John:
    Memorials 9
Wilkes, Benjamin:
    English moths 3886
Wilkes, John:
    History of England from the Revolution
    1609:57
    Letter to His Grace the Duke of Grafton
    1609:18
    Letter to Samuel Johnson 1609:25
    Letter to the Right Honourable George
    Grenville 1609:24
    Observations on the papers relative to the
    rupture with Spain 1609:5
    See Address 1609:24; *Authentick account*
    1609:6; *Battle* 1609:20; *Crisis* 3222:5;
    Dyson 1609:57; *England* 1609:55; *Essay*
    1609:25; *Fair* 1609:24; *False* 1609:25; *First*
    letter 1609:25; Foote 1810:15; *Grenville*
    1609:24; Hatchett 1810:4; Kidgell 1609:54;
    Letter 1609:6, 8, 54, 55; *Letters* 1609:6;
    Majesty misled 1810:16; Meredith 1609:23;
    North Briton 1576; *Reflections* 1609:20;
    Word 1609:24
Wilkes, an oratorio. See Foote 1810:15
Wilkie, William:
    Epigoniad 1883
Wilkins, John, Bishop:
    Essay towards a real character 1136

Wilkins, William:
  Essay 3836
Wilkinson, Tate:
  Memoirs 3479
Will of King Henry VII. See Henry VII 1609:
  58
Willes, Margaret, later Lady Beaumont. *See*
  Beaumont
Willet, Thomas:
  Buxom Joan 1810:29
William, Duke of Gloucester. *See* Lewis 1609:
  52
William I, King of England. *See* Tracts 1348:
  5
William II, King of England. *See* Caesar 2815
William III, King of England:
  Collection of all the speeches. See Tracts
    2769:11
  *Komste van Zyne Majesteit Willem III . . .
    in Holland* 3800
  Original letters 2035, 2779
  Relation du voyage 3529
  Royal diary 2036
  See Blount 1608:1; Boyer 1668; Kane 1608:
    50; Tillotson 1546
William IV, Prince of Orange. *See* Poems
  881:1
William of Newburgh:
  Historia 711
William Augustus, Duke of Cumberland. *See*
  Dialogue 1608:59; *Reasons* 1608:81; Town-
  shend 1608:32
William and Nanny. See Goodenough 1810:
  31, 35
Williams, Sir Charles Hanbury:
  Collection of poems 2050:22
  Place book. See Poems 881:8
  Orpheus and Hecate. See Poems 881:14
  Wife and the nurse. See Poems 881:6
Williams, Cooper. *See* Willyams
Williams, David:
  History of Monmouthshire 3218
  Royal recollections 1609:51
  See Letter 1810:18; *Orpheus* 3222:18
Williams, Edward:
  Poems 2988
Williams, Helen Maria:
  Poems 2989
Williams, Israel. *See Justice* 1609:13

Williams, John, Archbishop. *See* Philips 1717
Williams, John (1730?–1795):
  Account of ancient ruins 1609:39
Williams, John (1761–1818):
  Children of Thespis, parts I–III 3222:20–22
Williams, Rev. R.:
  The bard. See Gray 3222:14
Williamson, Captain. *See* Grose 2862
Williamson, Adam. *See* Turenne 1548
Willis, Browne:
  History . . . of . . . Buckingham 644
  History of the mitred parliamentary abbies
    670
  Survey of the Cathedral Church of Landaff
    2780
  Survey of the cathedrals 645
Willis, Henry Norton:
  Biographical sketches 2990
Willis, John:
  Art of stenography. See Tracts 210
Willoughby de Broke, Richard Verney,
  Baron:
  Poem on the Prince of Orange. See Poems
    881:1
Will's Coffee House. *See* Tracts 2146:3
Willyams, Cooper:
  History of Sudeley Castle 3558
Wilmot, John, Earl of Rochester. *See*
  Rochester
Wilson, Arthur:
  History of Great Britain 910
Wilson, Henry, Captain. *See* Keate 271
Wilson, Sir John. *See Examination* 1609:13
Wilson, Richard. *See Prints* 3460
Wilson, Thomas (1525?–1581):
  Vita et obitus duorum fratrum 402
Wilson, Rev. Thomas (1703–1784):
  Two letters. See Letters 2576
Wilton:
  Aedes Pembrochianae. See Guides 2387
  Hortus Pembrochianus 3667
  See Gambarini 297, 2378; Kennedy 1072
Wily beguilde. See Plays 2451:2
Winchester, Henry Beaufort, Bishop of. *See*
  Gloucester 2552
Winchester, John Paulet, 5th Marquess of.
  See Le Moyne 3279; Talon 97
Winchester, William Paulet, Marquess of:
  Lord Marques Idlenes 2499

Winchester:
  History and antiquities of Winchester 2991
Winchester Cathedral. *See* Gale 686
Winchester School. *See* Ken 1528
Winchilsea, Anne Finch, Countess of:
  Miscellany poems 61
  See Poems 175
Winchilsea, Daniel Finch, Earl of, later Earl of Nottingham. *See* Nottingham
Winchilsea, Heneage Finch, 2nd Earl of:
  True . . . relation of the late earthquake 102
Winckelmann, Johann Joachim:
  Description des pierres gravées du feu Baron de Stosch 3767
  Lettres familières 3061
  Reflections on the painting and sculpture of the Greeks 421
  Storia 36
Windham, Anne. *See* Wyndham
Windover, John:
  England's worthies 2627
Windsor:
  Windsor and its environs. See Guides 2387
  Windsor guide 2992
  See Hornby 692:1
  Windsor: an ode 3222:16
Windsor Castle. *See* Antiquities 3485:12; Pote 637
  Windsor Castle. See Pearce 1810:56
  Windsor guide. See Windsor 2992
Winefred, Saint. *See* Winifred
Winer, Robert. *See* Vyner
Winford, Miss. *See Hobby horses* 3222:17
Wingate, Edmund:
  Maximes of reason 2183
Winifred, Saint:
  Case of St. Winefred opened. See Detection 2677:7
  See Whiston 1727:2
Winnington, Thomas:
  Apology for the conduct of a . . . minister 1696
  Tracts about 1608:89
Winstanley, Hamlet:
  Portfolio of 20 engravings 3668
Winstanley, Henry:
  Ground-platts of Audley End 3480

Winstanley, William:
  Englands worthies 1769
  Historical rarities 403, 1808
  Lives of the most famous English poets 1923, 2781
Winter, Samuel:
  Life and death of Dr. Samuel Winter. See Sermons 2756:5
Winwood, Sir Ralph. *See* Sawyer 1100
Wisdom reputed folly. See Miscellaneous tracts 89:1
Wisdom the first spring of action. See Grove 1410
Wise, Francis:
  Further observations upon the White Horse. See Stukeley 668:3
  Letter to Dr. Mead. See Stukeley 668:2
  Nummorum antiquorum scriniis Bodleianis reconditorum catalogus 230
  Some enquiries. See Tracts 1348:9
Wishart, George, Bishop:
  History of the Kings Majesties affairs in Scotland 1770
Wishes of a free-people. See Hiffernan 1810:2
Wit, a poem. See Poems 3363:13
Wit and drollery 1994
Wit flying at St. James's. See Tracts 2146:3
Witenham-Hill. See Wittenham-Hill
Wither, Fabian. *See* Indagine 2017
Wither, George:
  Shepherd's hunting. See Overbury 2020
Withers, Philip:
  Alfred 1609:52
  Theodosius 1609:53
Withy, Robert:
  Twelve plates of English silver coins 259
Wits commonwealth. See Meres 1755
Wit's last stake. See King 1810:14
Wit's recreations 2037
Witt, Jan de:
  Political maxims 1350
Wittenham-Hill. See Pentycross 3222:14
Witt's recreations. See Wit's recreations 2037
Witty apophthegms 215
Woburn Abbey. *See* Walpole 2619
Wodenote, Theophilus:
  Hermes Theologus 2782

Wodhull, Michael:
  Equality of mankind 3222:7
Wogan, Charles:
  Female fortitude exemplify'd 1608:5
Wolcot, John:
  Apologetic postscript 3222:21
  Benevolent epistle 3222:22
  Bozzy and Piozzi 3222:21
  Brother Peter to Brother Tom 3222:22
  Expostulatory odes 3222:22
  Instructions to a celebrated laureat 3222:21
  Lousiad, Canto I 3222:20
  Lousiad, Canto II 3222:21
  Ode upon ode 3222:21
  Peter's pension 3222:22
  Peter's prophecy 3222:22
  Poetical and congratulatory epistle 3222:20
  Poetical epistle to a falling minister 3222:
  22
  Sir Joseph Banks and the Emperor of Morocco 3222:22
  Subjects for painters 3222:22
Wolf, Johann Christoph:
  Life and adventures, in Ceylon 2993
Wolff, Christian, Freiherr von:
  Real happiness of a people 1608:72
Wollaston, William:
  Religion of nature delineated 1363
Wolley, Edward:
  Loyalty amongst rebels 2783
Wollstonecraft, Mary:
  Historical . . . view . . . of the French Revolution 3177
  Vindication of the rights of women 3177
Wolseley, Sir William. See Victor 1805
Wolsey, Thomas, Cardinal. See More 2430
Wonderful wonder. See Tracts 3796:3
Wonders of Derbyshire. See Account 1810:30
Wood, Anthony à:
  Athenae Oxonienses 584
  History . . . of the colleges and halls of the University of Oxford 3219
  Modius salium. See Pope 1912:3
  See Huddesford 2875
Wood, John:
  Essay towards a description of Bath 2784
  Origin of building 537
  See Kirby 3858
Wood, Robert:
  Essay on Homer 37

Wood, Robert (*cont.*)
  Ruins of Balbec 3547
  Ruins of Palmyra 3548
  See Chandler 3534
Wood, Sir William:
  Bow-mans glory 774
Wood, William. *See* Swift 3984
Wood-cuts. *See* Saxony 2468
Woodbridge, Robert:
  The pad 1810:53
Woodchester. *See* Lysons 3434
Woodcock, Sarah. *See* Baltimore 3397
Woodfall, William:
  Sir Thomas Overbury 1810:27
Woodhead, Abraham:
  Two discourses 1635
Woodward, Henry:
  Letter to Dr. John Hill 1608:61
  Man's the master. See Davenant 1810:24
  Songs . . . of Harlequin's Jubilee 1810:15
Woodward, John:
  Art of getting into practice 1608:48
  See Freind 1608:50
Woollen manufacturers. *See* England. Woollen manufacturers
Woollett, William. *See* Drawings 3678
Woolston, Thomas:
  Discourse 1388
Wootton, John. *See* Drawings 3567
Worcester, Edward Somerset, 4th Earl of. *See* James I 2563
Worcester, Edward Somerset, 2d Marquess of:
  Century of inventions 1608:4
  Water-commanding engine. See Tracts 100:
  4
  See Birch 1665
Worcester, Henry Somerset, Marquess of. *See* Bayly 146; Cartwright 72
Worcester, William. *See* Tractatus 3383
Worcester. *See* Green 2697, 3855
Worcester, battle of. *See* Blount 1996; Charles II 2004
Worcester Cathedral. *See* Abingdon 671; Thomas 641
Worcestershire. *See* Nash 6
Word in behalf of the House of Commons 1609:24
Works of celebrated authors 1864
Works of the learned and pious author of the Whole Duty of Man. See Allestree 867

Works of the most celebrated minor poets. A supplement 184. *See Works of celebrated authors* 1864
The World 911, 2501
  Le Monde 2502
  The World. No. 190. *See Tracts* 2146:7
World, History of the. *See History* 2561
World as it goes 3222:16
World bewitch'd 1608:1
Worldly compliances 1608:7
Worms, Treaty of 1608:44
Worrall, John. *See Coke* 1847
Worsley, Sir Richard:
  History of the Isle of Wight 3220
Worthies of England. See Lloyd 1752; *Sandys* 1763; *Winstanley* 1769
Worthington, John:
  Doctrines of the Resurrection. See North 384:2
Worthington, William:
  Historical sense of the Mosaic account of the Fall. See Middleton 1379:9
Wotton, Sir Henry:
  Elements of architecture 103
  Reliquiae Wottonianae 1771
Wotton, Thomas. *See English baronetage* 655
Wotton, William:
  Reflections upon . . . learning 1498
  See Observations 1608:15
Woty, William:
  The graces 3222:13
Wouwerman, Philips:
  Oeuvres 3992
Wraxall, Sir Nathaniel William. *See Genuine review* 1609:50
Wreath of fashion. See Tickell 3222:16
Wree, Olivier de:
  Les sceaux des comtes de Flandre 646
Wren, Christopher:
  Numismatum antiquorum sylloge populis Graecis 2503
  One or more letters. *See Letters* 2576
  Parentalia 1137
Wright, J.:
  Elegia scripta in sepulchreto rustico 3222:21
Wright, James:
  History and antiquities of . . . Rutland 585
Wright, John. *See Seneca* 2028

Wright, John Michael:
  Account of Roger Earl of Castlemaine's embassy 3687
Wright, Samuel:
  Recommendation of Mr. Leland's answer. See Tracts 2049:5
Wright, Thomas:
  Clavis coelestis 473
  Louthiana 647
Wriothesley, Lady Rachel, Baroness Russell. *See Russell*
Writs. *See Reports* 2591
Wyat, Sir Thomas. *See Surrey* 58
Wyatt, James. *See Whitehead* 3222:14
Wyche, Sir Peter. *See Freire* 2172
Wycherley, William:
  Plays 1884
  See Bickerstaffe 1810:8; *Garrick* 1810:9; *Lee* 1810:7, 39
Wyck, Jan. *See Drawings* 3567
Wycliffe, John. *See Lewis* 1683
Wye River. *See Gilpin* 3854:4
Wykeham, William of, Bishop of Winchester. *See Lowth* 1684
Wyndham, Anne:
  Claustrum regale reservatum 2504
Wyndham, Charles, Earl of Egremont. *See Egremont*
Wyndham, Henry Penruddocke:
  Picture of the Isle of Wight 2994
  Tour through Monmouthshire and Wales 3221, 3481
  See Dodington 429, 2837
Wyner, Robert. *See Vyner*
Wyngate, Edmund. *See Wingate*
Wynn, Sir John:
  History of the Gwedir family 2785
Wynne, John. *See Locke* 1753
Wynne, Justine. *See Orsini* 3753
Wynstanley, William. *See Winstanley*
Wyrley, William:
  True use of armorie 712, 2505
Wyvill, Christopher:
  Summary explanation 1609:47

Xenophon:
  De Cyri institutione libri octo 2184
  Memorabilia 2229
  Memorable things of Socrates 1697
  Opera 2228

Xenophon, the Ephesian:
Ephesian history. See Egerton 1677

Yarico to Inkle. See Jerningham 3222:7
Yarmouth. *See* Swinden 2962, 3208
Yate, Richard:
Letter in defense of Dr. Middleton 1379:5
Yates, William. *See* Potter 3222:6
Yearsley, Ann:
Poems 3222:20
Yelverton, George Augustus, Earl of Sussex.
See Sussex
Yonge, Sir William:
Norfolk garland. See Strawberry Hill 3469:
2
Sedition and defamation display'd 1608:28
York, James, Duke of. *See* James II 51
York. *See* Drake 567; Torr 669
York, House of. *See* Halle 623
York Minster. *See* Drake 567; Halfpenny
3497
York mystery plays:
Cycle of 49 miracle or mystery plays 2628
Yorke, Mrs. Agneta (Johnson). *See* Etchings
3588
Yorke, Lady Amabel, Viscountess Polwarth.
See Polwarth
Yorke, Caroline. *See* Etchings 3588
Yorke, Hon. Charles:
Some considerations 1608:62
Yorke, James:
Union of honour 548
Yorke, Philip, Viscount Royston and later
Earl of Hardwicke. *See* Hardwicke
Yorkshire. *See* Bray 2345, 3400; Burton 562
Yorkshire Petition. *See* Hartley 1609:42;
Smelt 1609:41; *System* 1609:40
Yorkshire question 1609:40
Young, Arthur:
Six weeks tour 2995
Tour in Ireland 1364
Young, Edward:
Brothers 1818:12
Centaur not fabulous 1499
Conjectures 1609:85
Love of fame 3934-5
Two epistles 1818:3
Works 1885
See Dodington 3222:15

Young, John:
Criticism on the Elegy 1609:45
Young, Lucy, Countess of Rochford. *See*
Rochford
Young, Margaret Caroline, later Mrs. Rudd.
See Rudd
Young, Sir William. *See* Taylor 3830
Young Chevalier. See Charles Edward Stuart
Young senator. See Poems 280:7
Young woman in deep affliction:
Songs in the night. See Pye 2457
Youngson, Margaret Caroline, later Mrs.
Rudd. *See* Rudd
Yvery, House of. *See* Anderson 2328
Y-Worth, William:
Chymicus rationalis 2038

Zabdeel. *See* Book 1608:91
Zacchiroli, Francesco. *See* Florence 3570
Zampieri, Domenico, called Domenichino.
See Drawings 3568-9; Frey 3602
Zand-Avastá:
Zend Avesta, ouvrage de Zoroastre 3155
Zanetti, Antonio Maria:
*Delle antiche statue . . . della Libreria di
San Marco* 3559
XII teste e figure 3801
Zapata, B. *See* Castellamonte 3676
Zarah, Queen. *See* Secret history 1608:91
Zarathustra. *See* Zand-Avastá 3155
Zayde. See Segrais 1005
Zend-Avesta. *See* Zand-Avastá 3155
Zenger, John Peter, defendant:
Trial of John Peter Zenger 1609:10; 3459
Zenobia. *See* Murphy 1810:12
Zobeide. See Cradock 1810:18
Zocchi, Giuseppe:
Scelta di XXIV vedute 3583
Vedute delle ville 3530
Zoffany, Johann. *See* Prints 3460
Zoraida. See Hodson 1810:31
Zoroaster. *See* Zand-Avastá 3155
Zouch, Richard:
Elementa jurisprudentiae 3993
Zuccaro, Federigo. *See* Drawings 3567-8;
Zuccaro, T. 3560, 3615
Zuccaro, Taddeo:
Portfolio of 119 engravings 3615
Illustri fatti Farnesiani 3560
Zucchi, Francesco. *See* Venice 3662